Hail Mount Hermon!
A TRIBUTE

Hail Mount Hermon!
A TRIBUTE

Compiled & Edited by
Jigme N. Kazi

Also by Jigme N. Kazi:
INSIDE SIKKIM: Against The Tide
SIKKIM FOR SIKKIMESE: Distinct Identity Within The Union
THE LONE WARRIOR: Exiled In My Homeland
SONS OF SIKKIM: The Rise and Fall of the Namgyal Dynasty of Sikkim

Copyright © 2020, Jigme N. Kazi
All rights reserved.

No part of this publication may be reproduced or transmitted in any form or by any means, electronic or mechanical, including photocopy, recording or any information storage and retrieval system now known or to be invented, without permission in writing from the publisher, except by a reviewer who wishes to quote brief passages in connection with a review written for inclusion in a magazine, newspaper or broadcast.

Published by Prowess Publishing,
YRK Towers, Thadikara Swamy Koil St, Alandur,
Chennai, Tamil Nadu 600016

ISBN: 978-1-5457-5318-7

Library of Congress Cataloging in Publication

Contents

Introduction ix

HISTORY – Part I

1. Mount Hermon: Rising Up From The Ashes 3
2. By Faith They Built Mt. Hermon School 8
3. The Darjeeling Disaster Of 1899 17
4. The Lees And The Darjeeling Disaster 21
5. The Six Lee Children 27
6. "The House In Which Your Children Were Is Gone" 62
7. Letters Of Love And Support 77
8. The Lees And Their Work 88
9. The Lee Memorial Mission 95

FOUNDERS – Part II

10. The Founding Of Queen's Hill School 103
11. A Brief History Of Mount Hermon School 116
12. They Received The Call From Above 122
13. Keeping Alive The Spirit Of Queen's Hill School 128
14. Bishop Fisher Gave Us Our Estate And School Its Name 137
15. An Extraordinary Woman Of Courage 150
16. "May Thy Fair Name Live Forever" 167

PRINCIPALS – Part III

17. "I Feel At Home And I Belong To Mount Hermon" 175
18. David Stewart's Memoirs 194
19. Murray: A Rare Individual Full Of Life And Enthusiasm 204
20. My Tribute To A Revered Friend And Guide 225
21. Gardner Recollections: 1970-1984 253

MILESTONES – Part IV

22. Builders Of Tomorrow 263
23. Lila Gladys Kehm Enberg 268

24	William Wayne Jones: A Young Missionary From America	292
25	Cynthia Hawke: A Wonderful Time For Hawke In Sikkim	299
26	Rev. M.J. Eade: Mount Hermon Nearly Closed Down In 1943	308
27	Patricia Russell: She Made A Difference	312
28	Daniel Gyanendra Rongong: He Lived Out His Faith In Daily Life	318
29	Edna Williams: She Loved Mount Hermon And Mount Hermon Loved Her	323

MH FAMILIES – Part V

30	The Isons: Mount Hermon And The Ison Family	329
31	The Sarias: From Rajasthan's Lunkaransar To Darjeeling's Mt. Hermon School	339
32	The Mathais: We Had To Make A Huge Cultural Leap	359
33	The Moores: Mount Hermon: What It Means To Me	364
34	The Mapleys: From Homes to Hermon	370

MISCELLANY – Part VI

35	Mount Hermon In Israel	377
36	History Of Methodist Church In India	380
37	Darjeeling: Past And Present	395
38	MH Scores A Century	399
39	'Good Old Days' Club Formed By Alumni Of Darjeeling Schools In Sikkim	408
40	Defining Decades: '50s & '60s	415
41	Couples For Life: And They Called It Puppy Love	428
42	Mount Hermon Memories And Random Thoughts	440
43	Old Friends Are Loyal Friends	450

HERMONS ON THE MOUNT – Part VII

44	Madan Mohan Rasaily: The Jewel Of Sikkim	467
45	Tshering Dorji: Donning Many Hats	471
46	Altamas Kabir: "Mount Hermon Gave Me A Sound Foundation"	473
47	Amar Singh Rai: He Gave Us 'Darjeeling University'	476
48	Air Marshal Pratap Rao: Decades Of Dedicated Service	477
49	Sonam Dubal: "My Work Reflects Essence Of Northeast"	483
50	Tom Stoppard: British Playwright And Social Activist	486
51	Lodi Gyari: A Tireless Advocate For Tibet	493

MEMORIES – Part VIII

52	Looking Backwards To See Forwards	503
53	The Search For Queen's Hill: Romancing The Past	507

54	*Elkanah:* "Fire In Mr. Murray's House"	511
55	School Days In Darjeeling 1957	513
56	"Mount Hermon Fills My Heart With Special Things"	517
57	Walking Down Memory Lane	521
58	The Reunion	525
59	Making A Difference	527
60	A Himalayan Affair	530
61	The Life Of A Day Scholar	535
62	"I Love Darjeeling Because It Was My Home"	538
63	The Woods Are Lovely, Dark And Deep	540
64	Memories Of Another Time	545
65	Down Memory Lane	548
66	*Bhuntay* Will Be Missed	558
67	Hail Mount Hermon!	561

ALUMNI – Part IX

68	It's Springtime For The Hermonites	583
69	Sherab And Roslyn Spent An Afternoon At Mount Hermon School In 2012	592
70	Barbara's Barry In Leather Jacket	594
71	"Being The Principal's Daughter Had Its Advantages And Liabilities"	597
72	Whispering Pines And Misty Mountains	602
73	Renown British Playwright Tom Stoppard Studied In MH	607
74	MH Needs 'Reliable People' On The Ground	610
75	Friends Are Forever	618
76	My Return To India	624

GLOBAL HERMONITES – Part X

77	'MH Revival' Campaign 2012	631
78	MH Says 'No' To Global Hermonites After Assurance	791

Epilogue: 125th Anniversary and Beyond 829

Introduction

It was never my intention to publish this book this year (2020). Initially, I made concerted efforts to complete the book before the Hermonites' reunion in Kathmandu in 2017 but failed. It is just a happy and meaningful coincidence that this book is being published as Mount Hermon School celebrates its 125th birth anniversary in 2020. When you look back to this period when MH celebrates its 150th anniversary in 2045 this book would, hopefully, be a prized possession.

I have always been fascinated by history – history of any sort, individuals, communities, nations. A major part of the book records our school's past history. In 1978 when I edited the annual school magazine (Hermonite) my school friend and 1971 batch Hermonite Ved Prakash Agarwal and I did some research work on Queen's Hill School. What we discovered has been a very reliable and valuable source of our school's history of this period (1895-1930) for this book.

As mentioned in my writings MH has gone through a lot in these 125 years. The tragic beginning of the school (Arcadia Girls School) soon after its opening in 1895, when that terrible landslide of September 24, 1899, killed ten of our students, including six children of the Lee family, was a big blow to the school. This tragic incident has been fairly well documented in this book as a reminder for all Hermonites to look back in wonder and awe and derive strength from what happened and how we came through it. My friend and fellow Hermonite Uttam Pradhan (1973 batch) also helped me in compiling the much-needed materials of MH's early history.

The vision and determination of our school's Founder, Miss Emma Knowles, and her deputy Miss C.J. Stahl led to the founding of Queen's Hill School soon after the 1899 disaster in a new location just above the main road near the Darjeeling railway station in the town area. Miss Stahl deserves our gratitude. She was in Arcadia, Queen's Hill School and even lived at the present campus when the school was opened in 1926. She retired as Principal during the period when the school was renamed Mount Hermon School in 1930.

Though he was never our Principal, Bishop Fisher is considered one of our Founders for he was chiefly responsible for the purchase of the present Mount Hermon Estate, where the MH is located. The school was growing and needed more space for expansion. The Estate had around 100 acres in North Point facing Sikkim's mighty Kanchenjunga (Khangchendzonga), the third highest mountain in the world, and the Rangeet valley.

Not many people are aware of the role played by one of our Principals in helping MH sail through stormy times. I'm referring to our Principal Lila Enberg who in the mid-thirties restored a major portion of our main building after the devastating earthquake of January 15, 1934. As a reward the Managing Committee of our school failed to renew her tenure after her term came to an end in 1934! They wanted to get rid of her.

While trying to help the school with other Hermonites in the 2012, Lila's daughter Kitty Katzell (Mildred) got in touch with me from the US and sent me her mother's biography (*Lila*), which she authored. She took a lively interest in what was going on in MH and the involvement of the alumni. She was in her eighties then and, unfortunately, died soon after she showed us the way. I'm deeply indebted to her for all her help and inspiration. This book is a tribute to people such as Kitty.

Our fourth Founder, Rev. Halsey Dewey, did a wonderful job in holding on to MH when times were really very difficult after the 2nd World War, which saw the enrolment dip to its lowest level. The numbers were as low as 86 when Mr. David Stewart took over the school in 1953-54. In the ten years (1954-1964) of his leadership, MH soared to greater heights. Enrolment not only shot up to more than 300, MH was adjudged the best boarding school in India in 1960-61.

When Mr. Stewart's right-hand man, Mr. Graeme Murray, took over the reign in 1964 after Mr. Stewart retired MH was on an uphill swing. Mr. Murray built on the solid foundation laid down by his predecessor. One notable addition to MH's growing stature was the establishment of the Teachers' Training College (TTC) in its campus. TTC graduates not only played a significant role in improving the standard of education in Christian schools in Darjeeling, they have also done remarkably well while serving various schools in the rest of India as teachers and heads.

Due to unstable political situation in the region, Rev. John Johnston who took over after Mr. Murray in 1979 had a tough time in running MH. However, the soft-spoken preacher and Biology and Bible teacher kept the school going and MH sailed through smoothly. Much was expected from Mr. Jeff Gardner when he became the Principal in 1990 but due to many reasons, including internal 'staff politics', his tenure did not last long. This was most unfortunate as Mr. Gardner had worked under both Mr. Murray and Mr. Johnston as Senior Master for a long time and he was best suited for the job as Principal. Unfortunately, he left MH in 1994 just before the school celebrated its 100th year.

Those who took charge after Mr. Gardner, namely Mr. Gilbert Samuel, Mr. Pradip K. Das and Mr. George Fernandes, tried to keep MH flag flying but they faced many difficulties. It was the Hermonites from Sikkim, Siliguri and Darjeeling who persuaded the Managing Committee to appoint Mr. Fernandes as Principal mainly to stabilize the situation and to keep the school going. This worked well for sometime. But the downward slide that gradually started after Mr. Johnston and Mr. Gardner's departure was unstoppable and after Mr. Fernandes left in 2011 MH was heading towards a bleak and uncertain future.

Despite the enormous goodwill and sympathy and concern shown by the Hermonites to improve the situation the school authorities failed to respond positively. Mt. Hermon School is owned by the Methodist Church in India which runs the school with the help of the Managing Committee. For several years after the abrupt departure of its Principal, Mr. Terrance Wharton, the school was run without a Principal. Even now we don't have a Principal. In 2018 we came to know that there were only 51 boarders (18 boys and 33 girls) and a 100 odd dayscholars.

Introduction

The global Hermonites' concern for MH and the need to do something concrete is well-documented in the latter part of this book. Their love and concern for their alma mater is a profound reflection of the spirit that has not only founded the school but has kept the school going in the past 100 plus years through troubled times. I'm particularly proud and grateful to Roslyn (Rongong) Namgyal, Dipak Mirchandhani, Shiva Saria and Lucinda (Cindy) Gibbs for leading and managing the 'MH Revival' Campaign globally in 2012 and thereafter. A big 'Thank You' to all Hermonites for taking a deep interest in MH affairs and supporting my candidature as Principal. We have done our job sincerely and with good intentions. Leave the rest to God. "God moves in a mysterious way, His wonders to perform."

This book is a Tribute not only to our great Founders, Principals, Teachers, Students and Others, it is also a Tribute to all Hermonites of all ages who have lived, died and hoped so that MH lives on to reach greater heights. Bijay Palriwala, a Hermonite of the Stewart era from UK who started the 'MH Revival' movement in 2011 died in November 2019. This book is a Tribute to Hermonites such as Bijay. I wrote this in Facebook when Bijay passed away: "Bijay's efforts and hopes will not die in vain. May he rest in peace." Bijay's advice to us was: "Only combined, sustained effort can hope to improve the situation so I am hoping that others will join in the effort!" Hail Mt. Hermon!

Since the formation of Hermonites International (Hi!) in 2005, we have been very successful in forming/reviving alumni chapters all over the world, particularly in India, Nepal and Bhutan. Thanks to the MH spirit and communication technology, Hermonites are now closely united as never before. Here I would like to make a special mention of some of the active Hermonites who, over the years, have helped to connect Hermonites and cement their bonding. Some of them include the following: Krishna Goenka, Thinley Gyari, Mahesh Singh, Anita (Adhikari) Sahwney, Karan Anand (Delhi), Tshering Dorji, Thinley (Delma) Dem, Karma Khokor, Daw Penjo, Sonam Lhendup (Taki), Rinji Om (Bhutan), Pratap Rai, Anup Chachan, Sarthak Pradhan, Sunirmal Chakrabarti, Nima Thondup (Darjeeling), Charan Chabria, Sujit Singh, Prabir Manna, Hashib Mondol, Yasmin (Mukand) Chung, Shakti Shaw (Kolkata), Annie Gardner, Santosh Rijal, Ashok Pokharel, Ram Bhattarai, Pramod Shrestha 'Goofy', Jugesh Shrestha (Nepal), Ravi Agarwal, Moon Moon Singh, Sushil Mittal, Jagdish Saria, Narendra Sarogi, Jagjit Singh and Shiv Saria (Siliguri), Namgyal Wangdi, Prakash Mundra, Uttam Pradhan, Karma Bhutia, Suresh Sarda, Punam Agarwal, OT Bhutia, Thentok Lachungpa, Udai Sharma, Surendra Pal Singh Lamba (Sikkim), James Sinclair, Pradip Verma, Lucinda Gibbs, Dipak Mirchandhani, Bill Moore, Patricia Russell, Mary Ann Mackie, Ronen Ghose (UK), Ranjit Dasgupta and Pradip Singhania (Bangalore), Ashish Bhengra (Chennai), Walsa Mathai, Sherab Namgyal, Barry Ison, Johnstons, Glasbys (Australia), Dhruba Rai, Adrienne (Murray) Thompson (New Zealand), Puii, Rothang Rema, Robin Sengupta, Fui Chung Lee, Margaret Mapley, Sikdar Nirmal (US & Canada), Tony Sardjono, Barid Manna (Indonesia), Suresh Chatlani (Africa), Apok Jamir, Len Gangte, Bobby Roy, Thangi Rema, Jimmy Lowangcha, Zeena Singh, Ajit Singh, Ayinla Ao (Northeast), Frank Freese (Pune), Varongthip Lultanond (Thip), Navin (Khuria) Wongsejullarat, Aphichoti Chavengsaksongkram (Oak), Joy Nalinee Mishra, Nampung, Pornipha, Mantana (Thailand).

I may have forgotten to give due credit to photographs and other materials used in this book to all concerned persons. Please pardon me for this. But I do want to acknowledge my deep sense of gratitude to James Sinclair and late Hazel Craig of the UK alumnus for materials, including photographs, used in this book. Special thanks to Bangkok's Joy Nalinee Mishra for initially starting the ball rolling in her website on MH. It was an inspiration and a great help to us all.

The 125th Anniversary year will witness further bonding of Hermonites. We can only hope and pray that the alumni's wish and desire to start a new and fresh relationship with its alma mater will see the light of day in the days and months to come.

At this point of time we hope and pray that the Methodist Church leaders in India take a serious look in what is going on in MH. They must look within and introspect to find out what is really going on in this great institution, why it is sliding downhill and take timely and effective steps to restore MH to its former glory.

Carl Jung said, "Your vision will become clear when you look into your heart. Who looks outside, dreams. Who looks inside, awakens." The Bible is very clear as to what we should do when we are faced with a problem: "Trust in the Lord with all thine heart; and lean not unto thine own understanding. In all thy ways acknowledge him, and he shall direct thy paths." (Proverbs 3:5-6)

Amen!

Jigme N. Kazi
(MH: 1963-1979)

Gangtok (Sikkim), March 2020

HISTORY – Part I

1   Mount Hermon: Rising Up From The Ashes

"Inch by inch
Step by step
One day at a time
We Shall Overcome."

Jigme N. Kazi

KNOWLES
Founder: Emma L. Knowles (1840-1924, Principal: 1895-1917)

When Miss Emma L. Knowles, an educational missionary under the Women's Foreign Missionary Society of the Methodist Episcopal Church of the United States, founded Mount Hermon School on March 11, 1895, the school was called Arcadia Girls School and was located below Chowrasta facing Lebong in Darjeeling.

Miss Knowles had already spent many years in India as Principal of schools for European girls at Nainital (Uttarakhand) and Calcutta before coming to Darjeeling.

Emma Knowles played a major role in establishing the Wellesley Girls High School in Naini Tal and having worked at the Calcutta Girls School she realised the need for a similar school to be set up in Darjeeling's favourable climate.

She began 'Arcadia' with only 13 students. Deeply religious and a committed Christian, Miss Knowles was convinced that it was God's will to establish a school for girls in Darjeeling. Within three years of the founding of the school a terrible landslide in 1899 completely damaged the school building, killing ten of its students in the tragic incident.

Undaunted by the terrible disaster and faith in the Almighty, Miss Knowles purchased a piece of land near the railway station in Darjeeling town just above the Hill Cart Road and continued with the work. By 1902, the school had at least four dwelling houses and a three-storey building. The enrolment of the school rose to 50 and the school was renamed Queen's Hill School (QHS).

STAHL
Carolyn Josephine Stahl (Principal: 1918-1929)

From the beginning of the century till 1929, it was Miss Carolyn J. Stahl, who really served the school, first as an assistant to Miss Knowles, and then as the Principal from 1918 to 1929.

Queen's Hill School was nearly closed down in 1914 due to shortage of funds but because of the concern and dedication of both Miss Knowles and Miss Stahl the school survived. Miss Stahl, also from America and a member of Women's Foreign Missionary Society, believed that "any great task can be accomplished by the exercise of boundless faith, much intercessory prayer and ceaseless work."

By 1918, the enrolment rose to 163 and the school authorities felt the need to find a suitable site for expansion of the school. Queen's Hill School was primarily for the children of missionaries and other Europeans as most white people were called. The students were taught a British curriculum.

FISHER
Frederick Bohn Fisher (1882-1938)

Though he did not become Principal of the school, Bishop Frederick Bohn Fisher is regarded as one of the four Founders of Mt. Hermon School. Born in Pennsylvania in the US in 1882, Bishop Fisher was elected to the Episcopacy and came to India as a missionary and became the Bishop of Calcutta and served in the Thoburn Methodist Church in Calcutta.

As a prominent Methodist Church leader, Rev. Fisher took a live interest on Queen's Hill School. The present location of the school was purchased from Lebong Tea Company, Grand Hotel (Calcutta) and Mount Everest Hotel (Darjeeling) in 1920. Bishop Fisher played a vital role in the purchase of the new estate.

The inauguration of the new school building, which has been described as "one of the finest buildings in the Orient," was performed by Lord Lytton, then the Governor General of Bengal, in May 26, 1926. Initially, the school had around 100 acres.

In 1929-30, Rev. E.S. Johnson of the Thoburn Methodist Church (Calcutta) became Principal of the two schools located in the new campus – Queen's Hill School for Girls and Bishop Fisher School for Boys – and in the same year (1930) and for the third time the school was renamed Mount Hermon School and became a co-educational institution.

In their honour Mt. Hermon still continues the tradition of awarding best girl and boy students every year during its annual Speech Day: Miss Stahl Cup for Best Girl Student and Bishop Fisher Cup for Best Boy Student.

Bishop Fisher knew Mahatma Gandhi and Rabindranath Tagore on intimate terms. "He seemed to me to be one of the few Christians who walked in the fear of the Lord, and, therefore, feared no man," was Gandhi's comment on Bishop Fisher, who died of a heart attack in 1938.

Among the former principals of Mt. Hermon after Miss Stahl, Mrs. Lila Engberg (Principal – 1931-1935) needs a special mention mainly because it was she who helped and inspired MH to move forward after the devastating January 15, 1934 earthquake that caused severe damage to the main school building.

Mrs. Engberg not only managed to mobilize huge amount of funds to rebuild the school building but also made sure that repair and reconstruction works were done on time to enable the school to begin its next academic session in March 1935 without much difficulty.

DEWEY
Halsey E. Dewey (Principal: 1938-1952)

Mt. Hermon endured another major crisis in the early 1940s. The effect of the Second World War hit the school badly as most of its students were from abroad. The school was nearly closed down in 1943. Not only were the funds low the enrolment also dropped to only 120. The uncertainty of the future of the mission in India also had an adverse effect on the school.

But it was Rev. Halsey E. Dewey, who became the Principal in 1938, who was chiefly responsible for keeping the school going during one of its darkest periods. Rev. Dewey, who is one of the four Founders of the school, had heavy responsibilities for mission work in Bengal and as staff were hard to get, he found it increasingly difficult to keep the school going and was nearly closed down in 1952. Between 1938, when Rev. Dewey became the Principal, through to the 1940s and 1952, when Rev. Dewey left, MH had two other Principals: Rev. M.A. Clare (1942) and Mrs. R. Forsgren (1947).

STEWART
David Garth Stewart (Principal: 1954-1964)

Mt. Hermon really and truly emerged as a great educational institution in the sub-continent when Rev. David G. Stewart of the New Zealand Chinese Inland Mission (now renamed Overseas Missionary Fellowship) took over the school as its Principal in 1954.

From only about 100 students in early 1950s, the school grew to well over three hundred students by the time Rev. Stewart left at the end of 1963. The school grew not only in strength but in standards and character. In 1961-62, Mt. Hermon was adjudged the best boarding school in India.

By mid-1950s MH had a mix of children of different nationalities - American, Australian, New Zealanders, British, Europeans, Indians, Anglo-Indians, Tibetans, Sikkimese, Burmese, Bhutanese, Nepalese, Chinese and even students from Thailand who used to fly all the way out to India for the school term.

It was in 1960 that the school was divided into four Houses named after its Founders and Heads: Knowles (green), Stahl (red), Fisher (yellow) and Dewey (blue).

MURRAY
Graeme Armstrong Murray (Principal: 1964-1978)

Mr. Graeme A. Murray of New Zealand was already the Acting Principal during Rev. Stewart's last year in MH. He naturally took over the school as Principal in 1964 after Rev. Stewart's departure. Mr. Murray finally left MH after 24 years of service to the school in 1978.

Mr. Murray built on the solid foundation laid down by Rev. Stewart and Mt. Hermon blossomed and went from strength to strength during his tenure as Principal. Under Mr. Murray's leadership Mt. Hermon maintained its high standard in all spheres – academic, sports & games, music, plays & dramas etc.

Mr. Murray was blessed by a group of dedicated and competent members of the staff: Mrs. Joy Rongong, Mr. and Mrs. Mathai, Miss C. Hawke, Mr. and Mrs. W. Jones, Mr. and Mrs. Johnston, Mr. and Mrs. Jeff Gardner, Mrs. Alexandra, Miss P. Russell, Miss Bilcliffe, Mr. and Mrs. Lunnon, Mr. and Mrs. Ismail, Mr. and Mrs. West to name a few.

JOHNSTON
John Arcus Johnston (Principal: 1979-1989)

Rev. John Arcus Johnston, whose association with MH goes back to 1959, became the next Principal in 1979 after Mr. Murray left at the end of 1978. Rev. Johnston from Australia was a quiet, soft-spoken gentleman. During his tenure as Principal Darjeeling went through an uncertain political period when the main demand of the local Gorkha (Nepali) population was for creation of a separate state of 'Gorkhaland.'

Because of the new political environment most schools in Darjeeling, including MH, faced many difficulties during this period. However, Rev. Johnston somehow managed to stay the course and MH was able to pull through the turbulent period.

Uncertain future

Jeff Gardner, an ex-teacher of MH, who later became Rector of St. Paul's School, Darjeeling, took over the school in 1992 after Rev. Johnston left in 1989.

The school's future after Rev. Johnston's departure was uncertain. It may be recalled that most senior teachers of the school left MH in 1978 and this created a huge gap in the teaching faculty.

Mr. Gardner was already the Senior Master when Mr. Murray was the Principal. His taking over the school as Principal in 1992 gave much hope and confidence to all Hermonites and well-wishers of the school that the school was in good hands.

The manner in which the school was run after Mr. Johnston and Mr. Gardner left (1993-94!) prompted Hermonites in the region to urge the Managing Committee, which runs the school on behalf of the Methodist Church in India, to make Mr. George Fernandes, who was on the staff from 1977 during Mr. Murray's tenure, the Principal to ensure stability of the school. Mr. Fernandes and his wife Saroj (Pradhan) Fernandes (a Hermonite), who took charge of MH in 2000-01 have made much contribution to keep the school going and to stabilize the situation when it seemed MH was being troubled on all fronts.

'MH Revival' Campaign

In order to revitalize all aspects of the school's life Hermonites from all over the world from the beginning of 2012 have been unitedly urging the Managing Committee to appoint a competent Hermonite as Principal to set things in order so that the school regains its past glory and continues to give valuable service to society.

Despite overwhelming concern shown by global Hermonites throughout 2012 on the school's future survival and success the school authorities, Managing Committee Members and the Methodist Church in India did not respond to the Hermonites' call for 'MH Revival'.

The main building of the school has been badly damaged after the September 18, 2011 earthquake, staff cottages which were burnt down or in disrepair have not been rebuilt or maintained, school campus has been encroached and worse is the rapid fall in the enrolment…the present strength of boarders is said to be just over 200. There is also the justifiable apprehension that MH may be closed down in the near future or die a natural death if its problems are not properly addressed at the earliest.

(Jigme N. Kazi was a student in MHS (1963-1972), did his teacher's training (TTC) at Mt. Hermon (1974-75) and taught at MH (1976-1979). He was the Founder-President of Hermonite International (Hi!) and is now Chairman Emeritus of Hermonites International. He has written three books on Sikkim and is a journalist based in Gangtok, Sikkim, India. This piece (minus the first quote) was prepared for Hermonite Altamas Kabir, Chief Justice of India, who was the Chief Guest for MH's Speech Day, 2012.)

2 By Faith They Built Mt. Hermon School

FOUNDERS: (L to R) Knowles, Stahl, Fisher and Dewey.

Mount Hermon School is a co-educational school in the town of Darjeeling, in the Indian state of West Bengal. It is located in North Point, Singmari. It follows the American education style, rather than the British style in vogue in the other schools of the area. It has ICSE (for grade 10) and ISC (for grade 12) board.

The main school building of Queen's Hill School was opened in 1926.

Mt. Hermon is a renowned school in Darjeeling hills where facilities for both boys and girls from class KG to 12, day scholars and boarders are available including the facility of all three streams in classes 11 & 12, viz. Science, Commerce & Humanities.

History

The school was established in 1895 under the auspices of the Methodist Episcopal Church of America. Its founder and first Principal was Miss Emma Knowles, a missionary sent out to India with the Women's Foreign Missionary Society in 1881. Emma Knowles played a key role in establishing the Wellesley Girls High School in Nainital (Uttarakhand) and having worked at the Calcutta Girls' High School she embarked on a similar school to be set up in Darjeeling's cool climate. Her plan gained the approval of the Church authorities in the United States as well as in India, but no financial aid was forthcoming from either quarter. It was only by borrowing and by paying rent out of her missionary salary that she was able to open her school in 1895 in a rented house called Arcadia, in a long low building right in the heart of the town, with just 13 pupils on the rolls. The school was also called Arcadia at that time and was considered as a branch of the Calcutta Girls' High School.

By 1899 there were 37 boarders when Miss C.J. Stahl was the officiating Principal for Miss Knowles. On a late September evening, following a deluge from continuous rains, "the ledge in front of the school became a river of water." The children were evacuated to a home higher up. Some little ones had already fallen asleep in their new refuge when a great boulder hit the corner of the room destroying the two walls. The two children just moved to a place of safety were killed, all others went unhurt.

On the same night in a cottage not far from Arcadia, 6 children of Mr. and Mrs. Lee were living in the care of their older sister and trusted servants. They attended Arcadia as day scholars. The next morning revealed that there was not a vestige of the cottage or anything it held. Mrs. Ada Lee turned to God and wrote of her journey in pain in her book, *The Darjeeling Disaster*. It chronicles her struggles and her faith in converting her disaster to triumph. Out of this heart-wrenching engagement with God the Lee Memorial Mission was born to care for famine-stricken orphans, by providing for them food, education and a decent place to stay. Thus in Wellington Square, Calcutta, the Lee Memorial Building came into being in 1908, "In Answer to Prayer – Psalm 27:1".

In the disaster of 1899 ten students had died. Following the disaster Arcadia was closed and opened again on 1 March 1900 in two rented houses named Queen's Hill and The Repose, which were later purchased with a third house, Woodville, on ground leased from the Maharaja of Burdwan. These premises were above the railway station, and the school

By Faith They Built Mt. Hermon School

officially became Queen's Hill School for Girls. A new wing was added in 1902 with financial aid from the Women's Foreign Missionary Society and building grants from the Government of India.

Emma Knowles worked tirelessly for her school until 1915, and retired from active missionary service a few years later. Her greatest hope was to see her school established in a permanent building 'before her call should come'. She died in 1924 aged 84, but she got her wish when Miss Carolyn Josephine Stahl, who became Principal in 1918, was able to write and tell her of the purchase of the Mount Hermon Estate in 1920. A slump in the tea industry led to the sale of the large estate belonging to the Lebong Tea Company, an ill wind which blew some good for the Methodist missionaries looking for a site for the school. The site was bought for a bargain price of Rs. 50,000/- by Bishop Frederick Fisher of the Thoburn Memorial Methodist Church in Calcutta. Fred Fisher was the moving spirit behind the purchase of the site and the building of the new school.

Later he was instrumental in the purchase of Fernhill in 1927, which was to become the senior boys' living accommodation - again at a bargain price, a mere Rs. 35,000/-. Cottages sprang up on the new estate and the school itself was officially opened in 1926, still called Queen's Hill School. As early as 1899 only small boys were taken into the school and by 1903 there were 20 boys. In 1930 the school was renamed Mount Hermon School, incorporating the original Queen's Hill School for Girls and Bishop Fisher's School for Boys, eventually becoming the fully integrated co-educational boarding school.

By Faith They Built Mt. Hermon School

Fernhill 1932

The story goes that the school received its name during a prayer meeting of some of the missionaries, Bishop Fisher and Miss Stahl seated around Miss Stahl's fireplace. When they rose from their knees after praying, the name 'Mount Hermon' came to them of the snow-capped mountain 9,232 ft high in the northernmost part of present-day Israel.

Since the school was founded in 1895, for nearly 60 years it was run by the Methodist Episcopal Church of America through its Calcutta Christian Schools Society (CCSS), the Management comprising members of other non-conformist churches and missionary societies under the chairmanship of the Calcutta Methodist Bishop. In the early 1950s a new 'united' committee added with co-operating missions from the Australian, New Zealand and British Baptist societies, as well as British Methodists, the Presbyterian Church of Wales and the Church of Scotland. The religious ethos of the school remained evangelical, but the largely American influence became diminished for a short period with the appointment in

1954 of the Reverend D.G. Stewart, an Australian Baptist, as principal. David Stewart was Principal for ten years (1954-1964) and was then succeeded by Graeme Murray, a New Zealand Baptist, who held the post for 15 years. In 1979, Reverend John Johnston, an Australian Baptist and the school's Senior Master, became Principal, retiring in 1989 after 30 years' service on the school staff.

As the Methodist Episcopal Church decentralized it became the Methodist Church in Southern Asia, which included the territories of India, Burma, Malaysia and the Philippine Islands. In 1981 the Methodist Church in Southern Asia further decentralized and gave autonomy to the Church in India, which then became the Methodist Church in India. All its properties were transferred to the Methodist Church in India Trust Association (MCITA). Over all these years the governance of the school continued under the CCSS, and under the chairmanship of the Bishop of the Bengal Regional Conference and through the administrative jurisdiction of the Calcutta District.

Recently, on 4 May 2014, at the 31st Annual Session of the Bengal Regional Conference, the Presiding Bishop, Bishop Dr. Phillip Silas Masih, placed the Mt. Hermon School under the administrative jurisdiction of the North Bengal-Sikkim District providing it greater flexibility.

The school

The District Superintendent for this region is Rev. Noel Prabhuraj, Rev. Prabhuraj, Secretary and Chaplain of the school, is also the Vice-Chairman for the School. The present Principal, Mr. Terrence Wharton, was appointed in April 2013. Mr. Wharton took over from Mr. George William Fernandez who retired end of 2012. Mr. Norton Emmanuel took over from Mr. Wharton in April 2015 as the school's Administrator.

The student body is divided into four houses – Knowles, Stahl, Fisher and Dewey, which are named after previous principals/founders of the school.

The school has three departments – the Infant Department (KG to standard 2), the Junior School (standard 3 to standard 6), and the Senior School (standard 7 to standard 12).

The subjects taught in the school are English, Mathematics, Physics, Chemistry, Biology, History, Geography, Civics, Computers, Commerce, Accountancy, Political Science, Physical Education, Business Studies, Economics etc.

In standard 11 and 12 the stream is divided into Science, Commerce and Humanities.

Several languages are taught during the vernacular language classes - Hindi, Bengali, Nepali, Tibetan, Mizo (Lushai), Dzongkha and Thai.

Discipline

The discipline of the school is looked after by the Prefects of the school, who are usually chosen from a group of standard 12 students. House captains are elected from students of standard 9 to 12 by the Senior School students by way of vote among themselves to arrange for extra co-curricular activities. Every class has a Class Captain. Junior School students are looked after by their teachers in classrooms, matrons in the hostel and guarded by the Junior School Monitors selected from a group of standard 6 students when they play outside.

Co-curricular

Co-curricular activities include football, cricket, swimming, basketball, volleyball, throwball, badminton and table tennis.

Facilities

The school has a swimming pool, a playground named the Downfield, and a Top Flat for the Junior School. There is a playground for the infant department students with swings, merry-go-rounds, slides, sea saws, and monkey ladders.

Music

Singing classes from KG to Standard 8 are taken twice a week. Piano, violin, guitar lessons are individually given. The school has a grand piano in its chapel hall, seven upright pianos in the music room and several other upright pianos in the small lounge, big lounge, and cottages. Every year several students sit for the Trinity College of Music, London grade examinations ranging from Initial to Grade 8. The School has three choirs - Infant Choir, Junior Choir and Senior Choir.

Activities

- Every Saturday morning a class presents a Chapel Play based on a theological topic. Every Saturday evening a class presents a class play.

- The school major production over the years have included My Fair Lady, The King and I, Joseph and the Amazing Technicolor Dreamcoat, The Pied Piper of Hamelin, The Sound of Music, Fiddler on the Roof, She Stoops to Conquer, H.M.S. Pinafore, Scrooge, Salad Days and many more.

- Inter-house competition is organized among the students for quiz, debate, elocution, extempore, music competition, basketball, football, swimming, and cricket.

- For the Morning Chapel Service, every day at 7:40 A.M., the school assembles at the School's Chapel Hall where they sing a hymn accompanied by the music teacher on the grand piano, a reading is done from the scripture and a short prayer is made by the Chaplain. Thereafter, the Principal of the school makes announcements for the day.

- The students take part in various activities and play against various schools in Darjeeling, Kalimpong, Kurseong and Siliguri etc.

Notable alumni:

- Altamas Kabir - Justice Altamas Kabir, Chief Justice of India and Judge, Supreme Court of India.

- Emil Wolfgang Menzel, Jr. - primatologist and Professor of Psychology.

- Tom Stoppard - English playwright, attended the school from 1943 to 1946.

(Mt. Hermon School website, 2015.)

3 The Darjeeling Disaster Of 1899

On September 24th 1899, Darjeeling was devastated by a deluge of landslides in pouring rain, which wiped out many habitations. One such incident took place in a church school with little children as boarders, which was washed away killing almost all the children. This book, *The Darjeeling Disaster*, is about the aftermath for a family who lost their children to this disaster. This is the tale about a heroic mother, Ada Lee, with a small child who made the trip from Calcutta the next day of the landslides, when Darjeeling was totally cut off and there were no roads. This book was published in 1912.

David Hiram Lee spent his student days in Ohio and came to India in 1875, working alongside William Taylor. Ada Hildegarde Jones was born in West Virginia. At the age of fourteen an aunt took her to Ohio, where she went to Scio college. After a bout of typhoid fever she is said to have had a vision where God asked her to "live for India". A few weeks later a letter arrived from a certain Mrs. Doremous of the Union Missionary Society, "stating that Dr. Thoburn, in passing through on his return to India, had handed to her Miss Jones's name as a candidate for missionary work in India."

She arrived a year later as part of the Woman's Union Mission. A fairly sensationalist article in *The Milwaukee Journal* says, "[s]he was the first woman sent by other women to save women." The same article describes her as "a spunky type" and suggests that she was following "the man of her choice half-way round the world to marry him." The details are up for verification, but the two got married in Madras in 1881, after Ada apparently was rejected in Calcutta by "neglected sufferers" and inhabitants of harems, whose souls she was trying to save. When Hiram's health started to decline, they went back to Ohio, returning to India a few years later. It was during this phase that the tragic incident took place. On 24 September 1899, six of their children, Vida, Wilbur David, Ada Eunice, Esther Dennett, Lois Gertrude, and Herbert Wilson, who were studying at Queen's Hill School in Darjeeling, were swept away to death in one single landslide. The school had its premises in a building known as Arcadia where one Miss Emma Knowles served as the first principal. It was then supposedly regarded as a branch of the Calcutta Girls' High School (this is not surprising considering the American missionary connections). The school is known today as Mount Hermon School.

Wilbur was the only one who lived to tell his parents of their last moments, but he too died within a few days of the disaster. Along with the six, claimed by the landslide was also Jessudar, a Bengali girl who had become part of the family. Jessudar, Ada Lee tells us, was born of Hindu parents.

She lost her father early in life after which the family lived in great poverty. Throughout the narrative, the missionary tone strikes one as deeply problematic, but this is only to be expected I suppose. "A wicked man" tried to buy the little girl from her mother for eight rupees (translated in the account to 2 dollars 25 cents), but her mother resisted. Soon after the family converted to Christianity through some "native Christians of the village".

One day Jessudar was carried away by the wicked man, but she was rescued and deposited with the Lee family for safety. There is a highly dramatic story of how she decided once and for all to turn to God's service, discarding symbolically the Hindu bangle that she wore. The Lee family also used run a Sunday school, where Vida taught. A couple of photographs fascinated me from Ada Lee's book. The book by Ada Lee is a disturbing read, as it contains many of the letters exchanged with the children and an account by Wilbur of the fateful event.

Following the disaster, money flowed in and enabled the founding of the Lee Mission. Dr. and Mrs. Walter Griffiths took charge of the school from the late 1930s. (The rhetoric as reported by *The Milwaukee Journal* seems to have remained as problematic as ever even post-independence.) The Lee school in Darjeeling was reported by Gordon Sinclair (special correspondent for *The Milwaukee Journal*) as one of the best in the Himalayas. At the same time, around 1949, there were 400 students and a teacher's training programme for 30 and an orphan home in the Mission in Calcutta. It is also supposed to have provided accommodation for missionaries travelling in India.

Ada survived David Hiram and died in India in 1948. She is buried at the Lower Circular Road Cemetery. For now, I am quite grateful that they allow their premises to be used for diverse activities without interference.

(Blog: Calcutta Confusion)

Tragic beginning

Jigme N. Kazi

Arcadia Girls' School, Queen's Hill School, Mt. Hermon School

When Mt. Hermon School was first founded by an American missionary, Miss Emma Knowles, in Darjeeling in 1895 it was known as Arcadia Girls' School. Three years after its founding a devastating landslide in 1899 not only killed many of its students but destroyed the school building.

The Darjeeling Disaster Of 1899

Arcadia Girls' School was supposed to have been located on the Lebong side of Darjeeling's Chowrasta (see photos). The old photo of the area of 1880 shows a similar cottage (zoomed) on this side of the hill. Take a look at this cottage and the one taken by our Founder-Principal, Miss C.J. Stahl after the tragic incident.

In 1978 I edited the school's annual 'Hermonite' magazine and Hermonite Ved Agarwal ('71 batch) and I traced the school history of this era with articles and photographs on Queen's Hill School, located above the main road near the railway station. However, we could not locate the exact spot of the old school – Arcadia Girls' School.

The building at Darjeeling, India, in which the children were killed in the landslide 1898. Phobe & Ruth Wallace, Eric Anderson Noted by Carolyn Stahl

In the 1920s the school (QHS) was expanding and needed more space and the present school area was purchased and the school was renamed Mt. Hermon School in 1929.

Folks, we must all try to locate the exact spot of "Arcadia".

This is our school, not just one building but five, strung along the hill side down to the railway. Only three are showing. It is five minutes walk to the railway station. Has almost no playground. The tall building was built in 1902. The others were then old, forty years or more. It housed the school 1900 - 1925 (Carolyn Stahl)

(Jigme N. Kazi, Facebook. Photo of QHS from Hermonite 1978, annual school magazine.)

LEST WE FORGET

4 The Lees And The Darjeeling Disaster

Mr. and Mrs. D.H. Lee with their children in 1895.

On 24 September 1899, six children of the Lee family: Vida Maud, Wilbur David, Ada Eunice, Esther Dennett, Lois Gertrude, and Herbert Wilson, who were studying at Arcadia Girls' School in Darjeeling, were swept away to death in one single landslide.

Wilbur was the only one who lived to tell his parents of their last moments, but he too died within a few days of the disaster. Along with the six, claimed by the landslide, was also Jessudar, a Bengali girl who had become part of the family.

The school had its premises in a building known as Arcadia where Miss Emma Knowles served as the first principal. The school (founded on March 11, 1895, with 13 students), which was later renamed Queen's Hill School and finally Mt. Hermon School, was regarded as a branch of the Calcutta Girls' High School.

After the tragic death of their six children, their parents, David Hiram Lee and Ada Hildergarde Jones, with the help of generous donors, founded the Lee Memorial Mission School in Calcutta.

Mt. Hermon and the Hermonites will always remember the Lee family with love and gratitude even as the school celebrates its 125th anniversary in 2020.

Excerpts from Ada Lee's *The Darjeeling Disaster, Its Bright Side: The Triumph of the Six Lee Children* (published in 1912), highlighting the six Lee children who died during the tragic disaster of September 24, 1899:

Introductory

I esteem it a personal privilege to call the attention of the reading public to *The Darjeeling Disaster: Its Bright Side*, a book telling the story of the greatest tragedy in the life of any missionary family in all the history of missions. This book has passed through several editions and now a new edition is being published. I desire to express my abiding conviction that it would be of great benefit to have this book placed in the Sunday School libraries of the Christian world. It contains a story more thrilling than fiction, but it is not fiction. It is the story of the Christian living and marvellous triumphant translation of real children. I knew them well and loved them dearly. It sets forth an ideal Christian home, in which there were active, vigorous boys and girls, and earnest Christian parents. The story of this family presents a standard of Christian living for both parents and children. I have known lively boys and girls to read and re-read this book until the pages were worn and soiled, and in so doing their lives were transformed.

The book will tell its own story, but I wish in this introductory note to tell a comforting part of the story not contained in the book and not generally known. As the book will tell, I went with the Rev. D. H. and Mrs. Lee and their baby, Frank, from Calcutta to Darjeeling as soon as it was possible after the terrible disaster. After much walking and many difficulties in getting over the parts of the mountains where the rail-road had been washed away, we reached Darjeeling early on Friday morning. Wilbur, the one boy of the family who had been picked up alive after the disaster, was in the hospital and there was some hope for recovery. Almost immediately after his mother's arrival he begged the privilege of telling the story of the disaster, the mother urging him to wait until he was feeling better, but he insisted on telling it at once.

Shortly after the story was told he was taken with tetanus. If he had not told it that day, to the great loss of the Christian world, it never would have been told. His sufferings all day Saturday, Saturday night, Sunday, and Sunday night were heartrending for those who waited by him with the helpless parents. On toward midnight Sunday, J. Campbell White, and myself were waiting with the distressed parents. Mrs. Lee had not slept since her arrival on Friday morning, and was almost exhausted. After all hope of Wilbur's recovery was gone, we persuaded Mr. and Mrs. Lee to go into an adjoining room and rest, with the promise that we would call them when the end came. A more crushed and heart-broken couple could not easily be imagined than those bereaved parents were as we saw them go out of that room for rest.

This was about midnight, about half-past two in the morning the end was drawing near, and I went to call them, but when Sister Lee re-entered the dying-room the very form of her visage was changed. Her face was radiant with a light from another world, and she told us that while lying in the room there came to her a heavenly vision. She saw heaven's glories and the heavenly throne, and the other five children come out in glorified glory to meet, greet and embrace Wilbur and escort him into the heavenly home. With the vision there was given her a spiritual illumination that seemed to lift her so far above her unspeakable sorrow that she was really in spirit dwelling with her children in heavenly palaces.

I look back to that awful night and that manifestation of abundant grace as the greatest fulfilment of the promise - "My grace is sufficient," that I have ever been privileged to witness. The losing of Wilbur, the last of the six children who went down in that disaster, was a sorrow calling for superhuman comfort, and the grace manifested was sufficient for the almost incomparable emergency. My faith was marvellously strengthened as I witnessed the consoling power of grace sufficient.

I most sincerely believe that the reading of the story of the translated Lee Children will be very helpful to the family life of the Christian world, and I heartily commend the reading of this book to parents and children throughout the nations.

Frank W. Warne
Bishop, Methodist Episcopal Church in India.

The Darjeeling Disaster

On September 24, 1899, in the landslide at Darjeeling, India, God called upon us to return to Him the jewels He had loaned us; and took away that which was dearer to us than all the world besides - our six precious children.

We had rented in Darjeeling for the season a cozy little two-storied cottage where we spent, with our children, a few happy weeks of vacation. Leaving them where we returned to Calcutta where we had bought a property for the Mission. We were busy in our Mission work and in getting the house repaired and ready for their coming. We could hardly wait for their return, but they never came back to us.

After thirty-six hours of incessant rainfall the top of Observatory Hill (now known as Mahakal Dara – editor), around which is built the city of Darjeeling, broke away. The mountain side, on which was the little cottage where our children were, slipped off carrying everything before it into the abyss below. The children saw their danger and, realizing that the house was going, made an attempt to save themselves. The night was dark, the storm raging, trees were falling and boulders rolling down the mountain-side. The rain was falling in torrents and they could not find the road, so went back to the house hoping they might be saved.

Next morning not a vestige of the house remained, and our darlings lay buried beyond the reach of man. Lois' body was found almost buried in mud and water near her. Wilbur was found still living. Four kind men carried the bruised and suffering boy to the hospital where, after an awful journey, we found him a few days afterwards. He then told us of the brave, heroic way in which they met their death and of God's faithfulness to them in taking away all fear from their hearts and causing them to rejoice in the hope of Heaven. Then, he, too, having fulfilled his mission of coming back to comfort us, left us to join the others on October 2nd, just eight days after the landslide.

The motive which prompts the sending out of this little volume is the same that led us to write a sketch of their lives in the first place, viz., a desire to extend, as long as possible, the influence of their lives in the earth, hoping that other young people through reading of them, may be led to "seek first the kingdom of God and his righteousness;" and that other parents may, with God's blessing, be helped to realize their wondrous privileges and awful responsibilities before the golden days of opportunity are gone forever.

We also desire, through this little book, to be used, if possible, in comforting those who, like us, have had the heart-breaking sorrow of giving up their little ones, by the comfort where with God in His mercy has, and continues to comfort us. We are encouraged to publish this, because several thousand of the first edition, edited by Bishop Warne, under the title "The Darjeeling Disaster Its Bright Side," have gone out into the world; also another edition, entitled "Seven Heroic Children," gotten out by Morgan & Scott, of London, is nearly exhausted, and during the years we have had and continue to have letters telling of the help these sketches, under God's blessing, have been to others leading some to conversion, strengthening others in their Christian life, and comforting many a sorrowing mother.

The editor of the London edition asked us why, in writing the sketch of Vida's life, we had included her conflicts and sometime failures? My answer was, I must write of them as they really were a true story, or not at all. These sketches were written just after they left us, when the life of each was intensely vivid, when their sayings and actions and affectionate caresses were so a part of life, that I felt often, I could not live without them.

I have been thankful for having done as I was prompted, I believe, by God's Spirit. As Vida's struggles and victories have encouraged and helped many another who found it difficult to live the Christ life, and like her, has been led to triumph by faith in Jesus to save and keep. I wish hereto testify to the never-failing grace of God, which is sufficient for any sorrow and has sustained me during the years.

He, in mercy, spared to me my husband and "Baby Frank," who helped us to live and who seemed to think it his mission in life to cheer and comfort us. During that terrible march to Darjeeling, to reach Wilbur, he was our companion. Bishop Warne wrote of him at the time in the following words: "We came to a break in the railway line over which the ponies could not pass. We scrambled up the mountain side on our hands and feet and then picked our way over boulders and through slush down to the road again.

When we began to travel thus, a novel and interesting method was devised for carrying 'Baby Frank.' A little coolie girl who carries bundles on her back up the mountains, was secured, who had an inverted cone-shaped basket, which we cushioned with an over coat, and 'Baby Frank' sat in this, with his laughing-face above the brim. Throughout the journey this little man proved himself an excellent traveller, and soothed his parents with his smiles and baby talk. At this stage he appeared to the best advantage; for notwithstanding his new surroundings and mode of conveyance, he was full of fun, screaming with laughter, and kept one of us busy watching, that, in his dancing, baby glee, he did not jump out of his basket."

Two years later, in the same dark month of September, God gave us another bright, laughing baby boy - "Albert the good," as a friend called him. He has also greatly cheered and helped us. God has also given us numbers of forsaken and famine-stricken children to care for, and a great work to do for Jesus, which has given us no time to waste in thinking of ourselves and brooding over our own sorrow.

God has raised up innumerable friends, the salt of the earth, who have faithfully stood by us and aided us in the work we love. We wish also to praise Him for the commodious mission building he has given us large enough to house three hundred children, and which furnishes a comfortable home for us and a half dozen other missionaries. This building is called "The Lee Memorial," being dedicated to the memory of those dear children who expected to work with us for the salvation of India. They are working with us and seem very near to us, and maybe have accomplished more for Christ on the earth, in the higher service, than if their lives had been spared.

God has also given us those who faithfully work with us for the salvation of the people of India, and who have done much to comfort us in our home life. So we can say from our hearts: there has not failed one word of His good promises. We still go forward, our faces toward the "Morning Land," knowing that "there we will understand," and will prove that it was for some great purpose that He took our darlings and that it was best. "I know whom I have believed and am persuaded that he is able to keep that which I have committed unto him against that day."

"God knows the way He holds the key,
He guides us with unerring hand;
Sometimes with tearless eyes we'll see;
Yes, there, up there, we'll understand."

5 The Six Lee Children

In her book, *The Darjeeling Disaster, Its Bright Side: The Triumph of the Six Lee Children*, Ada Lee vividly describes her six children – Vida Maud, Wilbur David, Ada Eunice, Esther Dennett, Lois Gertrude, and Herbert Wilson – who died during the tragic disaster of September 24, 1899:

Vida Maud

In the clear morning of that other country
In paradise
With the same face that we have loved and cherished
She shall arise.
Let us be patient we who mourn, with weeping,
Her vanished face.
The Lord has taken but to add more beauty
And a diviner grace.
And we shall find once more beyond earth's sorrows
Beyond those skies.
In the fair city of the sure foundation
These heavenly eyes.

Vida Maud

The name of our first born, Vida Maud, would have been David had she been a boy. A friend suggested the feminine of David, which is Vida, so her name is that of her father's, and the pronunciation suggests the country of her birth - the Land of the Vedas. She opened her eyes first in a little mud cottage in the beautiful city of Bangalore, July 26, 1882. She was dedicated to God at her birth, and again publicly in baptism, September 10, the Rev. Ira A. Richards officiating.

She went to America with her parents, her—father being very ill, starting when only seven months old, by sailing vessel. The moon and the stars and the sea-birds were her first friends, in all of which she took a lively interest. After nearly four months on board she landed in the noisy bustle of New York City, which so frightened and bewildered her that she never was happy while there excepting the day we returned to the ship where she saw her friends, the sailors, and the only home she knew the dear old vessel which had brought her safely through many a storm.

She began her missionary work in travelling from place to place with her father and mother while they were speaking on India. After a few months she settled down as a preacher's baby, who is usually the centre of much loving attention and kind thought.

When only three years old her grandfather, who lived with us, and of whom she was very fond, died. As the funeral passed out of the church and she saw her grandma leaning on her father's arm weeping, she ran up to her, and catching her by the dress, called out, "Don't cry, grandma, Vida will take care of you now." Her little heart was almost broken to see her grandma's grief.

From infancy she was a child very difficult to control. One of strong passion, with a temper beyond any power to subdue, and yet a child with a most affectionate nature and of sterling honesty. She hated falsehood and deception with all the powers of her being.

Many times we knew not what to do, and confessed our inability to guide and control this strange child, and earnestly prayed for the day when Vida should find Jesus and the new nature He alone could impart. This was constantly kept before her, and she, too, became desperate about herself, and often sought earnestly. That blessed day came, and she was converted at a camp meeting held at Mountain Lake Park, Maryland, July 2, 1893, when eleven years old.

She and her sister Lois, two years younger, at an invitation for seekers, knelt at the altar together. The first meeting closed without her getting into the light. She came home deeply convicted of sin, and after prayer together and a bit of instruction she returned to the afternoon service and again went to the altar. She was brightly converted, and testified before a large audience to Jesus' saving power. Her face beamed with joy, and many hearts were moved by her sweet, childish testimony. She was a changed girl from that time, although she had much to contend with, and it was no easy thing for her to live out her high ideal of what a Christian life should be.

Shortly after this, in a holiness meeting, she sought definitely for the blessing of sanctification, and no one who knew her ever doubted her receiving it. Her joyous, childish simplicity in it only made her a greater blessing to others. She did not always retain this blessed experience, but she was never satisfied without it.

A young man, a backslider, came to that convention so dejected that he was almost in despair and ready to take his own life. He was a perfect stranger, but the child noticed his sad, hopeless face, and went to him with so much joy that the man was overpowered by her influence.

"You look so sad." she said; "it's because you want Jesus. Come along with me and find Him."

He went forward as a seeker, and never left the place of prayer until he too was happy in Jesus. He wrote of this to us after our return to India, saying he could not resist her, and that he felt she had been the means of his salvation.

She went to school but little in America, and found it difficult to get along with her studies, but being desirous of having a good education, she became a persevering student. She was especially fond of history and mathematics. She was also a great lover of the beautiful in nature as well as in character. Flowers and ferns were her delight; buttercups, daisies and wild flowers being special favorites. She had a passion for music and motion, and had she been thrown into such surroundings in her younger years she might have been led away by gaiety, dancing and dress.

She was a splendid letter writer for one of her age, and could write most interesting letters.

At twelve years of age she returned to India with her parents and soon entered on her school duties with a persistency which showed that she would win in the end. She had dedicated herself to God for mission work, so took up the study of the Bengali language, and living with the Bengali girls in our school she soon understood and spoke it very well. She was also able to read and write it. For a year she had been helping in mission work.

She had been conducting a native Sunday school, taking two of our Bengali girls with her to help in teaching the children. After the Sunday school she would go into the homes among the women and talk and sing with them. Her Sunday school numbered seventy-five children. She loved the children and women very much. They afterward gathered around and asked for her, and wondered why she did not come to them. She also helped me in the prayer meetings among the girls, and we had looked forward to her help in after years. She, at her own request, had been appointed the Sabbath school superintendent for the next year. How can we do without her!

The following is an extract from an unfinished letter written to a friend in America which we found in her writing desk:

"I am vice-president of our Epworth League and head of the Spiritual Department and working for the conversion of the young people."

"I know I am right with God myself, and do want others to feel the sweet peace I have in following Christ. There are very few young people who profess the baptism of the Holy Ghost. There are a good many converted, but they don't know that there is a higher life for them."

"I was talking of our English girls, but there are several of the girls in mamma's school (native girls) who have found that place in Jesus."

"I do want to tell you about a little Sunday school which mamma opened away out in a village where the people are very poor. I call this my Sunday School. I go there now on Sundays. First, we open with a hymn; and you should hear those dear children try to join us, one making awful faces, another holding the notes too long in one place and racing in another place, while most all are flat; but it is so touching. They are all little boys and girls, some with only a little cloth tied about their waists. We then have prayer, and it is pretty hard to keep their little tongues quiet and their eyes shut. I take two Bengali girls with me; then two boys from the boys' school come and help us.

"After the prayers we have the lesson; then the children receive a picture card. We use hundreds of picture cards every year — what a pity so many are lying unused in people's drawers at home."

"While Sunday school is going on, I take one of the girls and go to visit the zenanas where we meet such nice *bos* (young wives), and we sing and give them the lesson also. It is so nice, but I feel very sorry for the poor people, and wish that I could help them."

Vida was an earnest Bible student, — read her Bible from real enjoyment of it. She often read it as some girls read novels, — sitting down and finishing a whole book without putting it aside.

She at other times carried out prescribed plans for Bible study; was always anxious to attend Bible readings, working out subjects suggested, and had many verses memorized and their places fixed. The most enjoyable hour of the day of late years has been the evening hour, spent with the other members of the family in music, and in calling up old texts and learning new ones. Vida played the violin, but her special instrument was the guitar. She played sweetly, often accompanying with her voice, which was so adapted to its soft music.

Her sister Lois was the organist; and the two boys with their violins, together with Vida and Lois with their instruments, often formed a quartet whose home concerts made the evenings a delight. Now there is a blank in our home which can never again be filled. How perfectly they must play and sing together now! The piece which Vida and Lois often sang together, Lois singing the alto, was:

> *"In our Father's blessed keeping*
> *I am happy, safe and free:*
> *While His eye is on the sparrow*
> *I shall not forgotten be."*

Vida's plaintive soprano rings in our ears yet. They all sang together so often, "Behold the Bridegroom comes, be ready," "When the Roll is called up yonder I'll be there," these being the favorites of the boys. A favorite, and one sung so much during the past year, was, "Peace, Perfect Peace," and "There'll be no dark valley when Jesus comes," and "We'll never say goodbye in Heaven."

Oh, those darling children! How can we ever do without them! Some days the dreadful silence seems unbearable; but in the morning we will have them all again, praise His name.

For the encouragement of others trying to overcome evil dispositions and to live a true Christian life, there are many things in Vida's diary which should be known. In her diary for 1896; three years before she left us, she had written:

April 1st. "Had a nice talk with mamma. I am going to try to be a better girl and let my light shine. — 'Let your light so shine before men that they may see your good works.'"

May 5. "I solemnly promise, with God's help, to never speak another unkind word as long as I live. People may think it impossible, but I do believe with all my heart what God says: 'Things which are impossible with man are possible with God,' so I go to Him. . . .God helping me, I try. V. Lee."

She did pass; also passed her eighth standard in the final examination, to her great delight. This year (1998) she was taking the two years' course of high school examination in the one, and had set her heart on passing the "high school" in November, 1899, and the Entrance Examination of the Calcutta University the following March.

Vida from her childhood always had special love for old people. She liked to be with them, and in nearly every place we have had a home, she has had some old, blind or helpless person whom she visited regularly. When only five years old there was a crippled saint of His, to whom she and Lois used to carry their little basket of fruit, or flowers, or some other dainty, regularly. When only ten years old she used to take her Testament every Sunday afternoon and go over and read to an old blind lady.

Many of these old friends, we believe, gave them a warm welcome that night when the angels carried them through the gates of heaven. She was anxious that her old friend in Calcutta might be visited while she was away.

We all went to Darjeeling together, May 1, this year (1899), after much prayer about the selection of the house, and when we saw the beautiful two-storied building covered with ivy and surrounded with lovely flowers, we thanked God for selecting us such a beautiful place.

As we rejoiced over it, how little we thought it was to be our darlings' tomb, and that with this beautiful spot should perish our happy earthly home with so many of its delights. During the two months we remained Vida seemed to grow more affectionate and cling to her mother, and so much of the time wished to be with me.

About two weeks before I returned to Calcutta, she seemed so disturbed about herself, because she sometimes spoke impatiently and unkindly to the others.

One day she said, "Mamma, I feel I must get the victory over this habit, or I fear I will lose my religion. I must get back that blessing I once had, of full salvation, or I fear I will lose all."

I said, "Yes, Vida, you must get a victory or your life will be ruined. Why not get it today?"

It was Sunday, and neither she nor I were very well, so, while the others went to church, we got our Bibles and had a blessed search together.

After selecting a number of His promises on which to lean, we got down before Him and poured out our hearts to Him. We together sought for the fullness of His love.

Oh! that blessed hour together. I fear I did not fully realize all it meant. As we finished, I said, "Vida, dear, do you take your Saviour in all His fullness and trust Him to keep you at all times?"

"Yes, mamma, I do. I trust never to let go of Him again."

She arose so comforted and threw her arms about me, calling me her "sweet little mamma" (for she was so much taller than I and bigger in every way that of late this had become a favorite expression of hers — "my little mamma"), pressing her cheek to mine with a caress I shall never forget.

The next three weeks, which were my last with them, she was gentle and loving, and so helpful in every way that the joy of those days will linger until I clasp that dear, brave girl in my arms again in the Homeland.

After much prayer we decided that it was best to leave the children with Vida while we returned to our work in Calcutta, as we were buying property and altering the house there which would require three or four months.

It was so hard for us to leave them, but the children were so happy going to school together, and Vida was so proud of being trusted in charge of them, and all were so sure they could get on nicely together.

I remember the last night; I could hardly sleep, and kept praying that if it was not the right thing to leave them, the Lord would show us so plainly we could not be mistaken. I decided, should the Lord send us, before the train left that morning, a good cook-woman to stay with them night and day, I would go; if not, I would remain until we could make other arrangements. Next morning a nice hill woman came, and everything was arranged and we came away.

Vida and Lois fixed our tiffin, and then came to the station. I remember how erect and brave Vida looked as she bade us goodbye at the station, and how I had to harden my heart and call up all the courage I had, to leave them.

Many regrets have since come, but He whom we have always trusted, Who promises to lead in the way we shall go and to guide with His eye, must have guided us in leaving them, and it was a part of His great plan to prepare them for the higher work for which He felt He must take them at any cost.

Their papa returned in August and spent three delightful weeks with them, taking Esther back; whom it seemed advisable to leave with her brothers and sisters until we got settled. It was arranged even after her papa's return, to bring her down, but Vida felt it was so much better for her to remain, and we yielded. Sometimes we can hardly bear the regret for this decision, but the Lord had need of this dear child, too, and we believe we will understand why by and by.

By and by when our work here is finished
And the gates of the city appear,
And the beautiful songs of the Angels
Float out on our listening ear.
When all that now seems so mysterious,
Will be bright and as clear as the day.
Then the toils of the road will seem nothing
When we get to the end of the way.

Lois Gertrude

Lois, "Timothy's Grandmother," as she called herself — was born in Freeport, Ohio, U.S.A., July 2, 1884, and was baptized by our presiding elder, Dr. E. Hingsley, August 10. After the dear old man had baptized her he put her again in my arms, saying, "As Pharaoh's daughter said to Moses' mother, so the Lord says to you: 'Take this child away and nurse it for me, and I will give thee thy wages.'"

From that moment the care of this child became a sacred trust, a special work for God, and what a sweet, blessed work it has been. How I did enjoy that darling girl. She never gave me one hour of sorrow, not one moment of anxiety, in all the fifteen beautiful years of her life. She was our joy and sunshine, our never-failing comfort. Can it be possible any one so real, so full of life, so a part of my life, could be dead? Oh, I am so thankful she is not dead, only just crossed over ahead of us, and is living, rejoicing, and loving us just the same today.

Lois Gertrude

But the greatest wonder of all is that we still live and she gone. I had for a long time thought I could never part with her, not even for a few years to allow her to finish her education. I said over and over again, "It will kill me to send her home." The Lord knew He could not trust me to tell me beforehand what he intended to do, but did it without our knowledge; for our darlings were nearly twenty-four hours in heaven before we knew they had gone.

How can I portray her sweet, beautiful life! Oh, that I could tell the half of what her life was to us! She was unlike any other child we had. I seldom ever had to reprove her, and when it was necessary, just the mention of her fault was enough, and it nearly broke her heart to think she had done wrong or had in any way displeased us. Her sister Vida used to say, "Oh, it's nothing for Lois to do right; she is naturally good; but it means something when I succeed."

When our Lois was a baby, even then she was no trouble, and was so quiet and gentle. The winter she was a year and a half old I taught a Sunday school class. Every Sabbath morning, I would go into the Sunday school room and find the seats arranged for the class, with two chairs side by side facing it — one for myself and one for Baby Lois. Placing her in one she would sit quietly without a word for an hour, until I had finished my work; and yet she was anything but pokey. At other times she would run and romp: and play equal to any of them.

She was very bright and quick in her lessons as a little girl, and began the study of music when but seven years old. She used to play the organ for family prayers when her little feet could hardly reach the pedals. Her music was more the result of everyday home practice rather than constant work under a professor. She had about three terms of lessons at different times with the best professors to be had, but it was the everyday practice, and her playing for prayers and our times of singing in the evening in our home, that made music such an easy thing for her.

There were many girls who had taken more lessons, and upon whom more had been spent, who could not begin to play as well, in fact, who seemed unable to play much sacred music; but it was in this that Lois felt at home. I say this to encourage some parents who may regret not having the money to give their children a musical education. It is surprising what can be done by oneself in the home to stimulate in the children a taste for music, even though not a professional musician.

I believe we as parents are more responsible for our children's so-called talents than we think, and our children are much more what we make them than any of us has any idea. I loved music so much, though I had no special musical education, and I so longed for our children to be musicians. I used to sing a great deal myself, avid each baby that came was sung to sleep night after night. But we were disappointed to find that Vida and Lois seemed to have no gift in that direction. I tried to teach them the simple child-song, "Jesus loves me," singing it to them daily, and having them repeat strains with me, but they were neither of them ever able to carry a tune until Vida was about nine years old. At last they began to sing; and to play, and how rejoiced we were.

We had a desire that each should choose and learn to play a different instrument, and after the two girls could read notes they made their choice, Vida taking the guitar as hers, and Lois the piano and organ. We afterwards gave our boys each a violin, and by keeping them all at it a little each day they had become able to play a number of pieces together in such a way as to be a great joy to us. The evening hour of music was my rest hour, and their papa's interest in their music had much to do with cheering them on over the hard places.

It is wonderful what an effect even a child's toys will have in moulding the child, and the bent in life is often had from some familiar object seen daily or used in childhood. I have known instances where a desire to go to sea had been kindled in a boy's heart by the picture of a ship which hung on a wall in the home; also, a thirst for war and to be a soldier, by pictures of battles. If so, how careful we should be in choosing even our pictures and picture books for the home.

We found that our children got a love for the Bible in the same way. Illuminated wall-texts — very beautiful ones — were hung in the family room for this purpose, and those special texts they learned before they could speak plainly. They could tell where each text was to be found and also learned to love it, it being associated with their daily lives…

Lois, like the rest, was passionately fond of flowers. When a wee child she used to watch for the first dandelions and white clover. With the latter they used to weave great wreaths and play with them every day. Buttercups and daisies were her delight, and many were the offerings brought home to me, and a bouquet I must always wear, pinned on with her own hands. Pansies and chrysanthemums were other favorites of hers. Her favorite fruit, flowers, books and songs — all seem to suggest to us our great loss. Her songs we feel we can never sing without her, and everything about us seems changed because of her absence.

She was a natural elocutionist, and many were the home entertainments which she helped to make delightful with her witty or touching recitations, — one moment making us laugh with delight, and the next, cry. If this talent had been specially cultivated, certainly she would have excelled in it.

She was a most tender-hearted girl, and could not bear to give pain or see anyone in distress. This only increased as she grew older. She was converted in July, 1893, when but nine years old. She had been attending a meeting for children, at which her sister Vida had given herself to Jesus a few days before. Lois did not seem to have anything to repent of, as we could see, and we thought she was all right; but one evening on coming in from some gathering, instead of finding all the children asleep as I had expected, I found them in a great commotion.

Wilbur met me in his night-clothes, and said, "Mamma, what's the matter with Lois? She woke us up singing, and now she is laughing and crying." I went to her room and found her rejoicing in a most natural, childlike way. She threw her arms around my neck, her face just beaming with the light of heaven, and said, "Now, mamma, I'm ready to go to India, or anywhere God wants me to go." From that time, she reckoned herself a child of God, and was always ready to testify or pray in her sweet, child-like way. We have often known her to work for the conversion of others, praying for persons by name.

She and her sister Vida, although such opposites in disposition, were from childhood devoted to one another. They were together in everything, one not being able to enjoy anything without the other. If one's doll was broken, the doll of the other was carefully put away until the broken one was replaced. A box of sweets could not be enjoyed until the other one had them, too. One seemed to be the complement of the other. I am glad they were saved the sorrow of separation.

Lois was, as we called her, grandmother to all the children, and had a wonderful motherly way with the little ones, which was a great help in the home. She always said she was going to study medicine and be our medical missionary, a saying which during the last year or two had grown into a deep conviction. She loved her Bible, and read many chapters daily, as her diary shows, and had many uncommon verses which she had memorized and could tell where they were. She had special verses for every day in the month, and often gave us her "find" for the day. On the 9th of May, 1898, I find in her diary this entry, — "My verses for today are Matt. 9:29: 'According to your faith be it unto you'; Mark: 'Jesus said, if thou canst believe, all things are possible with him that believeth,' and 2 Cor. 9:8, 'God is able to make all grace abound toward you.'"

Once, when I was talking to them about their education, and regretting that we had not the money to send them home to finish their schooling, she said, "Mamma, 'the Lord is able to give thee much more than this;' this is my verse in 2 Chron. 25:9." Since that day it has been one of my anchor texts.

In her diary for 1896, we find several notes of great interest to us, such as, "My text for this week is, 'Blessed are those servants whom the Lord, when he cometh, shall find watching,' and in another place, 'I am sorry I was naughty today; I will try and never be so again'; "Believe on the Lord Jesus Christ and thou shalt be saved."

The following gives us a glimpse into her inner life: "I have been trying to be good and get full marks this week in conduct and in everything (this was about her school life). One of the girls put my name down when I never spoke, so one mark is off already. Mamma is away to the South Villages, so we all have to be mamma, and are trying our best. I read Psalm 20. I must go to bed now; so good-night, my dear old diary."

On her birthday in 1898, we find these verses, taken for the last year of her life, — Isaiah 54:10, 14: "For the mountains shall depart and the hills be removed, but my kindness shall not depart from thee, neither shall the covenant of my peace be removed, saith the Lord that hath mercy on thee."

The fourteenth verse is underscored: "In righteousness shall they be established. Thou shalt be far from oppression, for thou shalt not fear; and from terror, for it shall not come near thee."

These seem to us like prophecies fulfilled in her death. The mountains did depart, and the hills were removed, but I believe the Lord's kindness did not depart from that dear girl, and it was in the keeping of His covenant of peace that he snatched her out of the destruction caused by the fury of the elements on that awful night, and this prophecy was literally fulfilled in saving her from the fear and terror in the hour of death. He folded her in His loving arms and bore her away to be forever with Him.

A part of her diary for 1899 was dug out of the ruins. It has a few characteristic entries.

On June 1st, we read, "Today I made out a routine, and mean to keep it with God's help. I took the daily prayer-meeting this afternoon at the school. My verse was, 'Call upon me and I will answer thee and show thee great and mighty things which thou knowest not.'"

June 2nd. "I did not go to school today as it was very rainy, but wrote letters instead. I found out that my great-grandfather on mamma's side was a Methodist preacher; my grandpa on papa's side was a (local) Methodist preacher; my honorable dad is a Methodist preacher, and my kids will most likely be Methodist preacher's kids." This last shows how full of wit and mischief she was. No girl ever got more joy out of life than she.

She afterwards writes of the Fourth of July they had together, and the state dinner, as they called it, which they cooked and served themselves, having invited their principal, Miss Stahl, and Flora (her friend), to dine with them.

Her spiritual life seemed to develop rapidly this year, and to her joyousness there seemed no bounds. She had a way of getting around her papa; in fact, every one. It was difficult for anyone to refuse a request she made. She seemed to make only reasonable ones, and had such a loving, irresistible way about her that we would deny ourselves anything to please her. And gladly would we have given our lives to have saved her from pain and death.

Oh, how cruel it seems that her bright life should have been crushed out and that dear form bruised and mangled. Just think — thrown nearly 200 feet down the mountain side and found buried in the sand, all but her pretty white hand. She was dug out by friends, and carried to where kind strangers prepared her for the burial.

Then from the spot where she had often heard the Word of God, and had played the organ for Sunday school, and united her voice in the singing of the beautiful hymns of praise — from the little church in the hills, they bore her all covered with her favourite chrysanthemum, and laid her away, long before we could reach her. No "good-bye, mamma," nor parting word.

But our hearts would break should we dwell on this part of this awful mystery. So we try to drive it away and think only of her glorified spirit, happy with God in Heaven.

She wrote just a few weeks before: "Mamma — you have written to all the rest, but not to me for a long time. I think you have forgotten you have me." The thought of not having her would kill me — and the future without our darlings is so dark and dismal that today we feel we can never face tomorrow. But as we turn from the busy whirl of life to see the sunset each day, we say to ourselves: It is one day less until we shall go to them, — one day nearer home.

As we think of Christmas without them, it seems impossible for us to ever live through that once joyous tide again — and we catch ourselves breathing the prayer, "Come Lord Jesus, come not only for our sakes — but for others — and make this sad world glad. Usher in the time John spoke of when he said, "Behold the Tabernacle of God is with men, and he will dwell with them and they shall be his people, and God himself shall be with them and be their God. And God shall wipe away all tears from their eyes, and there shall be no more death, neither sorrow nor crying, neither shall there be any more pain, for the former things are passed away."

In her writing desk we found the following in her own handwriting. Surely her ambitions have been realized and she is now all she hoped to be.

> "My ambitions in life: —
> To be gentle and loving and loved by all.
> To have my secret hopes fulfilled.
> To be able to play the organ and piano perfectly.
> To be a doctor.
> To be the perfect model of a true woman."
>
> Lois Lee
> March 6, 1899.

How perfectly she must play and sing now. I remember on two occasions — once on my birthday anniversary, I was awakened from a sound sleep, by Vida playing her guitar at the door of my room. Another time, only a year ago, I had gone to sleep earlier than usual, and was awakened by Lois playing on the piano and she and Vida singing so sweetly.

I thought, at first, I was in Heaven — so sweet were the sounds, that it seemed the angels were singing. Tears of joy flowed down my cheeks. Methinks one day I will be thus awakened by their music, and will open my eyes in Heaven with them all about me — each one trying to be first to greet me.

> *When I shall meet with those that I have loved,*
> *Clasp in my arms the dear ones long removed,*
> *And find how faithful Thou to me hast proved,*
> *I shall be satisfied.*
>
> — Horatius Bonar

Wilbur David

Wilbur David

Wilbur was my little Samuel — asked of God. Mr. Lee's health had failed the year before, and he had to give up preaching and take a year's rest. I remember the test to our faith when the last of our year's salary came in and there was no prospect of more for another year. We had always given God His tenth. Should we tithe this, which was all we had, and it not half enough to support us and our two little girls for the three months ahead of us, let alone a whole year?

We hesitated only a moment, then said, "If we use God's tenth it will be taking what does not belong to us. It would also be doubting Him who has never failed us. We must live up to our principles." So we took the usual part and gave it to the Lord's work, as we had always done. It was not two weeks afterwards until God sent us, from a most unexpected source, ten times as much as we had given, and we were able to take the year's rest. This was one of the great lessons of my life. I never was afraid after that to take out our tenth for the Lord, even if it was our last penny. The Lord keeps His accounts balanced, and gives back in gospel measure. Mr. Lee was soon well and strong again, but our going back to India seemed doubtful.

On August 26th, 1886, (the year we were resting) in Mountain Lake Park, Maryland, U.S.A., Wilbur was born. How delighted we were with our Boy Baby! We gladly dedicated him to God for India, but soon after, he took ill, and was so ill, that he came near dying. Day and night he cried until it was almost unbearable. He was not able to retain nourishment, and went down, down every day until he was nothing but a skeleton. We called in an old doctor, who did everything that could be done. Finally, he told us nothing could save the child, and it was only a question of a few days, and then he left us.

Still I worked with the little fellow, hoping and praying, but he grew worse, until he weighed less than five pounds, and the skin seemed to dry on his bones. He was the most wretched sight I ever saw. For three months I never slept more than two hours at a time, and then usually with him in my arms. Many times I have prayed over him all night.

Finally, one morning after such a night, I laid him down to go and get the others something to eat. Suddenly the plaintive wail ceased, and I rushed back to my baby to find his eyes set, his arms and legs stiff, and he dying, as I thought. I took him in my arms and prayed for grace to give him up.

His papa said, "Shall I baptize him and name him before he dies?" I said "Yes," and not asking each other about the name, his papa took him in his arms and baptized him, calling him Wilbur. Although unable to draw his tongue into his mouth all day, still he lived.

Some kind friend came in to watch with him, and they sent me off to rest. While praying and waiting before God, I heard a little cry, and went to my baby, to find the change had come, and he was able to take nourishment. I got out his clothes again and went to work nursing him, saying to his papa, "Never mind; he'll live to be a man yet." A few days later an abscess seemed to break and come away, and the little fellow, although he looked to be a cripple, grew strong and became a nice, hearty child.

The old infidel doctor said: "If this child lives I will believe there is a God." When Wilbur was ten months old, I met him on the street one day, and he looking on our fat, bonny boy, said, "Well, I have seen one miracle in my life; there must be a God."

A year or two later Wilbur came nearly being washed away by a wave on the shore of Lake Erie. I caught him by the dress just as he was being swept under the water. He has had several other narrow escapes. Two or three times in his life he had been very ill, and we were very anxious about him; but I was always so sure he had a special mission that I never feared but that his life would be spared. Can it be he was born for the Darjeeling disaster? Was that his mission?

There is something mysterious about prayer. We are told it wields a wonderful power with God. I have had many wrestlings with God in prayer for the dear ones and the work, and great victories. Is it not strange that in this one awful hour of their lives we did not even know of their danger, and had no chance with God in prayer for them? Surely, this was also a part of His purpose.

After his recovery I added the name David to Wilbur, for his papa, and especially for the meaning — beloved of the Lord; and never was a boy dearer to his mother, too, than he.

I found him, when very young, a boy who could entertain himself. Always building little sand-houses, making mills and light-houses, and even to the last, always inventing play engines and machines, building forts and equipping them.

He was also ingenious in inventing or discovering ways of doing things. We noticed this on the last day of his life. When he could not get his jaws apart so as to drink from a glass or cup and we were all wondering what to do for him, he said, "Mamma, if I had a straw I could suck the water through it," and acting on this suggestion we got a glass tube with a rubber attached, and he was able to take nourishment for many hours. Then when he could no longer swallow such quantities, he suggested a sponge, and the dear boy used this to the last.

When the two brothers were old enough to play together, they seemed perfectly happy in each other's company. This was a great protection to both. Friends used to criticise our policy; for we never allowed them on the street, or to play with other boys. I have been told that in thus doing I was totally unfitting them for life's battles.

But I knew our Wilbur was so quick to imitate, that until stronger I must shield him from the sin about him, — this policy I would practice if I had a hundred boys.

He also learned at home; never having gone to school until eight years of age, so I am sure the boy never heard an oath until he was about nine years old, and then he did not know what it meant. When it was explained to him he thought it was an awful thing, and his whole nature revolted against the use of profane language.

He was naturally a brave boy, and I have known him to stand any amount of jeers and taunts rather than to do a mean thing. I was his confidant, as every mother should be to her son. There would not be so many boys go wrong if every mother insisted on knowing where her boy was and all about what he was doing, from the time of his infancy. She would be able to save him from many a snare, and I believe if we begin in time — we mothers — we can build so strongly around our boys' hearts that Satan and all his powers cannot invade successfully our domain.

He was frequently asked about how each hour was spent while out of the house, and was so in the habit of telling me everything, that should he do wrong or engage in anything he had been requested to keep from his mother, his conscience so troubled him, he could not long endure it without telling me all about it. He was also a great protection to his younger brother. Many a time the one might have been unable to withstand the temptation alone.

About a year ago some boys were trying to get him to fight another, and because he would not, called him a coward. He answered, "I am not a coward, but I was taught that it was wrong to fight; besides, this boy is smaller than I am, and a Bengali boy. I could never do so mean a thing as to hurt such a boy," and he took the sneers and cuffs of the boys, but would not yield.

He hated dishonesty and cruelty, and felt most indignant toward anyone who had robbed a bird's nest or injured a young bird. I have known them to hide and protect nests from other boys until the birds were ready to fly. Should any one destroy one of these birds he would cry bitterly; he could not bear to see anything suffer.

Notwithstanding this, he was a great, rollicking boy, full of play and mischief, even boisterous at times; but the moment he was alone with me, a place he liked so much to be, he was as gentle and manly as a boy could be, always ready to help me in whatever I was doing, — cooking, sewing, or whatever it might be. "Mamma, can't I help you?" rang out so merrily on my ears that the words themselves seemed to do half the work and lift the burden from everything. He was my right hand.

Oh! the companionship! I think we were more together than the others. His eyes not being very strong, I had always read much to him, and used to help him in his lessons, so that every day we had one or two hours alone together.

How I used to enter into their play. He and his brother were both very fond of soldiers, and much of their play was in imitation of them, — marching and drilling with all sorts of uniforms and make-believe swords and guns. The two little sisters were always ready to join in with all sorts of tin pans and broken bottles for drums and bugles, with streamers and flags flying — the trophies of many a battle.

In their play during the year of 1898, the Spanish were routed and Manila taken many times over. How fitting it was for the brave men of the Munster Regiment at Darjeeling to carry our boy to his last resting place! There were no others whom he would have preferred.

Wilbur, too, was a singer, and of late years his voice had become very strong and musical. He was also learning the violin, and played several pieces very well. One of his special songs was. "The hand-writing on the wall;" others, "Tell it to Jesus," and, "Someone will enter the pearly gates, Shall you, shall I?"

He was very fond of visiting the hospital and taking flowers and papers to the sick, and enjoyed distributing tracts.

I find an entry in Vida's diary of last year, as follows: "We were out in the square this evening, the boys distributing tracts as usual."

"Wilbur gave a gentleman one, and he, making fun, said, 'Where will this ticket take me, my lad?'"

"To heaven, I hope," said Wilbur, and walked on.

He was a very sociable boy. He liked to meet people, and had many friends among young and old. He had such a gentle way with little children, and he knew how to win them. Then, too, he was so full of play. He could amuse and interest others.

He was a great boy to tell stories and incidents, and if he ran out of those he actually knew, invented one for the occasion — such as a shipwreck.

If I would say, "Why, Wilbur, where did you read that interesting story?"

He would answer, "I did not read it, mamma; it's just one I made."

When I suggested a doubt as to its being the thing to do, he would say, "Why, mamma, people imagine these stories and write them in books; what harm is it for me to imagine a shipwreck and tell it to others?" Herbert would listen to him by the hour.

While he was a natural boy and enjoyed boys' toys and games, he was also very fond of dolls and girls' play. Only two years ago he was very ill, and had to be in bed two or three weeks. One of our missionary's daughters came to see him, and said, "Wilbur, what can I do for you? What can I send you?"

"Have you not a lot of dolls?" he said, "suppose you send me one of them."

She sent him one dressed as a sailor-boy. He then coaxed me for a wife for his sailor. A few days afterwards he saw a beautiful little baby doll only about three inches long, and said, "Let me have that for a baby for my sailor-boy; then I will have a whole family." These he kept among his treasures to be brought out whenever little friends came in, and we found them still among his things after he was gone.

He was very quick to understand that boys are sometimes unwelcome guests. He and his brother had a lady friend who often invited them to her place, and always seemed glad to see them. I overheard Wilbur remark one day concerning this friend, "She is a fine lady. She does not think boys are in the way."

Herbert chimed in and said, "Yes, and she knows what boys like, too."

Then "Hip! Hip! Hurray for Miss G!!" and all, little and big, joined in the three cheers.

Wilbur was very fond of flowers and ferns. He delighted in the mountains, and was continually finding some new flower or leaf to bring home to me. What jolly times they had climbing and racing! Could other children ever have a grander time together than they? During their two months' vacation, each hot season, for four years, they roamed those dear old hills over and over from Kurseong to Darjeeling! Oh! the freedom and the enjoyment of those times! Is it possible these days are gone forever?

This last year was also one full of joy. In spite of the excessive rains they would have their picnics and outings and days with their ponies, often coming home drenched. Wilbur was one to propose their staying up at the hills during the hot weather while we were getting their home ready for them in Calcutta, and he took no little share of the responsibility about the house. He looked after things, and he and Herbert did all the buying and keeping them in food. He was so helpful and kind that Vida often spoke of it in her letters.

He was also happy in his school relations, and seemed to be studying hard. In my last letter to him I said, "If you pass your examination this year, Wilbur, papa and I are going to give you a bicycle," the thing he so much coveted. He replied how pleased he was as he had so long wished for one, and assuring me he was trying to win it.

"But," he said, "mamma, do you know who deserves a bicycle more than I? It is Vida. She has been so good to us children ever since you went down — just like a mother to us. I think she ought to have a bicycle if no one else does."

Vida as the oldest sister was faithful to her trust until the last. So was our darling boy to his, and their reward — what can it be? Something far better than a bicycle, — something that fills them with joy supreme. Oh! how we long for one glimpse of their bliss! Just one look at our boys' cheery faces, how it would comfort our tired, aching hearts. But the Lord only took us at our word when we gave them to him, and had need of them on the other side. Instead of the strong arm of my boy that I had hoped to lean on, He puts underneath us His everlasting arms, and we just rest there until His time comes to bear us home:

> *There'll be songs of greeting when Jesus comes.*
> *There'll be songs of greeting when Jesus conies:*
> *And a glorious meeting when Jesus comes,*
> *To gather His children home.*
> *There'll be no dark valley when Jesus comes,*
> *To gather His children home.*

Herbert Wilson

With the birth of our fourth child, Herbert, dawned the busiest year in all my life as mother. With four little ones looking up into our faces, helpless, dependent, with no one to earn their support but their father, whose small salary required the most careful management to make it meet our necessities, and no others' hands but ours to provide for all the little wants and to do the work in the home, I found my moments full.

Herbert Wilson

How to keep the little bodies clean and comfortably clothed; the best way to keep them nourished with food suited to produce the best results in the healthy development of the entire physical structure; how best to execute that greatest of all missions — the caring for and training of the young minds and souls entrusted to our keeping by God Himself; these were all engrossing subjects, which kept me busy, and happy too, in that dear little country parsonage on the shore of one of America's greatest lakes.

I can remember how often my arms and back ached from the toil of the day and, when one was ill, from wakefulness and anxiety of the night; for, although a healthy lot of children, there came times now and then when disease would make its attack on one and another, and often for days, and even weeks, I have seemed to have to fight death in hand-to-hand struggles. With tears and prayers, and an anxious heart would I hold the little form all night; and yet how many times God heard and answered and gave us back our darlings again in health.

Sometimes there was a temptation to be irritable and displeased because, try ever so hard to keep them so, the once tidy rooms would become a chaos of books, slates, broken toys, dolls, baby garments, shoes and stockings, filling floor and chair, so that they looked as though (as their patient papa said) a cyclone had struck the room. But, oh! how little those things seem now, and how gladly we would welcome back the untidy rooms. How beautiful in our eyes would their torn shoes and stockings now appear; instead of the backache and armache we now have a heartache from which there seems no release.

We often catch ourselves listening for the rush of our darlings on the stairs to see who will beat up, and our lonely hearts long for the sound of their merry voices. We sometimes think if we could but feel their cheeks pressed to ours and their arms twined about us with the loving good-night kiss, we could work day and night, or dare anything, with a light heart.

It used to be a nightly habit before retiring, to go into their rooms and see that each one was safe and sleeping soundly; and at two o'clock to revisit the little beds and tuck each one in. Many a time have I dropped on my knees beside their beds and thanked God for them, and committed them to His keeping for the remainder of the night, and returned to my couch and slept such sound and peaceful sleep as only a tired, happy mother can.

Now the rooms and beds are empty, and everywhere we turn, the blank and silence seem to mock our yearnings, until we walk into the starlight and turn our tear-filled eyes to heaven. There they all seem to gather about us, their bright faces seeming to peer down at us, and we can almost hear them speak, so real is the vision, and we return to our couch comforted as only God can comfort, and we seem to rest on Jesus' bosom, "where nought but calm is found."

I have many things to regret; but how I thank God now that I never felt we had one too many; nor did I ever tire of their noise or of doing for them. I am glad that several years ago I wrote the lines, "The highest honor God has ever bestowed upon me in this life is that of motherhood and the privilege of living for the children He has given me. Next is the honor of being a missionary of the Cross, and the privilege of living for the women and children of Bengal."

Tired mothers, may God help you understand how rich you are, and how blessed your lot with all your little ones about your feet. Be thankful and murmur not, and do not let unnecessary work crowd out of your life the time you need to enjoy their prattle and play, and the time necessary to teach them to sing and to pray and to love God's Word while they are young.

I repeat, while they are young. I feel their first years are the most important of their lives to you. My antidotes for scolding and worry were singing and story-telling, Bible stories being the favorites. The hours spent thus did me as much good as it did the children, with whom it was a delight. Oh! the weight of the story, the value of the word of encouragement, the power of prayer and song upon the children, — yes, upon all. No one of us rightly realizes this, or we would use them more.

How proud I was when Herbert came and we had two boys — "a team," as Wilbur called them. He was born August 31, 1888 (on his grandmother's birthday, although but little chance did the dear boy ever have to enjoy a grandmother's love), at Saybrook, Ohio, U.S.A. He weighed eleven pounds, and seemed a baby almost three months old to begin with.

The Sabbath he was four weeks old I attempted to get all four children ready for Church, and told my husband I never could do it; I would have to give up going to church while they were so little. His answer was, "Well, dear, if you give up now I fear you will never go again." So I got ready and went, and did it every Sunday afterwards. I found about this, as everything else that was right to do, that there was a way, and the children need not be a hindrance, but if looked at in the right light, they were always a help and a blessing. He was dedicated in church that morning by the rite of baptism, we thinking the Lord had a great work for our baby boy to do, and praying for strength to guide him to it.

When six months old he came nearly dying with pneumonia. For twelve long hours one night he struggled for his breath. We were six miles from a doctor. The snow was so deep and the storm so great no one dared to venture out. We did all we knew; still he grew worse. We two bent over him all the night, with tears and prayers, begging our heavenly Father to spare his life. Near midnight the struggle for breath became desperate. I could hardly hold him in my arms. I felt relief must come soon, or our darling would leave us. We had done everything in our power.

In our helplessness, his papa flung himself down on the bed in desperation and my heart gave one agonizing cry to God for help. With this Mr. Lee sprang to his feet, saying, "Why, Ada, you forget that opossum oil the old lady brought you some weeks ago. It can do no harm; give him some." He handed it to me, and warming a spoonful I gave it to him, believing God had told us what to do, and in a few minutes the phlegm was thrown up. He was immediately relieved, and before morning was able to take nourishment and was soon well again.

Herbert was different from all the rest. From his boyhood he was a child with a determination seldom equalled. He would attempt the impossible, and it nearly killed him to fail or to have to give up anything he wished to do. This used to give us trouble, until we learned better how to manage him. There was no "give up" to him. I used to say to his papa, "The only thing to do with Herbert is to make the thing right that he wishes to do," so together we learnt to shift the little fellow about and to guide him into the right and then let him drive ahead.

He was the most tender-hearted child I ever knew. He was wonderfully fond of music, of which he had no little share in his make-up. There was a young lady who used to visit us who was a noted whistler. The little fellow caught it up, and used to creep about the floor whistling, and before he could walk he could hum the tune, "There is a land that is fairer than day." How I used to delight in singing to him, he humming with me the tune before he could talk. It was just as easy for him to learn his books, and no one ever taught him his letters, — he learned them by hearing the others recite them, and while only a wee tot used to surprise us by his achievements with his pencil on the nursery blackboard.

He was converted when only five years old. He deliberately and definitely gave himself to Jesus once and forever in a children's service held at a camp-meeting one Sunday afternoon. He dated his new birth from that hour, and never hesitated to tell anyone when and where he gave himself to Jesus. Ever after that day, his evening prayer was a settling up with God the accounts of the day.

Often it had to be done with tears, for his impetuous nature repeatedly got him into trouble with others, and the difficulty he had in yielding the point, or giving up what he had undertaken, used to lead to slight exaggerations or little stories, which he called his "besetting sin." Gaining the battle in discussions sometimes led to hot words. These all had to be repented of.

Our Sunday evening prayer-meeting with the children was the special time of reviewing the week's work, with its temptations and triumphs or failures. Such a time as this used to be! With Herbert it was usually a time of confession, with tears for failures to live up to the high standard we had before us, of what the Bible said our lives should be. So common was it for him, in praying, to break down and cry, that little Esther in late years used to say on Sunday evening, "Come, children, let's go to mamma now; it's time to pray and cry."

Herbert was so anxious to become a member of the Church, and to partake of the Lord's Supper that, often, his earnest entreaties bewildered us. After coming to Calcutta, he would give us no rest on Communion Sunday. I would say to him, "Herbert, I fear you do not understand what it means."

"Well, mamma, you tell me it's to remember Jesus' death. I love Him; do I not want to remember His death, too? I try to please Him every day, and I belong to Him. Why should I not take the sacrament with you?"

I could resist him no longer, and when he was but little past six years old he was permitted to kneel with us at the Lord's table and take Communion, a sacred privilege which we have all enjoyed together for the past five years.

I never saw two brothers more devoted to each other than he and Wilbur, and I have known months to pass without a single jar between them. They were together in everything; what one had the other had. Even in their lessons, they studied together, until during this last year, Wilbur failing in his examination led to Herbert's being promoted to a class higher, a state of things which we greatly regretted, and which required much wise management, on our part, on account of the thoughtless remarks dropped by others as to the younger being brighter than the older, etc. But even this God overruled, I believe, for good.

Herbert was full of life and activity. It was cruel to make him sit still. He was fond of his violin, and had learned to play many pieces for us. How proud I was of our boy and of his straight, manly little form as he stood up to play in concert with his brother, his sister Lois playing the organ, and Vida often joining them with her guitar.

"Blue Bells of Scotland," "Annie Laurie," "The Old Folks at Home," and "Home, Sweet Home," as well as many of the dear old hymns, such as "Oh for a thousand tongues to sing," and "What can wash away my sins?" used to make our home ring with joy and have become doubly sacred to us. It seems to me sometimes that I can never sing again until He comes and takes us home.

Herbert would take up a new piece and insist on playing it when he had not tried it before. Nothing would daunt or discourage him, and I used to silence the dissenting voices of the others by saying, "Let him try it, children, even if he fails." He would turn to me, so grateful, and say, "Mamma, they think I can't; but just listen: I will show them I can."

Sure enough, he would surprise us all with the degree of accuracy with which he was able to execute it. Oh, that darling boy! With what delight now that spirit, unfettered, must dive into the unknown and untried of heave! How I picture his beaming face as he succeeds up there! We had hoped he would be a preacher and do a wonderful work for God. The Lord will not disappoint us in spite of the mists which hang over us now.

He was so tender-hearted; he would give away almost his last penny, and he delighted to take out a card and write on it his regular gift of two annas each Sunday evening from his pocket money for the church collection. He could not bear to see others suffer, and had many friends among the poor, and the native people. He was a great boy for fun, and was tempted sometimes to go too far.

A year before they left us, the two boys went on top of the flat roof which was without balustrades, to play, a place where they had been forbidden to go. In their fun Herbert sprang back, not knowing he was so near the edge. He stepped off backwards, falling nearly twenty feet to the stone steps below. We were afraid to look at him, thinking, of course, he was dashed to pieces. He was greatly shaken up, but not a bone was broken, nor was there hardly a scratch or bruise.

As we laid him on the bed nearly wild with anxiety, he assured us he was not hurt; that God had sent an angel who caught him and saved him from falling hard. He quoted that verse in the 91st Psalm: "He shall give his angels charge over thee to keep thee in all thy ways; they shall bear thee up in their hands, lest thou dash thy foot against a stone," and said, "Mamma, that is my verse. How good God was to save me! 1 would not like to have died disobeying you and papa"; and he could not rest until he had sought and found pardon.

He had many verses so fixed that he could unhesitatingly repeat them and tell where they were found. He had a special liking for Malachi 3:16-17, "Then they that feared the Lord spake often one to another, and the Lord hearkened and heard it, and the book of remembrance was written before him .... And they shall be mine, saith the Lord of hosts, in that day when I make up my jewels." Another favorite was Rev. 22:17, "And the Spirit and the bride say come, and let him that heareth say come, and let him that is a thirst come, and whosoever will, let him take the water of life freely."

He was greatly interested in a concert given the Saturday evening before that terrible night, and was busy selling tickets and inviting friends to come. This was his last work of the kind. He was only eleven years old, but could be trusted to transact business, and helped us in many ways in our work. They were both naturally strong, healthy, rollicking boys, and it does not seem possible that we can live without them. I am thankful — oh! so thankful, for the assurance that they are living today, active and happy in the homeland, and are getting up many little surprises for us and counting the days, — not until they can come to us, but until we shall come home to them.

In our rambles they used to enjoy running up a *pakdandi* (a short cut) in the mountains and coming out ahead of us on some higher elevation, and then waiting for us, and greeting us with some new thing they had found — a flower, orchid or fern. They have only gone a shorter cut and beaten us home, and are waiting for our slower, weary feet to reach home by the longer way. Then — oh the greeting! We can hardly await the dawning of that bright morning, the beginning of that beautiful, endless day. Until then we shall travel with our eyes fixed on the eternal city, and our hearts rejoicing even here in the hope of the glory awaiting us.

> *"Some day," we say, and turn our eyes*
> *Toward the fair hills of Paradise;*
> *Some day, some time, a sweet new rest*
> *Shall blossom, flower-like, in each breast.*
> *Some day, some time, our eyes shall see*
> *The faces kept in memory;*
> *Some day their hand shall clasp our hand,*
> *Just over in the Morning-land —*
> *O Morning-land! O Morning-land!*
>
> — Edzvavd H. Phelps

Ada Eunice

Ada Eunice

Ada Eunice was named by her papa, — Ada for me. I called her Eunice, "Happy Victory," saying, "With her God will give me victory in raising our missionary fund for India." Ada, my name-sake, my little curly-head, how can I write about her! I can never picture her life so others can understand. We were so proud of her. If she were someone else's child I should say she seemed perfect, physically and mentally. She had feet and ankles like a deer; was as fleet as the wind; could climb like a squirrel, and was the companion of her two older brothers in all their walks and rambles, and they liked it because she could go wherever they could, and seemed perfectly fearless. She was full of play and mischief; entered into all their games and races; could ride or walk equal to any of them — just the kind of a sister brothers like to have about. She seemed gifted in many ways. For one so young she wrote a beautiful hand, was neat at sewing, and loved music and flowers passionately.

Oh, how much we hoped for this child in the future! I am glad for the faith we have that our dreams for her are not to be disappointed; that she will have unbounded opportunity for the development of those faculties we so admired, and when we see our beautiful Ada again we will be satisfied to a degree we never could have been here.

She was born in Dell Roy, Ohio, U.S.A., January 9th, 1891, and was baptized the following March 14th, by our presiding elder, Dr. R. M. Freshwater. She soon after began her work as my companion in holding missionary meetings in different parts of the country, helping more than others could ever understand. So good was she, that, night after night, she would go to sleep before the service and sleep until all was over, giving no trouble to anyone. One night after a longer service than usual, on returning and finding her sound asleep and happy, her uncle said to me, "Well, Ada, I think your babies are made to order; they seem never to interfere with your work." And so it seemed. It was during her babyhood that the fund for our return to India was raised, so she travelled many thousand miles with her mother during the first two years of her life.

When thirteen months old she took a trip of seven days, by train, to California. We had word that my mother was dying, and she wished so much to see me. Our engine broke down the night before we entered Denver, Colorado, and we were delayed several hours. I remember how earnestly I prayed that the train with which we were to connect in Denver might be detained so we might catch it. I felt so sure that the Lord was planning this trip for a purpose, and believed he would not let me and my baby miss the train.

When we arrived, to my great disappointment the train had left two hours before, and there was no other train until night, and I must spend the day in some strange hotel. I left it all with Jesus and sought out a hotel and sat down to think. I turned over the leaves of my address-book, and found the name of a gentleman whom I had never seen, but who had written to me sending an offering for our fund from his Sabbath-school class in Trinity Church. I found his office was just near the hotel. I sent him a note, and soon after he called. I asked him if there was anything I could do during the day. He told me that, not knowing beforehand, he could not leave his office, but he would give me a letter of introduction to two of the leading ladies of the church, and if I would call on them they would be able to open up work for me. It was a cold, stormy day, the snow filling the air, almost blinding one's eyes. While talking, he noticed my baby on the floor near me, and said, "Is this your baby, Mrs. Lee?" I answered in the affirmative. "Oh, then it will be impossible for you to go out."

"Oh, no," I said, "she is my partner in my mission work and always helps me."

So I went, and the baby, as well as I met friends who have ever since been active helpers in our work. From this opened up a whole week's campaign in Denver which we conducted on my return trip a month later. This campaign was characterized by two very large and influential gatherings which did more than we can ever tell for our mission work. With a fresh, delicious luncheon for the road, I returned in time to catch the train in the evening, and hastened on westward to California.

When I reached my mother I found her much better, all of which God knew and I did not, or I would not have murmured when the train broke down and my plans seemed frustrated. This taught me a lesson that I have learned many times over: that God leads us in the right way even when everything seems to be going wrong.

The Six Lee Children

The companionship of Ada, but little more than a year old, on that trip and during my missionary campaign in Southern California, I shall never forget. As we crossed the Great American Desert, and after long hours of confinement in the train, on reaching the stations, she would race from one end of the platform to the other so rapidly that she seemed almost to fly. She was such a mite that it attracted everyone's attention. Even the Indians and squaws who had gathered at the station to see the train, would call out, "Och! papoose, papoose!" ("The baby! the baby!") At another time during her second year she went with me on a missionary trip. After arranging the home affairs so they could get on without us for a few days, we drove five miles to catch a train.

We had agreed to be present at a certain place in time for a meeting in the afternoon, and had been praying much concerning it. When we drove up to the station, imagine our dismay to find the time-table had changed and our train had left two minutes before. Three or four hours must pass before another train would be due and this would take us in too late for our first engagement. It seemed at first God was against us. I said to my husband, "It will be so hard for Baby Ada to wait so long at the station. Drive us up to Mrs.----, whom I have met before, and I will wait at her house."

We drove up, and alighting with baby in my arms I mounted the steps and rang the door-bell. Mrs.----- met me herself, and exclaimed, "Oh, Mrs. Lee! who told you I was wanting to see you so badly? I was just about to write for you. Come in," and giving me a seat, she began to talk. I found her in great distress of mind. She had sometime before lost her only child, and Satan had taken advantage of her in time of sorrow and had gotten her to doubting God, and she had almost decided there was no hope of her own salvation.

We had a good time together with God's Word and in prayer, and she was greatly comforted and helped. She then told me she wished, in the name of this child whom God had taken, to build a room in our mission house for our native work in India, costing $300, (Rs. 900), to be paid in yearly instalments of $50 each. I thanked God for this, and hurried away to the train, and on arriving later in the afternoon I found that on account of some picnic the meeting had been arranged for the evening instead of the afternoon, and that I was in plenty of time for it.

All this God had arranged, and the missing of the train was only a part of his great plan that he might turn me aside to do another errand for him, and in doing this, accomplished more for the work itself than anything I had planned. Now, when He takes our darling girl, for whom we had planned so much, although it seems so hard and we cannot now see why, yet we do believe with all our hearts that our Father has planned it all, and that one day we will praise Him for all the way He has led us.

In all our travels before, and when on our way to India, Ada was the favorite with everyone, making friends both for herself and us wherever she went. She was so interested in all the sights, and shared in all the enjoyments along the way. In London she insisted on going with her papa and the other children wherever they went.

I got the benefit of the day's sight-seeing in her childish recitals to wee Esther, in baby talk, of all that had occurred while they were out: "I have been to see the great British Museum.

You ought to been 'ere too. We saw big kings and elephants, and pretty angels with wings. But mustn't touch; if you do, a great big policeman would take you away to jail. Then, too, we saw such lots of pigeons, and beautiful green grass — with no 'keep off the grass' on it either. We could roll and play all over it. Baby sister, wouldn't you like to see the British Museum?"

Her fearlessness often led her into trouble. Soon after we arrived in Calcutta, when she was only four years of age, a boy with his little drum and monkey came along. Ada was delighted with the tricks played, and the novelty of everything seemed to charm her. The next evening she heard him coming, but he did not stop. After a while our Ada was missing. The house and the compound were searched, but no trace could be found of her.

It began to grow dark; everyone was anxious, and we flew up and down the street in search of her. After a while she was found standing in a street in another part of the city, crying. Some gentleman gathered from what she said, something about the direction from which she had come, and led her down the street. After a while she espied the house, and turning to him said, "See! this is where my papa lives." We asked her where she had been. She began to cry, and said, "Mamma, I only went to find the monkey-boy, but I don't know where his house is."

She became interested in kindergarten work, and the kindergarten songs and plays were a part of our home life. A year ago she became very anxious to learn to read her Bible, and so determined was she that in a very few weeks she was able to read with us at prayer time. Her papa gave her a Bible of her own, of which she was very proud, and was constantly finding special verses in it, many of which she had beautifully memorized.

Her favorites were, "They that trust in the Lord shall be as Mount Zion, which cannot be removed, but abideth forever; as the mountains are round about Jerusalem, so the Lord is round about his people from henceforth, even forever." Ps. 125:1,2.

And another, "Thou wilt keep him in perfect peace whose mind is stayed on thee, because he trusteth in thee; trust ye in the Lord forever, for in the Lord Jehovah is everlasting strength." Isaiah 26:3,4.

The grand meaning of these verses must have flashed into the mind of this darling girl during that last hour on earth, when, having none else to whom they could look for help, that precious little group cast themselves on God, and His presence was so real that even the younger children rejoiced in Him, and that hour of terror was turned into an hour of joy and victory. He failed them not; He Himself became their refuge; and although all material things were utterly destroyed, our Ada abideth forever.

She had a joyful summer in school, romping and playing, climbing and racing all over those beautiful mountains. Her part in our little Sunday evening prayer-meeting was always very real and striking to me. She often asked God for a new heart, but she definitely sought Jesus one Sunday evening a few weeks before their translation, Vida and all the other children helping her with their prayers. She accepted Him and received such peace and joy that even her very countenance was changed.

In her last letter, written the day before the land slip, she speaks of her desire to have always a pure heart.

We do thank God that our darling is now like Jesus, rejoicing in His presence, and that when Jesus comes He will bring them all with Him, and when we see her glorified body we shall then be satisfied and she shall be ours forever.

> *"'Till He come!' Oh, let the words*
> *Linger on the trembling chords.*
> *Let the little while between*
> *In their golden light be seen.*
> *Let us think how heaven and home*
> *Lie beyond that — 'till He come.'*
>
> *When the weary ones we love*
> *Enter on their rest above,*
> *Seems the Earth so poor and vast,*
> *All our life joy overcast?*
> *Hush! Be every murmur dumb:*
> *It is only 'till He come.'*
>
> *See, the feast of love is spread.*
> *Drink the wine, and break the bread.*
> *Sweet memorials, — till the Lord*
> *Call us 'round His heavenly board:*
> *Some from Earth, from Glory some,*
> *Severed only 'till He come.'"*

Esther Dennett

Our little Queen Esther was born in Mountain Lake Park, Maryland, U.S.A., August 24, 1894. We were stopping in Hotel Dennett, a rest home for weary workers in the Lord's vineyard. We were there at the urgent request of its founder, — that noble man, A. W. Dennett. He wished us to spend our last four months in America in that delightful place, called by many "the nearest spot on earth to heaven." We had with us in the rest home about fifty missionaries and other workers, so Baby Esther had a warm welcome; and after we had named her Esther — saying surely "She had come to the kingdom for such a time as this" — our friends added the name Dennett.

She was baptized and dedicated to God September 10, the dear, white-headed "Bishop Thomson" performing the rite; and we all prayed that she might indeed be a Queen among Missionaries. She went to hold her first missionary meeting, with her mother,

Esther Dennett

when but four weeks old, and did very well. She sailed for India when seven weeks old, with her five brothers and sisters, and was the best sailor and gave the least trouble of them all.

After six weeks she reached Calcutta, still in a good humor with the world and all about her. Our native people called her *Ranee* (Queen). She was a hearty, healthy child with fair curls and a very affectionate disposition. Her short life seems like a flash of sunshine. She had a baby sister, whose name was Ruth, whom she had never seen, who went to heaven after being with us three short weeks. She had heard from the others about her, and she used to trouble us sometimes by her questions concerning her and heaven, often ending up by saying, "Mamma, I want to go up to heaven and play with Baby Ruth." What a grand time these angel babies must be having together these days!

She was very fond of the little Hindu girls who came to school at our house. She had a special favorite — a very dear little girl, Indu Bala, with whom she played nearly every day.

She could not bear to see a little child in distress or danger, and often came to me crying, begging me to go to the help of someone.

The year after our baby girl was in heaven, her little friend, Indu Bala, was married, only six years old. How our hearts ached for the lovely child; but, being a Hindu, our pleading for her was vain. She was taken away and not allowed to attend school. Her father's answer was that he must submit to the rules of his caste, which insisted on child marriage. Such a fate is worse than death. How much happier were the trio today, if together they roamed the fields of glory where there is "fullness of joy" and "pleasures forever more." This only strengthened my determination to spend my life in fighting these cruel customs, and in doing what I could to save innocent children from child marriage and widowhood.

Esther had taken part with us in a few lessons in physical exercise. From that time, she was continually reminding us to keep erect at the table, out walking, and wherever we might be together, by saying, "Hips back, mamma," "Maintain position, maintain position, mamma." Her wise little speeches — how we yearn to hear them again.

She was very original in her prayers, and it was a source of great joy to us — not unmingled with amusement — to hear her lead in prayer at the family circle or alone at her bedside. She used often to say, "Oh, Lord, don't bess the people only dat are good, but bess the bad people too — all the people in the whole world." She would tell God about everything. If her bunnie was hurt, or she had broken her dolly, she seemed to have great comfort in telling Him about it. Once while at the hills, she heard of my suffering with the heat in Calcutta, and that evening in her prayer she was heard to say, "Oh, God, send mamma lots of wind." In the last little Sunday evening prayer-meeting at which we all knelt as a family together, she prayed, "Oh, Lord, bless not only dis family, but all de families in de whole world."

She was a great singer. Her special favorites were, "Jesus Loves Me," "The Mothers of Salem," "Suffer little children to come unto Me," and "When He cometh to make up His jewels." She had several Scripture verses memorized. The last one she learned perfectly, was,

"Show me Thy ways, O Lord, teach me Thy paths." Psa. 25:4. Our darling baby girl! How far ahead of us is she today in understanding God's ways! We seem lost without her childish prattle, and long to feel again her arms twine about our neck.

She was with us in Calcutta until within a few weeks of that terrible disaster. She went up with her papa, as she said, to take care of him, when he went to visit the children, and she remained with them. We permitted her to stay, thinking it best for her, and afterwards every attempt to get her down seemed frustrated. It must be God had need of her and could not spare her to us. I shall never forget our last few moments together before she took the train for Darjeeling when she assured me she would not forget to say her prayers, neither would she quarrel with sister — "For, mamma, if I did those things, then God would not be pleased." Little did I think that was the last time I should ever see our darling. No wonder it nearly killed me to see her go.

Her little hand waving from the car window, as she smiled back "good-bye," was the last time we shall see that dear face — until after the night is over and we see her beckoning hands in the dawning of that eternal day, and when they will all run to meet us and welcome us home — then we shall have them all again, and forever.

> *O what are all my sufferings here*
> *If, Lord, thou count me meet*
> *With that enraptured host to appear*
> *And worship at Thy feet!*
> *Give joy or grief, give ease or pain,*
> *Take life or friends away,*
> *But let me find them all again*
> *In that eternal day.*

— Charles Wesley

WILBUR'S STORY

"The Mountain is Falling Down"

"And God shall wipe away all tears from their eyes, and there shall be no more death, neither sorrow nor crying, neither shall there be any more pain." Rev. 21:4.

"He shall swallow up death in victory, and the Lord shall wipe away tears from off all faces."
Isaiah 2:8.

The first telegram brought us the word that Wilbur had escaped. We were so benumbed by the awful news concerning the other children that we did not think of his being injured, and even expected him down on the next train with the other school children.

How little we knew of what that dear boy was passing through! It did not dawn upon us until some friend telegraphed, "I saw Wilbur Lee. Doing well." Then we began to fear he might be hurt. Not until two days after did we get the word that he was badly injured.

We then said we must go to him at once. Some said it would be impossible for me to go, the roads were so torn away; but I thought I must go to my boy; if he was suffering, I must be with him. The one thought of reaching him spurred me on through every difficulty.

All through that long, uncertain journey — walking, riding, climbing — nothing seemed too hard for me, if I could but reach him. All along the way everybody we met brought good tidings of Wilbur.

At last the journey was over, and at 1 o'clock on Friday, we reached the Sanatorium in Darjeeling. Oh, the joy of clasping him again in our arm! We found him propped up in bed, very bright and cheery, and seemingly getting well rapidly.

He was very much affected, and burst into tears of joy when he saw us; but we soothed and quieted him, and he was soon telling us all about what he had been doing, and asking us questions about home and ourselves.

He took his baby brother in his arms and played with him — so delighted was he to see him. Then he asked for his box, and, opening it, showed us his bottles of scent and handkerchiefs which many kind friends had given him. He told me how kind everyone had been to him, and seemed especially fond of the house doctor and the sister, who were untiring in their devotion to him.

He showed me the names of the ladies who had called on him, or had sent him some delicacy, or in any way had shown him a kindness. He had asked a friend to write down all the names, saying he would write to each one a letter of thanks after he got well.

I asked him about that night, and he said, "Mamma, let me begin at the first and tell you all about it."

I said, "No, son; you will have plenty of time to tell me, so do not tell me all today. But I wish so much to know if you tried to save yourselves."

He then told me that they first tried to escape from the south side and to get down to Nos. 4 and 5, [the nearest houses,] but they came to a flood of mud and water rushing down the hillside, as Wilbur said, "like the Ohio River." It was impossible for them to cross it.

They then went out the back way, going up the narrow foot-path to the road, and started to the house above toward the Mall, but they found the road washed away, and nothing left on which to tread.

Vida then led them back down toward Lebong, the opposite direction, but they were met by insurmountable piles of earth and debris.

Boulders were rolling down the mountain side, trees were falling and stones flying through the air. The rain poured in torrents; the roar of the cyclone and the pitch darkness were enough to terrify the bravest heart.

Vida found she could not keep them together, and said, "I am afraid we will get lost from one another, and I promised papa I would take care of Esther. Come, we will go back to the house, and, if the Lord wishes, he can save us together, and, if not, he will take us together."

So they returned and went upstairs and built a fire and began to dry their clothes. They knelt in prayer several times asking God to protect them.

Soon they heard someone knocking on the front door. They went down and found a poor native man, all crippled, and his face bleeding. He told them their house was going to fall; but he was so ill and shivering with the cold that the children became interested in him instead of themselves.

Vida took a cloth and wiped the blood from his face. They tried to lift him inside, but he fainted away. She then took the *durry* [large rug] from the floor nearby and wrapped him up in it. Two other native men passed the door, and said, "Children, the mountain is falling down, and you had better leave."

The children told them they had tried, — how could they get away? The men then passed on, not able to render them any assistance. The hill woman who cooked for them helped to get everything in from the out-houses, — the cooking utensils, etc.; and just as she came out of the cook-house the last time, it was washed away.

The native man lying at the door became conscious again, and said he must go to his master at Nos. 4 and 5, and went away, dragging himself along the ground. He says the last time he saw the children they were kneeling together in prayer.

Vida took them all back upstairs again to the fire, and while praying, the corner of the room cracked open.

I found it agitated Wilbur very much to tell me about it, so I checked him; but he said, "Mamma, I must tell you about Vida. She sprang to her feet, her face just beaming as she said, 'Children, the house is coming down, and we will soon be in heaven.'"

"But were you not afraid; Wilbur?" I said.

"No, mamma; God had taken all the fear away, and we were all so happy. We felt just as if we were in the train coming home to you. We said to each other, 'Now if papa and mamma and Baby Frank were only here, so we could all go to heaven together, how nice it would be.' Oh, Vida's face! Mamma, if you only could have seen her! How beautiful she looked! Her face shone like an angel's as she talked to us. She then led us into another room, and again we knelt about the bed, and we all prayed Jessudar (our Bengali girl) was kneeling with us, and with hands clasped and looking up to heaven, she said, "Oh, merciful God, take us now." These were her last words."

"Then there came a tremendous crash. I sprang to my feet with a lamp in my hand just in time to see the wall come in, and I knew nothing more until I awoke in the darkness in the mud and water below. It was still raining hard. I could see two lights in the distance, and I tried to get to the one I thought nearest me. I walked a little, and then fell down asleep."

Wilbur had been thrown more than a hundred feet down the mountain side. When daylight came there was not a vestige of the house left. The beautiful flower garden and trees were gone; nothing but fresh earth and roots of trees, and boulders piled up so high that no one could recognize the spot on which the house had stood.

In the house just near, only farther out on the mountain side, twenty-four persons had stayed all night unable to get away, and expecting every moment that their house would go, the stones rolling down on the roof all night. Two gentlemen attempted to get to our house several times, but the mud and water were so deep and the darkness so great that it seemed impossible.

As day dawned two ladies were looking out from the porch to see what had become of their servants, when on a little knoll some distance away they saw a muddy object rise up and throw up its arms, and then fall back. As it grew lighter, they discovered it was our Wilbur, and called to him to lie still, and they would send him help. What joyful words these must have been to the poor boy who had been trying so long to attract attention.

Some kind gentlemen went to him, wading in mud and water up to their waists. After a desperate struggle, an old gentleman reached him; the boy threw his arms about him, so grateful was he to him for coming. They carried him through much difficulty, to the house, where they washed the mud away, put on warm clothes and wrapped him in blankets, and then sent for the doctor.

He was very cold. In the meantime, they put hot bottles about him and brought him some brandy. This he refused to take, saying: "It's wrong to drink brand; I can't take that."

A lady said to him, "No, it's not wrong, Wilbur, for you to take it now as medicine. Do you not remember that verse where Paul told Timothy to take a little wine for his stomach's sake? So it's right for you to take it now."

"You are sure it will not be wrong?" he said. "Then I'll take it."

The doctor came and dressed the terrible wounds on his head and found, that, although badly cut and bruised, he had no bones broken. He was then sent to the Sanatorium, where all that kind friends and human sympathy could do was done.

That first day we arrived Wilbur seemed well and bright all day. What a blessed day it was! His sister Lois' ring, which had been taken from her finger, was handed to her papa soon after our arrival. He gave it to Wilbur, who showed it to me and was trying to clean the mud out of the sets. He asked me what we would do with it.

I said, "We give it to you, Wilbur, as no one deserves it more."

He thanked me, and with tears in his eyes, he put it on his finger, where it stayed until his death.

During the day he said to me, "Do you think I will be able to go up for my examination this year? I fear I will not earn my bicycle."

I assured him he should have his bicycle whether he took his examination or not, which seemed to greatly please him. He kept referring to the other children several times during the day.

He also asked about the house. "Is there none of the beautiful ivy left that covered the house?" If there were, he wished to take some of it to Calcutta. He told how well the two little children were, and how they had grown; also spoke of their all having gathered ferns and grass to take home to me.

I said to him, "Wilbur, there is one thing I wish you to tell me about. You know you could never quite say that you had been converted; that you had really been saved from your sins. How was it that night with you?"

"Oh, mamma!" he said, "I know I have been converted; that Jesus is my Saviour, I was not afraid to die. I knew it was all right. It has been a great blessing to me to help take care of the children this summer. It has made me a better boy. It has been good for us all; for we have lived for, and loved each other more than ever before."

Toward night he became restless, and complained of his head hurting him. He grew worse, and, after a troubled sleep awoke, screaming with pain, his jaws having shut, catching his tongue between his teeth. I then feared tetanus, which it proved to be. Oh, the awful suffering of the next two days and nights! Yet between the spasms he would be so bright and cheery.

Friday evening he asked me to read his chapter to him, and we read, "Let not your hearts be troubled....I go to prepare a place for you" (14th chapter of John), and prayed with him. The next evening, he had suffered so much during the day, that I suggested instead of reading we should repeat a few verses. We each repeated a verse.

He then repeated the one, "They that trust in the Lord shall be like Mount Zion, which cannot be removed, but abideth for ever," And he added, "This is Ada's verse, mamma."

We then prayed. He had just passed through a very severe paroxysm, but he prayed too. His prayer was, "Oh, Lord, I thank thee for not letting me die in the dark, that awful night. Bless papa, and mamma, and Baby Frank; take care of them. Bless me and take care of me, for Jesus' sake. Amen."

He had said to me during the day, "Oh, mamma, that awful pain! Why does God let me suffer so?"

I had been asking myself the same question all day, and the answer seemed to be given me as I said, "To make you perfect, I suppose, my darling. Be patient; there is a land where there will be no more pain. We will ask God to help you bear this terrible suffering. He will give you no more to bear than he will give you grace for."

He was very brave and patient. He would often put his arms around my neck and draw my head down on his pillow, and patting my cheek, would say, "My precious mamma; you are my sweetheart."

How these loving words linger with me yet! And another time he embraced his papa, and then asked for Baby Frank, and drew him down to him and kissed him. He seemed to know everyone, and had a word for everybody.

Sometimes he seemed to be gone, but would revive again after the paroxysm wore off. His papa said to him, "Wilbur, if you see Vida and Lois before I do, give them our love."

"Yes," he said, "I will; but why? Do you think I'm going now?"

We said, "You are very ill; it looks as if you would go to heaven soon."

"But," he said, "Did you not ask God to make me well, mamma, and don't you believe He will?"

I said, "Yes, I asked Him to make you well, but it may not be best."

"Yes," he answered, "God worked one miracle to save my life; and, if best. He can work another."

After another severe spell, I said, "Is Jesus with you, Wilbur?"

"Of course, mamma."

"Are you afraid?" I said.

"Oh, no; I am not afraid. Don't you and papa be afraid."

Once when I asked again if Jesus was with him, he answered me, "Of course," as he did so many times, and said, "You thought I was gone, mamma, but I am not."

"But are you afraid to die, Wilbur?" I asked.

"No, mamma, but I wish you and papa and Baby Frank could go, too?"

And, oh, how I wished we might go with him! A little later in the night I had to leave the room.

He drew his papa down, and said, "Papa, go and comfort mamma."

His papa said, "What shall I say to her, Wilbur?"

"Tell mamma I am so happy in Jesus."

I prayed constantly that the Lord would spare him, but we came to where we felt we must give him into God's hands, willing for Him to take him if it was His will.

A few hours before he left us it seemed to me it would kill me, and I went alone in my room, feeling that unless God wonderfully helped me, I never could meet it.

As I was praying that the Lord would take him out of the suffering, in my anguish God seemed to come so near, and gave me such a glimpse of heaven, with Wilbur just entering in and the other children greeting him — all so happy — that the awfulness of death seemed to be taken away, and I myself made to rejoice with them in their victory.

So real was the vision that I seemed to receive from its supernatural strength that bore me through those awful days that followed. The hour that Wilbur's spirit left the poor, bruised body to join his brothers and sisters, their spirits seemed to hover all about us. They seemed to come to take him home. It was an hour of victory for them, and also for us.

As we walked to the cemetery the day we laid his dear body away, the clouds hung over us all the morning; but, just as they lowered the casket into the earth, the sun burst forth in all its warmth and brightness, lighting up the grave and all about it.

It seemed to say to my heart:

"Oh, Death, where is thy sting.
Oh, Grave, where is thy victory?"

and I seemed to see beyond all this, when Jesus would come and bring them again, and we should be forever with the Lord.

"Thanks be to God which giveth us the victory through our Lord, Jesus Christ." Oh, that blessed day. How we rejoice even now in anticipation of its glory.

Oh, how sweet it will be in that beautiful land,
So free from all sorrow and pain,
With songs on our lips and with harps in our hands,
To meet one another again.

The Spirit Of A Man Can Endure All Things

So long Thy power hath blest me, sure it still —
Will lead me on
O'er moor and fen, o'er crag and torrent, till
The night is gone.
And with the morn those angel faces smile,
Which I have loved long since and lost awhile!

— John H. Nemman

For some months after our children had been taken — Satan often tempted me at prayer time, taunting me with the thought, "What is the use of your praying? What good does it do? You dedicated every one of those children to God for service in the mission field, and where are they now? You are trudging along trying to do what you thought the Lord had sent your children to do — without help, you are bearing the burdens alone. And there is Wilbur, your Samuel, as you called him, you definitely asked God for him to preach the Gospel, over whom you had prayed many an hour believing he was to be a preacher of power and lead many to Christ. How you pleaded for his life, and where is the answer? He is gone before he is fifteen years old. What good will it do for you to pray now?" I knew it was the adversary of my soul and fought him off — throwing myself upon God again and again.

It was the evening of the first birthday anniversary — little Ada's — I thought I could never live through the day; but I invited the little orphan girls of her age in for tea and a play, just as I had always done when she was with us, and spent the afternoon entertaining and trying to make happy these children, when my heart was breaking just for a glimpse of my own darling. At last the weary day was over, and I dropped on my knees at my bedside to plead for comfort and help, when, as usual, my old adversary appeared and again began taunting me.

I felt too weak and heartsick to fight him, but I turned to my Saviour with a heart-cry such as He only could understand, and said, "I know Thou dost answer prayer. How many times, in a wonderful way, hast Thou given me my heart's desire. Now give me deliverance once for all from Satan's daily insinuations. I am tired of fighting him."

Jesus drew so near to my heart, and seemed to say, "I know your sorrow, and I sorrow with you; but your sorrow can never be greater than I have borne for you. Your prayers are answered; your boy Wilbur has preached and accomplished as much as though he had lived and preached fifty years." Oh, the comfort that came into my soul, "the blessed assurance," the sweet fellowship of Christ, suffering with me. I arose so happy, — Satan was vanquished. I was sure my prayers were answered in a far better way than I thought, and one day I would see and understand.

A few days after a friend of position, whom we had never met, wrote from the homeland telling us Wilbur's story was being published in all the Christian papers in the land, and the story of their victory in death, as Wilbur told it, was being recited from thousands of pulpits in the land, moving many hearts to seek the blessed Saviour. "Your boy in the story of their triumph in that awful hour, is preaching all over this country." I believed it, because God had told me in my heart the night he comforted me. And from that day to this I have not doubted it; neither do I ever again have to fight that battle with Satan. I know God answers prayer.

Many friends seemed to fear that the Darjeeling disaster, which so suddenly crushed our home would also crush us and we would be compelled to give up our work. But, although the pruning has been most severe, God, in His mercy, has sent equal grace and strength, until, instead of crushing us, we believe it has better fitted us for this great work God has given us to do.

Many wonders at us and some have even said, "Oh, this mother does not realize her loss." But some days it seems that the weight of that terrible mountain in Darjeeling is upon my heart, and would crush out my life. As I think of the four lovely forms of those dearer than my own life, crushed and buried by it, and of the other two lying in the cemetery on the other side of the hill, it seems impossible to live.

There is another baby grave in the beautiful home land, making seven in Heaven, and two darlings left to share our loneliness. When the evening tide comes, the longing to hear their footsteps and their ringing laugh is greater than words can express. But I quickly turn away from these thoughts and with a cry, only Jesus can understand, I look to Him and He just seems to lift me above earth, and the loneliness, and even above that weariness which is caused by fighting sorrow, and which is different from all other kinds.

I sometimes seem to be all but in the heaven-land and see the loved ones so joyous and happy, that before I know it I seem to be sharing with them in the victory. The one heart desire of these days has been that God's purpose in all this stupendous mystery might be fulfilled in me.

So much has been accomplished already. It has enabled me to see life as never before, and to see my own weakness and nothingness. It also has put heaven in the right light — the one thing for which to live.

The Bible has become a new book, and its promises are my food and drink. Oh, how my soul feasts on them. Jesus has become my all in all as never before — and to know Him, whom to know aright is life eternal, has become my one study — and to be blameless in his sight my one aim.

"Only one day at a time — and one to please." Now while, with redoubled energy, I work to make Jesus known to those about me; and the desire to save as many as possible of his little ones in this heathen land, has became greater; still in it all I live like unto one who waits for his Lord. And while it seems almost impossible to rejoice and sing as once I did, my heart wells up with gratitude to God for His mercy in sparing to me my husband and our precious baby Frank, and permitting me the joy of still living for them and the work.

But above all I praise my Saviour for Himself and for the fulfilment of His promise: "Lo, I am with you always," and for His saving power. So I rest in Him and leave the future in His hands, but I have joy in the thought that one of these, days the end will come. "The silver cord will break." Then I shall see Him whom my soul loveth and shall have the unspeakable joy of presenting to Him those whom He gave me and those also whom He sent me to bring from India.

Some day the silver cord will break,
And I no more as now shall sing.
But, oh, the joy when I shall wake
Within the palace of the King!

Chorus
Then 1 shall see Him face to face,
And tell the story saved by grace.

Some day my earthly house will fall
I cannot tell how soon 'twill be;
But this I know, my all in all
Has now a place prepared for me.

Some day, when fades the golden sun.
Beneath the rosy-tinted West,
My blessed Lord shall say "Well done!"
And I shall enter into rest.

Some day; till then I'll watch and wait,
My lamp all trimmed and burning bright;
That, when my Saviour opens the gate,
My soul to Him may take it's flight.

6 "The House In Which Your Children Were Is Gone"

Villa Mall, **where the Lee children met their death on September 24, 1899.**

Apart from the six Lee children who died in the landslide, others who also passed away during the disaster were Violet Pringle, Eric Enderson, Ruth Wallace and Phoebe Wallace. They were all students of Arcadia Girls' School.

Along with the six Lee children, who died during the landslide, was Jessudar, a Bengali girl who had become part of the family.

Rev. Warne on the Lees

I have had the pleasure and honour of being the pastor of the "Lee family" since their return to India in 1894, and secretary to the Arcadia Girls' School from its beginning. I was with Mr. and Mrs. Lee through all the unspeakable experiences herein portrayed. I went with them to Darjeeling after the disaster; was with them as they waited with their son, Wilbur, while he told the story of the children's triumph; when he entered into rest, attended his funeral, and returned with them to their lonely Calcutta home.

Suggestions were made that someone should write an account of the Darjeeling disaster so far as it concerns the Lee children and the Arcadia School.

In this school and in "Mall Villa" (where the Lee children met their death) popular interest centred because in these buildings only were the lives of American and English children lost. My relation to the family and school singled me out as the one who should prepare the memorial volume. In endeavouring to carry out the suggestion, I have been happy in persuading Mrs. Lee to write the story of each of her bright, merry, Christian children, and these chapters will appear as written by her, a tribute of love to her darling children from their loving, sorrowing mother.

The Lee children in their religious life were exemplary, and their mother has told the story so as to reveal the secret of their training in such a way that it can be understood and may be imitated by other parents. If this book helps other parents and children to a higher ideal, and interests its readers in the salvation of the Bengali girls, a work to which this family was consecrated, and in which the parents are still actively engaged, the purpose for which it has been written will be accomplished.

With a prayer that they may aid in furthering the will of the Master in this mysterious providence, these hastily written pages are sent forth.

Frank W. Warne,
Pastor, Methodist Episcopal Church.
Calcutta, Feb. 6th, 1900

The first news of the disaster reach Calcutta

"Both Safe at Grand Hotel. Ida Villa Destroyed." Two gentlemen were waiting at my home for an explanation of the above telegram when I came in to dinner at 7 P.M. September 25th. They supposed I could explain how "Ida Villa" had been destroyed as it stood on the mountain side at Darjeeling, just above Arcadia, in which we had our Darjeeling Girls' School. It was my first intimation of anything out of the ordinary. I remember saying, as a first thought, "If there had been an earthquake we would have felt it, or would have had the news; there must have been a fire. "Ida Villa" could have burned and Arcadia could have escaped, I thought, and was only slightly anxious; but was anxious.

My servant came in and I asked: "Has a telegram come for me?" "Yes, sahib, but the man would not leave it without a receipt." I knew then that there was trouble, but what? While we stood bewildered, another gentleman, whose daughter was in Arcadia, arrived with a telegram he had received. It read, "Heavy landslide, Winnie safe, coming by first train."

"Winnie," his daughter, was in Arcadia; my own wife and daughter were in Arcadia. Are they safe? What is in the undelivered telegram? were the questions that came rushing to my mind. The cause of the destruction of "Ida Villa" had been explained, but 'how heavy the landslide' I did not know. I hastened to the telegraph office for the missing telegram, but could get no trace of it.

I then, with a burden of fear and uncertainty, hurried to several newspaper offices, and learned that the following telegram had been sent from the Commissioner at Darjeeling to the Lieutenant-Governor of Bengal: — "Mall Villas destroyed, lives lost as follows: D. H. Lee's children, eldest girl found dead, eldest boy saved, rest missing. At Ida Villa, Phoebe and Ruth Wallace, Eric Anderson, all dead."

These lost children were pupils of Arcadia, situated just below "Ida Villa." How they got to "Ida Villa," and what about the rest, was all a mystery. I mused. Lee's children all dead but one! How can I tell it? How can they bear it? My wife and child must be alive because their names are not among the dead. Then the many possible conditions between being dead and having escaped without injury were in my mind. Who else has suffered? I was not told of sweet Violet Pringle, and did not know of her death until next morning when her name appeared in the papers. I hastened toward home, and on my way met Rev. Herbert Anderson, India Secretary of the Baptist Mission. He had received a telegram stating that his "dear boy Eric" had been killed, but he was still hoping that it was not true. It was my painful duty in the darkness of the night to confirm the sad news, and see him clasp his head with both hands, and to hear him pray: "O God, help his poor mother." None but those who have had such news concerning their own can understand its crushing power. I had to hasten on to the Deaconess Home in which Mr. and Mrs. Lee were then living, and, how shall I tell them, was the uppermost thought.

When I arrived at the home, I met Miss Maxey and Miss Blair, two deaconesses, at the door. Let Miss Blair describe what followed: "A message had come for Mrs. Robinson, and Miss Maxey and I started out to take it across to her. Mr. Warne, just returned from the telegraph office, met us; his face was drawn, I thought, with anxiety for his own. He seized the envelope, tore it open, and read, 'Flora (Robinson) safe. Coming by first train.' No news of his family. Miss Maxey went in with the message, and Mr. Warne, motioning me aside, said in a voice trembling with emotion, 'All the Lee children, except Wilbur, are dead!' Oh, those terrible words it could not be — surely it could not be! My heart cried out against it. Vida, brave, womanly Vida, caring with a mother's tenderness for her younger brothers and sisters; Lois, the darling and joy of all their hearts; Herbert, and quaint, sweet little Ada; and baby Esther, just past her fifth birthday; that they had all gone, in a moment, like the puff of a candle, seemed beyond belief. But how to tell the poor parents, — should we tell them at once, or wait till the statement was verified?"

We went out. Miss Maxey and Miss Blair to take the good news to Mrs. Robinson, wife of the Editor of the *Indian Witness* while I hastened to my home, behind the church, to see if any other news had arrived, only to be disappointed. On my return, in the shade behind the church I met Mr. Lee. "Have you any news?" were his first words. "Yes," I said, "terrible landslips, Eric Anderson, Phoebe and Ruth Wallace killed, but no news of my people, and nothing definite about the rest in the school." His thought was of his own, and he at once asked: "Any news of our children?" The dreaded time when the terrible news must be told had come. By this time, we were out of the shade of the church and under the light of the street lamp. I tried to break it gently, and answered: "Yes, Brother Lee, there is some news. The house in which your children were is gone." He seemed to know the rest, for in an instant his erect and alert form was bowed, as if he were a man of eighty years, and with feeble, tottering steps, not uttering a word, he moved off through the darkness toward the Deaconess Home. Afterward he said to me: "I thought you would fall to the earth when you told me the house was gone."

At this moment, Miss Maxey and Miss Blair were coming across the street. I left them to follow Mr. Lee to their home, and I went to tell Miss Wi'ddifield, and to get news to Miss Craig, Mr. Chew, and other members of the mission. I will let Miss Blair describe what happened while I was giving the information to others: "We met Mr. Warne at the church gate, and saw Mr. Lee just turning away. "I have told him the house is gone" was whispered as we came up, I couldn't tell him the rest."

There was no need. The matter had been taken out of our hands; he knew. We overtook him in a moment, and Miss Maxey, thinking to reassure him, made some remark, but he walked on without a word. She spoke again; still no word did he say. He was like one stunned. Suddenly he stopped and said, 'All my children gone!'

Then it was we told him all we knew. He said no more but went directly upstairs to the room where sat poor Mrs. Lee by the side of her sleeping baby. There was no need to speak. She saw it written in our faces. Mr. Lee sat down and looked at her seeming still unable to shake off the spell which held him. 'Are the children all right?' she said, and when still no word was spoken, she cried out in agony, 'Oh, what is the matter! Are they safe? What is the matter!' 'Darling,' he said, they are all gone but 'Wilbur.' And then a cry, the cry of a mother's breaking heart rang though the room: 'Oh my God! Why didn't He take us all! Oh, what is there left to live for!' After having given the awful information to the other missionaries, I hastened to the Deaconess Home where all our mission people soon gathered, and where we together spent most of the night, giving what sympathy we could and praying with the sorrow-stricken parents.

On my arrival I found Sister Lee, in her husband's arms, looking as pale as death, her forehead cold, her breathing scarcely perceptible, her hands rising and falling at her side, and she moaning out: "My darling girls, Vida! Vid!! Vida!! Lois, precious Lois! Darling, cheerful Ada. Esther, — Esther, my baby girl — Esther — not a girl left! Not a girl left!! Not a girl left!!! O my God — not a girl left. What does it mean? Did I love them too much? Was 1 too proud of them? Have I sinned? My precious Herbert — no more hugs, no more kisses. Did they suffer? Did they all go together? They are happy, they are with Jesus. Why were we not all taken with them? 1 have lived too much for earth, and too little for heaven."

The husband and father — devoted husband and affectionate father, brave man — he held and comforted his heart-broken wife, as if he had not a sorrow of his own. He would say: "Darling, Jesus gave them to us. Jesus loved them. Jesus has taken his own. Don't weep, darling, they are with Jesus in heaven and we'll soon be with them." The rest of us looked on "dumb with silence." Such a providence would be mysterious under any circumstances, but to us, as missionaries, at first it seemed almost as if God discouraged missionaries and was frustrating the purposes of his best and most devoted workers. The Lee children had given themselves to mission work. Just about two weeks before, I remembered having gone in when Brother and Sister Lee were at tiffin, which was just after the arrival of the Darjeeling mail, and Brother Lee in his most cheerful and happy mood, sprang up and shook a letter which he had just received from Vida, his eldest daughter, and said: "No father ever received a better letter from a better daughter than I have received from Vida." He waved the letter in the air, and said, "It's worth a thousand dollars."

It was dated, September 7th, 1899: and in it she said: "My darling Papa, we were all talking the other night of what we would do for both, and I am sure Frank (a baby nine months old) would have joined if he had been here. Wilbur says he won't charge anything for your teeth rest of us, you know, aint so sure of our money as they two are. And Herbert, Professor Lee, will make home 'comfee.' I will try hard to keep up your work. I am sure God has called me to it, and will be with me. Now I have told you what I did not expect to. I have told you what is in my heart, I am God's for your work, trust me and believe me, your loving and affectionate daughter, Vida."

What a contrast between that scene and the one of which I now write! As the night wore on, and we prayed, and asked for light on the mystery, I began to think of that wonderful hymn of William Cowper's, on the text, — "Verily-thou art a God that hidest thyself."

God moves in a mysterious way
His wonders to perform:
He plants his footsteps in the sea,
And rides upon the storm.

Deep in unfathomable mines
Of never-failing skill,
He treasures up his bright designs,
And works his sovereign will.

Ye fearful saints, fresh courage take:
The clouds ye so much dread
Are big with mercy, and shall break
In blessings on your head.

Judge not the Lord by feeble sense,
But trust him for his grace;
Behind a frowning providence
He hides a smiling face.

His purposes will ripen fast,
Unfolding every hour:
The bud may have a bitter taste,
But sweet will be the flower.

> *Blind unbelief is sure to err,*
> *And scan his work in vain:*
> *God is his own interpreter,*
> *And he will make it plain.*

Then we began to understand that in God's infinite wisdom and love be could take those dear children, whom he loved so much and who had given themselves to him, all to heaven together, almost as painlessly as falling asleep, and use the story of their clear conversions, entire consecration, and triumph in darkness and storm on that terrible night, as it would be read around the world, to soften hard hearts, to open pocket books, and, through the story of their death, have not only six hearts opened and consecrated to his service, but six thousand or more. Thus as the night passed away, rays of light and hope began to glimmer through the darkness.

These rays, we are believing, were from the Revelation of the Spirit, the "Comforter," who was taking of the thoughts of Jesus Christ, and showing them unto us; and it is for the purpose of aiding in accomplishing what we believe to be the will of God in this otherwise very mysterious providence, that the story is being told in this form.

The journey to Darjeeling

Among the greatest wonders of the world are the Himalaya mountains, in which is situated Darjeeling, often called the "Children's Paradise;" which it certainly is to the children of a large portion of the Europeans of Bengal, for, when in the hot season the temperature on the plains is from 90° to 100°, in Darjeeling there is an average of 60°. It is about 450 miles from Calcutta, and at an elevation of about 7,000 feet above sea level. The first 400 miles out from Calcutta the train runs through the densely populated rice districts of Bengal, where sometimes there are nine hundred people living to the square mile, and during the last fifty miles there is an ascent of about one inch in every twenty-nine, and at some places one in every twenty-four.

The narrow-gauge light engines and small cars used on the road which ascends the mountain has given rise to the name "Toy Railway." A ride up the mountains on this railway with its spiral slopes, sudden reverses and sharp curves, passing places appropriately called "Sensation Point," and "Agony Point," as one is hurried up through forests, tea plantations, cloud and sunshine, with a change of mountain view at every turn, until he is higher than the very clouds and in full view of the "eternal snows," is considered by tourists to be one of the most delightful, exhilarating and inspiring experiences known in a journey around the world.

Darjeeling has been considered one of the safest resorts in the Himalaya mountains, there has not been a serious landslip in the memory of the oldest resident. "Arcadia," "Ida Villa" and "Mall Villa," the very houses in which the children suffered, have, without the slightest sign or suspicion of danger, been occupied every season for over thirty years; but an unusual rainfall began on Saturday, September 23rd, and did not cease till 4 a.m. on Monday the 25th between these hours 24-70 inches of rain fell.

The heaviest storm was between 4 P.M. Sunday, the 24th, and 4 A.M. Monday, the 25th, during which twelve hours fourteen inches of rain fell; but its severest fury was attained, and the greatest landslips occurred, between midnight and 2 A.M. Monday, when it would seem safe to assume that the rain was falling at about the rate of two inches per hour. Not only did the storm wash down the sides of the mountains in Darjeeling, but for many miles round the landslips were terrible.

On Monday, September 25th, before the news of the disaster at Darjeeling had reached Calcutta, Miss Fanny Perkins, a missionary from Than Daung, Burma, had left Calcutta for Darjeeling, taking with her a special parcel from Mrs. Lee for each of her children, prepared with great care by the mother, not knowing the children were already in heaven. Miss Perkins found two breaks in the road before reaching Kurseong, one necessitating a walk of a mile and a half, the other two miles. She reached Kurseong at 3 o'clock, Tuesday the 26th, and as she was one of the first party of Europeans who went over the road. I will let her tell her own story of bravery and endurance: — "The train did not go any farther and I knew nothing of broken telegraph connections and had decided to send Miss Stahl word that I had tried to visit her but could get no further; and I engaged a seat in the next train returning. I was standing watching four gentlemen who were preparing to walk through. One of them went to a shop across the street and soon returned and said to the others, 'That's terrible news from Darjeeling. The Rev. Mr. Lee and family have been swept down the mountain side and are lost.' I went out and said, 'That's a mistake so far as Mr. and Mrs. Lee are concerned: they are in Calcutta, but their children are living in Darjeeling. Are you sure it's true about the loss of the family?' 'Well, it's Mall Villa No. 2. Do you know their house?'

I went to the box and there I found the same name and number. The thought of returning to Mrs. Lee when so near and perhaps able to be of some service, seemed impossible, and I asked the gentlemen to permit me to go through with them. They looked a little doubtful, and I assured them I would cause them no delay as I was fully equal to the walk and they consented. I had my breakfast at 11 o'clock, but there was no time to get any food to take with me, as the others were ready to go, and it was late. Mr. Pascal secured me a coolie for my box and bundle and we started off, — Messrs. Pascal, Burke, Pymm, Macdonald and myself.

We had seven or eight coolies with us, one of whom had been over the road from Sonada that day. We left Kurseong at 4 P.M. The first washout was close to the town. They told us that there was a footpath, but we would find it very hard to get through as there was a very bad washout in the fortieth mile (the miles are numbered from Siliguri). We found several bad places before we reached Toong, but the ease with which we crossed them encouraged us to think that we would not find it impassable.

We rested at the Toong station five minutes, then hastened on in order to pass the bad washout before dark. We reached what we supposed answered the description, where the railway irons and ties hung like a suspension bridge over a space two hundred feet long. It was at a place where the road bent in, and from a point several hundred feet above there had been a great sweep of rocks, carrying away the railway bed. In the middle of the slip was a torrent of water.

The only sign of a footpath was a bridge made of small tree trunks thrown across the torrent. Climbing over the loose rocks on the steep mountain side we made for the bridge, which was about a foot wide. We crossed the break successfully and congratulated ourselves that we had been wise in passing it before dark. Daylight faded, the stars came out, and we found ourselves at the edge of a washout as large as the other and much worse, because the rocks were mixed with soft earth and water. We had no light save matches, Mr. Macdonald was ahead, then a coolie, Mr. Pascal and myself behind the others. The coolie called back that the "miss sahiba" could not come, and as we neared the torrent Mr. Pascal drew back saying, 'It's too bad. Miss Perkins; we can't go.' I heard Mr. Macdonald's voice across the torrent, and as the coolie reached down his hand and took it and went up and crossed the temporary bridge on my hands and feet.

The rest came over soon, and we made our way over fallen trees and rocks, through mud and water. Ofttimes when I sought a safe footing, my walking stick would sink to my hand in the soft mud. It was an awful place. But we came out on the railway again and found ourselves near a native hut. We aroused the inmates and purchased an old lantern (which did service for two miles or more) and some mustard oil. I had two towels in my hand-bag, one of which I tore and made torches which gave us light.

We found that instead of one washout there were many after the fortieth mile. Indeed, it was washout or washing most of the way to Ghoom. We had to walk in many places on a wet parapet, which on the top was only about a foot wide. A misstep might land a person hundreds of feet below. But our feet did not slip and we reached Sonada soon after nine o'clock. Here we rested for half an hour and the native postmaster made tea for us. We had some lunch with us and the hot tea refreshed us. We here secured four bottles of oil and my other towel was torn to serve as a torch. We had nine miles before us, and we found the road about the same as that over which we had passed. At Ghoom we rested for five minutes and then pushed on. The moon had risen in her fullness, and the walk up over Jalapahar was delightful.

From Kurseong to Ghoom there was the constant roar of falling water, but from here there was silence, because our path for a distance of five miles took us away from the railway track as we found its bed in the mountain side entirely swept away. We were compelled to climb a high mountain spur which carried us above Darjeeling. As we came down over the hill the challenge of the sentinel rang out in the stillness. We passed on and came to where we could see Darjeeling nestling in the mountain side. It was a beautiful sight! Death-like stillness reigned. I inquired of a policeman for "Arcadia," and was told that the school had moved out. The man said he knew the house and would take me to it. Bidding the others good-night, I went on my way. It was just three o'clock when we reached Darjeeling; but it was four before I found the house where Miss Stahl, Principal of Arcadia, was staying.

"The Arcadia Girls' School had been received by the Scotch Zenana Mission Ladies, and Miss Reid opened her door for me that morning and gave me a most cordial welcome.

Hail Mount Hermon! A Tribute

We were the first Europeans who had passed over the road, and our arrival was an omen of good. Cold and wet, I did not present a very pleasing picture. Miss Reid insisted on me going to bed at once while she prepared a cup of hot tea. This early chhota hazri (little breakfast) was exceedingly refreshing. I was then told to go to sleep, but closed eyes brought pictures of rocks, mud, fallen trees and hanging railway lines. At the usual hour for rising I was shown into Miss Stahl's room. It is needless to say that she was glad to see me, and we had much to say to each other. I learned that Wilbur Lee had been found and was still living, though his recovery was doubtful."

Just forty-eight hours later than the time Miss Perkins left Calcutta, another party left for Darjeeling, composed of the Rev. D. H. and Mrs. Lee, "baby Frank," J. W. Pringle (father of sweet Violet, who entered into rest from Ida Villa on that terrible night,) and the writer.

In the journey up to Kurseong there was nothing unusual, except the surprise at our going so soon after the disaster, and the sorrow that overshadowed us. In a conversation overheard between Mrs. Lee and Mr. Pringle, it was mutually decided that God had some very special blessing for each of them, or He would not have so afflicted, and both agreed that they would seek until they found the purposed blessing.

At Kurseong we procured ponies, but only rode five miles, and then reluctantly let them return because we came to a break in which over a hundred yards of the railway line was gone and over which the ponies could not pass. We scrambled up the mountain side on our hands and feet, and crossed a bridge consisting of two logs which had been thrown across the waterfall, and then picked our way over boulders and through slush down again to the railroad. Such experiences became common during the next ten miles. Over forty places were counted where the railroad was either washed away or buried. Then the one counting grew weary, but afterward estimated that forty other such places were crossed before reaching Ghoom? When we began to walk a novel and interesting method was devised for carrying "baby Frank." A little coolie girl who carries bundles on her back up the mountains, was secured, who had an inverted cone-shaped basket, which we cushioned with an overcoat, and "baby Frank" sat in this basket with his laughing face above the brim.

Throughout the journey this little man proved himself an excellent traveller, and soothed his parents with his smiles and baby talk. At this stage he appeared to the best advantage; for, notwithstanding his new surroundings and mode of conveyance, he was full of fun, screaming with laughter, and kept one of us busy watching that, in his dancing, baby glee, he did not jump out of his basket. The largest break on the line was about three hundred yards in a semi-circular form, and the iron rails were torn and twisted as if they had been made of iron threads. Huge boulders had been rolled down; in fact the hillside had been completely carried away, and perhaps more than anywhere else on the line was the mighty power of God manifested in the devastation the storm had wrought and we keenly felt the littleness and utter helplessness of man in the presence of such overwhelming destruction.

"The House In Which Your Children Were Is Gone"

At Sonada, ten miles from Darjeeling, night overtook us, and though we were intensely anxious to proceed, yet with Mrs. Lee and the baby in our party, we felt that to go forward in the night was neither wise nor safe; but we had nowhere to sleep. In this hour of extremity, a priest came down from one of the Roman Catholic sanitoriums situated close by and kindly offered us entertainment for the night, which offer we gladly and gratefully accepted and we were most delightfully entertained. On the following morning we rose much refreshed, ate a hearty breakfast, and started out on foot, feeling grateful to the kind-hearted priest. I noted that all hearts were touched when it was known that Mrs. Lee and "baby Frank" were in our party.

People vied with each other to see who could do the most for them. We had again reached a place where the journey could be made on ponies, and two ponies were ready to carry Mr. and Mrs. Lee into Darjeeling. A basket was specially prepared for "baby Frank" and a known and trusted servant sent to carry the precious baby. For this kindness Mrs. Lee is indebted to Mrs. Brown. Five miles further on at Ghoom a refreshing repast was given us at the home of the Rev. Mr. Frederickson, of the Scandinavian Mission. From Ghoom we ceased to even follow the railway line, for from there to Darjeeling we were told the railroad bed was almost entirely gone.

We ascended by a hard climb the Jalapahar mountain, and as we approached its summit the eternal snows in the golden glow of the early morning broke upon our view, and as we looked at the range, hundreds of miles in length, it seemed that nothing more beautiful and majestic could be seen until we see the King of kings in all His glory. Darjeeling was reached in a short time; and the party separated; the Rev. D. H. and Mrs. Lee to the bedside of their boy, Wilbur; Mr. Pringle to some friends; and I to where the Arcadia School was being kindly and gratuitously sheltered.

"Arcadia"

The death of the four children of the Arcadia Girls' School was caused by the falling in of the walls of the room in which they were at the time. The building was of stone, and a boulder coming down from the hill above struck the house with such force that the walls were collapsed without a moment's warning. There were nine ladies sitting in the room with the children when the walls fell, nearly all of whom were more or less injured. The story of the last day and night will be told by those who passed through it. Miss Stahl writes of the Last Sunday at Arcadia:

"There are two memories connected with our last Sunday at Arcadia. While the rain was falling in torrents outside we had a quiet, lovely day in the school, and no one thought of fear. The morning service in the church is at 11 o'clock, and Sunday-school immediately after. When the school-bell rang at 8 o'clock, as usual, for the study of the Sunday-school lesson, seeing that we would probably not be able to go to church I reviewed the lessons of the quarter with the older girls. Miss Brittain took the little girls, taught them the Golden Text, and read Bible verses to them until 9.30, the hour for morning prayers. On Sunday we always spent half an hour at prayers, sang several hymns, read the lesson for the day, and the little ones recited a psalm in concert. That morning they recited the 90th Psalm: "Lord, thou hast been our dwelling-place in all generations." The prayer closed the exercises, and then we had breakfast.

After breakfast the children played about or looked at picturebooks, and the older ones read for an hour or more. Then all were made to lie down on their beds and sleep or read, as they chose, until dinner time, which was at 2.30. The time for the Junior Christian Endeavour meeting was five o'clock, and I gave the Bible lesson that day, and the Lord gave me the verse, 'Suffer little children to come unto me' as the one to talk about. As I remember it now, if I had known that four little ones present at that meeting would be taken to heaven before morning, I could hardly have said anything more appropriate.

The Lord gave me the message. I knew it then but did not know why he had given me that particular message. The lesson was, first, the sweet story of how the words came to be spoken when the mothers brought their children to show them to Jesus. The disciples thought it would annoy Him, and tried to send them away, but Jesus said, 'Suffer the little children to come unto me, and forbid them not, for of such is the kingdom of heaven.' Then He took them in his arm and blessed them, which shows Jesus loves little children and loves to have them come to Him. That was the substance of the lesson, to which they all listened most attentively; they then sang the hymn about mothers bringing their children to Jesus. Tea was at 6.30, and after that the older girls gathered round the piano and we sang hymns, while the little ones sat quietly in another room and listened to a story.

At 7.30 they went to bed. Mrs. Warne, who had gone from Calcutta to spend some time in Arcadia, continues the story: 'About 8 o'clock in the evening we heard a peculiar roar which Edith, my only daughter, a child under fourteen years of age, said was thunder. I went down to see Miss Stahl and asked her if she had heard it, and she said it was the river roaring, in a lull in the storm, but I felt that it was a landslip. From 9.30 we sat with Miss Stahl and talked awhile. I then asked her if I could come to her room, as I was too nervous to sleep. She said, 'Yes, come.' We were just going to do this when there was the most awful roar, accompanied by the crash of stones on the roof of the room in which I lived at the end of the building. Miss Stahl asked, 'What is it?' I answered, 'A slide, and very near, too.'

We then went up to see how the girls were in the dormitory, and finding them all quiet, we came back to consult as to what to do next. I said, 'We are responsible for these girls, and I think we had better get them up the hill.' Just then we heard cries and pitiful screams from outside, and ongoing out, found all the school servants who had escaped, coming to the house. They said their houses had been swept away, one sweeper killed, the washerman, the watchman and his whole family covered (seven in all) by the debris. Miss Stahl took a lantern from the head bearer and went toward that end of the building to see what had happened, but before going two-thirds of the way she was over her ankles in water and mud, and was told she would be swept away if she went on.

We now felt that it was too much risk to remain in a building being undermined by a stream of water. The teachers were awakened; Miss Stahl went up the hill to Ida Villa to see if we could bring the children up there. While she was away Edith and I wakened the small children sleeping in a dormitory by themselves. We went to their room and soon quietly roused and dressed them. None were over nine years of age. Edith woke them, as she was a favourite, and could do it without alarming them. We soon had them dressed without arousing fear, some asking why we woke them so soon. We told them we were going up to Ida Villa, as a part of the hill had come down on the servants, and we wanted to go higher up. Eric Anderson was the last one I helped, and he dressed as if for the day, putting his little night-suit on his pillow as he would have done in the morning.

Phoebe Wallace, the school pet, laughed at me as I went round fastening a button here or a shoe string there that some child could not master. Her ayah put on her dress over her night-clothes and rolled her up in a blanket, leaving an opening through which we kissed her happy little face, but she knew nothing of the fear we had for her and the other little ones we had under our care. Miss Stahl returned and said we could go. Edith and I went with those whom we had dressed, and some of the older girls who were also ready. Miss Stahl came later with the others. We climbed by the sweeper's path, up the hill, the water coming down it as if in a drain and the rain pouring in torrents upon us. Mr. and Mrs. Lindeman gave us a kind welcome beside a good fire in a pleasant little drawing-room. We had the children take off their shoes and dry their feet, and after a time put them on the floor to have a sleep.

Miss Stahl and I went from group to group and talked with the older girls, who realized what had happened, and tried by being calm ourselves to keep them the same. The smaller children laughed and played, and one by one fell asleep with their heads under a round table and their feet sticking out, spoke fashion. Eric Anderson was full of fun and as he saw a hole in a stocking of a boy next to him, said, 'Mrs. Warne, I have found a potato.' As we were thus sitting and passing the time, without any warning, a slide came on the south and west ends of the room, filling it with the falling stones and dust. There was pitch darkness for a time, but when it subsided we saw the stones still falling; but to our joy the hanging lamp was burning as if nothing had happened. It seemed miraculous that the end of the beam on which the lamp hung should be saved and enough roof above it to protect the lamp from the rain. This lamp burned till morning. As soon as the dust cleared away we saw that all the teachers, except one, were wholly or partially covered with the falling debris. Miss Stahl and I got five children out by lifting stones off them.

It is still a marvel to me when I remember the large stones which we rolled off the children, that none of their bones were broken and no one seriously injured. This is probably accounted for, partly, by their having so strangely (which now seems providential) gone to sleep under the table. The next work was to get the teachers out. When we had released all we could, there was still covered Muriel Haskew, all but her head; but Violet Pringle, Ruth and Phoebe Wallace, the ayah, Eric Anderson and little Blanche Limpus, were entirely buried.

Finally, we could do no more, and Mrs. Lindeman came to me and said, 'Oh! Mrs. Warne; if someone could get out and bring help! My poor husband (an old gentleman) has not the strength to do all that is needed.'

Edith was standing near me, and said, 'Mamma, I think we can get out. I knew an old path two years ago when I roomed here.' I stood bewildered a moment, and she said again, 'We can get out that way, Mamma.' I could not refuse to go after this, even if it meant the end, so I said, 'We will try.' No one can ever know what it meant for me to take my dear girl out into that dark, stormy night alone. I got her where I could get a good, long look at her white, brave face, and gave her what I thought might be a goodbye kiss, and we started out. We could not get out at the end door as Edith wished, so left by a back bathroom door. At our first step we went into water to our knees.

Then followed an almost perpendicular climb on our hands and knees, the water striking us on the chest like a river, and the rain falling on us in torrents. This was between 12 and 1, the time of the fiercest storm. Umbrellas and cloaks we had none, as all were covered in the room we had left. We were dressed as we had been when helping the children. After we got on the first road above there came the most dreadful roar of falling hill that we had heard, or else we felt it more, being alone. The ground shook beneath our feet, and I put my arm around Edith and said, 'Darling, it is the end.' She answered, 'No, it is behind us; come on, mamma.'

I followed, and we soon came to where we had to cross the slide that had crushed the room in which we had been. Edith plunged in, and I followed as fast as my long, wet, clinging clothing would let me. I sank to the knees in mud, but got through the first slide; had a few feet of solid road, then came to another slide. I, fearing to go near the edge, kept toward the hill, and was soon in mud above the knees, which seemed to draw me down, and I thought I was in the mouth of a drain, as I could not get out. The earth and stones began to come from above, and I expected to be covered every minute, so I called to Edith, 'Go on; I can't get out.' I hoped she would be spared to her papa in Calcutta, even if I did not get out. She called back, 'If you can't come mamma, I am coming back to you.'

I knew she would, and gave another desperate struggle, found a little more solid footing, and reached her side of the slide. We had a few more feet of solid road, and came to the crossing of another slide. In this one Edith never left me, but kept hold of my hand, and we passed over safely and reached the level road on the top of the mountain. We soon found some native policemen, and told them our sad story of the children buried, and asked them to go down the hill and help dig them out. To comply with our request required more bravery than they possessed.

We had to pass on in the darkness without receiving from them any help. We called at other places on our way, but were disappointed in getting help. In our dire distress we thought of the Union Chapel Manse, half a mile farther on, and without a light we hurried on through the blinding rain, wading in water over our ankles, sometimes to the knees, sometimes running and then hardly able to walk, once climbing over a slide in which was a fallen tree. At last we reached the Manse, and were kindly taken in and tenderly cared for by Mrs. Campbell White. The Rev. Patrick McKay and Prof. Fleming, of Lahore, immediately left for the scene of disaster, and did excellent work." This rather full description of the

"The House In Which Your Children Were Is Gone"

experiences and difficulties of getting up the hill through that terrible cyclone and landslips, will reveal what Miss Stahl, the teachers, and the girls of the School, who came up the mountain side a few hours later, passed through in that terrible night.

At the house that had fallen in on the teachers and pupils, Miss Stahl continued, with Mr. Lindeman, working to rescue Muriel Haskew, but finding herself unequal to the task, she started out to find a way to take the remaining children of safety. Ten children followed her, among them the brother and sister of Ruth and Phoebe Wallace, who were under the stones. As she was climbing the hill, she saw a light, which proved to be Miss Reid guiding the rescue party to Ida Villa, and too much praise cannot be given to her for this brave act. The rescue party, on reaching the house, found Mr. Lindeman had gathered the frightened girls who had not gone up the hill with Miss Stahl, and was having prayer with them in one of the uninjured rooms. The first work was to rescue Muriel Haskew.

Beams had to be cut in three places, with a tiny meat-saw, and much rubbish removed before she was free. She was released after some three hours of waiting, not knowing when more hill might come down, hearing all the talk of the children and those who were working, and at last knowing she was given up till outside help came. After all this, when someone said, "Give her brandy," she said, "I can't take it; I'm a Band of Hope girl." Little hope remained that those in the far corner could be alive. The rescuers were wet and weary, and had about decided to give up for a time, when one young man thought he heard a cry, and said, "It's the baby. Come, one more trial," and they found Blanche Limpus, who had been sheltered by a chair and the organ in a most wonderful way. Great stones were all around her; she had thrown one tiny arm over her head as if to shield it from the falling walls. When taken up by one of the men, he said to her, "God bless you dear; we are glad to see you." She looked into his face and laughed a happy, childish laugh, and ran to the other children.

More help came at daylight, and the bodies of the following four children and a native ayah were recovered: Violet Pringle, who was the only daughter of Mr. J. W. Pringle, a wellknown Government servant of Calcutta. She had a slight head wound which the doctor thought gave her a painless death but was not at all disfigured. She was a sweet, quiet girl, loved by all. Eric Anderson, son of the Rev. Herbert Anderson, Secretary of the English Baptist Mission in India, a dear, bright, fun-loving boy. Ruth Wallace, a merry maiden of nine, one of the sweet singers of the school, full of music to her busy finger-tips; and dear baby Phoebe Wallace, the pet and darling of the School, whose rosy lips had been kissed when awakened a few hours before, but now were cold in death. She was found in her faithful ayah's arms covered with her *chadar*, as if she had tried to shield her darling from the stones. These two were the children of Dr. James R. Wallace, a widely-known physician in Calcutta. The bodies of these dear children were taken to the Union Chapel, where kind hands performed the last robing in earthly white, till they arise clothed in Christ's robes.

Dear Lois Lee, whose body was found below Mall Villa, and whose story will be told in another chapter of the book, soon rested in Union Chapel beside the others. At one side was placed the faithful *ayah* who had cared for Baby Wallace. On the day of the funeral many friends sent to the church baskets of flowers, wreaths and crosses of roses, lilies, chrysanthemums, ferns, and dainty creepers. These were sent by all who had a flower left after the storm. They came from the tiny garden of some quiet cottage on the hill-side as well as from the Maharani's and the Lieutenant-Governor's more beautiful grounds; but all alike bore a message of love and sympathy to the sad hearts of the parents away on the plains, and seemed to say, "These are also our children and in your place we pay the last tribute of love." Long before the time of service the church was crowded, and many had taken care to remove all bright colour from their clothing.

All sects were represented, Churchmen and Dissenters meeting on one common platform and joining in the service. The walk to the cemetery was an impressive one. The highest Government officials in Darjeeling, with the highest representatives of the Church of England and the Church of Rome, followed the coffins, which were borne by a detachment of soldiers of the Munster Fusiliers, led by the military band, and the procession extended half a mile. The simple hill people stood on either side of the road with their usually merry faces saddened and quiet, — not a murmur as the procession passed along. The five bodies were laid side by side on the quiet hillside in sight of the eternal snow in the beautiful "God's Acre," to rest till Christ shall call His own (for they were His), as their schoolmates sang, "Safe in the Arms of Jesus," and the Archdeacon read the beautiful words "I am the resurrection and the life."

The Master's call had again been given to mothers on earth: "Suffer little children to come unto me, and forbid them not, for of such is the kingdom of heaven."

7 Letters Of Love And Support

Extracts from letters

Most touching letters of sympathy have been received by Mr. and Mrs. Lee from the Secretaries of Temperance Unions, Conferences, Leagues, Boards, Missionary Bodies and Young People's organizations; from all denominations of Christian people and every part of the world — each containing beautiful and appropriate resolutions and tributes, but space will not permit their insertion here, nor allow the publication of but a very few of the hundreds of private letters from so many parts of the world.

LADY CURZON

Lady Curzon in a telegram to Mrs. Lee, said:

Will you allow me to express my deep sorrow and sympathy at the grievous blow that has fallen upon your family. Every woman and mother in India will be feeling for you.

THE METROPOLITAN OF INDIA

The Bishop of Calcutta expressed his sympathy in the following letter to Mr. Lee:

Reverend and Dear Sir: — The tragic news received from Darjeeling leads me to claim the Christian privilege of offering you my most true sympathy in your bereavement, which is so terrible that I can hardly write or think of it. I have so lately left Darjeeling, that the desolation in which it is plunged possesses for me a most vivid reality. But the tears are in my eyes when I think that your own home has in a moment been bereaved of all that had made it so bright and beautiful before. I can but commend you in faith and sympathy to the hands of Him who alone can send such wounds as yours and alone can heal them, praying that even now the light may spring up in your darkness and you may humbly and faithfully accept His ... and holy will.

Believe me. Reverend and Dear Sir,
Most faithfully yours,
E. C. Calcutta

BISHOP THOBURN

Dear Brother and Sister Lee: — The Advocate came to hand last night, bringing the news of the cablegram which had been sent, but which, for some reason, the people at the Mission Rooms did not forward to me. I have seldom been more shocked in my life than when we read that five of your dear children had perished in the landslide. It seemed to bring the awful calamity very near to us. Those children had become well known to us, and especially to my wife.

We have talked together about how useful they would become, and Vida seemed nearing the age when she could begin active mission work. We move in a sphere of mystery, but of all the mysterious events which have befallen us as a mission, this seems to me the most inscrutable, and this awful tragedy which has overtaken your family, is simply stunning to one's sensibilities and thoughts.

I do not suppose we will ever get much light on this problem until we rejoin the lost ones in the other world.

In some way, however, light in a measure will undoubtedly come to you. Instead of breaking up the work, or even putting it back to any great extent, I shall not be surprised if this becomes the means in God's hands of rousing our people to greater efforts than ever. It will undoubtedly produce a great effect in this country and it cannot but unite our people in a more determined way to establish the work of God on everlasting foundations in India.

The cablegrams distinctly state that a service for the dead has been held over the supposed entombment of your children. A note from Miss Knowles explains that you had taken a small house near Ida Villa, and that you had gone down, leaving Vida in charge of her brothers and sisters.

No doubt you were in Calcutta when it occurred, and it must have been an agonizing time to you to have been thus cut off from the children. I suppose also the telegraph line was interrupted so that some time must have elapsed before you knew the full measure of your loss.

In your sorrow you will have the sympathy, I may say, literally of a million souls. God help you and comfort you. The death, no doubt, was painless and although the grave seems a frightful one, it after all, I think, would not be saying too much to remark that God has buried them. We have laid away three of our little ones in quiet graves, and yet we cannot understand what it would have been if all three had been taken from us in a moment's time. The mysteries of life are many, the mystery of pain, the mystery of sorrow, the mystery of bereavement and separation. All these things belong to problems which cannot be solved this side the grave.

I arrived home last night after a very laborious campaign. If God wills I will see you in about three months. In the meanwhile may His grace sustain you. His love abound in you, and His everlasting arms uphold you. My God help you, I can say no more. I am sure He will help you and I am also sure that in the years to come when we all meet in the other world, we will be able to say with a depth of meaning which is impossible now, that God hath done all things well.

In great haste. Your sympathizing brother,
J. M. Thoburn

MRS. THOBURN

Dear Brother and Sister Lee: — What can I say. If I could sit down beside you and weep with you, it would be much more in keeping with my idea of showing sympathy.

How thankful we are to know that you know how to trust God in an hour like this, and that there will be no element of rebellion in either of your hearts.

What peace and comfort God can give to such! It has seemed to me like the burial of Moses — as I have thought that you could indeed say, that God himself did it. I have a peculiar feeling for your dear children. They were so much a part of the mission — and what blessed missionaries they would have made — nay, were already. But the higher service is better. God's best for you and yours.

If the dear people over here, who love you and your work would only have it in their hearts to put up a memorial building for your Bengali children, what a fitting thing it would be! Let us have the privilege of giving the first hundred dollars in the hope that many more hundreds will follow. May the Lord soothe and comfort as only He can. He knows what He is doing and we can afford to "wait patiently" for Him. Dear, dear friends, I am persuaded that riches of grace will abound toward you, and that you will be able to do more for India than you have ever done. "Call upon Me in the day of trouble, and I will deliver you and ye shall glorify me." I am sure this promise will be verified in your case.

With much love for you and tenderest sympathy.

Affectionately yours,
Anna J. Thoburn

LADY WOODBURN

The following was received from Lady Woodburn, wife of the Lieutenant-Governor of Bengal, on the morning of Wilbur's death:

Dear Mrs. Lee: — When the sad news, this morning, of your little son reached me, my first impulse was to write to you, and then I felt the words could not come to express all I felt for you, in your overwhelming sorrow.

You and Mr. Lee have been little out of my thoughts since we heard the terrible news of that Sunday night. The consolation must be so great to think how the dear children passed away, their hearts full of love and obedience to you, and their last conscious act — prayer.

My whole heart goes to you in sorrow and sympathy.

One knows where your darlings are, but the awful blank is with you, of where they are not. They are indeed in God's safe keeping and may you who are left, be comforted and supported till life's journey ends.

With deep, deep sympathy.

Yours sincerely,
W. WOODBURN

BISHOP CYRUS D. FOSS

My Dear and Most Sorely Bereaved Friends:
Since the tidings of your great trial sent a shock of pain through our whole church, and far beyond it, the bare thought of writing you a word of sympathy has paralyzed my pen

all the time, until I saw Mrs. Lee's letter in the Christian Advocate. For such a triumph of grace as that letter evinces, I thank God from the bottom of my heart.

I send up my prayer with thousands more that you may have measureless comforts of the Holy Spirit.

One of my jewels for forty years has been: "My God shall supply all your needs, according to his riches in Glory, by Christ Jesus."

Mrs. Foss joins me in kindest sympathy.

Yours most truly,
C. D. Foss

R. LAIDLAW, ESQ.

Dear Mrs. Lee: — I feel that I must send you a few more lines today, not that any words of mine can bring you any consolation, but I just want to say how very distressed we all feel. We have not passed a day or night since we got the terrible news without having the dear sweet faces of your children before us, and now poor Wilbur has gone too, to be with the others. The telegrams tell us how dear Vida told them all to pray; she knew where to seek strength in moments of trial. One was spared a few days to carry you a message of comfort and consolation.

You and Mr. Lee have the profound sympathy of many thousands in this country. May the little one that remains be spared to be a joy and a comfort to you, and may the Lord abundantly sustain and comfort you is the earnest prayer of your very sincere friend,

R. Laidlaw

REV. R. BURGES, Secretary of the L.S.S.U.

Mr. Burges was a special friend of the Lee children.

Dear Mr. and Mrs. Lee: — My heart's love to you! The God of our Father's be your God now. Words fail me. I have been in the Vale of Tears for eleven months, and I know, in some measure, your darkness of home and heart. But He is able. Your children, who were my friends, are with the King and see Him in His beauty. The grand re-union is not far off. They are safe and we are pressing on to the place where they are.

We now see parts of His way; this is why we grieve.

Love deep and strong,
Yours ever,
R. Burges

REV. W. S. MATTHEW, D.D., Editor, "California Christian Advocate"

My Dear Brother and Sister: — You can scarcely imagine in how many homes in America the sad story has been rehearsed, and at how many family altars you and sister Lee and the dear baby boy have been remembered. I think your dear wife's letter, published in last week's New York Advocate, is the most touchingly beautiful thing I ever read. As we all sat about the sitting room table, Tuesday evening, after upper, I undertook to read it aloud to the dear ones of my own family; but I broke down again and again.

Finally, I did manage to finish it, and we all wept together with you. Our hearts can only cry, God bless you and keep you. But what a glorious picture remains in our minds of those brave children praying together and trusting God amid the horrors of that awful storm! Surely their sweet faith and triumphant death must make a profound impression upon the people, wherever known.

Thank God for such examples of his saving power as are given us in the sweet lives and glorious translation of your six dear ones! And how glad are all our hearts that the Father above has spared you one sweet lamb of the flock to comfort you these days. God bless him.

Dear Brother and Sister, tears rain down my face as I try to write, and I can only say, God bless you. Surely, He will keep and comfort you. My wife joins me in all I would say.

Always your friend,
W. S. Matthew

WALTER DAVIES, ESQ.

My Dear Mr. Lee: — I never met a family of children which so charmed and interested me, and I shall never forget the happy afternoon we all spent together at our first meeting in Darjeeling. We looked forward to many happy days in their company, and had planned to find ponies for all the children and have a good day at Ghoom Rock on my return the following month.

My wife and I were strongly drawn to them all; their winning and natural manner appealed at once to our affections, and I feel I should like my own boy to grow up with such ideals as lived in yours. They will always live in our memories and we greatly prize the photographs you have so kindly given us.

Our hearts go out to you both in deepest sympathy.

Sincerely yours,
Walter Davies

C. M. D.

I cannot conceive of a more truly appropriate time, or a more beautifully appropriate attitude, to pass over, than that of prayer — the attitude in which your darlings received their last call "to go up higher." And may it not be possible that the incense and the fragrance of that beautiful prayer may linger round the eternal hills forever?

The whole picture of your dear Home is to me indescribably beautiful — so sweet, so bright, so divine. One evening your darlings form a miniature heavenly choir the next evening they are members of the Heavenly choir itself! How inspiring… "they were lovely and pleasant in their lives, and in death they were not divided".

And your brave, patient, darling little boy; how can words express the pathos and patience of his sufferings? His brightness, his thoughtfulness, on his sick bed, and, after all, to be called to join his dearly beloved sisters and brother in Glory! How unspeakably beautiful!

Just as if his special mission had been to come out of the gloom to tell how his dear sisters and brother had passed into their eternal home, and then joins them immediately himself! How angelic! What an unspeakable comfort it must be to you, my dear friend, to know that your darlings were like flowers in bloom fully ripe for the kingdom.

I sincerely and devoutly pray that our Heavenly Father may grant you both all grace, and faith, and strength and fortitude, to bear this grievous burden, and to enable you to say, "thy will be done". "The Lord giveth, the Lord taketh away, blessed be the name of the Lord."

Yours in the Lord,
C. M. D.

DR. W. W. WHITE

Dear Brother and Sister Lee: — May the Great Good God bind up your broken hearts. I know you will be brave in Him. We pray for the consolations of the one whose sorrow was greater than any sorrow.

Words are cheap and do not serve one's purpose at such a time as this. Be assured of the most cordial sympathy of us all. The children remember well your precious family.

Yours in Christ's behalf,
W. W. White

MRS. HOLCOMB

American Presbyterian Mission

Mrs. Holcomb was one of the first to suggest the memorial building in the following to Mrs. Lee:

My Dear Mr. and Mrs. Lee: — The measure of your awful grief God alone knows and He only can comfort you. "It is the Lord." How much of the brightness and the joy of earth has been quenched for you — how near has heaven come down to you! I have thanked.

God for the precious infant spared to you. When He committed to your keeping this dear child, He knew, though you dreamed not of it, that the other children lent to you were to be taken back to Him who gave them, and in tenderest love this little one was sent to be your comfort in your unfathomable grief.

In connection with you I have been thinking much of a dear friend at home — now with the Lord, who, when but twenty-two years of age, was called to give back to God her husband and her two children. While at the home of a brother, coming down late for breakfast she found on her plate a card on which has been written the following lines:

> "Enough! the dead have had thy tears.
> The living need thy care,
> A sinner in a dying world,
> No time hast thou to spare."

When we knew this lady she was seventy years of age, and her life had been spent in doing good. She told us that the message on the card seemed to her a message from the Lord himself. She felt a peculiar compassion for children. I do not know how many homes she had established, but through her efforts thousands of children had been rescued and trained up for God. I am sure that you will seek to ease your heartache by trying to bring brightness to other lives. I know how deeply interested you are in the children of India, and I have thought how suitable it would be, and how beautiful a memorial to the precious children God has taken, if an orphanage or a home bearing their name could be established. I am sending you by money order a small contribution toward this object now, but I may be able to send you something in addition later.

May the God of all comfort be with you in this time of sorest trial. My husband unites with me in this.

With deepest sympathy and much affection I subscribe myself

Your sincere friend,
Helen H. Holcomb

REV. J. H. BARROWS
President Obenlin College

My Dear Bereaved Brother: — Though *The Indian Witness* I have been made acquainted with your unspeakable affliction. The overwhelming loss which has drawn to you such world-wide sympathy. Your sorrows touch me very closely. The missionary circle in Calcutta are very dear to me. Be sure that my family have remembered you in our prayer to the God of all comfort.

Mrs. Barrows joins me in deepest sympathy for Mrs. Lee and yourself Your resignation and gracious acceptance of God's will are a wonderful evidence of the proof of that Gospel which you have gone to India to proclaim.

Believe me, dear brother,

Faithfully and affectionately yours,
John Henry Barrows

Extracts of letters from friends who knew the Lee children

W. ROSS, ESQ.
Superintendent of Government Printing in India

Air. Ross had them often in his house while in Calcutta. He was a friend to whom the children were greatly attached.

My Dear Mrs. Lee: — I know you will not think I am claiming too much to share your sorrow with you and your husband. The dear children. Of all the little ones in India, they had the biggest place in my heart and I am glad to think I had a big place in theirs. It seems today as if my own had been stricken down. May the Infinite Comfort which you have been privileged to carry to others in bereavement be yours at this time is the prayer of all in this house.

Yours Sincerely,
W. Ross

MRS. GORE

An old Quaker lady, who once lived with the children, writes:

How the dear ones were looking forward to helping you in your work. Lois said one day, 'Sister Gore, when you read of some big things we children are doing some day in India, you will be glad you knew us, and spent a winter with us.' Yes, I am glad I knew them.

MISSES FROST AND SIMPSON

The following is from two lady evangelists in the United States, who were present when the two older girls were converted:

Can it be our darling Vida and Lois are gone from us in such a fearful way. I am all broken up and can hardly write to you as I think of it.

Vida was a rare child. I never saw her equal. We did love all your children and were interested in all that concerned them, but Vida had a place peculiarly her own, perhaps it was because in one sense she loved and trusted us perfectly — and yet, other children love and confide in us, but no child has ever had the place in our hearts like Vida. It was her own rare beautiful nature, her spirituality.

MRS. J. E. ROBINSON

This letter is from the wife of the Editor of the *Indian Witness*, showing how the children were loved by our missionaries in Calcutta.

Their death was like a family grief to us all. My Dear Mrs. Lee: — Thank you very much for your kind invitation for the thanksgiving dinner on Thursday.

We shall be very glad to come and thank God with you for the precious memories of the dear ones. How I miss them every day I cannot tell you. But how wonderfully they have been just lifted into the beautiful life beyond, and I love to think of them there. It seems a fitting place for them — beyond the sin and sorrow of this world.

I thank God every day that we ever knew them and for you

*"Tis better to have loved and lost
Than never to have loved at all"*

and past memories are only a promise of future joy I believe.

I often tell Muriel that perhaps Esther talks to Jesus sometimes about her, and it is a very sweet thought to us both, to think of having friends before the throne.

With a great deal of love.

Yours affectionately,
Retta L. Robinson

MISS GARDNER
Union Missionary Society of America

Miss Gardner, who was a special friend of the boys, writes to Mrs. Lee, after having sent several telegrams:

How much it all means to you no one knows better than I do, who knew those dear children so well. I did so pray that God would spare Wilbur, but it was not His will, and so is not mine, and is not yours. I did not half realize how much I loved them. Their winning, coaxing ways, especially the boys, come to me over and over, night and day, and make me realize how great the desolation in your hearts. I could not read the account given by Wilbur before he joined the others. I try to think of them, as I know they are, brighter and happier than ever they were on earth, bright and happy as their lives were here, and I know you think of them that way, too, gone on only a little while before. Believing as I do in the speedy coming of Christ, it seems only a little while.

Always yours in this hope, and the deepest sympathy and love,
Sarah Gardner

MISS B. E. ROBINSON

My Dear Mrs. Lee: — The mail that brought the news of your great sorrow brought a sorrow to me. I don't need to tell you how I loved them all, from Vida down to dear little Esther. They always seemed like my own brothers and sisters.

Vida and I were like sisters and used to have such good times together. She was such a help to me and her sweet, Christian spirit will always be an inspiration to me. Dear Vida! How happy she must be now, and that thought takes all the sting out of the sorrow.

Lois, too, was such a dear, sweet child, always ready to help someone and to give a smile. She has all the music she wants now. I shall always love the guitar for Vida's sake, too.

Then there was Wilbur with his bright, boyish ways and his laughter-loving heart. I used to love to hear his hearty, infectious laugh; and Herbert, whom I always called "my little brother" especially. He and Wilbur used to play the violins so happily together, and — they have the harps now.

Then Ada and Esther whom I loved next to our own little Muriel. When I try to think of Calcutta and your home without the six dear ones, oh! I can't bear it.

I never thought when I said good-by on the 27th of March that it was the last we would see of them.

Mrs. Lee, if you only knew how I would love to put my arms around you and ask you to let me hug you for the sake of the dear children. This sorrow has come so close to me.

It is lovely to know that they were all ready, and that they are so happy now. I believe that my life will be, and has been, better for having known and loved your dear ones, and I feel as if I will need to work harder than ever to make up for what dear Vida longed so much to do in the mission field.

Dear little Frank! How I would love to sister him. Will you not think of me as one who loved your dear ones next to my own dear ones and as a second daughter as it were. If I were there and could, in a small measure, be another daughter to you, how gladly would I do it.

May the God of all comfort be your Guide and Stay — yours and Mr. Lee's — is my earnest prayer. With my sympathy, and love,

Ever lovingly and affectionately,
Bessie Ellice Robinson

MRS. TOMORY, Free Church of Scotland

My heart is sore for you when I think of your empty home and of those lovely children of yours. Of all your children I felt specially drawn to Lois, perhaps because I saw more of her than of the others, just a short time before I left Darjeeling she and Ada came to a Band of Hope meeting. I had a long chat with Lois. When they were leaving, Lois put her arms around me and kissed me, saying, "I want to kiss someone as I cannot get my Mama."

May God be very near to you in these dark days. We often pray for you and Mr. Lee.

With loving sympathy,
I am, yours very sincerely,
Mary C. Tomory

MRS. BROCKWAY, London Missionary Society

A friend of mine sitting behind the dear children in Church one day, inquired after service, "Who were those children with 'Holiness to the Lord' written so plainly on their faces?" This description fitted them exactly.

From the day I saw them on their arrival in India, to the last happy times we spent together in Darjeeling the impression left was a prayer that the same Holy Spirit, who was moulding these young lives so wondrously, would in like manner so deal with my own little ones in the far-off homeland.

J. CAMPBELL WHITE, ESQ.
Sec. of the College Y.M.C.A., Calcutta

My Dear Mr. and Mrs. Lee: — I have just returned this morning from Mussoorie. A telegram was handed to me from Mrs. White as I came in, saying, "We are safe." I cannot help thinking that your loved ones would like to send you a similar message this morning from the presence of the King; "Safe in the arms of Jesus." After joining a search party in Darjeeling composed of a number of prominent men, who did all they could to find the bodies of the children, he writes: — But we were glad we had gone, for we did all that seems possible to do, to find either the bodies or anything from the house.

It was a great blessing to me to be with you all during the closing days of Wilbur's presence here, and I feel that I shall always be a better man for the experiences I had. His own victory and yours were to me a fresh proof of the larger victory that God makes possible, to every one of us, in our daily life.

I was thinking much of you yesterday in connection with God's test to Abraham — Gen 22:2, 12. God knew how severe the test was — "thy son — thine only son, — whom thou lovest": — and He knows in your case also.

Some of us feel unable to sympathize as we want to, because of our lack of experience. You will probably never meet anyone who has had a greater sorrow, and you will therefore be prepared to sympathize, as few people can.

With fullest loving sympathy.

Yours most sincerely,
J. Campbell White

GRANTHAM GIDDY, ESQ.

Newcastle, N.S. Wales, Australia, Dec. 18th, 1899.

Dear Brother and Sister Lee: — Yours of 10th November to hand, together with the paper containing the sad, sad news. I can only partially realize its awful truth.

To say that I am sorry and sympathize with you in sorrow, would very inadequately express my feelings in the matter.

When I looked at the paper, and the full import of its contents dawned upon me, I had to close it for some time, so little did I previously realize how strong was that strange mysterious bond which bound us. It seemed as if it were my own brothers and sisters that had been so suddenly called into the Master's more immediate presence.

On Sunday morning I spoke to our Sabbath School, and the teachers and scholars in the afternoon passed the enclosed letter of sympathy. As I spoke, I saw many of our scholars in tears, and after the meeting some of the little ones belonging to the Junior Endeavour Society got together, and, of their own accord, drafted and wrote the other note of sympathy. I feel that their death has been blessed to the lasting benefit of many in these parts. And did I say death!! Nay, rather, "Translation." The Master has called upon you to lay your costliest gift on the altar of sacrifice, and you have obeyed.

I have tried to express my deepest sympathy with you in your loneliness, and have failed, and so must leave you in the hands of the "sympathising Jesus". God bless you my Brother, God bless you my Sister!! and prosper the work of your hands. Many a little one in these parts remembers you at the Throne of Grace.

Yours in His service,
Grantham Giddy

8 The Lees And Their Work

MR. AND MRS. D. H. LEE WITH THEIR CHILDREN FOUR YEARS BEFORE.

David H. Lee was born in Carroll County, Ohio, 1850. His father, Jonathan Lee, was a man eminent in the community for his deep piety and sterling Christian character. Young David was converted at eight years of age while kneeling in prayer with his godly mother, in the little old church on the hill, at Harlem Springs, Ohio.

Whilst his work has led him far from home to foreign lands, of this place he has often been heard to say:

> *There is a spot to me more dear,*
> *Than native vale or mountain;*
> *A spot for which affection's tear*
> *Flows grateful from its fountain.*
> *'Tis not where kindred souls abound,*
> *Though that were almost heaven;*
> *But where I first my Saviour found,*
> *And felt my sins forgiven.*

He was educated at Scio, Ohio, — at what was known then as the "one study university" — now Scio College. After preaching a year and a half in the North Ohio and Pittsburgh Conferences, Mr. Lee answered what he felt to be the call of the Spirit, and arranged to go to India as a missionary. He came out in connection with the pioneer work of the Methodist Episcopal Church, amongst the English-speaking people of India; and with no specified salary, shared some of the privations which are not now so necessary where the churches are built and the parsonages provide a home. He left home on the 2nd November with $50, which went towards paying his fare.

William Taylor, afterward Bishop, who was then Superintendent of the Bombay and Bengal Mission, provided the fare from London to Bombay, where he landed on December 18, 1875. He was kindly received by the members of the mission then working in the city, among whom was the revered George Bowen.

After a few days in Bombay, Mr. Lee came to Calcutta, where J. M. Thoburn, now Bishop, was beginning his work amongst the English-speaking people of the city, following up what had been inaugurated by William Taylor. Thus he became associated with the beginning of the work of our church in Bengal.

His first appointment was, however, to Agra, where he preached regularly twice on the Sabbath, and also during the week, and was, in addition, principal of the Agra Collegiate School. At Bombay, in the end of the year 1876, the South India Conference was formed, embracing that part of India not then included in the North India Conference. Mr. Lee became one of the charter members of the South India Conference, and served in its different stations until February, 1883, when a failure in health compelled his return to America with his wife, Miss Jones of the Union Missionary Society, whom he married in 1881 whilst at Bangalore.

By permission I use here the following sketch of Mrs. Lee's life taken from the appendix of her popular book "Chundra Lela": "I was born among the hills of West Virginia, of poor, but hard-working parents, and knew from the first what it was to suffer hardship. As early as possible I took my share of the daily toil. Very soon in life a longing, such as I can never describe, took possession of me to have an education. I have walked two miles in the deep snow day after day, over a rough road, to get to the little school house which afforded the only opportunity for learning in our part of the country. God sent a man to teach that little school who did much to encourage and help me, and also to lead me to seek in God the help I needed most. He has since become a great preacher, but his work began in that little school house." I soon got all I could in our country schools, still I could not be content, and longed more than ever for greater opportunity than West Virginia then afforded her daughters.

"My mother used to say I never shirked my work for anything but books; but no one could understand how hungry I was. Physically, I was frail; in disposition, gloomy, unhappy and discontented; yet God, in His mercy, led all the way through the darkness of these years.

"At the age of fourteen, an aunt came from Ohio to visit us, and offered to take me into her family if my father would let me go. Thus the way opened, and the fall of 1871, the time of the Chicago fire, found me attending college at Scio, Ohio. I worked for my board and studied as I could. I was so glad of the opportunity, I was willing to do anything that I might get on with my studies. Yet God only knows what a shrinking, timid, miserable creature I was.

"During the revival held early in the year 1872, the great turning point came in my life. The music teacher of Scio college, a soul-seeker, said to me: 'I am asking God to convert you at the beginning of these meetings, so you can help bring the other girls to Jesus.' She was the first one who had ever put hope into my heart. Such a thing seemed too high for me — too good to be possible!

"A few days later I was under deep conviction — so wretched I could not study, work or sleep. In the evening meeting, when the minister invited seekers, I felt I must go or be lost. I went, alone, and was the first to go. On the second evening, after such darkness and agony of soul, as, may be, but few ever experience, I was wondrously saved! My conversion was like coming out of the blackest of darkness, where I had been chained, a condemned criminal, into the bright sunlight and glorious liberty of the children of God. How I praise God that He ever, in His mercy, found my poor soul! At that time, I promised God to do His will, and life from that day was beautiful; and I, a changed, happy girl. The next three years were spent in college, planning for the future, doing what I could in the Church and Sunday School, seeing many of my classmates and college friends converted. But soon a settled conviction came over me that God wished me to go as a missionary to India. The place I knew very little about, and the work I felt very unfit for and unworthy of.

"I am sorry to say I fought against this conviction, more probably because I was afraid it was imagination, and yet, the more I fought, the farther away from God I seemed to get. In the meantime, I finished school and tried to settle down to teaching. But God troubled me, upset my plans and sent me sorrow, to let me see how much I needed His grace. In the midst of my first grief, at the loss of a dear girl friend, I fell on my knees in submission to God and said, 'Oh, Lord, I will go anywhere, if Thou wilt with Thine own hand open up the way that I make no mistake, and give me Thy presence and love in full measure.' I arose comforted, restful and happy, leaving it all with Jesus.

"One whom I had loved quietly, unknown to him or anyone else for several years, and to whom I had always been true, was a young minister in the Pittsburg Conference, and had formed a large part of the sacrifice I made, when I told the Lord I was ready to give up all and go to India. What was my surprise, when, a few weeks later, I returned home from my school work, to be told that this same person was going to India under William Taylor (now Bishop), and was to leave in a few days? I said "good-bye" and let him go away to India without ever telling him of the two years' struggle and the consecration I had made.

"The next six months were days of waiting in which my faith was put to some severe rests. With my consecration I had asked God to open up the way with His own hand,

and I had promised my mother I would never apply to any missionary society. I was back in the old homestead in West Virginia. Sometimes I wondered if I had been mistaken in the call, and would God ever open the way. One day after several weary weeks of suffering with typhoid fever, they all thought I was dying and were gathered about my bed.

"A cold shiver passed over my frame, and I said to a dear aunt who was bending over me, 'Is this death?'

"She answered softly, 'Yes, dear. Are you afraid?'

"I said, 'No.'

"And then God seemed to say to me, 'If you live, will you live for India?'

"I answered back, 'India or heaven, which ever be Thy will. Oh, my Father!' Then what peace filled my soul!

"A few moments later, God turned the whole course of that awful disease and I rapidly came back to health.

"A short time afterwards, I was sitting alone in the veranda pondering these things and wondering when God would open the way.

"Just then my uncle called to me from the road telling me he had a letter for me. The post-mark was 'New York;' the address in a strange hand-writing. I hurriedly broke the seal, feeling somehow it contained the light for which I was asking.

"It was a letter from the now sainted Mrs. Doremus, of the 'Union Missionary Society,' the first women's society in America. She stated that Dr. Thoburn, in passing through on his return to India, had handed her name as a candidate for missionary work in India, and enclosed was the list of questions I was expected to answer.

"I had never met Bishop Thoburn and knew very little about him, and how he had gotten my name I knew not. I afterwards found that he and my pastor at Scio had been school friends, and that the Bishop while visiting him had asked for young ladies likely to make missionaries, and from him obtained my name and address.

"My age, as well as other things, were against me, as I was not twenty-one, but in spite of all I was accepted by the Society, and on Nov. 4th, Centennial year, I stepped on board the steamer bound for India, the happiest soul the sun ever shone upon.

"Early in the voyage a deep conviction came over me of my unfitness for this holy calling. One of the parting gifts had been Dr. Steel's 'Love Enthroned;' the more I read and prayed and thought, the more wretched I became. Notwithstanding my bright conversion, my Christian life had been an 'up and down' sort of an experience; a constant struggle with evil tempers.

"Other members of the party seemed to be convicted at the same time and two or three entered into the blessing of perfect love. But I got more wretched until I felt that unless I got a clean heart and could find a place of constant victory over sin, I could never go on to India to preach the gospel to her sad daughters.

"At Liverpool, a noble man of God — an officer in the India army — came on board as a passenger. His face shone with the love of Jesus. One day he handed me a slip of paper on consecration, and asked me if I could take each step it marked out, and if so, to sign it.

"Among other things were the words: "I take the Holy Spirit as my Sanctifier." I prayed all day, and was determined I would not sleep until I could conscientiously sign that paper. I was worn out, so threw myself on my bunk, saying, 'Oh Lord! take temper and all else connected with sin and give me that for which my soul longs,' and a flood of peace came into my soul such as I could never describe.

"I lay there singing softly to myself — 'The great Physician now is near, Jesus, blessed Jesus,' until the waves of the Red Sea lulled me to sleep. I lived this life as best I understood it, for the first sermon I ever heard on sanctification was after I reached India, and preached by Bishop Thoburn. But oh! how much God has had to teach me!

"After reaching India, I began the study of the language, and to work among the Bengali women of Calcutta. For five years I went in and out among them, spending much of my time in their homes. God gave me to see some bright and definite conversions among the women in the zenanas. And yet how imperfectly I felt I did this work!

"The two paths which sometimes had been so near each other and at other times so wide apart that oceans rolled between, at last came together. God plainly led me, and the other part of my life, until the two became one by law, who had been so long one in soul. Thus, after five years of missionary service, I was married to David H. Lee, not to leave our work, but united to work together for the salvation of India.

"Two years later, on account of my husband's health, the Lord showed plainly He wished us to return to our native land.

"It was a sad day, the day I left Calcutta in a sailing vessel, with a wee baby in my arms and a sick husband by my side. It was a long, weary voyage of nearly four months, but our Father was still leading and brought us through storms and calms around the Cape of Good Hope, and safely home, at the cost of less than $200, and that not missionary money, but sent in answer to prayer. India was on our hearts at home, and while we tried to do faithfully what was intrusted to us by the church there, our hearts used to long for India. I would dream about the imprisoned women in the zenanas, and of sitting among them, telling them of Jesus, and would awake so disappointed to find I was so far away from them. How I prayed and waited! God had to give me a mighty baptism of freedom and of power before I was ever able to speak in public.

"After receiving this, wherever I went I pleaded for the Bengali people, that the gospel might be sent to them, for while some of the oldest mission stations are in this province, the millions are practically untouched. Wherever I told of the need of the people of India, God blessed me and persons became interested, but the different Societies said 'our old work fills our hands; we cannot enter new,' and wherever I turned, the way seemed blocked.

"God sent our children into our home, one after another; each one, in the eyes of the church and the world, making it more impossible than ever to return to India. Every one of them was, as soon as born, consecrated to God and laid on the altar of India.

"Whenever we spoke of our desire to return, we were commended for our interest and devotion to the work, but were frankly told that there was no money to send or support us.

Still the burden was upon me, until one night, after much prayer, my Father assured me that my work was not done in India, and that He was able to send us the means.

"I astonished my husband next morning by telling him that I was going to trust God for $20,000 for a missionary fund. Even he seemed a little doubtful, and thought I was beside myself, and would soon get over it, but I never did. I went on praying day and night, asking God to use me in any way He saw best to gather it. It is wonderful how He led and blessed me. At first I held meetings, taking my baby with me, but soon the Lord showed me that He had another plan, and put it into my heart to write about the people and the work I loved.

"My first article was, 'Jessudar, the Kidnapped Girl,' and was published first in the *Western Christian Advocate*, and afterwards in many other papers. Money began to come through the mail, and many very dear friends have been found thus. In 1893, the sum had reached $4,000, which came from persons of all denominations. One Sabbath, after weeks of earnest prayer, God gave me the answer in the verse—'Commit thy way unto the Lord, trust also in him, and he will bring it to pass.'

"I was so sure it would come that I arose from my knees and wrote to my husband to get ready to return to India. I, at the same time, wrote to several friends saying I believed the remaining 116,000 would soon come. In less than two months afterwards a Christian gentleman gave the fund $15,000!"

(Although this money has not yet been realized, the interest was paid for three years, which supported the Lees, and aided the work until the Lord raised up others, and the work goes on.)

"October, 1894, found the fund complete, and we and our six children on the good ship which carried us back to India. Our youngest, Esther Dennett, was a baby seven weeks old when we sailed from New York. It was with a heart full of thanksgiving to God for the privilege of going as His messenger to the lost ones, that I watched the 'Goddess of Liberty' fade in the distance, and again bade farewell to the dear home land. It was with joy of heart such as no words can express, that, after a voyage of six weeks, my eyes again looked upon the great plains, fern clad hills, and beautiful palm groves of dear, old India.

We believe God led us to begin our work in Calcutta, the metropolis of India, and a stronghold of idolatry. We live in the midst of the people and expect to spend the remainder of our lives for their salvation. Our one desire is to be completely in His hands that His will and way may be accomplished through us.

"We are opening up different departments of work just as God sends it to us, trusting Him for all we need. We are asking God for good substantial buildings, and a part of the money for this has come; we know He will send the rest. Children come to us without bread, others flee for protection from the awful curse of child marriage; others who have been sold into sin turn to us to be led back into the path of virtue.

"Some wish to prepare to preach the gospel, both young men and women, and we have had much joy in being the link connecting a number of these worthy cases with God's children at home, who feel specially led to educate these to represent them in India.

"To what proportions this work will grow we do not know. At present we have thirty-eight girls and sixteen boys in training. We take these trusting for their support. We believe this to be only the beginning of a great movement. There is no end to the evangelistic work among the hundreds of thousands of imprisoned zenana women of this city, and a vast field is open for "from house to house" medical work. The number who suffer and die for want of proper treatment is appalling!

"Eight millions die in India annually!

"Half of these are children who go home to Jesus. Of the other four millions ninety-nine out of every hundred go down to a Christless grave.

"Think of this great host of more than a quarter million marching into eternity from India every month without the gospel!"

The above was written by Mrs. Lee, at the request of a number of friends, in 1897. Since then their work has grown and opened up in many directions. They have in the Home and Training School over one hundred girls, besides about twenty boys.

During the past five years, twenty have gone out of the home into the work as teachers and Bible women. These teach in the schools and work in the zenanas — a work which has grown up around the home.

The Lees are now joining in the work of rescuing widows and children from the terrible famine. They have already taken in 30, which gives them a family of 150 souls. The Marwari widows saved from that famine district they hope to train for Bible work, and through them to reach the Marwari people, of which there are thousands in Calcutta with no mission work among them.

They also are opening up work in new parts through workers trained in the home. Already they have an interesting work in the suburbs of the city, day schools for girls, and a night school for boys who work in the shops all day; also Sunday schools and preaching. Mr. Lee has many interesting cases of inquirers among the Hindu students, of whom Calcutta now has over 15,000.

They also contemplate starting a branch school out of the city where the industrial department can be more successfully worked.

("The Darjeeling Disaster, Its Bright Side: The Triumph of the Six Lee Children"
Edited by Rev. F.W. Warne, The Methodist Publishing House, Calcutta, 1900.)

9   The Lee Memorial Mission

The Lee Memorial Mission, based in Kolkata India, is a home and educational center for destitute, orphaned and semi-orphaned children. The Mission aims to uplift children of all classes by providing child-care, education, Bible studies, general health and hygiene education, and evangelistic service. The school expands upon the missionary work of Rev. David H. Lee and Mrs. Ada Jones Lee, who founded the organization in 1894.

Though Lee Memorial Mission is a Christian Institution, its doors are open to the children of all religions. Any child who is need, poor, fatherless, or motherless is eligible for support. The organization especially welcomes children from the slums of Kolkata as well as the children of sex workers. Through the institution, many children in need have found shelter, security, and proper education that allow them to grow, develop, and go on to lead respectable adult lives.

Lee Memorial Mission operates out of a main building that is 118 years old. The building is in dire need of infrastructural renovations to make the building safe, operational, and a welcoming home environment for the students. Due to financial constraints, Lee Memorial is unable to self-finance these renovations. The Mission also hopes to expand by adding new classrooms, dorms, and bathrooms. Before these additions can take place, the organization must restore their current building so that the hundreds of students currently in their care have a comfortable and secure environment in which they can live, grow, and thrive.

This Giving Tuesday, Lee Memorial Mission aims to raise enough funds to make their building restoration a reality. Today, Lee Memorial is one of the oldest and most prestigious non-profit institutions in Kolkata and they hope to continue this legacy of quality care so that their students can graduate with healthy minds, bodies, and spirits that will support them as they pursue careers in their fields of choice and become active participants of the church 23, 2018.

(Lee Memorial Mission webpage)

"I the Lord do keep it, I will water it every moment."

Mrs. Ada Lee, Superintendent
13, Wellington Square, Calcutta, India.
Cable Address: "Vidalee"

Dear Friends,
    For this my 80th birthday, friends have suggested that I give a short synopsis of my life. If this kind of 'sharing' will bring glory to God, I gladly do so.

I was born among the beautiful hills of West Virginia, U.S.A. The first Spirit that moved me was an overwhelming desire for an education, such as these hills could not afford me. At an early age, I found myself in the little College of Scio, Ohio. There the most important was the night when, kneeling at the altar of the Church, I saw myself a sinner undone, and Jesus on the Cross suffering in my stead. God gave me faith to accept Him, and that wonderful change came that has affected my whole life. With this came a call to India, which any amount of resisting could not silence, and which led to the consecration of all and the dearest, and the putting of my life completely into my Father's hands. How wonderfully He opened the way!

The next was on board ship on my way to India under the American Mission. One of God's messengers, a Captain in the British Army, handed me a leaflet. On it was the question – 'Do you receive the Holy Spirit as your Sanctifier?' I could not answer, but when I did receive Him – Oh! the quiet of soul – the peace – the rest in Him which took place in my heart.

Sixty years ago, I came to India. After 5 years' service: One day in the Vepery Church of Madras, I found myself standing beside the young man, called of God to India – whom I had given up to come to India – given back to me, and we two became one 'Until death doth us part' – and forever. There we unitedly gave ourselves afresh to God and to India.

One by one God sent into our home the little ones to enrich our lives and to train for Heaven, until they numbered nine – seven of whom we brought back to India, except the little brown-eyed baby girl the Angels wanted and took home to live with them.

How wonderfully God led and answered prayer and sent the money to build the Lee Memorial Mission and buildings.

One day a message came, by Government wire, from Darjeeling, saying that a great storm had swept the mountain side – and our six children were not – for God had lifted them up out of the terrible crash to Himself where they were safe forever more.

Our empty home and hearts were still filled with His grace and mercy. Two boys were yet ours – given to comfort our hearts – and our home filled with one hundred famine skeletons to nurse back to life and to lead to God.

The Master of all willing hearts sent to work side by side with us some of the most devoted missionaries I have ever known, and I have had the honorable title 'Second Mother' to more than one young missionary. Another great gift has been the large number of poor girls and child widows – who in Him have found God and spent – and are spending their lives for Him.

From the Boys' School, two miles away, have gone out those who came idol worshipers, and others – now Colporteurs, teachers, preachers and self-supporting men in other walks of life. Our Colporteurs last year sold over 31,000 Gospels. Other devoted Indian workers, chosen of Him, still work with us for the uplift of India.

The fellowship (mostly through correspondence) with that large group of co-labourers – the givers and prayer helpers – has been most blessed. They have been and are the power behind the scene that has made this work a success. Some of these – God's dear children – have given yearly for thirty-five and forty years. Other younger ones are coming to take their places.

And now the doors of the Lee Memorial are still open, but every room full and running over, with many most promising girls – and others pressing for entrance, driven to us by want and desire for knowledge – whom we wish to lead to God and into usefulness. We are still praying for the next house, with precious gifts in hand and others waited for, which we believe the Great Giver intends to send, and complete the deal for us.

The furnace has been necessary many times, heated often seven times more than it was wont. But the form of the fourth like the Son of God was always present. 'Fear not thou worm Jacob' has often sounded in my ear. Once when the Life Companion went for his Coronation, all too soon we thought. But the Refiner has been the one present in every furnace of affliction. So I come forth as pure gold that He may see His likeness in me – here and now. And at last, that He may be able to present me, faultless before the presence of His glory with exceeding joy. That will be glory for me.

As I stand in the afterglow of the evening-tide of life, the question of years has been – What about the work? And the answer to me is – A faith that God has chosen and it preparing those who are to take our places. He has said to me concerning this vineyard of His planting – 'I the Lord do keep it, I will water it every moment: Lest any hurt it I will keep it night and day.' So with a heart full of peace and gratitude to all friends and to God, I am in His hands to occupy till He comes or calls.

Your fellow worker,
ADA LEE
March 23, 1936

LEE MEMORIAL SCHOOL, CALCUTTA

This must not be something new for those who have grown up in and around the Subodh Mullick Square area (or Wellington Square if you will). I am often amazed at how spaces open up in cities. You know what I mean? You see them from the roads as you pass them by, but when you enter them there's this entire world that unfolds. You feel stupid to have reduced this to a part of the map all this while. Anushka and I got involved recently with some work that took us to the Lee Memorial.

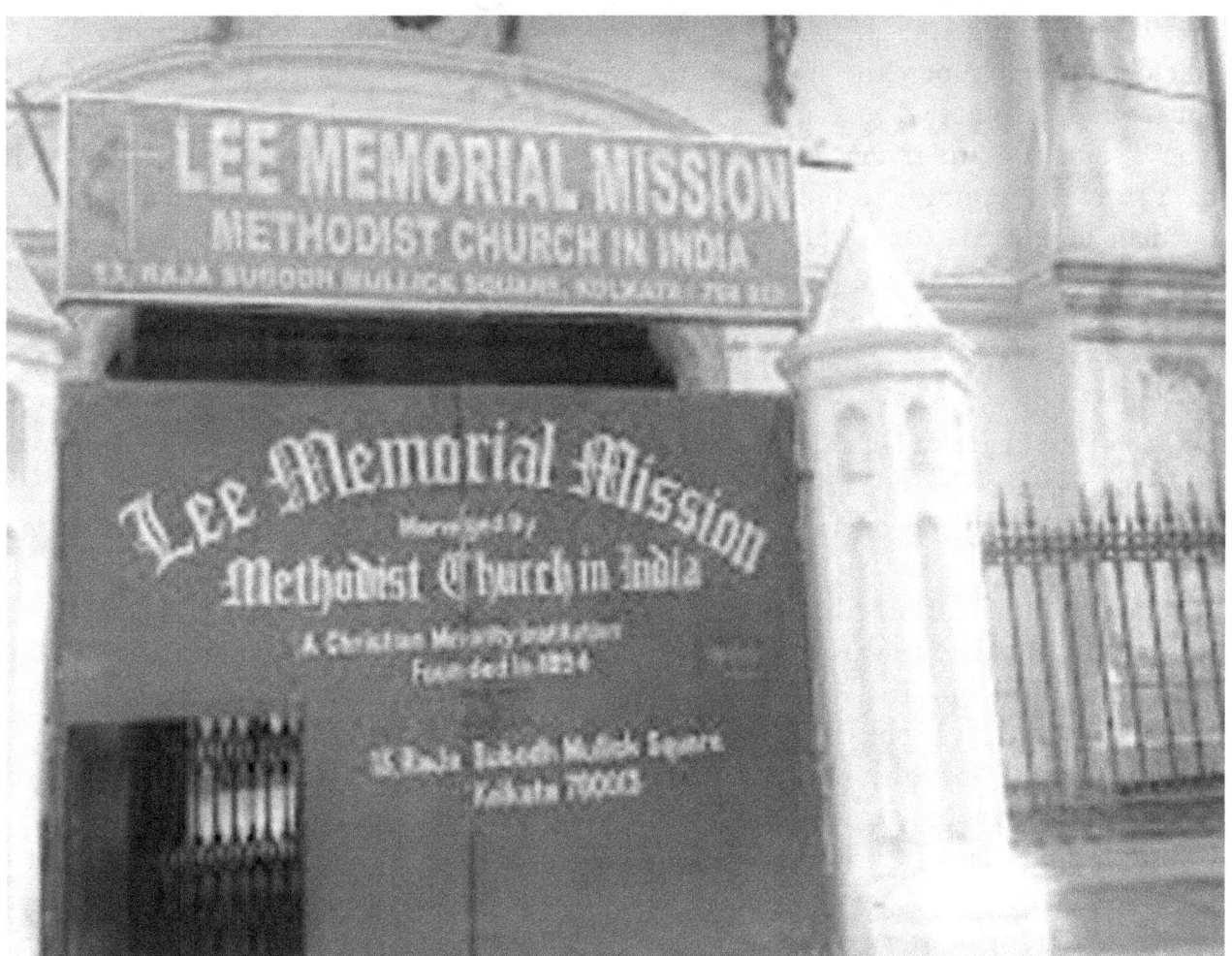

The old yellow building, just across the road from Subodh Mullick's palace, is fairly well maintained. I find it quite impressive. Upon entering the building, one sees a plaque describing in brief the lives of the founders of the Lee Mission, earlier known as the Bengal Mission. It was a great tragedy that led to the founding of the Mission, but first let's go back a bit.

David Hiram Lee spent his student days in Ohio and came to India in 1875, working alongside William Taylor. Ada Hildegarde Jones was born in West Virginia. At the age of fourteen an aunt took her to Ohio, where she went to Scio college. After a bout of typhoid fever she is said to have had a vision where God asked her to "live for India". A few weeks later a letter arrived from a certain Mrs. Doremous of the Union Missionary Society, "stating that Dr. Thoburn, in passing through on his return to India, had handed to her Miss Jones's name as a candidate for missionary work in India." (All photographs are from Ada Lee, Seven Heroic Children, London: Morgan and Scott, 1906, available at archive.org.)

She arrived a year later as part of the Woman's Union Mission. A fairly sensationalist article in *The Milwaukee Journal* says, "[s]he was the first woman sent by other women to save women." The same article describes her as "a spunky type" and suggests that she was following "the man of her choice half-way round the world to marry him." The details are up for verification, but the two got married in Madras in 1881, after Ada apparently was rejected in Calcutta by "neglected sufferers" and inhabitants of harems, whose souls she was trying to save. When Hiram's health started to decline, they went back to Ohio, returning to India a few years later. It was during this phase that the tragic incident took place. On 24 September 1899, six of their children, Vida, Wilbur David, Ada Eunice, Esther Dennett, Lois Gertrude, and Herbert Wilson, who were studying at Queen's Hill School (Arcadia Girls School – editor) in Darjeeling, were swept away to death in one single landslide. The school had its premises in a building known as Arcadia where one Miss Emma Knowles served as the first principal. It was then supposedly regarded as a branch of the Calcutta Girls' High School (this is not surprising considering the American missionary connections). The school is known today as Mount Hermon School.

Wilbur was the only one who lived to tell his parents of their last moments, but he too died within a few days of the disaster. Along with the six, claimed by the landslide was also Jessudar, a Bengali girl who had become part of the family.

Jessudar, Ada Lee tells us, was born of Hindu parents. She lost her father early in life after which the family lived in great poverty. Through out the narrative, the missionary tone strikes one as deeply problematic, but this is only to be expected I suppose. "A wicked man" tried to buy the little girl from her mother for eight rupees (translated in the account to 2 dollars 25 cents), but her mother resisted. Soon after the family converted to Christianity through some "native Christians of the village". One day Jessudar was carried away by the wicked man, but she was rescued and deposited with the Lee family for safety. There is a highly dramatic story of how she decided once and for all to turn to God's service, discarding symbolically the Hindu bangle that she wore. The Lee family also used run a Sunday school, where Vida taught. A couple of photographs fascinated me from Ada Lee's book. The book by Ada Lee is a disturbing read, as it contains many of the letters exchanged with the children and an account by Wilbur of the fateful event.

Following the disaster, money flowed in and enabled the founding of the Lee Mission. Dr. and Mrs. Walter Griffiths took charge of the school from the late 1930s. (The rhetoric as reported by *The Milwaukee Journal* seems to have remained as problematic as ever even post-independence.)

The Lee school in Darjeeling was reported by Gordon Sinclair (special correspondent for *The Milwaukee Journal*) as one of the best in the Himalayas. At the same time, around 1949, there were 400 students and a teacher's training programme for 30 and an orphan home in the Mission in Calcutta. It is also supposed to have provided accommodation for missionaries travelling in India.

Ada survived David Hiram and died in India in 1948. She is buried at the Lower Circular Road Cemetery. For now, I am quite grateful that they allow their premises to be used for diverse activities without interference.

(calcuttaconfusion.blogspot.in)

FOUNDERS – Part II

10 The Founding Of Queen's Hill School

Rev. D.H. Manley

Rev. D.H. Manley, one of the key figures of the school during its formative years in the 1920s, gives a vivid account on the purchase and development of the Mount Hermon Estate and the new Queen's Hill School.

This is our school, not just one building but five, strung along the hill side down to the railway. Only three are showing. It is five minutes walk to the railway station. Has almost no playground. The tall building was built in 1902. The others were then old, forty years or more. It housed the school 1900 - 1925 (Carolyn Stahl)

Queen's Hill School, located near the railway station, 1902.

Queen's Hill School was located for many years on the sides known as "Queen's Hill" and "Annandale" just above the Cart Road a few hundred yards to the West of the Darjeeling Railway Station. But the buildings were getting old and very inadequate for the accommodation of the School. Most of the buildings had been constructed as dwelling-houses before they were purchased and remodeled for the use of the School. And the Education Department of the Government was continually urging, and at last became almost imperative in their demand, that the School provide better quarters for itself.

Entrance of Queen's Hill School, 1907.

But it did not seem wise to put up new buildings on the old site. In the first place, the available level space for buildings was restricted and not adequate for such buildings as ought to be planned looking toward the future development of the School. And in the second place, the old site was a part of Burdwan Estate; the land being held only on leases from the Burdwan Raj. These leases had to be renewed every 30 years, and at each renewal the rate and conditions could be made more disadvantageous to the School, at the will of the Rajah of Burdwan.

For more than a dozen years earnest efforts were made to find a suitable new site for the School, with the requirements that if possible the site must not be on the Burdwan Estate, and that it must be adequate for possible future developments, having in mind that a Boys School also would probably be wanted at some future date. Properties in various and sundry parts of Darjeeling were investigated; and also along the road towards Ghum, and even as far as Sonada and Tung; but nothing that answered all the requirements turned up. The site at West Point now occupied by the Police Department was at one time decided upon and almost secured.

Likewise, other sites were seriously considered at various times. Dozens of committees made trips to Darjeeling in this matter but the way seemed always blocked for one reason or another; either the site was inadequate in size, or too high in price, or belonged to Burdwan, or there was some other serious difficulty. At times we seemed practically forced to the decision of building on the old site, even with all its hardships.

However, in 1919, Bishop Warne and the Committee got in touch with Mr. Paul, who owned what seemed to be a suitable site on the ridge just below the St. Paul's School grounds. The property was not on the Burdwan Estate, and for the requirements of a Girls School alone seemed adequate and suitable. There was a large Bungalow which could be temporarily used for the School; and there were perhaps four or five acres of level or nearly level ground which could be used for building purposes. The price being asked, however, was very high, three and half lakhs of rupees. The Committee practically decided to purchase this property. And Bishop Warne on his trip to America for the General Conference of 1920 was to interview the Ladies of the W.F.M.S. (Women's Foreign Missionary Society) with a view to securing their aid in its acquisition.

Picture of the new building when just finished. In the foreground is a native hut not yet cleared away. Taken from a tall scaffolding the contractors had on the lower flat for drying lumber. After that was removed, there was no way to get a view of the entire building. (Carolyn Stahl)

Queen's Hill School at the present location, 1926.

At the General Conference of 1920 Bishop Frederick B. Fisher was elected to the Episcopacy and assigned to the Calcutta Area. He came to the field having been informed by Bishop Warne of the situation at Darjeeling and fully alive to the urgency of securing a new site for Queen's Hill School. In December of 1920 Bishop Fisher came to Darjeeling accompanied by a small committee consisting of Rev. G.S. Henderson and Rev. D.H. Manley. Miss C.J. Stahl, then Principal of the School, had sent a word to the Bishop and the Committee that she hoped something definite could be accomplished immediately. She thought there had been enough "joy riding" by Committees to Darjeeling without tangible results. The Bishop and the Committee came with a determination, if possible, to make a decision.

Fernhill down the years

Fernhill Boys Hostel and the old swimming pool, 1932.

According to D.H. Manley, one of the prominent members of the committee set up to look into purchase of land for Queen's Hill School, in 1927 the Fernhill Estate, located below the main school building at North Point, was purchased from the Lebong Tea Company at a cost of Rs. 35,000/-. The area, containing 20 acres of land, belonged to Mr. Stephens, the Proprietor of the Grand Hotel in Calcutta and the Mount Everest Hotel in Darjeeling.

"On the Estate was the Bungalow which was used by Mr. Stephen as his summer home, also several other accessory buildings. Much of the ground was laid out beautifully in flower and vegetable gardens. The Fernhill bungalow is now used as a dormitory for the bigger boys of the School. Another building has been remodeled and is now known as Minton Dormitory, and is used as the home for intermediate sized boys."

Fernhill, 1939.

FERNHILL

Fernhill before the new swimming pool.

In between Fernhill and the swimming pool is the Round Building hostel.

Annual Swimming Gala

Accompanied by Miss Stahl, the Committee had several interviews with Mr. & Mrs. Paul, and though the price seemed very high, and although after paying such a price of the original property it was apparent that there would be great difficulty in raising the funds necessary for the erection of any new buildings, yet it was practically decided to accept Mr. Paul's terms for his property. But just at that moment, and by a mere chance, or shall we not believe by the leading of Providence, it was brought to the attention of the Committee that in the North part of town, on the ridge just beyond North Point there was a large plot of land being offered for sale by the Lebong Tea Company, which it was thought might possibly meet the requirements of a new site for Queen's Hill School.

Dawn Cottage, below Fernhill boys' hostel.

The Committee arranged with Mr. Christenson, Manager of the Company, to go with him over the property. The Bishop with Mr. Henderson, and Mr. Manley met Mr. Christenson on the ground the next day and a hasty view of the site was made. It was covered with forest and there was great difficulty in coming to any adequate conception as to its possibilities. The whole plot consisted of 63 acres of ground lying on both sides of the Tukvar Road, just to the North of St. Joseph's School. The plot lying to the East and above the Tukvar Road containing 18 acres was entirely "freehold". The plot lying to the West and below the

Tukvar Road, containing 45 acres, was held on a long lease direct from the Government. The Committee became convinced that this site was amply adequate and excellently well suited for the purpose in mind, and a decision was forthwith arrived at to make the purchase. The price agreed upon was Rs. 50,000, and at once a cheque was drawn for the money to bind the bargain.

It appeared evident then, and it has become more and more clear as time has gone on, that this was a Providential solution of the problem that had been before us for so many years. This was one of the rich blessings laid up by God awaiting the strategic moment for its manifestation. With the purchase of such a large piece of land it was certain that there was here the possibility not only of providing Queen's Hill Girls School but also for the development of a Boys School. Also there came to Bishop Fisher the idea and dream that there could be established an Indian "Northfield". There could be cottages for families on holiday and those having children attending the School, with religious and educational foundations and all the equipment for a great educational, recreational and spiritual centre along evangelical lines.

View of the main playground and Kanchenjunga (Khangchendzonga, Sikkim) from the main school building, 1941.

The land was purchased by the Financial Board of the Bengal Conference, and then an adequate plot was made over to Queen's Hill School on long lease for the erection of the new building.

When purchased the land was covered with forest. There was only the small house, formerly used as a Tea Godown, which was since then made over into what is now the "Dove Cottage". In May of 1921 a historic meeting was held in this house. It had been cleaned out a bit, but stars could be seen in many places through the roof. Cot beds were brought and here there assembled for the afternoon, evening and night, the following persons: Bishop F.W. Warne, Bishop J.W. Robinson, Bishop H. Lester-Smith, Bishop F.B. Fisher, Rev. G.S. Henderson, Mr. Fritchley, an architect from Bombay, and Rev. D.H. Manley.

In the evening, around a roaring camp fire, plans and dreams for the building of the new Queen's Hill School and the development of the community settlement were evolved. It was a memorable meeting, and in general future development of the School and the Estate has been largely along the lines discussed at that time.

On April of 1922, five cottages had been built. The site for the new school building was cleared, levelled, and made ready, during that season. Foundations were laid, and building work began in 1923, and continued through 1924 and 1925. Further cottages were also built during those years. In March of 1926 Queen's Hill School moved into its beautiful new building. By that time there were on the Estate more than a dozen cottages for families with children in the School and Missionaries on holiday.

In 1927 the Fernhill Estate containing 20 acres of land adjoining Mount Hermon Estate on the North was purchased for Rs. 35,000/- from Mr. Stephens, the Proprietor of the Grand Hotel in Calcutta and the Mount Everest Hotel in Darjeeling. On the Estate was the Bungalow which was used by Mr. Stephen as his summer home, also several other accessory buildings. Much of the ground was laid out beautifully in flower and vegetable gardens. The Fernhill bungalow is now used as a dormitory for the bigger boys of the School. Another building has been remodeled and is now known as Minton Dormitory, and is used as the home for intermediate sized boys.

The Mount Hermon Estate has been developed in a wonderful way. Roads and paths have been made, electrical and water installations have been laid on in all the cottages, and a number of the cottages have been fitted with sanitary equipment. At the present time, October 1930, there are on the Estate 34 cottages and suites, five of which have been put up by other Missions on leased land, and during the summer season there is a large community.

The School is the centre of the community life and is developing as a co-educational institution in the classes with separate dormitories for its growing boys' department. A Community Methodist Church has been organized and holds its services in the beautiful School Chapel. A Parent-Teachers Association is adding greatly to the mutual co-operation of the School and the Community lectures, teas, educational cinema entertainments etc., keep the life of the community interesting and helpful. A separate circulating library for the use of the cottages has been started.

(Hermonite 1978, annual school magazine.)

11 A Brief History Of Mount Hermon School

Hazel Craig

(Extracted from "Under the Old School Topee" with the kind permission of author Hazel (Innes) Craig)

I'm sure those early American Methodist missionaries who founded my old alma mater, Mount Hermon, originally named Queen's Hill School for Girls, would not have considered it a public school in the English sense of the word. They were totally without pretensions as to the provision of a socially *pukkah* school for the middle class and were primarily motivated to provide a secondary (High School) education for the 'children of missionaries and other English-speaking people in the land' (India). The school that was to become Mount Hermon was founded in 1895 under the auspices of the Methodist Episcopalian Church of America. Its founder and first Principal was Miss Emma Knowles, a missionary sent out to India with the Women's Foreign Missionary Society in 1881.

A Brief History Of Mount Hermon School

UK Reunion 2003: (L to R) Guest Terry Martin, Author of "Halfway To Heaven," a book on Darjeeling and its remarkable railway, Hazel Craig (Innes), Author: "Under The Old School Topee" and Secretary OMHSA, and Hon. Treasurer, James Sinclair. Taken at the Bombay Brasserie, London. (www.oldmhs.com)

Emma Knowles played a major role in establishing the Wellesley Girls High School in Naini Tal and having worked at the Calcutta Girls' School she realised the need for a similar school to be set up in Darjeeling's favourable climate. Her plan gained the approval of the Church authorities in the United States as well as in India, but no financial aid was forthcoming from either quarter. It was only by borrowing and by paying rent out of her missionary salary that she was able to open her school in 1895 in a rented house called 'Arcadia' in the heart of the town, with just 13 pupils on the rolls. Disaster struck in 1899 with the great landslip of that year, killing ten pupils. In 1900 the school re-opened in two rented houses named 'Queen's Hill' and 'The Repose', which were later purchased with a third house, 'Woodville', on ground leased from the Maharaja of Burdwan. These premises were above the railway station, and the school officially became 'Queen's Hill School for Girls'. A new wing was added in 1902 with financial aid from the Women's Foreign Missionary Society and building grants from the Government of India.

Queen's Hill School, located above the main road near the railway station in Darjeeling, 1901.

Emma Knowles worked tirelessly for her school until 1915, and retired from active missionary service a few years later. Her greatest hope was to see her school established in a permanent building 'before her call should come'. She died in 1924 aged 84, but she got her wish when Miss Carolyn Stahl, who became Principal in 1918, was able to write and tell her of the purchase of the Mount Hermon Estate in 1920. A slump in the tea industry led to the sale of the large estate belonging to the Lebong Tea Company, an ill wind which blew some good for the Methodist missionaries looking for a site for the school. The site was bought for a bargain price of Rs. 50,000/- by Bishop Frederick Fisher of the Thoburn Methodist Church in Calcutta. Fred Fisher was the moving spirit behind the purchase of the site and the building of the new school. Later he was to instigate the purchase of Fernhill in 1927, which was to become the senior boys' living accommodation - again at a bargain price, a mere Rs. 35,000/-. Cottages sprang up on the new estate and the school itself was officially opened in 1926, still called Queen's Hill and by then taking many more boys. In 1930 the school was renamed Mount Hermon School, incorporating the original Queen's Hill School for Girls and Bishop Fisher's School for Boys, eventually becoming the fully integrated co-educational boarding school that I knew in the 1940s.

The story goes that the school received its name during a prayer meeting of some of the missionaries, the Bishop and Miss Stahl seated around Miss Stahl's fireplace. 'When they rose from their knees after praying, the name 'Mount Hermon' came to them...' This is

Hail Mount Hermon! A Tribute

a snow-capped mountain 9,232 ft high on the Syrian Lebanese border, 25 miles west south west of Damascus, and I am struck by the fact that other non-conformist missionaries also named their school after a biblical place - the Hebron School down in Coonoor, later to move to Ootacamund. (Hebron lies in the biblical valley of Eshcol and is reputed to be one of the world's oldest towns and the burial place of Abraham, Isaac and Jacob.)

Since the school was founded in 1895, for nearly 60 years it was run by the Methodist Episcopal Church of America through its Calcutta Schools Society, the Management Committee comprising members of other non-conformist churches and missionary societies under the chairmanship of the Calcutta Methodist Bishop. In the early 1950s a new 'united' committee took over, with co-operating missions from the Australian, New Zealand and British Baptist societies, as well as British Methodists, the Presbyterian Church of Wales and the Church of Scotland. The religious ethos of the school remained evangelical, as it does today, but the largely American influence came to an end with the appointment in 1954 of the Reverend D.G. Stewart, an Australian Baptist, as principal. David Stewart was Principal for ten years and was then succeeded by Graeme Murray, a New Zealand Baptist, who held the post for 15 years. In 1979, the Reverend John Johnston, an Australian Baptist and the school's Senior Master, became Principal, retiring in 1989 after 30 years' service on the school staff.

Today Mount Hermon has an Indian Principal, Dr. Arun Nehemiah M.Sc., Ph.D., an Anglo-Indian Vice-Principal, Mr. A. L. Edgar, M.A., M.Ed., and a largely Indian staff coping with nearly 700 pupils. There is also a flourishing Teacher Training College on the Estate, until recently the responsibility of Mrs. Valerie Johnston. Many of its trainees are Anglo-Indian. The College was established in 1972 when the Undergraduate Men's Training College at St. Thomas's School at Kidderpore, Calcutta, was transferred to the management of the newly-formed Mount Hermon College of Education Society by Government order and with the co-operation of the Governing body of St. Thomas's School. The Mount Hermon T.T.C. is recognised by the Government of Bengal's Education Department and students are awarded their trained Teacher's Certificate for Anglo-Indian Schools after a two-year course. The College accepts both men and women students with hostel accommodation provided.

Some of the Former Principals of Queen's Hill and Mount Hermon School

1895 - Miss E. L. Knowles	1944 - Rev. J. R. Boyles
1918 - Miss C. J. Stahl	1945 - Rev. H. E. Dewey
1929 - Rev. E. S. Johnston	1947 - Mrs. R. Forsgren
1931 - Miss R. Field	1951 - Rev. H. E. Dewey
1931 - Mrs. L. Engberg	1953 - Rev. G. B. Workman
1935 - Miss R. Field	1954 - Rev. D. G. Stewart
1938 - Rev. H. E. Dewey	1964 - Mr. G. A. Murray
1942 - Rev. M. A. Clare	1979 - Rev. J. A. Johnston

12 They Received The Call From Above

MISS EMMA L. KNOWLES

KNOWLES
Emma L. Knowles (1840-1924, Principal: 1895-1917)

Stahl on Knowles: "She was God's Pathfinder"
"Her heart was in Darjeeling and Queen's Hill School"

C.J. Stahl

"Servant of God well done" must have been the thought in many minds on both sides of the earth when Miss Emma L. Knowles passed to her rest. Although eighty-four years of age she had retired from India only seven years before, having at the request of her fellow-worker remained on at Queen's Hill for three years after giving up active work.

Miss Knowles was born in New Jersey in 1840 and died at the sanitorium in Castile New York, March 28, 1924. She was from a family prominent in New York Methodism, contemporary with Dr. James Buckley, a classmate of her brothers in college.

Thirty-five years of her life was spent in India with only three short furloughs. At the time of her retirement in 1917, an article of appreciation appeared in the *Woman's Missionary Friend* with the heading, "A Pathfinder", in recognition of her career as the founder of our two schools in the Himalaya: Wellesley, Naini Tal; and Queen's Hill for Anglo-Indian girls, Darjeeling.

The need of such a good school at Naini Tal was early recognized and when Isabella Thoburn was at home on her first furlough in 1881, she advertised in the *New York Advocate* for a teacher of experience to go out and open such a school. Miss Knowles answered the advertisement ad accompanied Miss Thoburn on her return to India. But the founding of Queen's Hill was on Miss Knowles' own initiative. The first five years of her school term were spent in the Calcutta Girls' School. Having become familiar with conditions in Bengal, she realized the same need of a girls' school in the mountains here as there had been in North India, and proposed that instead of going home for her next furlough she would go to Darjeeling and start a school.

The plan met the approval of the mission authorities on the field and also of the ladies at home, who, however, could promise no financial aid. After weeks of heart searching and prayer often "with strong crying and tears", the final decision was made. She stepped out by faith on God's promises, borrowed one thousand rupees for necessary furnishings, paid the rent of a building out of her missionary salary, and on March 11th, 1895, opened the school with thirteen pupils, Vida and Lois Lee among the number.

For the next twenty years, except for two short periods when on furlough, Miss Knowles continued as Principal of the school, giving herself unstintedly to it, withholding nothing that would conduce to the well-being of the pupils and staff, physically, mentally, and spiritually. She possessed gifts of mind and heart that easily won the confidence of parents, and the school had a steady growth from the first among a class of people able to pay substantial fees, thus very soon becoming practically self-supporting.

In her contact with young people Miss Knowles was markedly a character builder. She had the ability in an unusual degree of bringing out and developing the best in a young girl's nature. Her pupils realized this and responded with lasting love and veneration. Scattered over many parts of India and Great Britain, are those who have received from Miss Knowles not only a good education through the schools but a lasting appreciation of the highest ideals of life and service.

A writer in the *Indian Witness* at the time of her death said, "A choice spirit entered within the gates when Emma L. Knowles received her "clear call". Her personality was alive, not full of life in the ordinary use of the term, but vital. Life appeared to be full of interest to her, full of surprising things. She had, to me, that rare thing an elusive and indefinable quality."

To me Miss Knowles was one of the great Women of India: such a perfect lady, like a piece of rare old china, or a bit of priceless lace. Hers was a deeply religious nature. She naturally shrank from expressions of excessive emotions, but her religious experience was like a steady deep flowing stream. She knew whom she believed and that was the strength and glory of her life.

Hail Mount Hermon! A Tribute

Knowles House 1970

All who have known Miss Knowles in these last years have known how her heart was bound up in Queen's Hill School. Her home was with her niece, Mrs. Charles Bateman, Somerville, N.J., who has written of her last days: "Her heart was in Darjeeling. She loved the work. It was her wish to leave her little to the school. She would have gone without what she needed many, many times had not my husband and I refused to permit it, all because she wanted to give more to the school."

For years her chief concern had been to see the school in a permanent building before her call should come. With this in view she had canvassed every possible and many times impossible sites in Darjeeling that might be available as a new property. It was a great joy, therefore, to write to her of the purchase of the Mount Hermon Estate and later of the appropriation of funds by the Women's Foreign Missionary Society that made the building possible.

And it is a joy to know that every young life passing through the school shall have, with God's blessing, the inspiration of this beautiful new building as a monument to a noble, courageous life.

(Hermonite 1978, annual school magazine.)

They Received The Call From Above

LIVING STONES OF GOD
"To strive, to seek, to find, and not to yield."
- Tennyson

Jigme N. Kazi

Hermonite Jigme N. Kazi at the main entrance of the school building where the portrait of the school's Founder, Miss. Emma L. Knowles, is hung.

Queen's Hill Girl's High School was first opened on March 11th, 1895, in a rented building known as 'Arcadia', located below the Chowrasta in Darjeeling. Its Founder-Principal was Miss Emma L. Knowles, an educational missionary under the Women's Foreign Missionary Society of the Methodist Episcopal Church of the USA. Miss Knowles had already spent a number of years in India as Principal of schools for European Girls in Nainital and Calcutta.

She felt the need of a similar school in the hills of Darjeeling. Her conviction that it was God's will helped her to initiate the first move. The Mission Board at home gave its approval to the plan but did not promise any financial assistance.

With a firm faith in God's promises, Miss Knowles borrowed from a friend one thousand rupees for furnishings, used her salary to pay the rent for a building and opened the school with thirteen pupils. Two years later it was recognized by the Education Department as a Lower Secondary School and received a grant.

The Darjeeling Disaster of 1899 caused severe damage to the school building. Miss Stahl was in charge of the school as Miss Knowles was granted a furlough. Many people doubted on the continuance of the school but Miss Knowles thought otherwise. She came back from New York in 1900 and continued her work. He faith was still high and the work went on.

A new site was purchased in the town area, near the railway station. The purchase of four dwelling houses had to be adapted for school use. In 1902, a three-storey building was constructed on the same site. The enrolment at that time was fifty. The name of the school was changed from Arcadia Girls School to Queen's Hill School.

As the years rolled by, the school authorities as well as all friends interested in the school, realized the need for adequate buildings for further development of the school. The old buildings were constantly giving trouble and this was a great hindrance to the school's progress. In December 1920, the Mission authorities, through the initiative of Bishop Fisher, purchased the present estate. It was Miss Stahl's sheer determination and her faith in God that helped the establishment of the present school building. Miss Stahl wrote, "Miss Knowles will tell you she never planned it should be a large school. Evidently the Lord's plans for the school were larger than ours."

The development of the school as a co-educational boarding school is due to the vision of Bishop F.B. Fisher, a great missionary leader. It was he who established a hostel for boys at Fernhill. The new name, Mount Hermon, was also the fruit of his labour.

Mr. H.E. Dewey became Principal of the school in 1938. As an educationist, a loyal friend, he did much for the school. During his stay the main playing field and a beautiful gymnasium were made. It was a very difficult period for the school. But he kept the school going and we owe much to his effort and devotion.

Since 1954, following a rather 'lean' period in the school's history, it has been a union of institutions, in which Baptist and Presbyterian Churches co-operate with the Methodist Church of Southern Asia in the running of the school. Rev. D.G. Stewart was appointed as Principal in 1953. Mr. Stewart's deep faith in God and the new challenge enabled him to lead Mount Hermon into a 'decade of achievement.'

The New Building and the Swimming Pool were constructed during his period. Mr. Murray stated that the new building would be named 'Stewart Building' as a memorial to the dedication of Mr. Stewart, Principal – 1954-1964. The school had grown from less than a 100 to 365 students. Mount Hermon was forging ahead.

Mr. Murray naturally became the Principal after Mr. Stewart's departure. He wrote, "…look forward to the future and be ready to build further upon the firm foundations that have been laid over many years…the best is yet to be." Under his leadership Mount Hermon witnessed many new changes. In 1972, a new Under Graduate College for Teachers' Training was established.

Mr. Murray is till the Principal of this college. Recently, a new college hostel and the Round Hostel for the school boys came into existence to accommodate the increasing number of students. We also have a new underground kitchen which was a real necessity as we have about 470 boarders. The total enrolment this year is 639. Compare this figure with the 13 students that we started with in 1895! What an example of the wonders of faith and human perseverance. Mr. Murray's friendly nature, his efficient organizational skills, zeal, energy and love for the school paved way for a greater future.

We come to the end of another chapter in the history of our school. The lives of these men (and women) who have faithfully served our school will ever remind us of our responsibility in making this world a better place to live. Let us, together, face the present crisis with confidence in ourselves and with faith in the Living God. Under the new leader who is appointment in Mr. Murray's place, let us all renew our pledge, dedicate ourselves anew, and remain faithful to the cause that has made our school great.

(Hermonite 1978, annual school magazine.)

13 Keeping Alive The Spirit Of Queen's Hill School

CAROLYN JOSEPHINE STAHL

STAHL
Carolyn J. Stahl (1860-1934, Principal: 1918-1929)

> "I believe that any great task van be accomplished but the excise of boundless faith, mush intercessory prayer and ceaseless work."
>
> - Carolyn J. Stahl

Neville P. Gardner

Miss Stahl also belonged to the Women's Foreign Missionary Society (WFMS) and came to India in 1893 as a member of the Methodist Church in Calcutta. Her tenure at the school as Principal dates back from 1914, though she did assist Miss Knowles from as early as 1900.

By 1914 the strain of too much hard work began to tell on Miss Knowles and she was persuaded to give up active service. Instead she decided to remain on in India till February 1915 to observe the development of the school.

Did you know that in 1914 the school nearly closed down? This came about due to a severe shortage of funds. The school needed more rooms badly and Miss Stahl wrote for 13,000 dollars from the WFMS, but since they couldn't raise the amount at short notice they wanted her to shut down the school. This she did not do, but succeeded in persuading the Government Educational Department, to see the necessity of a school like this in Darjeeling and the importance it played in the role of education. It was, and still is, the only nonconformist school in the hills of Bengal.

Stahl House 1962

Miss Carolyn Stahl

What sort of character did Miss Stahl possess? She was a person who did not yield to any one, missionary or otherwise, in her adherence to Christian principles as taught by the Methodist Church. We got to know a little about her childhood and upbringing through a letter dated July 1928, which she wrote to an acquaintance. "I was brought up in the Methodist Church in a country (Iowa) where the services were held in my grandfather's house and the first Methodist Church organized in his house, before there were enough people to build a church. When my knowledge of the place began there was a small country church, the charter members of which were mostly my relatives." The yearly "camp meetings" in the autumn were the joy of my life. Those were the days of the "Shouting Methodists" and I grew up in that church."

1918 – the total enrollment was 163 and there was an urgent need to find a suitable site for the peaceable expansion of the school.

1919 – people said about the school: "I think it is very remarkable that the children are so free in spirit and yet are so well governed and well behaved." The "Home atmosphere" others have called it. In one of her reports Miss Stahl has stated, "the prevailing influence about us, from the people we mingle with, from our recreations, from our reading, has far more to do with shaping our lives than the lessons of the classroom." Another time she wrote, "the greatest asset any school can have is the confidence and sympathy of the community it serves."

1920 – Bishop Fisher was elected to the Episcopacy and assigned to the Calcutta area. He became interested in the affairs of the school. It was his mission that purchased the present Mount Hermon estate.

1922 – Miss Stahl was on sick leave in America.

1925 – From her school report: "Six of our staff are former Queen's Hill pupils."

26th May, 1926 – Inauguration of the new school building, Mount Hermon, took place. Performed by Lord Lytton, then the Governor of Bengal.

1928 – Miss Stahl had become old and quite worn out physically, but she was still burning in spirit and kept up to her principles. She decided to retire in 1929.

1929 – She stated in her last report: "there is a spirit of harmony and goodwill among teachers and pupils, throughout."

Among the old files of the school is a letter (1929) from an ex-student who was in college in America, to her sister. "Carolyn, make good use of your last year at Queen's Hill. Bring home as much of the spirit and atmosphere of Queen's Hill as you can. Girls with the stamp of Queen's Hill are appreciated here." Thus Miss Stahl's reign as Principal came to a fitting end.

In 1930 the school was renamed – Mount Hermon School. Under this would be Queen's Hill School for Girls and Bishop Fisher School for Boys. Rev. E.S. Johnson of Thoburn Church, Calcutta, was appointed Principal for both the schools.

Today, Mount Hermon is co-educational and expanding even further on the best modes of education.

(Ref: Hermonite 1978, annual school magazine.)

The New York Times
Wednesday, September 29, 1899

DEATH IN THE INDIAN FLOODS

400 Persons Killed at Darjeeling
Many Drowned on the Plains
Great Havoc at Kurseong

CALCUTTA, Sept. 28. - Lieut. Gov. Sir John WOODBURN announced to the Council yesterday that 400 persons lost their lives through the floods at Darjeeling, capital of the district of that name, in addition to those drowned on the plains.

Great havoc has been caused at Kurseong. The Margaretschope estate lost 100 acres and the Mealand factory was destroyed. Some coolies were buried in the ruins of the manager's house, which was partly destroyed. The Avongrove estate lost thirty acres and 4,000 tea bushes. The coolie lines were swept away and many persons were killed, but the exact number is not known. A factory was also destroyed at this place.

A hug landslip below St. Mary's Seminary destroyed the railroad bridge and completely blocked the road. A breach thirty yards wide has been made and the rails are hanging in the air. It is thought the break cannot be repaired within thirty days.

Telegraphic communication between Calcutta and Darjeeling has been re-established, but railroad traffic beyond Kurseong is not likely to be resumed for a long time. The road is impassable for horses and travelers are only able to journey on foot and with much difficulty.

The Chicago Tribune
Chicago, Cook County, Illinois
October 2, 1899, Page 8

MISS C. J. STAHL, HEROINE OF INDIAN FLOODS

Miss C. J[osephine]. STAHL, Methodist missionary at Darjeeling, India, an Iowa gal and former student at the Northwestern University, Evanston, is the heroine of Darjeeling, where, as reported by cable, 400 lives were lost in the recent floods. Miss STAHL is a teacher in the Lela Villa branch of the Calcutta Girl's School. The flood brought on a landslide which left the building in momentary danger of collapse. Already nearly exhausted from her efforts in behalf of the flood sufferers, Miss STAHL left the building at the head of a long line of children and after a hard and perilous climb, succeeded in gathering her charges to a place of safety. Miss STAHL's courage saved her pupils from the death which overtook others at Lela Villa.

Miss STAHL's home is at Mount Ayr, Ia., and is one of four women representing Ringgold County Methodism in the missionary field. Miss STAHL is a member of one of the prominent pioneer families of the Iowa county. She was born about thirty-eight years ago, near the present Town of Delphos where her father, Michael STAHL, still lives. Miss STAHL was for some years a teacher in the schools of her home county and later in the city schools of Corning. Her college education was began at Simpson College, Indianola Ia., and graduated at the Northwestern University, Evanston [Illinois].

For twenty years she was an active helper in revivals. She went to India under the auspices of the Northwestern branch of the Women's Foreign Missionary society of the Methodist Church. She sailed from New York in the fall of 1896, and for about six years was a teacher in the Calcutta Girls' School. Within the last year she was put in charge of the school at Darjeeling. One sister, Miss Martha STAHL, is professor of Latin in Simpson College, and a brother, William STAHL, is an attorney with offices in the [illegible] building, Chicago.

C. Josephine STAHL wrote, "After the Darjeeling disaster, when the LEE children and four others from the school lost their lives in a landslide, there was a question whether the school should not be closed. After much prayer and consideration by the authorities in India, it was decided to continue it. Miss KNOWLES, who was in America at the time, returned with reinforcements for the staff. A site was purchased and the school entered upon a new phase of its history. The site contained two substantial dwelling houses, and a new building of moderate size was erected for class rooms. As the number of pupils has increased, additional room has been obtained by renting adjoining houses. This is obviously an unsatisfactory arrangement for a girls' school. The buildings originally on the site are old and in constant need of repairs.

"Notwithstanding the handicap of a lack of proper buildings, however, Queen's Hill has grown in favor with the community and with the local government, and the number of pupils has increased until it is almost entirely self-supporting. With proper buildings it would at once become entirely so."

Children of Missionaries at Queen's Hill

(Woman's Missionary Friend: Vol. 49 - 50. Pp. 349-51. Methodist Episcopal Church: Women's Foreign Missionary Society. 1917.)

Mission India - 2007 Vol. 1, Issue 2, Page 1
April, 2007

100 years from now - 100 years ago

What are you doing today that will matter 100 years from now? In 1892 Josephine STAHL journeyed from rural Iowa via trains, ships, ox cart, and foot to join a Methodist mission in Calcutta and then on to a school in Darjeeling, India. She taught there until 1930 when she returned to Iowa where she died in 1934.

I had the honor of accompanying her great-great-grand niece, Susan EASON, as we visited the Mount Hermon School. WOW!! Our team had completed a great week of evangelism in the villages around Siliguri. We took a side trip to Darjeeling. For most of the team it was a scenic trip on mountain roads but, for Susan EASON, it was also an answer to a dream. Could she possibly find the school her great-great-grand aunt (Aunt Josie) had been instrumental in establishing? The team visited a school on the original site, Queen's Hill School but, the headmaster said the original school by that name had relocated in the 1920's and was renamed Mount Hermon. Its location is a few miles away.

Leaving the team under the care of Temjen and with the assistance of our host, Chandan, we (Chandan, Susan, and Gary) took a taxi to the school. Susan had many old photos of the school which were plicated with our cameras. It was Good Friday so the school was closed (the good news is it is still a Christian school after more than 100 years of service), but we did meet the faculty member who was there to look after the students who had not returned home. We received a tour of the main building and looked around.

This story helps placed our short-term trip in a little different perspective; our 15+ hour airplane ride, staying in a hotel with irregular hot showers, and the rest compared to the effort and commitment of those who laid the foundation. Praise God for the Aunt Josie's and the 1000s of other Christian missionaries who went before us to prepare the landscape and plant the seeds we were able to harvest. 100 years from now, if the Lord doesn't return sooner, our decedents can look in on the work we have been involved in, thank you for also being involved in this work.

Transcriptions by Sharon R. Becker, September of 2009

The Blue and Gold, Pages 15-16

OUR PRINCIPAL, MISS STAHL

Miss C. J. Stahl.

To express on paper an appreciation of the work of our beloved principal is a pleasant task - but difficult. Miss STAHL is retiring and will make her home in America, but she will continue to live here in India, and especially in Queen's Hill School.

Miss STAHL has been a missionary in India and Burma for thirty-six years, and principal of Queen's Hill for sixteen years. She has given her best years of service working and praying over this school, and has seen it grow from the Arcadia of 1899 with its thirty-seven pupils to the present Queen's Hill with over two hundred boys and girls. She has left the mark of her influence upon hundreds of girls who have known and loved her. To be a genuine Queen's Hill pupil or teacher is to have absorbed not a little of Miss STAHL'S charming spirit.

To do justice in words to the character of our principal would require the inspiration of the Muses. She has done everything and has done it well. But to help old pupils and teachers recall the one we all love, let us reminisce a bit:-

What pupil can forget Miss STAHL'S keen sense of justice combined with a sense of humour? Do you remember when you were reported to her and you saw the twinkle in her eye, which foretold a just punishment? A little girl became rather exasperating and was told: "If you aren't good, I'll send you to Miss STAHL." Little Miss Four-Year Old replied: "I don't care. Miss STAHL likes me."

Yes, Miss STAHL loves her girls (and punishes in suit [of] the offense). It is not an uncommon sight to see the little ones hanging on her or following her to show a broken doll and get a word of sympathy. And pupils of any age do no quake with fear when they are told that Miss STAHL wants to see them. She is more apt to ask them if they are feeling well and to give them some medicine than to punish them.

Miss STAHL has an abundance of sympathy for her girls. One teacher remarked: "I'd rather be a pupil under Miss STAHL than a teacher, because she is always trying to make her pupils happy." The number of her pupils who apply for posts as teachers under her is proof of her remarkable spirit. After several rainy, dismal days, it is Miss STAHL who suggests a holiday "because it is a fine day and we do not know when we'll have another." Or she allows a juggler to do his tricks to amuse the pupils, who have not been out; or she plans a hike and picnic lunch. On these occasions, Miss STAHL leads the way, and when the others are so tired they are ready to drop, she is still alert and energetic. As she informed a new teacher who was being solicitous of her welfare, "you will have to learn, my dear, that my gray hairs do not mean anything." She is as young as the youngest and as full of fun.

Do you remember Miss STAHL'S illustrated lectures after morning prayers? Sometimes she would speak of proper enunciation, sometimes of carriage; on relaxing; how to sing, or, act, or speak; and annually she has taught the pupils how to receive their prizes.

What memories are awakened by the announcement: "Has any one seen my fountain pen?"

One pupil says: "Miss STAHL is not like other principals, who bury themselves in their offices, and whom pupils never see unless they are to be punished. She knows what every pupil is doing in school, and often she knows our parents and this helps her to understand us."

To her staff, Miss STAHL has always been loyal and kind. When the school was moved to Mt. Hermon, she sympathized with them because they were so far from town and she did all she could to make their lives pleasant and happy. If a teacher has some new ideas, Miss STAHL says, "try them out." No teacher can have too much enthusiasm for her work. Miss STAHL appreciates their suggestions and their efforts, and tries to mold the staff into a happy, united family. When a difficult situation arises, it is handled tactfully, and ironed out as only she can do it.

Some call our principal an autocrat, but she is a most loveable, charming autocrat. What loyal daughter of Queen's Hill was not proud to see her meet the queen of the Belgians so gracefully? And with what natural ease she meets and converses with those who are holding the highest positions in the city or state.

She is always mistress of any situation and seemingly at ease with those of high or low estate. When pupils talk of Miss STAHL'S leaving Queen's Hill, they mingle laughter with tears, for she has found her way into the hearts of the children, and has won the confidence and respect of parents and patrons by her unfaltering faithfulness to what is best for the pupils and her beloved Queen's Hill.

L. K. H.

Submission by Mike Avitt, April of 2011

Josephine STAHL was born December 2, 1860, and died October 8, 1934. Interment was at Bethel Cemetery, Diagonal, Ringgold County, Iowa. *"They rest from their labors and their works do follow them."*

· Mary B. (TALLEY) and Michael STAHL Biography

14 Bishop Fisher Gave Us Our Estate And School Its Name

BISHOP FREDERICK BOHN FISHER

FISHER
Bishop Frederick Bohn Fisher (1882-1938)

Frederick Bohn Fisher was the son of James Edward Fisher and Josephine Shirey. He married 1st Edith Jackson on 4th February 1903. He married 2nd Welthy Honsinger in 1924. The Rev. Fisher was the outspoken and somewhat unorthodox Methodist Bishop of Calcutta and Burma. With his friendly, unassuming ways, his ready laughter, his gift for reaching the hearts of his listeners, Fred made lifelong friends wherever he went. He was a friend of the poet Rabindranath Tagore and a supporter and friend of Gandhi, Nehru, and other leaders of India's independence movement. He resigned the Episcopacy in 1930 and returned to the U.S. to become pastor of First United Methodist Church, Ann Arbor, Michigan but still maintained strong ties to India. From 1934 to 1938 he served at Central United Methodist Church in Detroit, Michigan.

Faith Moves Mountains

"And when you had taken your leave, I found God's footprints on my floors."

Ashish Bhengra

Bishop Fred B. Fisher was born in 1882 in the State of Pennsylvania in the U.S.A., into a culture where religion was a predominant influence on everyday life. He was, even as a child, a bookworm; and although his family had to take a loan to have him educated, he attended Asbury College in Wilmore, Kentucky, a very 'holy' and puritanical institution, which laid the foundation of a man who was remarkably broad in his views and ranged even into Hindu religion in search of the deepest spiritual values.

Encouraged by the renowned Bishop Thoburn, young Fisher decided during his college days that he would go to India as a missionary. Accordingly, he came to Calcutta as a Bishop. There he served in the Thoburn Methodist Church. By this time, he was well established as an influential speaker, determined and self-assured fighter for his beliefs.

Fisher House 1962

He was also on intimate terms with Mahatma Gandhi and Rabindranath Tagore, two greatly admired friends who influenced him considerably. A man of intense energy and conviction, he was constantly looking to the future to build the present. The way to realize his visions was not always easy, but by sheer determination and faith, he would move mountains.

As you know, our school was formerly Queen's Hill School for girls, and the plea for a new site reached Bishop Fisher. The Estate was bought from Lebong Tea Company during a slump in the tea market at a price of Rs. 50,000. To accomplish this, Bishop Fisher had to make many trips to Darjeeling from Calcutta and search far and wide in this area – even in Sonada and Tung.

Bishop Fisher Gave Us Our Estate And School Its Name

Fernhill was acquired separately from an English man for the price of Rs. 35,000, a price which the seller would have preferred to be higher, but Fisher stood firm and was finally victorious. He had predicted many years earlier that Fernhill would come to Mt. Hermon because it was God's will. Though the owner refused to believe him, or to believe that God had fixed the price as low as Rs. 35,000, Bishop Fisher's faith was vindicated.

Bishop Fisher also gave our Estate and School its name. After purchasing the Estate and moving the school here – it was called 'Queen's Hill' – until one night when some of the missionaries held a prayer meeting with the Bishop around Miss Stahl's fire place. When they rose from their knees after praying, the name 'Mt. Hermon' came to them; and the Estate and School have been known by this name ever since.

Bishop Fisher died of a heart attack in 1938, but his work did not die with him, 'your old man shall dream dreams and your young men shall see visions.'

The Bishop was "adored by children", his wife wrote later. I think it is fitting that we children in this day do not forget this man to whom we owe so much. Bishop Fisher was a man who had a vision and sufficient faith and energy to begin a wonderful work. Let us pray that his efforts should not be in vain, but that our generation may accept this worthy challenge of creating and maintaining new opportunities for development of God's people.

(Ashish Bhegra was Fisher House Captain in 1978: Hermonite 1978, annual school magazine.)

Frederick Bohn Fisher: A Bishop with a difference

Frederick Bohn Fisher (14 February 1882 – 15 April 1938) was a bishop of the Methodist Episcopal Church, elected in 1920. He also gained notability as a pastor, missionary, author, and official in the Methodist missionary and men's movements.

Birth and family

Fisher was born in Greencastle, Pennsylvania. He was of English ancestry, the son of James Edward and Josephine (née Shirey) Fisher. He married Edith Jackson on 4 February 1903. In 1924 he married Welthy Honsinger.

Education

He graduated from Muncie, Indiana High School. He earned both B.S. and A.B. degrees from Asbury University in 1902. He studied at both Boston University and Harvard Divinity School, 1907-08.

Ordained ministry and missionary service

Rev. Fisher entered the North Indiana Annual Conference of the M.E. Church, serving as Pastor in Kokomo, Indiana (1903). He then went as a Missionary to Agra, India (the North West India Conference), serving 1904-05. He transferred his conference membership to the New England Annual Conference, serving the First M.E. Church in Boston (1907).

Rev. Fisher then became the Eastern Field Secretary for the Board of Foreign Missions of the M.E. Church (1911–12). He was then appointed the General Secretary of the Laymen's Missionary Movement of his denomination (1913–15), then the Associate General Secretary of the Laymen's Missionary Movement in the U.S. and Canada (beginning in 1916), transferring his conference membership back to the North Indiana Conference in 1913. His office was located at 1 Madison Avenue, New York City. He resided in Edgewater, New Jersey.

Rev. Fisher was a delegate to the World's Missionary Conference in Edinburgh, 1910. He was a Trustee of Asbury College, as well. In his official capacities, he organized conventions of Methodist Men in Indianapolis (1913), Boston (1914), and Columbus, Ohio (1915). The volumes Militant Methodism, New England Methodism, and The Challenge of Today were produced as a result.

Episcopal ministry

Rev. Fisher was elected to the Episcopacy in 1920 and assigned as Resident Bishop of the Calcutta episcopal area. He resigned the Episcopacy in 1930 and returned to the U.S. to become pastor of First United Methodist Church, Ann Arbor, Michigan. This is the only time on record that a Methodist bishop has resigned for other than health reasons, and he was the only bishop ever to return to the local pastoral work. In 1934 he accepted appointment as senior pastor of Central Methodist Church, Detroit.

While there, Woodward Avenue, the main street in the city, was widened. In order not to lose the steeple and west wall, a thirty-foot section was removed and the steeple and wall moved back to meet the rest of the church thus shortening the knave. Dr. Fisher designed a new recessed chancel including the new pulpit, reredos, mural of the apostles and had the ceiling painted with religious symbols from all over the world. He died 15 April 1938, Good Friday, in Detroit. His funeral was held on Easter Sunday in Central United Methodist Church, the only Easter funeral Detroit had ever known.

Selected writings

- Editor, *Militant Methodism*, New York: Methodist Book Concern, 1913.
- Editor, *New England Methodism*, New York: Methodist Book Concern, 1914.
- Editor, *The Challenge of Today*, New York: Methodist Book Concern, 1915.
- *The Way to Win*, New York: Methodist Book Concern, 1915.
- *The Man That Changed the World*. Nashville, TN: Cokesbury Press. 1917.
- *That Strange Little Brown Man Gandhi*. New York: Ray Long and Richard R. Smith Inc. 1932.

(Wikipedia)

Gandhi on Fisher: He Feared No Man

"He seemed to me to be one among the few Christians who walked in the fear of the Lord and therefore feared no man."

- Mahatma Gandhi on Bishop Fisher

Frederick Bohn Fisher (1882-1938) was a missionary in India from 1904 and Bishop of the Methodist Episcopal Church in Calcutta from 1920. He returned to the United States in 1930 and became Bishop of Ann Arbor, Michigan. He was the author of several books including *India's Silent Revolution* (New York, 1919) and *That Strange Little Brown Man Gandhi* (New York, 1932) which was banned by the British authorities in India.

He first met Gandhiji in 1917 and they became life-long friends. Bishop Fisher visited South Africa in 1925 and his report on the plight of Indians in that country was highly appreciated by Gandhiji.

His wife, Mrs. Welthy Honsinger Fisher, visited India in 1947 and met Gandhiji. Returning to India in 1952, she established the Literacy Village near Lucknow.

LETTERS

Ashram, Sabarmati,
February 11, 1926

Dear friend,

I was delighted to receive your letter just before your departure for America where I hope you and Mrs. Fisher will have a good time.

I have no doubt that whatever the present result of the South African struggle, the seed sown by you and now being watered by Mr. (C.F.) Andrews will bear ample fruit in its own time. I cannot be dislodged from my faith in the ultimate triumph of truth which to my mind is the only thing that counts. The downs of life on the way to it will have been all forgotten when we have attained the summit.

Mrs. Fisher asked me for a message. I can only repeat what I have been saying to so many American friends who have been calling on me, namely, what is required most is serious and careful study of the Indian movement. What I see happening in America is distressful, either an exaggerated view of the movement or a belittling of it. Both are like distortions. I regard the movement to be one of permanent interest and fraught with very important consequences. It therefore needs a diligent study, not a mere superficial newspaper glance. May your visit to America then result in the more accurate estimate of the movement in India.

Whenever you can come to the Ashram, you know you are sure of a welcome.

Yours sincerely,
Bishop Fisher
150 Fifth Avenue,
New York City

Letter, October 26, 1928

Bishop Fisher wrote in a letter to Gandhiji from Hingham, Massachusetts, on September 7, 1928: "Mother India has created a terrible sensation in America. It has been difficult to know just how to meet the situation... There is now coming off from the press a book by Gertrude Marvin Williams called *Understanding India*, which I believe will help in many ways to correct the wrong impressions which Miss Mayo has given..." He recommended that Gandhiji convey his opinion of the book to the author and perhaps review it in *Young India*. Miss Williams had assisted Bishop Fisher in writing his book, *India's Silent Revolution*.

Hail Mount Hermon! A Tribute

Satyagraha Ashram, Sabarmati,
October 26, 1928

Dear friend,

I had your letter from Hingham. I have got the book also, called *Understanding India*. I do not know when I shall get the time but as soon as I do, I shall read Mrs. Williams's book. I reciprocate the hope that we shall meet one another some time next year.

Yours sincerely,
Rev. F. B. Fisher
Methodist Episcopal Church,
3 Middleton Street,
Calcutta

C.F. Andrews: A friend of India

Group photograph taken at Marseilles in France 1931: C. F. Andrews, Gandhi, Miss Muriel Lester, Mahadev Desai, Madeleine Slade (Mirabehn), Pyarelal and an English friend. Mohandas Gandhi (1869 – 1948) was the preeminent leader of the Indian independence movement in British-ruled India.   (Courtesy: World History Archive/Alamy Stock Photo)

Letter, August 12, 1929

This is an appreciation of C.F. Andrews, a friend of Gandhiji and India. He had taken a special interest in investigating and publicising the conditions of Indians abroad and in assisting them in their struggles for their rights.

Sabarmati,
August 12, 1929

Dear friend,

What I think of Andrews is that India has no servant more devoted, more sincere and more hard-working than Deenabandhu Andrews. He is truly what the Fiji Indians, I think, called him, Deenabandhu, friend of the lowly.

Yours,
M.K. Gandhi

Letter, October 3, 1929

Bishop Fisher wrote to Gandhiji on September 25, 1929, that the Golden Rule Foundation of New York, which was interested in child welfare, had requested him to forward to Gandhiji a letter requesting information concerning specific ways in which American philanthropists might assist in meeting the economic limitations which surround Indian children. (The Golden Rule Foundation was the successor to the Near East Relief Association, which had donated millions of dollars after the First World War for relief in Mesopotamia, Palestine and Turkey.) He asked for Gandhiji's recommendation so that he could second it.

Camp Azamgarh,
October 3, 1929

Dear friend,

I thank you for your letter of the 25th ultimo. In the papers forwarded to me from Sabarmati I do not find the letter from the Golden Rule Foundation of New York referred to by you. But I can guess the purport of that letter from your letter. As I am dictating this, one thing does occur to me, namely, the scarcity of milk for Indian children. What American friends may do in giving constructive help is not to send doles of charity but to send expert knowledge in dairying, experts who are not exploiters in the disguise of philanthropists but true philanthropists who will give knowledge for the sake of giving it and who will study the condition of India's cattle and show us the way of improving our cattle breed and the supply of milk from the existing cattle. This idea, if it is entertained in a proper spirit, can be considerably amplified.

Yours sincerely,
Frederick B. Fisher, Esq.
Bishop's Residence
Methodist Episcopal Church
3 Middleton Street, Calcutta

Letter, September 29, 1931

Bishop Fisher sent a telegram on September 23, 1931, to Gandhiji, then in London, requesting him to send a "strong message to American Christians on world peace and disarmament."

88 Knightsbridge
London, W.1

September 29, 1931

Dear friend,

I was deeply touched by your prayerful greetings. My message to American Christians on World Peace and Disarmament is that Peace and Disarmament are not a matter of reciprocity. When real Peace and Disarmament come, they will be initiated by a strong nation like America - irrespective of the consent and cooperation of other nations.

An individual or a nation must have faith in oneself and in the protective power of God to find peace in the midst of strife, and to shed all arms by reason of feeling the loving power of God and His protective shield, and I hold such peace to be impossible so long as strong nations do not consider it to be sinful to exploit weak nations.

Yours sincerely,
M.K. Gandhi

The Right Reverend Bishop Fisher

C/o *Christian Herald*
New York
Letter, November 11, 1931

Bishop Fisher wrote to Gandhiji on October 1, 1931, enquiring whether he planned to visit the United States after the Round Table Conference in London. "If so, I want to be of every possible service to you. It would be a pleasure to meet you and to even travel with you, doing everything in my power, just as Andrews has so often done, to guarantee comfort and protection." He sent a cable on 9 October expressing the hope that Gandhiji would visit America. "Our country needs you dear friend please come." And another telegram on 11 October:

"Please come to America as my guest graciously permitting me to assume full financial responsibility for your trip leaving absolute freedom to choose your own programme of travel and work. Mrs. Fisher or I will accompany you on tour if desired to protect from inconvenience and lovingly try to surround you with ashram spirit. America needs you and will receive your message seriously. Five hundred Christian ministers at international convention of Disciples of Christ yesterday voted sincere welcome and assurance of spiritual cooperation." Dr. John Haynes Holmes and several other friends had advised Gandhiji not to undertake the visit at that time. Bishop Fisher wrote a long letter to Gandhiji answering their concerns and explaining the nature of his invitation.

"I want again to assure you of my deep prayers and my abiding interest in the ideals you represent. Your life has made a profound impression upon mine and I shall always look to you as my rare, spiritual guide and friend. I hope even yet that you may decide to come to America... I would then attempt to secure the cooperation of men like Holmes, Atkinson and others... Circumstances might alter their attitude because their hearts are deeply devoted to you and to your ideals."

88 Knightsbridge,
London, W.1,
November 11, 1931

Dear friend,

I have been receiving your very warm letters. I have time just to say this. With reference to the American visit, my own instinct was that the time had not arrived to visit America. That instinct still abides. I had made up my mind when the visit was first talked about that I would do as Dr. Haynes advised me. This was about 3 years ago or more when the visit was first talked about. As you know we have since met. He was in London just waiting for me, and I have told him that I would be guided entirely by him in connection with the pressing invitations that I received from America on my landing here.

Dr. Holmes and several other friends are decidedly of the opinion that it would be a mistake for me to go to America. Your decision therefore has come upon me as a surprise. You are just as dear a friend to me as Dr. Holmes; I shall therefore look forward to the result of your conversations with him. You know Richard Gregg too. He also supports Dr. Holmes and enforces the opinion by adding the winter will not be the proper season for me to visit America.

Yours sincerely,
The Right Reverend Bishop Fisher
The First Methodist Episcopal Church
Ann Arbor, Michigan

Message, November 17, 1931

This message was conveyed by telephone from London to Bishop Fisher, who was in Chicago. My friends in India, members of the Working Committee of the Congress, have cabled me to return to India, immediately the conference is over; so I must not go to America. It seems that there is still a long time before I could give any message to America. Perhaps God thinks that, though I would like to meet friends, I have no reason to go to America.

Letter, to Mrs. Fisher, December 28, 1941

Mrs. Fisher wrote to Gandhiji requesting a few words to be included in a biography of Bishop Fisher.

Bardoli,
December 28, 1941

Dear sister,

I have yours of October 17th received yesterday. To send you season's greetings is a mockery when hatred reigns supreme and God of Love and Truth is disowned.

Here are a few lines for your book.

"I had the privilege of coming in close contact with the late Bishop Fisher. He seemed to me to be one among the few Christians who walked in the fear of the Lord and therefore feared no man."

Yours sincerely,
M. K. Gandhi

OBITUARY

Fisher dies at 56 in Detroit

Rev. Frederick B. Fisher of Detroit, who attracted world-wide attention eight years ago when he resigned as a bishop of the Methodist church in India, to return to the pulpit and accepted the pastorate of the First Methodist church here, died suddenly this morning in Detroit, where he was pastor of Central Methodist church.

Coming to Ann Arbor in the fall of 1930, Dr. Fisher resigned the local pastorate four years later to accept the ministry of the Detroit congregation. His death, which came as a shock to his large circle of friends in Ann Arbor, was attributed to coronary thrombosis. He had gone to see his physician late yesterday and was advised to enter a hospital for rest and observation.

He died in Ford hospital in Detroit at 4:57 a.m. today, so suddenly that his wife and physician could not reach his side, although both were in the building.

Funeral services will be held at 4 o'clock Easter Sunday afternoon in Central Methodist church, Detroit, with Bishop Edgar Blake, head of the Detroit Methodist Episcopal area, in charge.

Dr. Fisher was 56 years old. A precedent was established when he stepped down from the bishopric to return to the pulpit. He was the youngest bishop in the church, and one elected to that position by one of the largest majorities. In petitioning for retirement to the council of bishops in Boston in 1930, he explained that he considered 10 years' experience in the judicial and administrative work of the church to be "enough for any prophetic preacher, for the pulpit is the great thing in any minister's life." He was elected a bishop in 1920.

Was Leader Here

In Ann Arbor, Dr. and Mrs. Fisher's vast knowledge of international affairs and their emphasis on religious education and international peace, established them immediately as leaders and gained for them many friends. Dr. Fisher, a personal friend of Mahatma Gandhi, published a book on the Indian leader and also edited a book of sermons while in Ann Arbor.

He was born in Greencastle, Pa., Feb. 14, 1882. He received B.Sc. and B.A. degrees from Asbury college in 1902 and 1903, and held a pastorate in Kokomo, Ind., in 1903. He later studied at Boston university and Harvard and held pastorates in North Cohasset, Mass., and Boston.

He served as a missionary in India from 1904 to 1906, and from 1910 to 1920 was secretary of the foreign missionary movement of the Methodist Episcopal church and the laymen's missionary movement. He was made bishop of India in 1920.

He was widely known as a lecturer and author, and received honorary degrees from Asbury college, Boston university, Depauw university, Wesleyan university and Hillsdale college.

The Rev. Mr. Fisher's first wife was Edith Jackson of Muncie, Ind., who died in 1921. In 1924 he married Welthy Honsinger of New York.

(*The Ann Arbor News*)

15 An Extraordinary Woman Of Courage

DR. WELTHY HONSINGER FISHER
(1879 – 1980)

Welthy Honsinger Fisher, left, meets with Indian Prime Minister Indira Gandhi. Fisher, a friend of the prime minister's father, was the first American to appear on an Indian postage stamp (1980).

An Extraordinary Woman Of Courage

Welthy Honsinger Fisher 1900, (1879-1980) was a teacher, philanthropist, and author. After volunteering for the YWCA in France during World War I, she traveled to Asia and devoted her life to promoting literacy. During the '20s, her personal friends included Gandhi and Sun Yat-sen. Through her organization, World Literacy Inc., Fisher created Literacy Houses, which trained thousands of dedicated teachers in India and China. Bearing special classroom equipment made to fit on bicycles (some of it designed by Fisher), her army of teachers pedaled to remote villages and taught thousands, who in turn taught millions, to read and write.

SU (Syracuse University) honored her with the George Arents Pioneer Medal for international culture in 1948. To celebrate her 100th birthday, Fisher traveled back to Asia. She was the oldest foreigner on record to visit China. In India, she accepted an honorary degree from Delhi University and the government issued a postage stamp bearing her likeness.

(Syracuse University Magazine)

Welthy Honsinger Fisher (1879-1980)

American Methodist educational missionary in China and India

Welthy Honsinger was born in Rome, New York, and grew up hoping to be an opera singer. But upon hearing a missionary speaker, Honsinger discarded her plan, completed her education as a teacher, and sailed to China in 1906. As headmistress of the Bao Lin school in Nanchang until 1917, she promoted higher academic standards and Chinese leadership. Upon choosing a Chinese to succeed her and then leaving, she was terminated by the (Methodist) Woman's Foreign Missionary Society. Back in the United States, she became a YWCA war worker and then edited *World Neighbors*, a Methodist mission magazine. In 1924, she married Frederick Bohn Fisher, American Methodist bishop of India and Burma and friend of Gandhi and Tagore.

The Fishers' commitment to indigenization caused Frederick to resign his bishopric in 1930 in favor of an Indian successor. After her husband died in 1938, Welthy Fisher wrote his biography and studied educational systems throughout the world. Stylish and articulate, she became a popular lecturer on missions, women's topics, and international friendship. She supported Chinese industrial cooperatives and was accused of being a communist. In 1948 she was chairman of the World Day of Prayer.

Six weeks before his death in 1947, Gandhi asked her to work for India's villages. In 1952 she returned to India to work with Frank Laubach, Christian literacy pioneer.

In 1953 she founded Literacy House at Allahabad. Breaking with Laubach, she developed secular methods to encourage functional literacy, linking it with agricultural and industrial development. Literacy House moved to Lucknow and became famous for its effectiveness and its House of Prayer for All People. Fisher was much-honored by the Indian government, which based its village literacy programs on her ideas. She returned to the United States in 1973 and died in Connecticut.

(Dana L. Robert, "Fisher, Welthy Honsinger," in Biographical Dictionary of Christian Missions, ed. Gerald H. Anderson (New York: Macmillan Reference USA, 1998), 212. This article is reprinted from Biographical Dictionary of Christian Missions, Macmillan Reference USA, copyright © 1998 Gerald H. Anderson, by permission of Macmillan Reference USA, New York, NY.)

ARCHIVES | 1978 New York Times

We'thy Fisher: Woman With a Mission

By SHARON JOHNSON APRIL 2, 1978

This is a digitized version of an article from The Times's print archive, before the start of online publication in 1996. To preserve these articles as they originally appeared, The Times does not alter, edit or update them.

Occasionally the digitization process introduces transcription errors or other problems. Please send reports of such problems to archive_feedback@nytimes.com.

LOS ANGELES — Welthy Honsinger Fisher, who first went to China as a Methodist missionary in 1906, didn't allow her 99 years, subzero temperatures, or a broken knee to interfere with a recent trio to China.

She traveled halfway around the world from her home in Southbury, Conn., so that she could visit old friends who share her interest in the education of women. One friend she met was Madame Sun Yat-sen, founder of the China Welfare Institute, who hosted a banquet for the tall, attractive widow of the Rev. Frederick Bohn Fisher, the late Bishop of India and Burma.

"We talked about the great progress that Chinese women have made," said Mrs. Fisher, who spent a few days in Los Angeles recuperating. "They are much better-educated today and are taking their places alongside men in all the professions."

When Mrs. Fisher arrived in Nanchang in 1905 to head the Ban Lin School, it was the only school for girls in the province of 45 million people.

"Young people were caught in the struggle between old and new," Mrs. Fisher reminisced. "Those who attempted to break with ancient tradition risked condemnation by their parents in the community. It was especially hard on women to assert their rights. Yet I found many girls who were determined to guide their own fortunes."

Mrs. Fisher helped them wherever she could. She shocked the Nanchang community by defending a student whose parents threatened to commit suicide because the girl refused to marry the young man they had selected for her. She persuaded the parents that 20th-century women should be allowed to select their own mates so that happier marriages would result. Mrs. Fisher, then a 26-year-old schoolteacher, also caused quite a stir in missionary circles because she adopted two Chinese infants, one of whom had been left on her doorstep.

'Never Regretted My Decision'

Mrs. Fisher's family and friends had opposed her decision to work in China. After graduating from Syracuse University in 1900, she had studied opera at Carnegie Hall. Her parents warned her that she was throwing her life away because they said she had a brilliant future as a performer.

"I never regretted my decision," Mrs. Fisher said. "Missionary work gave me satisfaction that would have been impossible to gain from a career in grand opera."

For 11 years, she taught in China and helped the Bao Lin School become the prototype for women's education. Even a fire that destroyed the school in 1911 didn't keep Mrs. Fisher from pursuing her dream of bringing education to Chinese women. With contributions from Methodists in the United States, she rebuilt the school.

When World War I broke out, Mrs. Fisher turned the administration of the school over to the Chinese and returned to America, where she joined the Y.W.C.A. She worked in Europe as a member of the War Work Council and after the war edited the Methodist magazine "World Neighbors" in New York. In 1924, at the age of 44, she married Mr. Fisher.

"I tell each generation of girls I meet not to fear leading independent lives," she said. "I generalize, of course, from me. The gamble was whether I could eat and have my cake, too. I wanted to do the work I did and I found, in the end, the man who loved me for this." Mr. Fisher died in 1938.

Worked With Illiterates

It is for her work as the founder of Literacy House, a grass-roots organization that teaches illiterates, that Mrs. Fisher is best remembered. As a widow, she visited India in December 1947, and met with Mahatma Gandhi, an old friend of her husband. The Indian leader asked her to help his country by teaching illiterate adult villagers to read and write.

"Gandhi told me to concentrate on the villages rather than the cities because he said the cities had everything," said Mrs. Fisher. "He said that if you do not help the villages, you do not help India because India is the villages."

Mrs. Fisher was reluctant to teach adults because she felt that her career of teaching children in China had not prepared her for the task.

But Gandhi told her to teach the adult villagers to read materials about things that concerned them: their work and their land.

Mrs. Fisher drew up a basic vocabulary list and wrote several books for adult readers. In 1956, she opened Literacy House's 23-acre campus in Lucknow, India.

Today the organization is part of World Education, which provides assistance to education programs in 30 countries, including the United States.

Mrs. Fisher now lives in Heritage House, a retirement community, with her secretary, Sally Swenson, who is writing a biography of Mrs. Fisher. In 1962, McGraw-Hill published Mrs. Fisher's autobiography, "To Light a Candle," a title she adapted from the Chinese model: It is better to light a candle than to curse the darkness.

"The publishers wanted to call it Born Welthy," said Mrs. Fisher, who was named for a Puritan ancestor who dropped the "a." "I said that title will prevent me from going around the world and raising money for things I believe in."

She attributes her long life to "deep breathing exercises and a good mental attitude."

"I could never manage to feel as I was supposed to about my chronological age," she said. "Maybe I was too busy. The future always seemed limitless and I have never stopped expecting something to happen, some invitation for another adventure."

An Extraordinary Woman Of Courage

155

Hail Mount Hermon! A Tribute

WELTHY HONSINGER FISHER: A VISIONARY

In her 70s, Welthy Honsinger Fisher begins literacy work: World Literacy of Canada is founded.

This year, at the age of 76, Welthy Honsinger Fisher (1879 – 1980), a tremendously innovative and dynamic woman, becomes the driving force for the establishment of the World Literacy of Canada. She served as its Honorary President from 1959 until her retirement in 1978.

At the time of its creation, the main goal of World Literacy of Canada was to support literacy initiatives in India through education and community development programs. Since 1955, WLC has supported literacy and development programs in Canada, Africa, Asia, Latin America and the Caribbean. WLC concentrates on programs that address the issue of adult literacy, and particularly on meeting the needs of women. The educators of WLC believe in a holistic, integrated approach to literacy and community development and try to develop programs with sensitivity to the needs and the cultural context of the communities where they work.

Welthy Honsinger Fisher was born in Rome, New York, in 1879. At 21, she embarked upon a teaching career. Her first job was in Haverstraw, New York, in a one-room school called Rosebud College where she was in charge of 15 students. "There she had her first experience with prejudice: the one Negro student ran away, fearing blame for the misdeed of a white student, and Welthy brought him back and defended him".

First day cover issued by Indian Postal Service
- An honour well deserved

Welthy's original experience in education in the developing world was as a teacher and headmistress of a school in China in the early 1900s. From the beginning, her approach to education emphasized the importance of local control and she was committed to the idea of women's independence through the tools of education.

Welthy Honsinger was drawn to overseas service after teaching for six years in the United States. In spite of the reservations of friends and family, in 1906 she travelled to China and became the headmistress of the Bao Lin School in Nanchang, and her years in China are vividly described in her autobiography, 'To Light A Candle' (published in 1962 by McGraw-Hill). Of her years in China, Welthy Fisher said, "I began to study larger maps... to question the exclusiveness of nationality, religion and race."

Back home from China, she edited a monthly magazine for young people called *World Neighbors*, received an honorary degree from Syracuse University, lectured, authored four books for children and two for adults (String of Chinese Pearls and Beyond the Moon Gate).

In June 1924, at age 44, Welthy Honsinger married Fred Fisher, a Methodist Bishop working in India. The Fishers were well-acquainted with and respected by Tagore, Nehru, Gandhi and other prominent leaders of the Indian Independence movement. Following her husband's death in 1938, Welthy Fisher travelled widely, returning to China and then to India. During the 1940s, she spent "semesters" studying the educational systems of Mexico, Peru, Bolivia, Brazil, India and the Middle East.

On a trip she took to India in 1947, Welthy was asked by Mahatma Gandhi to return permanently to India and continue her work in education there. In that occasion, on December 14, 1947, Gandhi took Welthy's hands and said: "When you come back to live in India, go to the villages and help them. India is the village." A month later, in January 1948 Gandhi was assassinated.

In 1952, fourteen years after her husband's death and four years after Gandhi's, Welthy Fisher returned to India to start a new life. She was 72 years of age but felt young and vigorous and, in the two-year-old Republic of India which neither her husband nor Gandhi had to lived to know, she looked for fresh inspiration. Her life came full circle, and it was at that time in India that she decided that literacy training was a key strategy to eradicate poverty. At that time, the newly independent India became the world's largest democracy, but the great majority of its population (320 million of its 435 million people) were illiterate.

It was unusual that a woman from the USA campaigned for women's literacy and women's independence in India in the 1950s. That Welthy Fisher began her literacy work at the age of 72 and launched a new life path that would include teaching and travelling on almost every continent for the next eighteen years, shows just how extraordinary she was. Not surprisingly, Welthy Fisher herself noted that she experienced several 'true reincarnations' within her long lifetime.

Dedicated to improving the people's lives in "new India" through education, in 1953 Welthy founded Literacy House, a small, non-formal school that combined literacy with vocational training. However, it was not long before Welthy and her fellow literacy pioneers realized that similar programs were needed throughout the world, and soon two non-profit organizations, the World Literacy of Canada (Toronto) and World Education (New York City) were founded with the purpose of providing literacy training to those who needed it most throughout the world.

Welthy Honsinger Fisher was deeply involved in both organizations for many years, either as President or advisor. Throughout her nineties she continued to travel widely and in 1978 she visited Peking as the oldest foreign guest of the Chinese government. She made two "farewell" trips to India in 1973 and 1977 but returned one last time in 1980 shortly before her death at the age of 101 in Southbury, Connecticut.

In March 1980, the Government of India issued a Welthy Honsinger Fisher commemorative postage stamp; she is the only American to be so honoured.

Part of Welthy Fisher's genius was that she understood the importance of learning on all fronts and she devoted much energy to educating and raising the consciousness of donors. Her strength, determination and stamina for literacy work in India seemed limitless and continued to be an inspiration for members.

Following her death in 1980, Indira Gandhi issued a message of condolence that stated:

"Mrs. Welthy Fisher was a wonderful woman. Beautiful, efficient, enthusiastic and energetic, she lived life to the hilt. At Gandhiji's request she threw herself wholeheartedly into literacy work and put hundreds of thousands of young women on their feet. She loved and served India. I am glad to have known her and count her amongst my friends.

Welthy Fisher's vision remains with World Literacy of Canada and her unique life is a testament to her faith and perseverance. Her motto, a Chinese proverb, was the guiding force of her own life: "It is better to light one candle than to curse the darkness."

Sources

Sally Swenson. Welthy Honsinger Fisher: Signals of a Century, by Three Decades for Literacy & Development: A History of World Literacy of Canada (http://www.worldlit.ca/history.html)

The 1964 Ramon Magsaysay Award for International Understanding. Biography of Welthy Honsinger Fisher (http://www.rmaf.org.ph/Awardees/Biography/BiographyFisher Wel.htm)

Prepared by World Literacy of Canada (Toronto) and Daniel Schugurensky (OISE/UT) (History of Education)

(The Ontario Institute for Studies in Education of the University of Toronto - OISE/UT)

An Extraordinary Woman Of Courage

First Among Many

Syracuse University alumnae have created pathways to progress that changed the world

By Christine Yackel

Generations of Syracuse University (SU) alumnae have been transformational trailblazers in a variety of fields—from aviation to zoology and almost everything in between. Their significant contributions were made possible by decades of progressive thinking when, from its very beginning in 1870, Syracuse was one of the few private institutions of higher learning to open its doors to women and people of color. For 145 years, SU's inclusive campus has created a learning environment that empowers women to find their own voices and thrive. Some have been honored for their notable accomplishments, while others are unsung heroines who have made the world a better place without recognition or praise. Here are the stories of just a few of SU's pioneering women who have had the strength of character and courage of conviction to forge their own destinies.

Welthy Honsinger Fisher: First Lady of Literacy in Asia

Welthy Honsinger Fisher 1900, (1879-1980) was a teacher, philanthropist, and author who believed the way to overcome poverty was through education. After volunteering for the YWCA in France during World War I, she traveled to Asia and devoted her life to promoting literacy in China and India. She trained thousands of teachers and came to be known in that part of the world as the "First Lady of Literacy." In 1951, she founded World Literacy Inc., an organization dedicated to providing literacy training to those who needed it most. In 1957, World Literacy became World Education, and today, the organization she began more than 60 years ago continues to carry on her vision to eradicate illiteracy both here and abroad. In honor of her work, the Indian government issued a postage stamp bearing her likeness.

(Syracuse University Magazine, New York, Spring 2017, Vol. 34, No. 1)

Our Founder: Welthy Honsinger Fisher

World Education Founder, Welthy Honsinger Fisher

If World Education is a tree, with branches currently reaching out all over the world, then its root, buried deep in the soil of Lucknow, India, is Literacy House. The light, heat, and water that nurtured its growth was Welthy Honsinger Fisher, the founder of Literacy House and World Education. That an American woman campaigned for women's literacy and women's independence in India in the 1950s is extraordinary. That Welthy Fisher began the enterprise that would become World Education at the age of 73, in the midst of a life that would include teaching and traveling on almost every continent for the next eighteen years, sheds light on just how extraordinary she was.

Welthy Honsinger began her life in 1879 in Rome, New York. After receiving her college education from Syracuse University, she traveled to China as a Methodist missionary to become principal of Bao Lin, a girls' school in Nanchang Province. The year was 1906, fourteen years before American women would have the right to vote. While there, she encouraged her girls to develop into new, modern Chinese women, often against the wishes of their more traditional parents. She was committed to the idea of women's independence, however, and knew that if she could give them the tools they needed through education, then there would be no stopping them from changing the face of China. In her words:

"To me there was virtue and grace in 'Old China' and virtue and hope in 'New China.' Proud of my own rich inheritance of freedom, I was trying to teach my southern Chinese children to 'know the truth.' My charges, ranging from babies to teen-agers, were the women of 'Young China's' future. In the happy assurance of my Christianity, my belief in Western progress and the emergence of women, I was sure that moral good could only beget good. When I was accused of encouraging young revolutionaries, a word I associated with 1776 and not with the ferment in Russia or the writings of Karl Marx, I agreed that indeed I was."

In fact, when the Chinese revolution occurred that put Chiang Kai-Shek in power, some of Welthy's female students were there to help make it happen.

Prime Minister Indira Gandhi, Governor of Uttar Pradesh, Mr. Akbar Ali Khan, and Welthy Fisher celebrating the 20th Founder Day of Literacy House, Lucknow, 1973.

In 1924, after working for the YWCA during World War I and traveling the world for pleasure, Welthy married Frederick Bohn Fisher, a Methodist bishop with a passion for life, freedom, and mutual respect among all peoples. For the next fourteen years these two amazing personalities joined forces to campaign for cooperation among peoples and cultures in order to eradicate suffering and promote peace. Throughout their travels, they came to realize that lack of education and poverty were the cause of much suffering in the world, and they both spoke publicly throughout the U.S. to raise awareness of such problems.

The Fishers spent much of their time in India, where Fred's sermons drew standing-room-only crowds. Despite Fred's powerful Christian message, and both Fred and Welthy's dedication to their Christian faith, they had the ability to see beyond the boundaries of individual religions. They embraced all races, cultures, and faiths equally. It was this "spiritual color-blindness" that drew the attention of Gandhi, a man who would remain both friend and inspiration to the Fishers throughout their lives. In the times they met with Gandhi, they engaged in philosophical debate and discussed how best to solve the multitudes of problems India was facing in the twentieth century. Welthy was impressed with Gandhi's dedication and self-sacrifice. "There was no one with whom I could compare him except Christ himself," she once said.

An Extraordinary Woman Of Courage

While traveling in the U.S. in 1938, Welthy, at 59 years of age, lost her favorite companion and great love when Fred Fisher died of heart complications. Although she felt an overwhelming sense of loss and loneliness, she carried on her life's work with the positive outlook that characterized every aspect of her life. Once again, she was off to make her place in the world, first traveling to China and India as a journalist, and then to South America and the Middle East to study women and educational systems. On a trip to India in 1947, she was asked by Gandhi himself to return permanently to India and continue her work in education there. Her life came full circle, as it was in India that she decided beyond all doubt that the only way to eradicate poverty was through literacy training. As Welthy said at that time:

"Illiteracy is a real tragedy for a modern man. ...As a nation becomes democratic and industrial, there's no time for the wise men, for the cultured illiteracy of simpler civilizations, where remembered words were handed down in the village square. Now a man who can't read is cut off from participation in his own government, in choosing his leaders. He can't progress or improve himself because he can't read directions or handle the workings of machines. In this new India, men and women needed to read as never before."

Dedicated to improving the chances of men and women's survival, advancement and independence in "new India" through education, Welthy began Literacy House, a small, nonformal school that would combine literacy with agricultural training. However, it was not long before Welthy and other literacy pioneers realized that "new India" could be replaced with "new Asia," "new Africa" or even "new America," and World Education was born in New York City, dedicated to providing literacy training to those who needed it most throughout the world.

Welthy Honsinger Fisher was deeply involved with World Education either as president or advisor from 1951 until 1972, when she gave up all official duties. At the age of 93 she was once again free to travel as she pleased. In 1973 she visited China for the first time in years, and returned to Peking in 1978 as the oldest foreign guest of the government. She made two "farewell" trips to India in 1973 and 1977, but returned one last time in 1980 before dying at the age of 101 in Southbury, Connecticut. (Read her memoriam.)

Two things are certain about Welthy: she was a woman of action, and she had a personality so large and multi-faceted it is almost impossible to portray accurately in words. While she fought tirelessly for education for the poor and was dedicated to the notion of Christian charity, she never gave up her personal pleasures, including her collection of stylish dresses and hats, her desire to be hopelessly in love with her husband, and her delight in singing in her renowned voice. She had an amazing ability as a fundraiser, yet she paid her own way every time she traveled internationally. She lived her entire life on the very modest wages she made through working for various organizations, yet she never wanted for anything. Above all else, she was ready at a moment's notice to speak, campaign, raise money, or travel for the people she helped in India. She had an amazing energy that persisted until the day she died of natural old age. World Education still benefits from that energy. Thanks to the tireless efforts of Welthy Fisher, World Education was built with enough vision and strength to carry on her work into the twenty-first century, and to expand to reach larger numbers of women, girls, and men. As Welthy knew, there is still much work in the world to be done—she herself was planning for a century.

(Sally Swenson, Welthy Honsinger Fisher: Signals of a Century, 1988.)

MAGSAYSAY AWARD
Welthy Honsinger Fisher

"It is better to light a candle than to curse the darkness"

The 1964 Magsaysay Award for Peace and International Understanding was awarded to Dr. Welthy Honsinger Fisher.

An Extraordinary Woman Of Courage

The Ramon Magsaysay award was established in April, 1957. This award was created to commemorate Ramon Magsaysay, the late president of Philippines. The Ramon Magsaysay Award, Asia's premier prize and highest honour, celebrates greatness of spirit and transformative leadership in Asia. The Award is presented in formal ceremonies in Manila, Philippines on August 31st, the birth anniversary of the much-esteemed Philippines President whose ideals inspired the Award's creation. This award is given in 6 categories.

The Ramon Magsaysay Award is considered as the Asia's Nobel prize. In the past five decades, the award has been bestowed on over 300 outstanding men, women and organizations whose selfless service has provided solutions to some of the most uncivilized problems of human development.

These categories are:
1. Government services (GS)
2. Public services (PS)
3. Community leadership (CL)
4. Journalism, literature & creative communication arts (JLCCA)
5. Peace and International Understanding (PIU)
6. Emergent leadership (EL)

From the year 2009, The Ramon Magsaysay award foundation has done away with the practice of awarding the award in the above six categories.

"I accept the Ramon Magsaysay Award with the humility of one who has tried to light a candle for physical, mental and spiritual enlightening in some of the far corners of the earth, for I have discovered that illiteracy is darkness."

WELTHY HONSINGER FISHER
1964 Ramon Magsaysay Awardee
August 31, 1964

FISHER ON FISHER:
"Fred taught me that living was an adventure"

Dr. Mrs. Welthy Honsinger Fisher with Mt. Hermon Principal, Mr. G.A. Murray and Mrs. Patricia Murray during Speech Day at Mt. Hermon School, November 1967.

Dr. Mrs. Welthy Honsinger Fisher wrote:

"Fourteen years with Fred Fisher convinced me that living was an adventure. He was interested in the smallest creature and the most insignificant happening in our day, and wove them into the rich tapestry of his enjoyment. He taught me nothing is unbearable – unless we ourselves permit it to be. When we were riding on the hot dusty trains of India, the screeching of the flat wheels dinned into our years all day long. But Fred would say, "Now, Welthy, just get into the rhythm of hot squeak!"

"Don't you think it is wonderful that I can work so much even at this age? You see, I have never been without a goal in my life. Every night I feel awfully tired, but some new idea, some new hope, some new plan refreshes me and I get to work again with joy and enthusiasm. This keeps me going and I am so happy."

"I hope to be alive as long as I live. I love to be curious. If you take a cynical view of the world, you feel very old and spiritually dead, even if you are young. But if you take a bright and hopeful view of things, you feel young and enthusiastic."

"I am just a member of the human race. I got this idea from a Negro boy. Racial discrimination is obnoxious. Better to light a candle than to curse the darkness."

"O God, help me to keep my sanity and not to live in the past, for I am sure Fred is still living in the future, as he always did here."

MH SPEECH DAY 1967: A Great Honour

Junior School Dewey House captains, Soni Lama and Jigme N. Kazi, receiving Dr. Master's shield from Chief Guest Mrs. Welthy Honsinger Fisher on Speech Day function at Mt. Hermon School, Darjeeling, 1967.

Bishop Fisher's wife, Dr. Mrs. Welthy Honsinger Fisher, a noted educationist in her own right, visited MH in November 1967 when I was in class 7. We had the privilege of hearing her speak on the annual Speech Day as the Chief Guest. During the prize distribution on the Speech Day, I, as, Junior School Captain of Dewey House, received the Dr. Master's trophy for the best House in the junior school on behalf of Dewey House from Dr. Fisher. It was indeed an exciting moment in my life which I shall ever cherish. In 1972, Sherab Namgyal, my friend and classmate from Sikkim, and I shared the Bishop Fisher Cup, a prestigious annual award of the school for the best boy student of the school. The award is given in recognition of the student's character, leadership and sportsmanship.

(*Inside Sikkim: Against The Tide*, Jigme N. Kazi, Hill Media Publications, 1993.)

16 "May Thy Fair Name Live Forever"

HALSEY E. DEWEY

DEWEY
Helsey E. Dewey (Principal, 1936-1942)

The school's main playground was built during Dewey's tenure
Each one of us who has or has had a part in Mount Hermon, has a responsibility placed upon us to continue to promote not only education but peace and goodwill everywhere, says Rev. Halsey E. Dewey, who was the school's Principal during the 1930s and 1940s.

Reverend Dewey is the most recent of the Four House heroes and he is the only one who is living today. He was a great missionary leader and spent 42 years in India, working mainly in Bihar and in Bengal; with the Santhal people. So he had two jobs, one in the plains for his missionary work, and the other at school as a Principal and it is not surprising that Reverend Dewey was constantly moving from the plains up to Darjeeling and vice versa.

When problems arose, he would come up to M.H. to solve them. He would not leave M.H. until the school was running smoothly again. Sometimes, if the problems were serious, he would raise funds in the U.S.A. Thus, he was able to pull out the school from its dark and troublesome period.

The Second World War put a lot of pressure on the school. Many staff and students from Britain left the school. Rev. M. J. Eade of the Managing Committee tells us this experience:

"Did you know the school nearly closed down towards the end of World War II – about 1943? The future of the Mission seemed uncertain. The student roll dropped to 120 – staff was difficult to obtain. Funds were low. Mr. Dewey, the American Methodist Principal, came to us when my wife and I were on holiday in Mount Hermon, and gave us a terrible shock when after telling us all about this, said the school will have to close unless something drastic is done – "I want you to call a meeting of all missionaries and parents and advise me about the future: Mt. Hermon School; To Be or Not To Be?"

Today, M.H. is a dream come true of our Founders and others who helped to establish this great institution. Thank you, Mr. Dewey, for all your efforts and perseverance in keeping the school going. We are the fruit of your labour.

Recently, the Hermonite Editorial Committee wrote a letter to Mr. Dewey. Let him tell you his story:

"I went to India in 1919 and spent part of my one month summer breaks ordered by the Missionary Society 1920-21-22 on the then newly named Mount Hermon Estate where the new school building was taking shape, built largely from the rock mined in the wooded area of the land.

Missionaries, seeking relief from the heart of the plains were purchasing plots within the borders of the Estate, and building cottages where they could go and live for a time near their children, who were or were to be students in the school.

During the winter vacation 1935, the devastating earthquake did tremendous damage to the school and some other buildings, and I went with the Bishop to visit, and was appointed Principal from March 1936, taking the school party up by train at that time and carrying on extensive repairs from the time of my arrival there. Of course, I became very well acquainted with the parents as well as the students during the first close connection which lasted till the spring of 1942 when my furlough became due, and with my wife and daughter, I came on one of those converted passenger steamers from Bombay to New York City.

I should state that it was probably the rapid increase in male students in a school which had catered largely to girls up the time of moving to Mount Hermon Estate, that caused a man to be appointed Principal.

During the years '36-'41 while the upper flat served as a playing field, a large hilltop standing between the school and Fernhill was cut down to make the present playing field, and allow the interschool competition in many games to be developed.

It was customary for many parents, mostly missionary wives to come to spend a part of the school year in one or other of the cottages to be near their children, and some of the groups of missionaries purchased plots on which to build cottages for year-round use.

Hail Mount Hermon! A Tribute

Dewey House 1962

Dewey House 1977

"May Thy Fair Name Live Forever"

The years 1945, and 1946, and 1951 and 1952 again found me with appointment to leadership of Mount Hermon, and I look back upon my close association with a multitude of missionaries from many parts of the globe as special blessings that came my way. Slowly, but very surely, developments beyond our power to resist, took more and more of the foreign missionaries back to their home-lands, until today the student body is very different from that which I knew from my days.

As the school reaches out as it does through its students, and faculty to many places around the world, we can rejoice in new opportunities, and perhaps new responsibilities, resting up our shoulders. Each one of us who has or has had a part in Mount Hermon, has a responsibility placed upon us to continue to promote not only education but peace and goodwill everywhere.

"Beloved Mount Hermon, we greet thee,
Thy daughters, and sons from afar,
As oft as we pause in our toiling,
To Hail Thee, whose children we are.

O, may thy fair name live forever,
Be deeply impressed on each heart,
That we in our trials, and triumphs,
May ne'er from thy guidance depart."

(Hermonite 1978, annual school magazine.)

PRINCIPALS – Part III

17 "I Feel At Home And I Belong To Mount Hermon"

DAVID GARTH STEWART
Principal, 1953-1963

THE SPIRIT OF MH: INITIATIVE, WHOLENESS, INTEGRITY

It's always a scary thing to come back. Especially, to come back to a place that has bound close ties around your heart. After fifteen years there won't be, of course, be any students who know you. The customs will have changed. Even the buildings will be different. Well you seem to the new generation a strange oddity stepping out from pages of the past, like a Rip Van Winkle waking up in a world where life has passed him by, and he is a quaint old man (rather than like a sleeping beauty, awakened by the kiss of a Prince Charming!)

And particularly scary to come back alone, without the partner by my side who shared all my life at Mount Hermon with me, and who would know and understand how I felt. But costs and home responsibilities ruled that out as a possibility.

In some ways the place has changed. The school has grown, almost twice the number of pupils when we left in 1964 (and five times the number when we came in 1954), and classrooms have sprung up here and there, taking over from former dorms. So, new dorms have come into being, notably the Round Hostel (alias the Doughnut). New offices, staff room, library, dining room and kitchen are to be viewed. And yet it is unmistakably still M.H.S., the same old school, the same old friendly walls and shadowed arches grey that we sang about, and my sentimental solitary wander down every corridor and around the grounds brought vivid memories at every turn.

I don't know whether the students thought me strange or not, but I felt at home. A school is not, of course, buildings and playing fields and wooded hillsides, memorable as they all may be. A school is people, and a school is a shared spirit and philosophy. It has been so good to meet my old students, in Bangkok, Calcutta, Gangtok and Darjeeling, to feel proud of their achievements in many and varied spheres of life, and to be surrounded by their warm affection and gratitude for what the school has done, to find nine of them now serving on the staff, together with quite a number whom I appointed 15-25 years ago. It has been good to see well-remembered faced of school servants, some now showing signs of age. And the hosts of students now, the present generation of Hermonites? They are just the same, and I belong.

Rev. D. G. Stewart: Chief Guest Speech Day 1978
Presenting the Stewart Shield for Juniors

And how can one describe the spirit and philosophy which lies at the core of Mount Hermon School? I think it may perhaps be summed up in three words; *initiative*, *wholeness* and *integrity*. Mount Hermon has never been a school stuck hopelessly in the mud of its own traditions, fearful of experiment, fearful of change. I am thrilled to see that continuing *initiative*, as exemplified in the new Teachers Training College, which is making such a worthy contribution, with support of so many other schools, to the future of education in the whole country.

Mount Hermon has always believed in an all-round education for the *whole* of life, physical, social, cultural, mental, spiritual. Every aspect of life is important.

The School maintains an all-round programme. Sports, studies, music, art, drama, involvement in social welfare programmes all have their place. And central to all is the spiritual dimension of life, a right recognition of God, and a striving for the highest ideals, as taught by a Christian school such as Mount Hermon.

Several ex-students have told me that what they gained from M.H. most of all was to recognize the need for *integrity*. To be true to themselves and their inner convictions, to be honest in business, loyal in friendship, trustworthy in word and deed, to be real people and not phonies. And as I talk with a newer generation, I believe that same emphasis is coming through still.

Yes, this is still the spirit of our beloved Mount Hermon. God has been good to the school, and I have rejoiced to see it. God has been good to me.

Ex-students on the staff with Mr. Stewart in 1978

Standing (Left to Right): Robin Sengupta, Dhruba Rai, Richard Tamang, Mr. D.G. Stewart, John Glasby, Jigme Kazi, Sherab Namgyal, Benu Chaterjee (not on the staff)
Seated (Left to Right): Shanta Mathai, Roxana Gardner, Roslyn Namgyal, Walsa Mathai, Pratap Singh Rai (not on the staff)   (Hermonite 1978, annual school magazine.)

David G. Stewart's 92nd Birth Anniversary
THE 'BOSS' LIVES ON

Today, February 19, 2015, is the 92nd birth anniversary of our former Principal, David Garth Stewart. Had he lived he would have been 92 today. Rev. Stewart, who was referred to as 'Boss' in MH (Mt. Hermon School, Darjeeling), died in Auckland on December 12, 2014 at the age of 91.

Though Rev. Stewart is no more yet he lives on...in our hearts.

A Tribute to David Stewart

Kamal Haque

It has come as very sad news that our dear "Boss," David Stewart, passed away peacefully today (12th December 2014). He was Headmaster of Mount Hermon between 1954 and 1963. I know he had recently been very ill, but he lived to a good age and led a fulfilled life.

"I Feel At Home And I Belong To Mount Hermon"

Kamal Haque, a student of MHS between 1954 and '61, wrote this very fine tribute when he first heard "Boss" was so seriously ill:

"Boss" was full of life, optimistic, always active. I do not remember him ever falling ill. He would inquire about every student and was known to visit the sick in the School Dispensary. His sense of humour never left him. I shall mention below, some of these that I remember.

His faith was very strong and he derived inspiration and strength from his noble mission, to spread the "message", do good to all, assist those who needed

Kamal Haque

help. As a teacher, he felt imparting "Christian" values was just as important as motivating students to achieve high academic and moral standards, so that they would be leaders to their communities. He set an example for his students to follow. I think this was one of his greatest gifts to his students and all those who were associated with him.

David Stewart's contribution to MHS was immense. He developed the small school, in 1954/55, to become a large, multi-national, multi-ethnic institution, with students from Thailand, East Pakistan, Burma, Singapore, Nepal, Sikkim, Bhutan, Finland, besides India, Australia, New Zealand, Britain, Canada, United States, Sweden and other countries. MHS was the only co-educational school in Darjeeling, which was more difficult to manage than single gender schools. "Boss" managed this very well. True, there were a few "incidents". He handled these with skill and firmness, and set a high standard for co-educational schools in other locations. He was kind, considerate but also firm. He did not hesitate to cane offenders for "serious" offenses. He later delegated this task to his deputy who had a "strong right arm."

"Boss" believed in the saying "All work and no play makes Jack a dull boy." He placed great emphasis on sports and culture, which was necessary to develop a "complete, all-rounder" individual. MHS had teachers for piano, violin and other musical instruments, (I learnt to play the violin from Ms. O'Hara). MHS was active in Choir singing, orchestra, piano recitals, debates, talent quest, plays of popular novels etc. "Boss" invited John Randell's Shakespeare Company (in which Shashi Kapoor was an actor/member) to stay in MHS. A number of Shakespeare plays were performed at the School stage, which was witnessed by guests from Darjeeling/other schools.

"Boss" was very keen to promote sports and encourage students to play games. He was an experienced football referee and led several trekking/hiking trips. (I was in one that went to Sikkim). "Boss" developed these standards/values which was followed by his able successors.

As I mentioned earlier, "Boss" had a sense of humour. I remember him telling students sitting on the garden fence "You birds, hop off the fence". He liked students to be clean cut and would tell some to scrape the "fungus" from their faces. He related that some friends decided to seek "guidance" from the Holy Bible. One person closed his eyes, opened the Bible and placed the pencil on a line. It was ".......and Judas went out and hanged himself...."

The friends thought that was not suitable, so they tried again. This time the pencil rested on the line that said "..........and do so likewise."

He will live for ever in my heart. God bless David Stewart.

(Humayun A. Kamal, former Bangladesh secretary and ambassador. Known as "Kamal Haque" in MHS – courtesy: UK alumni website: www.oldmhs.com)

Eulogy given at David Stewart's funeral by his niece Roz Namgyal

We have come today to mourn our loss of this beloved man David Stewart. I speak today on behalf of his extended family members who live in Australia and cannot be here. Heather, Michael, Indira and Sherina; Sherab, Debbie, Daniel, and Marley; Danny, Ayesha and Nuri, Becky and Lochie. John and Wendy Williamson, Graham and Annette Williamson, and Alan and Wendy Williamson and all of their families. It is, however, lovely to have Jennie, my daughter here with us today from Fiji.

The first thing I want to say about my Uncle David was that he was brother, father and grandfather to many more than just those of us privileged to have been born into his family. Today I speak to many of you here. I want to acknowledge how much you enriched his life – from his childhood, from the mission field, Mount Hermon School in India, the Bible College of NZ – later Laidlaw College, friends and brothers from his prison ministry, and others who have come into his life over the years. At this point I do want to make special mention of you, Darcy, and his church family here in Henderson Baptist. You have been the community that has faithfully and lovingly stood by him through the good as well as the bad, and often exasperating times for the past 50 years. You have been with him right to the end of his life. We want you to know how grateful we are for your love and care of Uncle especially in these later years through declining health and the loss of his beloved Dorothy and his son, John.

"I Feel At Home And I Belong To Mount Hermon"

Although an imposing man physically, possessing both a charismatic personality and a towering intellect, my Uncle David was to me quintessentially simple and uncomplicated at heart. As a child I had a much loved Christopher Robin book complete with the little ink drawings by E. Shepherd. In my child's mind it was always quite clear to me that Uncle David and Pooh Bear were interchangeable. My favourite pictures were those of Pooh and Piglet holding hands and ambling along the road talking, or the one where Pooh braves the brunt of the wind for little Piglet. In many ways I think my childish perception was remarkably correct. David has always held out a hand to us when we have found ourselves small, weak, vulnerable and marginalised, and drawn us into his larger than usual orbit of life. He was safe, loveable, present, kind. He was fun and funny - a good listener and always sharing what he had. He hated seeing people left out - and of course he also loved honey. The one thing I got totally wrong was the size of his brain - he was most certainly not a bear of small brain!

Hospitality and generosity were hallmarks of his life, but I cannot talk of this without mentioning his beautiful wife Dorothy, his sisters Joy Rongong and Heather Williamson and his brothers in law - Gyanendra Rongong and David Williamson. As children, we in the family, grew up with the expectation that people were only ever strangers for an instant. Invariably they would become companions at the dinner table and very often guests in the home as well. These encounters always brought joy and interest - They expanded our horizons and remain one of the most treasured legacies these elders in our family leave us. Most recently, while he was bed-ridden, I read him emails and letters from people all over the world who remember him sharing his money with them, bringing them home with him, advocating for them or simply listening to them and hearing what they were saying. It's testimony to the man that quite often he'd forgotten he'd ever done these things.....

Uncle was always learning-right to the end. A word he loved to use was cogitate, which means to reflect upon, think deeply about and mull over. On his death bed he received a phone call from a nephew who talked about Asperger's syndrome. After the call he asked Darcy and me if we knew about it and what it was.....Sick as he was, I saw him cogitating as he lay there after our little conversation.

David was also gentle with those in pain - and for me this became most noticeable after his own brush with death in 1987 after his massive stroke. He would become so choked up it caused rather extended periods of uncomfortable silence for his listeners. However, I also noticed that his tears never seemed to be for himself - in any form of self-pity - but were evidence of the depth of his feeling of compassion for the other. Stories relating to forgiveness, compassion, restitution and healing are the ones that would stop him short. I am no Biblical scholar, and I am quite happy to be corrected after the service, but I believe that the Hebrew word for compassion isn't just a kindly thought or attitude, but describes a visceral feeling experienced in one's body - Not dissimilar to the protective feeling and love one feels towards an unborn child. I believe David grew in his depth of understanding the other person's physical, emotional and spiritual pain after his own stroke and it moved him profoundly. His ability and willingness to stand alongside the other person in their pain and weakness is to me one of the things I have most loved and admired about him.

David loved camping and the outdoors – but his secret passion was fishing. Initially, as a naïve 18-year-old, I joined Uncle and 8-year-old John in a little dinghy, but sea sickness and uncle's never ending resolve to catch something – anything, put paid to any joy in the ventures! I do remember once that he was absolutely determined to catch a huge fish, and popped the appropriately sized bait on a large hook, stood up in the dinghy and cast it. There was a squawk as a bird dived for the bait, and the next thing we knew he had caught a very large, very cranky albatross by its wing.

David was fun loving and filled with the joy of life right to the very end. He could laugh - with that dry sense of humour sweeping us up into his bad jokes - for almost for as long as he could talk. One morning after he'd started to have trouble swallowing, I came in and brightly asked if he'd had breakfast. He replied somewhat dryly with a twinkle in his eye - "I've had a spoonful of porridge, half a glass of milk, and lots of spittle."

David was always breaking boundaries, and skating close to the wind taking risks. This was never more evident than behind the wheel of a car. My personal experiences include - being in a Jeep stuck on tea bushes in Darjeeling above a hairpin bend with a chasm of 100 feet or so just under our airborne front wheels, a cow lying on the bonnet of the jeep with its horn through the windshield, being stopped by cops in Auckland for speeding on our way to church where he was the speaker and we were already late....and so the litany continues. The family heaved a collective sigh of relief when Uncle's driving career came to an undignified end in a final prang outside Waitakere hospital....

However, he also took on risks and challenges in other life matters and stood beside people who had to make difficult challenging decisions themselves. Against much cautionary advice from the missionary community in India, he encouraged his sister, my mother, to embark on a marriage with a man from a different culture, years younger than her, and with the physical handicap of blindness. For this, my own sister Heather and I – and I'm sure our families - are profoundly grateful!

He and Dorothy took us, his two nieces into his already full home for a total period of 8 years (probably without consulting their two sons!) And today I'd like to say to you, young David - never once were we made to feel that it wasn't our home too. You and John are the brothers we never had – and you were the most beloved sons of David and Dorothy. You both brought such joy to them – They were so proud of you – of your individuality and differences, of your achievements and the wonderful men you became. It goes without saying that that same love flowed through to your families – to Sue and Jude and to David, Mark, Chloe, Jack and Joshua.

David rose to the heart-breaking challenge of trying to support and take care of Dorothy in her long battle with Alzheimer's, and most recently he took on the challenge of dying. He did this, as he did most other things, with grace, dignity and courage and without a shred of bitterness or anger.

While, as you know, he did have extremely comprehensive answers for many of life's questions, in later years I found Uncle to have a much deeper capacity to acknowledge the mysterious, and serendipitous. His iconic phrase "Ah well....." Could mean either he was ending the conversation, or he'd come to a point where there were no black and white certainties, and he really had nothing more to add... This seemed to apply especially to those situations where people may have found themselves excluded, or left out. He always hoped the best for people - sometimes exasperatingly so - sometimes long after they had stopped having any hope for themselves. He embodied for me verse 7 from 1 Corinthians 13 – "love bears all things, believes all things, hopes all things, endures all things, love never ends". Dare I say that one of the really precious things he said to me during these last 7 weeks was that he felt that deep down he was a bit of a universalist at heart. He could not believe that anyone - anyone at all - could be lost or left outside the love, grace and mercy of God.

Uncle David - in your life you Walked the Talk. You loved The Lord your God with all your heart and mind and soul and strength, and you loved your neighbour as yourself. You did this, and we witnessed it. What a legacy!

"Stewart embodied the spirit and ethos of Mt. Hermon"

Wendy Ann Morrow

PRINCIPAL & PREFECTS 1954
Back (L to R) Abu Rauff, Hans Klimkeit, Brang Sen, Arun Das. Front Ruth Isaacs, The Principal, Peggy Murtough.

What better name than "D.G. Stewart" to encapsulate the heritage, spirit and ethos of the wonderful Institution up in the hills - Mount Hermon School, Darjeeling, where Mr. Stewart was the Principal in the 1950s. I was very fortunate to be a part of this great Institution during his tenure as Principal.

A man of stature and a formidable figure who commanded respect from one and all, he inculcated high moral and ethical values to his students. Known for his great academic prowess, he was also actively involved in all aspects of the normal functioning of the school, be it sporting, drama, operettas, art exhibitions, debating, entertainment - he was part of it all. Discipline was very much on his agenda when he took over as Principal and he was able to accomplish this to a large degree with the help of his staff, prefects and the like.

Hail Mount Hermon! A Tribute

It is well over 50 years since I studied at Mount Hermon, but I would like to share a few little mundane memories that are still vivid in my brain up to this day:-

I remember him replete in his black graduation attire conducting the prayer services at the Assembly Hall every morning while his feet would tap along to the beat of the Marches so ably performed on the piano by Miss Tegal and Mrs. Murray.

It would be remiss if I did not mention about the delicious hot dogs that he would prepare with generous dashings of ketchup and mustard at our annual Sale Day held in May, at picnics in the woods nearby and last but not least at treks to Tiger Hill at crack of dawn with the hope of sightings of Mount Everest on a clear day.

Due to normal progression and successorship, it was possible to take Mr. Stewart out of Mount Hermon but I am sure it would not be possible for Mount Hermon to be taken out of Mr. Stewart!!

A very Happy 90th Birthday with good health, peace and happiness always.

Wendy Ann Morrow
(student from 1952 to 1957)

(UK alumni website: www.oldmhs.com)

Stewart built one of India's greatest educational institutions

Ronen Ghose

I will say just a few words about our BELOVED BOSS, the Rev. David Stewart who was Principal of Mount Hermon School, Darjeeling and during his tenure, I was most fortunate to have been associated with one of India's greatest educational institutions.

"I Feel At Home And I Belong To Mount Hermon"

MH | Staff & Teachers | 1962 |

Back Row | Standing | L to R | Mr. R. N. Dutt, Mr. J. Mapley, Mr. J. Darr, Mr. Kelvin Hendry, Mr. D. Lloyd, Mr. D. Logan, Mr. M. Manaen, Mr. E. Stemberg

3rd Row | Standing | L to R | Mr. M. Mathai, Ms. N. Raichoudhury, Mrs. M. Wilde, Miss C. Williams, Mrs. Barbara Hendry, Mrs. E. Logan, Ms. Netta Bilcliffe, Mrs. O. Alexander, Mr. P. Rai

2nd Row | Standing | L to R | Miss Rona Dawson, Mrs. I. Raichoudhury, Mrs. E. West, Mrs. E. Williams, Miss B. Cann, Sister J. Digby, Mrs. A. Lloyd, Miss C. Hawke, Miss P. Page, Mrs. E. Martin

Sitting | Front | L to R | Mrs. V. Johnston, Mr. J. Johnston, Mrs. J. Rongong, Rev. D. G. Stewart, Mrs. D. Stewart, Mr. G. A. Murray, Mrs. P. N. Murray

Absent | Ms. Leith MacGillivray |

Point of Interest | Mr. Jim Darr |

It was David Stewart's infinite capacity to be a perfectionist as a Principal, combining his deeply religious Christian beliefs with his academic and intellectual insight into which he was well versed and this was adequately shown throughout the school in all aspects of education where he had to control and manage students from different cultures, countries, religions and blend all of them into one beautiful mix of vibrant boys and girls imparting superb education as the end result.

We in Mount Hermon were being prepared for the outside world and the BOSS took great care to ensure that each one of us who left, would be in a position to face the trials, tribulations and challenges of life that lay ahead and for this I am greatly indebted to this great man of Jesus Christ.

David Stewart was one of the greatest CHRISTIAN MISSIONARIES TO HAVE EVER WALKED THE CORRIDORS OF MOUNT HERMON SCHOOL, DARJEELING. He left a legacy so great that it still permeates the very walls and corridors of the school to this day. David Stewart our BOSS will always be remembered with love and affection and it is evident from messages already sent by P.S. Rai, Bijay Palriwalla and so many more in the pipeline that I take this opportunity of saluting a great human being, a missionary of unrivalled proportions, on his 90th birthday on the 23 February 2013 in New Zealand. We shall all pray for his welfare and health and he must remember that there are hundreds if not thousands of Hermonites all over the world who share my sentiments.

His 'total package' prepared us for life

Sujit Kumar

THE STAFF 1963

Back Row: Messrs. M. Mathai, J.O. Wilde, J. Darr, D. Wainwright, D.N. Pradhan, K. Hendry, B. Byrne, M.S. Manaen, P. Rai, I. Sampson.
Middle Row: Mrs. I. Dam, Mrs. Sampson, Miss F. Gaunt, Mrs. O. Alexander, Sister J. Digby, Miss. L. MacGillivray, Miss N. Bilcliffe, Miss C. Hawke, Mrs. M. Wilde, Mrs. I. Raichoudhury, Mrs. E. Martin.
Front Row: Mrs. E. West, Rev. & Mrs. J.A. Johnston, Rev. & Mrs. D.G. Stewart, Mrs. J. Rongong, Mr. & Mrs. G.A. Murray, Mrs. E. Williams.

The 'Stewart' years (1954-1963) will be remembered as a time when Mt. Hermon School (MH), Darjeeling consolidated and expanded.

I was but a child of ten when admitted (to MH) in 1958; I grew with the numerous initiatives Mr. Stewart took to make our school a better learning place. He put together a team of teachers who were not only specialists in their respective disciplines, but took us beyond our syllabi and made us what we are today.

He recognized a need to develop facilities to keep pace with the rapid progress in contemporary education in India and worked to see the creation of our swimming pool and soon thereafter, a new multipurpose building (later, Stewart Building) with classrooms, better equipped laboratories and dorms above.

He was particularly involved in drama, music and debating and encouraged student participation – a favourite highlight in the MH calendar was Talent Quest night, wherein songs, musical pieces and skits were performed with enthusiasm by students. Weekend extra-curricular activities like photography, scouts and guides developed our level of communication and taught us to work as a team. We learned to live outdoors with limited resources on camps and treks organized during summer and autumn. The total package was structured to enhance our learning experience not just for school but for life!

I was a less-than-mediocre student in school but privileged to have been taught by Mr. Stewart, albeit just for a year. I remember him as a disciplinarian, who loved a game of soccer, but left little room for nonsense and lived up to his nickname – Boss!

(Sujit Kumar MHS: 1958-1965)

Sikkim Hermonites pay rich tributes to former Mt. Hermon School Principal D.G. Stewart

Sikkim Hermonites paid rich tributes to their former Principal Rev. David Garth Stewart, who passed away peacefully in Auckland, New Zealand, on December 12, 2014.

At a condolence meeting held in Gangtok (Sikkim) on December 16, 2014, grateful Hermonites, alumni of Darjeeling's Mt. Hermon School (founded in 1895), said Rev. Stewart who passed away at the age of 91 was a 'man of God', whose dedication and commitment to the school when he was its Principal (1953-1963) raised the standard of the school and brought it to becoming the best boarding school in India in 1961-62.

These photos are of Sikkim Hermonites during their condolence meeting in Gangtok on Dec 16, 2014 of former Mt. Hermon School Principal, Late Rev. David Garth Stewart, who passed away in Auckland, New Zealand, on Dec 12, 2014.

(L to R) Jigme N. Kazi, Arthur Pazo, Raaj Bangar, Punam Agarwal, Uttam Pradhan, N.K. Pradhan, Tempo Bhutia, Udai P. Sharma, Ram Gopal Pradhan, Shuva Pradhan and O.T. Bhutia. (Pix by Tashi R.N. Kazi)

1967 batch Hermonite Narendra K. Pradhan.

"I Feel At Home And I Belong To Mount Hermon"

Former Minister and senior Hermonite N.K. Pradhan said Rev. Stewart was not only a towering personality, a great orator, but cared for each and every individual in the school. "We are what we are because of MH (Mt. Hermon) and we are grateful to Mr. Stewart for his love, affection and care."

Reading from the Bible (Psalm 23), Jigme N. Kazi, President of Hermonite International, said Rev. Stewart, like King David in the Bible, was a "man after God's own heart".

1973 batch Hermonite Uttam Pradhan.

1972 batch Hermonite Udai P. Sharma.

1972 batch Hermonite Arthur Pazo.

Kazi, who also taught in MH, said, "God sent him to MH in the 1950s when the school was floundering and by the time he left it in 1963 our school was adjudged the best boarding school in India." He added, "If we as Hermonites have contributed anything significant to society it is because we have been touched by this mighty man of God."

RNI No. 40958/89 ESTD 1986 Vol XXIII No. 21 Gangtok, Wednesday, December 31, 2014 Rs. 3 Regd. No. WB/SKM/116/2015-2017

Sikkim OBSERVER

The VOICE OF SIKKIM

China deepens Nepal *engagement* PAGE 3

Sikkim Hermonites pay rich *tributes to former Principal* PAGE 4

Chief Minister Pawan Chamling with Brand Ambassador of Winter Carnival and actress Geetanjali Thapa during the launch of Sikkim Winter Carnival 2014 in Gangtok recently.

PDP floats 'grand alliance' for stable govt in JK

Hill Media *Network*

Srinagar, Dec 29: The PDP on Monday came out with the idea of a "grand alliance" with its arch-rival National Conference (NC) and the Congress to form the new government in Jammu and Kashmir, introducing a new element in the power sweepstakes.

Amid reports that the PDP, the single largest party with 28 members in the 87-strong Assembly, was warming up to BJP, second with 25 MLAs in the hung House, for the first time it spoke of the possibility of a tie up with NC and Congress both of whom have extended support to it, PTI reported.

Making a bid for getting into power for the first time in the Muslim-majority state, BJP has held talks with both the PDP as well as the NC, which has verbally promised its support to keep out the saffron party.

PDP chief spokesman Nayeem Akthar's statement that a grand alliance between the party, NC and Congress "was also an option" to form a stable government led to speculation on whether it was a tactic to put pressure on BJP to which PDP has set tough conditions including retention of Art 370 that grants special status to the State.

Meanwhile, Nirmal Singh, MLA who was Chairman of BJP's campaign committee during the elections, said in New Delhi that his party is in talks with other parties and "all our options are open".

Meanwhile, PDP president Mehbooba Mufti is slated to meet Jammu and Kashmir Governor N N Vohra on Wednesday for discussing government formation.

"The meeting of Mehbooba Mufti, Member of Parliament and President of Jammu and Kashmir Peoples Democratic Party (PDP), with the Governor has been advanced to take place on Wednesday at the Raj Bhavan in Jammu," a Raj Bhavan spokesman said today.

Vohra had on Friday invited Mehbooba and BJP state unit president Jugal Kishore Sharma for separate meetings to hold discussion on formation of government in the state.

At the end of two days of informal consultations with the party MLAs, PDP patron Mufti Mohammad Sayeed told them that they should go back to their respective areas to sense the mood of the people on the possibility of allying with the BJP for formation of the next government, PDP sources said.

The sources said the PDP patron wants to build a consensus within the party before Mehbooba Mufti meets the Governor.

NEWSLINE

Observer News Service

US ends war in Afghanistan

WASHINGTON: President Obama has hailed the end of U.S. combat operations in Afghanistan, saying that a Sunday ceremony in Kabul "marks a milestone" for the United States.

"Now, thanks to the extraordinary sacrifices of our men and women in uniform, our combat mission in Afghanistan is ending, and the longest war in American history is coming to a responsible conclusion," Obama said in a statement.

Koirala confident on constitution

KATHMANDU: Nepal Prime Minister Sushil Koirala is still confident that the political parties will promulgate the constitution before the January 22 deadline expires.

Koirala expressed his confidence while addressing a programme here yesterday.

Warning for Oz PM

CANBERRA: Tony Abbott is facing a rout in southern Australia as voters shun the Prime Minister's policies and style, prompting nervous Coalition MPs to call for a clearer and more compassionate strategy to market the government.

Private universities in Sikkim set up illegally: former Chief Secy

Observer News Service

Gangtok, Dec 29: Reacting to a report on establishment of educational institutions in Sikkim, former Chief Secretary Sonam Wangdi says the Sikkim Manipal University Bill did not have the mandatory assent of the President of India.

"Since 'education' is in Concurrent List, the President's assent is compulsory which is corroborated by the fact that Sikkim Education Act [No 11 of 2002] Sikkim Government Gazette No 310 of 2002 was assented to by President K R Narayanan on July 5, 2002," the former Chief Secretary said in Facebook.

"Unconfirmed reports state that the President refused to assent to the so-called unprecedented "Sikkim-Manipal University" Bill. The Bill was made into law without President' assent. The 2002 Sikkim Act is about education in Sikkim up to the college level," Wangdi said.

"Now the question arises why did the President assent to the SKM Edn Act? Obviously the assent was required. Since education up to college level required the assent, it is a common sense - and not a legal sense necessitating a legal luminary - to hold that State Bills for establishing universities shall be compulsorily assented to by the President. In other States, Private University Bills are invariably concurred by the President.

I would be delighted to be informed of any State Bill, setting up private universities, which did not require President's assent. Hence, all private universities in Sikkim are 'illegal' as pointed out in my three papers on Private Universities in Sikkim and seven on The Sikkim Manipal Saga which appeared in *Sikkim Express* and *Himalayan Mirror* during 8 May 2012-2013. Since there was no rebuttal, I am confirmed in my view. Nevertheless I welcome contrary opinion to arrive at the ultimate truth notwithstanding my deep conviction."

Wangdi further states that the EIILM University - like all other universities except the Central - is illegal since there is no President's assent which is absolutely mandatory. The Bill for the EILLM was passed in the Assembly [proceedings 20-25 February, 2006].

Sino-India ties set to soar after roller coaster 2014

Observer News Service

Modi to inaugurate Kailash Manasarovar Yatra route through Nathula in Sikkim

Beijing, Dec 29: Sino-India relations experienced both highs and lows in 2014 which saw President Xi Jinping's visit to India amid concerns over Chinese border incursions but bilateral ties are set to soar with Prime Minister Narendra Modi's slated trip to Beijing in the coming months.

Modi is expected to make a high-profile visit here in the next few months following up on September trip of President Xi to India during which the two countries signed several agreements including setting up of two industrial parks in India with USD 20 billion Chinese investment besides cooperation to modernise Indian railways.

He is expected to formally inaugurate a new route for the Kailash Manasarovar Yatra through Nathu La in Sikkim which would for the first time enable Indian pilgrims to travel to highly popular religious places by buses without undertaking an arduous journey by trekking or on mules.

Indian Ambassador to China Ashok K Kantha accompanied by top Chinese officials has already made a tour of Tibet to finalise the arrangements before Prime Minister's visit here.

This year has ended on a positive note with an Indian railways team holding comprehensive talks with Chinese counterparts on conducting a feasibility study of the high speed rail line between Delhi and Chennai besides track upgradation.

India currently is considering two corridors for high speed trains. While Japan is conducting a feasibility study for the bullet train project on the Mumbai-Ahmadabad corridor, China will do the same for the Delhi-Chennai route which is expected to begin by early next year.

If it materialises, the Indian bullet train project is a major gain for China which is making an aggressive pitch to market its high speed train technology outside the country.

Besides the high speed train, India and China have agreed to cooperate to identify the technical inputs required to increase speeds on the existing railway line from Chennai to Mysore via Bangalore.

All these projects are expected to take shape during Modi's visit, including the operationalisation of the two industrial corridors that China has agreed to set up in Gujarat and Maharashtra with an investment of USD 20 billion.

RSS has Sikkim in mind, holds session

Observer News Service

Gangtok, Dec 29: The Rashtriya Swayamsevak Sangh (RSS) has not forgotten Sikkim. It is also aware of the recent tie-up between the BJP and Sikkim Krantikari Morcha (SKM), which has ten MLAs in the House of 32.

Last week, RSS chief Dr Mohan Madhukar Bhagwat held brainstorming sessions with Sangha members of Odisha, West Bengal, Sikkim, Andaman and Nicobar in Bhubaneshwar. His five-day-long session ended on Monday, sources said.

Bhagwat discussed about strengthening of the Sangh in the eastern States through different RSS works. He also emphasised on protection of Indian traditions, specifically Hindu religion and traditions, by creating awareness among the people through different programmes, sources said. The Sarasanghachalak conducted internal meetings with 200-300 Sangh members at Utkal Bipanna Sahayata Sammiti in Bhubaneshwar on Sunday.

Dalai Lama concedes he may be the last

Observer News Service

London, Dec 29: The Dalai Lama, Tibet's exiled spiritual leader, has said he thinks his traditional religious role should cease with his death rather than a "stupid" successor replace him and disgrace himself.

He told the BBC in an interview recently that the Tibetan people should decide whether to continue the spiritual line, which dates back to the 15th century, Reuters reported. In Tibetan Buddhism, the soul of a senior lama is traditionally believed to be reincarnated in the body of a child on his death. China says the tradition must continue and it must approve the next Dalai Lama.

In another interview with France24 television, the Dalai Lama said hardliners in the Chinese government were holding back President Xi Jinping from granting genuine autonomy to Tibet.

Beijing accuses the Buddhist leader of being a violent separatist. He denies the charges, saying he only wants real autonomy for Tibet, a remote region ruled by the Communist Party since its troops marched in 1950.

"The Dalai Lama institution will cease one day," he told the BBC. "There is no guarantee that some stupid Dalai Lama won't come next, who will disgrace himself or herself. That would be very sad. So, much better that a centuries-old tradition should cease at the time of a quite popular Dalai Lama."

The exiled Tibetan, 79, said he expected to live for another 15 or 20 years.

The Dalai Lama said he took heart from hearing Xi talking about Buddhism recently. "This is something very unusual," he told France24. "A communist, usually, we consider atheist."

Asked if the remarks led him to believe Xi was ready to discuss genuine autonomy for Tibet, the spiritual leader said there were "some indications".

"But at the same time, among the establishment, there is a lot of hardliner thinking still there. So he himself sometimes finds it's a difficult situation," he said.

Representatives of the Nobel Peace laureate held rounds of talks with China until 2010, but formal dialogue has stalled amid leadership changes in Beijing and a crackdown in Tibet. Many Tibetans feel their intensely Buddhist culture is at risk of annihilation by Beijing's political and economic domination and a regional influx of majority Han Chinese. China denies these are risks.

Arthur Pazo, grandson of Gangtok's Pastor, Late C.T. Pazo, and Ram Gopal Pradhan led the prayers in offering thanks to GOD for the exemplary Christian life of the late Rev. D.G. Stewart, while Udai P. Sharma and Sikkim Hermonite Association (SHA) Vice-President Uttam K. Pradhan also spoke on the occasion.

Among those present during the condolence meeting, where a two-minute silence was also observed, were Tempo Bhutia, Raaj Kumar Bangar, Punam Agarwal, O.T. Bhutia and Shuva Pradhan.

SHA President Karma Bhutia attended the funeral service in Auckland on December 16.

(*Sikkim Observer*, December, 2014)

Rev. D.G. Stewart: A Man After God's Own Heart
Jigme N. Kazi

"Surely goodness and mercy shall follow me all the days of my life; and I shall dwell in the house of the Lord for ever." (Psalm: 23)

1972 batch Hermonite Jigme N. Kazi.

"Jigme, can you tell me anything about the present situation? I seem bereft of information. I heard an indirect report that the school had started again this year, but with only 100 boarders, and that it was deeply in debt."

This is what Mr. Stewart wrote to me on June 27, 2012 in my email. He was concerned about Mt. Hermon (MH) thereafter, too, and perhaps till the very end.

I am happy and proud of the fact that I was in MH in class 2 during his last year as Principal in 1963. I believe it was him or Mr. Murray who asked me, "Do you like the school?" when I entered the school building for the first time in 1963 from the front porch. I said, "Yes."

And for 16 short years (1963-1972 – student, 1974-1975 – TTC and 1976-1979 – teacher) I lived in MH and had a good time. I am a part of MH and MH is a part of me.

My family (wife Tsering, son Tashi and daughters, Yangchen, Sonam and Kunga - only the head is seen) with Mr. Stewart at the Planters Club, Darjeeling, during the Centenary celebrations of Mt. Hermon in November 1995.

I remember him as a football referee – he was very strict – and when he used to come to the school dining room to announce the name of the Saturday night movie. When he used to say, "And the movie is technicolour" he used to get a loud applause from us. Those days most of the movies were black & white.

When Mr. Stewart visited MH in the latter part of 1970s he spoke about the need to have men and women of 'integrity' in today's world in the school chapel. He was a great speaker and he spoke with much conviction.

I spent more time with him when he came for the school's centenary celebrations in 1995. Mr. Stewart, along with other former teachers and students, wanted the school Managing Committee to seek induction of Hermonites in the Committee to help the school to forge ahead. Thereafter, we kept in touch with each other till the very end.

When I think of Mr. Stewart I often compare him with King David of the Old Testament. Like the warrior-king of Israel Mr. David Stewart, too, was "a man after God's own heart".

God sent him to MH in the 1950s when the school was floundering and by the time he left it in 1963 our school was adjudged the best boarding school in India.

If we as Hermonites have contributed anything significant to society it is because we have been touched by this mighty man of God.

Psalm 23: A Psalm of David

The LORD is my shepherd; I shall not want.
He maketh me to lie down in green pastures: he leadeth me
beside the still waters.
He restoreth my soul: he leadeth me in the paths of righteousness
for his name's sake.
Yea, though I walk through the valley of the shadow of death,
I will fear no evil: for thou art with me; thy rod and thy staff they comfort me.
Thou preparest a table before me in the presence of mine enemies:
thou anointest my head with oil; my cup runneth over.
Surely goodness and mercy shall follow me all the days of my life:
and I will dwell in the house of the LORD for ever.

18 David Stewart's Memoirs
DAVID STEWART: Mount Hermon School 1954-1964

"We Both Loved Our Time In Mount Hermon"

David Stewart went to China to become a missionary in 1948. He loved China, and believed God had prepared him to work there. However, in 1951 he and his band of missionaries were expelled from China as Mao Tse Tung's Communist reign began. He left in tears, and never went back.

When he returned to Australia in 1951, he married Dorothy Jury, and worked as a Pastor for some time. In mid-1952 he went to New Zealand to conduct a series of missions. Very significantly for Mount Hermon School, that was when he met Graeme Murray at Victoria University, and Patricia North at Teacher's College in Wellington.

In 1953 he was then asked to join All Saints Anglican School, Bathurst, Australia, as Deputy Head and Dorothy became the Matron and Nurse. As a boarding school it was a wonderful training ground for his time in Mount Hermon School. He resigned from there at the end of 1953, but did not have another job lined up at the time.

Then out of the blue he received two letters. One was from his sister Joy Rongong telling him that Mount Hermon School was likely to close down and that the Methodist owners had appointed a Managing Committee made up of five missionary groups to see if they could save the school. She asked if she could give the Managing Committee his name as a possible candidate, to which he agreed. An hour after he accepted the offer to become Principal of MHS, an old friend Merie Tegel (a music teacher) wrote to him confiding that she wanted to go as a missionary teacher to India, and she had heard of a school called Mount Hermon! He burst out laughing... "Merie, an hour ago I was appointed Principal of Mount Hermon School (at a joint salary of Rupees 500 a month - $50 Australian), plus a full board!"

So they set sail for India and arrived at Calcutta. There on the wharf was Bill Jones, a 3-year missionary internee.

The following comes from David Stewart's Memoirs dedicated to a friend during his last months of life during the latter half of 2014:

"Bill took us overnight to Lee Memorial, and the next day by two trains to Siliguri, where we had breakfast topped off by our first taste of real Darjeeling tea – the best in the world. Then we went in a land rover up the winding hill through Kurseong, Sonada, Ghum (the highest point) and downhill to Darjeeling. We drove through the bazaar, then down to North Point where St. Joseph's Catholic school is situated. We turned left down the road, and eventually got our first sight of Mount Hermon. It was a magnificent building of local stone, and around to the north side (the main entrance) was a welcoming committee of Lulu Bowles (an American missionary), Buddiman (the Chowkidar or night watchman) in his marvellous attire, and Mr. Manaen (the Cashier) whose Office was just opposite mine. He was an enormous help to me, translating English into Nepali or Hindi. What a wise, helpful man he was! I could fulminate to him in English, and I know he'd put it all in courteous modified language for his listeners.

The school was run down. A succession of American missionary Heads had done their best to run it like an American School, but geared to a Cambridge, English examination syndicate, it didn't work well. A magnificent school, built for 300 boarders, the numbers were down to 86 returning students. The accounts were a mess and there had been no audit or over two years. As far as numbers were concerned, Bill and Lulu made a recruitment trip to Calcutta, and we actually grew to 128 in 1954. At the end of 1954 I had a recruitment drive in Calcutta and Bangkok (courtesy of the father of one of our Thai students). We reorganised the school into four Houses in 1960 and named them after four Americans. Knowles (after Miss Knowles who founded the school in 1895 as Queen's Hill School in Darjeeling town); Stahl (after Miss Stahl who was Miss Knowles' Deputy and successor as Principal until after the move to North Point); Fisher (after Bishop Fisher who along with Miss Stahl, raised the enormous sum needed to build the school, as well as obtaining Fern Hill for the Senior Boy's Hostel); and Dewey (after Hal Dewey who managed the beautiful estate for about 70 acres).

This estate boasted a magnificent Cryptomaria Pine forest, and the better half of 20 Missionary cottages plus Community Hall.

Mr. Stewart at school chapel service.

Mr. Dewey also held the school together as Principal during its difficult times in the 1940s and early 1950s. Four Houses were better for competition, and the award of House Points for sports, academics and other achievements. We also introduced a Prefect system. The Prefects were chosen by the Senior School. I nominated everybody, and the seniors all had a preferential vote. We gave each Prefect an honours Blazer (pale blue), and an honour point for their Houses. Each Sunday we invited the Prefects to a supper in our little three-room flat on the top floor, north-east corner of the main building. We made a boo-boo the first Sunday evening. We invited them to "supper", which they thought was a main meal, so they all refused school dinner in anticipation. Dorothy produced some cream cakes etc., she had made, but when they wolfed them down she realised my mistake. So with the help of the Head Bearer, she rustled up some toast and scrambled eggs, I think it was, and fed the multitudes! Our School had three-quarters boys and one quarter girls, so we elected 2 girls and 6 boys that first year. The Prefects were always a loyal band, and to my knowledge never misused their position.

THE STAFF

Back Row: (L to R) Mrs. Armstrong, Miss Menzies, Mrs. Hamer, Mr. Jones, Mr. Law, The Principal, Mr. Manaen, Mr. Vanghan, Mrs. von Rauch, Miss Madhaven, Mrs. Gleaves.

Front Row: Miss Pradhan, Miss King, Miss Macclesfield, Mrs. Williams, Miss Kessop, Mrs. Stewart, Mrs. Daniel, Mrs. Vanghan, Miss Block, Miss Morris, Mrs. Martin, (Absent: Miss Hutley).

My father died suddenly of heart failure in 1954. Even though I did not follow in his footsteps, I think he was proud of me. When I went to China, he was proud of my dedication to a cause, and when I went to India, he was proud that his only son had come into a significant educational position.

There was a good spirit between the Hills' schools, especially the four of us in Darjeeling. St. Paul's, an Anglican school, was located the highest at about 7,000 feet on the upper road to Ghum. Leslie Goddard had been Rector there for over twenty years – a real *pukka* English gentleman, who sometimes spoke of St. Paul's as the Eton of the East. I knew I was accepted when a few years down the track he said to me: "We've got to know each other, so from now on I'll call you Stewart and you call me Goddard!" I preached a few times at their Sunday evening Chapel. They invited me to speak at their end of the year dinner and bring the boy prefects with me. Fortunately, the speech was before dinner, where I unwittingly scoffed a prawn cocktail to which I was allergic. I had to leave in a hurry and vomit by the side of the road!

The second school was Loreto Convent. Mother Antoinette was from Melbourne and had been there for sixty years. When she was offered her first trip home at that point, she refused because Melbourne would be strange to her and her own family had passed on. About the time we left India, they had put her for retirement in a Loreto Convent in Calcutta, and I was able to visit her. They called he out of Vespers to see me and she slipped around the corner and whispered like naughty child "I can miss Vespers! Under the more liberated rules now, I can have a cup of tea with you!" And so we did to her great delight.

The third school was St. Joseph's School and University College. Father Maurice Stanford was in a position of leadership then. Let me blow the gaffe on three stories of Father Stanford. When the Pope announced the Canonical belief in the bodily assumption of the Virgin Mary, there was quite an uproar – especially in America. Father Stanford lent me his copy of the somewhat heretical American Jesuit magazine which had an article saying that the Vatican maintains that all its pronouncement ex cathedra are based ultimately on the Bible, but (tongue in cheek) the author said "???" – Where is this in the Bible??" I returned the magazine and we never referred to it again! The second incident was when at the end of 1964 Dorothy and I planned a world trip. Maurice's brother had died of a heart attack when attempting an ascent of Mount Sinai in the Holy Land, and Maurice asked that we visit his mother and sister in Quebec in Canada. We could and we did. They showed us the grand Cathedral and Quebec's beautiful countryside. In his latter years, Maurice suffered extreme deafness. He asked me several times to pray for him but neither prayer nor advanced audio-aides did any good. The last time I saw him he was on his death bed at St. Joseph's. He spoke fluidly and lucidly, and I wrote my contributions on a little pad beside his bed. When I about to leave he said, "David, would you pray for me?" and thrust the pad and pencil towards me. I never prayed like that before, and for a very dear Roman Catholic Priest. It was laboured, but he ended with a fervent "Amen".

There were three major building efforts during my time. The first was a swimming pool. It took me years to persuade the Managing Committee that a swimming pool would ever get used at 6,300 feet above sea level, particularly when our sister school Woodstock, had had a tragedy in their pool at Mussoorie, the other side of India. They had a covered pool with deep diving pit. I insisted on a pool open to the skies, on the level stretch between Fern Hill and the playing field. I agreed that it must have a re-circulating filter, and slope down from 4 feet to 6 feet. But Darjeeling was chronically shot of water – how could we ever fill it?? Kevin Henry, from West Australia, solved the problem. Over the winter months, when the school was not occupied, he rigged up a pipe from the main school right over the playing field into the empty pool. The water was a dirty brown, but we ran the re-circulating filter non-stop for a month, and it reflected the cerulean blue of the sky! But used at 6,300 feet?? It became the most popular amenity! We let St. Joseph's boys come down at 5 a.m. to use it. Since then a number of schools have built their own swimming pools. Only Dr. Graham's Homes (at 4,000 feet) had a pool before we did. John Johnston coached swimming and water polo, and the Swimming Gala and Inter-School Galas were very popular.

Fernhill, barbar's shop and swimming pool. (Mr. Brian L. Byrne, MH teacher, 1957-65).

The second building task was when the school roll topped 300. We simply had to find more accommodation. I looked at the attic covering three quarters of the building and only used for storage and missionaries' junk. With the help of Major Plant, a local architect and builder, we built in about eight new dormer windows, and created a small boys' dormitory and a small girls' dormitory, each with a matron's attached suite. The attic rooms were very popular having the best view of the mountains.

In 1959, the Inspector of the Anglo-Indian Schools for West Bengal, Austin D'Souza, a put up two more propositions to me:

1. That Mount Hermon School build an All Indian Teacher Training College with a Managing Committee for the rich Anglo-Indian High schools of the Darjeeling, Kurseong, Kalimpong area, to train for Primary school Teaching.

2. That we accept a very large grant from the Central Government of India to build an all-purpose High School building catering for Humanities, Commerce, Science (including Physics, Chemistry and Biology).

Regretfully I declined the first offer as I felt there would be too much on Mount Hermon's plate in one go, but I enthusiastically, and with the Managing Committee, accepted the second proposal. Once again, with the help of Major Plant, we planned a five-storey reinforced concrete structure at the back of the west-side playground, level with the main building. The ground floor comprised six classrooms, the second floor, Physics, Chemistry and Biology Labs, and the third a Warden's flat. There were dormitories on the upper floors and the attic dormer windows matched the main building attic. There was also a short passage linking the top floor or the main building to the top floor of the new building – a most convenient connection for staff and inspections! There was a sub-warden's flat also built there. The new building was opened in 1963, and in 1964, while Dorothy and I had a year off, Graeme Murray and the Managing Committee re-named it Stewart Building.

The main school building with the Stewart Building.

My sister Joy Rongong joined us in 1961 – coming across from Dr. Graham's Homes. She came with her two delightful daughters Roslyn and Heather and they occupied a cottage on the north-east of the playing field. Joy became Junior School Head Mistress. Mr. D'Souza was impressed by Joy's junior (school) teaching methods and her linguistic flair. She spoke Tamil, Hindi and Nepali. He was concerned that the Anglo-Indian schools now had to teach Bengali as the State language, and he felt that the teachers, with their bookish approach needed help. He offered to pay Joy's salary for three months to enable her to learn enough Bengali to prepare a "play-type" syllabus to start off the Kindergarten children with Bengali. Joy knew no Bengali! Anyhow she did so, using well-known English Nursery rhymes translated into Bengali along with all the appropriate hand gestures!

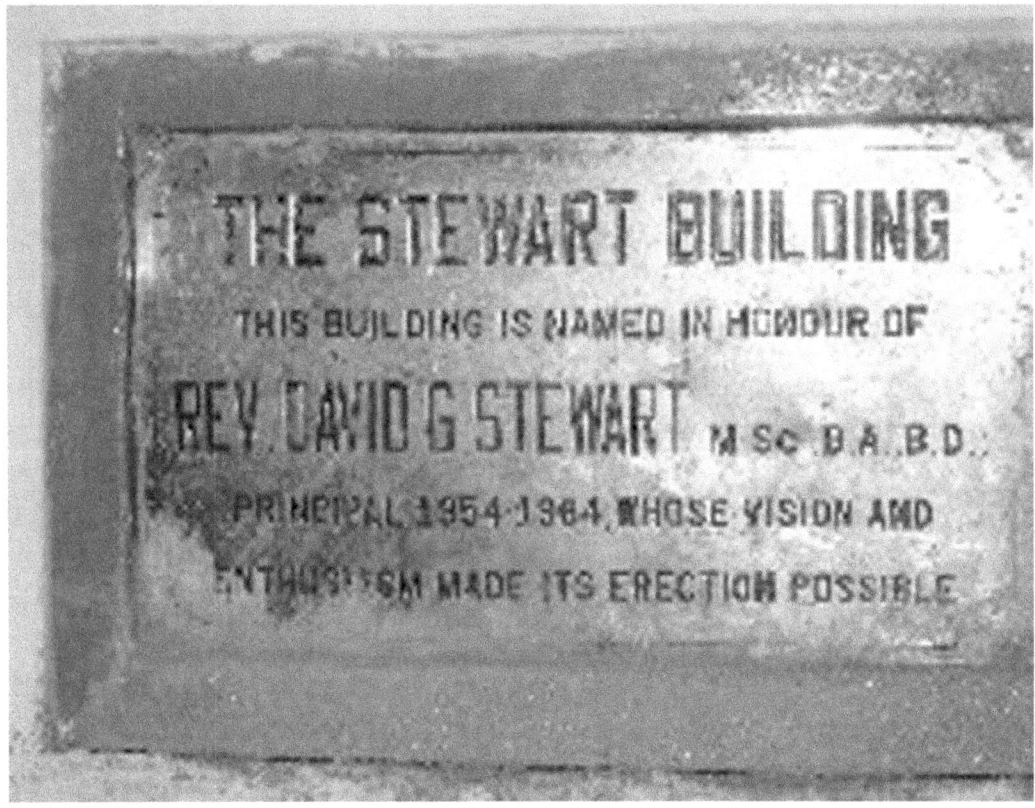

Incidentally, the Inspector's first proposal to me did not get lost! After Graeme Murray succeeded me as Principal, Mr. D'Souza again approached him with the same proposal, and Graeme courageously accepted! The Eight Hills schools warmly co-operated and buildings were constructed on the Mount Hermon Estate for the Mount Hermon Teachers' Training College (TTC). The eight schools provided the Board, with Graeme Murray as the first Principal and Joy Rongong as Lecturer-in-Charge. Joy designed the whole two-year course emphasising good teaching methods. (Later there was great input from Val Johnston and Neena West who took up the reigns after Joy left). It was a fairly small cottage (40 students altogether), but with a vast influence on teacher training. Many students went on to do further education studies, and become the Heads of prestigious Primary and High schools across India.

The Inspector conveyed another amazing offer from the Central Government of India. India was concerned about offering support to its neighbouring countries, Bhutan and Sikkim. It awarded ten school-long boarding scholarships to Bhutan (ten boys went to St. Joseph's) and Sikkim (ten boys went to Mount Hermon). Needless to say, there was huge competition for such large scholarships, and 400 applied from Sikkim. The Sikkim government weeded the number down to 50, and he sent Edna William (KG Mistress) and Joy Rongong (Junior School Headmistress) to make the final selection. They sensed the burden, and my sister asked me to pray especially that they would choose aright, and that some might become Christians. They felt they had to depend largely on non-verbal tests, for fairness. I certainly believe God guided their choice. At least three went on to become Christians. Jigme went on to do TTC and taught at Mount Hermon for a few years before becoming an editor of a newspaper in Sikkim. He was a strong voice against corruption. Dhruba is now the Deputy Head of a large Primary School in Auckland, and the third, Sherab, became Joy's son-in-law and is now living with Roslyn in Canberra with their four adult children, Jennie, Debbie, Danny and Becky. And of course, Joy's second daughter Heather is not far away in another suburb of Canberra with her and Michael's two daughters, Indira and Sherina. Sadly, however, Michael has developed Alzheimers.

We both loved our time in Mount Hermon. I love teaching Math, and especially Scripture to the upper classes, and Dorothy was marvellously busy with household affairs, looking after our Dormitory Matrons, the tuck-shop and the clothing department. But we had a personal disappointment – no children. We decided in 1959 that we should arrange to adopt, and on our short leave in Sydney in 1960, we adopted David Ian Stewart. At eight days old we flew him back to Darjeeling where he spent his first four years. He was utterly spoiled, not only by his doting parents, but everybody, especially some of the senior boys who seemed to enjoy hosting him up on their shoulders and walking around the school grounds.

One of the problems of a Hills Boarding School is that the school has responsibility for nearly all of its students for nine months straight. So we had two "between term" holidays in May and August, as well as the Government required days off for the main Puja (Hindu worship) days in October when we had to entertain our students. A number of teachers helped in this, with games and competitions, outings to town and scenic spots, occasional film evenings, talent quests and party games. Several ran treks and camps. I personally organised at least one trek or camp for several days each year for the senior boys. The highest trek was to the Kanchenjunga Trek Base Camp. Kanchenjunga, 28,000 feet, was first climbed (to with 10 feet off the summit) in 1955. Two boys and I were puffing at 14,500 feet, so we rested a day while the others made it to Base Camp and back. The longest trek we made was in September/October 1957. We drove to Tonglu by school jeep, and hiked from there the 14 miles to Sandakphu (11,979 feet) where we stayed in the Youth Hostel after an excellent succulent meal cooked for the ten of us by our cooks Ying and Nat. The next morning, we had an excellent view of Mount Everest, and then moved on past Singalila (12,095 feet) to Temi where we were infested by leeches. We went on to various places in Sikkim, and I remember a lively game of "chook chook" after another Ying and Nat's dinners. Finally, we begged a lift on the back of a friendly loaded truck to Gangtok, the capital of Sikkim, where two of our school parents had arranged most comfortable bungalows for us. The next day the school land rover came to fetch us and bring us back to school by 7.30 p.m. We had several camping trips, the most notable ones being to Rungphu just within Sikkim with a good swimming spot in the river.

In 1963 I asked the Managing Committee to grant us a year's furlough. I was not sure whether we should return, and Dorothy felt more so, therefore, the Board asked us to let them know by September 1964 if we were returning or not."

(David Stewart's reminisces stop at this point. They did not return to Mount Hermon School as teachers again, but I know that for the rest of their lives they carried their love for the school deep within their heart - Roslyn Namgyal, November 2019.)

19 Murray: A Rare Individual Full Of Life And Enthusiasm

GRAEME ARMSTRONG MURRAY
Principal, 1964-1978

Rev. J.A. Johnston

I arrived with my family in Darjeeling in 1959 at the same time as the Murrays returned from their furlough. Within the first weeks we shared a dedication service for the babies, Kristine and Stephen. Over the years since then, our friendship has grown, along with the growth of our Hermonite children and our absorption into the life of M.H. So this is a personal appreciation and farewell to our Principal.

Graeme Murray is one of those people who cannot be easily fitted into any neat category. Some may say, "he is mad on sport"- which no doubt would be true, but hardly adequate as a description of someone who is also mad on History and a walking encyclopaedia on the causes and pattern of current affairs. He is always busy in the wider community – Chairman and the guiding spirit of such diverse activities as the Gold Cup and the Darjeeling and Dooars Medical Association. But he is also the man willing to lay aside his business to give individual attention and loving counsel to someone in need.

Murray: A Rare Individual Full Of Life And Enthusiasm

As a schoolmaster, every aspect of school life has felt the impact of his rollicking enthusiasm – whether politely informing a footballer he is a "brainless idiot" or gently coaching a cricketer by telling him he is "as nutty as a fruit cake", explaining carefully to a hockey player that "he doesn't know a bee from a bull's foot", he has usually been able to make his meaning clear! From his earliest days as a teacher and hostel warden to Senior Master and finally Principal, he has left his mark on two complete generations of Mount Hermon students.

He has worked not only as coach of Cricket, Football, Hockey and other games – but as Scout Master, camping enthusiast, leader of Geography excursions, and as a teacher he has cheerfully put up with students who are "as cunning as a Mao-dog" or "useless as a one-armed paper-hanger!"

We shall miss the whirlwind car rides, the orders bellowing down our corridors, the radiogram needle jumping off the record as he stamps into a room. But most of all we shall miss a friend and guide. One seldom finds a boss so little concerned about his own status or "prestige" and so ready to be a friend, and to see the best in others.

This is part of that awareness of others which is the most endearing characteristic. We have all at sometime been aware of how he strives to say or do the thing that might necessarily be hurtful. In such a way, that most of the sting is taken out of the hurt. He is a great gossip whose gossip is always healthy and often involves a truly remarkable grasp of the web of personal connections surrounding a student or staff member, which allows the individual to be viewed with the utmost sympathy and understanding.

Yes, we shall certainly miss all this but just as certainly we shall not forget.

The Chairman's dream: Hermonites must fulfill Mt. Hermon's mission

'The Murrays wherever they roam, we will find them and claim them and bring them back home'

A.B. Singh

It is a long cry from 1962, that is when I first came on the Managing Committee and a year or two later, I was elected as the Chairman of the Managing Committee and continued as such till the nineteenth of May this year (1978). Since those days terrific changes have come over our country in general and Mount Hermon in particular. We have dreamt daring dreams and our achievements in Mount Hermon will go down in the history of the school for which we of the present generation, and those following us, can truly be thankful and happy.

Murray: A Rare Individual Full Of Life And Enthusiasm

The thought uppermost in my mind today as I look back is, "This is the Lord's doing, it is marvelous in our eyes." From the old Queen's Hill School to the Mount Hermon of today will make an interesting history and I am sure someone will be found to write it.

As Mt. Hermon was in those early years, it was a source of embarrassment to the Methodist Board in New York. The enrolment had gone down with expenses rising sky high. They had to look out for a more suitable set up. And it started on a union venture. Mr. David Stewart was our first whole time and 100% Principal and we saw new light. It happened that he had to leave soon after, leaving a yawning gap to fill. That made us sit up and think.

If I could remember anything with real satisfaction and joy, it is in the fact that we luckily hit upon a Green Horn, Mr. Graeme Murray who was a Godsend to take the place of Mr. Stewart. I had the satisfaction of accepting the resignation letter of Mr. Stewart and of appointing Mr. Murray. Since then things began to happen. Mr. Murray had the needed leadership and the courage to risk impossible things. He soon became the idol of the students and was highly popular with the staff, Class IV employees and guardians.

The Managing Committee backed him unitedly and they never differed with him. After Mr. Stewart left we were in the red to the tune of several lakhs. Timid people prophesied disaster. Against all this we had the substantial Stewart Building and helpful, generous Methodist loan of three hundred thousand rupees. During my tenure the loan was almost repaid and the school plant was enriched by valuable additions worth many lakhs.

We have the Stewart Building as a memorial to the last Principal. Some of you may be wondering as to a suitable memorial to Mr. Murray who is leaving at the end of this year. To them I would say, "Just look around, you will find him everywhere in his work."

When I left as your Chairman on 19th May I was given a beautiful picture of Mt. Kanchanjunga, in all its beauty and majesty looking upon Mount Hermon. Kanchanjunga is a part of Mount Hermon and Mount Hermon has soulful relations with Kanchanjunga. Each is a part of the other. It hurts to feel that we have said the final farewell. The spiritual link will last.

The Murrays wherever they roam, we will find them and claim them and bring them back home. We had another lucky break with regard to the Murrays. In appreciation of his services and spirit of co-operation with the Methodist Church they were accepted as Board Missionaries with support provided. We hope that this link will continue with the Board and the school.

The products of Mt. Hermon School, budding leaders of tomorrow, will continue as a tower of strength to Mt. Hermon School and some enterprising dreamer will organize them in India and abroad and yoke them to the job of developing the school still further, and spreading its message and accomplishing its mission in the years to come. God bless you.

(Mr. A.B. Singh was the Chairman of the Managing Committee)

Mount Hermon (1955-1977): Warm memories of the great times

Patricia Murray

What a host of memories for me as I look back over these years. How impossible it is to express the honour due to the school, the staff and students and to this wonderful place that has given Graeme and me, and our family, so much. So often we have agreed that our lives have been immeasurably enriched by our Darjeeling and M.H.S. experiences.

It wasn't all easy – homesickness and illness made early responsibilities as Matron of Fern Hill and Class 4 teacher quite a strain. Later there were those endless attempts to dry off children's washing over a kerosene stove, or conversely during the dry dusty months, the anxious search for water as we begged a bucketful from neighbours, and rationed it for our family of six. Coping with electric power failure of course is still commonplace – just so inconvenient when one has popped a cake in the oven or is taking a night rehearsal in the Hall.

But whatever happened, we knew we were all part of a community that cared and shared. This friendship and fellowship amongst staff and their families, along with the trust and affection of our school children, are the most treasured memories for me as I think of M.H.S. Even more than the constantly changing, uplifting beauty of the mountains and valleys that I loved so much, is this memory of these very precious relationships which, I believe, are true expression of Christian love. How I would love to write of the many, many dear friends we made. These would include people who are sometimes forgotten, our servants, who so cheerfully and capably keep the routine going in our homes as well as in the school. To write adequately about beloved Mount Hermon, I would need to be a much more skilful writer and would need a year at least to express even a fraction of what life there meant to us individually and as a family. So instead I will select just one aspect of M.H. life.

Inevitably, perhaps, it was the sound of singing and of music-making that brought me some of my deepest joys. What a procession of small students and bigger ones for music classes, some so suspicious, some so eager; they came for choir practices, orchestra, piano, voice or violin lessons; for recorder groups, theory lessons, music club, major production rehearsals; for Indian and Asian Music, for folk dancing, and on Sundays for Sunday School, Scripture Union and Crusaders. In recent years, the Teachers College students added their voices too; "Let every good fellow now join in a song".

How hard we worked at Choir – well usually! On warm sunny Wednesday afternoons, it was difficult for footballers to concentrate on their tenor or bass parts when shouts from the playing field interrupted us, but it was all well worth it, especially when our efforts culminated in higher musical standards and later in those great Choir expeditions to Calcutta and Shillong. More important still, many of us found a much deeper and more personal understanding of the Christian life through the hymns and anthems that we learnt.

How much the sound of singing marked the different activities at M.H.S. From the lusty thumping out of old favourites such as "She'll be coming round the mountain", as the school jeep whirled round those corners; to the soulful outpourings and strumming of guitars from certain dormitories after night study; to the latest pop song bellowing from the showers in Fern Hill after a football match; for, far from the busy routine, campers and trekkers expressing their companionship in songs, hummed or strummed beside many a camp fire. Bedtime in the Little Girls' dorm, often meant an impromptu concert when our smallest children sang and danced the songs they had learnt in their homes and villages. A very special delight for an invited guest.

The regular school programme provided for singers of all ages in the various choirs, from the little 'Blue Angel' in the Junior Choir who were always so fresh and sweet, to the "Red Demons" (?) in the Intermediate Choir and the "White" of the Senior Choir. Their regular practice and loyalty resulted in memorable Chapel Services, Concerts and Carol Services.

A yearly event in the Inter-House Music Competition, Western or Asian, when House Captains and other Seniors really showed their abilities to persuade or bully every member to do their best in the "Set Piece", and for other more able musicians to perform on instruments, in solos or vocal duets and groups. Despite the sometimes painful preparations (despair, indignation, frustration etc.) these competitions became a highlight of the M.H. year. Not only did we enjoy the great excitement, the colourful House uniforms, and an extremely varied and attractive programme, but we heard much from instrumentalists and singers that was of a very fine musical standard, far better than one hears or even expects in an average New Zealand school.

Hail Mount Hermon! A Tribute

How can one attempt to cover the musical life of M.H. in a few paragraphs? For me, one of the greatest treats was to relax as our talented girls and boys performed their songs and dances and dramas on Vernacular Talent night, particularly on Festival occasions when we experienced a wonderful variety of cultural items from many different countries. Nepal, Sikkim, Tibet, Bhutan, Thailand and several of the states of India were always represented, with songs in many languages. I will never forget the intricate rhythms of the table or the exquisite dancing in national costume of some of our beautiful girls, along with the vigorous efforts of our boys. Neither will I forget the achievements of soloists, choruses, pianists, and orchestra in class musicals and Major Productions. Surely those who sang and acted in "H.M.S. Pinafore", "Salad Days", "The Little Sweep", "Oliver", "Fiddler on the Roof", "Amahl and the Night Visitors", and many others, will always have warm memories of the great times we shared making these productions a success.

For Crusaders and Hi-C groups, this sharing in song is a vital part of their growth in their understanding of each other and of God. This in fact was perhaps what made the times when we all sang, staff and students together, in Chapel Services, on National occasions, and in our Carol Services the best times of all, not forgetting those often tear-jerking final goodbyes in our much-loved G.H.D. songs.

Sir Henry Wood provides my musical hope and prayer for my M.H.S. "children" from 1955-1977:

"If you will allow it to do so, music will be a comfort in sorrow, a solace in affliction, an endless source of pleasure and joy and hope and inspiration, and it will help you to find your soul."

(Hermonite 1978, annual school magazine.)

HERMONITE *Archives*

G.A. MURRAY: He lives in each one of us

"A journey of a thousand miles begins with a single step"
　　　　　　　　　　　　　　-Lao Tzu

Jigme N. Kazi

In honour and fond memory of our beloved Principal Mr. G.A. Murray, who passed away at this time last year on April 7, 2015, I have decided to begin recording and documenting the rich and unique heritage of our alma mater, Mount Hermon School.

Murray: A Rare Individual Full Of Life And Enthusiasm

Introducing "HERMONITE Archives" is our first 'single step' towards a thousand miles journey. I hope Hermonites from all over the world, particularly the older ones, will take this initiative seriously and begin setting aside some time for themselves and MH and start using this page to record of their times spent around the 'old and friendly walls' of Mt. Hermon.

I'm honoured and delighted to formally begin a serious attempt to document our school's history and its rich tradition and renown personalities. I joined MH as a Class 2 student in 1963, finished Senior Cambridge in 1972, joined Mt. Hermon's Teachers Training College (TTC) for two years in 1974-75, and finally taught in MH between 1976-1979. Therefore, I'm perhaps one of the very few fortunate ones who worked under Mr. Murray for such a long time.

Mr. Graeme Armstrong Murray began his teaching career in MH in 1955 when Rev. David G. Stewart was the school Principal. He later became the Senior Master and finally the Principal in 1964. Before he left MH at the end of 1978, MH was one of the best boarding schools in India.

Most Hermonites of my generation last saw Mr. Murray in 1995 during the school's centenary celebrations. Some of us last saw Mr. and Mrs. Murray in Darjeeling a few years after 1995. I had hoped to visit him and his family in New Zealand thereafter but sadly that was not to be.

Hail Mount Hermon! A Tribute

> When Mr. Murray passed away at this time last year something in each one of who knew him so dearly and fondly also died. But a part of him also lives in each one of us and we rejoice in knowing this. Hail Mt. Hermon!
>
> (Jigme N. Kazi, MH – 1963-1979)

REMEMBERING
Our Murray on his 86th birth anniversary

Vedprakash Agarwal, SC 1971

Graeme Armstrong Murray
24 August 1931 – 7 April 2015

Therefore, since we are surrounded by so great a cloud of witnesses, let us also lay aside every weight, and sin which clings so closely, and let us run with perseverance the race that is set before us, looking to Jesus the pioneer and perfecter of our faith. For here we have no lasting city, but we seek the city which is to come.

In MH (Mount Hermon School) we used to get a holiday on August 24th because it was Mr. Murray's birthday. On this day we recall the days of our youth in MH when Mr. Murray was there – 1955-1978.

A former student, Ved Prakash Agarwal (SC 1971), paid a brief tribute to Mr. Murray in 1978, the year he left MH after serving for 24 years:

"I did not know that this would be his last year, but somehow I was not surprised. I respected him as most children respected their teachers, and I suppose I was a bit infatuated with him. As a man I liked him and I hope I look at him honestly, good points, warts and all. I have never known him anything but honest, abrasive certainly, aggressive and blunt always, be it on the cricket field, in the classroom, or in the chapel where he is expounding a theory on the current trends of discipline among students.

Mr. Murray is one of those most casual and immediately likable persons I have ever met. He knows character instinctively and is always in a hurry to impose the force of his own which is considerable. Perhaps the secret of his rugged good nature is that he is an incurable individualist, certain of himself that he can afford to be sure of others. This trait has always invited comments and he has been described by an NP (St. Joseph's School) teacher as petulant, rude and stubborn. However, there is one yardstick about people I know. The ones who don't change are the genuine ones. *Bhuntay* (a Nepali term for a fat person) has not bothered to change. He is always going to be his own man and do his own thing. He is loved by his students and although he endangers more arguments, more fury, more passing than others, he definitely is the most intriguing man I have ever met.

Mr. Murray has been here for twenty-four years now. Thousands studied at his feet, united in reverence and love for him. I don't know what he taught us and I don't really care. He taught us to think and that was enough. That was the heart of it all, *Bhuntay* made us think. He was his own man. Non Scholae Sed Vitae Discimus (*Not* for school but for life we learn). That was his legacy to us – he made each of us what to be his own man."

In his final year at Mount Hermon, 1978, Mr. G.A. Murray in his Annual Principal's Report on Speech Day, urged staff and students of the need to keep alive the spirit of Mount Hermon School.

"Overall, I think, three things characterise what Mount Hermon is for me. I hope that they also speak to you of what is at the heart of our school, and that they will ever continue to do so. They are Friendship, Fellowship, and Worship. Perhaps I should have put Worship first, for it is in the worship and praise of God that we first find that friendship and fellowship which must characterise all we do in the Mount Hermon community.

These are things I found at Mount Hermon when I came first with my wife, way back in 1955. These are things which I trust I have tried to cherish and develop through the years that have followed. These are now those values which I pass on to you, staff and students alike, for you to cherish and preserve and strengthen through the years that remain to you at Mount Hermon, that they may by you in your time be transmitted to many others in the years to come."

On this special day we also remember – with love, thanks and gratitude – Mrs. Murray, Adrienne, Stephen, Bronwyn and Johnny for their service and friendship.

"May the Lord bless you and keep you. May the Lord make his face to shine upon you, and be gracious to you. May the Lord lift up his countenance upon you, and give you peace." (Numbers 6:24-26, Bible)

Hail Mt. Hermon!

Edinburough Shield team, 1968.

Hail Mount Hermon! A Tribute

Live one day at a time

G.A. Murray

"If you can live fully, gladly, joyfully in the present – one day at a time, then you will have no fears for the future, and a wonderfully satisfying past to look back upon."

Ladies and Gentlemen, and School,

Since our Chief Guest (Mr. B.T. Brooks, Principal of Dr. Graham's Homes, Kalimpong) cannot be with us after all, I want to take a few minutes to talk with you about my personal experience in the days since the 'Elkanah' fire.

I can only hope that by sharing these thoughts with you that our fellowship within Mount Hermon community will be further strengthened because for me, Mount Hermon first of all is not a school or an institution but a community of people, adults and children, who share a common life and work together for common goals which include such things as games, studies and socials: first above all else our concern is with our understanding of God and His purposes for us in the world and in our individual lives.

As I have already told a number of you, I was giving advice to a student on the night before the fire, and the point that I was making was that we have to live one day at a time, for we do not know what the future holds and we cannot be always living in the past. Little did I know that within a few hours I would have very little left in material terms of what I had accumulated through the last 22 years at Mount Hermon. What then has this experience taught me: first of all it has taught me that I must live up my own advice and live one day at a time asking God for strength for each day because that is really what is going to count, not what might be nor what is past; but what is today.

Secondly, I have learnt that one's dependence must be on God and one's trust must be in Him, no matter what may happen. It has been surprisingly easy to live this way once the blow has fallen and I would recommend to all of you, who are weighed down by the cares of life to "put a match", not literally of course, but certainly in your mind, to those things which are holding you back from being fully yourself and enjoying the love that God alone can give, through His Son.

Thirdly, and also very important: I have experienced in great measure, what I have already referred to when I began, the love and concern of people which they have shared fully and freely so that I can say that the compensations have been far greater than the losses, especially in spiritual things and also in some materials things for while I still do not have any reliable potato peelers for Yanki to use, I do have 5 new suits.

More than fifty of our seniors will be leaving school this year. You are, I'm sure, looking forward to all the excitement and challenge of the future, and dreaming of what great things you may accomplish.

Soon however, if you follow the pattern of former students who have talked with me, you will become disillusioned with life in all its freedom outside these walls and you will be tempted to look back in nostalgia to the past, to your time here, and you may even begin to bore your friends with talk about "the good old days."

But neither looking forward, nor looking back will solve your problems – for it is the present that really counts. If you can live fully, gladly, joyfully in the present – one day at a time, then you will have no fears for the future, and a wonderfully satisfying past to look back upon.

Did you note some of the words of the anthem which Barbara sang just now – repeated several times in a minor Key!

Hail Mount Hermon! A Tribute

"Without Thee all is dark – I have no guide." I can best sum up all that I want to say in these words for truly a pathway though life without God's hand upon us as our guide is truly dark and we will often lose our Path. My experience in recent days, which can be yours too, is that God, through His Son Jesus Christ, is that guide which we can have, for in Him is light for every step of the way.

(Mount Hermon Principal, Mr. G.A. Murray's address on Speech Day, 1976: Hermonite 1978, annual school magazine.)

The Cup Runneth Over

To our dear friends and family.   February, 2011

A VERY HAPPY NEW YEAR TO YOU ALL.

Thank you very much for your welcome cards and letters, messages, photos, electronic cards, and greetings over the Christmas New Year Season. It is always heartwarming to once again receive news of yourselves and your families and to be aware of your times of happiness and sadness too. We wish we could see you and talk together. A general letter seems so inadequate, but be assured we do think of you often and many others who have not been in touch very recently.

For us, 2010 had its ups and downs, healthwise with periods in hospital for me, (Tricia), but our family and friends once again were wonderfully kind and helpful and now as I write, we are both quite well and loving these warm sunny days by the sea and sometimes, in the sea for refreshing swims. As always, Adrienne and Paul with their adult family have been a wonderful support to us.

However, the highlight of our year was the family wedding, when Adrienne and Paul's third daughter Philippa married Dr. Brendan Ng, a N.Z. Chinese whose family settled in N.Z. back in 1907. They were married on Easter Saturday, last April on a beautiful bright sunny day in our family church, Central Baptist, Wellington, where my Father was the minister in the 1940s and 1950s.

To our immense delight, for the first time since 1979, all our four "children" with eight of our ten grandchildren met here to celebrate this special occasion. Bronwen with daughter, Becky (19) came from Germany for two weeks, Stephen, with his wife Amanda and Cameron Elizabeth (12) and James (6) flew from London, for one week, Jonathan with daughter, Devon (18), drove from Auckland, for 4 days and with Adrienne's four; Emily (29), Anna (25), Pip (24) and Daniel (18), we were over flowing with happiness to have all these beautiful young cousins together and having such a riotous time laughing and singing and having so much fun.

Everyone contributed to the joy of the day, especially Adrienne and all her family and Pip and Brendan who had worked so hard and imaginatively to create a combination of symbols from their Asian and N.Z. backgrounds and to make everyone so welcome. Philippa looked gorgeous in a red silk dress, in accordance with both Chinese and Indian (and Bangladesh) marriage custom. Her two sisters, Emily and Anna wore contrasting coloured dresses and her two friends also were in different colours, as you will see in the photos. The wedding ceremony and the reception represented their different cultural backgrounds. Pip chose flax as her bouquet and for the table decorations, and saris to decorate the hall. Adrienne and Paul wore their lovely Bangladesh outfits. At the wedding service, all the Thompson family escorted Philippa down the aisle and all the Ng family did the same for Brendan.

Bronnie played the organ as they walked in and Bronnie and I played a piano duet as they signed the register. After the entire congregation had signed as witnesses to their vows, the 'Stillwaters' community in which Philippa and Brendan have lived for several years sang them out of the church with 'Lean on me'.

The sun shone, the sea sparkled as the young and older later wandered by the waves, or ran in for swims over the next few days. Graeme and I felt "our cup running over!" We really missed Wolfgang and Patrick (22), Bronnie's husband and son, and Eleanor (19), Stephen's eldest daughter.

Now the family has scattered again - but we are all grateful for Skype, email and the telephone as ways to keep in touch with them.

> Having just recently re-read your letters cards and messages, many with pictures of you, I realise again how blessed we are to have you as our friends over these many years. We hope that this year 2011 will bring you new joys and blessings and that there will indeed be increasingly, Peace and Goodwill amongst all the peoples of this beautiful world.
>
> With our thanks and love,
> Patricia and Graeme Murray.

MH - 1955-1978
Mr. and Mrs. Murray's tribute to Mt. Hermon

Mr. and Mrs. Murray, finally left Mt. Hermon at the end of 1978 after 24 glorious years (1955-1978) in Mt. Hermon. In this article they pay their tribute to the school which meant so much to them and to all Hermonites.

Mr. Murray took over as Principal from Mr. Stewart in 1964. The Murray-era saw further development in MH in more than one way. He successfully built on the solid foundation laid by Mr. Stewart. When he finally retired in 1978, he was succeeded by his long-term friend and colleague, Rev. John Johnston:

We count it an honour to write this brief tribute to the Staff, Students, Parents, School Board members, and all those other people, especially those of Darjeeling, who welcomed us, worked with us, learnt from us, taught us so much of their own lives and cultures, helped us raise our own children, and so enriched our lives over the 24 years that we were part of Mount Hermon.

We also want to set out the basic facts about ourselves and our experiences at MHS; this will, we trust, ensure that those interested in us, looking back with the nostalgia that Hermonites seem to have about most aspects of their years at MHS, will not allow the passing years to make us larger than life! Robin Sengupta as already begun this in his memoir, we note, by adding 2 inches to Graeme's height - alas, he was only 6'0".

So first, the facts:

Patricia Noeline (North) Murray b. Christchurch, NZ, 25 December 1931. Attended primary schools in NSW (Australia), Christchurch and Wellington, then Wellington Girls' College 1945-49. LRSM (Performance in Piano) 1950, Wellington Teachers' College 1951-53. Taught at Wellington East Girls' College, 1954.

Graeme Armstrong Murray b. Otahuhu, NZ, 24 August 1931. Attended primary schools in Auckland, Wellington and Napier, then Napier Boys' High School 1945-46; Hutt Valley High School 1947-49. Victoria University College 1950-52 and 1954 [MA in History]; Auckland Teachers' College, 1953.

We were married on 22 January 1955, sailed for India on 1 February, and arrived in Darjeeling (by train from Bombay via Calcutta to Siliguri), on 10 March, the day before Mount Hermon's 60th birthday. We lived in Fernhill for our first three years, as Warden and Matron of about 60-70 boys in addition to our teaching roles; Patricia taught Class 4, and Graeme's subjects in the senior school were English Language and Literature, plus some PE. During our first three years, Adrienne was born in November 1955, and Bronwen in September 1957.

We spent 1958 in New Zealand, Patricia, with two little girls at home, did not teach; Graeme taught English and History at his old school, Hutt Valley High. We returned to India in January 1959, going to Agartala (Tripura) for Stephen's birth, before joining school. Graeme appointed Senior Master, and Patricia took up the leadership of the school's music, taking over from Merle Tegel, soon to become Merle Ingram and settle in the UK. Jonathan was born on 1 May 1961. In November 1963 Mr. & Mrs. Stewart began a year's leave, having completed ten years at MH; Graeme was appointed Acting Principal, and John Johnston Acting Senior Master. The Stewarts resigned at the end of 1964, and in 1965 Mr. Stewart became Principal of the Bible College of New Zealand, where he continued until his retirement in 1988. Graeme and John Johnston were appointed officially as Principal and Senior Master in May 1965.

School Staff 1964

Left to Right—M. K. Lama, L. Chonzin, I. E. Sampson, P. Appadurai, B. L. Byrne, J. S. Darr, W. D. Logan, D. Wainwright, D. N. Pradhan, M. S. Manaen, J. Ismail, M. Mathai, J. O. Wilde, S. S. Basil.

Mrs. D. Pradhan, Miss P Sen, Mrs. I. Dam, Mrs. J. Davidson, Mrs. T. Petersen, Miss D. Ritchie, Mrs. O. Alexander, Mrs. M. Byrne, Miss N. Bilcliffe, Mrs. M. Wilde, Miss S. Raju, Miss F. Gaunt, Mrs. S. Thapa, Mrs. E. Martin

Mrs. E. West, Miss C. Hawke, Sister J. Digby, Mrs. J. Rongong, Rev. J. Johnston, Mrs. V. Johnston, Mr. G. A Murray (Principal), Mrs. P. Murray, Mrs. E Williams, Miss L. MacGillivray, Mrs. J. Wainwright, Mrs. E. Logan, Miss J. Hames.

At the end of 1968 Mount Hermon Managing Committee granted us a year's study leave; we returned to New Zealand where Graeme completed a Diploma in Educational Administration at Victoria University, and Patricia taught music part-time at her old school, Wellington Girls' College. Our return to Darjeeling was by ship from Auckland to San Francisco, then across the USA to the UK, then Switzerland, and finally arriving in Darjeeling on 4 March 1970. The Johnston family left MH in December 1970, and settled in Hobart, Tasmania - but they were to return due course.

Bill and Beulah Jones rejoined MHS in 1971, Bill as Vice-Principal, with Jeff Gardner being appointed Senior Master. The Jones had met as young teachers on the MH staff in the early 50s, so this was very much a 'homecoming' for them. Through 1971 Graeme was increasingly involved in planning and preparing the establishment of the Mount Hermon College of Education - an under-graduate teacher training programme for primary teachers in Anglo-Indian Schools; this officially commenced in April 1972, when the students

arrived, having been transferred to Darjeeling from St. Thomas's School, Kidderpore, [Calcutta] where they had previously been training. [The TTC is still going strong, now under the leadership of Neena West, whom older Hermonites will remember as Mandira Dam, a Hermonite with twinkling feet and usually winning her races far in advance of her competitors].

The British Council in Calcutta gave considerable material and personal help in the establishment of the TTC and also, early in 1973, organised a visit for us to the UK, organising a programme to see different schools and colleges of education in England and Scotland, from London as far north as Durham and Edinburgh. Before getting to London to start this visit, however, we had flown from India directly to the USA, and spent several weeks there visiting churches and talking about MHS and education in India, as well as visiting a number of schools and colleges.

Our last four years at MHS were rather difficult as we had to compromise between the conflicting needs of our children's post-school education and our commitment to Mount Hermon. In 1974 Adrienne began university in Wellington, and Bronwen had a year at school there, but then returned to MHS for a final HSC year in 1975. In 1976 Patricia stayed in NZ with the three older children, while Jonathan remained in Darjeeling with Graeme.

After Adrienne was married in January 1977, Patricia returned for our final year together at Mount Hermon. It was rather a sad return for her as, in October 1976, our Darjeeling home, 'Elkanah', had been totally destroyed by fire [caused by an electrical fault]. This was the notable occasion when Graeme went to morning chapel wearing only his pyjamas and a borrowed dressing gown - all other clothing having been destroyed in the blaze! Patricia took Jonathan back to Wellington at the beginning of 1978, while Graeme remained to complete his final term, before also leaving, in early December 1978. Bill and Beulah Jones had moved on to Woodstock School at the end of 1977, for a six-year term as Principal there; John and Val Johnston returned to MHS in 1978, with John following Bill Jones as Vice-Principal, and then succeeding Graeme as Principal in December 1978.

(Courtesy: www.success.co.th)

20 My Tribute To A Revered Friend And Guide

JOHN ARCUS JOHNSTON
Principal, 1979-1989

Thomas D'Souza

"Whether we live or we die, we belong to the Lord" (Rom 14:8). As I think of the life and death of Rev. John Johnston, I feel that these words of St. Paul beautifully summarize his entire journey of life. Indeed, he always belonged to the Lord as much as he belonged to all who knew him as a family member or a teacher or friend.

I was privileged to know him from the early eighties when we both appeared for a qualifying examination necessary to be the Head of an Educational Institution. His vast knowledge and experience in life helped me learn many things including the academic curriculum! His simplicity, cheerfulness, laughter and serene countenance reminded me of a man of God, a missionary and a friend of all.

When the Johnstons left Darjeeling after retirement, their nostalgia for Mount Hermon School and friends was palpable in their regular visits to Darjeeling, Siliguri and Calcutta. Supported by Mrs. Val Johnston, Mr. Johnston would always visit me, even for a short time, wherever I was. It was this warmth and affection of a friend to another friend that soon became a strong bond for many years until his death.

His unassuming and joyful nature endeared him to all. Anyone needing help could approach him without fear. His availability and readiness to help made many a student and friend come to him and listen to his sound advice. John's sense of humour made all around him burst into peals of laughter and thus maintain that balance of joy even in the midst of a burdensome life.

This quality of being human had its roots in the Christian Faith which John professed and in the Person of Jesus for whom John lived all the days of his life on earth! This Jesus gave him the gift of a sense of proportion in life and this won him many friends from all walks of life, especially from the student community he guided and served.

As we bid a final farewell to our dear friend and guide, Rev. John Johnston, I remember the words of the great poet of Bengal and a Nobel laureate – Gurudev Rabindranath Tagore:

"On the day when death will knock at thy door, what wilt thou offer to him?
Oh, I will set before my guest the full vessel of my life –
I will never let him go with empty hands.
All the sweet vintage of all my autumn days and summer nights,
All the earnings and gleanings of my busy life will I place before him
At the close of my days when death will knock at my door."

My Tribute To A Revered Friend And Guide

Rev. John Johnston has gone to the Father's House as Jesus promised, setting before God the full vessel of his life, placing before him all the earnings and gleanings of his life, and I pray that the merciful Lord Jesus may purify him fully and transform his mortality into immortality in heaven for ever.

I offer my heartfelt condolences to Mrs. Val Johnston and family members and assure all of them of my prayerful support in this hour of sorrow. Good bye, dear friend and guide! May you rest in peace.

(Thomas D'Souza, Archbishop, Calcutta.)

MH Forever: 1953-1989

Val Johnston

Hail Mount Hermon! A Tribute

We first made contact with India in November 1952 (on Nehru's birthday – a good omen!) when we arrived by ship from Australia at Bombay, on our way to Assam as Missionary probationers with the Australian Baptist Missionary Society. Soon, in March 1953, we made contact with MH, because the Mission required us to attend the Language School, then located at MH, using Fernhill and some of the cottages.

Val Hutchinson, as she was then, was already a trained teacher so she became even more involved with the school. The American Methodist Mission to which Miss Knowles etc., belonged had almost decided to close the school because they no longer had children to send there (they started using Woodstock in Mussoorie). But several other Missions wanted it to keep going, so a new committee was formed, to make MH a United Mission school. The last American Principal, Rev. George Workman, was there in 1953 and did a good job keeping the school together, and reorganising the accounts etc., (not many people know about him I find). Interestingly, in the light of Mrs. Murray's later well-known musical gifts, Mrs. Workman too was a very good musician, and a lovely lady. Part of the new arrangements was for the supporting missions to provide either a subsidy, or a staff member. So Val found herself "loaned" to the school, and spent a very satisfying year, teaching senior English and being senior girls' matron.

We were engaged to be married at the end of the year, so naturally I took an interest in what was going on in the school, as much as in doing Bengali! This also meant I came to know some of the students, and became interested in the idea of making "teaching" my contribution to the Mission. We can look back on that year, to remember some of the old timers among old scholars when they were children! So to cut a long story short, soon after our marriage in Calcutta, we returned to Australia, and I did teacher training until 1959, when we accepted an invitation to join Mr. Stewart at Mount Hermon.

By the time we returned to Darjeeling there were 3 little Johnstons, Michael, Carol and Christine, and they, with Jenni born in 1961, and Lyndy in 1965, became very much part of MH. They all look back on their years there as among the best of their lives. When we left after 12 years to "retire" to Australia in 1971, first Christine in 1975 and then Jenni in 1976, asked to be allowed to go back for a year on their own. So when I returned to become Principal in 1978, we had connections which had never really been severed for 25 years. The years 1978 to 1989 have quite different memories from our first period and I find myself getting confused about what happened when!! But it was a moving experience to visit the school from our "voluntary" year with Dr. Graham's Homes in 2000, and find some of the ISC class were the last I had enrolled in KG back in 1989! I realized, when we visited again in 2001, that it was the first time since 1953 that there were no students at all in the assembly whom we had known….very sad! Even then, I did know Mr. Fernandez' son Anil who had been a baby boy in 1989, but not a "student" then!

1959 to 1970 and 1978 to 1989

Mr. Stewart placed us in charge of the boys' dorms at Fernhill, along with Mr. & Mrs. Mathai, who became our very good friends – and their children Shantha, Walsa, Mon, George and Nilima, were our children's constant playmates. I was made class teacher of class 9 and retained that job until 1963, when I was made Senior Master. I can look at the class 9 photos of those years and remember almost all the faces…..a very warm, happy period of my life.. Mrs. Johnston too had some classes as well as being very busy with the dorm work, dhobi etc., and looking after the family. My teaching also involved alternating the 10/11 Bio classes with Mrs. Dam, and scripture with Mr. Stewart. The great feature of MH in those years, and for many years to come right up to the 80s, was the variety of out-of-class activities in which all the staff seemed to be involved. Trekking and Camping were popular because many of the boarders did not go home for the May and Sept Holidays, in the days before easy "Plane Parties".

One of the first big events around then was the building of the swimming pool in 1960. Being put in charge of Swimming gave me a satisfying "sporting" interest, which suited my blind-eye lack of skill with ball games! And of course, the Swimming Gala became a major feature over the years. Mr. Stewart became famous in the district as a football umpire, and Mr. Murray played both football and cricket. Mr. Mathai was keen on table tennis and basketball, and I think all of us had sessions of trekking and camping. Mr. Hendry made a big contribution to woodwork and other hobbies and Mr. Burn was famous for his photography interest. And I must not forget the ladies who looked after girls' sports… athletics, basketball, netball, Bulbuls and Guides, camps and treks…. in the hand of Mrs. Rongong, Miss Bilcliffe, Miss McGillivray, Sister Digby and others.

Another feature which flourished every year was the "MAJOR PRODUCTION". I think almost every staff member in those years had some part to play in producing quite outstanding stage shows….costumes, make-up, sets etc. This was true right up until 1989, when "The Winslow Boy" was put on by Mrs. Johnston and Mr. Mervyn Baptist in the midst of the difficulties caused by the GNLF movement. Naturally I can remember all the shows of the 80s when I was "in charge" and therefore responsible to see all went well. How fortunate I was to have Mr. Blackmore as director of many of them, and Roslyn Rongong/Namgyal and Raj David as musicians for the great Musicals we had.

The list includes:- 1979: *A Quite Fantastic Concert* (starring John Glasby, Raj David, Digby Barrow, Sara Bunce among others); 1980: *Sound of Music* (Emma Masand a star soloist as Maria); 1981: *Anne of Green Gables* (Many will remember John Duncan's dramatic death in the role of old Matthew); 1982: *She Stoops to Conquer*, (directed by Steve Lewis while Mr. Blackmore was away); 1983: *Scrooge* (Mr. Blackmore's version of Dickens' "Christmas Carol", with music composed by Christopher Masand); 1984: *Ruddigore* (somewhat disrupted by the beginnings of the GNLF disturbances); 1985: *Summer Song* (for which I actually got to be the pianist! and Rajashri Basumatari was discovered as a brilliant soloist); 1986: *My Fair Lady* (one of the best in all my 25 years at MH); 1987: *Brigadoon*; 1988: *Carousel* (which yielded the going home day song "Don't be afraid of the storm"); 1989: The Winslow Boy… I remember Firdausi Rahman having the leading girl's role in no less than three years 1986, 1987 and 1988.

For those who were at MH in the 60s & 70s I can't supply all the titles, but those that come to mind include: *HMS Pinafore*; *See How They Run*; *Iolanthe*; *School and Crossbones*; *MacBeth* (in Tibetan costumes); *Oliver*; *Midsummer Night's Dream*; *The Prodigious Snob*; *Salad Days* (which yielded the going home day song, "We said we wouldn't look back"); *The Mikado*; *Gondoliers*; *King and I*; *Fiddler on the Roof* …. and there must be two or three others I did not see during our gap away in Australia and Mussoorie, 1971 to 1977. In the 50s and early 60s we had the benefit of Mr. Stewart's friendship with Geoffrey and Laura Kendal and their later famous daughters, Jennifer and Felicity. Their company, known as Shakespeareana, put on such classics as Hamlet, Othello, Merchant of Venus, Twelfth Night and Shaw's "St. Joan" and, to the great delight of everyone, actually lived at the school (in the hospital) and gave valuable advice to our efforts. All the big boys were in love with Felicity! Jennifer later married Sashi Kapoor and brought him to MH on one occasion.

Almost as important as the "MP" were the Class plays and Chapel plays, where many of the stars of the MPs had their first try on stage. I experienced these first hand as Class 9 teacher, and later when I became Principal was able to appreciate how much I owed to the staff in this area. Other equally important activities were the Quizzes, Debates, Elocutions, and House Singing, all of which depended so much on the gifts and willing spirit of the staff. (I think Miss Mitchell's beautifully painted "magic piano" for Salad Days is still in the school somewhere, and Henry Soggee's backdrop paintings remained from year to year). Singing and Elocution alternated between "vernacular" and "English", so even the "dayscholar" language teachers had an active role and were always willing helpers. Even to mention these things throws up a host of memories of individuals and special items. I can still picture my Nines doing "The summoning of Everyman" as a Chapel Play which almost matched an MP (I think Anjali was "Faith"!) ……… how often we saw "The Monkey's Paw" as a Class Play!!

The other big excitement in our early years was the construction of the Stewart Building in 1963, which provided lovely new labs for Mr. Darr (Physics), Mr. Mathai (Chem.), Mr. Murray (Geog - with Miss Russell and Mr. Blackmore later) and Mrs. Dam and myself (Bio). Our family had to say a sad farewell to Fernhill in order to take charge of the new dorms. I had quite an argument with "Boss" over that!! It was called the "New Block" at first, but when Mr. Stewart left it was rightly named in his honour.

When we returned in 1978, we found the *dhobi ghat* spring had been tapped by Mr. Murray, and to make full use of this benefit, over the next few years we constructed additional tanks, which made MH among the best off among Darjeeling schools in the dry season. (Boarders will say "wow! How bad they must have been!!") Another new arrival in those years was the "Round Building" set up as an additional boys' dorm over the Rose Garden. Here too I was fortunate to gain the services of Mr. Wadkar as Sports Master, and to be able to place him and Mrs. Wadkar in charge of Round Building…..if you visit MH you will find them still there doing a great job! A powerful generator and a genuine 35 mm Movie Projector were other important additions in the late 70s and early 80s.

They served us well: at the centre is Kishore, who also played for the school's 1st XI football.

One of the most important aspects of my purpose in being in India was to share the message of Life I believed I had found for myself in Jesus Christ. In this connection it was always a joy to see how children of every faith cheerfully took part in "Christian" activities like Chapel and HiC. On the other hand, I too came to appreciate what the culture and beliefs of India had to offer me, and to love my Hindu, Buddhist, Muslim, Sikh, Parsi and Jain students and friends. I think fondly our Parsi friend and counsellor, Dr. Master. Our own family have always maintained they were given a great gift in this modern world, to know first-hand that the important thing about people is not what their background is, but what kind of people they are.

Robert and Dattaram: helped with the boys at Fernhill hostel.

Four items in this connection stand out in my memory – 1) The Easter Play on Good Friday morning, before Easter holidays officially started; 2) Some marvellous Carol Services put on by Mrs. Murray, then later Raj David and others; 3) I always had to make the class play roster work out so KG, 1 & 2 would do the Christmas play, under Mrs. Williams, (then later Mrs. Masand and Mrs. Rongong); 4) The marvellous succession of music teachers who were responsible for the Chapel Choirs.. and for myself, the sheer joy of the morning hymn at assemblies.

One other personal memory for me and the family involves the dwellings we had at MH……first Fernhill, then Stewart building, then Trees and finally Grace Cottage. Every one of these could warrant a paragraph to itself, since each had a special connection with the lives of our children as they grew up. All the cottages on the estate held personal memories. For example, I recall the time in 1968 when the terrible floods washed away the Anderson bridge, and Mt. Hermon Estate suffered a lot of damage. Mr. Daniels was nearly washed away with Boronia cottage that night, and I only just managed to escape being drowned in a mudslide from the road above!

No account of the things that were special to us over the years would be complete without coming to the Teachers' Training College (TTC), begun by Mr. Murray in the early 70s, and coming to its full flourishing when we arrived in 1978. Mrs. Johnston in particular found her most rewarding efforts there, and more than 200 teachers all over India look back with gratitude to the solid training in methods and classroom management they received from her. I was officially "Principal" of the College, and took a great deal of pleasure in the association I was able to have with so many fine young men and women.

When I finally left MH at the end of 1989, ALL my staff in the Junior School were our own graduates from the TTC. Later it was a big thrill to work "under" Henry Soggee as Principal of Mount Home School, Coonoor, in my retirement years' work between 1994 and 2000.

He was the first TTC boy I met, as he joined in 1978, and has done a fine job at my other "MHS". We arrived in the thick of the changes that followed Mr. Murray's establishment of the College; new College building where log cabin cottage used to be; the Murray Hostel below the road to town; and the reorganising of the kitchen and dining room, which was needed to accommodate young men and women separately from the school. Although the arrangement later came under criticism from some old scholars, I can confidently say the underground dining room and kitchen worked well while Mr. Gardner was in charge, and I actively kept an eye on things "down under".

One final matter is lying before me here in my notes; the list of over 200 boys and girls who were PREFECTS during the years I was Principal, and I know Mr. Stewart and Mr. Murray would each have similar lists for the decades of their care. I cannot go into that on this occasion, but later may post a list of those to whom I am ever grateful for their loyalty and hard work. We would have found it much harder to manage during the upsets of the GNLF agitation without their solid, sensible, support.

Now if I think of any more this will be much too long! Sufficient to say you will gather that the word "regret" is not in the vocabulary of our thinking about MH – except regret at having to leave! Perhaps if enough old scholars bother to read it all, we may get a flood of reminiscences, adding to and correcting what I have said.

JOHNSTONS' *TRAVELOGUE*
Reaching out, touching lives

The Johnstons in Gangtok, 2010.

Dear Friends around the world……

This may not be of great interest to everyone who received my "Christmas" letter last November; but I did promise to make a "report" of the expedition outlined then. Many of the 'reportees' are those whom we met in India between Nov 24 and March 8, so it's easier to go back to the email IDs I used before, and I trust others in UK etc., will enjoy the ride!

I realised after some working of the old memory, that mostly this is a Hermonite report….. In our notes I can make out over 100 Hermonites, students, staff and TTCs with whom it has been our privilege to make connections… so you will appreciate too much detail would be overwhelming! and I apologise to any who may feel "left out!" During the course of these weeks we have covered a history going all the way from Val's first contact in 1953, until our final visits from DGH in 2002….almost exactly 50 years of beloved Mount Hermon. Also, I find there are nearly a dozen "places" where these connections were made. We started in Perth when a touchdown there enabled us to meet Ranjit's lovely daughter Shaheen (one of my junior monitors in 1986) and her daughter Rachael.

The next bit of course is part of more recent history, when we spent the first weeks at our last Indian home, Barnes School, Devlali. Even here MH caught up with us, as the new Principal Bryan Martin, V-Principal Trevor Jacob, and long-time staff member, Brian Fernandez are all ex-TTC. It was part of our "working holiday" to enter into the Barnes activities….chapels, dorm prayers, matrons' meetings, blessing of new dorms and swimming pool, rehearsals for a splendid Christmas programme, Sports Day heats, and of course lots of interest in our former 8s and 10s who were getting ready for this year's ICSE and ISC.

Mr. and Mrs. Johnston with 1971 batch Hermonite Namgyal Wangdi in Gangtok, 2010.

Taking an outing from Devlali we enjoyed meeting up with former staff, Frank and Val Freese in Pune, and inspecting Frank's two wonderful new schools, extensions of Bishops, where Hermonite TTCs and staff, Henry & Hema Soggee, and Ferdinand Bunyan are in charge. Also mention should be made of Shalini (another of my 80s monitors) and her "little" sister, and Mrs. DeSousa (widow of Norbert) and old MH and Darjeeling friend, Mrs. Nuges Madan.

From Devlali we went to South India for almost a week with Mrs. Mathai and Shanta, and latterly meeting George and his family, and former staff, P. C. Mathews and his family. That week deserves a whole letter to itself, it gave so much pleasure!

But then it was off to Kolkata via Cochin and Bangalore (sad not to be able to meet up there with a whole list of friends from Coonoor days). It was wonderful to be met by Sujit and Dipak from the plane at midnight. Courtesy of Sujit (via Manoj's P.O. connection) and Dipak's India Oil connection we enjoyed first-rate guest house accommodation in Kolkata. Our Christmas day visit to St. Paul's was a lovely experience and even there MH cropped up! Anjali's choir (sadly for the occasion without Anjali) lifted our spirits, and a bit of old Darjeeling came up there when we met Jogen Khan (ex-St. Paul's) and Mary Ann Das Gupta (ex-Calcutta Girls).

For years Kolkata Hermonites depended on Anup and then Santosh, so it is great to see Sujit, Dipak, Sajan, Dipkantha and Dibyendu carrying on the good work. Sujit, with much help from many others, finally got dates from us (!) and later organised a great get-together on Jan 9th. There must have been between 40 and 50 at Hathi's place, and Sujit has prepared a full set of pics of that occasion, and a complete list of Kolkata Hermonites.....thanks Sujit! As usual we also enjoyed a lovely meal at Sajan's with the old timers, including Rajeev; Singhanias have a 2-generation connection with MH! Prabir mounted a great outing to his ancestral home for several of us, including Anjana, Anup's sister, who was one of Mrs. J's senior girls in 1953....time goes by!

In between the two sessions at Kal we went to Siliguri, from where we were able to visit Kalimpong - only 4 hours thanks to the Gurkha agitation, but time to visit Gyanu Rongong, Binod Yonzon and his fine son Sidarth, Gandhi Ashram (sadly now without Fr. McGuire) and the sisters at St. Joseph's Convent . The Siliguri visit in the hands of Ravi and his sons, along with Rajendra, Kavita and family, and Sushil was really wonderful ... how proud we are of these fine young (?) people.

After Kalimpong the Lakhotia vehicle took us on to Gangtok to be guests at the famous Tashi Delek Hotel. A sensational morning visit to Hanumantok with Motilal Lakhotia left us with wonderful images of the Kanchenjunga range for our digitals! The next day was one of the highlights of our travels, when no less than 17 Sikkim Hermonites enjoyed dinner at the Hotel....among all the boys it was special to have Nim and Yanki Shipmo! A great experience to see "my" students from the 80/90s mixing with our old timers from the 60/70s. We were also proud to be the guests of Sikkim's new Minister for Education, Narendra Pradhan, at a conference for his teachers, supported by another Hermonite, Roshni Pradhan......Dr. Uttam, and several others came again to the hotel next morning....... a feast of memories.

My Tribute To A Revered Friend And Guide

My wife Tsering with the Johnstons (Jenni, Christie and Lyndy) in Gangtok.

Besides the Reunion during the second session in Kal, other highlights were meetings with the S. K. Agarwals (Parents of Rashmi, Divya and Priya), Ramdin and Mridula, Yasmin Mukand, old Committee member Alfred Martin (and Arpita), and DGH ex-Principal Bernard Brooks. Also, Dipkantha was able to fix a meet with Sunirmal Chakraborty, now Principal of La Marts, where we also met Anjali who teaches there too. A final meeting was with Aparna, and a ride with Runa to see Carol & Benu's new apartment and meet Anuva. Senior girls from the 80s will be interested to know of Ma'am's visits with Sr. Decklen (St. Joseph's K/P) in Siliguri, Sr. Stella (Loreto Dj.) in Kolkata Loreto (both of them now very unwell) and Sr. Cyril at Sealdah Loreto. Then all too soon Sujit and Dipak saw us onto the train for Delhi, and all we had planned was history.

Mrs. Johnston with Ramesh and wife Kavita Lakhotia in Gangtok, 2018.

The Delhi phase is very much Firdausi's story! From her first appearance at the Station to whisk us off to her apartment (if anyone can whisk anybody in Delhi!!) until we left nearly a month later, she was our guardian angel. (Firdausi Rahman was the star of 4 musicals in the 80s!). As with Kolkata the Delhi visit was in two parts…a week of various visits…. Dr. Navreet Singh; ex-TTC Troy Calvert, Head at Frank Anthony School; the Lalls from Soom Tea Estate; ex-TTC sisters at Ashok Vihar school, courtesy Thinleys' taxi; meals with Rajendra's family (sadly in Delhi because of Anand's accident); with Ritesh and his lovely wife and daughter; and an outing with Lance Fuller – ex-TTC and ex-DGH Principal. Then a quite wonderful luncheon Firdausi organised for nearly 20 Hermonites at a very smart hotel at the end of the week……Sashikala, Ayinla, Pema, Anita, Beauty, Jasmina, Naveen, Harsh, Dipak, Gita,…..even ex-TTC Andrew Hoffland, and so many others (photos in Facebook) not least Firdausi's beautiful little girl, and her honorary Hermonite husband Matthew, and Beauty's daughter who is ditto her mum.. Then Mehaboob took us for two nights to stay in Meerut with his family. There we also met Patricia Ismail and her family…..

My Tribute To A Revered Friend And Guide

Then the scene shifted to Dehra Dun, for a week with ex-TTC/staff Tashi and Tsering Dhondup, and 10 days with Namla Tsarong, where Ma'am did a workshop for the Monks and Nuns of the Tibetan centre where Namla has been director with Norzin assisting…… what a thrill also to welcome Rigzin all the way from Dharamsala (for many years Secretary to His Holiness), and have tea with him and Sopal Tethong (Matron in 1953), and also with Namla's

brothers and parents. Tashi & Tsering organised a meal for us to meet Rockey Gardner and Charlotte, Debasis Brahma with his wife… Thinley and his wife…..wonderful! I also managed to squeeze in a visit with Debasis to Doon School, where he works, and a visit with Barnes ex-Principal and ex-DGH, Albert Temple to see his new school.

A very special item at this stage was a 3-day visit to Wynberg Allen in Mussoorie… (where we were happily settled in 1977 until Mr. Murray came and called us back to MH!). The new Principal, Leslie Tindale was our student in class 7 and 8… and our art teacher Mr. Misra and steward Terence Cashmore are still there. Mussoorie holds many happy memories for us with Jenni and Lyndy…..I think I took most pics of Mussoorie!!

Then a few more days with Firdausi, where she hosted visits from Krishna, Shibesh and Narottam, and Joysree & A.K.; then we were on our way to Devlali to finish where we started, at Barnes. There a special visit from Pune by Jayanta kept MH in sight. Finally a couple of days in Mumbai to have a meal with Indranil and his new wife Sweta (all the way from Patna)….and a time with Tehmi Master, daughter of Dr. Master whom Hermonites of the 60s will remember…..a bitter sweet meeting since it was the first time seeing Tehmi since Mrs. Master passed away last year at 92.

Now if you think "this is more than enough", find room for two more days….. in Singapore with 80s ex-staff Sunny Mathai and his delightful family…but after 4 months it was nice to land in Melbourne, to be met by Kris and Jenni's big girl Annie, for whose graduation we remained a few weeks more in Melbourne until finally reaching Tasmania in April...

Now greetings to all…. And the last question, when and where next??!!

John & Val, April, 2010

Dear friends around the world….

I am in a bit of a quandary because my dear wife has already done about 50 Greeting Cards….. so, what to put in an email ??? However, looking over all the items in my "in box", I am reminded of so many who have been in touch through 2010, and will pick out a few from the several hundred in our "Contacts" page to say

Happy Christmas and blessings for 2011

The highlight of 2010 was of course its beginning, as we tripped around meeting friends in India. I did do a full report on that, which went individually, and to the Hermonites and Facebook websites, so will not load you with repeat details.

Tasmania has been good to come back to, although rather too cold for our liking after our weeks away in India. We are blessed to be able to have regular contact with Michael, Jenni and Lyndy with their families by living here in Launceston…. and it's an easy place for the "Australians" to come to for a quiet rest! The Tas Symphony in which Michael plays comes here regularly, and in any case it's not a big trip to Hobart. His new grandchildren (and our great-grandchildren) Myra and Atticus are growing quickly, and there are plenty of other activities at Jenni's place to keep up with too. Annie had her B.Sc. graduation just as we arrived home in March…so we now follow 3 graduates with loving interest…Annie, plus Snehala B.A., LL.B., and Dr. Laurin all make us very proud…and there are more in the pipeline…Carol's Barun, Kris' Miriam and Camilla, Jenni's Liz and Andrew, Lyndy's Toby, and Sherap's Derek & Jordan are all now in Tertiary courses.

My Tribute To A Revered Friend And Guide

We gave ourselves a most enjoyable trip to Queensland in July to celebrate Val's birthday, catching up with several Hermonite contacts…Brian Lee, Soma Baidya, Alex Thomas, the Isons, the Canberra mob…Ros & Sherap, Heather & Michael, Walsa & Stephen and Nilima, as well as enjoying the warmth of Maroochydore! This was followed by a second celebration at Jenni's place with nearly all the family there. Unfortunately, the chief guest tripped over Tammy the dog, and ended up having to cut the birthday cake in hospital, with a broken arm!! Fortunately, it's mending fairly well, although still a nuisance as 12 weeks have now gone by.

We were sad to lose our parallel grandparents and long-time friends, Peg Glasby from Kris family, Bruce Rose from Jenni's and David Aldridge from Lyndy's earlier in the year. But we do have cause to be grateful that otherwise all the extended family seem to be carrying on without significant problems.

I do look at my Facebook page from time to time… have collected over 650 "friends" but don't know how to do much with them! over 100 sent birthday greetings in October, mostly from MHS and Coonoor. Very satisfying not to be forgotten in one's declining years!! Now this is enough!

Loving greetings,
John & Val

JOHNSTONS *INDIA VISIT*: DEC 2011-JAN 2012

"I do want to acknowledge the help and friendship of so many during our 8 weeks 'back home'"

Dear friends around the world,

It has taken a little while to collect myself after our return from India. Most importantly, we had the pleasure of delaying our return to Tasmania in order to attend the wedding of our son Sherap Dorjee on the Gold Coast on Jan 30. He has married a lass from Gangtok, now Australian, whose family we met during our visit there in Dec.

This "report" may not be of great interest to some on my list, but I do want to acknowledge the help and friendship of so many during our 8 weeks "back home". So many places and people I had better enumerate!

1. Firdaus, as so often before, took charge after we arrived in Delhi on Nov.14. Her place in Greater Kailash has become a second home....thanks Firdaus! From here we were able visit people and places on our list....including Karen and "Quack", the Lalls, and Tenzing Norbu's family, Manish Chaturvedi and family, and Wallace Shah from Wynberg Allen days.. We tried to show granddaughter Emma something of Delhi, which is even more crowded and congested with traffic than 2 years ago!

2. A day in the train brought us to Dehra Dun where Tashi met us and took us to our second "home" in India, the Sambhota Orphanage and Educational Institution. It is a great privilege to feel so much part of the place with Tashi and Tshering, and to be able to relive happy days with them in MH during the 80s. Including the days after we had been in Mussoorie, we were able to meet other friends in D.D.....Beryl & Irwin Sealy, Ruth and Jeff Gardner, Namla Tsarong, and friends in Clement Town. Dehra is still a great place to visit, but becoming horribly crowded since it is now the new capital.

3. The chief purpose of our visit was to take charge of granddaughter Beth, after she finished her term at Wynberg Allen, so our next move was to Mussoorie WA was our happy home there in 1976, and it was great to see how well it has progressed..... under the present leadership of Leslie Tindale who was one our "boys" back in '76. We were proud to see Beth go forward on Prize Day, and to observe how well she had been received in our old school. Kris was able to join us for a few days, after completing her trek in Sikkim, so together we all enjoyed Mussoorie. How lucky we were to have cloudless days to enjoy the views we remembered too well. It was the icing on the cake to return and have another week with Tashi and Tshering in D.D.

4. Firdaus welcomed us back in Delhi after Dehra Dun and saw us on our way to Kolkata for the next major part of our visit. (our train was 12 hours late!!!) Kolkata came in two bits! Dec. 8 to 16 and Jan 3 to 8, with the intervening weeks

occupied by our trips to Siliguri, Kalimpong and Gangtok. Each day seemed to have something interesting for us to do, while enjoying the generous hospitality of Iqbal Khan and his lovely wife Ruksana. Old friends included Bernard Brooks, Ramdin & Mridula, S.K. Agarwal's family, my companion Thomas D'Sousa, now Archibishop of Kolkata, Aparna Chaturvedi, Sajan Singhania, Dipkantha, Clayton Moses, ex-TTC, Zeena and Mr. Behera at Lower Circular Rd. Church, a number of Sisters who were our friends in the Convents and especially the farewell assembly for Sr. Cyril of Sealdah School.

5. On Dec.15 we took the train to Sealdah and began another major part of our journey. Rahul Lakhotia met us at NJP and looked after us in Siliguri, in the midst of the Lakhotia family mourning the loss of Anand (who was one of my Prefects in 1986). Special features of Siliguri were to meet Ravi and his 3 fine sons and smart new grandson, and to visit the Sealdah Sisters including ex-TTC Marcelene (now in charge of Bethany in Darjeeling). We were grateful to score a ride to Darjeeling with Marcelene and to stay at Bethany school for our 3 days there. This gave us the chance to explore Darjeeling...and meet old friends such at Habib Mullick, Durga Das, Fr. Van of NJP, and meet George, Saroj and Eddie from MH. Its sad to have to say that nothing in Darj seems to be as attractive as it was in the "old days"..... and this is not the place to express opinions about what is going on at MH!

6. From Siliguri we moved to Kalimpong to spend 4 great days as guests of Amode Yonzone in his fine Park Hotel (a great place to stay if you are in Kalimpong!!). Part of the visit to Kalimpong was to share in Christmas celebrations in the home of our old friend Gyanu Rongong, where nearly all of Roslyn's tribe were also involved. It was a special privilege to attend the Christmas service in the Homes Chapel, (which I knew so well) led by ex-TTC Henry Simon, now Rev. and chaplain of the Homes. Another special visit was with Manikumar, son of our loved ayah Chandra, in his new house in 12th mile.

7. Our days in Gangtok would justify a letter to themselves... sufficient to say we were fortunate indeed to have cloudless days and clear views of the snows. The Tashi Delek Hotel is THE place to stay. How wonderful to meet Gangtok Hermonites, including all the Lakhotias, Tashi and Cherry Densapa, Jikme Kazi & family, Arthur Pazo, the family of our new "daughter-in-law" Kalsang, Kunsang Khangsarpa and his family and many more. Gangtok needs to be on the list for another visit!!!

Mr. and Mrs. Johnston with Arthur, Jigme, Roslyn and Sherab in Gangtok, 2011.

8. The highlight of our return to Kolkata was of course the Hermonite re-union on Jan 5th...when about 70 Hermonites gathered at the Kolkata Rowing club rooms..... thanks to the great organising by Sujit, Iqbal and several others. It was especially good to see a lot of "my boys and girls" from the 80s meeting older characters from previous decades. Two of the oldies...Dibyendu and Sajan...extended their hospitality for dinners on 4th and 6th.....all greatly appreciated.

9. At the risk of making this too long I must conclude with our final week in Chennai, where Subrangshu and is lovely wife Soma provided such wonderful hospitality... a time in which we were also able to enjoy meeting Mr. Varughese and the Raj Davids, and a meal with Ashish Bhengra and George Mathai at Chennai Cricket Club. On the last night we were able to spend time with Drs. Susie and Sam Samuels...all of which leaves feeling there has be at least one more outing!!! There will be some pics eventually in Facebook...no more now.

Love to all John & Val

Loving memories of TTC days

Stuart D'Costa

"Pa J". That's what he was affectionately referred to by all TTC students, and rightfully so. He changed my life and gave it direction at a time when, after my schooling, I felt I was adrift in the doldrums like a ship with no sails. He interviewed me at the Calcutta Boys' School in 1979, and must have been appalled to hear my "speech impediment" with words like "mudda" and "fadda" and other "howlers" that probably spewed out of my mouth. Yet, he saw something in me, and in admitting me to the Teachers' Training College the following year, he put wind in my sails and set me on a course of new adventures. Later at our TTC graduation, he affectionately explained how he was impressed with my big smile and flashing white teeth at the admissions interview. My life has gained so much momentum since, and words can never do justice in expressing my gratitude to someone so tender, and fatherly to us all at MHTTC.

The main TTC building, located below the school.

"Pa J and Ma J" knew we were hundreds of miles away from home, and would have us over at "Trees", their residence almost every Tuesday, where we were served refreshments, and harmoniously sang spirituals. It was their way of making us feel at home, and it truly felt so. Pa J added a verse to the spiritual, "Give me oil in my lamp, keep me burning" which made him appear so human to me, and it always cracked me up. It went something like, "Give me umption, in my gumption, help me function." Another regular, and favorite at "Trees" was:

From left: Aubrey Mc, James Roberts, Peter D'Souza, Raymond Perry, George Shepherd, Brian Christensen and sitting, Darryl Bloud.

"Because He lives, I can face tomorrow. Because He lives, all fear is gone. Because I know, He holds the future. And life is worth living, just, because He lives."

Pa J will always live on in our hearts. Through his lessons on life, he has given direction to the lives of so many young TTC students, and in doing so, has helped us touch the lives of hundreds and thousands of children who passed through our classes.

TTC: batch of 1973-74 (David Hilton)

Ma J and Pa J truly were like parents to us all at TTC and would encourage us to share our problems with them whenever they sensed we were troubled. We will always cherish every loving memories of them we so fondly hold in our hearts. Our prayers and love go out to Ma J and the girls.

It is with great honor and sadness that I thank you for giving me this opportunity to share my memories of the Johnston family.

Hail Mount Hermon! A Tribute

"He was loved by all the students"

Bhaskar Paul

I am deeply saddened to hear about the news of our honourable and beloved ex-principal Mr. John Johnston. It was he who got me admitted to MHS in the first place. I still remember when he was taking attendance during admission and it was the first time I heard him speak. He had to call out my name three times before I answered "yes". I couldn't understand English very well then, and for someone as well spoken and refined as Mr. Johnston, I couldn't make head or tail of his accent. I was getting admitted to class 3 then. I was frightened and afraid. He did say something to me for my late response but again I didn't understand a single word of what he had said. All I could make out was the laughter in the room after he finished whatever he was saying. He must have said a few words of advice for me, which the others could comprehend but which I couldn't. He was really an inspiration and loved by almost all the students.

I remember him playing the piano full of energy and enthusiasm, and singing the morning hymns along with us. When we were in class 3, 4 and 5 we usually got the front benches, and occasionally we got the side front benches putting us directly on the righthand side of the piano and the piano player. This is when we got the best view of him. I can't remember him using any lyrics from the music script while playing, and we just sang a little louder than him at the piano. His energy and joy inspired us to sing better.

I still remember when we bid farewell to him. We lined up on both sides of the drive way from the main gate (Kangchenjunga side) till the exit gate of the school, holding flowers in our hand, and as the old Ambassador car passed by we threw the flowers on the vehicle. The vehicle was moving very slowly as if to allow us just a few extra minutes of his presence. I think both Mr. Johnston, his wife and many of us were crying. Finally, the car exited the gate, climbed up the hill, and disappeared from our view. I think we still stood there for the while just to make sure that he really had gone. We wanted to see him as long as we could. We wanted to be there with him as long as we could. During my 7 to 8 years in MHS (class 3 to class 10) never did we have such a farewell again. Although we did say goodbye to many after Mr. Johnston.

TTC: batch of 1973-1974 (David Hilton)

I am not very religious but I do firmly believe in God and I believe the spirit never dies. Based on our Karma (deeds) the good Lord decides what to do with our spirit and if our deeds are good then the good Lord rewards our spirit and we have nothing to worry about. I am sure Mr. Johnston is going to be taken good care by the Lord and we have nothing to worry about. This is just a journey and like everyone else he has passed from one stage to the next.

May God give strength to his family and friends to overcome this little hard phase of life. May God grant us the wisdom to have faith in the Lord and understand that even things such as these are part of his plan and happen for reasons best known only to the Lord. May our "Sir" Mr. Johnston rest in peace.

(UK alumnus)

Hail Mount Hermon! A Tribute

Coming Home

For 14 years Darjeeling had been our home and even the 5 years 'abroad' were years of "homesickness."

Val Johnston

Yes! We have come home! For most of you, G.H.D. is the most exciting day of the year, but for us – the Johnston family, coming home to M.H.S. was the most exciting day.

My Tribute To A Revered Friend And Guide

For 14 years Darjeeling had been our home and even the 5 years 'abroad' were years of "homesickness." Why? Because India has become so much part of us, since we first placed our feet near the Gateway of India, Bombay in November 1952.

Here we find most friends are true friends – and most people are 'real' that is unless they've been tarnished by a Western facade. Values are different, personal values are respected, there's courtesy, a dignity, sincerity amongst the poor that one finds nowhere else in the world; a generosity toward the stranger even to the sharing of a last simple meal of rice. People don't build fences around their houses in true India – their problems are everyone's problems for the finding; their joys – everyone's joys. A person has time to talk to his neighbour – to share the evening twilight, to mediate on life – and death – of creation and creator. There's time to think – to look, to absorb – even the spices and incense of the evening air of the bazaar penetrate one's whole being and prayer comes easily to the heart.

For us at Mount Hermon, our friends here are important and condition our thinking wherever we may go. We shall always remember Laskari, who still carries his battered broom after 37 years – who for 37 years has trailed his wet cloth down the main corridor and led the sweepers in preparing the field for Sports Day – with systematic sweeps only to discover next day their only prize – another heap of litter. Kishore, his son with a 'lucky hand' sings at his work, be it a septic tank to be cleaned or 'emergency' after hours – a young man who has worked out his priorities more wisely than many "graduates." There's Kalooram, who seldom has the clothes delivered on time but who is always so agreeable and tries to be honest. And Mr. Manaen – the most gracious, truly 'educated' of our Nepali staff over many years, who still takes his daily slow climb to North Point.

We lose our most trusted friend and brother when Mr. Murray leaves – he can never be replaced in our hearts but our brothers and sisters from Kerala – the Mathai family were here to welcome us back with the assurance that they will stay – they are true friends with whom we lived and played for 10 years with never a cross word; we love and understand each other.

These and so many other things – big and small – make this our home. Even Addie Gardner's 'Chapel' flowers and polished brass give the human touch to so much of our institutional life.

But on the broader scale – students, friends, parents from all corners of India – from all creeds and communities make up our big family to which we have come home. We pray that nothing of self-seeking, misunderstanding, barriers or resentment may enter this sacred 'campus' to spoil the family unity that has been the greatest feature of Mount Hermon over the past 25 years.

May God bless us all!

(Hermonite 1978, annual school magazine.)

21 Gardner Recollections: 1970-1984

JEFFERSON GARDNER
Principal, 1990-1994

'Big Jake' Was Loved And Respected

Ruth Gardner

"We'll never be able to break the spell,
The magic will hold us still,
Sometimes we may pretend to forget
But of course we never will!
We've broken the ties,
We've said our "Goodbyes"…..

But our resolution is oft times slack,
For try as we will
Mem'ries remain with us still,
And yes, oh yes, we often look back!"

The earliest memory I have goes back to 1970 when my husband, Jeff, and I first joined Mount Hermon. We were met at Siliguri by Jeff's brother, Rocky, Winston Lunnon and George Daniels who had driven down in the school jeep to take us up the hill. On reaching Ghoom we were told, "We're almost there now." We were told the same when we reached the Lower Market, then again at North Point, till I began to wonder when "…..there" would finally come! I remember sitting at the edge of my seat with my heart in my mouth as George Daniels manoeuvred the turn at what I later came to know was termed Pooh Corner and where we were again told, "We're almost there.", then drove down that awful slope with our luggage in the trailer behind and wondering what would happen if the brakes failed! They didn't - and wasn't I relieved to see the gates of the school loom ahead out of the mist! But alas, George drove right passed them down yet another uncomfortable slope saying he was taking us right to our cottage, Woodbank. Finally, we arrived - and didn't I send up a prayer of thanks!

Mr. and Mrs. Gardner with Glenn and Aprille, 1971.

After our luggage had been unloaded, Rocky took the four of us across to Trees where we received a warm welcome from the Johnstons whose house, at that evening hour, seemed crawling with kids. Then, on our way up to Stewart Building where Adelaide was waiting with a warm, well-cooked dinner, we got our first glimpse of the main school building from across the field. What a fine impressive building it was - awe-inspiring in the gathering dark. We began to look forward with eager anticipation to working in our new environment.

Our first meeting with other members of Staff (Darrs, Wainwrights, Mathais, Wests, Mapleys, Mathews, Ishmaels, Mrs. Joy Rongong, Miss. Williams, Davidson, Alexander, Mukand, Wasson, and Misses Hawke, Russel, Meagher, David, Rungard - to name only a few) at the opening gathering to break the ice with games, fellowship and dedication to a new year of service, like subsequent fellowship evenings, left a lasting impression of an atmosphere of warmth, helpfulness and common Christian commitment which we had not experienced to the same degree in other schools where we had worked earlier, and which we still associate with Mount Hermon. It is indeed that atmosphere of caring concern that shaped the attitudes and values of so many impressionable young folk and our own two children, Glenn and Aprille, in particular, which we cherish even today.

The following year Joyce Wainwright saw a need to open in her little cottage, Rosebank, a nursery class for staff pre-schoolers which our daughter attended, while Glenn, now a 'big boy,' joined Hilda David's K.G. in the Main Building at the end of the 2nd floor. The nursery fee to cover cost of paper, pencils, crayons etc., amounted to the paltry sum of 50 p! Mrs. Wainwright, with her boundless enthusiasm, kept these little ones profitably occupied through the morning with rhymes, songs, drawing and nature walks which the now grown Wainwrights, Darrs, Wests and Gardners must look back on with fond remembrance.

In our second year, sunrise at Tiger Hill followed by a breakfast of sausages, baked beans and buns brought up by Mr. Murray in the jeep, was another occasion we look back to nostalgically. Staff and children trekked from school at 3.00 a.m. to be in time for the spectacular scene as the sun rose over the majestic mountains and tinted them pink. Soon after, with great excitement, about two centimeters of the tip of Everest was pointed out to us and we in turn pointed it out to others on subsequent visits!

The Duke of Edinburgh Award Scheme, started in 1971, became Jeff's responsibility. The associated activities included camps and treks to picturesque places in the district and neighbouring tea gardens, Rangaroon, Mungpoo, Singla, Sandakhphu among others. Participation increased and the Scheme gathered momentum as its participants felt a sense of achievement when they received their bronze, silver or gold awards.

As I look back to those years when I taught Class 2 in the Infant Department, I think of Mrs. Williams and the warm appreciation for work done under her and of the luxury of a bright and spacious classroom in which, for the first time, I felt the freedom to break away from the traditional arrangement of tables in neat rows, and work with children in groups instead. We could even spill out onto the terrace for activity periods and have Nature and Painting Corners. Singing and Percussion were done in the Class 1 room where there was a piano and when Jillain Johnson had taken her Class 1 swimming.

Class Plays sent everyone into a panic! The emphasis was on encouraging more children to participate publicly than on polished perfection. Indeed, for the latter there was little time as there was such a constant flow of activity for children and teachers to contend with! I recall using Mrs. Davidson's Linen Room in the Little Boys' Corridor to iron costumes and lay them out in readiness for the great day. Imagine my consternation when I was teaching in the Junior School a few years later, to find on the morning of my Class Play that the main 'prop' - a large window on a movable frame which was usually left in the wings between practices, was untraceable. On reporting the loss to the boss, Mr. Murray, he just laughed and said he didn't know it was being used and had lent it to the Convent as they needed it for their play! Of course, he got the Maintenance Department to produce another one by that afternoon. Poor Richard Tamang! I bet he had a few nasty things to say of that!

The Gardners with the Wasons and Mrs. Daniels (extreme right) during the school's Centenary celebrations in November 1995.

Gardner Recollections: 1970-1984

Some Major Performances that come to mind are Salad Days (from which the Leavers' Song is taken and in which Jeff took part), The Gondoliers (performed by the Training College and the school Staff and in which I took part), The King and I with Barbara Nichols-Roy in the lead role. Glenn was little Prince Chulalongkorn and Aprille had her first part in a Major Production, Fiddler on the Roof with Stephen Murray as Tevye (and the Rev. Bill Jones literally fiddling on the roof!), The Sound of Music with Emma Masand as Maria, Pygmalion with Johnny Murray as Henry Higgins and songs from My Fair Lady, Anne of Green Gables with Aprille as Josy Pie, A Christmas Carol and so many others - most directed by Geoff Blackmore. Staff entertainment on Children's Day in 1978 had the Junior School Staff singing Three Blind Mice and Mrs. Joy Rongong, knife in hand, prancing about on the stage! Those were the days of fun and healthy camaraderie----would that they could return!

In 197? a group of Americans from Pennsylvania paid the school a visit. Jeff, assistant master at the time, helped organize a social in their honour. They taught the current seniors some vigorous square dancing which even the usually shy students made bold to join in, and which they, like the rest, thoroughly enjoyed. The visitors left the records with the school and square dancing became a regular feature at socials till 1984 when we left to join St. Paul's up at Jalpahar. Much to the chagrin of the Paulite community our loyalty and affection for Mont Hermon became obvious and we would happily have returned to take over from the Johnstons when they returned to New Zealand had the powers that be so wished. (As it turned out it was only when Jeff resigned from St. Paul's to join me, now looking after my aged mother in Dehra Dun, that the school committee prevailed on him to hold the fort at M.H. till a new Principal was appointed. So it was then he took over temporarily, this time as Principal from May 1990 to March 1994 - to contend with the disturbances that resulted from the Gorkhaland agitation.)

When Jeff became Senior Master in 1977, he was soon named Big Jake by the Seniors who came to respect and love him because of the way he disciplined them with his own special blend of firmness and caring, always keeping in mind the days when he was himself their age. That year Jeff and I, along with Glenn and Aprille, accompanied a group of middle and senior school students to attend a 21-day ski course in Gulmarg, Srinagar. For some of the group it was the first time they had seen snow. We occupied two chalets which were warmed by smokey 'bukharis' and visited the Highland Park Hotel where, because everything else was so expensive, a few of the bolder ones in the group, on the pretext of using the toilets, surreptitiously had the occasional hot bath until the doorkeeper jumped to it and firmly ticked them off! At the end of the course when all in the group had become proud possessors of bronze medals we were snow-bound. So as to catch the last flight out of Srinagar on which we had been booked, we had to be transported in an army truck that was going down and had special chains round the wheels so as to cut through the snow which had frozen!

When there was water in it the Swimming Pool gave all Gardners a chance to learn swimming. As Glenn and Aprille gained confidence, and later shone in their events, their mother, who had long wanted to learn swimming but had never had the opportunity, learned to float and flop across the pool and Big Jake enoyed early morning sessions with school teams and new learners and even set a time for enthusiastic but self-conscious staff while children were at study.

On Mrs. Rongong's retirement at the end of 1978 I took over as Junior School Supervisor. Clubs and Corridor displays were started the following year and it wasn't long before wall space ran out as displays became more elaborate and each class tried to outdo the other. Goats became the bane of the Gardening Club run by Henry Soggee who was also artistic and offered to paint in oils the two animal pictures that were hung in the Junior Corridor when complete (I wonder if they are still there!). General Knowledge Quizzes for which the winning class received a small cup, became a monthly feature after Junior Chapel on Thursdays - with Kevin Martin being the Quiz Master. A third banner was added to the existing two (for Spelling and Tables - started in Mrs. Rongong's time) for the Best-Kept Classroom of the Week.

Litter outside the Tuck Shop, in the Corridor and on the playfield inspired a 'Clean Mount Hermon Week'. Junior classes got busy making slogan badges for distribution and posters for display. The week was formally opened after chapel on a Monday morning with a 'pep talk' by representatives from Class 5 and the 'introduction' to the three Garbos (garbage bins) made by the Maintenance Department and painted brightly by Henry Soggee, with smiling faces and open mouths. After chapel each morning through that week a junior class read an appropriate portion of Scripture to do with cleanliness (found by Trish Russell) and repeated the exhortation to the assembly to 'Keep Mount Hermon Clean'. Class 3 concluded the Week with a song to the tune of Old Macdonald but with the words suitably changed for the occasion to 'Papa Johnston had a School'.

Environmental Studies - EVS - introduced in Mrs. Rongong's era, became a much-enjoyed learning experience in the Junior School. I remember, when 'Time' was our topic, taking my Class 3 children up into the Clock Tower above the Capitol Cinema. How jumpy I was lest they touch or trip over the many cables and wires at the top of the rickety staircase, and instructions and admonitions to 'take care' were oft repeated! A week later the clock stopped and, to my knowledge, has never worked since! Great was my relief on being assured by Mr. Avari, the then owner of the Capitol, that the clock had in fact been running down and had needed attention for some time, and Class 3 was definitely not responsible! Till then however it had given me many uncomfortable thoughts!

A highlight in the school calendar was Sale Day - always held on 1st May. The Fancy Stall began with good but unused household items contributed by members of the staff. Encouraged by good sales and dwindling contributions, material was later purchased and Staff either volunteered or were coerced into embroidering, painting or making articles for sale. It became a source of good-natured chaffing in the staff-room when, as the day approached, for the benefit of the inevitable procrastinators, I put up reminders '2 weeks left to Sale Day', '13 days left....', '12 days left....' and so on! Heart-warming it was indeed when staff members occasionally even bought back the very item they had themselves made. Some will even remember the ever popular, practical and pretty aprons and pot-holders (made by Yours Truly) which were often booked in advance.

Jaldapara - this time accompanied by 'the other Gardners', the Glasbys the Johnston children and some others was another happy memory despite the fact that on the way down the trailer carrying our supplies overturned at a bend and the many eggs, cushioned in the rice, broke! At the Sanctuary itself a friend of the Johnstons, Dusty, had the group in peals of laughter when he dismounted with stiff, bowed legs from the elephant he'd been riding astride for five hours in search of the rhino which we did eventually track down - but not before the lead elephant had fought its way through the tall, thick elephant grass, by repeatedly using its great forehead like a battering ram.

As I look back there is such a volume of memories and wealth of experiences which I felt couldn't be left out, and so this article has grown. That however, is in keeping with the original aim of Mount Hermon, isn't it? To encourage growth and development by just such exposure to a variety of experiences, for at MH we both learned and taught….'not just for school but for life.' So……

'We mustn't look back, no we mustn't look back,
Whatever our memories are,
We mustn't say "Those were our happiest days."
But "……our happiest days so far."!'

(Mrs. Ruth Gardner was the school's Junior Head Mistress.)

MILESTONES – Part IV

22 Builders Of Tomorrow

The Realization Is Greater Than The Dream

Johnston-Murray-Stewart era (1953-1989)

"We have gathered today to formally open this beautiful building for the purposes of Christian Education. With sincere gratitude to Almighty God, who has singly blessed his servants in this enterprise, we would devote this school to the development of Truth, Character, Godliness, Faithfulness, Purity and Service. We remember with gratitude all those who have given liberally of their means, their thought, their skill, their time and labor, that this enterprise might be brought to a successful issue."

Chairman D.H. Manley, Wednesday, 26th May, 1926: 3 p.m.
Formal Opening of the New Building.

"I was very pleased at the opportunity afforded to me by the inauguration ceremony to see the fine new building of this admirable school. I sincerely hope that the school will have a period of increased prosperity and success."

Lord Lytton, Governor of Bengal, 26th May, 1926.

"I have watched the development of Mt. Hermon and the new Queen's Hill School, with keen pleasure, deep interest and high hopes. The realization is greater than the dream. The wholesome atmosphere, the scholastic attainments, the wonderful buildings, all bring me joy. The end is not yet! Greater blessings lie ahead."

Fredrick B. Fisher, April 1927.

"Our daughters were among the group with which Queen's Hill was organized in 1895. From that time to this, 1927, I have had a very deep interest in the school. God bless each member of the staff and every girl who enters its portals."

Ada Lee, Founder of Lee Memorial School, Calcutta.

"You are pioneers about to begin the adventures of real life. Many trackless wildernesses lie before you, but you are experienced pioneers. You are accustomed to blazing new trials, to facing hardships or defeats, and to overcoming seemingly insurmountable obstacles during these years of preparation…Life with its opportunities, its difficulties and its dangers lies before you…"Non Scholae Sed Vitae Discimus" – the future will be the test of how well you have learned these lessons…As you are about to begin this greatest of all adventures, I beg of you – do not simply drift among the streams of life. Continue to blaze your trials but keep your minds always upon some purpose, richer and nobler and broader than yourselves. Live!"

Mrs. L. Enberg, Principal's Message to the Senior Class of 1932.

"Our school is growing. Growing in numbers obviously. Growing we trust, also in tradition, in spirit, in service. Great is the task presented to us, of training for life…May we each, grateful to God for the opportunities and talents He has bestowed upon us, go forward to do our best to bring honour to our school, to our country and community…

As we think of our present building, it is only fitting that we pause and pay tribute to builders of the past. Here in Mount Hermon we have a splendid heritage. One has only to look at the construction of this building in which we are today, which I believe is second to none in the district, to realize that our forbears built solidly and well. Not only did they build a building such as this, but they have left us a heritage of tradition and character up to which we of the present have to live.

It is fitting that during 1960 our school has been reorganized into four Houses, and these four Houses have been named after the Founders, and Heads of our school, to remind us of those who have gone before and built well. Miss Knowles who commenced our school in 1895, and remained as Headmistress of the Queen's Hill School until 1917 is revered as our Founder. Miss Stahl joined Miss Knowles right at the inception of our school in 1895, and remained as Miss Knowles' assistant, and later, after Miss Knowles retired, took over the task of Principalship, and remained as Principal of our school until 1933.

Thirdly, we remember Bishop Fisher. Owing largely to his drive and vision and enthusiasm this splendid Mount Hermon property was acquired, and this school built. Lastly, there is Mr. Dewey, who was Principal of our school for 7 or 8 years, and who has given so much effort to the development, not only of our school, but of this beautiful one hundred acres of property in which we are pleased to dwell. May the Four Houses each seek to bring honour to the name of the founders after whom they have been called…In our school where we are builders together with God, we are building not a building of wood and stone or bricks and mortar, but of flesh and blood, of mind and spirit."

D.G. Stewart, Principal's Report, Speech Day, 15th November, 1960.

"When I think over 1961…I come to the question which I believe is the final judgement of the worth of our work as a Christian school – what contribution have we made in the individual lives of our students – with how many have we succeeded in laying a good foundation of true and sincere Christian faith and character?…The greatest joy I have as this year is concluded is the knowledge that here in Mount Hermon God has been adding living stones one by one to that house which He is building."

D.G. Stewart, Principal's Report, 1961.

The swimming pool near Fernhill Boys Hostel came up in 1961.

"We will always seek to retain the happy, 'family' atmosphere that has characterized Mount Hermon's growth over the years…In 1926 our school was described as 'The finest school in the Orient'…As we take our 'look into the future' we know, finally, that Mount Hermon will continue to stand at all times for the development of true Christian character and ideals or service. We are made more aware each day of the need for such dedicated men and women whose lives truly reflect the love and compassion of Christ. It is our earnest hope and prayer that in the future, as in the past, Mount Hermon will send them forth."

G.A. Murray, Mid-Term Hermonite Magazine, 1964.

"Nineteen hundred and sixty four in Mount Hermon has been the passing of an era in the resignation of Rev. D.G. Stewart, who has served us here as Principal since February, 1954…We have a long history as a school, going back to 1895, so that this is our 70th Speech Day but I am sure that these ten years have been the most effective in our history, as we have seen so much done under Mr. Stewart's wise guidance to raise standards, attract and hold good staff and improve the quality and extent of our physical plant…Together Mr. and Mrs. Stewart have made a tremendous contribution to Christian Education in India, and they will not be forgotten by Mount Hermon.

May I conclude therefore by drawing your attention for a moment to that which is central in everything we do at Mount Hermon – our love for God and our desire for His purposes in our own lives and in the lives of all our students. We represent here a very privileged section of our great land of India, a group to whom much has been given which is denied to so many others, and constantly crossing my mind as I think about this are the words: "Of them to whom much is given, much shall be required." It is the prayer of the staff therefore that we may be able to give to our students not only our worldly knowledge which will lead to success in the affairs of the world, but above and beyond that we want to impart a knowledge and understanding of God's purposes for all His creation, so that those who learnt their lessons for life as well as for school here may be able to serve others and share with others the good things they have been given. Only in this way will our work have been truly well done, and our purposes as a school justified."

G.A. Murray, Principal's Report, 1964.

"Mount Hermon is a vigorous, growing community and we are proud of the record of achievements…The school…has need of people who will give their best in any task to which they find themselves committed. We have a favourite hymn in Chapel – 'Give of your best to the Master'…This, of course, is reminding those who belong to Christ to know Him in every kind of task or service, but it is surely the sentiment that needs to find expression in every individual's life. 'Give of your best' to your school, your games, your friends, your study, you work, your country."

Rev. J.A. Johnston, Acting Principal, 1970.

23 Lila Gladys Kehm Enberg
Principal, 1931-1934

"The Latter Glory Is Greater Than The Former"

Lilly: A Biography
Author: **Kitty Katzell**

"Lila" is the biography of the author's mother. Born in a small town in Iowa and raised in early 20th century South Dakota, Lila lived a Cinderella childhood with a cruel stepmother. After attending Dakota Wesleyan University, she worked in a bank and then taught school until she met and married Royce Engberg. They had one child, a daughter, before Royce died.

Lila then became a missionary and taught in India for nine years. During that period, the school (Mt. Hermon) of which she had become the principal (1931-1934), was destroyed in an earthquake in 1934. She saw to its reconstruction before returning to the United States and building a new career for herself by working toward higher degrees which led to a career in higher education.

In time, she was married again to a professor of Philosophy and Religion (Dr. Raymond Frank Piper) at Syracuse University, New York. She became a leader in Syracuse, heading up various community organizations. At the end of her life, she developed alzheimer's disease. She died peacefully on March 26, 1986, six and half months short of her 90th birthday.

In her book *Lila*, Lila's daughter Kitty Katzell writes: "On April 6, 1986, a memorial service was conducted at the University United Methodist Church in Syracuse, again in accordance with her instructions. The Pastor and Assistant Pastor spoke in the course of the service, those assembled sang "All Hail the Power of Jesus' Name" and "Abide With Me". The scriptures were Psalm 23 (The Lord is my shepherd), Psalm 121 ("I will lift my eyes unto the hills"); Ecclesiastes 3 (To everything there is a season); and selections from John 1 and 14, Romans 8, and Revelations 21. A soloist sang "How Great Thou Art" and "Crossing the Bar." The congregation recited the Lord's Prayer."

Kitty Katzell, daughter of MH Principal, Mrs. Lila Enberg.

Two chapters of the book – "To India" and "Earthquake" – reveal how Mrs. Enberg (Lila) struggled and succeeded in rebuilding a portion of the main building of Mt. Hermon School after the devastating earthquake of 1934.

Another chapter, "Second Marriage", tells the story of her life with her second husband, Dr. Raymond Piper.

To India

After closing the apartment in Chicago, Lila returned to Mitchell, South Dakota, to stay with her sister and her husband, Elsie and Fred Rolfe. Both Elsie and Fred worked in a local florist, so Lila took care of Mildred (Lila's daughter from her first husband, Dr. Royce Enberg, who died of pneumonia on April 1, 1925, aged 27) and kept house for them. They had a small home and they raised a few chickens and had a small garden. Lila kept hoping and praying that she would be able to go to India, where she could take care of her baby and earn her living as a missionary.

Meantime, their sister Alta had gone to India in 1924 to manage a girls' school in Lahore in what is now in Pakistan. Alta had also studied at Dakota Wesleyan University and had signed up to be a missionary so she could travel. After Royce died, Lila was distraught. She wrote pathetic letters to Alta telling how upset she was, how she was suffering with boils that made her really ill. During the summer of 1925, Alta went to the mountains for her vacation, and had a chance to talk with the India-Secretary of the Woman's Foreign Missionary Society (WFMS) about Lila and the fact that she wanted to go to India. The president of Lila's alma mater, Dakota Wesleyan University, Dr. Schermerhorn, had also been a missionary in India, and he, too, was trying to help her.

Suddenly, through the combined efforts of Lila, Alta in India, and Dr. Schermerhorn in South Dakota, Lila was told that there was a place for her to teach in an English boarding school in Darjeeling, up in the Himalaya mountains. This was 1925, so it took a month for the letter to reach her from India and another month for her reply to reach them, but Lila was exuberant when she learnt that she might go.

But there were still hurdles. "Send a widow and baby to India?" The WFWS knew they were taking a chance. Arrangements were made for Lila and Mildred to have physical examinations in Minneapolis, since it was from that branch of the WFMS that she would be sent out. Lila knew she was not in best physical condition, and, when the physician hesitated and then asked if she really wanted to go to India, she broke down and cried. He had found a slight heart murmur and that was why he was hesitating, but when he saw that she was really anxious to go, he passed her.

Friends and relatives in the U.S. thought she was crazy to take Mildred to heathen India. They predicted all sorts of dire consequences, but Lila believed that it was God's will and that He would give her the strength she would need. One relative told her point blank that it was stupid or worse, and that if anything ever happened to Mildred, it be Lila's own fault. She never forgot those words.

She signed a three-year contract with the Woman's Foreign Missionary Society of the Methodist Church, and on January 1, 1926, Lila and Mildred set sail from New York on the S.S. Homeric. Mildred had her second birthday on the Atlantic (Incidentally, she had her seventh birthday on the Pacific in 1931, when they were returning to India after a six-month furlough in the U.S.) It was a rough crossing, and nearly everyone was seasick, but not Lila. She would put the two-year-old Mildred on the floor and as the ship rolled back and forth, Mildred would roll from one side of the room to the other. They were travelling with another missionary family all of who were ill all the way to Cherbourg. From Cherbourg, they crossed Europe and took another ship from Marseilles to Bombay via the Suez Canal.

Although Alta was already living in India, she didn't know Lila was on her way until she received Lila's cable from Port Said. Immediately, she sent off a letter which was awaiting Lila's arrival in Bombay the end of January. There, Lila and Mildred stayed at the Methodist Mission, while they cleared customs and made arrangements to join Alta in Lahore until school opened the beginning of March.

From Lahore, they went to Arrah, in Bihar province, to visit another missionary friend who was also a graduate of Dakota Wesleyan. That evening at dinner, Lila asked about the humming sound she heard. "Mosquitoes!" she was told. Right after dinner, she and Mildred went to bed - in a single bed. Lila had never seen a mosquito net, so she didn't know that one must tuck them in all four sides of the bed. Toward morning, she was wakened by Mildred's restlessness. It was getting light, so she sat up and saw that the inside of the net was black with mosquitoes. Mildred looked like she had measles; she was covered with mosquito bites! Lila drew a circle the size of a dime on her own knuckle and counted 64 bites within the circle. She was tough, so her bites dried up and faded away pretty soon. Mildred's became infected and she got malaria, which Lila had to fight periodically over the next few years. Eventually, she read about Esanophele tablets, which she bought, and after the first few, Mildred's malaria left her and she never had another attack. (During World War II, Mildred tried to donate blood but was refused as a donor because she had malaria.)

They took the train from Arrah to Calcutta. In order to be thrifty, Lila took third class, not knowing anything about the conditions in which they would be travelling. The train was noisy, crowded, and dirty, but they finally reached Calcutta, having picked up head lice on the way. Before lunch the first day at the mission house in Calcutta, Lila washed Mildred's hair with a suggested treatment for the lice, and they went down to lunch Mildred's hair bundled in a towel. One of the other missionaries at the lunch table commended, "Did the little girl have her hair washed?" to which Mildred responded gaily, "Yes. I have lice!" To treat her own case of head lice, Lila sprayed her head with Flit, a common treatment for all sorts of household vermin in those days. The Flit killed the lice, but it also caused her hair to fall out in handfuls.

The trip from Calcutta to Darjeeling was another unique experience. They took trains north to reach Darjeeling. They left Calcutta late in the afternoon on regular wide gauge train, changed in the night to a medium gauge train, and, in the morning, got into a rear car on the Darjeeling Himalayan Railway, the so-called Toy Train, because it runs on a narrow 24" gauge. The train winds around the mountains, sometimes backing up to go higher and higher and often positioned so that the front of the train overlapped the rear.

There were no restrooms on the train, and there came a time when two-year-old Mildred needed one. Since there was no alternative, Lila held her out the train window to do what was necessary. It happened to be one of the times when the front of the train overlapped the rear of the train as it circled the mountain, so everyone on the train was able to see what was going on. After a six-hour ride, they arrived in bitter cold Darjeeling. Miss Stahl, the principal of the school where Lila was to teach, met them at the station, took one look at Mildred, and said, "What has she got?" Mosquito bites.

Later, Lila understood her concern, Miss Stahl was the principal of a boarding school, Queen's Hill, where the children lived in close proximity to each other in dormitories, so any contagious disease was a serious threat. There was a full-time nurse on the staff, and the English Civil Surgeon was always on call from Darjeeling. In fact, he came to the school every Monday morning to provide routine medical care.

In India, Mildred lived through pneumonia twice, flu, tonsillitis, whooping cough, malaria, and epidemics of measles, chicken pox, and mumps. She started whooping with the whooping cough while she was on the operating table having her tonsils removed. The one epidemic that Mildred avoided was diphtheria. To avoid that, she had given an antitoxin to which it turned out she was allergic. She developed a rash that was only relieved by the continuous application of compresses of witch hazel and baking soda. Lila often wondered if it would have been better for her to get diphtheria, since the treatment of the rash lasted for weeks. One long-term benefit of Mildred's many illnesses was that she learned to knit while she was confined, a hobby that she continued to enjoy for the rest of her life.

Lila's first job in Darjeeling, before school started, was to engage an ayah to take care of Mildred while she was teaching and on duty. Lila had talked to Mildred every day about Darjeeling and what she would be doing, and how there would be an ayah to be with her all the time when Lila was working. Every time Mildred saw an India woman, she would ask, "Is this my ayah?" until it became embarrassing. They all wanted to be her ayah.

Lila talked with Miss Stahl, the principal, about getting an ayah who would be clean, competent, and dependable. Finally, Miss Stahl picked out the small Nepalese wife of one of the school servants. She was clean and very bright, had children of her own, and she loved Mildred. Almost overnight, she learned to understand Mildred, and soon Mildred was speaking Nepalese and serving as Lila's interpreter. One day, Lila told Mildred to ask the ayah something. They conversed and went back to their play. When Lila asked Mildred what the ayah had said, Mildred replied, "You heard her."

When they first went to Darjeeling, Mildred never saw any men except the Indian servants. One day, she heard a man's voice in the hall and she went running to Lila and slammed the door behind her, screaming, "Mummy, a man, a man!" Seeing that she was afraid of men, Lila cultivated married friends and also managed to have Mildred spend a few weeks of every year in a normal home away from her mother.

Although Lila had been sent to Darjeeling as a "Contract Teacher" for a three-year term, she stayed four years. In a boarding school, a missionary teacher is on duty 24 hours a day, seven days a week. Her specific responsibilities included being in charge of the older girls' dormitory, which was next to the room that she and Mildred shared. She also conducted morning worship services; took her turn at various duties, such as supervision in study halls and dining rooms; and taught English, Scripture, Algebra, and other subjects.

Queen's Hill School was primarily for the children of missionaries and other Europeans, as most white people were called. The students were taught a British curriculum, which prepared them to take Junior and Senior Cambridge Examinations, sent out from England. The examinations were administered each December following the end of the school year, which ran from March through November. One year, Lila discovered at the end of the year that one of the classes preparing for the Cambridge Examinations had not been taught by the correct syllabus in their Scripture course. With only two weeks until the examination, she taught the students what they were supposed to have learned during the year, and not one of them failed the examination.

The school was also associated with The Associated Board of the Royal Schools of Music in London, which sent examiners to evaluate the music achievement of individual students seeking their certification. Mildred took piano lessons at the school from the age of four, and took the associated examinations the last two years that they lived in India.

The credentials provided by the two aforementioned institutions were accepted worldwide when the students returned to their home countries.

When Lila and Mildred first arrived in Darjeeling, Mildred was in the habit of calling her mother by her first name. After all, everyone who knew her called her "Lila." But many of the other missionaries thought it was highly inappropriate for a 2-year-old to call her mother by her first name. So Lila sat down with Mildred and explained the situation to her. Most of the other children in the school called their mothers "Mummy" so Lila suggested Mildred adopt that practice. During the transition, Mildred used "Mummy-Lila" but eventually she grew comfortable calling Lila "Mummy".

Other teachers would sometimes ask Lila to wake them in the morning so they would be on time for classes. So Lila would send Mildred on the errand with instructions to tell the teacher it was half-past-seven. Mildred could then be heard going down the hall from Lila's room to the teacher's room, chanting all the way, "Mummy says it's half-past-seven, Mummy says it's half-past-seven."

Being in charge of the older girls' dormitory also meant meting out discipline when it was needed. On one occasion, Lila was summoned because one of the girls had "fainted." When Lila arrived on the scene, she was told that the girl, who was lying on the floor, often fainted. After hearing the other girl's explanation of the situation, Lila asked someone to bring a glass of water, which she calmly poured on the girl's face. For some reason, the girl never fainted again.

One time, the girls were eating tinned fruits in the dormitory and got sticky syrup all over the floor. When Lila came into the room, she stepped into it. She sent one of the girls to get a pail of water and another to get a supply of rags. Then she had the girls wash the floor.

Other examples of discipline were equally colorful. Shen students had been flicking spoonfuls of water at each other in the dining room, Lila had them come out to the playground after the meal wearing their raincoats. Each of the guilty students was given a teaspoon and a pitcher of water, with instructions to stand there and flick the water at each other.

In a similar vein, in a study hall that Lila was supervising, some of the students were whispering instead of studying for an upcoming examination. Lila took their books away from them and wouldn't let them study. She soon got a reputation as being a firm but fair disciplinarian and she rarely had problems with the students.

The year 1926, when Lila arrived in Darjeeling, was the year that Queen's Hill School moved to the Mount Hermon estate. The school was in a brand new fieldstone, three-storey building with a basement which housed the kitchen and a large area used for a variety of activities. The previous school building had been nearer to the city of Darjeeling, but it had been destroyed, with much loss of life, in a landslide.

The year 1926 was also the first year of co-education at Queen's Hill. Up to that time, only small boys under the age of ten had been accepted; above that age, they went to a boys' school. Most of the teachers were Anglo-Indians, and Lila was the only person on the staff who had ever taught boys before. As result, she had the older boys in her room and she was responsible for their discipline. The boys were American, English, and Anglo-Indian. The boys soon got to know Lila.

As an illustration, one day the boys, aged 13 and 14, did something for which they had to be punished. They were turned over to Lila. When she dismissed the other children from the dining room after tiffin (a light meal served at 3 p.m.), Lila asked the boys to stay. As she talked with them, they admitted that they had to be punished, "But none of that girl stuff!" they said. "OK, so what shall your punishment be?" she asked. "Cane us!" came the reply, almost defiantly. Lila agreed and told them to go out and bring their switches but they'd have to tell her how to do it. When they returned, they bent over, hands clasping their ankles, and said, "Do it hard!" So she did it "hard" till they told her to stop. Then they shook hands and thanked her. Thereafter, they could face the boys in the All-Boys schools and brag about having been caned.

Another time, one of the small American boys had been sent to Lila's office to be punished. She asked him what kind of punishment he thought she should give him, and he asked for a spanking. So she bent him over his knee and spanked him, after which he climbed into her lap, put his arms around her neck and said, "Thank you, Mrs. Engberg."

Students in one class had been cheating, and someone tattled to the teacher, Mrs. Ryan. Mrs. Ryan was very strict and stern so the students expected severe punishment when she came to class. As a prank, they all had reversed tangerine skins covering their teeth. When Mrs. Ryan saw them, she stormed out of the room and went to get Lila. Lila came to the class and asked for their side of the story. Then she made them promise never to cheat again, and she would deal with Mrs. Ryan.

What the students had no way of knowing was that Mrs. Ryan hated teaching. She had gotten married to get out of it. She had a child, but her husband and child were both killed in a boating accident. She had to resume teaching to support herself. Lila tried to work with her and help her to deal with her personal situation.

Since the school had a kindergarten, Mildred started attending it right away and continued for the next four years. She loved school and, despite being sick much of the time, she progressed. She was able to read when she was three years old and could write her name when she was four. The kindergarten taught much of what American children were learning in the first two grades.

As already noted, during Alta's fourth year in Lahore, she was sent to Ajmer to fill a vacancy there. In Ajmer, she met Cecil Harris to whom she became engaged after a year, and married early in 1930. Lila and Mildred were present for the wedding, with Mildred serving as flower girl.

Soon after the wedding, in January 1930, after four happy years in Darjeeling, Lila and Mildred left India for a furlough in America. On the trip, they were accompanied by Miss Stahl, the retiring principal of the school. The three of them shared a cabin on a lower deck. When the ship was passing through the Red Sea, the sea was rough and Miss Stahl had the berth under the porthole. A wave poured through the open porthole bringing live fish and drenching Miss Stahl and all her belongings, which she had left on the floor.

While sight-seeing in Egypt, Lila was spat upon. She asked the guide if he understood what had happened. His response was, "They thought you were Jewish." The travelers also visited other countries in northern Africa and Europe on their home, with Mildred and Lila compiling scrapbooks of the sites they visited.

In the U.S., Lila was occupied with traveling for the WFMS, telling the church groups about mission work in India and throughout the world. She left Mildred with her friends in Minnesota, and Mildred went to school there for four months. Initially, when Lila took Mildred to enrol her in the school, because Mildred was six years old, the school wanted to put her in the first grade. Lila would have none of that. So they said they would try Mildred in the second grade. After a few days of that, the school decided she was too far advanced to stay in the second grade, so they put her in the third grade, which was a bit more difficult but still not challenging enough to keep her occupied. Finally, she was put in the fourth grade, to the dismay of the principal who could not condone having a 6-year-old in the 4th grade. But Mildred worked hard and did reasonably well.

It was in Minnesota that Mildred first learned to trust dogs. The friend with whom they were staying had a black cocker spaniel called "Nigger". Nigger would escort Mildred to school and then return to escort her home at the end of the day. He could sleep on the floor of her bed, but when he heard Lila coming to bed, he would get off Mildred's bed and hide underneath till Lila had settled down. From that point on, Mildred never had a fear of dogs.

Lila and Mildred had been in the U.S. less than a year when Lila received a cable asking her to return as the principal of Queen's Hill School. They returned early 1931. As principal, Lila had a suite of rooms on the third floor of the school building, with windows looking north toward the Kinchenjunga range. Mildred shared her rooms, until 1934, when she was 10 years old and moved into the girls' dormitory. Lila's suite consisted of four rooms: a living room, bed-room, bathroom, and sewing room. In the living room, there was a fireplace, and the cement floor was covered with 9"×12" Chinese rug. In the sewing room, she had her electric sewing machine, which she had brought from America, and her American iron. She also had an American electric waffle iron. To use these appliances, she had a transformer, since Indian electric outlets did not accommodate the American plugs.

Lila often entertained visiting dignitaries for tea in her living quarters. On such occasions, she would have a fire in the fireplace, and serve Darjeeling tea, accompanied by waffles. The waffles were sometimes flavored with cheese or chocolate, but even ordinary waffles were an unfamiliar treat for anyone in India.

Lila used her sewing machine to make many of her own clothes and all of Mildred's clothes, except for school uniforms. Even after they returned to America, and when Mildred went away to college and then married, Lila continued to make clothes for her.

Lila's position as principal of the school was a very responsible position with a good deal of authority, and Lila very much enjoyed it. She lacked self-confidence but she loved the feeling of power. She liked being able to do things to make the school and its pupils grow and develop. She was quite popular; she had a position of respect and responsibility, and she felt that she did her work well; the teachers, pupils, and parents all cooperated and the future looked bright.

Then, in January 1934, the earthquake struck and everything changed.

"It Shall Be Rebuilt!"

Under the guidance and leadership of Mt. Hermon School Principal, Mrs. Lila Enberg, the school successfully completed the task of restoring a major portion of the main building of the school which was destroyed during the devastating earthquake of January 15, 1934.

Seven months to the day after the earthquake, on August 15th, the new Assembly Hall was re-dedicated. To quote from the dedicatory speech: "We need not mourn for the greater glory of the former building that was shattered by the earthquake. Instead we all rejoice that the latter glory is greater than the former. The Assembly Hall is now more firmly constructed, more strongly bound together than before. We would now, therefore, render hearts full of thanksgiving to your Gracious God who, of His infinite mercy and goodness, has made all this possible. It was He who gave the faith and courage that enabled us to say: "It shall be rebuilt!"

A tribute to Mrs. Lila Enberg (Principal 1931-34) by Hermonite Ujjawal Chettri.

Lila Gladys Kehm Enberg

SNAPS OF THE BUILDING
BETWEEN JANUARY 15th
AND AUGUST 15th

Earthquake

Lila and Mildred were in Calcutta on January 15, 1934 taking their usual afternoon rest when there was a major earthquake in India. In Calcutta it lasted for eight minutes. They followed the usual evacuation procedures, which meant going outdoors and leaning against the building. The theory was that if anything fell off the building, it was not likely to fall straight down.

The next day, the newspapers were full of news of the earthquake. There were places where the earth had opened up and people had fallen in. Buildings had collapsed, crushing people to death. People were sleeping in the parks because they feared more tremors. The damage to the Himalayas nearer the epicentre had been even more severe, although it had been felt for little more than a minute.

Lila received a telegram from Darjeeling, which read: "School extensively damaged. Come immediately." So she went, leaving Mildred with missionaries in Calcutta. School was scheduled to open the first week of March. Was the school going to be usable? What would she do? What could she do?

Queen's Hill School was built in the shape of a large U, with a quadrangle play-ground between the two wings. In one wing of the U there was the Assembly Hall, which was two stories high, and below it the Kindergarten. The other wing was three stories high with teachers' rooms on the top floor, dormitories on the second floor, and classrooms on the first floor. Both wings had been virtually destroyed and all of the interior partitions in the building had fallen like blocks. There were six weeks in which to get the place habitable before school was to have opened.

The school was already in debt and the managing committee said they could not afford to rebuild it because it was estimated that it would cost $35,000, a lot of money in India at any time and certainly in 1934. Lila insisted that the school had to be rebuilt and that they would get the money somehow. That was the beginning of a year that was a nightmare for Lila.

School opened only 10 days later than had been planned. It was exactly two months to the day since the earthquake, but all partitions were in. Work continued on the outside walls until August. Lila had made friends and had a good reputation among Indian government officials who thought highly of her ability and her efficiency. She used her connections to get a substantial amount of earthquake relief money to rebuild the school.

Meantime, what about the students who were going to attend the school? They had seen newspaper stories of damage in Darjeeling, so they wondered what would happen to them. Little by little, word spread among the students that Lila had been summoned and that the school was seriously damaged. Eventually, Lila was able to send letters to all the students' families describing the situation she had found and the plans as she saw them. She said that the school had been judged to be structurally sound and it was expected that it could be repaired sufficiently to open it but later than originally planned.

Some parents were worried about sending their children to Darjeeling, so they took a trip up to see for themselves. They returned to tell others how all the partition walls in the two upper storeys had been dismantled where the living quarters were located, and they were being rebuilt with reinforced concrete, so the building would be quite new and entirely safe. Until the building was done, the staff would live in cottages on the school grounds that were usually occupied by parents visiting their children during the school year.

When the students arrived on March 15th, there were piles of stones; mounds of broken plaster, sand, and other debris; a forest of scaffoldings; the broken ends of the school's two wings; hundreds of broken windows; bent and twisted steel girders. Many saw it as a picture of desolation and destruction. Inside, the building reeked of new paint, new plaster, and varnish. It was cold and damp. The floors were not their usual spotlessly clean. There was evidence of fresh cement everywhere. The building looked quite safe, but depressing.

Some students tried surreptitiously to make arrangements to go back to their homes. Others stood rooted to the spot, not knowing how they could adjust to what stood before them. Some went directly to Lila and asked her to let them go home at once. Lila gave each of them her time and attention and asked them to try for two weeks. If, at the end of two weeks, they still wanted to go home, she would make the arrangements. Apparently, it worked. No one went home.

School was organised and classes began immediately. They were held wherever space could be found: in the library, an unoccupied office, the sewing room, the art room, anywhere. Two dormitories had been destroyed, so sleeping arrangements were created by crowding beds into the usable dormitories. The next morning, the bell rang as usual for students to attend morning prayers – but the Assembly Hall had been destroyed. They were crowded into what had been the teacher's parlor, where benches had been placed. Everyone had a seat, but their knees were up to their chins and they looked like a tin of sardines.

That temporary arrangement proved to be unsatisfactory so after a couple of weeks, a divider curtain was hung in the children's dining room and the benches were put there for church and chapel services. The arrangements made the dining tables very close together causing problems for the bearers serving food, but it was manageable.

Classes began in earnest despite the pounding, coolies singing, chipping stones, etc. Teachers developed strong lungs in order to be heard above the din. Daily the work continued, and daily everyone watched the progress. When the children had arrived on March 15th, the Assembly Hall and Kindergarten wing had already been dismantled, the roof was off, the walls had been torn down to the foundation, and they were already rebuilding. They were still dismantling the classroom and dormitory wing. Day by day, the reconstruction progressed.

It was a tradition at the school to hold an annual Sale Day in May. To this event, parents and other guests were invited. There were speeches, entertainment, and concerts. In 1934, Sale Day was held on Saturday, May 26. The Assembly Hall, though still incomplete, was used for the first time, despite the fact that it resembled a huge barn with a tin roof.

Soon after Sale Day, the Kindergarten was able to move down to their old quarters. Gradually, the hammering, pounding, and scrapping diminished. The scaffolding was removed from the exterior and the finishing touches commenced. Now, in place of the sand and debris on the playgrounds, there were resurfaced tennis courts, new swings, and new playground equipment. The Assembly Hall had a big beautiful stage in place of the inadequate one of the past. The acoustics of the hall had been improved by the installation of a special ceiling and stage. The exterior, too, was more imposing, with the seat of the school at the top gable and the name "Mount Hermon School" across the end of the wind where it could be seen as one approached the school.

Today, this part of the main building, which was destroyed during the devastating 1934 earthquake, has the chapel (first floor) and the study hall (ground floor).

A word about the name of the school. When it opened in 1926, it had the same name as its predecessor, Queen's Hill School. It was built on land known as the Mount Hermon Estate. Over the years, as the number of male students increased, many of them expressed their disapproval of the name "Queen's Hill School". It sounded sissy. Gradually, the name "Mount Hermon School" had crept into general usage. So when the school was rebuilt, the name was officially changed to Mount Hermon and that name was emblazoned on the end of one wing.

During the 1934 school year, Lila arranged for the publication and distribution of a little booklet (3 1/2 × 4 3/4") entitled "What is an Educated Heart?" In January of that year, the *Reader's Digest* magazine had printed an article, "The Educated Heart" by Gilbett Burgess, from which the booklet was developed. The Preface, signed by Lila, said: "This booklet is presented to you in order to help you to lay solid foundations for Christian Characters. I hope it will help you to form good habits, attitudes and relationships in the life and work of the school, and in your later life. Remember, boys and girls, that the only human example we have of a Perfect Educated Heart is found in our Bible. I would urge each of you to take Jesus as your example and try to develop an Educated Heart." Each page of the booklet presented a set of rules and a familiar quotation related to one of the following characteristics on an Educated Heart: Reverence, Loyalty, Truth, Social Attitudes, Obedience, Punctuality, Stick-To-It-Iveness, Self-control, Initiative, Judgment, Thrift, and Good Sportsmanship. Throughout the year, Chapel services addressed the various rules and their application in students' lives.

Seven months to the day after the earthquake, on August 15th, the new Assembly Hall was re-dedicated. To quote from the dedicatory speech: "We need not mourn for the greater glory of the former building that was shattered by the earthquake. Instead we all rejoice that the latter glory is greater than the former. The Assembly Hall is now more firmly constructed, more strongly bound together than before. We would now, therefore, render hearts full of thanksgiving to your Gracious God who, of His infinite mercy and goodness, has made all this possible. It was He who gave the faith and courage that enabled us to say: "It shall be rebuilt!"

So the school was rebuilt; it was well regarded by the parents and by the Indian government; the children were happy. It seemed that what Lila had done had turned out well. But the building committee and the people in charge in the mission were displeased. Lila's success in raising the money and getting the school rebuilt, when they had thought it couldn't be done, did not please them. They wanted to get rid of her, so when her four-year contract expired, they refused to renew it. Lila had given what she considered nine of the best years of her life to the school and she had loved it. She believed she had done were work well, that she had many friends and few enemies, but the enemies had the real power.

School closed in December, so Lila and Mildred left India later that winter. On their way back to the United States, they stopped in England and spent three months with Alta, Cecil, and their two children, Lenore, born in 1930, and Alfred, born in 1933. Mildred attended school in London during the time they were there.

In May, 1935, Lila and Mildred sailed from Southampton to New York on Cunard's Berengaria.

Second marriage

It was customary, when Lila lived in India, for her to entertain guests from America who came to Darjeeling. Weather permitting, she would take them to Tiger Hill, the nearest site from which the tip of Mount Everest could be seen. She also generally exchanged Christmas cards with such visitors in the years that followed.

One such visitor was a professor of Philosophy and Religion from Syracuse University, Raymond Piper. Dr. Piper was traveling to various locations in the orient visiting the sites associated with the

Lila with her second husband Raymond Piper.

oriental religions. One of the missionaries in Calcutta brought him up to Darjeeling and asked Lila to take him to see the sunrise on Mt. Everest. This was not an unusual request. Lila had the use of the school car, and she would drive with her guests to Ghoom, a hill station where they would leave the car and start the climb.

She told the missionary to have Dr. Piper at the car at 2.30 a.m. He was there, and as they drove, Lila learned that he was a professor of Philosophy at Syracuse University and that he was primarily interested in religions of the people. The people of Darjeeling and the surrounding area were mostly Buddhists, but a very different form of Buddhism from that found in Japan, China, and the Eastern Orient, which he had already visited and studied.

At that time, the population of Mt. Hermon School included not only Americans, British, and other Europeans, but also Anglo-Indians, a few Chinese and Tibetans, many of mixed parentage, and a few Indian children.

Learning of his interest, Lila suggested that he might like to visit a lamasery. There were two Tibetan girls in the upper classes at Mt. Hermon and they had taken Lila to observe various rituals in a local lamasery. On one occasion during a Pujah, a major religious celebration, they had invited her to go with them to their lamasery when the Dalai Lama was to be in Ghoom to baptize their baby brother. On that occasion, Lila had met the Dalai Lama. The occasion was especially memorable to her because she was privileged to be the only white woman to have this rare opportunity.

The climb up to the place from which the peak of Mt. Everest can been seen is a long, arduous climb, but they reached their destination before the sun was up. They opened their lunch bags, ate, and exercised to keep warm, all the time watching the sky gradually brightening and finally the clouds clearing. It was a gloriously beautiful sunrise. First the sunbeams touched Kinchenjunga, then other peaks, and finally there was Mt. Everest. The mountain has been reported to be 29,002 feet high and, from Tiger Hill, people say they can see the top two feet.

Lila had made the trip to Tiger Hill to see the sunrise on Mt. Everest on many occasions. Others had sometimes gone up and the cloud cover hid the mountain, but when Lila went up, it never failed to make its glorious appearance. She always found it an awesome sight, which made her feel uplifted and yet very humble. Dr. Piper was exalted by the sight! Lila said it was one of the really perfect sunrises on Mt. Everest that she had seen, and she had taken groups to Tiger Hill in everyone one of the nine years she was in India.

An interesting side note: During Lila's last year in India, one of the students in the group going to Tiger Hill suffered an epileptic seizure when the group was still at the Ghoom station. Lila sent the group on ahead to Tiger Hill while she stayed at the station with the student. On that occasion, the group did not see Mt. Everest.

After seeing the sunrise, Lila took Dr. Piper to the Bazaar in Darjeeling where she helped him buy some very unusual and lovely curios. Little did she know that a few years later, they would be added to her own collection of Indian and Tibetan curios.

While she was teaching at Drew Seminary in 1935-36, one of her senior students said that she was going to study at Syracuse after graduating from Drew. Lila told her that if she ever took a course with Dr. Piper, she should tell him she had been a student of Lila's. Not only did she take a course with Dr. Piper, she took every course he taught and she was instrumental in bringing them back together.

On June 7, 1940, Lila married Dr. Raymond Frank Piper, professor of Philosophy at Syracuse University at Iowa Wesleyan chapel with Mildred as her maid-of-honour. Mildred had just graduated from Mount Pleasant High School. That marked the end of Lila's career as a Dean of Women and the end of her doctoral studies. She had completed her course work, passed the required language exams, and had dissertation topic, so she became what is known as an ABD – All But Dissertation. She moved to Syracuse, New York, and the next chapter of her life began.

Dr. Piper had been married before and divorced from his first wife. They had two adopted children, a girl named Laurine and a boy named Edward, who had both left home by the time Lila and Raymond were married. Mildred was away attending Carleton College in Minnesota, so Lila and Raymond rented a one-bedroom apartment at 606 University Avenue within walking distance of the University. The apartment also had an alcove where they put a studio couch, dresser, and desk for Mildred's use when she was home from college.

At first Lila was busy getting acquainted and involved in her new community. She and Raymond were both active in University United Methodist Church, the church in which Norman Vincent Peale had formerly been the pastor. Raymond often taught the adult section of Sunday School. Lila also taught Sunday School, and eventually became the Sunday School Superintendent and a member of the Church's Board.

On one early occasion at the church, the woman who was president of the Women's Christian Temperance Union (WCTU) approached Lila about becoming a member. While Lila did not smoke or drink, her response to the president was, "I believe in Temperance in ALL things, but that does not mean abstinence." Needless to say, she did not join.

Lila loved the stained glass windows of the church, which depicted stories from the Bible. She enjoyed taking visitors on tours of the church and explaining the windows to them. Later in her life, she recorded her narrative describing the windows and it was published and re-published by the church.

As a professor, Raymond was very conscientious about his research and teaching. He and a colleague of Syracuse had published a book, *The Fields and Methods of Knowledge*, and when he married Lila he had started gathering materials for another book to be called *Cosmic Art*. He always carried a pencil stub and some 3×5 cards in his jacket pocket. They were used cards that he got either from the University Library or from the Registrar's Office. When an idea struck him that might be of late use in a class or in his book, he would pull out the pencil and a card and make a note of it in Gregg shorthand. He was very skilled in shorthand.

Raymond had a nervous habit of clearing his throat frequently when he spoke before groups. This was true in his classes at the University and also in other settings, such as the Sunday School classes that he taught. But he was a popular professor, generally patient with his students and always interested in their progress.

Another of Raymond's characteristics was his deep interest in ESP and spiritualism. He would visit a spiritual medium from time to time, and sometimes give full credence to their comments and suggestions. In one instance, when there were two candidates for an open position in the Philosophy Department, he visited the medium and then pursued the candidate that she had recommended. He read all of Edgar Cayce's books and his thinking was influenced by them.

Lila and Mildred had not had to share each other from the time Royce died in 1925 until Mildred came home from her first year of college in 1941. By then, Lila and Raymond had worked out a pattern of living into which Mildred had to fit. There were stresses and strains and life was not always peaceful, but Mildred's part in the friction was not continuous. She returned to Carleton College in Minnesota for her sophomore year in 1941-41. By the fall of 1942, World War II was in full swing, travel was difficult, and she could receive free tuition at Syracuse University as Raymond's step-daughter, so she transferred. At Syracuse, she lived in one of the women's dormitories the first semester of her junior year, until the need for housing for other students forced her to move back to Lila and Raymond's apartment. In her senior year, she lived in the Alpha Chi Omega sorority house, a sorority she had joined during her junior year.

Jobs in Syracuse

Syracuse University, New York.

In March, 1941, Lila was appointed Secretary of Civilian Mobilization. At that time, the Volunteers Service Bureau of the Syracuse Council of Social Agencies began its program of expansion to build up the civilian protection organization. Later, the program became the Civil Defence Volunteer Office (SDVO) of the Syracuse War Council. In that job, Lila was responsible for over-seeing the recruitment, training, and assignment of civilian volunteers.

No clippings are available to describe Lila's work during the first nine months of her work in that job, but at a special luncheon meeting, on December 5, 1941, over 200 men and women gathered to hear a report on progress of the office in its first year. At the luncheon, a telegram was read from Mrs. Eleanor Roosevelt, wife of the President, in which she congratulated Syracuse office on being one of the first in the country and on having a long record of achievements. In Lila's report at the luncheon, she said that from a registration of 130 volunteers in the year before, the enrolment had jumped to 6,000. She reported that 2,000 of these had taken a first aid course with 44 new instructors for additional teaching already trained. In addition, 250 people had completed home nursing, with 30 teachers trained; 141 had completed the "Gray Ladies" course, 25 the nutrition course, and 60 were currently enrolled in the Nurses' Aid course.

Other courses being conducted under the auspices of the volunteer office included a recreation leaders' course, a motor corps and motor mechanics' course, a staff assistants' course, knitting, office work, and surgical dressing work. There were 1,500 wardens registered, 800 more were in training, and 3,000 were needed. There were 700 volunteer policemen, 325 in training, and 1,000 more needed.

For her job as Director of the CDVO, Lila had a military-type uniform, which she often wore when she made her frequent speeches throughout the country. Her topic on many occasions was "Women's Place in the War Effort." In one of her speeches, she said: "There is something for everyone to do to win the war. We must feel that the job we are doing is important and significant in the war effort. Sometimes it takes imagination to see where we fit into the total effort, but every man, woman and child can have a part. We must be articulate about what we are fighting for. It is the war of the people and we must make the peace."…..

As a result of Lila's experience with the day care program in Syracuse, she was hired by the State of New York to take charge of day care centres for the children of women in the work force throughout the State, from Montauk Point to Buffalo. Travel was extremely difficult in those days. Trains and buses were crowded and often without schedules because of military needs. Gas was rationed, so she couldn't drive her own car the length and breadth of the State. Her solution to this was interesting. She rented a room in Albany, where she had her office, returning home only on weekends. Mildred, who had transferred to Syracuse University by that time, kept house for Raymond. With all the time Lila had to wait for trains and buses, she resumed one of her youthful pursuits, crocheting. She crocheted over 100 very attractive and very popular corde purses during the war for friends, for family, and for sale.

During one of her winters in Albany, Lila slipped on the ice and broker her ankle. When it had been set, she resumed her work and travel. Since she used public transportation anyway, her inability to drive with cast failed to limit her productivity. By the time the war was over, she was Director of the Child Care Division of the New York State Youth Commission.

After the war, Lila returned to Syracuse where she continued working. In the spring of 1948, she was appointed Director of the Onondaga Council of Campfire Girls, Inc. which served Syracuse and Onondaga Country. Lila was very skilful at many crafts and she applied those skills in her work with the Campfire groups.

When Lila started working with Campfire Girls, their total membership in the county was 500 girls and 20 active leaders. By March of 1952, when she resigned, there were 1800 girls and 150 active leaders. One of the major improvements made under her leadership was in the camping facilities, which were enlarged to accommodate more than twice as many campers as before, with nine new cabins, new docks, and better sports and game facilities. Another major improvement was a much sounder financial position….

In early 1951, Lila and Raymond bought a home at 1310 Comstock Avenue, in Syracuse. It was the first time Lila had owned a home and she loved it. It had basement, where she did the wash and stored her canned goods and frozen foods. It even had a fruit cellar under the garage which she filled with her products. She also produced dozens of crafts in her basement.

The ground floor of the house had a living room, dining area, kitchen, two bedrooms, one bathroom, and an attached garage. The upper floor had a study and an attic. Raymond had his study on the upper floor where he worked on his *Cosmic Art*.

When Lila and Raymond moved to their new home, Mildred (then known as Mickey) and her husband, Jim Leonard, moved into the apartment at 606 University Avenue. They had been married in 1947, and their marriage broke up in 1951. Mickey stayed in the apartment and another graduate student, Adaleen Burnett, moved in with her to share expenses.

In August, 1952, Lila became Executive Director of Syracuse Girls Club. When Lila joined the staff, the club was meeting at the Vocational High School. Under her leadership, many changes took place and the program was expanded. By the time she resigned in August 1957, the club was meeting five days a week in its own building, to which a recreation room had been added through the generosity of one of the city's women's service groups. The Club's membership was over 300, a Mothers Club had been formed, and Day Camps had been developed to meet a need during the summer months.

In 1953, Mildred (by then known as Kitty) was married to Raymond A. Katzell, an industrial psychologist. They lived in an apartment in Jackson Heights, Queens, New York. Kitty, who had earned an M.A. in Counselling Psychology at Syracuse, had a job at Macy's as Supervisor of Employee Testing. From 1954 to 1973, she worked for the National League Nursing in their Division of Measurement and Evaluation. While working there, she completed a Ph.D. in Psychological Measurement and Evaluation at Columbia University in 1967. In 1973 she became vice-president of the Professional Examination Service, another testing company in New York. Later that year, and until her retirement in 1981, she was on the staff of the Professional Examinations Division of The Psychological Corporation.

It might be noted that Lila adapted to Mildred's various name changes. When Mildred became "Mickey" in high school, and later when Ray nick-named her "Kitty", Lila accepted each of the new names and used them in correspondence and in personal conversations.

At that time of their marriage, Kitty's husband, Ray, was Vice-President of Richardson, Bellows, Hendry & Co., an industrial psychological consulting organization. From 1957 until his retirement as a professor emeritus in 1984, he was a Professor of Psychology at New York University, during nine years of which he served as Head of the Psychology Department. In 1956, he and Kitty bought a home in Glen Cove, New York, where they lived until 1989 when they moved to a continuing care retirement community, Medford Leas, in Medford, New Jersey. From 1965 to 1981, they also had an apartment in Greenwich Village from which Ray could walk to his office at the University, and

Kitty could get the subway at the corner of their block to reach her office. Ray died in 2003....

Throughout Lila and Raymond's married life, Raymond continued working on his book, *Cosmic Art*. His objective at first was to determine if there were living artists who were objectifying their philosophical, religious, and later, psychic insights in aesthetic forms. He corresponded with over 2,000 artists from 64 countries and gathered over 2,500 prints of their work, supported artists' statements, personal histories, and inspirational writings....

Ingo Swan, who assisted with the publication of *Cosmic Art*, reported that all of the 850 artists "whose works form the nexus of (Raymond's) inquiry" reported at length on their special experiences which, as the years proceeded, gave rise to their particular visions.

Lila and Raymond's home was decorated with some of the cosmic paintings and he talked about this interest of his at every opportunity. In preparation for *Cosmic Art* and to generate interest in the subject, he first wrote and published a smaller volume, *The Hungry Eye*. While it was never a best-seller, in a sense it paved the way for *Cosmic Art*. At this writing, in 2006, both books are listed with Amazon.com.

Raymond died on December 31, 1962. He and Lila had spent a pleasant Christmas holiday with Mildred and her husband in Glen Cove, New York. On December 31, Lila was in the kitchen and Raymond was lying on the couch in the living room when she thought she heard him say something to her. He often spoke from the living room when she was in the kitchen and she often asked him not to do that because she couldn't always hear what he was saying. When she went into the living room to ask what he had said, she discovered that he had died. He apparently had suffered a massive stroke. The mailman arrived at that precise moment and stayed with Lila despite her protestations that he should be about his duties.

Lila and Raymond had both arranged that their bodies should be given to the Syracuse University medical school, so there were no funeral arrangements to be made. Kitty came and stayed with Lila for a few days to help her with some of the many details to be handled at such a time.

In 1968, Lila started losing weight. She was having trouble with here digestion. Her physician put her in Maalox, but it didn't seem to solve the problem. One Sunday in church one of her friends, a physician, commented on her weight loss. She told him what had been going on and he asked her to come and see him.

He discovered that she had intestinal cancer. She had successful surgery, and returned to her usual busy life in her own home, but never regained the weight she had lost. Kitty came from New York and stayed with her for a time during her hospitalization and her convalescence.

Lila had become very well known in Syracuse and Onondaga County and was named one of the eleven "Women of Achievement" by the Syracuse *Post-Standard* newspaper in 1963, when she was recognized for her contribution to international friendship. Beginning in 1966, she was listed in *Who's Who of American Women*. She was a member of Pi Lambda

Theta, women's education honorary society. Among her many local activities, Lila was a member of the Syracuse Business and Professional Women's Club, Zonta, the National League of American Pen Women, Friends of Reading, International Platform Association, and AARP, serving as president of each at some time. She was the only woman member of the Monarch Club, a local men's service club, and she served as president of the Women's Society for Christian Service of the University United Methodist Church.

After Raymond's death at the end of 1962, Lila determined to pursue the completion of *Cosmic Art*. He had devoted many hours over many years to the book and she felt that it needed to be finished. With the cooperation and assistance of a friend, Ingo Swan, the book was finally published by Hawthorn Books in 1975. It contains 152 pages, with 18 color plates and 94 black and white illustrations. In its initial printing, it sold for $16.50.

The final chapter

In the 1970s, Lila completed Raymond's *Cosmic Art* book and continued to teach classes in Graphoanalysis, but her friends and neighbours began to notice changes in her behavior. She sometimes failed to keep appointment; she telephoned people at ungodly hours in the middle of the night; she drove at 25 mph in the left lane on the super high-way. After a time, one of her neighbors wrote and told Mildred something was wrong. Mildred was still working full time and had not been seeing Lila often enough to realize how much she had changed.

When Mildred visited, she found that Lila was not eating properly, so she ordered Meals-on-Wheels to be delivered. A week later, when she phoned Lila to find out how it was going, Lila reported that she had cancelled the delivery. Mildred scolded her and told her she needed to eat those meals, but Lila explained that they regularly served peas and she didn't like peas.

Next, Mildred found that Lila had designated someone in her church to have Power-of-Attorney for her. She had also sold some of the treasures she had brought back from India. Members of her first husband's family came to visit one time, having phoned the day before so say they would be there. When they arrived, Lila was surprised to see them. Also, Lila's appearance had changed so much that they would not have recognized her but for her smile.

Lila was aware that memory was failing. Every day, she forced herself to do the crossroad puzzle in the daily paper. She would sit on the couch in her living room with dictionary beside her and work for as long as it took to do each puzzle. On occasion, when she was with Mildred, she would say, "Oh, how I miss my mind."

In 1977, Lila moved from her beloved house to an apartment at 753 James Street in Syracuse. Friends helped her move and settle, and her designated power-of-attorney handles the sale of her house. When Mildred visited her in the apartment, she found four cans of copper polish under Lila's kitchen sink. Lila had a large Tibetan copper tea kettle which she kept polished so she must have thought she needed copper polish. Lila had a sofa bed for Mildred to sleep on which she visited. Mildred would wake in the night to find Lila standing over her not knowing who was sleeping on the sofa bed. Lila would order items from catalogs and, when they came, she would leave the packages outside her door to be returned, not knowing that she had ordered them. A dear friend at the church kept tabs on Lila, visiting almost daily. One time she wrote a note with lipstick on Lila's mirror, saying "Call Nancy." When Nancy returned the next time she found that Lila had written lipstick, under the earlier message, "Who's Nancy?"

By this time, it was obvious that Lila needed closer supervision and that friend, Nancy, facilitated her move to a temporary facility until Mildred could make other arrangements. There was a fine nursing home in Glen Cove, where Mildred and her husband lived, and they were able to arrange for Lila to move there during 1978. She had a private room in the nursing home with a few pieces of her own furnishings, as well as pictures and books of her choosing. Lila accepted the arrangement quite graciously, perhaps because she knew she would be able to see Mildred at least once a week, whereas in Syracuse, she saw her infrequently.

Mildred and her husband tried to arrange stimulating activities to share with Lila on the weekends when they were in Glen Cove. Mildred would take Lila to the supermarket when she did her shopping. They would take Lila out for dinner and to their home. Mildred took care of Lila's laundry, which provided another topic for conversation.

The nursing home also provided some of the typical activities for the residents, Bingo, group singing, entertainers, and the like. But Lila missed some of the things that had been part of her life when she had lived alone. She had worked in a bank after college and she had always had a bank account. There was a bank across the street from the nursing home and one day she crossed the street and went in to open an account. Another time, she wandered away from the nursing home and was brought back by the local police who had found her down town in Glen Cove. The local physician who attended to Lila eventually told Mildred that the diagnosis was Alzheimer's. It was the first she had heard the term.

At this time, Mildred and her husband were still working in New York, where they had an apartment that they occupied during the week, returning to Glen Cove on weekends. They also had a pet cat, Snowflake, who was always kept indoors or on a leash, so she would be there when it was time to go to their other abode. One Sunday afternoon, when Lila was visiting at their home, she opened the back door and let Snowflake go out in the yard. The cat wandered about until Mildred realized what had happened. When she went out to bring the cat back, Snowflake went up the nearest tree. Eventually, of course, she was brought down, but that episode showed Mildred that Lila needed constant supervision.

After Lila died, Mildred found a packet of notes Lila had written, seemingly to members of her family. The noted had been written in ink on 4x6" pieces of paper.

The handwriting was tiny and quite unlike her former writing. In her Graphoanalysis talks, she had often said that very small handwriting indicated deep concentration. The second notes reproduced below was the date August 31, 1978 on it, and Lila comments that the next week she would become an octogenarian. Her birthday was October 9, and she turned 80 in 1976. The fourth note starts with the comment, "Today I am 90 years old"; she died in 1986 at the age of 89. The sixth note starts thus: "Sunday, I think And I think it is Saturday the 8th and my birthday" but her birthday was the 9th of October. ....

It is worth noting that she refers in some of the notes to her father, who was long since died, and in one she says "my sister is a missionary," apparently referring to Alta who was teaching in India in the 1920s. She also refers more than once to the WFMS, the Women's Foreign Missionary Society, which had sponsored her work in India 50 years earlier. On the other hand, she speaks of Kitty, whom she had only called by that name in the more recent past.

On one occasion, one of Lila's former students came to visit her. The women's father had been a bishop in India. Lila apparently recognized her and, although she didn't call the visitor by name, she did say something about the "bishop." But, as her memory worsened, Lila came to think that Mildred was her baby sister, Anna, who had died in 1918. On the other hand, one of the aides at the nursing home used to sing Negro spirituals to Lila when she was bathing her, and Lila would sing along, remembering all the words. Memory is a strange and wonderful thing.

Physicians will tell you that no one dies "of" Alzheimer's; they die "with" Alzheimer's. At Mildred's request, Lila's physician had recorded "DNR" on her records at the nursing home so she would not be resuscitated if she were to suffer cardiac arrest. In March 1986, Mildred and her husband went on a Caribbean cruise and, when they returned, found that Lila had developed pneumonia. She died peacefully on March 26, 1986, six and half months short of her 90th birthday. Her body was donated, in accordance with her instructions, for medical education. When she was moved from Syracuse to the New York area, arrangements were made for her body to go to the Medical School of New York University.

On April 6, 1986, a memorial service was conducted at the University United Methodist Church in Syracuse, again in accordance with her instructions. The Pastor and Assistant Pastor spoke in the course of the service, those assembled sang "All Hail the Power of Jesus' Name" and "Abide With Me." The scriptures were Psalm 23 ("The Lord is my Shepherd"), Psalm 121 (I will lift my eyes unto the hills); Ecclesiastes 3 (To everything there is a season); and selections from John 1 and 14, Romans 8, and Revelations 21. A soloist sang "How Great Thou Art" and "Crossing the Bar." The congregation recited the Lord's Prayer.

24 William Wayne Jones
Vice-Principal, 1973-1977

A Young Missionary From America Lands In Darjeeling And Falls In Love With MH

"During the winter of 1951, Mr. Dewey had seriously wondered if the School could be reopened for the 1952 session."

Rev. W.W. Jones, who was the school's Vice-Principal (1973-1977), recalls his early days in Mount Hermon and says, "Mount Hermon has given me more than it ever gave any other person on earth in all its 83 glorious years."

Dear Hermonites,

I think many of you will remember the six years during the 1970s when Mr. and Mrs. Jones were working at the school; but there aren't many people who will remember the 1950s. So I will let others tell the stories of our recent days, and give you a few "yarns" from the '50s.

I signed up for service in India with the Board of Missions of the Methodist Church during my last year of College; and I was told by the Indian Secretary of the Board, James Mathews (now Bishop of the United Methodist Church in Washington D.C.) that I would be assigned to Woodstock School in the Himalayas. I wasn't sure what 'Himalayas' were, but I started reading about Woodstock School and these and the mountains.

In May, 1951 just when I was about to leave College and begin three months of training for foreign mission work, Mr. Mathews told me that there really wasn't much point in planning to work in India; because the Government there had stopped giving visas to missionaries. He wondered if I would go to Africa for my mission service. I replied that, if I would not go to India as I had planned and dreamt, then I would have to think all over again about mission service. I certainly couldn't reconcile myself easily to service anywhere else. Seeing my disappointment, Mr. Mathews said he would try to get a visa for me from India, but obviously he couldn't assure me that the Government would grant it.

Well, the Government did. They allowed very few people to go to India as missionaries that year, the fewest of any year right up to the '70s, I've been told. But they let me into India, and I have always thanked God as well as the Mission Board and the Indian Government for that. (Other people at various times in my career must have thought that was one mistake the Indian Government made; but I have never had anything but considerate treatment from them – though their speed at times did help me immensely to cultivate the great values of forbearance and patience, virtues in which I have never naturally excelled.)

While I was training in Hartford, Connecticut in the summer of 1951, I got further news from Mr. Mathews that I wouldn't be going to Woodstock School, because there was an urgent need for help at Mount Hermon School in Darjeeling. Mr. Dewey was the Principal, and he was barely able to keep the school open. Staff were hard to get, the student enrolment was low (less than 150 in the whole school) and Mr. Dewey had heavy responsibilities for mission work in Bengal as well as in the school. I was reassigned to Mount Hermon, and set off at the end of August from New York. I missed the ship that was supposed to take me: the Queen Mary. I caught my next ship, the P&O Ship Himalaya, on time and had a wonderful trip to Bombay.

The harbour was so beautiful when we steamed in at night that tears filled my eyes, (yes, even as a very young man I often "choked up"). I was met on shipboard and taken care of for two days in Bombay, by our mission staff in Bombay; and then they put me on a train for Lucknow. In Lucknow I spent several wonderful days with Bishop Rockey, who gave me a feeling for the great land of India and some advice also. He told me to be careful of the lovely young women I would find at Mount Hermon! I won't comment on how well I followed that advice. The Bishop put me on the train for Katihar, where I would change trains for Siliguri. At Katihar, I was surprised to find a kind Mennonite Missionary waiting for me – Amos Dick, who not only escorted me to Darjeeling but also opened his home and the mysteries of the Hindi language to me. (The Dicks lived in Trees (MH campus at Fernhill), upstairs).

My first home at Mount Hermon was Snow View. I had thought I would live in a mud hut in India, but here was a lovely cottage for me. (It was in that cottage that I had my first experience of healing through prayer.) I thought that Mr. Dewey would give me several days to settle, to observe the work and the people in the school, and then give me something to do. I was wrong! He told me, as he left me on that first afternoon to unpack my bags in Snow View, "I have a class for you to take over tomorrow; the third class teacher is ill." I stammered that I had never had any teaching training or teaching experience, and everything looked very different from what I was used to in the U.S.A. He just asked me, "Have you had any good teachers?" I assured him I had. He then grunted, "Well, just do what they did." That is the sum total teacher training; and now those of you who wondered why I wasn't a better teacher can wonder how I ever managed to teach anything at all. But teach I did: English, Latin, British Imperial History (which was an entirely new field for me) for S.C. and pre-S.C. classes, and music (orchestra, choir and violin) throughout the school.

I met Mr. and Mrs. Johnston who were in the Language School in those days (still unmarried at that time, and was she giving him confused signals!!). Kancha Rai was in charge of maintenance, and I worked a lot with him during the winters. I was also a general handyman for fixing fuses, water taps etc...during the school term. In fact, I got a personal introduction to a new teacher in 1954, Beulah Kessop, by being called to her room to fix an electrical fuse. She discreetly left the room when I arrived to do the work; but I had other chances to do little things for and with her. Since – as you know – Mount Hermon has always been a friendly school.

Teachers came and went pretty rapidly in 1952 and 1953. By 1954 when Mr. Stewart came to take over as Principal, I was the "senior teacher", in terms of seniority, though I was at 24 years of age and too young and untrained to be designated senior master. Fortunately, Mr. Stewart himself was an expert teacher, and a versatile school head who began immediately by the strength of his mind and character to pull up the school.

During the winter of 1951, Mr. Dewey had seriously wondered if the School could be reopened for the 1952 session. He decided we could reopen if 100 paying borders could be enrolled. We did open in 1952 with about 110. I still can't imagine how we did the things we did, with such a small student body. He fielded teams in Senior, Junior divisions against St. Joseph's and St. Paul's, in cricket, football and hockey. (Actually, we were more afraid of St. Joseph's competition for the attention of our senior girls than we were afraid of them on the sports field) We fielded a girl's hockey team against the Convent (Loreto Convent) and defeated them once when Julie Dunne was captain (having transferred from Dow Hill to M.H.S.). I had to learn hockey, so I could coach the junior boys, who lost only to St. Joseph's in 1954, as I recall.

The senior teams did well too, with chaps like Brang Seng, Mawu Naga, and Ram Bahadur making M.H.S. a real football power. We came to the finals one year, and I made problems for the District Sports Association by preparing the whole school for American-style cheering, complete with drums, horns, tin cans and lids to be beaten, and organised cheers completely distracting the opponents. Unfortunately, this *hulla* also distracted the officials, who had to stop play until I would agree to stop the din.

Of course, I remember well the period when I decided to neglect Bishop Rockey's advice that I would be equally pleasant and distant with all the Mount Hermon staff women. The geography teacher Miss Kessop, obviously needed special attention from me. I'll never forget that day in the mountains when God told me so clearly, as I trekked along all alone at about 13,000 feet on my way back to School from Dzongri, that I should go ahead with a commitment to that young woman. On my return I let her know what was on my mind by warning her that she should get used to the way I stank when I came back from the mountains!

When I left school at the end of 1954, I was sure I would return. I wasn't sure how or when but the certainty of coming back struck me on the curve at Batasia Loop. I remember riding out the School driveway and up the hill on a truck with my luggage, headed for the U.S.A. with very mixed emotions. But before catching the ship in Bombay I would have to stop in U.P. at the family home of Miss Kessop and get them to agree that she should marry me. I did; and they did; and she did. You may say I'm biased, but I honestly believe Mount Hermon has given me more than it ever gave any other person on earth in all its 83 glorious years.

(Hermonite 1978, annual school magazine.)

WILLIAM WAYNE JONES

He will be long remembered at Mt. Hermon School

James Sinclair

I apologise for the brief announcement on the News Update page of the sad death of Bill Jones (William Wayne Jones). I was prompted by Mrs. Murray (Patricia Murray - wife of Headmaster, Graeme Murray), to say a bit more about Bill Jones and the contribution he made towards Mount Hermon School during his three-year term there. In truth, I did not know Mr. Jones very well, as I was a day-scholar for a few brief months of his final year, and the only time I had any contact with him was during PE.

So I had to look up extracts from the Blue & Gold Yearbook for 1954 which had been very kindly sent to me by Headmaster David Stewart, and I found out a bit more about him from the School Notes for 1954 - the year of Mr. Jones' leaving - in which the Headmaster had paid him a tribute for all the work he had put in during his years at MHS. So, I have added that bit in the News Update page for 2014, and also corrected some errors in the initial announcement. I have also added in a piece he had written about his memories of Mount Hermon under the tab Memories of 1954. Unfortunately, it is incomplete as I did not have the second page of what he had written. My most vivid memory of Bill Jones was what a wonderful violin player he was, when he performed at one of our concerts.

I have also added a page "Growing up in India" which Kitty Katzell (Mildred Engberg - daughter of Headmistress Lila Engberg) had sent me recently of her memories of growing up and schooling in India, which I am sure will revive memories of the school back in the 1940s.

It is with sadness that I have to announce the death of Bill Jones (William Wayne Jones), who died on 15th June (2014) at home after a long illness. He leaves behind his widow (Beulah Kessop Jones), sons Arun and Kenny and daughters Sharon and Nalinee. His son Kenny said his end was peaceful and the family are thankful that he is finally at rest.

Mr. and Mrs. Murray with Mr. Bill Jones (centre) and the Hermonites in the US.

In the Headmaster's Notes published in the Blue and Gold 1954 Yearbook, Rev. David Stewart paid this tribute to Mr. Jones on his leaving MHS.

"It is a very sorrowful farewell we say to Mr. Jones. Mr. Jones has served three years on the staff, and has contributed a tremendous amount to the school. He has always been not only capable and efficient, but continually cheerful, encouraging, enthusiastic, and helpful. He has not only taught English, History, Latin, and Violin, he has also conducted choir and orchestra, coached games, has been Scout Captain and Warden of Fern Hill. He has earned the affection of staff and students alike, and will be long remembered at Mount Hermon. His three-year term is, however, ended, and we must say farewell. Mr. Jones goes to Yale Divinity School, where he will complete his theological studies. If in a few years' time he again returns to India, there are many of us who hope we might again see him in Mount Hermon School."

Mr. Jones was back in Mt. Hermon in mid-1970s and served the school as its Vice-Principal.

(James Sinclair is Treasurer of Old Mount Hermon Students' Association (UK)).

A memorable Choir Practice
Thangi Chhangte (Rema)

For the class of SC74 Arun was 'Jones' and his father was 'Talu'. This distinction was kept for identification purposes and I don't think anything derogatory was ever implied.

One of my lasting memories of Talu Jones was at Senior Choir practice. On this particular day in question Talu was in charge of the choir practice as Mrs. M was away. It was a warm day and he was wearing a white short-sleeved shirt. As soon as he raised his arms to conduct the choir, it revealed the tear in his underarm (I will leave the visuals to your imaginations). This provoked giggles from the teenagers (that we were then) and no amount of 'dirty looks' could scare us into keeping a straight face. To make things worse, the madder Talu got, the redder his 'talu' became until we were all a hopeless mess. The practice hour (if you could call it that) ended finally and Talu stomped off muttering dire threats. I'm sure he'd have given us all house marks right there and then.

The following week, it was choir practice time again and we all sat sheepishly waiting for Talu (and imagining the horrors he might visit upon us). As he strode into the very quiet practice room, he raised his arms and said, "See, no holes!" I don't think any of us dared laugh - if we did, it was very polite.

For me this is a perfect illustration of who Mr. Jones was - a man who could laugh at himself, put everyone else at ease with his broad smile and "Ya'll." He introduced us to America by bringing kids our age. Square dancing - I don't think people in India know what that is.

For our class he was special as he made a big deal of inviting the whole class to his son Arun's birthday party - at his house, no less. That is how we got to know the man who was extremely proud of his family and was not afraid to say so.

Sunrise, sunset, swiftly fly the years....

Jones inspired me to write: Jigme

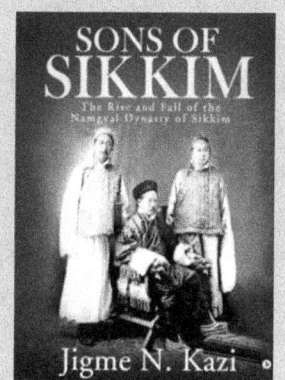

I think if was in 1978, my third year as a teacher in MH, when Mr. Jones, reacting to Sikkim Crown Prince Tenzing's death in a car accident in Gangtok on March 11, 1978, said psychologically those who drive fast have a 'death wish'. Prince Tenzing loved to drive fast.

It was also Mr. Jones who, perhaps noticing my interest on Sikkim, said I should write something about L.D. Kazi, Sikkim's first Chief Minister. The country seller, I thought!!! But I wrote a poem on Sikkim's political situation of that period. This was also in 1978. It was in the same year that I got down to doing some research on Sikkim history. My book on Sikkim history is almost complete. I, therefore, owe something to Mr. Jones for nudging me into the literary career. Love him, miss him. May his soul rest in everlasting peace.

(My two books: Sikkim history and MH tribute, are being published simultaneously in 2020.)

Hail Mount Hermon! A Tribute

OBITUARIES/Rev. William Wayne Jones, June 22, 2014

His love for music led him to many directions

DURHAM — Rev. William ("Bill") Wayne Jones was born on November 3, 1929 in Sharon, Pennsylvania, the elder child of Anthony Wayne Jones and Margaret Aebi Jones. His brother, Donald Alan Jones, was born in 1934. Bill grew up in Franklin, PA, attending Franklin High School and excelling in scouting, music, oratory, debating, and academics. In 1947 he received a Pennsylvania State Senatorial Scholarship to study at the University of Pennsylvania, from where he was graduated with a B.A. with Honors in History. He was the only non-Music major to play in the University String Quartet.

In 1951 Bill went to India as a missionary. There he met Beulah Kessop, and they were married in 1956. Bill received his Master of Divinity degree, and Beulah her Master in Religious Education degree, from Yale Divinity School in 1958. Their first child, Arun Wayne, was born that year, and they returned to India the next year to begin their ministry as Methodist missionaries, from which they retired in 1998. While they were in India, they had three more children: a daughter, Sharon Anjali; a son, Kenneth Lalit; and a daughter, Nalini Lillian. One other daughter was stillborn in New Haven, Connecticut.

Bill served in a number of capacities in several locations in North India: as school teacher, district missionary, pastor, school administrator, church leadership trainer and historian, in the states of Bihar, Uttar Pradesh, Uttarakhand and West Bengal. His expertise in and love for music led him to direct choirs in all of the churches and schools that he served, as well as occasional performances with the symphony orchestras of Calcutta, Delhi, and the University of North Carolina at Chapel Hill. He was an accomplished violinist.

In 1998 Bill and Beulah moved into retirement in Durham, North Carolina, and to faithful, active membership at Trinity United Methodist Church.

Bill was predeceased by his parents, Anthony Wayne Jones and Margaret Aebi Jones; a brother, Donald Alan Jones; and a grandchild, Roshni Antoinette Joseph. Surviving are his wife, Beulah Kessop Jones of Durham; two daughters, Sharon Anjali Jones of Durham and Nalini Lillian Joseph and husband, Jude A.B. Joseph of Salisbury; two sons, Rev. Dr. Arun Wayne Jones and wife, Yolanda R. Jones of Atlanta, GA, and Kenneth Lalit Jones and wife, Sunita Jones of Durham; a friend, James D. Hamerlee and wife, Elizabeth S. Hammerlee of Meadville, PA; and five grandchildren, Suresh Paolo Jones, Amihan Shireen Jones, Christopher Ashwin Jones, Daniel Avinash Jones and Rohan Anthony Joseph.

A memorial service will be held on Saturday, June 28th at 1:00 P.M. in Trinity United Methodist Church officiated by Rev. Taylor Mills.

The family is being assisted by Clements Funeral Service, Inc., in Durham, N.C. Online condolences may be made at www.clementsfuneralservice.com.

25 Cynthia Hawke
1962-1978

A Wonderful Time For Hawke In Sikkim

Gangtok, Nov 9: Miss Cynthia Hawke (75), former teacher of Mount Hermon School, Darjeeling, now living in retirement in Australia, had a "wonderful" time in the State last week.

Miss Hawke speaking at North Sikkim Academy, Mangan, north Sikkim, November 2010. The school then belonged to 1971 batch Hermonite Namgyal Wangdi's family.

After the reunion dinner, hosted by Sikkim Hermonites Association (SHA) on October 31, on the day of her arrival from Kalimpong, Hawke visited North Sikkim after a day's sight-seeing in the capital.

On November 2, students of North Sikkim Academy (NSA) in Mangan, North Sikkim headquarters, gave her a grand reception in traditional Nepalese attire. During a cultural function at the Academy, depicting the rich ethnic traditions in the State, the Principal, Namgyal P. Kazi, while welcoming Hawke and her friend Jill, said Hermonites in the State have contributed a great deal to the State.

Miss Hawke with Namgyal Wangdi in Mangan, North Sikkim.

During the two-day North Sikkim tour, Hawke was accompanied by Hermonite Namgyal Wangdi and Jigme N. Kazi. She stayed at Hermonite Pintso Chopel's newly-opened Apple Orchard resort in Lachen. She also visited Kazi's ancestral home in Lachen for a cup of tea.

Miss Hawke and friend Jill at the kitchen of Jigme N. Kazi's ancestral home, Lachen, North Sikkim.

The visits to Lachen and Lachung's Yumthang valley was "most wonderful", said Hawke after the hectic-non-stop trip.

Hawke, who taught English literature in Mt. Hermon for 15 years (1962-1978), left for Darjeeling last Friday accompanied by Hermonite Rajendra Lakhotia. She is presently in Thimphu, capital of the Druk Kingdom, where she will stay with Hermonite Sonam Lhendup (Taki), President of Bhutan Hermonites Association.

Miss Hawke with Udai Sharma in Gangtok.

SIKKIM HERMONITES ASSOCIATION

Miss C. Hawke's Visit: Tentative Schedule

27th October, 2010 - Wednesday
Arrival Bagdogra. Lakhotias will receive at airport. Hermonites get-together dinner at Lakhotia residence (Siliguri).

28th October - Thursday
Visit to tea garden around Siliguri with Shiv Saria & Co.
Will stay overnight at tea garden with Shiv Saria as host.

29th October - Friday
Departure for Kalimpong. Transportation by Lakhotias (Rajendra & Kavita) and escorted by Lakhotias. Kalimpong host will be Binod Yonzone at Cloud 9.

30th October - Saturday
Visiting Mr. Rongong and Dr. Graham's Homes.
Seeing Hermonites. Dinner at Cloud 9 with Hermonites.
Kalimpong Coordinators: Binod Yonzone & Amod Yonzone

31st October - Sunday
Travel from Kalimpong to Gangtok with Lakhotias. Stay at Hotel Tashi Delek, Gangtok. Hermonites get-together dinner at Hotel Tashi Delek.

1st November - Monday
Gangtok local sightseeing around Gangtok (Tibetology, monasteries, handicraft centre – N. K. Pradhan, Tempo Bhutia & Co.)
Sikkim Coordinators: Karma Bhutia, Uttam Pradhan, Punam Agarwal & Udai P. Sharma

2nd November – Tuesday
Visit to North Sikkim (Mangan, Lachen & Lachung) – Namgyal Wangdi, Jigme N. Kazi, Phintso Chopel & Co.

3rd November - Wednesday
North Sikkim visit continued.

4th November - Thursday
Return to Gangtok from North Sikkim. Stay at Hotel Tashi Delek. Farewell by Sikkim Hermonites.

5th November – Friday

Leave Gangtok for Darjeeling. (Possibly via Jorethang as a Hermonite Vikas Gajmer of Barnesberg Tea Estate has offered to provide a night stay at the Garden)

Kisan Memani has offered to host a tea at Jorethang if Hermonites want to get together at this time in Jorethang etc. (Rudramani Gurung, Tsering Bhutia and Jayang Bhutia could join us there if they miss Gangtok reunion)

Stay planned in Darjeeling from 5th or 6th till 8th November.

Stay confirmed at Villa Everest — Owned by Surendra Rongong who used to teach at MHS.

MH Principal George Fernandez has invited Ms. Hawke (and any other Hermonites) for lunch on Saturday the 6th Nov at MHS.

Pratap Rai wants a visit to his School and Chachans also want to host a lunch.

Mr. Fernandez has offered to host Miss Hawke at the school for at least one day and night if she wants.

Probable Darjeeling Programme:

Visits: Darjeeling Zoo, Mountaineering Institute, Tibetan Centre and MHS. Shopping. Possibly Tiger Hill and definitely Carol service at MH, even if it is a practice session.

Hermonites get-together at Anup Chachan's Apsara Hotel.

Miss Hawkes special diet: gluten-free, i.e. no cereals except for rice and sweet corn, which means no chapatis, shingharas or puris.

9th November - Tuesday

Darjeeling-Phuentsholing (Stopover at Maikabari tea estate with Rajah Banerjee as host.)

Stay at Phuentsholing — Residence of Dr. Sonam Wangyal.

10th November – Wednesday

Phuentsholing to Thimphu: Stay at Sonam Lhendup (Taki) and wife Barbara – email address: sbyts5@gmail.com. Postal address is PM 600, Thimphu, Bhutan.

16th November - Tuesday
Thimphu – Paro-Kolkata

1. Calcutta Hermonites receive at airport.

2. Living arrangements made at Indian Oil Guest House at Alipur.

3. Hermonites reunion on 16th.

17th November - Wednesday

Departure for Singapore. Calcutta Hermonites see off.
Calcutta Coordinators: Sujit Kumar and Deepak Datta

Travel Dates:

27th	Oct	Delhi-Bagdogra
29th	"	Siliguri-Kalimpong
31st	"	Kalimpong-Gangtok
5th	Nov	Gangtok-Darjeeling
9th	"	Darjeeling-Phuentsholing
10th	"	Phuentsholing-Thimphu
16th	"	Thimphu-Calcutta
17th	"	Calcutta-Singapore

Please add suggestions. Contact:

Rajendra Lakhotia - sikkim@gmail.com.
Shiv Saria (94340-01526)
Karma Bhutia - karmapb@rediffmail.com
Jigme N. Kazi - jigmekazi@gmail.com
Anup Chachan - apsaras@sancharnet.com
Binod Yonzone - cloud9kpg@yahoo.com
Sonam Lhendup (Taki) - sbyts5@gmail.com

HERMONITES INTERNATIONAL
SIKKIM HERMONITES ASSOCIATION
DARJEELING HERMONITES ASSOCIATION
FOOTHILLS HERMONITES
KALIMPONG HERMONITES ASSOCIATION
BHUTAN HERMONITES ASSOCIATION

(Himalayan Guardian Nov 11, 2010; Editor-Proprietor:
Jigme N. Kazi (MH, 1963-1979)

Cynthia Hawke

4/16 Bridge St.
Victor Harbor,
SA 5211
28-7-2017

Dear MHS Crew,

Thank you so so much for the lovely flowers you sent me. I was really puzzled when I saw the flowers at my door. Who could be sending me flowers? My puzzlement only increased when I read "From the MHS Crew". "MHS" That could only mean one thing, Mt Hermon School! Had they really been sent all the way from India? As you'll know, I contacted the local florist who contacted the Sydney florist who contacted you. Hurra! The mystery was solved. It really was from the Mt Hermon crew.

How absolutely wonderful! How many 82-year old teachers receive flowers from students they taught 50 years ago! You have given me such joy and blessing.

I thank God for each one of you. You'll know each one of you has a special place in my heart and always will have.

God bless and keep you in His care.

Love,
from
Miss Hunter.

And thank you, David, for all your part in this.

"GOD'S BEST — JESUS' CHRIST'S BLESSINGS ON YOU!"
PROFESSOR F.S. FREEMAN

A letter of appreciation from Miss Hawke.

26 Rev. M.J. Eade

Mount Hermon Nearly Closed Down In 1943

Rev. M.J. Eade and Mrs. Cath Eade, New Zealand Baptist Missionary Society

So many happenings and names come to hand. Our personal link with Mount Hermon School began in 1934-35 when we first went to India to work in East Bengal. Language School in 1935-36 in Darjeeling enabled us to find out about the school when we visited on Sundays for Church Services and during the week for various school programmes. Already my brother (Bun and Lois Eade and family) had linked up with Mount Hermon School. Eventually their four children (Don, Joy, Judie and Mike) attended there. Our children (Patricia and John) began their school about 1950 and continued, except for furloughs in New Zealand, until they completed Higher Cambridge in 1960 and 1965. We found their education in Darjeeling enabled them to merge easily into the N.Z. system of education.

So many names! My brother Bun, his wife and family introduced us to the school at various levels.

The Saturday morning individual and class concerts stir our hearts and minds. There was the occasion when our John and Ruth West played a piano duet which brought the house down when they finished playing the March Militaire with a crash of chords together. My comment was 'Dead Heat'. One Assembly morning our Pat read the Scriptures and said a brief word about them. My brother later commented to us, "We have a budding parson in sight." We had...she still talks (like Dad). The plays and concerts lifted our hearts as some 300 missionaries were on holiday in May and September.

Helen Brown (her parents from the Baptist Mission, England) and our Pat sitting at a desk outside and swatting (?) together made a picture when the dark hair of Pat and Helen's fair hair caught the sun as they bent over their books.

The shock that we got when we heard John had broken his wrist during a football match, but the relief we experienced when we knew the school nurse and doctor were caring for him. Remember Sister Digby, Australia and Dr. Master of India?

And do you remember Thongtip from Thailand...who delighted us with her singing and exhibitions of Royal Dances, and charm (we notice so many girls with charm who frequently broke "forever" the hearts of certain boys...it is remarkable how over the years they recovered and married someone else!). Thongtip's friendship with our daughter was delightful and later this enabled us to visit her home in Thailand in 1973...a great and happy experience.

Then there was Nath Indrapana...Phys. Ed. Zealot from Thailand. He kept us all fighting but not really fighting it.

The international nature of the staff proved an inspiration to students and parents. Asia, Europe and British Commonwealth were all represented. What musicians some were...violinists, pianists, singers, actors. All cultures learned to live together in a rather remarkable way.

POLICIES? Did you know the School nearly closed down towards the end of World War II, about 1943? The future of Missions seemed uncertain...students rolls dropped to about 120 (today about 640). Staff was difficult to obtain. Funds were at a low ebb. Mr. Dewey the American Methodist Principal, came to us when my wife and I were on holiday in Mount Hermon, and gave us a terrible shock when after telling us all about this, said the school will have to close down unless something drastic was done. "I want you to call a meeting of all missionaries and parents and advise me about the future: Mt. Hermon School...To be or not to Be?"

I finally accepted the challenge with a good deal of fear in my heart. However, after a full review over two days, we all agreed that the school must continue. We also felt it could best continue as a Union School and be supported by the united efforts of all Missions in North East India. After a few years this was achieved. How glad we are now that these decisions were made as we have seen the School develop over the years as a strong institution with a Teacher Training College attached. Its influence is felt in many lands as students have gone to all parts of the world we serve.

But again an amusing incident occurred as one result of the Union plan. I became Chairman of the Board for some time and during that time our daughter said, she had something special to say. What was that? A large boarding section of the school had to be fed of course. They have one main complaint...the hot dinner was often cold by the time it reached them, so would I take immediate steps to ensure the meal was served hot? Well, eventually this crisis was dealt with and proved again the old word, "It's the people you know that counts!"

Where have students gone? Our son John has become Vice Consul and Third Secretary (Admin) in N.Z. High Commission in New Delhi. Thongtip became a Professor of Physics in a Thai University; our Patricia is just now (October 1978) in China visiting with a team of N.Z. Community workers. They hope to find out how China now sustains her vast population and that makes them "tick" as a nation...what an experience. Many returned to be good citizens round the world.

Remember the great crowd of missionaries of many countries? Mount Hermon was a great centre for people to meet, when on holiday to relax, play tennis, and confer together, and generally to be uplifted in spirit during the holidays. The students entertained us in many ways and visitors also shared their talents in the various school programmes and concerts.

There were also inspiring Sunday Church Services which uplifted all of us. Gifted speakers gave of their best and the school Orchestra and Choir helped and encouraged us in so many ways. Remember the special talk of that original Australian, Rex Glasby? I mention his name because he is not in New Zealand!! He spoke one day about Jonah and the big fish, and at the dramatic moment when the fish swallowed Jonah he said something which brought the "house" down: "Then Jonah went down the slippery dip into the breakfast room."

So Mr. W. W. Jones (Vice-Principal for some years) moved this year to become Superintendent at Woodstock School in Mussoorie. How he inspired us with his violin. And do you remember his special sermon about the use of our talents? He told us when he first came to India from the United States of America that he expected he would have to give up all his talents and especially music. Instead, he said, "I have used everything I ever learned." Best Wishes Bill!

Remember Sale Days? When the community circle members made up of parents and Language School students from different countries shared together to make the various stalls attractive with home-made sweets, cakes, novelties, doll clothes. Some worked for weeks to stock the stalls.

That Community House (often called Log Cabin) gave mothers from different countries (e.g. Scandinavia, Germany, Britain, U.S.A., India, Australia and New Zealand) living on the Estate to insure some home-life for their children, providing mutual support and developing the community spirit. The M.H. Community Circle for some yeas maintained the Log Cabin which housed a small library and the kitchen equipment for parties and functions. Sunday Services and weekly prayer meetings were held regularly under the auspices of the Community Circle. It was a lively body…and the Log Cabin helped greatly.

Music and drama. Several good productions were staged by the School and enjoyed by all. An outstanding performance in 1956 was "The Little Sweep" by Benjamin Britten when there was audience participation conducted by Miss Tegel (then), a first experience for some of us from jungle stations…and very effective it was.

Many will remember today with great affection, Miss Hebblethwaite, the Kindergarten Headmistress with Mrs. Williams as Assistant. I shared the music (says Mrs. Eade) with them for five years and it was a privilege indeed. Many delightful programmes were given by the children. Who can forget the Percussion Band and the sweet singing of little children?

We near the end of memorising but not quite!

Remember Mrs.Von Roche (pronounced Rock)? She was a refugee from Austria. Alas her husband had been killed in the war. Her English was not too good for teaching but she helped the school in various ways. She had one especially lovely expression. After explaining something she would ask: "Understoodst?" This became famous for many.

To modernise it…do you wonder that we are so vitally interested in Mount Hermon? And sing: "Beloved Mount Hermon, we love you!"

Understoodst?!

(Hermonite 1978, annual school magazine.)

Tripura Baptist Christian Union

The Tripura Baptist Christian Union (TBCU) is the largest protestant church body in the Indian state of Tripura. It has its head office in Agartala, the state capital. The TBCU is affiliated to the Asia Pacific Baptist Federation (APBF) and the Baptist World Alliance (BWA). It is also a member church in the North East India Christian Council (NEICC), a regional church body of the National Council of Churches in India (NCCI). As of 2015, TBCU had 84,795 members in 845 churches.

History

The union was formed under the leadership of Rev. M. J. Eade in December 1938 in Lakshmilunga, a village six miles from Agartala. TBCU was supported and funded from the beginning by the New Zealand Baptist Missionary Society (NZBMS) and they provided most of the staff till the 1960s. Since then TBCU has now become an independent indigenous self-supporting church organisation. Rev. M. J. Eade was appointed as the first General Secretary of the Tripura Baptist Christian Union. Rev. Lalhuala Darlong was the first national General Secretary.

TBCU employs many pastors and evangelists and runs community programs such as schools and dispensaries. Since the early 80s, it has been working in partnerships with the Baptist Church of Mizoram (BCM) and also with the Evangelical Church of Maraland (ECM) from Mizoram. Both BCM and ECM have many workers in Tripura working as missionaries and evangelist/teachers in various TBCU churches and schools.

TBCU celebrated its Golden Jubilee and Diamond Jubilees in 1988 and 1998 respectively with much fanfare.

(Wikipedia)

27 Patricia Russell
1968-1991

She Made A Difference

Jigme N. Kazi

Sikkim's 1970 batch Hermonite Prava Rai with Miss Russell at the Bangkok reunion in 2016. (pic: Ian Reid)

Tempo Bhutia (1969 batch) took the initiative when he at our (Hermonites) pre-Christmas dinner in 2019 at Hotel Tashi Delek said he would like to invite Miss Russell for the school's 125th birth Anniversary...and that he would pay for her fare. Fantastic! And then I took my own initiative and told Tempo that we, the 1972 batch, would pay her fare one way. He agreed. Miss Russell loved us so much (!!!) that she was our class teacher for three consecutive years! (1970-1972 – class 9, 10 and 11) And so it was apt that we share the financial burden for her trip to India from England. As expected, the few Hermonites of my 1972 batch whom I contacted agreed to my idea. The question is when would she come.

When I wrote to her about the invitation, she was very happy, almost ecstatic, and said "Yes". She emailed me: "My apologies that I have been busy with friends and prayer groups especially during the holiday period (in December), and sadly missed your msg because it got so buried beneath all the other items that I have only just seen it."

She added, "Of course I can think of no greater privilege than to come and see all of you. So the answer is Yes, please, I'd love to come, and just await hearing the details of dates etc., and it will be wonderful. Thank you beyond words for your generosity."

Tempo Bhutia with Miss Russell and Miss Hawke in Gangtok, early 1991-92.

She wants to come in November and not in March. November is a long way off and she is now nearly 83-84, I believe. Its a dicey situation but we are hoping she will make it. In our correspondences she complained of her ill health. The last I saw of her was in Darjeeling in the spring of 2018. She was walking slowly down the main road near Capitol Hall with the help of a walking stick and a helper, a former staff member of MH. But despite her feeble condition, Uttam Pradhan and I were there to take her for a brief visit to Gangtok. She is a tough and also an adventurous lady. When we were all packed and ready to go she says, "I'm sorry. I have left my passport at Saroj's (Rongong) in Siliguri. I can't go, so sad." And that was that. Uttam, always a quiet risk taker, told me, "Jigs, I think we can take her. We will put her at the back of the vehicle and cover her with a bed sheet." Uttam meant what he said. Had I agreed Miss Russell would have been in Gangtok that evening. But this time, I surprised myself. I said no!

Miss Russell's Class of '72

Hopefully, she will make it in November to Darjeeling and Sikkim. We will take special care of her. The good news is that several old teachers of MH, including Mr. Moore and Mr. Ison, will also be there for the Carol Service function in the school to round up the year-long celebrations. I have already invited the three of them to stay at my house in Gangtok, which I hope will be ready by then. Presently its under construction/renovation.

During this period my Facebook message was:

Miss Russell with Bhutan Hermonite Thinley Delma.

"HAIL HERMONITES!

My brief visit to Darj with Sikkim Hermonite Uttam Pradhan (1973 batch and Sikkim Hermonites Prez) this week was very rewarding. We could not bring Miss Russell (MH - 1968-1992) to Gangtok as she left her passport at Saroj Rongong's in Siliguri! She, however, has postponed her visit to Sikkim till 2020 when MH celebrates its 125th anniversary. She is 80 now.

Thank you Tempo for taking the initiative to bring her to Gangtok, to Ramesh for her proposed stay at your hotel, to Lamba for agreeing to take her to Siliguri and to OT for his readiness to take her around in Gangtok.

Thank you Chuck for the breakfast feed at Keventers, Mukesh for the coffee and to Jagjit and Pratap for the help. Wonderful meeting Sinee and Deoprakash.

The short visit to MH, where we met members of the staff, students and others gave us a glimpse of our beloved school. For the first time after a long time I felt positive about MH. We enjoyed the school-made cakes, biscuits and tea in the school kitchen. Thank you all!

In Siliguri Miss Russell met Jagdish and Punam. She will have dinner at Shiv Saria's tonight with Surendra and Saroj Rongong, both ex-teachers. She leaves for Cal on March 24 and from there to UK on March 28. Thank you for the visit, Miss Russell and Godspeed. Hail Mt. Hermon! Hail Hermonites!"

"MH Revival" campaign started again after six years gap during Miss Russell's visit to Darjeeling in spring of 2018. Cheers to the grand old lady who never fails to fascinate us! She reminds me of Miss Stahl, one of our four Founders. She has a lot of energy, push and optimism.

"Well done Jigs and all of you" was how she reacted when we informed her of our efforts to help MH again. "As you perhaps know, I met Mr. Partha Dey on my visit in March 2018, and his wife, as well as several other concerned staff members, and was much impressed with all of them. We'll pray God's will in the matter."

Despite the fact that she was an excellent Geography teacher, Miss Russell was not an administrator. We know that very well, especially the 1972 batch. And yet after her retirement in 1991-92 she came back to MH to help in the administration but without much success. She candidly blames the church leaders and a section of the staff for this.

In class 10 she taught us Geography and as I recall she was an alumnus of Oxford University. In one of her test questions we were asked to explain the meaning of 'hanging valley', to which I answered, "A hanging valley is a valley hanging between two mountains/hills!" The Oxford dictionary describes 'hanging valley' as "a valley that joins a deeper valley, often with a waterfall where the two valleys join". Did I get 5 out of 10! In the final examination of Senior Cambridge in 1972 I got grade 3 in Geography. Hail Miss Russell!

Besides being an excellent Geography teacher, Miss Russell's main passion was the Bible. She wanted and wished all of us to turn to Jesus Christ and be saved. She gave me a small leather-bound Bible which I still have and use every once in a while. During one of her visits to Sikkim I asked her to scribble something on this Bible, which she did. I would love to add here what she wrote but alas after the state authorities pounced on my building in March 2015 and broke down several rooms my precious Bible (I think it was my favourite King James Version) cannot be traced. It is somewhere tucked away safe and sound.

Miss Russell with Jagjit Singh.

I would like to end this short note on my class teacher with what I wrote in my first book (*Inside Sikkim: Against the Tide*):

"It was my class teacher, Miss Patricia Russell, who got me into trouble on another occasion. Our class had decided to go for a picnic all by ourselves without being accompanied by any member of the staff. Some of us were quite apprehensive that Miss Russell may barge in. If she did this, we would not be able to stop her. We had nothing against her but wanted to be on our own. While some of us were casually talking over the picnic programme in the Geography lab during the change of period, Miss Russell overheard us and wanted to know what was going on. When no one wanted to tell her what we were discussing, I spoke up, "Miss, we are planning to go for a picnic and we don't want you to come with us." She seemed a bit surprised and disappointed over what I said but didn't react straightaway or make any fuss in the classroom. But later in the day I was called to Murray's office. She had obviously reported the matter to *Bhuntay* (Murray's nickname).

"You are being rude to Miss Russell, I hear," said Murray starring at me sternly over his glasses. "Sir, that's what the boys were feeling. We didn't want her to accompany us for the picnic. I told her how we felt and if that means I'm rude then I guess I'm rude." This was followed by a ten-minute lecture from him on 'being rude'.

When I came out from Murray's office, Miss Russell was at the door. "I'm sorry. I didn't mean to get you into trouble," she told me. I was in no mood to listen to her consolation after Murray's lecture and I walked off – rude again?"

Rude or not the two of us keep bumping into each other in the past five decades. Cannot wait to see her again in November 2020. MH had great women of vision and character to build its foundation and sustain it for a long time. Miss Russell is one of them.

28 Daniel Gyanendra Rongong
A TRIBUTE

He Lived Out His Faith In Daily Life

In her eulogy, Roslyn Namgyal, former student-cum-teacher of Mt. Hermon School (Darjeeling) and former teacher of Tashi Namgyal Academy (Gangtok), says her late father Daniel Gyanendra Kumar Rongong, who passed away peacefully in Kalimpong (India) on July 3, 2014, was a simple man who lived out his faith in daily life. His compassionate nature and creativity have impressed his near and dear ones who will surely miss him dearly. He was 80 and is survived by his two daughters, Roslyn and Heather Prickett, and their families who are now settled in Australia.

Good afternoon and welcome to you all. Thank you very much for coming today. Many of you have travelled from far places in bad weather and on difficult roads. Thank you. Many tributes have come in from around the world and there are messages that can be viewed on *Facebook* under my name Roslyn Namgyal if you are interested.

We have come today to mourn the loss of our beloved father Daniel Gyanendra Kumar Rongong - Gyanu. But along with the tears we have also come to celebrate his extraordinary life. I speak today on behalf of his immediate family members who love him dearly and most of whom cannot be here today. Today I want to acknowledge his younger daughter Heather Joy, his brother-in-law David Stewart, his sons-in-law Sherab Namgyal and Michael Prickett. His beloved grandchildren Jennifer Zangmu, Deborah Rinzing, Daniel David, Rebekah Joy, Indira Joy and Sherina Ruth, their partners Daniel, Ayesha and Lochie. And lastly, I want to mention his two darling great granddaughters Nuri Elly Namgyal and Marley Rinchen Ram.

Mr. and Mrs. Rongong.

I think the first thing I want to say about dad was that he was brother, father and grandfather to many more than simply those of us privileged to have been born into his family. I speak of you who have become extended family to him and to us too - who became his sons and daughters, especially later in his life. From the blind school, from Albella and many other places. To you all from this unique, extended Tirpai family - we want you to know how grateful we are for your love and care of dad especially in these later years after we moved to Australia. He loved you and chose to be with you right to the end.

Sherab Namgyal with wife Roslyn, Heather, Late Mr. Rongong's sister and Hermonite Shiv Saria (behind Roslyn) at the funeral in Tirpai, Kalimpong, on July 6, 2014. Hermonites P.J. Pradhan, Udai P. Sharma, Amode Yonzone, Palden Gyamtso and Jigme N. Kazi were also present during the funeral.

Heather and I always felt we had the best dad in the world. He was a brilliant story teller - in his stories everything came alive and he fired up the imaginations of his listeners. He could build us anything we wanted. A cute little play house with thatched roof that was the envy of our friends in Mount Hermon School - a dolls house, a rocking horse...he could fix anything that had stopped working - washing machines, sewing machines, jeeps, piano accordions and broken toys. He made the best and most comfortable beds we have ever slept in - all tucked in and warm and cosy.

He had amazingly clever hands and a wonderful sense of design. He could see the finished product mapped out in his minds eye and so often it was we who were the blind ones as we stood beside him passing him the screw driver while he fiddled under the car or inside the bowels of the washing machine. I often think he "saw" things much more clearly that the rest of us.

He created beauty and order around him - everywhere he could. Flowers - gladioli, orchids, cacti. Beautiful weaving in cane work and with wire. Even on the day he died we hear he was outside polishing up the panes of glass in the house - a task he did faithfully every day as he imagined the sunlight and colours that the clear, sparkling glass would allow inside.

Dad could pack a suitcase so that it looked like a work of art - he would fit large numbers of different shaped objects into the smallest of spaces - there was a space and a place for everything. And this reminds me of another tremendous gift he had - the wonderful ability to include people who have been left out or didn't quite fit in and so became marginalised from the mainstream of life. It was people most in need who found the largest space in dad's huge compassionate heart and very often right beside him in his own home.

He was one of those rare people with an infinite capacity to see the best in everyone and to hope for and work towards fullness of life for everyone around him. Many of us remember his business ventures - the 5-star chicken houses complete with saw dust on the floor and special egg laying trays. His beehives and all of us chasing swarms of bees in unlikely and dangerous places. His orchids, cacti and gladioli business deals. His *phing*-making days and his numerous taxis......Many of us also remember he never seemed to make any money out of any of these ventures but he pursued them passionately and we were all swept along for the ride.

Another thing I loved about dad was that he never sat and "counted the cost" - he gave freely from whatever he had - his generosity was legendary - very like that of his beautiful mother - our Aji. He was known to literally give away the shirt off his back and certainly his last rupee!

He shared with our mother Joy Rongong a remarkable gift as a teacher, a leader and a guide. Together they inspired and guided several generations of young people. Their ability to really see what was important in life has guided many of us through their visionary leadership.

Junior School Monitors: Standing (L to R): N. Shilu Ao, E. Zair, N. Choden. Sitting (L to R): P. Changte, N. Todi, A. Rahman, J. Alam, Mrs. J. Rongong, K. Kokhor, G. Tharchin, M. Ahmed.

Above all dad would want to be remembered for his deep faith in Jesus Christ. I understand that in the original language of the New Testament, the word for faith is not actually a noun - it is not a static word describing a thing we can possess, but is actually used more like a verb – a "doing" word. It describes faith as an activity - a living and a way of being - not simply an idea in our heads. I love that meaning - and I especially love what it means in my dad's life. For we know he actually lived out his faith in humble daily acts of love, kindness, thoughtfulness, loyalty, generosity and humour. He prayed often and deeply - he also cared for the widow and the orphan, the fatherless and the dispossessed. These words from Micah 6:8 I feel describe him well. Let me read them to you.

"He has shown you O man what is good: and what does The Lord require of you but to do justly, to love mercy, and to walk humbly with your God."

Although we now feel and will continue to feel, the terrible void of his absence, although there will be tears, his legacy of love, faith, hope and joy lives on in us because he loved us and showed us the Way of Jesus by his own living and loving.

I therefore say with tremendous pride and love - What a magnificent life! And I venture to believe that at the portals of heaven they too will be saying – "Well done, thou good and faithful servant."

29 Edna Williams
1953-1972

"She Loved Mount Hermon And Mount Hermon Loved Her"

Many will remember "Ma Willie" either as their KG teacher or Dormitory Matron. MHS was her beloved home from 1953 to 1972. I am her daughter Cherry and am submitting this in memory of a teacher who loved her work and students.

Below is a tribute I received from Mr. Stewart after her passing in 2008.

"Dorothy and I remember vividly when we first met Edna Williams. It was 1954, and we had just come to Mount Hermon School, Darjeeling, as the newly appointed Principal. We were new to India, and new to the task of Headmaster.

Class of 1972 in 1963 with Miss Williams.

In that first year we were so greatly helped to work out our job by some half-dozen of the staff who were there before us. Of these, Edna was one of the best. She was Kindergarten Supervisor, and she was also Matron of the Senior Girl's Dormitory.

Both of these were demanding jobs, and she did both superbly throughout our 11 years. In later years, she was Matron of the little girls in the renovated attic dorm. In the Kindergarten, she cared for each little boy or girl, even those who were well below the minimum age of 5 when they came!

It was wonderful to see how she helped them settle in, learn their work (some of them, their English!) and made their lives away from home, happy. And at the other end of the student scale, she always showed understanding of those teen-age girls, was able to adjust, and yet control and exercise gentle but firm discipline. Her class play productions were a joy to watch. She taught the little children to speak out so clearly, strongly, distinctly. "She loved Mount Hermon and Mount Hermon loved her."

Mrs. Williams (left) at her daughter Cherry Williams's wedding, 1962.

Jigme,

I am hoping that you will be able to include the above in the "MH Souvenir" book. This is such a wonderful idea and I look forward to getting a copy once you have completed the huge task. Please change the format in any way you see best.

Kindly let me know how your plans for the school in Paro Valley are progressing.

Wishing you all the very best.
Cherry (Williams) Hall
thehalls62@hotmail.com

MH FAMILIES – Part V

THE ISONS

30 Mount Hermon And The Ison Family

Barry Ison

Mount Hermon School has been a significant part of my life dating back to the early 1950s and all the way to the present. I first became a genuine Hermonite at the age of 6. Apparently, I had started earlier, attending the youngest KG class, but the teacher, Mrs. Heppelthwaite, asked my mother to withdraw me as I was becoming a nuisance. I only know one story relating to this and it goes like – whenever the teacher handed things out to the class, I would go around and collect them up and give them back to her. So it seems I was a helper from a tender age, but that kind of help was not appreciated.

My next earliest teacher was Mrs. Williams. I have only the best memoires of that time and, as many will agree, she was a wonderful person in every way. Her daughter, Ruth, was a successful student and an amazing athlete. She would take the field from any girl of Dow Hill, St. Helen's, Dr. Graham's Homes, or Loreto.

I entered boarding school at the age of eight or nine. Up to that time, my mother would bring my brother and myself to stay in one of the cottages (I remember the house's name was Wattle) and we would walk up the hill to school. My mother did try and home school us, but we were rather impossible to keep still and in the end she gave in and my parents opted for boarding school. My first experience of boarding was as a room guest of Mrs. Johnston. Miss Hutchinson, as she was then called, agreed to look after me for a few months at the end of a school year, so I stayed in her room which was the Senior Girl's Mistress's room next to the senior girl's dormitory. At that time, Mr. Johnston was courting Miss Hutchinson and, I believe, would frequently visit her in her room. But in my innocence, I cannot recall any of those occasions.

My day's as a student in MH were similar to most other Hermonites; up early for breakfast, later it was even earlier for study hall, breakfast, chapel; classes, recess, classes again, lunch, classes and finally play time – and later, during the regime of Mr. Stewart, compulsory sport. The evening included evening study, dinner, late night study and finally to the dorm and bed. I'm sure others will write more about their particular experiences under this regime.

Mount Hermon And The Ison Family

Over the years, I have been a student, a teacher and, more recently, a parent in Mount Hermon. I was a student from 1951 until 1961 when I completed my O levels. Then in 1971/72, I was the MH Art teacher. Many of you will also remember our refugee program in 1971 when we, as a school, contributed ourselves to helping refugees fleeing persecution and a civil war in Bangladesh and settling along the Indian border. That was an amazing time and we gained more than we contributed in being able to experience the suffering as well as the endurance of families who had lost everything, except their exceptional will to live. Much later, in 2005, I became the guardian of an orphan in Bangladesh. His name was Shapan and he took my name – Shapan Douglas Ison. My attempts to have him schooled in Dhaka only resulted in a waste of time, so I placed Shapan in MH. Although he had not completed class 6 in the village and knew no English, he was placed in class 8. I thought this would also end in failure, but by the time he had progressed into class 10, he was first in his class and, by the time he was in class 12, he was appointed Chairman of the prefects, which was the same as school captain in my era.

Because of my many years of a close association with Mount Hermon, there is obviously a lot to write, but I will leave the more interesting day-to-day events to other Hermonites to recount. I do want to add a short recounting of the Ison family and our contributions to Mount Hermon. My parents initially came up to Darjeeling over a period of two years during the late 1940s for language school. I was talking to my mother, still living in Brisbane at the age of 97, about the Ison involvement in MH, and she told me that the person who was probably the instigator of the appointment of Mr. Stewart as principal of Mount Hermon was Rev. George Watterson, an Australian Baptist missionary working in East Pakistan. The Australian Baptists had taken a significant interest in Mount Hermon from way back before WW II. It seems that on one occasion, a conversation took place among some of these missionaries to wondering about the future leadership in the school. Most people don't know this, but the American Methodist Church, which owned Mount Hermon, were thinking of closing the school because they could not find a suitable Principal.

My father, before he became a missionary in East Bengal (later East Pakistan), had been pastor of a church in Australia which was attended by Mrs. Stewart – nee Jury. Then Mr. Stewart came into the picture when he started courting his wife-to-be (Ms. Jury). So my parents knew both Mr. and Mrs. Stewart from way back. During the conversation mentioned in the previous paragraph, my mother shared the fact that she and my father were friends of Rev. Stewart, and while he had been a missionary in China, knew that he had been smuggled out of the country by the other missionaries to avoid the Chinese Government forcing him to become involved in one of their new universities. So Rev. Stewart was now in Australia, very capable and probably available. Rev. Watterson had studied with Mr. Stewart in Bible College, so he, apparently, wrote to Rev. Stewart and other friends and it all began from there.

The rest, as they say, is history. Mr. Stewart (as we knew him, though he was a Reverend) – 'Boss' for most seniors - was recruited to become the principal who really put Mount Hermon on the map of Darjeeling schools. Unfortunately, not that many of my (and earlier) vintage Hermonites are involved in various MH associations, websites and blogs so the Stewart era is less covered these days. But, as Ronen Ghose will testify, it was Boss who raised the quality of everything about Mount Hermon, recruited Mr. Murray and of course Mrs. Murray, brought in Miss Teagle (our very talented music Mistress), and Miss Hutchinson (later Mrs. Johnston) – and a large number of very talented and committed teachers from Australia, New Zealand, the UK and the US and molded them into a team that raised Mount Hermon from near extinction to the phenomenal institution that continued like that for many decades. I was a student before Rev. Stewart came to MH and, though young, was also somewhat aware of the rather lax administration.

My first Principal was Mr. Dewey and his contribution was quite significant especially in establishing the Mount Hermon Estate. After he left, we had a short time under the leadership of Mr. Workman – also an American. This was a time when senior students would touch the heart strings of Mr. Workman and appeal for a sunshine holiday – on a pretty regular basis. So these become quite common as we all loved being out in the sunshine looking at the snows. Then Boss came into the picture, the senior students only ever once tried the sunshine holiday appeal on him – his reply was quite simple and straightforward. "When your results are of the highest standard, I will think about it". From then on – it was work and harder work in the class room and on the playing field and with the result that MH became known for, arguably, the best academic and sports results in Darjeeling.

Back to my family and their involvement. For several years my father sat on the Management Committee and when he became Field Secretary of the Australian Baptist Mission in East Pakistan, he also became Chairman of the Management Committee. He was also a pretty good cricketer – as some of our older vintage – like Prabir Manna – may remember. There was an 'Estate cricket team' – made up, principally, of Australian and NZ Baptist missionaries, though we also had a great cricketer in Rev. Swan, from the British Baptists. This team really helped shape the MH school team into something quite formidable.

Mount Hermon And The Ison Family

335

Meanwhile, my mother, who was frequently left to fend for herself in a huge home with several servants in Mymensingh, East Pakistan, (though that was about the only perk of being an Australian Baptist missionary – as other support was pretty Spartan) would become fed up being left alone while her husband (my father) went on Mafusol (which was the British term for a tour of villages). So my mother would come up to Darjeeling and take my brother and myself out of boarding. We appreciated this much more as we got older as my mother is a very good cook and the food in MH was never anything to write home about. During the mid to late 1950s, my mother also served as matron for the middle school boys' dormitory. Some of the readers may remember.

Mr. Barry Ison (seated right) with Hermonites during MH's Centenary celebrations, November 1995.

I've written this piece to add to the many stories that, I am sure, have been contributed by our amazing MH alumni. By doing so, and focusing on the Ison family contribution, I wanted to provide an additional focus on the very valuable input into Mount Hermon's development into a school of excellence by missionaries from the Baptists of Australia, NZ, the UK as well as other missionary agencies such as the one in which the Whyte family, the Hudson family, the Hastings family and many other families worked.

Overall, it was a labor of love by many missionaries, who, apart from their primary responsibilities in the plains of India and East Pakistan, provided the Principals of Mount Hermon with professional, personal and spiritual support that enabled them to focus on the task of administering the school and its staff and students without worrying about personnel, financial, political and physical issues that have plagued Mount Hermon in more recent years. When the various missions left the sub-continent and involvement in the Management Committee the rot started setting in and we know what has been the result.

We, the student alumni of many generations have offered to assist the nationalized Management Committee. We did not want to take over – we simply wanted to do whatever we could to maintain the quality of education and life skills that we grew up with. Unfortunately, the Management Committee and the Indian Methodist Church could not lift their heads out of the sand and decided to continue in their self-centered, self-serving involvement – and now we know where all this has led.

If, in fact, Mount Hermon is forced to close down, it will not be because of the current demand by local people in Darjeeling for an independent state. The blame will be totally that of the Methodist Church and its MH Management Committee, which have refused to accept the resource offered by the Hermonite alumni. This contribution would have prioritized the mobilization of local support for the school and, given this support (which would have also included scholarships) the potential built on the sacrificial lives of so many over past decades, would have continued. Mount Hermon could have, again been rejuvenated and been able to serve through its excellent development of students in the various field of academia, sports, human endeavor and positive international relations. So let us continue to pray and hope that God will intervene and that everything that Darjeeling and, more specifically, Mount Hermon has stood for over so many decades, will not be lost.

THE SARIAS
31 From Rajasthan's Lunkaransar To Darjeeling's Mt. Hermon School

Balkrishna Saria, 1969 batch

Hailing from Lunkaransar a small village in the District of Bikaner, Rajasthan the Sarias migrated to Pokhariabong, a small village in the District of Darjeeling (Many a time we were asked "Your Great Grandpa didn't have any brakes. He kept walking from one end of India to the other till there was no further land??"). Great Grandpa was like a Zamindar with a large moustache and a huge six plus foot frame very well respected in the village (nobody dared to pass in front of our house if drunk, they would slink from a small road above and behind the house).

Our family business in Pokhariabong in Darjeeling was to act as agents for six Tea Estates in the area. An agent was required to do everything for the tea estates as the then owners/managers of these estates were the high and mighty English who didn't even tie their own shoe laces when living in grandeur in the Indian Tea Estates.

Everything included carrying coal tea chest spares and other stores from the nearest rail head/town to their factory. Drawing money from far off banks and delivering to the estate and sometimes smuggling a few whisky bottles to the more adventurous was part of the job. We were called "Kaiya" (meaning Marwaris in Nepali) by them.

Early memories included the ration distribution to the labourers of two estates every Sunday from our house to the estate labourers. We had a large godown where hundreds of sacks of rice and atta were stored and distributed. Coins needed counting and stacking on trays for easy distribution to the labourers. An estate clerk would come and call name/amount and we paid them from the trays.

"We were agents for some tea estates surrounding Pokhariabong. We carried their stores, tea, ration, coal etc., from Ghoom to the estate. We were there bankers, as well or basically Man Friday for the Englishman manager of the estate," recalls my younger brother, Shiv Saria (1972 batch).

"Our house was on the boarder of Sungma TE and on Sunday (holiday) workers (labourers) would come to Pokhariabong to buy provisions and also take their quota of subsidised rations at 0.47 per kg," adds Shiv.

My elder brother and I used to study in Selimbong Tea Estate in a school run by the estate. It was a hilly 3 kilometre walk from our house. Daily pocket money was half anna (three old paise) sometimes one anna if the munimji (munimji is the very well-respected clerk of the family, sometimes acting like a second father) was in a good mood. He would pay and write the amount in the books of account which he had to tally daily – each paise was accounted for.

Meanwhile, Mr. Rai, a manager in Sungma Tea Estate, (whose agent or Kaiya we were – they used to give us live electricity from their generators for our house which was like a seven-star facility in those days for our village) decided he needed to have a talk with Daddy. The conversation, in 1959, followed something like this in Nepali which was virtually our mother tongue then. "*Aye* Dalchand (my father, God bless his soul, left us so well-off and educated) *key yo thero keta horoo lai Kaman ko school ma parhai garne. Inarlai pani kaiya banaoune. English School ma halnoo parcha.*" (Translated – "Mr. Dalchand, are you going to keep your kids in these estate schools and not educate them properly. You must put them in English Schools and not make them Kaiyas for estates.")

Balkrishna Saria

Dad thought about it and agreed. Hence MHS was chosen and I was shipped to MHS in 1960.

So started the journey from a house in Pokhariabong, a short description here – We enter the main room called the gaddi (doubles up as the office in day and sleeping quarters at night). This is closed at night with wooden planks (called JHARAP in Marwari) which fit into grooves on the top and bottom. The opening is 15 feet wide. On the right is the godown of rations and behind it is the dark stairs (no daylight and no electricity hence dark) up which we climb to our living area. Take the left and we go to the Chowka (a kitchen-cum-dining-room with a big attached store with a mud Chula (a chula burns logs with pots resting above the flames for heating) and five concrete squares earmarked for squatting in lotus pose and eating lunch and dinner).

The Sarias' bungalow at Pokhariabong, Darjeeling.

Opposite the stairs are the two Indian toilets (with minimum light and running water for washing) and beside it is the bathing room with a big 100 litter drum of water which is always hot – heated by another big Chula. You scoop water into a bucket, mix with cold water, squat on a wooden pata (a low wide wooden stool) and bathe. Ladies had a separate bathing room, hot water supply was common. Clothes were washed here and dried in the sun on the slanting tin roof. Clothes of course were limited; we normally owned two sets of underwear two shirts and pants. They better dry next day or you wear yesterday's clothes.

Shiv Saria and Saroj with Mr. and Mrs. Murray, November 1995.

The tin roof of course had another important function – sun bathing Indian style. In the cold of Darjeeling it was a great comfort and enjoyment to lie in the sun and take our dose of Vitamin D, a side benefit to the enjoyment provided. A lot of back biting and other mind games were played on this roof. (there was no TV and WhatsApp or mobiles to pass the time – Thank God)

Opposite the roof was the small kitchen garden where naturally organic cucumbers and corn were grown. The corn cobs roasted in the wooden fires can beat the modern popcorn any day. Take a right from the stairs and you end up in a corridor leading to the chimney room and the main hall. The chimney room is called that because it had a fireplace for the cold winter. Children's entry was restricted as it had furniture which was not to be sullied. I remember Shiv was given a bicycle which he refused to share with me. I used to plead with Mom who used to put me in the chimney room with the bicycle to ride around. The door was shut to keep me away from his prying eyes.

Led by Shiv Saria, the Saria brothers have built on the tea industry established by their father and expanded their tea garden business beyond the frontiers of their native Pokhariabong in Darjeeling.

The hall led to 4 rooms – Room 1, Labour Room – where we were born in darkness because it was believed light and air would harm the mother after childbirth. Opposite was the room where we brothers slept. There were three beds where four of us slept. We have fond memories of talks and getting up early in the morning to reserve the favorite seats for lunch in the chowka. Next to it was Dad's room – from where he would call out my name to give him a foot massage sometimes at 5 in the morning. Opposite it was the guest room (later allotted to elder brother after he was married).

Shiv Saria

Lunch was at 10 a.m. in the Chowka followed by dinner at 5 p.m. A glass of milk at 7 p.m., sometimes in the gaddi and sometimes in the hall and off to bed at 7.30 p.m. after the radio news if interested. Simple healthy life.

Now School – grand buildings, huge dining halls, study halls, 400 students, foreign teachers from England with huge playgrounds and sinister big boys. AND most important a row of toilets with English commodes and NO running water but toilet paper instead. I could not balance myself on the commodes (as I refused to sit on them) and do my morning absolutions for 7 whole days and I finally ended up doing it in the pants before I learnt to adjust.

It was a nightmare and I don't remember crying but I must have cried very hard in the first week. Bread, dhal, aloo without any spices; chapattis and rice which even our servants won't have eaten. It was a huge transition from a school of Nepali-speaking students and teachers to one where only English was spoken but with the grace of God and the fear of Daddy we survived and got the education and foundation for life which our father's friend Mr. Rai had envisioned for us.

Jagdish Saria

Shiv followed me to school. Jagdish and Gordhan who were living in Lunkaransar were shipped to Pokhariabong and put into Mount Hermon. For them it was a trauma as they were older by then and also Rajasthan and Darjeeling are like Moon and Mars. Jagdish was a little chubby then and the boys used to tease him about that a lot and he came home down in the dumps and teary eyed during the holidays. "I refuse to return to MHS", he said. Dad had a simple chat with him in Marwari. "*Mai mota hoo to tero thori khayo hai Apnee ga go dud peeyo hai. Koi isme sharam koni.*" (So what if I am a little plump. It is the milk from our own cows and I have not taken anything from you. There is nothing to be ashamed of.) Argument ends and back to school after holidays!

So glad it ended that way for the school has given us a lot and I am very grateful to my Father and Mr. Rai who guided him to put us there. *Non Scholae Sed Vitae Discimus,* NOT FOR SCHOOL BUT FOR LIFE WE LEARN. The school did exactly that to our characters. It has added and strengthened what we were taught at home and we cannot distinguish and demarcate exactly where we got our traits but MHS had a big part to play in this.

- We were never converted to Christianity but we learnt all the good it had to offer us.
- I feel we are honest (to the best extent possible in today's world of good, bad and the ugly).
- I feel we do not harm others even if it hurts us sometimes.
- We respect our elders and have full faith and obedience to them (a trait fast going downhill in today's world of lightning quick alliances and relationships).
- Today I can eat any vegetarian food and enjoy most of them (school did not teach me to eat non-veg).
- I could sleep under the most difficult conditions, now I have softened up a lot.

Why migrate from Rajasthan?

Lunkaransar was a village without water – only *khara pani*, meaning salt water, no fresh water at all. The family did get rain water whenever it rained (sometimes the clouds forgot that we existed and suddenly remembered after two years and came to bless us with rains) and stored this in a Kund (a big flat land cobbled with stones/bricks etc., with a natural slant to a big well into which the rain water would flow.) The whole area was kept safe with a 10 ft high wall. Water was as precious as the air we breathe in Lunkaransar. The family had a cart on which was mounted a 500 litre tank of steel. This tank was filled with the kund water and taken home by the friendly bullock pulling the cart. Many a trip have we brothers made – drawing water from the kund, filling the tank, riding home in the cart and unloading the water into another well at home. Those were fun days and better than the video games we play today.

Later on, the Government started bringing water from Bikaner town in a tanker attached to the local train for the residents. At 1 p.m. you could see all the women lined up with their gharas to take water home. The waterman of India could have learnt a lot from us if he was in Lunkaransar during those days – now the story has changed as canal water has reached our village.

There were no roads and no toilets in the village. The vast dunes were the only option. Washing of utensils was a luxury. They were cleverly cleaned by rubbing fresh sand on them and clearing the soiled food and oil which of course was used in plenty in the cooking along with red chilly powder – if this curry was eaten by any of us today, we would probably fly to the moon, it was so potent.

Gordhan Saria

I do not recall any business we had there. Funds were sent from earnings in Pokhariabong to sustain the life there. The only business was shop keeping and dairy farming.

I presume the question as to why migrate is answered but things are different today and the day is not far off when backward migration may start taking place.

After school ended for me in 1970, I went to Delhi and took coaching for IIT which led me to joining IIT Kanpur.

BIKANER BREAK WITH 'JAGGUBHAI'

During our long winter vacations, I often used to correspond with my classmate, Jagdish Saria (Jaggubhai), who spent some time in his native village in Rajasthan. We were good friends, and still are. All I remember is the word BIKANER in his address. So when in the winter of 2016 I had a chance to visit Bikaner along with Jagdish I grabbed the opportunity. I was staying with my daughters in Delhi and it was only a night's train journey to reach my destination, Lunkaransar, Bikaner.

What a wonderful break it was – sunrise and sunset from my terrace room of the Saria's ancestral house, peacocks hovering around the house, a camel ride, visit to a farm/fort, shopping around the busy streets, morning walks and generally relaxing and having a good time. One more thing, for the first time I touched 'sand'! And I was thrilled.

I made many young friends there, some of whom still stay in touch with me through WhatsApp. Bikaner? Now its not just an address, its a destination.

Hail Mount Hermon! A Tribute

Jagdish comes out of his ancestral house at Lunkaransar, Bikaner, Rajasthan.

From Rajasthan's Lunkaransar To Darjeeling's Mt. Hermon School

'MH' FAMILIES

ALEXANDER the Great

Epitome of discipline and mannerism, Mrs. O. Alexandra, our beloved metron who was loved and feared by most of us who went through her in AB and C boys' dormitories in the main building during our childhood days in MH, died sometime in 1978. She not only taught us how and why to sleep during daytime after lunch but also taught us how to eat properly using fork, spoon and knife in the dining room.

Most of us got a good spanking from her with her wooden brush if we misbehaved in our dormitories. She will always be remembered as one of the main pillars of MH.

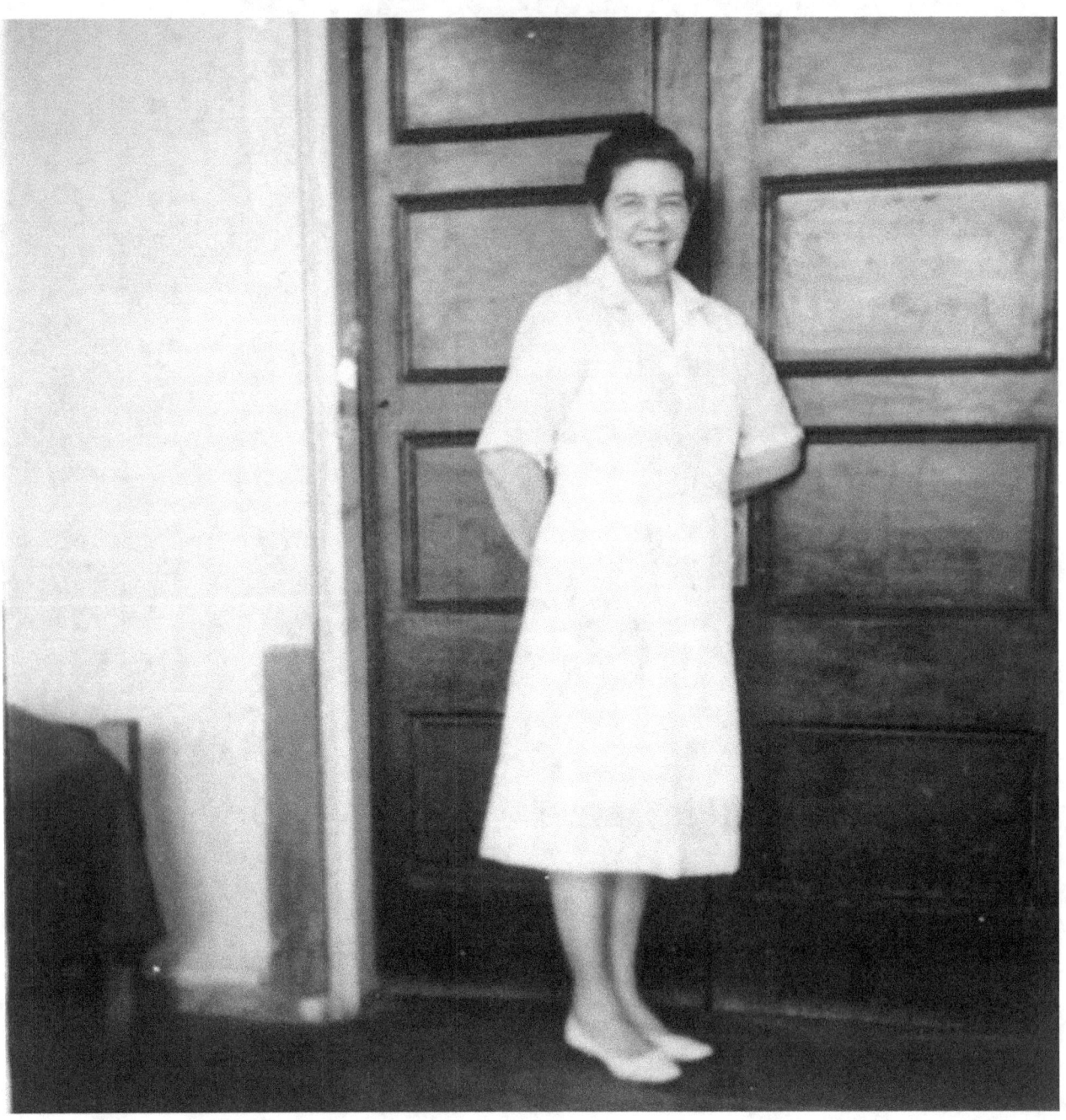

From Rajasthan's Lunkaransar To Darjeeling's Mt. Hermon School

Mrs. Alexander (second from left) with her friends: Mrs. Davidson, Mrs. Ghomes and Mrs. D'Rozario.

Sister DIGBY

Staff kids at MH

The TOPDENS

The Topdens: (L to R) Tashi, Lhundup, Champa, Lobsang and Tseten.

From Rajasthan's Lunkaransar To Darjeeling's Mt. Hermon School

The GLASBYS

Hail Mount Hermon! A Tribute

The ISHMAILS

352

The WASONS

Mrs. Wason's class

Hail Mount Hermon! A Tribute

The REMAS

From Rajasthan's Lunkaransar To Darjeeling's Mt. Hermon School

The GARDNERS

Hail Mount Hermon! A Tribute

The HAGENS

356

From Rajasthan's Lunkaransar To Darjeeling's Mt. Hermon School

Karl, Sulee and Kenny.

32 The Mathais
1958-1987
"We Had To Make A Huge Cultural Leap"

Walsa (Mathai) Matilda

Judging from old school photos, Mount Hermon was mainly staffed by European teachers in the early years. This started to change when Rev. Stewart became the principal of the school and the decision was made to add more Indians to the staff body. One of his earliest Indian appointees was Mr. Mathai, and talking to Rev. Stewart, this was a decision he seemed to take some pride in. Mr. Mathai was appointed as Chemistry teacher and Senior boys' warden and to this end, the Mathai family arrived in Darjeeling at the beginning of 1958 - and there they remained until retirement 30 years later at the end of 1987.

Travelling to Darjeeling from Kerala in the early days was not for the faint-hearted. It took about a week and involved travel in 1 boat, 1 ferry, 7 taxis, 6 trains and overnight stays in Madras and Calcutta! Booking seats for such an epic journey was another feat in itself. As soon as bookings opened for that date, Mr. Mathai would be at the booking station while it was still dark, just to be able to get far enough forward in the queue to ensure each person got a reserved seat. For a further bit of spice, the number of children in the family grew from 2 to 5 over the years, there was always a mountain of luggage, and the intense haggling with the numerous coolies along the way was just another part of the ritual! Over the years, the journey gradually became more streamlined and by the time my parents retired, they could catch just one train all the way from New Jalpaiguri to Kottayam, their final destination. We could only marvel at this newfound ease.

Back: Benu Chatterjee, Nat Indrapana, Ronen Ghose, Noel Long, Akbar Sadique, Cyrus Ruttonsha, Aulis Aho, Kishore Gandhi, Ho Shan Ying. Middle: Somkiat Gantanant, Menno Ziessen, Gordon Whyte, Anup Banerjee, Ram Bahadur, Suraphat Krisadaphong, Lim Hong Tatt. Front: Lynda Martin, Chhanda Datta, Rev. D. Stewart, Mr. M. Mathai, Rosalind Thutyakul, Anne Hunt, Nilima Raichoudhury.

Not only were Darjeeling (Mount Hermon in particular) and Kerala at opposite physical ends of India, they were also worlds apart in thinking styles, cultural norms, styles of dress, language, food, temperature, the lot. Kerala was extremely traditional with relatively little exposure to the West. The result was that my parents had to make a huge cultural leap, adapt to different styles of thinking and behaving, and one big concern was – would the children be able to adapt back to their culture if they grew up here? As can be expected, this created challenges not only for the parents, but for the children as well.

Mr. Mathai had a range of interests. He performed magic shows, kept bees for many years, enjoyed photography and then got into photo development, heading a photography club at one point where students could try their hand at developing their own photos.

Another possible little-known fact was his ventures into tailoring - he decided at one point that tailoring was not beyond him, so he bought a sewing machine and a book on how to cut your own patterns and next thing, we had home-made clothes! Other interests included chess and bridge, which he would play regularly with his friends at different times.

He didn't play the 'big' games of MH – cricket and football – but he was very interested in a different set of sports. He had been on the university basketball team in his university days and his enthusiasm for this continued when he came to MH. When there was little scope

to participate in this, he would join the ladies in netball, participate in volleyball, table tennis, badminton and even water polo when he could. In fact, Mr. Darr told me very enthusiastically how Mr. Mathai was the water polo star of MH.

Mr. Mathai's career included a stint of teaching at his old high school in Kerala, a few years teaching in Ceylon, some work at a bank and a year of teaching in New Zealand. He initially joined Mount Hermon as chemistry teacher and senior boys' warden, but later became Senior Master for a little while before taking on the position of Bursar at a point when the school finances were going through a crisis. He reversed that state of affairs and maintained a very healthy budget throughout his tenure. He ensured all creditors were paid in timely fashion, he managed the funds for smooth execution of all Mr. Murray's various projects – the round hostel, the TTC buildings and various renovations – and when he left, the school finances were probably at the healthiest they had ever been. His financial prowess seems to have been passed on to his sons, both of whom have excelled in that field – one entering the upper echelons of the Indian banking system and the other as a chartered accountant with various prominent organisations, including Jaguar in England.

Mr. Mathai, Chief Guest, at the Murray Cup Cricket Tournament, organized by Sikkim Cricket Association, in Gangtok in the 1980s.

Mrs. Mathai looked after the Stockroom for a while, but she was mainly a homemaker and in that role, she was a bedrock for the emotional and spiritual health of the family. All the Mathai children did their schooling at MH and three of them even taught there for various lengths of time, Shanta contributing the most in this area.

Mount Hermon was and still is home to the whole Mathai family - physically for many years, and in the depths of our souls for ever.

33 The Moores
1970-1973

Mount Hermon: What It Means To Me

W.D. Moore

The Moores at Mt. Hermon School, Darjeeling, 1970s.

The year was 1970. The month was June - the second week in June to be precise and I was still a student. My beautiful fiancé, Liz, had worked all night in a Belfast Hospital on night-duty. I had picked her up at 7.00 a.m. after a very tough night, but she said to me "I would like to go to the Portstewart convention". This is a very well-known religious jamboree type gathering which takes place every year in a seaside town in Northern Ireland. I protested that she MUST be too tired but she just said "I will sleep in the car". So off we went in the car on a two-hour journey to the convention.

I had been in touch with a gentleman called Jim Barton for a number of years while I had been studying for my Bachelor of Divinity Degree at University. My plan was to go to Wilson College in Mumbai to do the degree there, as a way of getting into that wonderful country India. Missionaries were not welcomed by the Central Government so I was hoping to get in as a student. It had really only been talk and nothing came of it. But that day at Portstewart was a day of destiny. As we left the convention tent, Jim Barton, (whom we did not know was in Northern Ireland on Furlough) met me and simply said "are you still keen to go to India"? Without hesitation I said "yes".

He was in a great hurry and briefly told us he knew a school that needed a Chaplain, then his face changed slightly and he added "but they want a nurse as well. The authorities will make it difficult for a Minister, but a teacher and a nurse would have no problem". I pointed to my fiancé and said "Meet Liz, she is a Nursing Sister in the Royal Maternity Hospital in Belfast". (She had also done her General Nursing and was the youngest Sister ever in that prestigious hospital so was well prepared for anything that the future would throw up as regards nursing). She later proved that for four years and I still joke that I sneaked into India in her luggage, as the nurse was more acceptable officials issuing permits than a teacher. True to his word Jim send me the address of the famous Mount Herman School and I can say "the rest is history!"

I suppose a good question could be "How did I come to this position in the first place?" Well it is a long story and some of the many details are long forgotten. In my two years HSC in grammar school I had read "A Passage to India", by E.M. Forster, my geography course had been India and South East Asia, and at University I had met a person who studied in Mount Hermon as the daughter of a missionary. (Of course, I had never even heard of MH until Jim gave me the address years later). Her love of India rubbed off when she had us round for tea. We sat on the ground, and ate with our fingers! There was also another Minister in a local church who had spent many years in India and also had a terrific love for the country. He influenced me greatly as a teenager. Then there were so many little incidents (newspaper articles, chance remarks, names etc.) that brought me to a realisation that God was directing me to India and that would be my destiny.

My mother didn't want us to go, but my father was very enthusiastic and he believed that if God was directing me then there was nothing else to be said. Elizabeth's parents were great folk who also gave us their blessing. Mum told me that I would never see my father alive again - and she was correct. Some of the students will remember the fact that my father died in my second year in the school and shared my loss. It was him who supplied the football team with our famous yellow socks...remember? We really looked and felt special.

Liz and I were married in September. Our meeting was, like the meeting with Jim Barton, another God incident. (We call these moments "God incidence" rather than "coincidence" because they have been so pivotal in our lives). The first night Liz and I went out together she tells everyone that I said to her "Are you prepared to go to India? If not we are wasting each other's time with this friendship, because that is where I am going". Strangely enough she had called, just that very week, at an Office in Belfast, enquiring about vacancies in Africa for a nurse! She did not see any problem changing continents so the answer was "yes" and the friendship developed.

I postponed my ordination as a minister which should have taken place in September and so I came to India as a teacher. My B.A. was a teaching Degree so it was not dishonest to have it on my passport. It meant that I had a much smoother entry at Mumbai than it might have been. The official insisted that I was a missionary, and three times I pointed to my passport and said I was a teacher. It was an awkward moment!

We stayed with the Bartons in Mumbai and it was fitting that they introduced me to my first taste of India. They laughed when I thought that beetle juice was blood, that I closed my eyes when the taxi met other cars on blind bridges, and heard strange noises at night in their bathroom - which they told me was made by rats who like to eat soap! They were a terrific couple - even though he finished as principal of a rival school, Woodstock.

Mr. John Johnston met us in Siliguri after a never to be forgotten "first journey on our own" and we had many incidents on the way. However, we made it, and quickly settled in to our home for the next four years – Mount Hermon School.

My title is "The day that changed our lives", but really it was the next four years that really changed them and the memories have stayed with us until today, forty-seven years later. I was at the inauguration of the Church of North India in Nagpur the following year and was ordained in the fledgling Church by the godly Bishop Pradan in the School Chapel was a special memory.

The Moores with the Murrays, Darrs and Miss Hawke in Wellington (NZ).

David Thomas PEMBA and Esther Mary CHANDRA were born in Planters Hospital, Darjeeling - delivered by the great man, Dr. Pemba – and that doubled the Moore family during the next four years. They were much loved by the Hermonites who never used their English names. The boys of Fernhill were wakened earlier that expected at week-ends when "Pemba" was quietly pushed in to the dorm on his squeaky little tricycle to trundle up the open space. (It meant Liz and I, the wardens, had a short lie-in after the 6.30 a.m. football practices before study in the other mornings). He was the little brother of every student and I remember some senior boys taking him for a toy-train ride to Ghoom on a Sunshine Holiday. He also claims to remember it, although he was only three years old when he left India, and he has a framed picture of the train on his wall.

"If we liked India so much why did you only stay four years?" you might ask. The answer is… that while we liked India, India didn't always like us! I had dysentery and hepatitis (at the same time) shortly before we went back to Ireland. The "nurse" said I needed time to recuperate, and the school wanted an immediate answer if I was going back, otherwise they needed a permit for a replacement. So the Blackwoods (Blackmoores) replaced the Moores. We also had a strong sense that our time in India was over and other God incidents shaped our post-India future.

When anyone asks "Did you like India?" we simply smile and say "Our children are called Pemba and Chandra". There is no more to be said.

34 The Mapleys
1959-1971

From Homes to Hermon

Margaret Mapley

Rachel Mapley (nee Selfridge) moved to Bombay in 1953 to nurse at Breach Candy Hospital. Jeffrey Mapley followed her out in June of 1954, they married in October 1954.

They took positions at Dr. Graham's Homes in 1956, Rachel as the house mother for Wellingdon Cottage and Jeffrey the maintenance manager for the homes. Here they met and worked with Miss Stewart (later Mrs. Rongong). It is deducted that it was through Miss Stewart's connection to her brother David Stewart (principal of Mount Hermon School in Darjeeling) that the Mapley's took positions at Mount Hermon in 1959.

Rachel took the position of nurse in the MH school hospital, and helped with the kindergarten children. Jeffrey took the position of maintenance manager for MH. They moved as a family with one daughter, Margaret, who was born in Darjeeling at the Planter's Hospital in 1958. Rachel soon took on the managing of the Ailina Guest House, and providing home economic classes for senior students in the kitchen of Wayside. They went on to have two more daughters, Rosemary and Phyllis-Joy, both born in Darjeeling. A son, Philip, was born in 1967.

Jeffrey played 'footie' and cricket on many of the staff teams that played against the students. He built and repaired many of the facilities that are still in existence today

(2017) – the lockers and night tables in the dorms, the water towers on the hill behind the hospital, the desks many of us sat in, the swimming pool. He created many of the props used in the school plays – the piano in Salad Days.

Mr. and Mrs. Mapley, 1954.   Jeffrey and Rachel Mapley, 2010.

Mrs. Mapley and Margaret, 1962.   Rosemary, Phyllis-Joy, Margaret and Philip, 1968.

Rachel Mapley, Mrs. Williams, Mrs. Gardner and Margaret Mapley.

The Mapley's left Mount Hermon in May 1971. Rachel and Jeffrey left India after serving their Lord for 18 years. The children left the only home they had known. They spent six months in the UK before immigrating to Pefferlaw, Ontario, Canada in October 1971. The education that Mount Hermon provided was above the Canadian standard of the time, and Margaret was placed into grade 9 in high school. Rosemary entered elementary school, while Phyllis-Joy and Philip remained at home until they were old enough to attend school. Jeffrey worked as a plumber in Toronto for a couple of years before he took on the role of maintenance manager at River Glenhaven in Sutton, Ontario. Rachel was hired as head nurse at River Glenhaven shortly after arriving in Canada. Both Rachel and Jeffrey worked at River Glenhaven until they retired.

Jeffrey Mapley passed away after a short battle with acute leukemia on February 14, 2011. Rachel Mapley passed away on October 13, 2014. Margaret, Rosemary, Phyllis-Joy and Philip all live in Ontario, Canada.

Mount Hermon School was home for the most impressionable years of our lives. Our family consisted of the other staff children during school holidays, and classmates

Ailina guest house

during the school year. The workers at both Ailina and the workshop looked out for our well-being, and helped us learn more than any book could ever teach us. Our lives in Darjeeling have impacted who we are today – our world view, acceptance of differences in religious beliefs, an understanding of the struggles that are faced by many around the world. Our family of friends have become a way to stay connected to a place and time that will forever remain etched in our memories and hearts.

MISCELLANY – Part VI

35   Mount Hermon In Israel

The Hermonites

Wayne Blank

Mount Hermon, from the Hebrew word pronounced ker-mone, meaning abrupt, is the eastern extension of the Anti-Lebanon mountain range. Consisting of a ridge about 20 miles (32 kilometers) long with three peaks rising up to 9,200 feet (2,800 meters) above The Mediterranean Sea, it marked the northern boundary of Israel (Deuteronomy 3:8, 4:48, Joshua 11:3, 11:17, 12:1, 13:11).

The Hermonites

Mount Hermon's majestic snow-covered peaks can be seen from far south into Israel, to the west in Lebanon, and to the east in Syria. About 20 miles (32 kilometers) north of the Sea of Galilee, it would have been a well-known sight for Jesus Christ all of His life, from Nazareth, and then later from Capernaum.

Before the invention of modern refrigeration, Mount Hermon was a source of ice, as indicated by another name that it is known by - ice mountain. In modern times, many people go skiing on its slopes in season.

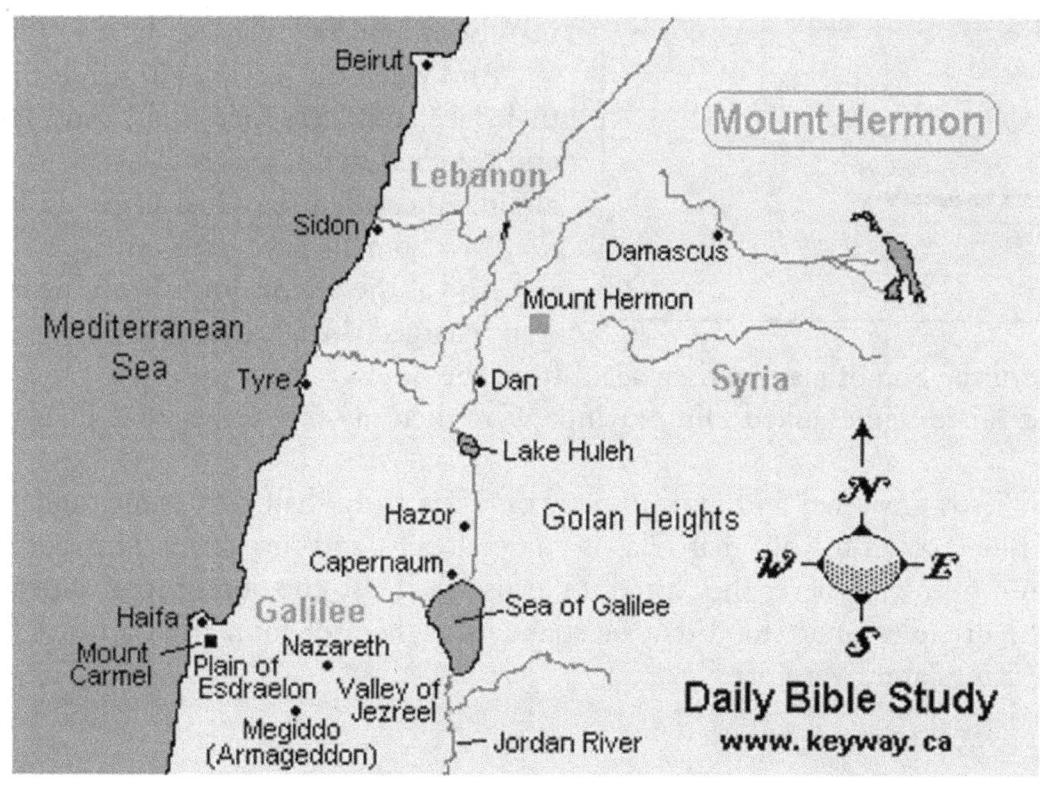

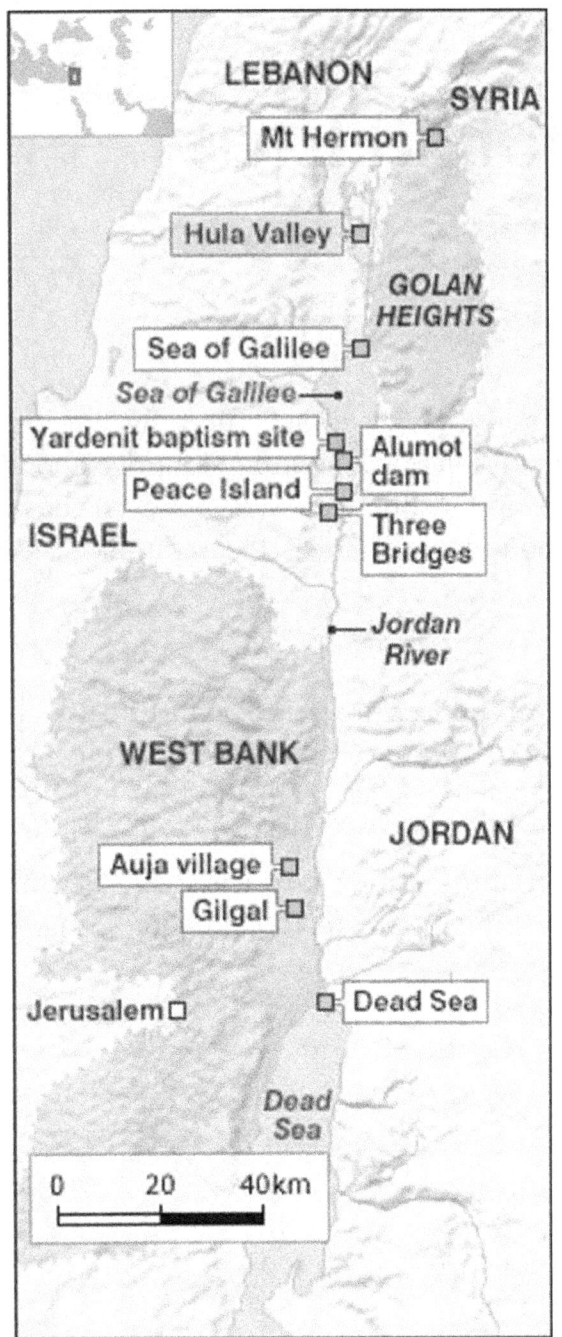

Throughout Bible History, Mount Hermon was known variously as "the Hermonites" (Psalm 42:6 KJV) because of its multiple summits. It was known to the Sidonians as "Sirion," and to the Amorites as "Senir" or "Shenir" (Deuteronomy 3:9). Others called it "Baal-Hermon" (Judges 3:3, 1 Chronicles 5:23) and "Sion" or "Siyon" (Deuteronomy 4:48).

Many believe that the occurred somewhere on Mount Hermon:

"And after six days Jesus taketh Peter, James, and John his brother, and bringeth them up into an high mountain apart, and was transfigured before them: and His face did shine as the sun, and His raiment was white as the light. And, behold, there appeared unto them Moses and Elias [i.e. Elijah] talking with Him."

"Then answered Peter, and said unto Jesus, Lord, it is good for us to be here: if Thou wilt, let us make here three tabernacles; one for Thee, and one for Moses, and one for Elias."

"While he yet spake, behold, a bright cloud overshadowed them: and behold a Voice out of the cloud, which said, This is My beloved Son, in Whom I am well pleased; hear ye Him."

"And when the disciples heard it, they fell on their face, and were sore afraid. And Jesus came and touched them, and said, Arise, and be not afraid. And when they had lifted up their eyes, they saw no man, save Jesus only."

"And as they came down from the mountain, Jesus charged them, saying, Tell the vision to no man, until the Son of man be risen again from the dead."

"And His disciples asked Him, saying, Why then say the scribes that Elias must first come?"

"And Jesus answered and said unto them, Elias truly shall first come, and restore all things. But I say unto you, that Elias is come already, and they knew him not, but have done unto him whatsoever they listed. Likewise shall also the Son of man suffer of them. Then the disciples understood that he spake unto them of John the Baptist." (Matthew 17:1-13 King James Version)

Hebrew - Hermonites, Hermon

Mount Hermon in northern Israel. The River Jordan springs from this mountain, Mt. Hermon.

PSALM 42:6 O my God, my soul is cast down within me: therefore will I remember thee from the land of Jordan, and of the Hermonites, from the hill Mizar.

A peak, the eastern prolongation of the Anti-Lebanon range, reaching to the height of about 9,200 feet above the Mediterranean. It marks the north boundary of Palestine (Deuteronomy 3:8, 4:48; Joshua 11:3, 17; 13:11; 12:1), and is seen from a great distance. It is about 40 miles north of the Sea of Galilee. It is called "the Hermonites" (Psalms 42:6) because it has more than one summit.

The Sidonians called it Sirion, and the Amorites Shenir (Deuteronomy 3:9; Cant 4:8). It is also called Baal-Hermon (Judges 3:3; 1 Chronicles 5:23) and Sion (Deuteronomy 4:48). There is every probability that one of its three summits was the scene of the transfiguration (q.v.). The "dew of Hermon" is referred to (Psalms 89:12). Its modern name is Jebel-esh-Sheikh, "the chief mountain."

It is one of the most conspicuous mountains in Palestine or Syria. "In whatever part of Palestine, the Israelite turned his eye northward, Hermon was there, terminating the view. From the plain along the coast, from the Jordan valley, from the heights of Moab and Gilead, from the plateau of Bashan, the pale, blue, snow-capped cone forms the one feature in the northern horizon."

Our Lord and his disciples climbed this "high mountain apart" one day, and remained on its summit all night, "weary after their long and toilsome ascent." During the night "he was transfigured before them; and his face did shine as the sun." The next day they descended to Caesarea Philippi.

36 History Of Methodist Church In India

Methodist Church in India is a Methodist Christian denomination of India. Its seat is in Mumbai. The Church of South India and the Church of North India are the results of mergers involving Methodist Churches. It has hundreds of thousands of members. It is a member of the World Council of Churches, Christian Conference of Asia, the National Council of Churches in India and World Methodist Council. It runs schools. The Methodist Church in India (MCI), is an "autonomous affiliated" Church in relation to the United Methodist Church.

In 1856, the Methodist Episcopal Church from America started mission in India. The Methodist Episcopal Church began its work in India in 1856, when William Butler came from America. He selected Oudh and Rohilkhand as the field of effort, and being unable to secure a residence at Lucknow, began work at Bareilly. The first War of Independence broke up the work at Bareilly, but in 1858 Lucknow was occupied and Bareilly re-occupied and the work of the Mission started anew.

By the year 1864 the work had grown to such an extent that it was organized under the name of the India Mission Conference. Additional stations were occupied in Oudh, Rohilkhand, Garhwal and Kumaon, and by the year 1876 The Methodist Episcopal Church had established work both along evangelistic and educational lines, that was to furnish the foundation for the largest and most successful Mission of the Church. Methodist Churches were established in cities such as Mumbai, Kolkata, Chennai, and Bangalore. Special revival meetings were held which led the church out of its boundaries and gave it a national status.

The year 1870 is remarkable in Indian Methodism's history not only because of William Taylor's visit but for another reason as well. It was the year that marked the coming of the first missionaries of the Woman's foreign Missionary Society of the Methodist Episcopal Church. Two young ladies arrived that year: Isabella Thoburn, to start her wonderful work of education among India's girls and women; and Clara Swain, to inaugurate our medical work among the women of this land, she being the first lady doctor to undertake such work in Asia.

It was fitting that the first missionaries of the Woman's Foreign Missionary Society should come to India, for Mrs. Lois S. Parker, who with her husband Edwin W. Parker had come to India in 1859 and Mrs. William Butler who had served in India still earlier were the leading spirits in the organization of the Woman's Society in Boston, U.S.A., in 1869. The growth of the work supported by our Woman's Division (formerly Woman's Foreign Missionary Society) has been even more phenomenal than that of our Board of Foreign Missions, and in all lines of missionary endeavour it has met with remarkable success.

Evangelistic work in the villages of northern India resulted the baptism of large numbers of people from the deprived classes. Thus it began the mass movement work, which has brought thousands of converts into the Methodist Church in rural areas.

Thus began the mass movement work, which has brought several hundreds of thousands of converts into the Methodist Church in the rural areas. In 1920 the Methodist Missionary Society was organized to supervise the missionary work in India. In 1930 the Central Conference of Southern Asia elected the first national bishop. Since the independence of India in 1947 all bishops have been Indian nationals. Missionaries were sent to Borneo in 1956 and to the Fiji islands in 1963.

Since 1928, the MCI was engaged in union negotiations in North India. In 1970 the Central Conference voted against the plan of union, but dialogue with the Church of North India has been continued. In 1981 the Methodist Church in India was established as an "autonomous affiliated" church in relation with the United Methodist Church. This ushered in a new era for Indian Methodism. The church is now independent in its life and organization and has adopted its own constitution and Book of Discipline and Articles of Faith. The Methodist Church in India understands itself as the body of Christ in and for the world as part of the church universal. Its purpose is to understand the love of God as revealed in Jesus Christ, to bear witness of this love to all people and to make them his disciples.

The MCI runs 102 day boarding schools and 155 village schools in which over 60,000 children are enrolled; 89 residential hostels provide Christian care for 6,540 boys and girls. The church also operates 19 colleges and vocational training institutions, 25 hospitals and health care centres, and many community welfare and development programmes in the country.

(Wikipedia, 2006)

METHODIST CHURCH IN INDIA (MCI)

I have no problem with Christ; my problem is with church: Mahatma Gandhi

India Methodists celebrate 150 years of ministry

By James S. Murthy*

Mahatma Gandhi and E. Stanley Jones.

LUCKNOW, India (UMNS)—Nearly 700 Indians and dignitaries from other nations celebrated 150 years of ministry in this South Asian nation.

Meeting Oct. 20-23 at Isabella Thoburn College, delegates from the 12 regional conferences of the Indian church and Methodist leaders from other nations celebrated the 25th anniversary of the Methodist Church of India, a 649,000-member autonomous denomination affiliated with the United Methodist Church.

Dignitaries came from Hong Kong, Singapore, Malaysia, Myanmar, the United Kingdom and the United States.

Retired United Methodist Bishop S. Clifton Ives spoke at the opening service of thanksgiving and Holy Communion. "Give thanks to God for he has placed us to bring the Gospel – the love and peace of Jesus Christ – to this fractured world and to people living in a multi-religious milieu," he said.

Earlier in the morning, Mulayam Singh Yadav, chief minister of the state, lauded Methodist schools and colleges for educating the masses, especially illiterate girls and women. A member of the Uttar Pradesh legislative assembly since 1965, Yadav noted that, since 1956, Methodist institutions and churches "have played an important role in spreading the message of brotherhood, peace and humanity in India."

Yadav told the assembly that he wants to make sure the status of Isabella Thoburn College is changed to a university. "I am aware of the great service being rendered by IT College under the dynamic leadership of its president, Dr. E.S. Charles," he said.

The college was begun in 1870 by Isabella Thoburn, a missionary sponsored by the Women's Society of the Methodist Episcopal Church.

Founders recalled

The Rev. William and Clementina Butler arrived in India in 1856 and began ministry at Bareilly near Lucknow. They later moved to Nainital. "India shall yet be one of the brightest gems in the diadem of Christ," William Butler said.

James M. Thoburn became a missionary to India in 1859. In 1888, General Conference elected him missionary bishop for India, a role he filled until 1908.

William Taylor, a preacher at spiritual revival meetings, won many souls for Christ and organized followers into Methodist congregations in Bareilly, Nainital, Poona, Madras, Bangalore, Calcutta, Baroda, Hyderabad, Jabalpur and Khandwa.

Another renowned evangelist, the Rev. E.A. Seamonds, came to Bidar near Hyderabad and started mass spiritual revival meetings; these revivals at Dharur continue after 83 years.

The first women missionaries from the Methodist Episcopal Church arrived in 1870; they included Isabella Thoburn and Clara Swain, who was the first female doctor in Asia.

E. Stanley Jones

E. Stanley Jones, perhaps the best-known Methodist missionary, arrived in India in 1907. His innovations in proclaiming the Gospel caught the attention of high-caste Hindus who wished to learn about Jesus Christ. In 1930, "Brother Stanley," as he was addressed, founded the "ashram" or "forest retreat" at Sat Tal, at the foot of the Himalayan mountains. It was there that people of all faiths could join in a common quest to experience the spirit of Jesus Christ.

Judges, bureaucrats, lawyers, doctors and administrators went to Sat Tal Ashram, and many accepted Jesus as savior though the experience. The confession, "Jesus is Lord," was used as a greeting by Jones and is now used throughout the International Movement of Ashrams in 40 countries.

Jai Singh, 74, is a Methodist who converted from Hinduism. At the assembly, he described how he accepted Jesus Christ after attending the Sat Tal Ashram in 1963. "The Lord has led me to share his blessings with three Methodist churches in and around Lucknow," said Singh. "I have found peace and joy in Jesus Christ."

In a keynote address at the three-day gathering, Bishop Robert Solomon of Singapore related an incident from Jones' life. Brother Stanley told Mahatma Gandhi, father of the Indian nation, "You are an ardent practitioner of Jesus' Sermon on the Mount; why don't you join the church?"

Gandhi replied: "I have no problem with Christ; my problem is with church."

Solomon encouraged his listeners to follow Jones' example by reflecting Christ in their lives. The bishop said Jones' life and spirit will continue to invite people to experience the love of God.

Church growth

At the assembly, Bishop S.V. Sampath Kumar of the Bangalore Area celebrated the growth of Methodism in India. The Madras Regional Conference, the youngest of the 12 regional conferences of the denomination, had only two churches in 1974 and now is a separate conference.

Kumar said the growth is an eloquent testimony to the commitment to evangelism and mission of the Emmanuel Methodist Church and the Tamil Methodist Church. "It is true that God moves in mysterious ways, his wonders to perform, and his ways are not our ways," the bishop said.

The denomination has six episcopal areas with 12 conferences. It has 2,500 local churches with a membership close to 649,000, served by 2,200 clergy, 10 of whom are female.

Murder and violence

While the denomination continues to witness to the prince of peace, India has experienced a rise in unprovoked violence.

Australian Baptist missionary Graham Staines and his two sons were burned to death in a remote village in the Indian state of Orissa for allegedly engaging in conversion activities.

Father Ignazio Bara, an Indian Catholic priest, was killed when he tried to intervene during an attack by Hindu fundamentalists on Christian villagers in Simdega, India.

Methodist pastors have been beaten during worship services.

These ugly acts were premeditated and carried out by the so-called guardians of Chauvinist Hindu ideology. Their slogan is "Hindu India," a challenge to the church in India.

Indian political and educational leaders who were educated in Methodist schools, colleges and institutions disapprove of Hindu hegemony. They participate in interfaith dialogue, where they gain better understanding of Methodist goals. These Indian leaders join Methodists in efforts to aid nearly 45 percent of the Indian population who live in poverty, irrespective of their creed, class and ethnicity.

The future

Elizabeth S. Charles, president of Isabella Thoburn College, says she foresees the Methodist Church growing stronger in the next 25 years. "Education is important as India is poised to become a global power for education opens the mind." She said the denomination is aware of India's social, political and economic problems.

"I shall work for removing gender bias and many social problems, (such) as girl infanticide, promoting women literacy and empowerment, which I believe were also envisioned by pioneer educationist Isabella Thoburn," Charles said. "I endorse the recent government legislation to protect the Indian women from domestic and external violence."

In addition to empowering women, Methodist leaders want to focus on young people in the church.

"My predecessors of the past five generations ministered in Methodist congregations starting in 1863, when the first convert in the family was ordained a local deacon," said the Rev. Isaac P. Mann, a pastor in the Delhi Regional Conference. "My vision is to lead the youth of the Methodist Church to Jesus Christ through biblical values in these changing situations of our society."

*Murthy is a freelance writer based in Lucknow, India.
(Ref: newsdesk@umcom.org., 2006)

SIBLING SYNERGY:
James and Isabella Thoburn

STORY BY EARNEST LAU
PHOTOS FROM
THE METHODIST CHURCH ARCHIVES

Isabella accepted James' call to teach in India

James and Isabella Thoburn

IMAGINE being sent off by your mother to college at the age of 15 with $162.50, her blessing and the advice to "spend this carefully".

This is the moving beginning of a story of a poor but bright young lad who was later to become a dynamic Methodist missionary and bishop, James Mills Thoburn, who led the team which opened Methodist work in Singapore, and provided episcopal supervision after 1888.

Born on March 7, 1836 in St. Clairsville, Ohio, James was the son of Irish immigrants, the eldest of nine children. In 1850, a year after the death of his father, James enrolled in Allegheny College and graduated in 1857, after having to seek temporary employment as a teacher for a few years because he was short of funds.

He was converted at a church meeting, and although he continued in a "twilight of the soul", his potential was noticed by his pastor who appointed him as a leader of their obligatory class meetings. Forcing himself to lead and pray publicly, his efforts were apparently effective, and resulted in the doubling of the class enrolment - leading to his being encouraged to enter the Christian ministry, even though he was only 19 at the time.

He resolved, however, to complete his college education, joined the Pittsburgh Conference of the Methodist Episcopal Church and was ordained in 1858.

On Jan 1, 1859, James answered the call to be a missionary to India and sailed in July. Coming close to the beginnings of the Methodist Mission in India, set up by William Butler in 1857, James' career paralleled the remarkable growth of the work in India in the second half of the 19th century.

Two almost revolutionary developments were the direct result of his leadership. He was one of the first to start work among India's women and work among the low-caste and untouchables.

It was he who first opened the possibility of his sister, Isabella, taking part in a promising future for India which included educating women and girls, but finances did not exist for a school in every village where there were Christians.

Without much thought, he penned a letter to Isabella, asking if she would like to teach in India. Drawn by the "law of service" which her mother inculcated in her from young, Isabella accepted without hesitation and when the Woman's Foreign Missionary Society (WFMS) was formed in 1869, together with Dr. Clara Swain, they became the first two Methodist women missionaries to be sponsored by the WFMS. Both were the forerunners of a small army of workers who served in India.

Isabella Thoburn College for Women in Lucknow, India.

While Dr. Swain pioneered medical work among women, Isabella was to provide an education for the women who were confined to the zenanas, starting in a one-room schoolhouse in 1870, and expanding to the stately and respected Isabella Thoburn College for Women in Lucknow in 1890 that carries on her work to this day.

One beneficiary was our Mrs. Ellice Handy (née Zuberbuhler) who attended the college in 1917 after completing her Senior Cambridge at Methodist Girls' School (MGS) at the tender age of 14. But she had to spend one year studying Latin before being allowed to start on her BA programme. She returned to Singapore to teach at MGS for the next 25 years, and became the first Asian Principal of the school.

Meanwhile, Isabella's brother, the Rev. James Thoburn's remarkable missionary career in India, which started with preaching to both British soldiers and low-caste folk, included establishing the "Centennial School" in Lucknow, the Lucknow Christian College, Sunday Schools which grew strongly from 34 in 1870 (with 116 students) to 344 in 1881 (with 15,397 students) and editing the Lucknow Witness, a weekly Christian paper. In addition, he was involved in numerous building projects - church sanctuaries, college and school buildings.

As a dynamic speaker and a staunch believer in evangelistic work, he invited the American evangelist William Taylor, widely known as "California Taylor", from his courageous and successful work among the saloons and gambling dens of San Francisco, to preach in India - one result being the conversion of a young man, William F. Oldham, who was to be a key player when the Singapore Mission was started in 1885.

James Thoburn brought Methodism to Southeast Asia

In 1876, James was appointed the Presiding Elder of the South India Conference, and his vision about projects away from India, independent of the "home" Conference in America began to take shape. When he was appointed to take charge of the English-speaking congregation in Calcutta, he accepted an invitation by one of them to open work in Rangoon, where the first Methodist Church was organised in 1882.

But James' vision went beyond Rangoon. As perhaps the most well-known evangelist in India, his reputation had reached the attention of Charles Phillips who headed the Singapore Seamen's Institute. James' vision and Charles Phillips' invitation resulted in the historic voyage to Singapore in 1885 and the establishing of the Methodist Mission in February. From Singapore, James looked east and, having been elected missionary Bishop of South India and Malaysia in 1888, personally visited Manila on March 6, 1900 to hold the first Methodist service shortly after the end of the Spanish colonial regime.

More than a visionary, Bishop James Thoburn was a gifted preacher, administrator and leader who initiated Methodist work in South-east Asia. He died in Meadville, Pennsylvania, on Nov 28, 1922.

History of the Methodist Church in India

According to Mr. P. Dayanand, a leading researcher on the subject, Methodism first came to India with the arrival of Rev. James Lynch to Madras (now Chennai), at a place called Black Town (Broadway), later known as George Town, in 1817. Lynch conducted the first Methodist Missionary service on 2nd March, 1817 in a stable. The first Methodist church was dedicated in 1819 at Royapettah. A chapel was later built and dedicated on 25th April, 1822 at George Town. This church was rebuilt in 1844 since the earlier structure was collapsing. At this time there were around 100 Methodist members in Chennai, all of them either European or of Eurasian descent.

In 1856, William Butler, a missionary from America, heading the Methodist Episcopal Church came to India and began work at Bareilly. However, it was only in 1870, with the arrival of William Taylor, the famous evangelist, who led revival meetings in India that, Methodism became a national factor. Evangelistic work among the deprived classes led to a large number of converts into the Methodist Church in the rural areas. In 1920, the Methodist Missionary Society was organized to supervise the missionary work in India. In 1930, the Central Conference of southern Asia elected the first national Bishop. Since the Independence of India in 1947 all bishops have been Indian nationals. Missionaries were sent to Borneo in 1956 and to the Fiji islands in 1963.

On 7th January, 1981, the Methodist Church in India (MCI) was established as an "autonomous affiliated", church in relation with the United Methodist Church. Bishop Dr. Kariappa Samuel was the first elected bishop of the MCI. The church is now independent in its life and organization and has adopted its own constitution and Book of Discipline and Articles of Faith. The MCI understands itself as the body of Christ in and for the world as part of the church universal. Its purpose is to understand the love of God as revealed in Jesus Christ, to bear witness of this love to all people and to make them his disciples. It has hundreds of thousands of members. It is a member of the World Council of Churches, Christian Conference of Asia, the National Council of Churches in India and World Methodist Council. It runs schools, hostels, colleges, vocational training centres, hospitals and health care centres and many community welfare and development programmes in the country.

Functioning of MCI

The Supreme legislative body of the Church is the General Conference, which meets once in four years.

General Conference takes all major decisions including the appointment of bishops. Bishops are elected by General Conference from among the pastors. The retirement age is 65. Ministerial laymen and deaconess delegates are members of the General Conference.

The Church is divided into six Episcopal areas. It has an Episcopal Conference and Bishops Cabinet. Each Episcopal area is divided into two regional conferences and they are divided into districts. Pastorates form the basic units. Each division has its Conference. Besides ordained ministers, deaconess and laymen are members of the conference.

There are licensed laymen as lay preachers. They are for voluntary preaching in the pastorate. The deaconess renders full time service to the church. A deaconess is a person who is committed to Christ and commissioned by the bishop of the regional Conference.

The MCI has a three-tier judicial system. There is a Judicial Council at the General Conference level. Every Regional Conference has a regional court and at the bottom level there are committees on conciliation at the district conference and pastorate conference level.

The six Episcopal areas of the Church are Bangalore, Bareilly, Mumbai, Delhi, Hyderabad and Lucknow. The strength of the Church is around 7,00,000. All bishops are chairmen of the meeting. Among them one is elected as the President of Council of Bishops.

No.	Episcopal Areas	Regional Conferences	Current Bishops
1	Bangalore	South India	Bishop Dr. Tarnath Sagar
		Madras	
2	Bareilly	North India	Bishop Dr. Samuel Sunder Singh
		Moradabad	
3	Bombay	Bombay	Bishop Dr. Elia Pradeep Samuel
		Gujarat	
4	Delhi	Delhi	Bishop Dr. Samuel Sunder Singh
		Agra	
5	Hyderabad	Hyderabad	Bishop Dr. M. V. Khisti
		Madhya Pradesh	
6	Lucknow	Lucknow	Bishop Dr. Tarnath Sagar
		Bengal	Bishop Dr. M. V. Khisti

References
1. *http://indianchristianity.org/methodist.html*
2. *http://en.wikipedia.org/wiki/Methodist_Church_in_Indi*
3. *http://www.facebook.com/pages/Methodist-Church-in-India/132967530076579*
4. *http://www.oikoumene.org/member-churches/regions/asia/india/methodist-church-in-india.html*
5. http://www.brcmci.org
6. http://gbgm-umc.org/global_news/full_article.cfm?articleid=3174

(Wikipedia)

History of Bengal Regional Conference

The Lucknow Area
This area includes the Bengal, Lucknow and Burma Conference. When Burma joined the South East Asia Central Conference, the Lucknow Area was left with only the Lucknow Conference and the Bengal Conference.

Bengal Conference
Asansol District
In 1926 **James Lyon** was the Presiding Elder of this district. He reported that in spite of sickness, lack of finances and workers the district had grown. By 1926 there were 2,893 Christians in the district. The foundations were laid 40 years ago with the Railway Chaplaincy, English Church and a parsonage. Lyon then turned to Institutions, which no one else had dreamed of.

In Asansol there was a community school under **Dr. and Mrs. Fred Williams,** a large **Bengali Girls' School** under **Miss Carpenter,** a Hindi school and a Bengali school for girls under **Miss Boles** and **Mrs. D'Cruz.** In the Community School, which was outside the city, courses in agriculture, irrigation, carpentry, care of cattle and building abode houses were offered in addition to the regular curriculum. The school was called **Ushagram, "Village of the New Day".** Soon the Bengali Girls' School at Ashabaree also joined Ushagram. The girls learnt cooking, gardening, weaving, arts, music and village work apart from regular studies. **Miss Horshabala Biswas** was the first Bengali woman to become Principal here. Around 1947 **H. E. Dewey** became Director of Ushagram.

Pakur District

After property was purchased in Pakur, the Calcutta Boys' and Girls' Orphanages moved to Pakur. Santals, Muslims and Bengalis studied together. In 1891 two boys from this school became District Conference Members. As the number of Santals increased to a large extent and their official language was Hindi, therefore Hindi became the language of their schools. In the year 1924-25, a separate school was made for the Santal children. **Miss Mildred Pierce** laid the foundations of this school, which would keep the children connected with their simple village life. Ultimately the Women's Foreign Mission Property from the Board of Missions and set up the Santal school project.

As the school made constant and quick progress, it was called **"Jidator"** meaning **"Village of Persistent Advance."** Later it became a High School. It was co-educational and its Principal was **Miss Premi Lee.** She was one of the 2 students who first graduated from Johnson Girls' Training Institute.

During the District Conference in 1941 a large school building was dedicated by **Bishop Rockey.** This has existed as a small school at Sangrampur for many years, it showed signs of growth in 1941. The younger Santal children attended this school, where as the older Santal children went to study at Asansol.

The Bengali Girls' Boarding School at Pakur was at that time called **Alma Jacobson – Keventer School.** Later it became a co-educational Middle school in the Birbhum District. **Rev. and Mrs. K. Das** were the Principals. **Henry Swan** reported that a dispensary had been opened in Pakur before 1898. **Miss Hilda Swan** carried on the work here in 1913. **Miss Marnie Reilley** expanded the work of this dispensary. In 1919 there had been 235 in-patients and 13,825 out patients. **Miss Alley** was a most faithfully worker and a splendid physician – she not only won the confidence but also the hearts of the people.

In the summer of 1923, **Bishop Fisher** transferred the **Edith Jackson Memorial Dispensary** from Calcutta to Pakur. Later **Dr. Mrs. R. N. Peters** took charge.

Calcutta District

A "Native Department" was opened in 1893 under the Principalship of **G.S. Bomwetch.** It was called American Methodist Institute and later renamed The Collins Institute. After **B. J. Chew** and **J.E. Jobinson** served as Principal, **Lolit B. Chatterji** was the first Indian Principal of the school to take charge **S.K. Mondal** was in-charge of the Boarding and Training school. Both of them had served long and efficiently and had won the confidence of Bishop Fisher. Chatterji died in 1925. S. K. Mondol became Assistant Superintendent of the Calcutta Bengali District and later he became District Superintendent. (He was elected Bishop in 1940) **A. B. Singh** was one of the Principals of this school. This school had a total of 780 students in 1954. The original purpose of this school was to supply leaders to the Conference.

The Lee Memorial was an important part of the Calcutta Bengali District. **Dr. Lee** died in 1924. **Mrs. Lee** continued to serve till 1940. Later she gave charge to **Dr. Walter** and **Mabelle Griffiths.** Mrs. Lee passed way in 1948. The Lee Memorial Mission owned a School, a Training Centre at Wellington Square, small Orphanages and schools and some work at Beliaghata and other centers. The representatives of this Mission were also involved in evangelistic work and directed the Church at Beliaghata. In 1906, **Mr. and Mrs. Lee** had deeded the property to Trustees representing the Methodist Church of Southern Asia, the Divisions the Board of Missions, and the Bengal Conference.

Mr. H. C. Fritchley served the Calcutta Boys' School. After 31 years his service came to an end in 1951. He was succeeded by **Clifford Hicks.** It was strongly felt that Christian English-speaking schools were serving the communities of free India in a way that no others had done. The school celebrated its 75th, Anniversary in March 1952.

The Calcutta Girls High School always maintained high standards of character and scholarship. In 1954 there were a total of 529 students. In March 1942, the boarding department was evacuated to Kanpur.

Dhanbad District

In 1926, Dhanbad was a circuit in the Asansol District. Total number of Methodists in Dhanbad, Jerria and all the coal fields was 564. **Benjamin A. Mott** was in charge of this coal-field circuit for a long time. He was strongly supported by the Quarterly Conference. He was the only Hindi preacher in the District in 1948. **J.E. Titus** was the D.S. Gomoh was the District Headquarters for a short while, and B.A. Mott was the resident Pastor. The Bishop Rockey High School in Gomoh had an enrolment of 384 students in 1954.

(The Church of North India)

Church of North India

The Church of North India (CNI), the dominant Protestant denomination in northern India, is a united church established on 29 November 1970 by bringing together the main Protestant churches working in northern India. The merger, which had been in discussions since 1929, came eventually between the Church of India, Pakistan, Burma and Ceylon (Anglican), the United Church of Northern India (Congregationalist and Presbyterian), the Baptist Churches of Northern India (British Baptists), the Church of the Brethren in India, which withdrew in 2006, the Methodist Church (British and Australia Conferences) and the Disciples of Christ denominations.

CNI's jurisdiction covers all states of the Indian Union with the exception of the four states in the south (Andhra Pradesh, Karnataka, Kerala and Tamil Nadu) and has approximately 1,250,000 members in 3,000 pastorates.[3]

History

Ecumenical discussions with a view to a unified church was initiated by the Australian Churches of Christ Mission, Australian Methodist Church, the Wesleyan Methodist Church, the Methodist Episcopal Church and United Church of Northern India during a round table meeting in Lucknow in 1929.

A negotiation committee was set up in 1951 using the plan of Church Union that resulted from the earlier consultations as its basis. The committee was composed of representatives from the Baptist Churches in Northern India, the Church of India, Pakistan, Burma and Ceylon, the Methodist Church (British and Australia Conferences), the Methodist Church in Southern Asia and the United Church of Northern India.[4][5] In 1957, the Church of the Brethren in India and the Disciples of Christ denominations joined in the negotiations as well.

A new negotiation committee was set up in 1961 with representatives from all the above-mentioned denominations. In 1965, a finalised plan of Church Union, known as the "White Paper", was made. The union was formalised on 29 November 1970, when all the negotiating churches were united as the Church of North India with the exception of the Methodist Church in Southern Asia which decided not to join the union.

In 1994 at a synod in Etah, a decision was made by some members of the then dioceses of Agra and Lucknow to withdraw from the CNI and revive the United Church of Northern India, to which they belonged prior to the union.

Beliefs and practices

The CNI is a trinitarian church that draws from the traditions and heritage of its constituent denominations. The basic creeds of the CNI are the Apostle's Creed and the Nicene Creed of 381 AD.

Liturgy

The liturgy of the CNI is of particular interest, as it combines many traditions, including that of the Methodists and such smaller churches as the Church of the Brethren and the Disciples of Christ. Provision is given for diverse liturgical practices and understandings of the divine revelation.

Governance

The polity of the CNI brings together the Episcopacy, the Presbytery and the Laity in an effort to reflect the polity of the Churches that entered into union. The Episcopacy of the CNI is both historical as well as constitutional. There are 26 dioceses, each under the supervision of a bishop. The main administrative and legislative body is the Synod, which meets once every three years to elect a presiding bishop, called a Moderator, and an Executive Committee. The Moderator acts as the head of the church.

Social involvement

Social involvement is a major emphasis in the CNI. There are synodal boards in charge of various ministries: Secondary, Higher, Technical and Theological Education, Health Services, Social Services, Rural Development, Literature and Media. There is also a synodal Programme Office which seeks to protect and promote peace, justice, harmony and dignity of life.

The CNI currently operates 65 hospitals, nine nursing schools, 250 educational institutions and three technical schools. Some of the oldest and well-respected educational institutions in India like Scottish Church College, Calcutta, Wilson College, Mumbai, Hislop College, Nagpur, St. Paul's School, Darjeeling, St. John's College, Agra and St. Stephen's College in Delhi are affiliated to or administered by the CNI.

Ecumenism

The CNI participates in many ecumenical bodies as a reflection of its commitment towards church unity. Domestically it participates in a joint council with the Church of South India and the Mar Thoma Syrian Church known as the Communion of Churches in India. It is also a member of the National Council of Churches in India. Regionally, the CNI participates in the Christian Conference of Asia and on an international level it is a member of the World Council of Churches, the Council for World Mission, World Alliance of Reformed Churches, World Methodist Council and in full communion with the Anglican Communion. The CNI is also in partnership with many other domestic, regional and international Christian agencies.

(Wikipedia)

37 Darjeeling: Past And Present

Darjeeling is a Himalayan city in the Indian state of West Bengal. It is internationally renowned as a tourist destination, along with its tea industry and the Darjeeling Himalayan Railway, a UNESCO World Heritage Site. It is "hill town headquarters" of Darjeeling district with a partially autonomous status within the state of West Bengal. The town is located in the Mahabharat Range or Lesser Himalaya at an average elevation of 6,710 ft (2,050 m).

The development of the town dates back to the mid-19th century, when the British set up a sanatorium and a military depot. Subsequently, extensive tea plantation was done in the region, and tea growers developed distinctive hybrids of black tea and created new fermenting techniques. The resultant distinctive Darjeeling tea is internationally recognised and ranks among the most popular of the black teas.

The Darjeeling Himalayan Railway connects the town with the plains and has one of the few steam locomotives still in service in India. Darjeeling also has several British-style public schools, which attract students from throughout India and neighbouring countries. The town, with its neighbouring town of Kalimpong, was a center for the demand of the Gorkhaland movement in the 1980s. The present movement for a separate state of Gorkhaland is also centered in Darjeeling town. In recent years, the town's fragile ecology has been threatened by a rising demand for environmental resources, stemming from growing tourist traffic and poorly planned urbanisation.

History of Darjeeling

The history of Darjeeling is intertwined with that of Bengal, Sikkim and Nepal. Until the early 19th century, the hilly area around Darjeeling was historically controlled by the kingdom of Sikkim, while the plains around Siliguri were intermittently occupied by the kingdom of Nepal, with settlement consisting of a few villages of Lepcha, Bhutia and Nepalis people. It is also known that Nepal once expanded its kingdom up to the Teesta River after the establishment of the Shah Dynasty in Nepal in the latter part of the 18th century.

The Kingdom of Sikkim was established by the Namgyal Dynasty in 1642. After the Anglo-Nepal war in 1814-15, a delegation of British East India Company officials on its way to Nepal-Sikkim border stayed in Darjeeling in 1828 and decided that the region was a suitable site for a sanatorium for British soldiers. The company negotiated a lease of the area west of the Mahananda River from the Chogyal of Sikkim in 1835.

In 1849, the British East India Company (BEIC) director Arthur Campbell and the explorer and botanist Joseph Dalton Hooker were imprisoned in the region by the Sikkim Chogyal. The East India Company sent a force to free them. Continued friction between the East India Company and the Sikkim authorities resulted in the annexation of 640 square miles (1,700 km²) of territory in 1860.

In 1864, the Bhutanese rulers and the British signed the Treaty of Sinchula that ceded the passes leading through the hills and Kalimpong to the British. The continuing discord between Sikkim and the British resulted in a war, culminating in the signing of a treaty and the annexation by the British of the area east of the Teesta River in 1865. By 1866, Darjeeling district had assumed its current shape and size, covering an area of 1,234 square miles (3,200 km^2).

During the British Raj, Darjeeling's temperate climate led to its development as a hill station for British residents seeking to escape the summer heat of the plains, and its becoming the informal summer capital of the Bengal Presidency in 1840, a practice that was formalised after 1864.

The development of Darjeeling as a sanatorium and health resort proceeded briskly. Arthur Campbell, a surgeon with the Company, and Lieutenant Robert Napier were responsible for establishing a hill station there. Campbell's efforts to develop the station, attract immigrants to cultivate the slopes and stimulate trade resulted in a hundredfold increase in the population of Darjeeling between 1835 and 1849.

The first road connecting the town with the plains was constructed between 1839 and 1842. In 1848, a military depot was set up for British soldiers, and the town became a municipality in 1850. Commercial cultivation of tea in the district began in 1856, and induced a number of British planters to settle there.

Scottish missionaries undertook the construction of schools and welfare centres for the British residents, laying the foundation for Darjeeling's notability as a centre of education. The opening of the Darjeeling Himalayan Railway in 1881 further hastened the development of the region. In 1899, Darjeeling was rocked by major landslides that caused severe damage to the town and the native population.

Under British rule, the Darjeeling area was initially a Non-Regulation District, a scheme of administration applicable to economically less advanced districts in the British Raj, and acts and regulations of the British Raj did not automatically apply to the district in line with rest of the country. In 1919, the area was declared a "backward tract".

During the Indian independence movement, the Non-cooperation Movement spread through the tea estates of Darjeeling. There was also a failed assassination attempt by revolutionaries on Sir John Anderson, the Governor of Bengal in 1934. Subsequently, during the 1940s, Communist activists continued the nationalist movement against the British by mobilising the plantation workers and the peasants of the district.

Socio-economic problems of the region that had not been addressed during British rule continued to linger and were reflected in a representation made to the Constituent Assembly of India in 1947, which highlighted the issues of regional autonomy and Nepali nationality in Darjeeling and adjacent areas. After the independence of India in 1947, Darjeeling was merged with the state of West Bengal. A separate district of Darjeeling was established consisting of the hill towns of Darjeeling, Kurseong, Kalimpong and some parts of the Terai region.

While the hill population included mainly of ethnic Nepalis who had migrated there during British rule, the plains harboured a large ethnic Bengali population who were refugees from the Partition of India. A cautious and non-receptive response by the West Bengal government to most demands of the ethnic Nepali population led to increased calls, in the 1950s and 1960s, for Darjeeling's autonomy and for the recognition of the Nepali language; the state government acceded to the latter demand in 1961.

The creation of a new state of Sikkim in 1975, along with the reluctance of the Government of India to recognise Nepali as an official language under the Constitution of India, brought the issue of a separate state of Gorkhaland to the forefront. Agitation for a separate state continued through the 1980s, included violent protests during the 1986–88 period. The agitation ceased only after an agreement between the government and the Gorkha National Liberation Front (GNLF), resulting in the establishment of an elected body in 1988 called the Darjeeling Gorkha Hill Council (DGHC), which received autonomy to govern the district.

Though Darjeeling became peaceful, the issue of a separate state lingered, fueled in part by the lack of comprehensive economic development in the region even after the formation of the DGHC. New protests erupted in 2008–09, but both the Union and State governments rejected Gorkha Janmukti Morcha's demand for a separate state. In July 2011, a pact was signed between Gorkha Janmukti Morcha (GJM), the Government of West Bengal and the Government of India which includes the formation of a new autonomous, elected Gorkhaland Territorial Administration (GTA), a hill council armed with more powers than its predecessor Darjeeling Gorkha Hill Council.

Besides the demand for creation of a separate State for the Gorkhas/Nepalis in Darjeeling, a vocal section of the Nepali leadership in the hills have been demanding Darjeeling's merger with Sikkim.

(Wikipedia with edition)

38 MH Scores A Century

Jigme N. Kazi

OUR PRINCIPALS during the Centenary Celebrations at Mt. Hermon School in November 1995: (L to R) Mr. & Mrs. Gardner, Mr. & Mrs. Johnston, Mr. & Mrs. Murray and Mr. & Mrs. Stewart.

"It is better to light a candle than curse the darkness," reminded Welthy Honsinger Fisher, wife of Bishop Frederick Fisher, one of the Founders of Mount Hermon School, Darjeeling, which celebrates its Centenary Year this year.

Emma L. Knowles, an educational missionary under the Women's Foreign Missionary Society of the Methodist Episcopal Church of the US, started the Queen's Hill Girls' High School in Darjeeling on March 11, 1895 with only 13 pupils and one thousand rupees.

Knowles, who had already spent some years in India as Principal of schools for European Girls at Nainital (UP) and Calcutta, started Queen's Hill School in a rented house known as 'Arcadia', located below the mall at Chowrasta in Darjeeling.

Mr. John West with the 1973 batch at the Centenary celebrations.

Knowles was a woman of strong faith and devotion to her work. Unmoved by the disastrous earthquake in 1898, which killed many of her pupils, Knowles purchased another plot of land for the school above the railway station on the Hill Cart Road. There she constructed her new school building and continued with her work in 1900.

Twenty years later, the school was shifted to the present location which is several miles away from the town. In 1930, the school was renamed Mt. Hermon School. The present building, which was opened by Lord Lytton, Governor-General of Bengal, was described as "one of the finest buildings in the orient".

"I was very pleased at the opportunity afforded to me by the inauguration ceremony to see the fine new building of this admirable school. I sincerely hope that the school will have a period of increased prosperity and success," stated Lord Lytton during the inaugural ceremony of the new school building on May 26, 1926.

Ada Lee, Founder of Lee Memorial School of Calcutta, had this to say about the new school: "Our two daughters were among the group with which Queen's Hill was organised in 1895. From that time... I have had a deep interest in this school."

The boy's section of the school started only after Bishop Frederick Bohn Fisher, Bishop of Calcutta (Thoburn Church), started taking a deep interest in the school. In fact, Bishop Fisher played a key role in the purchase of the new site which was bought from the Lebong Tea Company and the proprietor of the Grand Hotel in Calcutta and Mount Everest Hotel in Darjeeling.

Bishop Fisher School for Boys, which came up soon after the school building was opened in 1926, was later amalgamated with the Queen's Hill School for Girls. Mount Hermon School was the new name chosen for the school in 1930.

The Darrs, Johnstons, Gardners, Murrays and Stewarts all at my (Jigme N. Kazi) house in Gangtok during the Centenary Celebrations in November 1995. (Hermonite Anup Banerjee took this shot.)

Today, Mt. Hermon has 750 pupils in its roll. Compare this with the 13 students it started with. Besides Knowles and Fisher, among those who played a vital role in setting a strong foundation for the school during its early days were Carolyn J. Stahl and Rev. Halsey E. Dewey. Stahl, Knowles' assistant, took over the school as its Principal in 1914. Referring to her predecessor, Stahl wrote: "...Miss Knowles will tell you she never planned it should be a large school. Evidently, the Lord's plans for the school were larger than ours."

Mt. Hermon (MH) went through a very difficult period in the early 1940s. Because of the Second World War many students and staff from Britain left the school. The future of the mission also seemed uncertain. The enrolment of the school dropped to 120 and the school nearly closed down in 1943.

But somehow Rev. Dewey, the school Principal, kept the school going. Mt. Hermon actually grew in size and substance when Rev. David G. Stewart of the New Zealand and Chinese Inland Mission (now renamed Overseas Missionary Fellowship) took over the school in 1954. Graeme A. Murray, who succeeded Rev. Stewart in 1964, had this to say about his 'boss': "1964 in Mount Hermon School has been the passing of an era in the resignation of Rev. D. G. Stewart, who served us here as the Principal since February 1954...We have a long history as a school, going back to 1895...but I am sure that these

ten years (1954-1964) have been the most effective in our history, as we have seen so much done under Mr. Stewart's wise guidance to raise standards, attract and hold good staff and improve the quality and extent of our physical plant...Together Mr. and Mrs. Stewart have made tremendous contribution to Christian Education in India, and they will not be forgotten by Mount Hermon."

When Stewart took over the school, the enrolment of the school was less than 100 but over the years more students came to study in Mt. Hermon and by the time he left in 1964 the strength of the school had shot up to 365. During the Murray-era (1964-1978), Mt. Hermon became one of the most distinguished co-educational schools in the country. Of the total of 639 students in 1978, 470 were boarders.

MH distinguished itself in both academic and co-curricular activities. Mrs. Murray's contribution added to the school's rich musical heritage. Rev. William Jones and Rev. John A. Johnston built on the foundation laid by their predecessors.

As with many great institutions, MH is going through a difficult period today. The absence of dedicated teachers and the departure of many of its old staff members, particularly those from abroad, coupled with frequent changes in the leadership, have been the main reasons why the school is going through another crisis.

But most Hermonites and well-wishers of the school, who are conscious of the school's long history and its inherent ability to overcome difficulties, believe that this is just a passing phase and sooner or later it will pull through. The need for schools such as MH is greater now than it was a hundred years back. Perhaps it is at times such as these that we ought to remind ourselves of the need to press on and remember Mrs. Fisher's advice: "It is better to light a candle than curse the darkness."

(*Hill People*, July 1995.)

MOUNT HERMON SCHOOL

CONGRATULATIONS: 100 YEARS!!!

We rejoice with you on this special day, 11 March 1995, as you celebrate in Darjeeling the centenary of the founding of "Arcadia", the small seed which has grown, developed and changed through years, becoming in turn "Queen's Hill" and finally our "Beloved Mount Hermon".

It was exactly 40 years, on March 1955, that we arrived, two very young, newly married, inexperienced teachers from New Zealand, to begin our service at Mount Hermon.

We gladly recall all that we were able to share, along with so many others, during the next 24 years, until 1978. Mount Hermon gave us, from its long traditions, just as much, if not more, than we were able to contribute in return. We have so many wonderful memories of colleagues on the staff, students, employees, parents, and people of the Darjeeling community which continue to enrich our lives here in our retirement in Wellington.

And our children, three of whom were born in Darjeeling, had their formative years and most of their schooling as Hermonites; they too rejoice with us in all that they have gained from their Mount Hermon years, and join their greeting with ours on this great occasion.

We wish you all, staff, and students and community, a wonderfully positive time during this Year of centenary celebrations; we have already experienced, at reunions during January in Canberra, Siliguri, Calcutta and Bangkok, just what Mount Hermon means to its "daughters and sons from afar". We hope to be with you in November, along with many other Hermonites from all over the world.

So a very, very,
HAPPY BIRTHDAY, MOUNT HERMON
and every blessing throughout your 1995 centenary year!

Patricia and Graeme Murray
Adrienne (Thompson), Bronwen (Berg),
Stephen & Jonathan

(This was a message from the Murrays for March 11, 1995, and the Centenary Year)

CENTENARY CELEBRATIONS OF
MOUNT HERMON SCHOOL, DARJEELING.
Address by: Shri K.V. Raghunatha Reddy, Governor of West Bengal, 13th November, 1995.

Mount Hermon is a Rare and Unique Educational Institution: West Bengal Governor

I am happy to be with you today for the Centenary Celebrations of Mount Hermon School. It is indeed a great event in the history of the school which has distinguished itself as one of the premier temples of learning not only in our State but in the entire country. I congratulate the school authorities, teachers, staff and students – both past and present – on this occasion and wish the Institution all the best in the service of the society through the spread of education.

Your School has come a long way in the last 100 years. It had a small beginning in 1895 but due to the sincere efforts of various distinguished educationists and personages of vision it soon acquired a reputation which, I must say, has remained quite unique and rare. It would be a befitting occasion to pay our humble homage to these great personages who worried selflessly to give the School the shape and stature which it now enjoys. It is also an occasion which calls for reiteration of their resolve by the teachers and the students alike to work for the sustenance and promotion of the values which were so dear to Emma Knowles and others who founded and nurtured this great Institution. I am sure they will all measure to the occasion and take the school further on its path of glory.

May I, on this solemn occasion, say that the nation expects a great deal from the teachers. The teaching community has to live up to these expectations and imbue the students with the qualities desirable of a responsible citizen. It is the teachers who, through their dedication and selfless service, can help the cause of nation building. Since the teaching community through its own example in professional and social domains can mould the character not only of the students but also of the society its role in frustrating and defeating the evil forces of communalism, separatism and racialism is paramount.

An occasion like this reminds us of the necessity of evaluating our achievements and failures in pursuing our educational goals. The education system in our country this made great strides in offering education to substantial numbers. However, a lot remains to be done. We have not yet fully succeeded in providing quality education to all our people. At times, we even have a feeling of being involved in a losing battle against ignorance and illiteracy.

Our higher education, in particular, is often criticised for its inadequacy in developing proper linkages commensurate with our social and economic needs. If we have to meet the goal of providing a better quality of life to our people, we have to use Science and Technology as an effective instrument of economic growth and social change. Science and Technology should be recognized as an important tool in the development process.

It was Pandit Jawaharlal Nehru's desire to free the Indian mind from the shackles of prejudice and superstition. His vision was to build a nation based on science and socialism and not on fanaticism and monopoly. He, therefore, laid great stress on balanced development of youth which would require a meticulous blending of two currents of thought, viz. the scientific and the spiritual. According to him, "scientific knowledge of the world is essential for the proper education of the youth. A mere study of science, however, without a study of humanities may lead to de-humanisation."

Education is the primary need for promoting human values, improving the quality of human resources and inculcating among the people an attitude to respect our rich cultural diversity. Education to be meaningful cannot remain indifferent to the concern for propagating true humanism which involves tolerance and amity between people of different persuasions in the context of caste, religion, culture and language. These concepts have been a part of our ethos since time immemorial.

While science and technology strive to make a man's existence on earth easier and more comfortable, education in its truest sense should, as Swami Vivekananda said, aim at "life-building, man-making and character-making". It should cater to the development of mind and the spirit or else we would have enormous power without any over-riding ethical purpose.

Parents and teachers have to bear in mind that it is only in the formative years that the values of democracy, secularism, equality and social justice can be successfully inculcated in the students. Similarly, pride in our heritage and nurturing of diversity, if taught in early stages of life, become part of their nature. Here I may quote our respected President Shri Shanker Dayal Sharmaji who said, "Education is more than transfer of information from the teacher to the students. It becomes meaningful only when it creates a value system in which knowledge is received and assimilated. Its importance is in providing the moral and ethical bearings to assess and appreciate developments of life."

Lord Lytton during his visit to your School in May 1926 said, "I sincerely hope that the school will have a period of increased prosperity and success". I echo his sentiments and wish you all the best.

Jai Hind.

ADDRESS BY MR. K.N. RAI, MINISTER OF EDUCATION, GOVERNMENT OF SIKKIM, ON MOUNT HERMON SCHOOL'S CENTENARY CELEBRATIONS, NOVEMBER 22, 1995.

"May Mt. Hermon go from strength to strength"

Mr. and Mrs. Stewart, Mr. and Mrs. Murray, Mr. and Mrs. Johnston, Mr. and Mrs. Gardner, Mr. and Mrs. Samuel, Ex-Hermonites, distinguished guests, staff and students of the school.

It gives me immense pleasure to be here today on this historic occasion of the Centenary Celebrations of this great institution.

First of all, I would like to thank the Sikkim Hermonites Association for inviting me here today.

The school, in the past so many decades, have given a firm educational foundation to many of our youngsters in Sikkim. Many of them are making great contributions to the people in the State today. We are indeed grateful to all ex-principals and staff members of the school for giving an all-round educational development to all Hermonites.

As in the past, I believe Mt. Hermon School will continue to maintain its rich heritage and standards in the field of education and in imparting human values to all those who have spent some part of their life in the school.

The year-long Centenary Celebrations will come to an end tomorrow, but we believe that all those who are present here today will not go back with only fond and happy memories but will continue to take an active part in all spheres of life in the school.

Let this day be not just a mere celebration of a glorious hundred years of Mt. Hermon School. But let this day be the Dawn of a new era – the beginning of a new relationship with the school. I make a fervent appeal to all Hermonites to continue to live up to the motto of the school "Not for school but for life we learn".

May Mt. Hermon go from strength to strength and may the dreams of its Founders and all those who have devoted their life to the school become a reality today and in the years to come.

"Hail Mount Hermon!"

Delhi Hermonites reunion, 1995.

'Good Old Days' Club Formed By Alumni Of Darjeeling Schools In Sikkim

Alumni of Darjeeling, Kalimpong and Kurseong's renowned missionary (public) schools residing in Sikkim on August 15, 2014 formed the 'Good Old Days Club' (GODc) in Gangtok.

"The main purpose of the body is to renew old bonds and have a good time together," said one of the members at the informal launch of the Club.

The members of the Club will be ex-students of St. Paul's School, St. Joseph's School, Mt. Hermon School, Loteto Convent (Darjeeling), Goethal's Memorial School, Dow Hill School, St. Helen's Convent, Victoria School (Kurseong), Dr. Graham's Homes, St. Augustine's School, St. Joseph's Convent (Kalimpong).

These schools were founded by foreign missionaries in Darjeeling hills in the 19th century, when the region came under the British Raj in India.

Initially conceived by Sikkim Hermonites Association a few years back, the Club will reach out to all alumni of these schools in the State to make the association an active forum for renewal of friendship and preservation/celebration of the unique spirit of camaraderie that alumni of these schools enjoy.

"One of the main reasons for the alumni of these schools to come together on a regular basis is that no matter who we are or what we do our 'hard disk' is the same! We started our life together, lets end it in the same spirit," said Hermonite Jigme N. Kazi.

Those who were present at the historic dinner get-together on August 15 at Hotel Tashi Delek were: Ashwin Oberoi and Govind Alley (Goethal's Memorial School), A. Dutta (Victoria School), Sonam Dorji (St. Augustine's School), Navin Prasad

(Dr. Graham's Homes), Wangyal Topden and Tashi Gyatso (St. Joseph's School) and O.T. Bhutia, Surendrapal Singh Lamba, Uttam Pradhan, Ramesh Lakhotia and Jigme N. Kazi (Mt. Hermon School).

A formal launch of the GODc will take place in Gangtok shortly with a larger body, followed by the keenly-awaited 'bash' to set the ball rolling.

NP's Mohan Pradhan takes a walk around the Mall, Darjeeling.

Hail Mount Hermon! A Tribute

The North Pointers

HERITAGE SCHOOLS IN DARJEELING

Dow Hill School, Kurseong.

Dr. Graham's Homes, Kalimpong.

St. Paul's School, Darjeeling.

Goethal's Memorial School, Kurseong.

St. Joseph's Convent, Kalimpong.

St. Joseph's School, Darjeeling.

Loreto Convent, Darjeeling.

Victoria School, Kurseong.

GOOD OLD DAYS *Club* (GODc)

Friends,

We are coming together again and forming our own exclusive club. Its going to be called GOOD OLD DAYS *Club* (GODc) and you are invited.

But you have to be an alumni of these schools: St. Paul's School, St. Joseph's School, Mt. Hermon School, Loteto Convent (Darjeeling), Goethal's Memorial School, Dow Hill School, St. Helens School, Victoria School (Kurseong), Dr. Graham's Homes, St. Augustine's School, St. Joseph's Convent (Kalimpong).

These schools in Darjeeling hills were basically missionary schools when it began in the 19th century. Now, we are the 21st century missionaries! And GOD has called us to come together again...and we have arrived!!!

The first get-together will be a small one on August 15, 2014 in Gangtok. Later on, we will have a grand bash in Gangtok.

GODc is an idea whose time has come. Take advantage of it, folks and see you soon!

(Jigme N. Kazi)
August 13, 2014

40 Defining Decades: '50s & '60s

Hail Mount Hermon! A Tribute

Hail Mount Hermon! A Tribute

Defining Decades: '50s & '60s

Hail Mount Hermon! A Tribute

Defining Decades: '50s & '60s

421

Defining Decades: '50s & '60s

Hail Mount Hermon! A Tribute

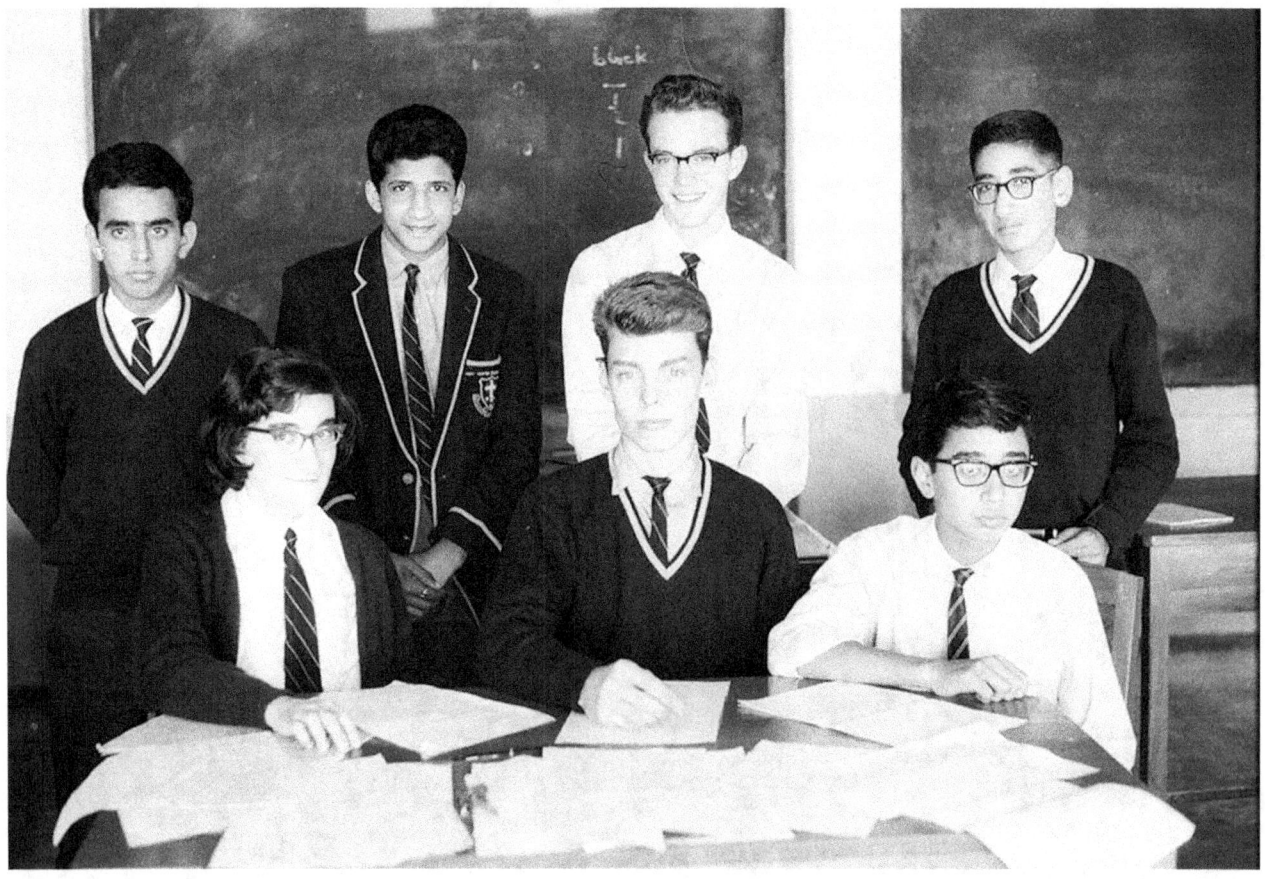

Hail Mount Hermon! A Tribute

Defining Decades: '50s & '60s

COUPLES FOR LIFE!

41 And They Called It Puppy Love

Dedicated to Sherab & Roslyn

Stephen Murray, SC 1974

Sherab Namgyal and Roslyn Rongong were pairs in school. After they left school in early 1970s the couple met in Australia, where Roslyn lived and where Sherab had gone for higher studies (actually he studied at Papua New Guinea University). However, both of them came back to Mt. Hermon to teach and love blossomed, ending in their marriage in MH in 1977!! They now live with their family in Canberra, Australia.

And They Called It Puppy Love

Mount Hermon has been described in *Time* magazine as an International School. The description is surely apt for the school students come from a wide range of social, racial and religious backgrounds both from within Indian and from overseas as well. No doubt other schools in the district could similarly lay claim to such a title.

What really sets Mount Hermon apart from other schools in the hills and indeed the vast majority of schools in India is the fact that it is a co-educational boarding school. In a country where the relationship between the sexes is often regulated by rigid social roles it is not surprising that this should be reflected in the social world. However, there are other influences mainly what some have called the Western ideal of romantic love and the inevitable influence, where young teenagers are concerned, of popular culture. These combine to form a subtle style of "love" that belongs to Mount Hermon uniquely.

Fencing or what?

If a stranger asked who the boy and girl sitting near the monkey ladder were, he would probably be told that they were a couple. A couple? Well what is a couple? How is that status attained? Mr. Moore – the teacher which a football took away the little bit of sense he had – called the phenomena "fencing". A sport it almost is – each generation of Hermonites has its own idiosyncrasies and I can only write from the experience of my peers although I do believe that certain traditions are firmly established.

You've got a friend

As in any honourable society a boy at Mount Hermon who wishes to get to know a girl must declare his intentions either to be her brother or her boyfriend. To be a brother is to be a close friend. These brother-sister relationships extend right through the school and I think are largely responsible for the close family atmosphere in the school. I remember being big brother to some very junior school girls whom I would have died for. To become a boyfriend is an operation fraught with risk although the risk can be substantially diminished if the operation is carefully executed.

Tell Laura I love her

I will leave aside the description of the first realization of love to poets and pop singers. Now I need some hypothetical boys and girls – so since $X+Y=Yom?$ – let X, Y be the boy and his best friend respectively. X tells Y that he "likes" P and then the object immediately becomes to discover what P thinks. P may suddenly find herself being teased about X by all his friends. X will of course vehemently deny that he has anything to do with it although secretly he will be watching her reaction closely for some favourable sign. If actually confronted by her, his beautiful blush may give the whole game away. The lesson for every girl in this predicament is that there is no smoke without fire.

As I write this letter

We all know about writing notes in the study hall although some of us shouldn't. Here is where the final drama takes place. X tells Y to write to P in his name; this is his protective device. The standard form note reads something like this:

"Dear P,

I like you. Do you like me? Do you want to start off walking around the school?

X

P.S. Don't show to anyone O.K. TEAR IT UP"

An acceptance is namely immediately forthcoming. The standard form of refusal generally reads:

"Dear X,

Don't mind please my daddy will kill me if I don't study hard. Everybody is my friend O.K.

P

In which case X replies:

"Dear P,

What are you trying? I didn't write boy. Also everyone is my friend.

P.S. Don't be so proud."

This note hopefully exonerates him unless it is intercepted by a staff member. Mr. West was always particularly adept at this. Not only did he leave the study hall doors open so that the tell-tale door opening did not give him away but he also sat near the back of the room which made beating him extremely difficult. If something ever did give him away it was the clatter of one of his numerous cups of tea.

Are you going to Scarborough fair?

The traditional day for a couple to start off is Sale Day. This is a perfect occasion for a couple. Not too near the beginning of the year so people will think them "fast" and not too late in the year when boys are more likely receive I-have-to-study-hard refusals. Furthermore, it is a day of great festivity and colour with everybody in their "fancies" and crowds of people everywhere making the new couple less conspicuous. The boy can show off his strength and agility by "killing the rat", or attempt the even more difficult task of knocking coconuts off their holders which are embedded more firmly in the ground each year as the stock of coconuts dwindles. Couples usually end up in the cafe stall which was always set up in the lounge and run by the pop music gurus of the time, where they dedicate songs to each other. I recall songs like "Don't let me down" by the Beatles, "Let me be there" by Olivia Newton John, "Everything I own" by Bread, "Until the Twelfth of..." by the Osmonds and many others.

We've only just begun

The status of being a couple is however incomplete until the pains of having walked around the school on an ordinary evening. The phrase "walking around the school" is actually innocent. Firstly because it is forbidden to walk right around the school and secondly because couples tend to stand along the fences running on either side of the steps leading down to the gymnasium or in between the Old and New Building – hence Mr. Moore's "fencing". Once the step has been taken both staff and students give the two recognition as a couple. From then on, the staff keep a watchful but parental eye on them.

It takes two baby

Couples should never be described without some mention of their particular friends Y-Q, on in fencing terms, their seconds. They play a vital role carrying notes and messages patching up quarrels and rendering advice with wisdom beyond their years. One of the benefits of being a second is the opportunity to share "leave day" spoils, the cakes from Glen's, chowmein from Shang's or the latest knick knacks from Das Studio. Frequently this constant interaction between the seconds (most surprisingly) leads them to pair off too!

The things we do for love

There were the dainty patterned umbrellas which the girls lent to the boys in the monsoon for the walk to and from Fernhill. Sewing Sports Day numbers on vests was a task which generous girlfriends performed for less practical boys like myself. Then there were the notes, coloured, scented, in all shapes and sizes. An interesting aspect of these notes were the geographical acronyms – one for each fold. Examples are INDIA – I'll never do it again, ITALY – I trust and love you, FRANCE – friendship remains and never can end etc. Finally, there were the autograph books. At one time charts of best boy/best girl/best food/best actor etc., were very popular but they later disappeared and the proverbial message columns took this place.

I'll never fall in love again?

While writing I have necessarily had to typify the events I have tried to describe. But the basic traditions serve to protect the fragile feelings of Hermonite teenagers as they encounter students from a host of backgrounds with varying social attitudes. Moreover, they draw the students into the heart of school life rather than rejecting them. Ort staff take a caring approach to the couples and on the whole handle them sensitively when they could so easily crush any notion of their feelings. For this they deserve a great deal of respect. Here one catches a glimpse of the humanity of the school which cover every activity. Some might question the propriety of writing about "couples" but surely it is hardly surprising when you consider the startling beauty of our girls. I should say it definitely makes up for their netball!! and this rather prolix piece of prose will end with a nostalgic verse from a song by the Bee Gees:

"Now we are tall, and Christmas trees are small
And we don't ask the time of day
But you and I, our love will never die
And guess we'll cry come first of May!!!"

(Hermonite 1978, annual school magazine.)

For Life!

Tenzing Tethong and Bina Lama with Hemant Lama, March 2017. (autumnbrave)

Hail Mount Hermon! A Tribute

"NON SCHOLAE SED VITAE DISCIMUS"! That bold motto is so solemnly followed by the pupils and so successfully achieved here in the same place. Mount Hermon has been responsible for the ringing of many wedding bells. Not for school but for life. Let us step closer and get a better look at her work of match-making.

Mr. W.W. Jones came to Mount Hermon with a violin and an innocent heart. He taught his pupils to master the art of producing music with the aid of metal strings and hair from horses' tails. Suddenly the tune changed. His eyes jumped from the music to Miss Beulah Kessop and rested there. Within a few weeks his art of whistling left his fiddling in the shade as each night he stood under the window of Miss Kessop and conveyed his love through whistles. Cupid had converted a violinist to an outstanding whistler. Miss Kessop soon occupied the place of the violin. M.H. took the two love-laden hearts to the altar and has kept them together – for life.

Two people from the continent of Australia came as complete strangers to each other and then got to know each other on the tennis court of M.H. Thus, began the romance of Mr. Jim Darr and Miss Judy McCallum. The same two people who were hitting tennis balls at each other soon were exchanging wedding rings. Score – LOVE ALL.

M.H. then witnessed the Hindi teacher, Mr. Das, being swept away by Miss Waters. Once again two people from the staff agreed to spend their lives together as wife and husband. The tennis court at the same time kept on attracting more players two of which were Mr. George Daniells and Miss Yeoline Massey. It was there they fell in love and decided to quit the game of singles and instead play "doubles". The bells of St. Andrews soon announced the wedding of Mr. Daniells and Miss Massey.

We saw the beautiful paintings and other work of art and heard the melodious voice of the Hindi master, Mr. Bhatt. Miss David, Head of the Infant Department, saw things from a different point of view and Mr. Bhatt acknowledged her views most approvingly. The "Yes" had been uttered and their engagement was announced in chapel. The end of 1975 saw Miss David change her name to Mrs. Bhatt.

For about 80 years of her life, M.H. had heard of only one case where two ex-students were bound in matrimony. It seemed that that was going to be the first and the last. Suddenly news arrived saying that Rajendra Lakhotia was getting married to Kavita Palriwala, both ex-students. Now they are together – not for school but for life. When would M.H. see the marriage of two of her ex-students next?

Staff and students wondered why Mr. Francis Borges, teacher of class 5, made so many visits to the school office every day. The suspense ended when they saw Miss Prava Khaling, Mr. Jones' private secretary, frequently walking around with Mr. Borges. M.H. saw them go away to get married and live together.

"When would M.H. see the marriage of two of her ex-students next?" was the question that went unanswered. 1977 answered the question. 1972 had seen two shy young lovers still in school, Sherab Namgyal and Roslyn Rongong. After school Roslyn went to New Zealand and Sherab to New Guinea. They remained friends but couldn't see much of each other.

And They Called It Puppy Love

Rajendra Lakhotia and Kavita Palriwala.

As coincidence would have it, Sherab returned to Sikkim in 1976 and Roslyn came back to M.H. in 1977. Suddenly the line went hot and on Sale Day, word of "Yes" went around. They were married in the school chapel on 30th December 1977. The third couple of ex-students to come to the altar.

Along with Miss Namgyal had come a friend of hers from Aotearoa (New Zealand). Miss Sandra Riley had come to see the mountains but she found the Yeti more attractive.

Mr. Dhruba Rai's keen yeti-eyes soon fell on the young Kiwi. They were engaged in October 1977 and December 1978 will see them walking down the aisle, hand in hand.

Who said there is a vast difference between History and Science? Not Mr. George Fernandes and Miss Saroj Pradhan. They too became Cupid's victims and announced their engagement in October 1978. Wedding bells are waiting to be rung.

Al these are a reflection of the homely and family atmosphere of M.H. She will put more hearts together I'm sure – not for school but for life.

-Anon

(Hermonite 1978, annual school magazine.)

Hail Mount Hermon! A Tribute

Thupden and Rinchen

Thupden and Rinchen.

And They Called It Puppy Love

Two Sikkimese Hermonites, Thupden Gyatso Bhutia and Rinchen Gensapa, both batches of 2002, have been married for over 23 years now. Thupden is a lawyer while Rinchen, a physiotherapist and presently a lecturer, in live in Gangtok.

"We were together since 1996....that's when we were in grade seven. Today, it's been 23 long years, still going strong and blessed with a baby girl!," says Rinchen. She adds, "Thankyou Mount Hermon for playing cupid to this beautiful union!!"

The couple made outstanding performances in school. Rinchen was intelligent and was awarded 1st Prize in every class, while Thupden was not only the recipient of Dr. Master's Cup for Service while passing class XII but was also the holder of Blue Coat for games and sports.

Mick Glasby and Khristine Johnston.

Hail Mount Hermon! A Tribute

Dhruba Rai and Sandra Riley.

Ramesh Lakhotia and Kavita Chainwala.

Hashib Mondol and Mafida Rehman.

'JOHNNY' AT THE 'GARDEN OF REMEMBRANCE'

Mount Hermon Memories And Random Thoughts

Ranjit Dasgupta, 1953 to 1963

So, here we go, a glass of Single Malt by my side, and a walk back to my childhood, school days.

I started boarding school when I was five, a year in St. Paul's (Darjeeling); no real memories except for the Principal Mr. Goddard (I think) and a lady who taught piano who had a little girl with leg braces. Then two years in Goethal's (Kurseong); no memories, except for the Conifer trees opposite the dorm on fire!!

1953, Mount Hermon, secluded in a wooded countryside. I guess the difference between the other two schools and MH was the feeling of Peace & Warmth, to an eight-year-old boy who came from a Tea Estate background.

Names pop-up, Mrs. Martin, the matron. Her son Derek Martin, with his cream-role hairstyle, the in-thing then!! Elvis was alive & well!! Mrs. Alexandra and her son Robin.

Sneaking up through Top Flat to "Hafees" the shop for "churpi" and peanuts (which we hid inside our beds and munched after lights out!!)

Years go by, the cricket season matches. I was in Dewey House playing against Fisher (unlike Ronen Ghosh, I was not a cricketer!!), went in to bat, the ball missed my bat but struck true, in my crotch! I dropped to the ground, writhing in pain. Mr. Murray came up and asked, "Aren't you wearing a guard?" "No!" "Idiot it's your own fault!!" AND that was the end of my cricketing career!

TRIBUTE TO MR. JOHNSTON BY RANJIT DASGUPTA

"Mr. Johnston touched our lives by the ordinary things he did"

The power of a man's virtue should not be measured by his special efforts, but by his ordinary doings. People can argue with your faith, your doctrine, and even your convictions, but one thing they can never successfully dispute is a life well lived.

And so, it was for my Fernhill Warden, for the Senior Master and Principal of our daughters Jasmina and Shaheen.

Ranjit Dasgupta (front right) is with the Johnstons during a function in honour of Mr. Johnston at the 'Garden of Remembrance' at Dr. Graham's Homes, Kalimpong, 2018.

Mr. Johnston, or Johnny, as he was affectionately called, along with Mrs. Johnston, touched our lives, by the "ordinary things they did", that in later life we look back as "extraordinary teaching".

To love, to have empathy, to help those less fortunate, to laugh, to sing and always, always to give thanks to God each and every day.

Ordinary things make a caring human being. "Ordinary things" that have made us what we are today.

I came to Mount Hermon in 1953, after me came our daughters Jasmina and then Shaheen. Our girls were treated as grandchildren of the school, perhaps the first children of an ex-student to enroll. Most especially by Mr. and Mrs. Johnston.

Jasmina was the first recipient of the Johnston Cup for excellence. She would have been here today, but is still in Perth with our younger daughter Shaheen.

Hot chocolate seems to be one of the binding factors both for Jasmina and myself to the Johnstons!!! Mr. Johnston used to take Jasmina swimming at 5.30 a.m. to improve her kicking ability. Mrs. Johnston turned up later with hot chocolate.

Shiv, Uttam, Roshan and Jigme at the 'Garden of Remembrance', Kalimpong, 2018.

Today is a celebration of Mr. Johnston's life, today is to say "Thank You" for being such an important part of our lives, and today is to say "Thank You" to Mrs. Johnson for making it possible for all of us to be a part of your family in laying rest the ashes of Mr. Johnston in these beautiful hills.

To Mr. Johnson, a man who made the ordinary, extraordinary.

Athletics and Hockey were more my style. Preparing for Sports Day, the after-dinner laps in the field (I was by then in Fern Hill), building up stamina and speed. High-Jump with my Eastern Roll! Hockey Practice, played Goalie. The finals against Goethal's, no backs in sight, the ball whipped into the top corner of the goal, no option but to head it out and in the process knocked myself out!! Saved the day and earned my Blues!!

Sundays, digging the swimming pool (I was in Minton then) took months but it got done. The first water, brown & dirty, but what a swim! The senior years, as a Prefect. My first lessons in man-management!! The realisation as to how easy it is to whip up emotions and how difficult to control them thereafter. The food at times had taken a major drop in quality, bread was stale and hard and we were being served brain curry!!

As a Prefect started a protest, (by ringing the dining room bell with a stale bread crust!!) which quickly got out of hand and guys started throwing *dekchis* of curry out the window!! Net result: my Dad was called up and I got a good talking too, but the food improved and I retained my Prefect status!! Now That was The Boss, handling the situation. The greatest Principal MH has ever had, David Stewart!

Compared to St Paul's & Goethal's, the only time I ever got caned was by Mr. Murray!! It was Sale Day (Sale Day was held in the Quad) and I won a coconut from the coconut-shy. Question was how to break the coconut? So I went up to the toilets in the boy's dorm and smashed the coconut in the wash basin! The basin shattered and the coconut remained whole! Some kid reported me and there I was bending over in Mr. Murray's office!!

Fern Hill, first with Mr. Mathai as warden and then the Johnstons. Ovaltine and cookies for babysitting their kids. Best Ovaltine I ever had! Thinking back, so many faces (now thanks to Face Book, being able to reconnect).

Relaxing at our favourites haunt, Hotel Tashi Delek, Gangtok.

Tommy Creese, my first devoted friend! But how we met; he was a Tea Owner's son (Lopchu Estate) and me from a Tea family. I guess this kicked it off. Anyways I remember he had a new football and we were kicking it round near the monkey ladder and I kicked it over the fence and down the Khud! A wrestle in the mud, some tears at the lost ball and friends forever!! Tom is one of the most gifted people I have ever come across. Give him any musical instrument and in half a day he will play it. Brainy without trying, did his Senior Cambridge with me in Arts, stayed back to do it over in Science the next year.

We later teamed up with David Hunt and Yusuf Hussain and became the gang of four! One of my fondest memories was sitting on the first-floor ledge outside Fern Hill, Dave with only the mouth piece of his trumpet, and Tom with his guitar, overlooking the valley, a clear crisp night with Kanchenjunga in all her glory, simmering in the moonlight, and these two making music!!

My younger Dilip, has his own tale to tell of his years in MH. Our two daughters, Jasmina and Shaheen, followed my foot steps into MH. Same teachers, different students, as one of them said Jasmina & Shaheen were like grandchildren to them!! Possibly they were the first children of a former student to pass through the walls of Mount Hermon.

Friends and lovers never to be forgotten, memories may grow dim but are encased in that warm light that glows in the depths of one's soul.

Hail Mount Hermon!!

THANK YOU ALL: VAL JOHNSTON

Very dear Jigme,

Three weeks have passed since Lyndy and I reached Tasmania after that extra week in South India meeting up with staff and ex-students once more. It is not easy to come to terms again with the empty house but all the love and support you all spread amongst the 7 family members and the comfort of CLOSURE for us and MHS/DGH ex-staffs and students as his mortal remains rest in peace, is truly a Blessing. I believe his spirit is with us and his prayers for you all continue.

Thank you so very much for all you did to make the journey for us so perfect amid underlying sadness. You were present at MHS, DGH and again at Gangtok and I appreciate what you expressed as did many others. It was humbling and gratifying to hear some of the sincere insights the students had experienced over the years - in the 50s, all the 60s, beginning and late 70s and all the 80s. They were well represented and I felt a bonding of all - no matter what Faith, Creed or Caste - we are all Hermonites sharing the same love and values.

Whatever happens to the bricks and mortar, the original and renewed Admin, which may change as change does, we are all together in honouring those wonderful years that 'filled the gap' and changed many lives. To have been so welcomed back HOME was gift enough for us wherever we went. Thank you for the generous gifts at Gangtok. There was no need but we appreciated the love and thought.

Siliguri Hermonite Ravi Agarwal with Mrs. Johnston.

I was especially thrilled that so many girls from the 70s and TTC etc., were present. If you could let me have the contact IDs for Prava, Pasankit, Karma, Roshni, Dalamu, and any TTCs I would appreciate it. I think I have most other ex-Hermonites' IDs in Gangtok.

Ravi, did a great job in organising Siliguri Darjeeling and DGH gatherings, also with transport and the Plaque at the Garden of Remembrance, Amode in Kalimpong, also Sunirmal and Choten for accommodation in Darj and their participation.

I found Henry Simon so sincere, self-effacing and well prepared suitable to the occasion as with the children singing and the few words from Michael and Lyndy. Thanks for your contribution in your sincere speech. I noted with delight your reference to the Bible verse Sir gave you to encourage and live by Acts 10 verses 34 and 35. In whatever circumstances you have found yourself, this commitment you made so many years ago in the 60s. God honours for Eternity. It was always the simple Truth Sir shared with all - 'God loves you God forgives you' - Jesus came to tell us. I see Sir has underlined that and hundreds more verses in his small Good News NT he carried always and which is rather falling apart if I am not careful! I remember occasions when he had to punish some misdemeanours - all class 9 boys! He put way the cane and shook hands with them; never held a grudge. It made such a difference to the whole student body.

Mrs. Johnston with Motilal Lakhotia at Hotel Tashi Delek, Gangtok, 2018.

Kristine and Jenni will probably make their 'pilgrimage' to Kalimpong and Gangtok late February. They are trying to persuade me to come again but I have to see how old age and finances can allow, nevertheless, it will always be 'coming home' for us when we cross the equator and step on to Indian soil.

God Bless you.
My love and prayerful remembrances always.
Val J

THAI HERMONITES AT THE 'GARDEN OF REMEMBRANCE', March 2020

43 Old Friends Are Loyal Friends

OLD WALLS

Old walls are friendly walls
Friendly walls, farewell!
Old walls hold memories
That breathe a kindly spell.
Breathe then your benison
On me as I depart,
I'll keep your memory
Warm in my heart.

Old shadowed arches grey,
Long have we been friends.
We can no longer stay
Where your kind shade extends
Breathe then your benison
On me as I depart,
I'll keep your memory
Warm in my heart.

Old friends are loyal friends,
Friends of happy days.
Now we must say goodbye
And go dividing ways
Breathe then your benison
On me as I depart,
I'll keep your memory
Warm in my heart.

Friends of happy days: Dhruba, Sherab, Sandra, Roslyn and Walsa.

(L to R) Namgyal, Uttam, Rocky Gardner and Jigme, 2018.

MH Family: Anands, Glabsys and Namgyals.

Mr. Murray with the Hermonite staff on the way to Gangtok in late 1970s.

Adrienne and Roslyn.

Old Friends Are Loyal Friends

Sonam (centre) with Namgyal and Jigme.

Varongthip's daughter's wedding, Calcutta, 2019.

Tshering with Thinley.

The Class of 1972: Sherab, Jigme, Ongeytob and Udai.

1973 batch reunion, Kalimpong.

UK Hermonites: Ian, Neena, Mitti, Mary Ann Mackie and Ronald Alcorn.

Mahesh, Apok and Charan.

Krishna with Deki.

MH 1977: Brenda, Annie, Karen, Mala and Corinne.

Hail Mount Hermon! A Tribute

Thip, Joe, Bronwyn, Navin and Ravi, 2013.

Old Friends Are Loyal Friends

Hermonites reunion, Pattaya.

1969 batch reunion, Kaziranga, 2019.

Daars with Dubs, New Zealand.

Edinburgh Shield team

1968 batch reunion, Kurseong, 2018.

1972 batch: Jagdish, Sunirmal and Sushil.

HERMONS ON THE MOUNT – Part VII

44 The Jewel Of Sikkim

Madan Mohan Rasaily

Born on 22nd September 1928, the fourth son of Manbir Singh Rasaily, Finance Secretary to His Highness, the Maharaja of Sikkim, Sir Tashi Namgyal, Madan Mohan Rasaily studied up to Class IV at Sir Tashi Namgyal High School, Gangtok, and went to join Mt. Hermon School, Darjeeling, as a boarder, from where he completed his Senior Cambridge in 1943.

He pursued his B.Sc. at St. Xavier's College, Calcutta, and later shifted to the Government College, Darjeeling, when they introduced the subject Botany. Before going for his higher studies, he taught Science and Geography at Sir Tashi Namgyal High School for sometime as there was no subject teacher available at that time.

From the year 1955-58 he underwent Higher Forestry training at Indian Forest College, Dehradun. After successful completion of his training he came back and joined the Sikkim Forest Department as Assistant Conservator of Forest on 1st of March 1960. He became DFO, East when Arjan Singh was the Conservator of Forest on deputation from Punjab. He took the charge as Head of Forest Department as Conservator of Forest after the tenure of Dakman Lama.

He served as a bureaucrat for 35 years. Working in tandem with the vision of the 12th Chogyal of Sikkim, His Highness, Palden Thondup Namgyal, he helped to set up the State Trading Corporation of Sikkim, the State Lottery (for aiding Development Plans), the Sikkim Jewels, the Sikkim Time Corporation and the Sikkim Supreme Factory at Singtam. At the time of Chinese invasion in 1962, he was entrusted with the work of Civil Defence Commissioner.

He was also the Auditor General of Sikkim till 1974. During his tenure he held the responsibilities of Auditor General as well as Secretaries of different Departments like Trade, Industries and Commerce, Tourism, Education, Motor Vehicle, Home and also as Director Vigilance. He retired from the service in 1988 when he was posted as Home Secretary. Apart from the committed service to Sikkim, he was also involved in other activities. He was one of the founding members of the Rotary Club in Sikkim.

He was an avid footballer and played for the school team, college team and also the town team which consisted of officers serving the Chogyal of Sikkim. He accompanied the Chogyal Palden Thondup Namgyal in his visits to Switzerland, UK and also Birendra of Nepal.

He also helped strengthen the Sri Satya Sai organization of Sikkim as its President and also helped in designing and completion of the Sai Mandir at Baluwakhani, Gangtok. He was conferred the Denzong Thu ki Norbu (The Jewel of Sikkim), the highest civilian award of the then Kingdom of Sikkim. He received this award in the year 1974 from His Highness, the Chogyal Palden Thondup Namgyal. He also conferred the Pema Dorjee medal, for his dedicated service. He retired from Government service in 1988 when he was Additional Chief Secretary-cum-Home Secretary.

Tributes to a true and loyal 'Son of Sikkim'
Rasaily was an upright man: Chief Minister

The Chief Minister Pawan Chamling in his condolence message said that MM Rasaily, who held the high esteemed post of Secretary Home and many other departments in his service career, was known for his professionalism and his able administration.

"Shri Rasaily was an upright person with impeccable integrity and his demise is an irreparable loss to the state" the Chief Minister said.

He was loyal to his motherland Sikkim

With all respect and veneration, we the monks of Sikkim remember great son of Sikkim, Madan Mohan Rasaily on his passing away, early morning today.

The monks and people of Sikkim shall always remember late MM Rasaily with fond memory of his love for Sikkim. We believe he preceded every Sikkimese official, both amongst his contemporaries and present as far as loyalty and love for the motherland is concerned.

Sherab Tenzing Lepcha
General Secretary
Monks of Sikkim

His love and loyalty for Sikkim inspires us

"On the passing away of Shri Madan Mohan Rasaily ('Denzong Thuki Norbu' and 'Pema Dorje'), former Home Secretary of Sikkim and Ven Dorje Loben Sonam Angay Lama of Sumin Monastery early morning today, I express my heartfelt condolences to the members of the family of the deceased.

Shri MM Rasaily's contribution and sincerity towards the delivery of his duties are legends in our Sikkimese society. A blue-eyed figure of Sikkim, his loyalty to his duty and motherland shall surely become a source of inspiration for all of us."

Sonam Lama
Sangha MLA

He stood firm, we salute him

"The passing away of Mr. MM Rasaily has left an irreparable vacuum in the Sikkimese society, particularly the one who loves Sikkim. The conferring of Sikkim's highest Civilian Award of Sikkim 'Denzong Thuki Norbu' and others as 'Pema Dorje' simply speaks the volume of the very principles and ordeals with which he delivered his responsibilities in high public office, officially and socially.

We particularly appreciate his love for the Sikkim and the Sikkimese people by means of never accepting the coveted IAS which otherwise would have had invited three more non-Sikkimese officials, an exemplary act which abundantly lacks amongst all his contemporaries as well as that of today's.

We salute the pious stand that he undertook as Sikkim's Home Secretary during the hour of her trials in the mid-1970s.

On the passing away of Mr. MM Rasaily, 'Denzong Thuki Norbu' and 'Pema Dorje', this organization bow it's held in high veneration and respect.

Pintso Bhutia
President
National Sikkimese Bhutia Organisation (NASBO)

(*Sikkim Observer*, September 2014.)

Rasaily hailed as a 'Great Son of Sikkim'

Gangtok, Sept 5 (2014): Forty years after he was sidelined and punished by anti-Sikkim, pro-India authorities in Gangtok for his principle stand against Sikkim's 'merger', Madan Mohan Rasaily, who passed away here on Wednesday, is being hailed as an "upright person" and a "great son of Sikkim".

Chief Minister Pawan Chamling described Rasaily (89) as "an upright person with impeccable integrity". He said Rasaily's demise is "an irreparable loss" to Sikkim.

Recipient of Denzong Thu ki Norbu (The Jewel of Sikkim), the highest civilian award of the then Kingdom of Sikkim, and Pema Dorjee (for dedicated service), conferred by the Late Chogyal Palden Thondup Namgyal in 1974, Rasaily studied in Mt. Hermon School and completed his Senior Cambridge (class 11) in 1943.

He held many posts in the State Government, including Additional Chief Secretary-cum-Home Secretary. He was with the ruling Sikkim Democratic Front for a brief while in the 1990s after his retirement from service in 1988.

He is survived by his wife Rani Mala Rasaily, two sons and two daughters.

(*Sikkim Observer*, September 2014)

45 Tshering Dorji
Donning Many Hats

In a career spanning 32 years, Tshering Dorji has served Bhutan as the Home Secretary, Foreign Secretary and as an Ambassador to Thailand and Bangladesh. He also served as the Managing Director of National Housing Development Corporation and Dzongda of Samtse and Pemagatshel, among others.

After his retirement from government service, Tshering tried his luck in politics and joined the Druk Kingdom's ruling People's Democratic Party (PDP) and fought the 2018 general elections. Tshering was successful in winning from his constituency but could not be a member of the National Council since his party lost the polls.

One of Tshering's main motive for joining the ruling party was: "In 2013 we all know the people of Bhutan elected PDP and gave it the responsibility of running the country and we have seen how the government has functioned. I have worked closely at the highest levels in two ministries for four years and I was very impressed with the way the government functioned. The government has done very well for itself by all standards, with the leader of the party, Lyonchhen Tshering Tobgay, ably assisted by the Cabinet Ministers and MPs."

"I saw a very well established and proven leader supported by a good party and decided to join. PDP has done really well in serving the country, Their Majesties and the people and deserve another term. I wanted to be part of such a team to support then in running the country," says the former Ambassador.

Tshering, a thorough gentleman, and his charming wife Deki (alumnus of Kalimpong's Dr. Graham's Homes) are the main pillars of the Hermonite community in Bhutan and with their help and guidance there have been many memorable reunions of the Hermonites in Bhutan in the recent past.

Members of the Bhutan Hermonites Association led by Home Secretary Tshering Dorji and Sonam Gyaltsen (Taki) successfully organised the 2014 reunion in Bhutan. Dheera Sujan, who came all the way from the Netherlands, says she had a wonderful time and wants to come back again.

Altamas Kabir
"Mount Hermon Gave Me A Sound Foundation"

Darjeeling, Nov 27 (2012): Chief Justice of India Justice Altamas Kabir candidly acknowledged that he owed much to his alma mater for what he is today. "What we are today is because of the basic grounding that we got from Mount Hermon School," Justice Kabir said during his brief address at the school's annual Speech Day function here on Saturday.

"The values that you inculcate stand in good stead throughout life," he said while adding that he was "extremely honoured" to be back after 56 years.

Justice Kabir spoke fondly of his three years in Mt. Hermon, where he remembers having 'basmati rice and mutton balls for lunch' not forgetting the 'toy train rides and Going Home Day songs.' He also recollected that David G. Stewart was the Principal when he was in school. He said former Principal G.A. Murray, who became Principal in 1964 when Stewart left, was "large as life."

More than 150 ex-students and teachers attended the function. Prominent among them were P. Russell (UK), Rocky Gardner, Amar Rai (Chairman of Darjeeling Municipality), Justice Indrajit Mohanti, Tshering Dorji (Home Secretary, Bhutan), Karma Bhutia (Sports Secretary, Sikkim) and Mr. and Mrs. S. Rongong. Several ex-teachers were felicitated during the function.

Several Managing Committee members of the school, including Bishop Dr. Philip Masih, and Gorkha Territorial Administration's executive member Roshan Giri were also present during the occasion.

The outgoing Principal George Fernandes, who served the school for 35 years, appealed to all Hermonites to look after their alma mater. Bishop Masih announced that a 'Hermonite' has been selected as the next Principal of the school. For almost a year now Hermonites from all over the world have been urging the school authorities to appoint a credible Hermonite as the next Principal to ensure that the school regains its past glory.

Following Justice Kabir's elevation to the high post on September 29 this year (2012), a delegation of Sikkim and Delhi Hermonites called on him at his residence in New Delhi to felicitate him. (The delegation also invited the CJI for the Speech Day function)

Justice Kabir's visit to his alma mater is significant as the school is going through a tough period in all respect. Global Hermonites, including past principals and teachers, have urged the owners of the school, the Methodist Church in India, to take strong measures to strengthen the school with a view to regain its past glory.

Justice Altamas Kabir has been sworn in as the 39th Chief Justice of India (CJI) on Saturday, Sept 29, 2012. President Pranab Mukherjee administered the oath of office of Justice Kabir at Rashtrapati Bhawan.

The oath taking ceremony was attended by a host of dignitaries, including Prime Minister Manmohan Singh.

Justice Kabir, 64, has succeeded Justice Sarosh Homi Kapadia. The new CJI's tenure will end on July 18, 2013. The 39th CJI was born on Jul 19, 1948 in Kolkata, West Bengal.

He did his MA and LLB from the University of Calcutta. Justice Kabir was admitted to the bar in 1973 and practiced civil and criminal law in Kolkata at the district court and the Calcutta High Court, Kolkata. He became a judge in the same court on Aug 6, 1990.

He became the Acting Chief Justice of the Jharkhand High Court on 3 Jan 2005, an elevation made permanent on Mar 1, 2005. He was elevated to the Supreme Court of India as Justice on Sept 9, 2005.

(*Himalayan Guardian, Sikkim Observer,* **November 2012.**)

HERMONITES FELICITATE CHIEF JUSTICE OF INDIA

CJI to visit Darjeeling for Mt. Hermon School function

Gangtok, Oct 19: A delegation of Sikkim and Delhi Hermonites called on Chief Justice of India Justice Altamas Kabir at his residence in New Delhi on October 6.

During his hour-long chat with fellow Hermonites, alumni of Mt. Hermon School, Darjeeling, the CJI confirmed that he would be coming for the school's annual Speech Day on November 24 next month. Justice Kabir, who was sworn in as the new CJI here on September 29, fondly recollected his school days at Mt. Hermon in mid-fifties.

The Hermonites called on the CJI to felicitate him for heading the country's judiciary as the CJI. Sikkim Hermonites Association President Karma Bhutia, also Secretary of Sports Department, had sought the appointment with the CJI to felicitate him.

Two members of Sikkim Hermonites Association (SHA), Udai P. Sharma and Jigme N. Kazi, were part of the eight-member delegation who met the Chief Justice.

The Delhi Hermonites Association (DHA) were represented by Mahesh Singh, Krishna Goenka and his daughter Ratika Goenka – also a Hermonite, Karan Anand, Anita (Adhikari) Sawhney and Shibesh Singh.

"Mount Hermon Gave Me A Sound Foundation"

Senior Sikkim lawyer and Hermonite Udai P. Sharma felicitating Chief Justice of India Hermonite Justice Altamas Kabir in New Delhi on October 6, 2012. Also present at the function are (L to R) Mahesh Singh, Jigme N. Kazi, Krishna Goenka and Karan Anand.

More than 150 Hermonites have confirmed their participation during the week-long reunions in Darjeeling in the third week of next month. "We are going to have a good time. At least 40 1979 batch will be present in Darjeeling for the reunion," said Thinley Gyari, a Delhi-based Hermonite, in New Delhi.

Alumni from Bhutan, Nepal and also from abroad, including Miss P. Russell, an ex-teacher, will be present during the "grand reunion."

(*Sikkim Observer*, Oct 20, 2012.)

47 — Amar Singh Rai
He Gave Us 'Darjeeling University'

The credit for renaming of the proposed "Greenfield University" to "Darjeeling University" goes to Darjeeling MLA Amar Singh Rai. When the bill for the new university was tabled in the Bengal Assembly in the summer of 2018, Rai urged the Bengal Government to rename it as "Darjeeling University."

The University will be located at Mungpo, about 30 km from Darjeeling.

The need for a university in the hills was first raised in 1955. The establishment of the North Bengal University (NBU) in the plains in Siliguri in 1962 did not fully cater to the needs of the hill people.

Amar Rai, an alumnus (Hermonite) of Mt. Hermon School (brother of Hermonite Pratap Singh Rai), has been asked to head a special committee to oversee the development work in the hills. The decision to form this committee was taken on September 4, 2018 during a meeting chaired by the Bengal Chief Minister Mamata Banerjee.

"We want to develop the hills for which we have to make new plans and projects," Mamata said. She said all aspects of development in the hills, including tourism and education, would be taken up by the new committee, whose members include MLAs of Kalimpong and Kurseong.

In 2019, the Gorkha Janmukti Morcha-Trinamul Congress chose Rai as its candidate for the Darjeeling Lok Sabha seat in line with demands from some sections for a "son-of-the-soil" nominee.

Morcha leader Binay Tamang dwelt on the "son-of-the-soil" theme. "We have selected a son-of-the-soil candidate, as demanded in the hills," Tamang said. But the Gorkha National Liberation Front (GNLF), the Morcha's main Opposition in the hills, objected to a Morcha MLA contesting on a Trinamul symbol. Unfortunately, Rai lost to Bharatiya Janata Party's Raju Bista, a non-local candidate.

The soft-spoken Rai is a former vice-principal of Loreto College—now christened Southfield College. In 2011, he won the Darjeeling municipality election and was made chairman.

After his term as civic chief, he won the Assembly seat as a Morcha nominee in 2016.

While being MLA, Rai was appointed to the board of administrators of the Tamang-headed Gorkhaland Territorial Administration (GTA) as a member in charge of education.

48 Air Marshal Pratap Rao
Decades Of Dedicated Service

"Air Marshal Pratap Rao has rendered distinguished service of most exceptional order"

It was a great pleasure and privilege meeting Pratap Rao (retired Air Marshal) over dinner yesterday in Gangtok. I had a very lively and interesting 3-hour chat with him, his wife Suman, son Ajay and wife Sonali.

Rao was in MH between 1941-1947, when our Principal was Mr. H. Dewey. They will make a short trip to Lachung, North Sikkim (unfortunately, not my native village of Lachen) today and then head to MH in Darj.

I hope Darj Hermonites and school authorities will make their stay there enjoyable as they travel down memory lane. (You may contact him at 99228 28846.) Hail Mt. Hermon! His service record has this to say:

"Air Marshal Pratap Rao was commissioned as a fighter pilot on 25 August 1956. He has held numerous important command and staff appointments. Being an A2 Qualified Flying Instructor, he was sent on deputation to a friendly country to impart training to its pilots. Subsequently, he was posted to Aircrew Examining Board where he was awarded Vayu Sena Medal in 1975 for utmost devotion to duty. He was also specially selected for the appointment of Military, Naval and Air Attache to Bangkok. On return he was appointed as Air Officer Commanding (AOC) of a major fighter base in the Western Sector, where for his distinguished service of an exceptional order, he was awarded Ati Vishisht Seva Medal in 1989. He has also held important assignments such as Planning Officer in the Department of Defence Production, Director Intelligence and Assistant Chief of the Air Staff (Inspection).

On promotion to the rank of Air Marshal, the Air Officer was appointed Senior Air Staff Officer (SASO) of the Western Air Command (WAC). In this assignment the Air Officer made significant contributions to the operational plans and their execution. The Air Officer was then appointed as Air Officer Commanding-in-Chief of WAC. In a very short time, the Air Officer was able to appreciate the priorities of Govt and dovetail them with the Command plans, which increased the operational potential of the Command without any additional resources or expenditure.

The Air Officer is presently holding the vital appointment of Vice Chief of the Air Staff. In this assignment, the Air Officer brings to bear his best operational and staff experience. He has left an indelible imprint in the appointments that he has held during his chequered career spanning nearly four decades of dedicated service,

Decades Of Dedicated Service

Air Marshal Pratap Rao, AVSM, VM has thus rendered distinguished service of most exceptional order."

(Hermonites International, Facebook, Jigme N. Kazi, 2018.)

MH: 1941 and 1996

Pratap Rao's collection of Mount Hermon U.S. Alumnus Reunion, Sept 27-29, 1996, and class photos of 1941, where his family members are seen.

Hail Mount Hermon! A Tribute

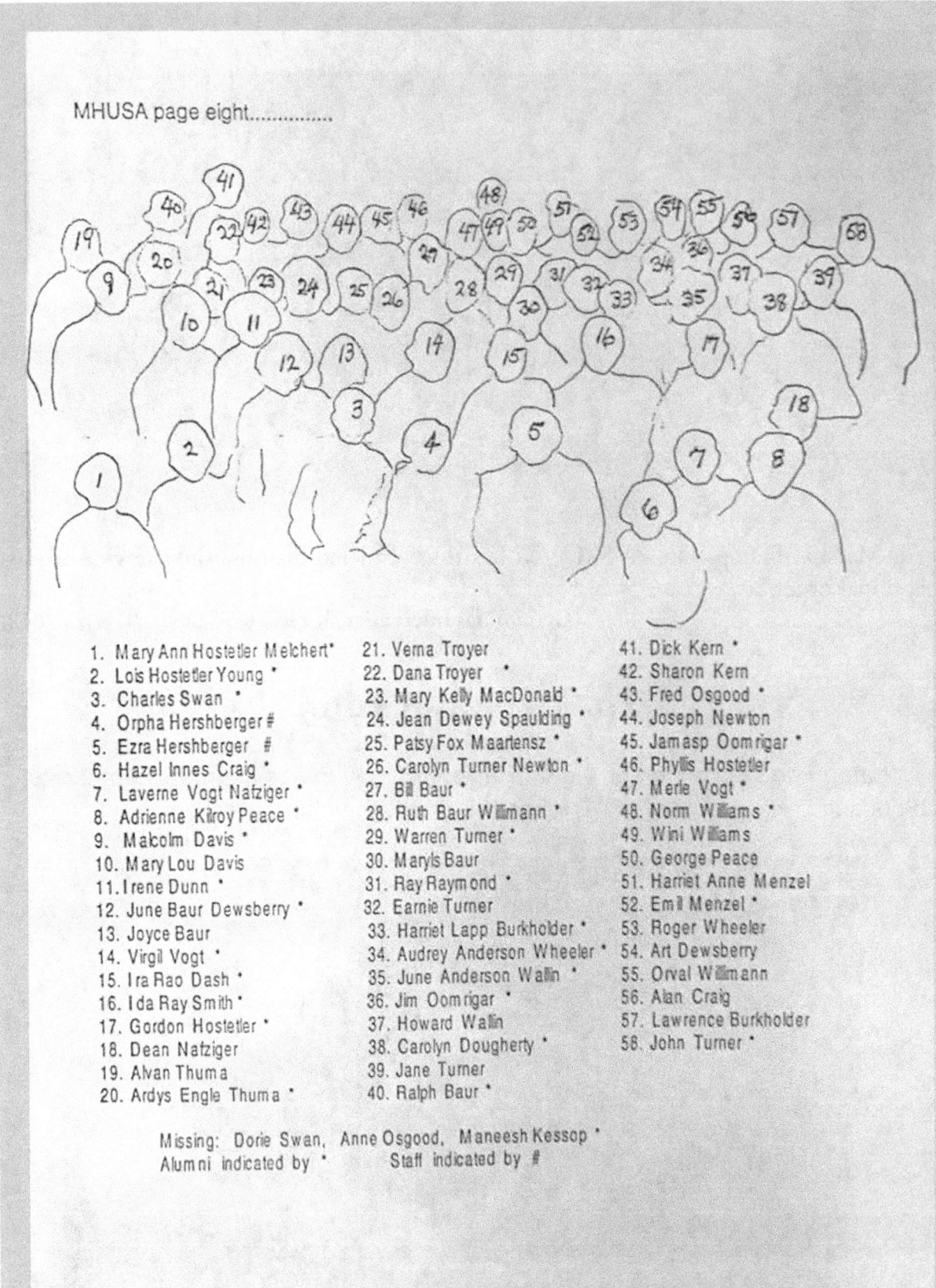

MHUSA page eight................

1. Mary Ann Hostetler Melchert*
2. Lois Hostetler Young *
3. Charles Swan *
4. Orpha Hershberger #
5. Ezra Hershberger #
6. Hazel Innes Craig *
7. Laverne Vogt Nafziger *
8. Adrienne Kilroy Peace *
9. Malcolm Davis *
10. Mary Lou Davis
11. Irene Dunn *
12. June Baur Dewsberry *
13. Joyce Baur
14. Virgil Vogt *
15. Ira Rao Dash *
16. Ida Ray Smith *
17. Gordon Hostetler *
18. Dean Nafziger
19. Alvan Thuma
20. Ardys Engle Thuma *
21. Verna Troyer
22. Dana Troyer *
23. Mary Kelly MacDonald *
24. Jean Dewey Spaulding *
25. Patsy Fox Maartensz *
26. Carolyn Turner Newton *
27. Bill Baur *
28. Ruth Baur Willmann *
29. Warren Turner *
30. Maryls Baur
31. Ray Raymond *
32. Earnie Turner
33. Harriet Lapp Burkholder *
34. Audrey Anderson Wheeler *
35. June Anderson Wallin *
36. Jim Oomrigar *
37. Howard Wallin
38. Carolyn Dougherty *
39. Jane Turner
40. Ralph Baur *
41. Dick Kern *
42. Sharon Kern
43. Fred Osgood *
44. Joseph Newton
45. Jamasp Oomrigar *
46. Phyllis Hostetler
47. Merle Vogt *
48. Norm Williams *
49. Wini Williams
50. George Peace
51. Harriet Anne Menzel
52. Emil Menzel *
53. Roger Wheeler
54. Art Dewsberry
55. Orval Willmann
56. Alan Craig
57. Lawrence Burkholder *
58. John Turner *

Missing: Dorie Swan, Anne Osgood, Maneesh Kessop *
Alumni indicated by *   Staff indicated by #

Mt. Hermon U.S. Alumnus Reunion, September 1996.

Decades Of Dedicated Service

TEACHERS: Miss Howie, Miss Cox, Mrs. Vicary.
TOP ROW: Stanley Russell, Clifford Addison, Gerald Bradshaw, David Musselwhite, Sydney McLaughlin, Desmond Pilkington, Davis Kniss, John Vicary, Peter Eldridge.
MIDDLE ROW: Shirley Solomon, Ivan Pilkington, Ida Ray, James Hershberger, Ira Rao, Richard Brown, Keith Brown, Joan Snook, Gordon Hostetler, Virgil Vogt, Penelope Shebbeare, Heather Watson.
BOTTOM ROW: Hugh Rolfe, Sheila West, Moira West, Patrick Moore, Ruth Thomson, Michael Eade, Douglas Brymer, David Baechtiger, Theodore Johnsrude.

Kindergarten (?), 1941.

TOP ROW:— Donald Schultz, Herbert Russell, Janice Ellicott, Ruth Feierabend, Mrs. Brown, Teacher, Amy Badal, Elizabeth Halden, Alan Swan, Stuart Watson.
MIDDLE ROW:— Joan North, Sheila Boyden, Joan Robinson, Jill Terrell, Myra Murgatroyd, Joy Callow, Hilary Archer, Margaret West, Mona Ryrie, Judith Eade, Alice Nadjarian.
BOTTOM ROW:— Nariman Kutar, George Ward, Mackie Palamkote, Ajoy Gupta, Arun Rao, Maneck Vatchagandhy, Nicholas Wibmer, Michael Killick.

2nd Standard, 1941.

Hail Mount Hermon! A Tribute

TOP ROW:—Herbert Feierabend, Faith Russell James Irwin, Gordon Roadarmel, Dina Farbstein, Grace Niblett, Elizabeth Dodd, Usha Rao.
MIDDLE ROW:—Doris Davis, Joy Wade, Daphne Bowen, Lois Hostetler, Georgnia Ward, Miss Murphy, Teacher, Esther Kniss, Laverne Vogt, June Solomon, Anne Curlender, Jean Gilson.
BOTTOM ROW:—Peter Ghey, Robert Bowen, Bernard Maddison, Phyllis Engle, Pauline Wade, Joy Eade, Ruth Calhoon.

4th Standard, 1941.

Sonam Dubal

49 "My Work Reflects Essence Of Northeast"

Delhi-based fashion designer, Sonam Dubal, though born in Assam, is of Sikkimese and Maharashtrian descent, and wears his lineage and cultural background on the sleeves of his kimono jacket. Indo-Asian silhouettes, vibrant indigenous fabrics and recycling stories make Sonam Dubal's label Sanskar, launched in 1999, stand apart in an over-fraught fashion industry.

An alumnus of Mount Hermon School (Darjeeling) and National Institute of Fashion Technology (NIFT - New Delhi), Sonam began his career with the vanguard of Indian fashion - Rohit Khosla. Thereafter, journeying into the world of Theatre Design and Advertising, while travelling extensively, enriching his creative experience. His cultural background is largely responsible for the creation of his signature style, which emotes a fusion of Eastern traditions, with Western aesthetics giving rise to silhouettes that are Pan-Asian in essence.

Hail Mount Hermon! A Tribute

Says Sonam, "The craftsmanship of the region is an ecological treasure that needs to be highlighted and preserved. Events like these not only focus on under-appreciated skills but are also a wonderful way to encourage exchange of ideas between designers, artists, craftspeople and writers. Not only will they introduce the rest of India to the region's indigenous textile crafts, they will also ignite conversations on protecting these practices and keeping them alive. I've committed myself to this cause."

He returned to mainstream fashion in 1999 with the launch of Sanskar label. Since then he has been awarded the Elle global award for 2007 and was also the recipient of the 'Top 50 Achievers in Global Mainstream Media' in the Fashion category at the University of Leicester Law School in 2006.

His collections on the ramp have been widely appreciated by designers and artists and have been drawing the attention of eminent personalities in the fashion industry. He would ensure to create a different and out-of-the-box look just for you so that you look beautiful and flawless from inside as well as outside.

"I did show my collection at Amazon India Fashion Week in 2015 and then participated in the Eco Fashion Week in Vancouver, Canada, in 2016 and 2017," says Sonam, who has lately stayed away from fashion weeks because he wanted to set up his business, make a conscious move towards a sustainable economy and redefine his work vis-a-vis the ecological shift in fashion. "I also wanted to expand my international market and set up Maison Sanskar in Vancouver in April 2016."

(*Indian Express*/www.maisonsanskar.com/asiastore.org)

50
Tom Stoppard
British Playwright And Social Activist

In 2008, Stoppard was voted number 76 on the *Time* 100, *Time* magazine's list of the most influential people in the world.

Sir Tom Stoppard OM CBE FRSL (born Tomáš Straussler; 3 July 1937) is a Czech-born British playwright and screenwriter. He has written prolifically for TV, radio, film and stage, finding prominence with plays such as *Arcadia*, *The Coast of Utopia*, *Every Good Boy Deserves Favour*, *Professional Foul*, *The Real Thing*, *Travesties*, *The Invention of Love*, and *Rosencrantz and Guildenstern Are Dead*. He co-wrote the screenplays for Brazil, *The Russia House*, and *Shakespeare in Love*, and has received an Academy Award and four Tony Awards. His work covers the themes of human rights, censorship and political freedom, often delving into the deeper philosophical thematics of society. Stoppard has been a key playwright of the National Theatre and is one of the most internationally performed dramatists of his generation. In 2008, *The Daily Telegraph* ranked him number 11 in their list of the "100 most powerful people in British culture".

Born in Czechoslovakia, Stoppard left as a child refugee, fleeing imminent Nazi occupation. He settled with his family in Britain after the war, in 1946, having spent the three years prior (1943–1946) in a boarding school in Darjeeling in the Indian Himalayas. After being educated at schools in Nottingham and Yorkshire, Stoppard became a journalist, a drama critic and then, in 1960, a playwright.

It was announced in June 2019 that he had written a new play, *Leopoldstadt*, set in the Jewish community of early 20th Century Vienna. The play premiered in January 2020 at Wyndham's Theatre with Patrick Marber directing.

We aren't drones. We're born to fulfil our unique destinies: Stoppard

Speaking of his childhood in Darjeeling, Tom Stoppard, the 80-year-old playwright of *The Real Thing*, said he has "huge" nostalgia for his life in India.

British Playwright And Social Activist

Tom Stoppard, the 80-year-old playwright who came up with some great lines during his conversation with Sanjna Kapoor at the Jaipur Literature Festival, charmed the audience and made them break into spontaneous applause again and again.

"Last year I invested in hearing aids and by the way, I forgot to wear them today," Tom Stoppard says to a giggling audience. With expressive hand gestures, Sanjna Kapoor -- daughter of Shashi Kapoor and Jennifer Kendal, whose sister Felicity was the English playwright's long-time companion -- quizzes him about childhood memories, his India connection and his advice for playwrights.

"I approached the subject of the British empire in a positive manner," Stoppard said, when asked if he would change something in his play The Real Thing.

"If I have to do it again, I would take things into account of what has entered my consciousness," he added. He concedes Henry's character in *The Real Thing* is similar to him, not "in an autobiographical sense" but in an intellectual sense. "I've given him a lot of lines that I would actually have liked to say myself."

Speaking of his childhood in Darjeeling, Stoppard said he has "huge" nostalgia for his life in India. Perhaps that's why he keeps coming back. "It made me a touch more exotic than the farmers' sons of Nottinghshire," he says, charming the audience.

The conversation shifted to theatre, with the 80-year-old saying he is "text-driven" in his approach to plays. "When you write a play, it is an illusion that the play is a private enterprise... but when you hand it over (for production), the play is reliant on synonymous technological achievements that make it a play," he says. It's the sort of line that theatre enthusiasts thrill to.

Stoppard is, of course, well known for his film scripts too with *Shakespeare in Love* being everyone's favourite. Clearly, though, like the Kapoors (the Shashi wing of the family) with whom he has been closely associated down the years, he is a theatre person first. "I think of myself as a theatre writer who does other things."

Stoppard, whose *Rosencrantz and Guildenstern Are Dead* is often compared to Samuel Beckett's *Waiting for Godot*, believes a society is all about the artists. Without them, the physical world would be a "dystopia". "We are all believers. We aren't drones... we're born to fulfil our unique destinies," he claims with conviction.

The audience erupts in loud applause and cheers, probably the loudest of the day, as the session concludes with his advice to aspiring playwrights: "It doesn't actually happen unless you have a pen in your hand."

(*Hindustan Times*, 2018)

Life and career

Stoppard was born Tomáš Straussler, in Zlín, a city dominated by the shoe manufacturing industry, in the Moravia region of Czechoslovakia. He is the son of Martha Becková and Eugen Straussler, a doctor employed by the Bata shoe company. His parents were non-observant Jews, members of a long-established community. Just before the German occupation of Czechoslovakia, the town's patron, Jan Antonín Bat'a, transferred his Jewish employees, mostly physicians, to branches of his firm outside Europe. On 15 March 1939, the day the Nazis invaded Czechoslovakia, the Straussler family fled to Singapore, where Bat'a had a factory.

Before the Japanese occupation of Singapore (February 1942), Stoppard, his brother, and their mother were sent on to Australia. Stoppard's father remained in Singapore as a British army volunteer, knowing that, as a doctor, he would be needed in its defence. Stoppard was four years old when his father died. In the book *Tom Stoppard in Conversation*, Stoppard tells how his father died in Japanese captivity, a prisoner of war but has said that he subsequently discovered that Straussler was reported to have drowned on board a ship bombed by Japanese forces whilst trying to flee Singapore in 1942.

In 1941, when Tomas was five, the three were evacuated to Darjeeling, India. The boys attended Mount Hermon School, an American multi-racial school, where Tomas became Tom and his brother Petr became Peter.

In 1945, his mother, Martha, married British army major Kenneth Stoppard, who gave the boys his English surname and, in 1946, moved the family to England. Stoppard's stepfather believed strongly that "to be born an Englishman was to have drawn first prize in the lottery of life"—a quote from Cecil Rhodes—telling his 9-year-old stepson: "Don't you realise that I made you British?" setting up Stoppard's desire as a child to become "an honorary Englishman".

"I fairly often find I'm with people who forget I don't quite belong in the world we're in", he says. "I find I put a foot wrong—it could be pronunciation, an arcane bit of English history—and suddenly I'm there naked, as someone with a pass, a press ticket." This is reflected in his characters, he notes, who are "constantly being addressed by the wrong name, with jokes and false trails to do with the confusion of having two names". Stoppard attended the Dolphin School in Nottinghamshire, and later completed his education at Pocklington School in East Riding, Yorkshire, which he hated.

Stoppard left school at seventeen and began work as a journalist for the *Western Daily Press* in Bristol, never receiving a university education. Years later, he came to regret not going to university, but at the time he loved his work as a journalist and felt passionately about his career. He worked at the paper from 1954 until 1958, when the *Bristol Evening World* offered Stoppard the position of feature writer, humour columnist, and secondary drama critic, which took Stoppard into the world of theatre. At the Bristol Old Vic, at the time a well-regarded regional repertory company, Stoppard formed friendships with director John Boorman and actor Peter O'Toole early in their careers. In Bristol, he became known more for his strained attempts at humour and unstylish clothes than for his writing.

Career

Stoppard wrote short radio plays in 1953–54 and by 1960 he had completed his first stage play, *A Walk on the Water*, which was later re-titled *Enter a Free Man* (1968). He noted that the work owed much to Robert Bolt's *Flowering Cherry* and Arthur Miller's *Death of a Salesman*.

Within a week after sending *A Walk on the Water* to an agent, Stoppard received his version of the "Hollywood-style telegrams that change struggling young artists' lives." His first play was optioned, staged in Hamburg, then broadcast on British Independent Television in 1963.

From September 1962 until April 1963, Stoppard worked in London as a drama critic for *Scene* magazine, writing reviews and interviews both under his name and the pseudonym William Boot (taken from Evelyn Waugh's Scoop). In 1964, a Ford Foundation grant enabled Stoppard to spend 5 months writing in a Berlin mansion, emerging with a one-act play titled *Rosencrantz and Guildenstern Meet King Lear*, which later evolved into his Tony-winning play *Rosencrantz and Guildenstern Are Dead*.

In the following years, Stoppard produced several works for radio, television and the theatre, including "M" is for *Moon Among Other Things* (1964), *A Separate Peace* (1966) and *If You're Glad I'll Be Frank* (1966). On 11 April 1967 – following acclaim at the 1966 Edinburgh Festival – the opening of *Rosencrantz and Guildenstern Are Dead* in a National Theatre production at the Old Vic made Stoppard an overnight success. *Jumpers* (1972) places a professor of moral philosophy in a murder mystery thriller alongside a slew of radical gymnasts, and *Travesties* (1974) explored the 'Wildean' possibilities arising from the fact that Vladimir Lenin, James Joyce, and Tristan Tzara had all been in Zurich during the First World War.

In his early years, he also wrote extensively for BBC radio, often introducing surrealist themes. He has also adapted many of his stage works for radio, film and television winning extensive awards and honours from the start of his career. His latest original radio production, *Darkside* (2013), has been written for BBC Radio 2 to celebrate the 40th anniversary of Pink Floyd's album, *The Dark Side of the Moon*.

Stoppard has written one novel, *Lord Malquist and Mr. Moon* (1966), set in contemporary London. Its cast includes the 18th-century figure of the dandified Malquist and his ineffectual Boswell, Moon, and also cowboys, a lion (banned from the Ritz) and a donkey-borne Irishman claiming to be the Risen Christ.

In the 1980s, in addition to writing his own works, Stoppard translated many plays into English, including works by Sławomir Mrożek, Johann Nestroy, Arthur Schnitzler, and Václav Havel. It was at this time that Stoppard became influenced by the works of Polish and Czech absurdists. He has been co-opted into the Outrapo group, a far-from-serious French movement to improve actors' stage technique through science.

Stoppard has also co-written screenplays including *Shakespeare in Love* and *Indiana Jones and the Last Crusade*. Spielberg states that though Stoppard was uncredited, "he was responsible for almost every line of dialogue in the film". Stoppard also worked on *Star Wars: Episode III – Revenge of the Sith*, though again Stoppard received no official or formal credit in this role. He worked in a similar capacity with Tim Burton on his film *Sleepy Hollow*.

In 2008, Stoppard was voted number 76 on the *Time* 100, *Time* magazine's list of the most influential people in the world.

Stoppard serves on the advisory board of the magazine *Standpoint*, and was instrumental in its foundation, giving the opening speech at its launch. He is also a patron of the Shakespeare Schools Festival, a charity that enables school children across the UK to perform Shakespeare in professional theatres.

In July 2013, Stoppard was awarded the PEN Pinter Prize for "determination to tell things as they are." Stoppard was appointed president of the London Library in 2002 and Vice-President in 2017 following the election of Sir Tim Rice as President.

In July 2017, Stoppard was elected an Honorary Fellow of the British Academy (Hon FBA), the United Kingdom's national academy for the humanities and social sciences. Stoppard was appointed Cameron Mackintosh Visiting Professor of Contemporary Theatre, St. Catherine's College, Oxford, for the academic year 2017–2018.

The accusations of favouring intellectuality over political commitment or commentary were met with a change of tack, as Stoppard produced increasingly socially engaged work. From 1977, he became personally involved with human-rights issues, in particular with the situation of political dissidents in Central and Eastern Europe. In February 1977, he visited the Soviet Union and several Eastern European countries with a member of Amnesty International.

In June, Stoppard met Vladimir Bukovsky in London and travelled to Czechoslovakia (then under communist control), where he met dissident playwright and future president Václav Havel, whose writing he greatly admires. Stoppard became involved with Index on Censorship, Amnesty International, and the Committee Against Psychiatric Abuse and wrote various newspaper articles and letters about human rights. He was also instrumental in translating Havel's works into English. *Every Good Boy Deserves Favour* (1977), 'a play for actors and orchestra' was based on a request by composer André Previn; inspired by a meeting with a Russian exile. This play as well as Dogg's *Hamlet*, Cahoot's *Macbeth* (1979), The Coast of Utopia (2002), Rock 'n' Roll (2006), and two works for television Professional Foul (1977) and *Squaring the Circle* (1984) all concern themes of censorship, rights abuses, and state repression.

Personal life

Stoppard has been married three times. His first marriage was to Josie Ingle (1965–1972), a nurse; his second marriage was to Miriam Stern (1972–92), whom he left to begin a relationship with actress Felicity Kendal. He has two sons from each of his first two marriages: Oliver Stoppard, Barnaby Stoppard, the actor Ed Stoppard, and Will Stoppard, who is married to violinist Linzi Stoppard.[26] In 2014 he married Sabrina Guinness.

Stoppard's mother died in 1996. The family had not talked about their history and neither brother knew what had happened to the family left behind in Czechoslovakia. In the early 1990s, with the fall of communism, Stoppard found out that all four of his grandparents had been Jewish and had died in Terezin, Auschwitz and other camps, along with three of his mother's sisters. In 1998, following the deaths of his parents he returned to Zlín for the first time in over 50 years. He has expressed grief both for a lost father and a missing past, but he has no sense of being a survivor, at whatever remove. "I feel incredibly lucky not to have had to survive or die. It's a conspicuous part of what might be termed a charmed life."

In 1979, the year of Margaret Thatcher's election, Stoppard noted to Paul Delaney: "I'm a conservative with a small-c. I am a conservative in politics, literature, education and theatre." In 2007, Stoppard described himself as a "timid libertarian". The Tom Stoppard

Prize (Czech: Cena Toma Stopparda) was created in 1983 under the Charter 77 Foundation and is awarded to authors of Czech origin.

Stoppard, Kevin Spacey, Jude Law, and others, joined protests against the regime of Alexander Lukashenko in March 2011, showing their support for the Belarusian democracy movement.

In 2014, Stoppard publicly backed "Hacked Off" and its campaign towards press self-regulation by "safeguarding the press from political interference while also giving vital protection to the vulnerable."

Awards and honours

Tom Stoppard has won awards and honors like Evening Standard Award for Most Promising Playwright, UK, 1967, London Theatre Critics Award *Rosencrantz and Guildenstern Are Dead* (UK), Prix Italia, 1968, Evening Standard Award for Best Comedy of the Year (UK), 1974, Giles Award, The Pen Pinter Prize, 2013, four Tony Awards and an Academy Award. He was elected as a Fellow of the Royal Society of Literature 1972, CBE 1978, Knight Bachelor, 1997, Honorary Doctor of Letters, University of Cambridge, 2000, President of The London Library, 2002 and Honorary Doctor of Letters, University of Oxford.

(Encyclopaedia Britannica/Wikipedia)

Stoppard with Carey Perloff, American theatre director and author, 2012.

Sir Stoppard to receive PEN award in March 2020

British playwright Sir Tom Stoppard is set to be honoured this month (March 2020) by PEN America, the literary and human rights organisation.

PEN America has announced the winners of their 2020 literary awards, including two playwrights. This year's winners are playwright Tom Stoppard, author Rigoberto González, playwright Tanya Barfield, and poet, novelist, and essayist M. NourbeSe Philip.

PEN announced that Sir Stoppard will receive the 25,000 US dollars (£19,000) PEN/Mike Nichols Writing for Performance Award for Leopoldstadt, a new work set in the Jewish quarter of early 20th century Vienna that the 82-year-old has said may be his last play.

The Nichols prize, established last year and named after the late film and stage director, was previously given to the playwright-filmmaker Kenneth Lonergan.

"Fostering and celebrating international literature is central to the mission of the PEN America Literary Awards," said PEN America director of literary programs Clarisse Rosaz Shariyf in a statement. "We seek to champion original and promising writers of the global community and promote their work to an American audience. This year, we are incredibly proud to honor such urgent and diverse voices, which we know have the power to awaken empathy and redefine public discourse."

51 Lodi Gyari
A Tireless Advocate For Tibet

Lodi Gyari, second from left, and the Dalai Lama in a 1993 meeting with President Bill Clinton, right, and Vice President Al Gore. (International Campaign for Tibet)

Lodi Gyari, who escaped Chinese oppression in Tibet as a child, then spent his life as a tireless advocate for his native land and people, becoming an emissary of the Dalai Lama in negotiations with the government of China, died Oct. 29 (2018) at a hospital in San Francisco. He was 69.

The cause was liver cancer, said Lesley Friedell Rich, an official with the International Campaign for Tibet, which Mr. Gyari once led.

Born in a tent surrounded by snowcapped mountains, Mr. Gyari (pronounced "Gary") was descended from a long line of chieftains and resistance fighters, including his grandmother and an aunt who raised him. He was considered a reincarnated lama in the Buddhist religion and, as a child, helped guide his family out of their homeland after China seized control of Tibet in the 1950s.

Hail Mount Hermon! A Tribute

He and his family fled to northern India, where many Tibetans formed an exile community in Dharamsala, under the spiritual guidance of the Dalai Lama. Mr. Gyari, who studied in monasteries in Tibet and India, was drawn from an early age — like his ancestors — to the cause of Tibetan freedom.

Lodi Gyari. (International Campaign for Tibet)

In 1970, he helped found the Tibetan Youth Congress, which remains the largest political organization of Tibetans in exile. Mr. Gyari, who became a skilled English-language writer and speaker, was a translator for Tibetan resistance fighters training in the United States, then became the editor of a Tibetan-language newspaper and an English-language publication, now known as the *Tibetan Review*.

At first, he was an advocate of complete sovereignty for Tibet, which had been an independent nation before China's Communist-led revolution of the late 1940s. He became active in the Tibetan government-in-exile in India and, at age 30, became the speaker of its parliament and later a cabinet officer.

The exile government — the Central Tibetan Administration — is not an officially recognized body, but it carries considerable moral authority in the West. Mr. Gyari became, in effect, the leading diplomat of the global Tibetan exile community.

As China tightened its control over Tibet, Mr. Gyari sought to draw attention to the plight of his people, first at the United Nations and later in Washington, where he was posted as the Dalai Lama's special envoy in 1990.

Tempering his earlier calls for Tibetan independence, Mr. Gyari became a champion of the Dalai Lama's more moderate "Middle Way" approach, which sought political and cultural autonomy for the Tibetan people within the framework of the Chinese constitution.

In Washington, Mr. Gyari coordinated the Dalai Lama's visits to the United States, including meetings with several presidents. He also carried Tibet's message to the State Department and Congress.

He helped secure congressional funding for the Tibetan people and their causes, totalling almost $200 million from 1991 to 2011. He was also a leading advocate for the Tibetan Policy Act of 2002, which established a special coordinator for Tibetan affairs at the State Department and called for a dialogue between China and representatives of the Dalai Lama.

"He was instrumental in putting Tibet at the center of U.S.-China relations," Bhuchung K. Tsering, vice president of the International Campaign for Tibet and a member of Mr. Gyari's negotiating team, said in an interview. "I found that Mr. Lodi Gyari worked steadfastly to foster the aspirations of the Dalai Lama, and he was able to do that in ways I haven't seen in others."

At the Dalai Lama's request, Mr. Gyari opened discussions with Chinese officials, holding nine rounds of talks between 2002 and 2010. He considered the Chinese responses to his pleas for Tibetan self-determination to be inflexible, if not hostile.

Mr. Gyari, who was allowed to return to Tibet only under close monitoring by Chinese officials, described his homeland as "in every sense, an occupied nation, brutally occupied."

In 2008, China imposed a deadly crackdown on a Tibetan uprising and charged the Dalai Lama with attempting to foment an insurrection.

"The more you suppress, the more the resentment," Mr. Gyari told NPR at the time. "We can provide them legitimacy, but if and only if the Tibetans are also given the opportunity to live in dignity."

His discussions produced few lasting results, except for greater recognition of the Tibetan language in what is called the Tibet Autonomous Region. In 2011, when the Dalai Lama yielded political authority to the democratically elected government-in-exile, Mr. Gyari resigned as special envoy.

Hail Mount Hermon! A Tribute

Jigme N. Kazi at one of the funeral rites of Lodi Gyari Tulku in Dehradun, India, 2018.

"Far from fading away," Mr. Gyari wrote in the *South China Morning* Post in 2010, "the Tibetan political movement will reinvent itself in the absence of the current, Fourteenth Dalai Lama, and become something far more complex and unmanageable in the process."

Lodi Gyaltsen Gyari was born Aug. 25, 1949, in the Nyarong region of Tibet. His father was a local chieftain who was imprisoned for a time by the Chinese government.

His grandmother, Gyari Chime Dolma, was executed after fighting against Chinese warlords at the turn of the 20th century. She was later was honored in song and became an inspiration to future generations of Tibetan freedom fighters.

At age 3, Mr. Gyari was identified as the reincarnation of a Tibetan lama and began his schooling in monasteries. During the 1950s, his aunt — who he considered his mother because she cared for him as a child — led a group of Tibetan resistance fighters on horseback raids against Chinese forces.

In 1957, Mr. Gyari was pulled out of a monastery as his family and others began a long journey into exile. They traveled at night to escape detection by Chinese forces.

Despite his young age, Mr. Gyari was held in a position of respect because of his standing as a monk. He conducted religious rituals and "performed divinations regarding the most auspicious time to travel and recited mantras to stop the blizzards," he wrote in the 2016 book "Himalaya: Personal Stories of Grandeur, Challenge, and Hope."

"Chinese troops pursued us and I witnessed many violent gun battles," he wrote. "On two occasions, in the darkness and through whirling snow, men riding ahead of me were shot before my eyes and crashed from their horses to the ground. We couldn't stop, or we would all have been lost."

He and his family crossed the Himalayas on foot. When they finally reached the border of India, Mr. Gyari had only one shoe, the other having been left behind in the mud of his homeland.

Survivors include his wife of more than 40 years, Dawa Chokyi of McLean, Va.; six children; his mother; three sisters; four brothers; and five grandchildren.

While serving as the Dalai Lama's special envoy, Mr. Gyari was also president of the International Campaign for Tibet from 1991 to 1999. He later was chairman of the board before being succeeded in 2014 by actor Richard Gere.

In addition to his work on behalf of Tibet, Mr. Gyari helped found the Allied Committee, which aims to draw attention to the repression of minority groups in China, including Tibetans, Uighurs and Mongolians. He was also a founder of the Unrepresented Nations and Peoples Organization, which seeks to give a voice to ethnic minorities and stateless groups and to spread democratic principles throughout the world.

Before his death, Mr. Gyari spent time in Thailand, writing his memoirs.

"It is because of the tragic loss of the cultural identity of my people in Tibet," he wrote in "Himalaya" in 2016, "that I feel there is such importance and urgency in doing whatever one can to restore it, in whatever way possible."

(The Washington Post, Nov 18, 2018.)

HERMONITES CELEBRATE LODI GYARI'S LIFE!

Jigme N. Kazi

On November 18, 2018, several Hermonites were present at the funeral of senior Hermonite Lodi Gyari at Clement Town, Dehradun.

For Gyari Rinpoche, who passed away in California on Oct 29, 2018, aged 69, Mt. Hermon School (1960-62) was his second home. He fled Tibet in 1959 after the Chinese occupation of his country.

Among Hermonites present at the funeral at the premises of Mindrolling Monastery were Rinpoche's younger brothers - Pema Gyalpo and Thinlay Gyari.

Hermonites at Lodi Gyari's funeral at Dehradun, November 2018.

After the funeral ceremony was over, Thinlay rounded up the Hermonites for a photo session (see pix). Pema said the occasion was a 'celebration' of the life of his late brother.

When I took a last look at the funeral pyre to say my last goodbye, these words from our school song filled my mind:

> "Breathe then your benison
> On me as I depart,
> I'll keep your memory
> Warm in my heart."

Lodi Gyari and Jigme N. Kazi at Gyari's daughter's wedding in Thimphu, 2008.

Lodi Gyari Rinpoche, former special envoy of His Holiness the Dalai Lama, who died in California yesterday (October 29, 2018), was a Hermonite. He was in Mt. Hermon in the latter part of 1950s and early 1960s. The photo of Dewey House here may be in 1961-62 and Lodi Gyari may be placed 7th from top loft near Tom Crees.

Gyari Tulku's passing away is a personal loss to me and my family. My wife Tsering is closely related to him. We have many precious memories of him in Sikkim, Bhutan, Nepal and Delhi.

Hail Mount Hermon! A Tribute

Gyari Tulku and his wife Domala with Jigme N. Kazi and wife Tsering in Gangtok in 2012 during a wedding of their daughter.

Gyari Tulku is not only a great human being but has devoted his whole life for the Tibetan cause. While we mourn his passing away, we rejoice and celebrate his life and achievements. Hail Mt. Hermon! Hail Gyari Tulku!

MEMORIES – Part VIII

52 Looking Backwards To See Forwards

Dr. Charles L. Swan

Charles Swan

Dr. Charles L. Swan joined Queen's Hill School (QHS) in K.G. on May 15, 1914, when Miss Emma Knowles, the school's Founder, was the Principal. He later taught at Mt. Hermon between 1929-1936. Dr. Charles is best remembered by the school and the Hermonites for his famous 'Going Home Day' (GHD) songs.

When I was a small boy in old Queen's Hill, Miss Knowles, the founder of the school, was still Principal, and Miss Stahl was Vice-Principal. When I was appointed to teach at Mt. Hermon, Miss Stahl had only just retired from the principalship. So my memory leads me to think of the original purposes of the school. It was patterned after the Public Boarding Schools of England, but the pattern was given an American flare, and some major adjustments were made to fit to the Indian scene.

The school was started primarily to meet the needs of the Protestant and Evangelical families of the Anglo-Indian community, many of whom had been touched by Methodist revivals of the period. The children of missionaries were served well by the school but their needs were secondary.

Instruction was based on the standards of British education. At that time, Britain was taking a leading role in the educational developments needed for a new age of industry, science and world perspectives. In this role, however, British educators generally retained their concern for the traditional values of the Judeo-Christian heritage and the moral experience of the Church. Mt. Hermon, even today, is deeply rooted in that original setting.

There are aspects in the "old system" which I have come to value very highly, and some things I wish had been different. Most of my pre-collegiate education was received in that system, and my early experience in teaching gave me some deeper understandings of its worth.

I am particularly glad for the many hours I spent in 'study hall' and the much work assigned as 'homework'. Some of my best learning was done when the teacher on duty

Hail Mount Hermon! A Tribute

gave me a bit of help or when some of the brighter students in my class explained things more clearly than my teacher could (at least for me). I hope teachers on duty in after-supper study hours still permit 'student conferences' as some of my teachers did – and I hope students will not 'take unfair advantages' of the privilege!

The curriculum which offers all subjects simultaneously throughout the school years is one I feel gave me many advantages. We took Geography and History, Maths and Science, Scripture and English, all subjects every year and every week. I have seen students try to 'gobble down' Algebra in a single 'semester'. They suffer intense mental indigestion and then they proceed – most of them – to forget the subject; they have earned a 'credit' but they have little else. Our way meant that we wove all our learning into an integrated fabric of learning which made us more inclined to think carefully, including all aspects of a problem in our decisions.

Supervised sports involving every student in the school brought many blessings to me. I grew up clumsy and never made higher than the 'B' team in our House System. But pushed to the limit by my friends in my House, I learned the lessons of team play and a healthy attitude towards both victories and defeats.

Of course, growing up in the Himalayas was a privilege. The majesties of the clear days when the snow stood high in the sky; the bursting of plant life in the Monsoons, the vigor of animal life – especially of the insects – all made for a keen awareness of the Creator and His creations.

Teachers played no little role in making life good and growth joyful. With so many of our teachers we were part of a family. (After all, our parents didn't see much of us, nor we of them!) Some teachers were feared. Sometimes a teacher was distrusted. But most of the time teachers were kin-folk, and I know this is so in Mt. Hermon today. Children cannot really grow up fully without the warmth and support of parents or their substitutes given on a day-to-day basis.

Many other memories of the 'old system' are remembered with deep appreciation. But one regret troubles me. I never had a chance to learn to be a handy man. My house needs a versatile householder who has tools and knows how to use them, who is not terrified by the misbehaviour of gadgets and structures. There were many hours of idleness in my boarding school days. In those days, 'vocational training' was thought suitable only for dull students or those with no ambition. But if there had been a workshop available and a teacher – a man of great patience would have been necessary – the empty hours would have been enriched with very useful experiences, useful to any normal householder in this modern day.

People well along in years – as I must reckon myself to be – are often inclined to cast an aura of glory over the days gone by. To me, that aura still hangs over the present-day Mt. Hermon, where enormous changes have taken place to meet unprecedented changes in the world, for Mt. Hermon still preserves the eternal and unchangeable varieties and works under the blessing of the divine Master whose kingdom is the surest future.

(Hermonite 1978, annual school magazine.)

CHARLES SWAN: A 'HERMON KNIGHT'

Dr. Charles L. Swan and I share something in common. Both went to school, MH college (he, the Language School and me TTC) and later joined the staff. He joined our Queen's Hill School, then located above the Railway Station, Darjeeling, way back in 1914 in KG, and later taught in the present Mt. Hermon School - 1929-1936.

He is most remembered by us for his 'Going Home Day' songs. I met him in MH when I was teaching there in mid-'70s. I still remember how, one fine day in the staff room, he thundered: "You are APPOINTED to write!" What? He later sent me two thick books on anthropology from the US.

Was he a prophet? I have written three books already and am now preparing a souvenir on MH as a Tribute to these giants of MH - I refer to them as "Hermon Knights".

When I edited the school's annual Hermonite magazine in 1978, this is what he said in the magazine:

"When I was a small boy in old Queen's Hill, Miss Knowles, the founder of the school, was still Principal, and Miss Stahl was Vice-Principal. When I was appointed to teach at Mt. Hermon, Miss Stahl had only just retired from the principalship. So my memory leads me to think of the original purposes of the school. It was patterned after the Public Boarding Schools of England, but the pattern was given an American flare, and some major adjustments were made to fit to the Indian scene."

Dr. Swan died many years back. May he rest in peace. Hail Mt. Hermon!

53 The Search For Queen's Hill: Romancing The Past

"We walked on hallowed ground"

Vedprakash Agarwal, SC 1971

This is our school, not just one building but five, strung along the hill side down to the railway. Only three are showing. It is five minutes walk to the railway station. Has almost no playground. The tall building was built in 1902. The others were then old, forty years or more. It housed the school 1900-1925 (Carolyn Stahl).

Mount Hermon School owes its genesis to a woman missionary, Miss Emma Knowles. She started the school in a building called 'Arcadia,' but following a devastating earthquake she was forced to shift to two rented buildings. The new school was named 'Queen's Hill' and she served as its first Principal. Whilst working together on a school magazine, of which Jigme Kazi was the editor, the two of us decided to locate the location of the school when it first commenced way back in 1895. We had little information to go on other than the chitchat that the school is now a residential building and the only way we could narrow down where the school could be located was by the suggested landmarks, that it was above the railway station, towards Kakjhora, near Tenzing Norgay's House and that it bordered a popular hotel. Finding a building that was built almost a century ago, without an address was not going to be an easy task but Jigs and I decided that we were going to give it our best shot.

We were overwhelmed to find that a charming lady by the name of Mrs. Tenduf La, a Sikkimese of Tibetan descent, now the owner of the delightful Windamere Hotel, renowned for its unique ambience and charm had been a student of the school and studied at Queen's Hill under Miss Emma Knowles. This was too good an opportunity to miss and both us trooped to her hotel, after taking a prior appointment. She welcomed us with gracious charm and seated us in a lounge whose walls were lined with photographs of important guests, the King of Thailand, the King of Greece and Denmark, Begum Aga Khan, Hollywood Actress Vivian Leigh all share space on the walls. This was the place where in 1959, the Chogyal, then the Crown Prince of Sikkim met his future wife Hope Cooke for the first time.

Mrs. Tenduf La served us tea from the Makaibari Tea Estate and it was accompanied by sandwiches and scones. She spoke about how kind and loving Miss Knowles was. She told us where the school had been but was unable to pinpoint the exact spot as she said that lots of new buildings had mushroomed in the area and that it was a pity that the playground was long gone and most of the hills had been constructed upon. She said that it was a veritable maze and wished us luck. Reminiscing about the school she said that they sat at long desks with inkwells in them and wrote with quills that had sharp nibs that "we dipped into the inkwells." Discipline in the school was very strict. Girls who misbehaved or did not learn their lessons were hit with a cane. Girls had to learn needlework. Some teachers had a "Dunce's Corner", any child who missed a question had to stand there. As day scholars "we paid around 6 to 8 annas per month as fees". When we asked her if she remembered Miss Knowles she said that she was genial lady who wanted to use her skills and talents for God. She wanted to make the world a better place and it was her desire to bring God's goodness in the lives of people through education. She challenged and encouraged us to become closer to God, she added.

Embarking on this emotional pilgrimage a gamut of inexplicable emotions engulfed our heart. There was no way either of us could have predicted how deeply the search for our school would affect us. We took a cab up to Kakjhora and from there stepped on to the slippery and uneven path up the hill dotted with houses. We could hear the incessant chattering of the inmates and the occasional muffled barking of the pet dogs that nearly every single household seemed to possess. Nervously we knocked on the door of a house and spoke briefly to the elderly man who opened the door. Not only did he say that he had never heard of any Queen's Hill but was certain that none existed in this area.

We talked to various people who we felt were geriatric enough to remember what their forefathers would have told them. Every time we met with answers that were vague and muddled and with each passing minute the disillusionment and disappointment was digging deeper into our hearts. It was then that someone suggested we talk to the 'boju' who lives in "that house yonder" and with hope reignited we traced our way to the house. Nepalese are an affectionate and warm people and there wasn't a single house that looked upon our intrusion as trespassing or annoying…this house was no different. After the initial namastes, the nonagenarian lady, she must surely have been in her late 90s warmed up to the conversation and very convincingly and credibly told us that there was a house up the hill that used to be a school and was run by white foreigners. She was gracious enough to walk out of her house and actually point out the building to us. Our relief and gratitude knew no bounds…..perhaps the moment had arrived; perhaps the wait would be over?

Seeing the building for the first time was cathartic. There was no doubt that it was the one, for "Queen's Hill" was embossed right on top of the building. The sight invoked the school's glorious past. It presented a past which instilled nostalgic longing, something being stuck in a time warp. For us Hermonites, this is a heritage site, but ravaged by time and no formal restoration ever taking place, the grand old school was barely recognizable. The only hint that the school ever existed was the arched façade where the name "Queens Hill" was etched into its stone. The colour and the paint had long gone but the empty furrows and an inkling of dried out tint proudly proclaimed "Queen's Hill" and for a long time Jigme and I stood their mesmerized and fascinated and soaking in the moment.

> *Queen's Hill - you make me smile,*
> *You make the effort worthwhile,*
> *Finding you, a dream come true*
> *An old bond, we choose to renew*
> *So this is the womb from which*
> *Beloved Mount Hermon grew.*
> *The old stone walls still the same*
> *Hallowed still thy fair name.*
> *The trees whispering in the breeze*
> *Your wonders will never cease.*
> *The scent of roses in the air*
> *Children playing here and there*
> *Frozen virtues warm again*
> *Walking down memory lane*

We opened a creaky gate and for a moment paused. Did we hear the sounds of tiny footsteps as they ran from their classrooms towards the playground? There was a vacant threshold waiting for us to cross. Echoes from a distant past were tugging at our heartstrings. Could we be accused of trespassing? Would we offend someone? Or would a friendly ghost from those bygone days manifest itself and offer us a comforting sanctuary and relive the glorious past. We stood transfixed caught in a state of heavenly trance. We stared at the name incised on the walls. We went back into time….we could see the mason chiselling the school's name for future generations to witness, record and remember that this was where it all started….this was Queen's Hill. We were on hallowed ground.

Hail Mount Hermon! A Tribute

The emotions that caroused within our body were perhaps similar to the ones that Edmund Hillary and Tenzing Norgay must have felt when they summitted Mount Everest. The building was large – its colours faded, two large 'Deodhars' trees grew in the compound. Perhaps they were there when the school started. Who knows maybe, Emma Knowles herself had planted them. From the patio, encircled by a wooden fence, lined by little patches of green and marigold flowers, we could see the magnificent Kanchenjunga in the distance. At least there was something that was common between the current site and the original site…the magnificent mountain has always been a source of awe, grandeur and opulence. It is one of the most serene, scenic and picturesque sights and we Hermonites were blessed that it has been guarding and protecting us ever since the school's humble beginnings…it was truly overwhelming.

After talking to a few people in the building, we made our way back. Our memorable expedition now captured in photographs. A void creeps into us and fills our hearts as we bid adieu to Miss Emma Knowles legacy. A feeling of accomplishment, a sense of reclaiming our heritage and history engulfs us. It was important to understand where we started from and what shaped the identity of the school as it stands today….perhaps our expedition helped in recovering a part of that identity, reclaim pieces that have been lost with the passage of time, things that have been left undocumented and left a void in the schools knowledge of itself……perhaps we have helped fill in some of those gaps in the school's history pages.

54   *Elkanah:* "Fire In Mr. Murray's House"

Ann Gardner, Class 11

I awoke with a start. There was a loud banging on the door. I heard Daddy stir, got up and rushed to open the door. The night guard was shouting hysterically, "Fire in Mr. Murray's house."

Hurriedly Daddy got dressed and went off. Puzzled at all the commotion, I got out of bed curiously and went outside. The first thing that struck me was how pink the sky was. It was bright pink in colour – reflecting a glow somewhere. I ran down to school and stood above Mr. Murray's house. I stared in utter amazement at the large grey clouds bellowing up from there. The sky was an intense orange hue and high flames licked the sky.

Early next day, instead of our usual hour of study from 6.30 to 7.30 all students flocked down to see the remnants of last night's fire. The tall chimney stood out desolately against the blue sky. Cinder and ashes were all around. The tub, all charred stood where the downstairs bathroom had once been.

The lovely, warm, homely house had gone…only memories lingered.

Later, I got the inside story to the fire.

Date: Monday, 18th October, 1976.
Place: Mount Hermon School, Darjeeling.
Weather: Cold clear night.

Mr. Murray, who was alone without his wife and family except for Jhonny (one of his sons), went to bed at about 9.00 p.m. on that unfortunate night. He slept soundly for three hours, but was suddenly awakened. He heard a crackling sound and movement upstairs. The smell of smoke reached him.

"Fire!" the shout came down to him from the upstairs bedroom. On joining Mr. David Hampshire they found out that the fire had evidently started in the wiring leading to the immersion heater in the hot water cylinder in the bedroom.

After phoning the fire brigade, Mr. Murray's immediate reaction was to get the fire extinguisher. It worked well but was not of much use as the ceiling was already alight and the bathroom walls were in flames. They finally gave up and decided to save what they could from downstairs. They escaped from the upstairs furnace just in time, and the staircase collapsed.

Mr. Hampshire got his wife Christina and four children out. By this time three of our teachers at Mount Hermon had come over on seeing the flames from Grace Cottage which was below Elkanah. They immediately and effectively took charge of the children and helped in moving things out.

The record player and a few records were taken out, plus two mountain pictures. Working fast, but getting warmer by the minute, they managed to get out the refrigerator, kitchen stove, furniture from the sitting room and a big yellow carpet. Nothing more could be saved because by this time the whole house was on fire. Suddenly, with a shock Mr. Murray realized that he had left the gas cylinder inside. This could pose a serious problem and a dangerous one at that. Onlookers would not let Mr. Murray go in as they considered it too dangerous. So everything else was lost.

The next morning found Mr. Murray at college (TTC) assembly looking most comical in pyjamas and a borrowed *bakhu* of Mrs. Larsen's. Everyone was very kind and helped Mr. Murray in numerous ways.

"He brought us through water and fire." (Psalm 66)

(Hermonite 1978, annual school magazine.)

55 School Days In Darjeeling 1957

Arup Sengupta

Arup Sengupta

So early March from Dim Dima Tea Estate 4 steel trucks were tied up in the tea garden, Willy's jeep to take our belongings up into Darjeeling. Our Tea Estate Manager Uncle Austin had two children, George and Gwen who were my seniors by a few years already were students of Mount Hermon and my elder sister and me were joining the new session hence all our belongings were loaded and shipped off early in the morning.

Baba decided to take the old Ford Prefect 1928 model into the hills as he wanted to show off that he too owned a car. We left Dalgaon at 8 a.m. post a hearty but tearful breakfast with Didibhai howling away and me in tears. We took 3 hours just to get into Siliguri as our car heated up and we had to fill up the radiator time and again which in itself was a long story.

We had packed lunch in Sukna forest area and then we started the climb into Tung, and our car really struggled on the road. Our refill were much more and thankfully the mountainside had these cute bamboo water connection so getting water was not a problem but wearing a suit and then doing the exercise was an ordeal. By the time we hit Kurseong our car and Didibhai both got sick. My sister started puking all over and our car refused to move and needed longer cooling down time. By the time we hit school it was late evening and children from all over the world were checking in. The car just broke down near the school gates and we walked the last few steps into the compound tired and hungry.

Mrs. Williams who was going to be our teacher was there to greet us as was Mr. and Mrs. Murray as well as Mr. and Mrs. Stewart and a host of pretty looking teachers all from New Zealand and UK etc. I was in shock as the school was huge. I mean huge with kids like me running around wild and screaming or crying as the case may be and my sister who was two years older than me holding my hand and telling me to run back to the car.

A matron took us inside and took me to the boy's dormitory while someone else took my sister to her dormitory and soon we assembled for dinner. The dining room was like a palace to me… so much food and so many kids eating all at once. This was fascinating for me as I came from a middle class joint family back ground and now rubbing shoulders with the "who is who" of the world was just a dream. Their English was pure while mine was just about adequate and the first friend I made was Sonam Wangyal and Shankar Dev. Sonam is still with me in FB and that night as I lay down tucked in my blankets I felt cold, confused and scared and felt that my parents had abandoned us and run off.

Next morning at 6 a.m. while it was still dark, we were woken up and I went to the locker room and took out my tooth brush and paste and was helped by a beautiful Angel Tara who was the Ayah under the matron. Tara spoke fluent Bengali so conversation was not difficult and she helped me with my new uniform and slipped on the tie and soon I was ready for breakfast.

I was taken to my new class and saw Mrs. William there and I think it was class 2 and soon I was given a huge pile of books and brown paper and labels and everything smelt new. I never had new books before and a school bag too and my own seat and chair. Wow and an angel sat beside me. She was Sasi Boonloog from Siam (Thailand) and I fell in love with her instantly….. Maybe I still am. She was stunningly beautiful and we became great friends too.

The day passed off well and we had PT for one period and what I did not do during class I made up in the PT class. I was very, very good in sports as it came naturally and whatever sports task was given to me I did well and became a pet with PT Ma'am Miss Samson. Post classes we were allowed to play in the front of the school ground reserved for the juniors and now I had good cricket equipment to play with and wooden wickets too and a real bat. My sporting career got shaped up here.

In meanwhile my homesickness was getting cured but whenever I met my sister and saw her cry as she never got over her sadness I too would hold into her and cry too.

In fact, Ma had to come back for her the following Saturday and the 3 of us stayed in Planter's Club for the weekend and things got slightly better as for the next one month we were allowed to go out on weekends.

I loved the swimming pool as we had 2 days of swimming which was great. We really had a blast and in spite of the cold it was fun. Open air and the Queen of mountains Kanchenjunga right in front of us with her peak covered with a huge blanket of clean snow and I never got tired of that view ever.

We had forests all around us and Mrs. William would take the class out on walks during classes and show us nature and we saw how spiders spun webs and how seeds became flowers. We grew flowers in beds dug by us and we planted the seeds and watered it too and my learning was more outdoors than books and today if I love nature and mountains it was because of Mrs. Williams. We went for picnics to Lebong Race Course and had our own adventure with monkeys. We invented adventures too and Robin Hood was my favourite.

We saw movies in school and John Wayne was my hero as was Tarzan and other movie characters. Comics were read and reread so many times and I never got bored. We were taken to town once a month I think and were given Re.1/ to spend and I would use it on pony rides and toffees. We could not leave Mrs. Williams reach and she kept a great watch over us as would some of our seniors too.

I don't remember which House I was allotted to but our leader was Benu Chatterjee who was the hero of every one. My heroics in the sports field got our team points and in junior school I was quite popular. Organised games in cricket, football and hockey happened as per season and I learnt the fundamentals through good players and Robin Sir. Mr. Murray played for New Zealand in cricket and he was a great wicket keeper and my first sports hero. Although I was fond of bowling, I wanted to keep wickets as that is what my hero would do. He would stand right up to the stumps even to fast bowlers and that was exciting. We never were allowed net practice as I was only in class 2 but he would come to our junior school compound and show us the correct way to hold the bat and also help me with my bowling etc.

Within the end of first term my grades improved and my English was good and when Baba came for a weekend visit he was so surprised with my progress and Mrs. William had good things to say about me and my report card showed good marks. This excited my father as I came from a Bengali medium school to an upper lip English medium school and one of the best too and I did well. He pampered me in town and I got to take my first photograph with school uniform and cap in Das Studio and Baba got many prints to send back to his family. He was so proud of his children and it showed. In Calcutta Baba was very strict and I feared him but on this visit he was so different, kind hearted and full of humour and he remained like that till his untimely death in 1966.

He had gone out of his way to get a good job in the tea garden and as part of the perks Didibhai and me were given education by the organisation and he felt proud to see simple children running around with the rich kids who were giving that much respect back to us….. Baba never understood that in school all were equal.

Soon monsoons came to Darjeeling and for days and weeks it just poured. I never saw so much rain in my life and this weather fascinated me and even today I love rains. Life carried on for us and we even had swimming classes in the rain and it was quite comical to wear our swim suits and on top of it wear our rain coats and then swim….. Come back in rain coats……Don't ask me why???

I remember North Point School and other schools come and play matches and we would all stand in the sidelines and our cheer leaders would go…1-2-3-4 who are we for…5-6-7-8 who do we appreciate and we would howl and enjoy ourselves in the side line - win or lose. And we had our class matches too and it would be fun.

Weather changed again and it was October and in another month we would be home. Now school sports practice had started and I was entered in various events and my House captain made us practise our events over and over again and we spent hours perfecting our craft. D-day came and I remember it was so colourful. The whole area was marked by huge flags and ropes and tracks were coloured in white and whole of Darjeeling came to see our events. My parents were there too and I remember I got 3 prizes in running and spoon and marble race and sack race. Standing on the podium to get a prize was a great high.

We would now sing some songs about going home and I can still hum the tunes but have forgotten the words but it used to be great singing together and having a blast.

Group class photo and school photo sessions was a new experience for me and my sister and we had a holiday as we changed dresses so many times for various group activities and I really admire uncle from Das Studio who used to come to photograph a bunch of co-ed naughty but fun loving brats.

Hail Mount Hermon! A Tribute

The day school closed for us juniors and we went to Darjeeling Station and boarded the toy train to Siliguri and "Boy Oh Boy" was it thrilling or what….. No one could stop us from singing Do Da Do Da Day on the top of our voices and running all over the small compartment and at times even sneaked on to the road when the train was climbing slowly to Ghoom. Batasiya Loop saw us stop our sing and dance as someone told us we were going back to school….Oops!!!!! What a ride we had and I did not want it to end…… We chug chugged into Siliguri and there was Baba and Ma ready to take us into their arms. Our Ford Prefect car "Jagarnath" was waiting for us and also the Willey's jeep and we returned back in style as Baba being an engineer and Duar Garage Uncle Dhatt did things to the car and she ran quite well. No filling up water in the radiator every 10 k.m. and soon by evening we were home.

A great first year in a boarding school in new surroundings and I came out better and strong. Thank you Mrs. William and my friends for teaching me to live together and share things….. Sonam, if you ever read this Thank You brother for being there for me.

56 "Mount Hermon Fills My Heart With Special Things"

Aphichoti Chavengsaksongkram (Oak)

Aphichoti Chavengsaksongkram (Oak), 1974 batch Hermonite from Thailand, gets entertained on his first journey to Mount Hermon School in mid-1960s. He encounters cows, dogs, rickshaws ..... and 'gods'.

I have a dreadful long-term memory. Where do I begin. To tell the story of how great Mount Hermon School has been to me. She fills my heart with very special things. With angel's songs, with wild imaginings. She fills my soul with so much love. That anywhere I go I'm never lonely. Who could be lonely I reach for her she's always there within my heart, for all the days of my life.

Oak with wife Nantana and son Ben.

Where do I start. March 1966 two fat boys age eleven, and ten with cheeks to the brim my elder brother and I. Our bags packed and ready to go. We were all very excited to make our first journey oversea. Mom was taking us to see an English boarding school somewhere high above the clouds in Himalaya mountains of India.

Hail Mount Hermon! A Tribute

Travelling with us was an ex-Thai student, 'Sasithorn Boonlong' whose parents were mom's friends. Flying those days was for few fortunate people so everybody was excited. At the airport grandmother, uncle, aunties, cousins, neighbours, our three servants, the gardener, the chauffeur, several mom's friends, and even mom's favourite massager came by train all the way from eastern Thailand to see us of. Everybody's putting garlands on my neck and I've that lovely feeling of a movie star.

Hello Calcutta, it's now that I remember that India was like Wonderland. In this other universe everyone seems crazy and everything was upside down, back to front and infuriating bizarre. I get off the plane to be embraced by the hot and clammy smog. The cocktail of damp diesel fumes, swirling dust, burning cow dung, toxic chemicals, spicy sweat and sandalwood wraps me in memories.

A different tarmac welcoming committee emerges from the mist - five men with massive mustaches, machine guns and moronic stares, each of them clutching scratching his own balls.

We spend hours inching along an impossibly passport queue. It takes half an hour to find our bags in the midst of a screaming and jumping porter mosh and another twenty minutes to have our bags checked open by customs. Exiting the arrival hall, dazed, disoriented and dusty, I sense a strange sight and sound emerging from the smog. A huge hurricane fence appears to be alive. It's rocking and writhing – fingers, toes, and small arms reach through wire gaps, heads poke over the barbed wire, and mouth pressed to the steel groan and moan "taxieee, taxieee, madam, taxiee, baksheesh, money."

Thai Hermonites: Oak is standing second right in back row.

"Mount Hermon Fills My Heart With Special Things"

We checked in the old Grand hotel. The next morning, we wake wrapped in noxious cloud of smog and dirty diesel fumes. The ceiling fans struggled to cool the hotel room. The whirl barely covered the cawing of large crows on trees outside. I move to the deck to watch a roaring rough sea of traffic wildlife. Blokes – and a friend or two – perch atop tall, rusty bicycles. Entire families share motorcycles; toddlers stand between dads' knees or clutch his back, wives sit side saddle while snuggling babies.

The incessant honking horns from the black-and-canary-yellow Ambassador cars – Indian made half Rolls Royce and half Russian tanks rules the roads with class. Huge tinsel-decorated trucks rumble and groan, filthy lime-green buses fly around like kamikaze cans squeezing out a chunky sauce of arms and legs. Shoes dangle from back bumpers and black demonic face poke out red tongues from windshields; these are for good luck. But it's probably the holy mantra written on the backs of vehicles that keep things moving. It's not Baby On Board, or Jesus Saves. Instead, hand-painted in swirling childish capital letters is: HORN PLEASE.

Everyone seems to drive with one finger on the horn and another shoved high up a nostril. The highway soundtrack is a chaotic cocktail of deep blasts, staccato honks, high pitched beeps, musical notes and bicycles bells. It's as if Calcutta is blind and driving by sound – except it seems many are deaf. Pedestrians are on the bottom and run out of the way of everything, bicycles make way for cycle-rickshaws, which gives way to auto-rickshaws, which stop for cars, which are subservient to trucks. Buses stop for one thing and one thing only. Not customers – they jump on while the buses are still moving. The only thing that can stop a bus is the king of the road, the lord of the jungle. The holy cow.

Next morning, we catch a domestic airplane which had an Indian name I can't recall. Parked way off from the Dum Dum airport building we had to walk under the scorching sun all the way to the old classic World War II plane James Bond piloted a DC-3. Indiana Jones hopped a ride on one for his last crusade. The rusty old plane was a three-wheeler like all plane except this one had a tiny center wheel at the back, so the nose is tilted up as though it's taking off standing still. It was rather small with just two seats each side of a center aisle.

One of the most memorial flight where one can fly without seat belts, and smoking seems compulsory. There was no cockpit door so we can see the two pilots smoking little brown Bidi cigarettes all the way. A couple of frail thin men pulled down the propellers to jump start as the engine coughed and sputtered to life with smokes and backfires. The plane began to roll as I look back there was no door to close, and a man in white *dhoti* without shirts seems like Gandhi himself came running with a pot in one hand and a goat in another arm. He got on just as the plane roared down the runway.

As a ten-year-old boy I was enjoying the flight. It didn't fly high like today's plane, and I could always look down to see people, cows, kids running, and dogs chasing us. As we levelled a smoke started to fill the cabin. The *dhot*-clad man started a fire in a stove to boil tea for passengers. The little goat was used to add milk. The entire flight was a roller coaster as the plane keep hitting air pockets, and we scream when it suddenly drops a few thousand feet.

Hail Mount Hermon! A Tribute

As we reached the destination the plane swooped down at an attack angle the *dhoti-wallah* at the back door was hollering out, and I looked through the square window seeing that he was chasing some cows which was feeding on the grass runway. The plane made a sharp circle and came around to make a landing. After three hours' dreadful flight with lots of pukes (in this world we applaud a dreadful landing that's as fast and steep as a takeoff) we jump up to tackle fellow passengers in a crush at the door while the plane is still moving, and the *dhoti-wallah* gets off first. Bagdogra airport, here we come!

Stepping down the narrow stairs and across the tarmac, with fresh tar painted in broad strokes along its weathered cracks, to Bagdogra's low, white terminal, the sharp glare makes disembarking passengers' wince, and the heat smacks with heat unsettling force of an open palm. After an hour's waiting, we came across some taxi rest stop and find our driver holding hand with another man. The two darlings of Siliguri pretending they were here two hours ago. But their vintage World War II Land Rover rut put cab makes up for their shortcoming. It had an orange roof and a back-window curtain of purple paisley, and it doubles as mobile temple. The dashboard had a fluorescent Ganesh (the elephant head God), an orange toy cow, a snow dome of Sathya Sai Baba (the Afro-haired living God of Bangalore) and a blue plastic Shiva bouncing on a spring. A brown, four-armed Barbie in a *sari* stands on lotus and she had an aura of tiny lights that flash when we brake. Kumar stated that she's Lakshmi, goddess of money as his boyfriend who was sitting on his lap adds that she's their favorite. Below is a faded photo of the driver's parents, a tiny national flag saying, "Proud to be Indian". Within half an hour we were almost a convert – praying to all these Gods and more – because Kumar, the most annoying man in the world, drives like the maddest, playing chicken with everything on the road.

Only later in years I learnt that Darjeeling was just fifty miles by road. But it took us more than four hours to reach. Fields of tea are immediately around the airport, seven or eight slow miles brought us to Siliguri, as traffic braids around potholes that would shake off tooth fillings, bicycles and cycles rickshaw, goat, dogs, rusted buses, high-riding military trucks, and pale cows. Schoolgirls with pigtails tied in colored ribbons walk along the uneven lip of the blacktop. Boys in boiled white shirts, their uniforms jacket dangling jauntily by a thumb over the shoulder, follow behind. Rusted corrugated-tin roofs cover small houses. (This article will be continued in the next edition of the book – author)

57 Walking Down Memory Lane

Rita Farhat Kurian (Rita Mukand)

Growing up in the 70s in the hills of Darjeeling was a life-drawing experience like inhaling in cool clear air under a bright blue sky. Sharp memories like a fragmented kaleidoscope color up my mind whenever I remember school.

Why was it so hard, so special, and so easy? Mount Hermon School to me was an oxymoron, all packed in one parcel, joyously sad, crazily sane, or the baddish good days! Back then, my mother, Mrs. Mukand was a teacher. Teaching was part of the flow of her life - and before marriage, she taught in Wynberg-Allen School, Mussoorie. Destiny always brought her to the mountains. So here we grew up, Yasmin, Anita, me, perhaps not realizing that we had stumbled across a treasure-mine-in mountain, metaphorically speaking.

Mount Hermon School lavished in luxury of wide fields, forested thickets, grand gray-brick school and other yellow buildings, football/tennis courts/pool/gym, and cottages for teachers sprawling over a 100 acres of land. When I was six, one evening, the Bailey twins, Pam and Judith, originally from Australia, teachers of the Kindergarten invited me for their nature walk down the road below Fernhill. The summer evening was mellow with croaking frogs, fireflies shooting through the greenery, and crickets singing merrily. I guess our school was famous for its nature walks we went for hundreds of those! Later, we took an 11 kilometre walk to Tiger Hill, starting before dawn to see the exquisite sunrise. Only I did not see any sunrise because I was squashed between a sea of squabbling tourists. I actually got a better sunrise from our cottage veranda at home!

While music, sports, and much more flourished in this co-educational school, some memories that flood my mind are a folk-dance event hosted by our musically gifted Mrs. Murray, where girls dressed adorned with red lipstick, makeup, long silky black hair or wavy ringlets, wearing long skirts came floating into the quadrangle that night and danced exuberantly to a very merry folk dance and enacted a drama, I remember there was a kind of night feast with stalls set up. The melody of the music resounded in my head for days.

Winter holidays could be very lonely on the campus for staff kids if we did not go home, and a few times we stayed in Darjeeling for Christmas and one cold lone winter, on a particularly bright night, a few staff, us and the Johnstons met in Ailina Guest House. (Incidentally, the big rumour floating around was that Ailina Guest House was haunted, it has a terrible heavy air of smoky darkness). That winter, our family, trudged up to Ailina Guest House with the others and had a glorious time, with bright lights glowing all over amidst the glimmer of tiny coloured-Christmas lights. My father who loved cooking exotic

Mughal food was there, taking a short break from New Glencoe Tea Estate. He had made his famous shammi kebabs and everyone gushed "Ohh, it's delicious." We relished the potlucks and unity that the staff held in those days along with the Wednesday night prayer meetings. The old saying goes, people who pray together stay together.

Talking about food, we all remember Mr. Rocky Gardner's unforgettable egg-and-bacon pie, shortbread and banana cakes and his other edible wonders. *"Those were the days my friends,"* Hermonites crooned gustily, with misty eyes. Thinking of sentiment, at the drawing near of winter holidays, the entire school would croak sentimentally, "Old Walls Are Friendly Walls" amidst rolling tears and clasped hands.

In the 2000s, we walked into Mount Hermon and a wave of nostalgia hit us when we realized Mr. Mannon's tuck shop was shut and gone forever, Mr. Mannon himself tucked in another corner of Darjeeling was a bit heartbroken. You may ask what was so special about that tuck shop? Well, it fed our souls with its manna that one finds in a desert depleted of food shops or any shops; comfort foods of singhara and bun, egg and bun, bun and chops, red-hot chips, plain chips, tea, and the walks. An oasis in a desert, students and staff flocked to the tuck shop during break and after tea to get nourished, and Mr. Mannon only ventured back up the mountain, over valley and hill back home after 6 p.m.

Night drops swiftly like a black blanket swiftly and unless the stars and moon brightened our skies, we were pretty much in the dark with nocturnal power-electricity cuts that visited us faithfully each evening. Some hardships of life were scarcity of water, where Mom would get up at dawn to fill the drums with water. We learned the value of water through those water-grilling years, sweet lessons learned of valuing water. Talking of sweetness, there is nothing like sweet spring water above the tasteless slightly chlorinated-tinged water given by our governments.

Wonderful class teachers always shine out to help us, like knights in armours, like a certain Mr. Jigme Kazi, my class 4 teacher, kind dark eyes framed in a handsome face was a great encouraging teacher. I never heard him shout, rail, look irritated or smear us with deriding comments.

Unfortunately, there are memories of some teachers that did that. Well, humans are not perfect, so forgiven. Ms. Russell was another inspiration, always encouraging me, building up my broken morale. Our principals were a class of their own. Like in one incident, Yasmin, my sister, along with friends bunked school to go to North Point Singamari to eat aloo dum and parathas, when Mr. Murray drove along in car, and his keen-blue eyes caught them. He silently opened the door, motioned them to hop in and didn't say a word to them. His cold silence was steel and did its deep work to grip their consciences to true repentance.

On this reflection back to Mount Hermon, I am grateful for the rich depth, joy among some tough times that this school poured upon me. Sometimes, we may not realize it then, but the days we considered our toughest were shaping us in unseen ways, preparing us for an unknown future path that enables us to break caged bars and climb higher mountains to see the silver lining in the horizon, for that, I am grateful to Mount Hermon School!

Rita Mukand pays tributes to Russell and Kazi

Hi All, I am taking the plunge here!!!! Mount Hermon School has a rich heritage and most kids shone in the school because of the umpteen opportunities. However, there are the backbenches who did not rise and shine, and I speak for them and me. Down the road of my life, there are two wonderful teachers I never forgot. I was thrilled to reconnect with them, and now, I think this is the moment I should let them know. Hopefully, this will be a blessing to others too. I know we can never make it perfect for everyone and I appreciate all the teachers.

A student's honest confessions to two great inspirational teachers!

I grew up amidst the rolling hills of Darjeeling
With view of the snow Kanchenjunga Mountains
Pine trees towered amidst waterfalls and fountains
In summer, tiny fireflies fluttered golden and bright
Diamond stars sparkled on the clear winter's nights

Our grey-brick walled school stood expansive and great
Honesty for me, I lugged behind and caught the train late!
I was a shy kid, alone a lot and often felt dejected
I did not blossom in school as other kids, and felt rejected.

Hail Mount Hermon! A Tribute

In class 4, I suddenly got a wonderful class teacher
He was a teacher who did not deride, sneer or jeer
But in kindness and wisdom, he washed away fear
I felt a sense of belonging and peace in his class
His words strong and warm, not sounding hollow brass

Jigme Kazi saw us as we were, took off our defensive lids
In kindness and creativity, taught with passion and grid
I never saw him blow his top or get angry or mad!
He was patient with kids that were a little shy and sad.
It was Jigme Kazi who helped me out at that stage
The most inspirational teacher at the tenderest age...

Then the years rolled by in some misty darkness
Then another teacher rose out of the barren starkness
With golden green eyes and golden brown hair
A heart of kindness, she tucked me under her care
Patricia Russel, an engaging lively teacher from Britain
A great lady whose life story was little known or written
She helped many kids all along the winding road
Personally for me, it was the higher way she showed

Teachers may not realize the colossal power they carry in life
How their words can build, shape, mould or even cut like a knife!
Thank you, Sir Jigme Kazi
For being the teacher to build, mold, nurture and repair
Thank you, Ma'am Patricia Russell for being the teacher
To help me climb up the rickety creaking stairs!
And thank you too, all the other teachers
That taught me and I met along the way!
Some of those shaping are here in life to stay...

Rita F. Kurian (aka Rita Mukand)

58 The Reunion

Rekha Samuel

'Non Scholae Sed Vitae Discimus
Not for School
But for life we learn'
Her mind was restless
She had abruptly left school
Three decades ago
Thanks to a political revolution
That shook the
Queen of the hills
Darjeeling

The climb had started
From 'Sila'
She told an amused taxi driver
That this was her first visit back
To Mount Hermon School in 30 years
"Ehhhhhhhh ho hajoor?" He asked
His kind wrinkled face
And toothless grin with 'khaini' stains
He politely turned down the volume
To listen to her banter

The language warmed her heart
Phrases and mannerisms
That the Nepali speaking
People convey with ease
The 'namaste'
Dai, didi, bhaini, daju
Deep respect
'Mariyada' in Tamil

The music on the radio
took her back to
Singing in school

The Chapel
Morning has broken
Master the Tempest
Kumbaya my Lord
Beloved Mount Hermon we greet thee
Going Home day has come at last

Hey 'Jilli Milli Jilli Milli duese re!'

Kurseong-Sonada-Ghoom
She glanced at the toy train
A UNESCO world heritage site
Chugging slowly alongside
She could hear the slow whisper
"I think I can, I think I can"
Unchanged
In a landscape
Where several roofs
camouflaged the erstwhile vast green hills

Flashes of designated sacrosanct areas
Came to her mind
Pairs: the 'fence' or around school
Romance initiators: study hall
The recently broken hearted: everywhere

Where 'Jhaaps' were exchanged: Top flat
Bunkers: anywhere out of bounds
Smokers during class hours: the 'bogs'

Non dining room food:
tuck shop, 'boxsi wallah'
someone's tuck parcel

Hail Mount Hermon! A Tribute

Punishment: Principals office
And the deceptively brave walk back
with sore gluteus maximus
along the long corridor to class

Several cars had stopped at a turn
'It's the best momo place' the driver said
'would you like to try'
How could the driver know?
That this question was like
Asking a Hermonite
"would you like some oxygen?"

She was delighted!
Perfectly sculpted dumplings
Of Heaven on a plate
With the 'Dalle' ko achar
Darjeeling tea
Alu dum!

The wander luster in her
Had never found food comparable
And she knew 'Darj' was closer

It reminded her of 'town leave'
Where hungry students would flock
To the famous haunts
'Sungur' momos were most popular
At New Dish or Penangs
Or the calorific good value – for - money
Sausages, eggs, toast and the milkshake
Brunch at Keventers

The rich went to Glenarys
The poor sacrificed the extra momo plate
To buy pastries from 'Glens' for the
    pretty girl
They wanted to impress
Or just ate from Boxi wallah!
The music lovers stopped at Das studio
The fashionable went to 'Annies'

The Simple Life
The Contented Life

59 Making A Difference

Jigme N. Kazi, SC 1972

My *alma mater*, Mount Hermon School (MHS, often referred to as MH), Darjeeling, did not start with a bang. For Miss Emma Knowles, a Christian missionary from the US, who founded Queen's Hill School in Darjeeling way back in the latter part of the 19th century, it was an uphill task. Funds were low and competent and dedicated teachers were even more scarce.

MH was first called 'Arcadia' when it was first established in a bungalow below Chowrasta facing Lebong in 1895. Four years after its founding a massive landslide in 1899 killed thirteen of its students when the school building collapsed. Failures did not deter Knowles. She had faith in God Almighty to provide for all her needs.

A few years later, Knowles shifted the location of the school to below Mt. Everest Hotel near the railway station and renamed the school – Queen's Hill School (QHS). In the turn of the 20th century, QHS (the old school buildings are still there) shifted to the present location below Singamari at North Point. The school was expanding and needed more space. It was again renamed Mt. Hermon School in 1930. The present MH campus originally had 100 acres. It has now only about 80 acres. The rest is history.

I have great love, affection and regard for my *alma mater*. Even after nearly three decades since leaving MH my passion for the school has not diminished. MH not only gave me a sound educational foundation but also gave me the much-needed training and experience to become a qualified teacher. What MH taught me has withstood the test of time. And that is why I recently dedicated my second book, "*Sikkim For Sikkimese: Distinct Identity Within The Union*" to "My teachers who taught me how to read and write and aim for higher things in life."

Hermonites: We Hermonites are a peculiar breed. Commented a NorthPointer, who at times get invited to our 'reunions': "Your get-togethers are very different and informal. I enjoy it. We get stuck in protocols." My reaction to this has been: "We are Protestants, you chaps follow the Jesuit Order. We are comfortable with disorder!"

When Hermonite N.K. Pradhan was recently inducted into the Chamling Cabinet as Human Resources Development (HRD) Minister it was time to party again. "NK" (Senior Cambridge 1968), fourth time winner of the Assembly elections, during our get-together in Hotel Tashi Delek (one of our favourite haunts) rightly acknowledged, "We Hermonites should feel proud that we have many Hermonites in high places."

One of the oldest active members of the Sikkim Hermonites Association (SHA), formed in 1985, is former Secretary, Tashi Densapa, who is presently the Director of the world-renowned Namgyal Institute of Tibetology (NIT), which is one of the three such institutions in the world for study and research on Tibetology and the Himalayan region.

Jigme N. Kazi, Tenzing Tethong and Tashi Densapa in Gangtok, 2012.

Hermonites, by and large, are a versatile lot. Our definition of "high places" is not confined to "government service." Even on this count we have several big shots. Our Association's President, Karma Bhutia (Senior Cambridge '72), is Principal Secretary and Chief Engineer. Senior Hermonite Nim Lhamu Ethenpa is also a Secretary and another senior Hermonite Tempo Bhutia is not only the Managing Director of SITCO but also the President of the Sikkim Football Association. And the list could go on and on…

Besides myself, one of the Hermonites who has been giving a tough time to the establishment is Athup Lepcha, former Minister who now heads the Affected Citizens of Teesta (ACT) as its President. The ACT is against big hydel projects in the Dzongu region of North Sikkim, largely inhabited by the Lepchas, widely regarded as the original inhabitants of Sikkim. The Lepchas are now a fast-vanishing tribe and a prominent Hermonite is leading the movement fighting for their survival in the land of their origin.

Karma Bhutia rightly noted during the dinner hosted by the Hermonites to felicitate "NK": "Where in Sikkim would you find a member of the Opposition like Jigme enjoying the company of a Cabinet member of the ruling party?" Even if others don't follow our example we still need to set the right trend.

"NK *daju*" must recall the times he used to lead groups in singing patriotic songs during Independence Day (August 15) functions in MH. The song sung in Hindi went like this: "*Insafki dagarape/Bacho dekhao chalke/Ye desh hai hamara/Neta tume ho kala ke*" (the song exhorts children, who are the future leaders, to tread the path of justice).

Now that "NK" himself has become a *pucca neta* he must try to always tread the path of justice. We, particularly the Hermonites, will judge "NK" not only by his loyalty to his government, party leadership, and the people but by his commitment to ideals and principles that give birth to great institutions and nations. What is the use of our unique educational background and experience if we cannot set high standards in public life?

White House connection: Luckily, Hermonites now have a live connection with the most powerful man on earth – the US President, Barack Hermonite Obama! Only last week Obama appointed Hermonite Barbara Nichols-Roy's South Indian husband (now settled in the US), Vinai K. Thummalapally, as the US Ambassador to the small Central American country of Belize. (see page 1 for details).

The Nichols-Roys, originally from Shillong, are known to most Hermonites of the '60s, '70s and '80s. "NK" is familiar with Marian Nichols-Roy, the eldest daughter of Stanley and Helen Nichols-Roy.

For Barbara and Vinai, Obama is not only their former college classmate but they also helped to raise funds and campaigned for him.

Says Barbara, "We are very honoured and privileged, proud and humbled, all at the same time, to have been a part of it and to know that we played a part in Obama's historic success." Vinai's appointment naturally gave an opportunity for global Hermonites to get in touch with each other. I've already congratulated Vinai and Barbara on behalf of Sikkim Hermonites and Hermonite International (Hi!) and also hinted for a global Hermonites' meet at Belize to which she replied, "Thank you, Jigme."

(This is an article by Jigme N. Kazi published in his
Sikkim Observer in May-June, 2009.)

60   A Himalayan Affair

Karl Hagen, SC 1972

Karl, Kenny and their mother, Mrs. Hagen.

For three years in the mid-to-late 1960s, I went to boarding school in Darjeeling, six thousand feet above sea-level in the Himalayan foothills. Every March I would take a small plane from the plains down in Calcutta (Kolkata) to Bagdogra airport in Siliguri. From Siliguri it was six hours of winding vertiginously up into the mountains by jeep or bus or, for the lucky ones, narrow-gauge railway. Our school's main building was an unheated stone castle, wreathed in mist most of the time. We slept under three blankets throughout the school year, which lasted until November, when the school closed down for the winter months and most of the students made the long journey back down to the plains.

A Himalayan Affair

For a month beforehand we all sang GHD (Going Home Day) songs rich with school slang; one of our favorites, sung to the tune of "The Camptown Races", went:

Going Home Day has come at last, doo-dah, doo-dah/Going Home Day has come at last, Oh, doo-dah day/We travel all the night, we travel all the day/We spend our money on the DHR (Darjeeling Himalayan Railway), *doo-dah doo-dah day. Down from old Mount Hermon, on a rutphut* (ramshackle) *bus/After nine months mugging* (studying), *back to home again, to fuss/Teachers are so bucky* (trouble-making), *prefects are the same/Everybody's happy, waiting for the train. Ghoom, Sonada, Kurseong, all are left behind/Though our journey's very long, I'm sure we do not mind* (all shout: *We do!*)/*When we reach Sealdah* (railway station in Calcutta), *hail it with a shout/Paan, bidi, cigret* (the cries of the station-vendors), *kick the teachers out!*

All the English-medium boarding schools in Darjeeling were run by Christians of various denominations, on the model of British public schools. There was St. Joseph's and St. Paul's, both boys-only schools, and the all-girls' Loreto Convent. Mount Hermon, the youngest of the four, was unique in being coeducational and was run by Baptist missionaries from Australia and New Zealand (although it had been founded by American Methodists). The schools had been established during the days of the British Raj, when Darjeeling (originally Dorje Ling) became a summer getaway for wives and children of the British civil servants stationed in the sweltering plains.

Twenty years after independence, the quaint little town was inhabited by Indians, Nepalis, Tibetan refugees, Sikkimese, Bhutanese, and a few Britishers who had stayed on. There were still vestiges of the colonial days in the Mall, where tourists could get pony rides, buy cakes and milk-shakes at Glenary's, go for a drink at the Planters Club, and—if they could afford it—stay at the elegant, old-world Windamere Hotel, where afternoon tea and sandwiches were still served in the British style. By our day, though, one could just as easily find salt-and-buttered Tibetan tea in Darjeeling.

Despite our school's mostly-non-Indian staff and its British boarding-school traditions such as the house system, school ties, and the tuck shop, the students themselves were mostly Indian, with a few each from Nepal, Sikkim, Tibet, Thailand, Australia, England, and the United States (three American exchange students from Chicago who initially shocked us with their cigarette-smoking but became good friends). I still remember our lively discussions about Christianity with our missionary teachers, coming as so many of us did from Hindu, Muslim, or Buddhist families. Isolated on the school grounds (except when we "bunked" to Hafiz' shop at North Point for *momos*, steamed meat dumplings, or to Black Rock (*While preparing to write this piece, I looked up Black Rock on the Internet, and learned, to my sorrow, that in November 2009 Mount Hermon student Romel Ropuia fell to his death from the rock as he and two schoolmates, bunking from the school grounds, were returning for dinner. My deepest sympathies go out to his family. According to the current Principal, plans are now underway to fence the entire 74-acre school campus.*), the spot among the tea bushes where as teenagers we once arranged a secret—and completely innocent—meeting with our boy- and girl-friends), we were far removed from the turmoil of the outside world,

from the Marxist-Leninist Naxalite movement exploding nearby in our own Marxist state of West Bengal, from the Nepali separatist movement that would erupt into violence in Darjeeling just a few years later, and from the civil rights, anti-Vietnam War, and Flower-Power movements flourishing in the United States.

Surrounded by swirling mists and tea estates terraced on the steeply sloping hillsides, our one immovable frame of reference was the mountain range. On days when the mists cleared, we looked out of our dormitory windows upon the snows of Kanchenjunga, the third-highest peak in the world. We were told that it was fully fifty miles away, but it appeared to be just across the valley. Since our headmaster's wife was a passionate music-lover, Mount Hermon was known as the singing boarding school. We sang our hearts out morning, noon and night: in morning chapel, in daytime music classes and choir practice,

Paul Hagen and Jigme N. Kazi in Gangtok, 2018.

in evening rehearsals for the annual—and legendary—school musicals. When the choir sang the anthem, "Lift thine eyes, Oh lift thine eyes, to the mountains, whence co-meth, whence co-o-meth, whence co-o-meth help," we lifted our eyes and souls to the Himalayas alone. The song must have been written with other, faraway mountains in mind, but for us there were no others.

When we were taken into Darjeeling town to see *The Sound of Music*, Maria's echoing hills were, naturally, the Himalayas only. And when we learned a song called, "Oh India, Mother India," our hearts swelled with pride at the natural beauty of our country, a beauty that we could not fail to see around us wherever we turned our heads. The words are engraved in my mind:

O beautiful for azure skies, for amber waves of grain/For snow-capped mountain majesties, above the fruited plain.

O India, Mother India, God shed his grace on thee/And crown thy good with brotherhood from sea to shining sea.

Later, when my family emigrated to the United States, I encountered another version of this song, which the Americans had had the cheek to rename "America the Beautiful." The mountains in their version were not snow-capped, but bare and purple with cold.

Today, I have little use for nationalist sentiment, but the thought and even the sound of the word Himalaya remains powerfully evocative for me. Himalayan—as in the often-used Indian English phrase, Himalayan blunder—has passed into the English language as an adjective of extremes. Abode of the snows and the Everest-climbing Sherpas, the Himalayas are the source of the River Ganges, place of myth and legend, danger, awesome beauty and unimaginably lofty heights. For me they are still the only real mountains.

(Tell Me Another: josna.wordpress.com)

61 The Life Of A Day Scholar

James Sinclair

Although I was happy enough being a day-boy, I felt I missed out a lot on school life, says James Sinclair, Treasurer & Web of the UK Alumni.

I am sure there are many stories of boarding school life at dear old Mount Hermon. But I was never a boarder, and instead was a day scholar and used to travel to the school and back in the old school Jeep.

I used to be up at 6.30 a.m. then walk down the hill to the old John's Taxi stand where I would wait for the Jeep which arrived to pick me up at 7.30 a.m. There were I think, eight of us who used to squeeze into that Jeep – Thomas Ghosh, Prem Singh, Charles MacGilchrist, Le Thung Foo, the two Mustapha brothers, Dilip and Depak, and the eldest of us all, Jagdish Agarwal who was in the SC. He, Thomas, Prem and Charles were already on board when the Jeep came to collect me, and we picked Foo and the two Mustapha brothers on the way down. I could see the Jeep down in the bazaar as it came to fetch me, and a short while later it climbed up Laden La Road, past the Capitol Cinema to the motor stand.

We got to school by 8 a.m., just in time for Assembly and prayers. I remember one day we were late, and instead of going up to Assembly, we went to our respective classrooms, and caught up with a bit of homework. This went on for about 4 days, but one day Mr. Stewart noticed the absence of day boys at Assembly and sent for us in his office. We thought we were all due to get the cane, but Thomas pleaded our cause (I think Mr. Stewart had a soft spot for him) and he let us off with a warning!

At lunch time, we day boys used to go up to the flat just above the Infirmary, and have our respective packed lunches. I loved Jagdish's parathas and lime pickle, and he loved the Marmite sandwiches my grandmother made for me, so we often used to exchange meals.

After classes ended, we day boys used to hang round till the boarders had their tea and changed for games. Then it was hockey or football on the playing field. I was usually an observer, as no one wanted me on their team, I was such a lousy player. So I used to sit on the bank of the hill and watch the others play, sometimes sitting in drizzle or not being able to see the field because of the mist. Then afterwards, at about 5.30 p.m. we would all clamber back into the Jeep and the driver – a dear old soul he was – would drop us off at our respective destinations in town. I hated this, as I would be too late to go to the pictures at the Capitol or Rink cinemas. So being pretty fed-up with the long school day, I got my mother to write to Mr. Stewart to exempt me from games, saying I had a weak heart. I was checked out at the Infirmary by Dr. Masters, who found I was palpitating when he examined my chest, and he signed me off.

So then, I was able to return home earlier than the rest of the day scholars, much to their disgust. I climbed the steep hill, past the North Point playing ground to Singamari, where (if I had a four anna bit) I would take a seat in a taxi to the Darjeeling Bazaar. Otherwise, I would walk all the way back to town via the Birch Hill West Road, which took me about 45 minutes. Sometimes, for variety, I would walk along the East Birch Hill Road on the opposite side, looking out towards Lebong, and then climb up the steep Hermitage Road which would bring me near the gates of Government House.

I remember so well my first week at school in the 5th Standard. It was on a Saturday where I had been invited to spend the day with my American friend, David Shoemaker, whose family lived in one of the cottages on the Mount Hermon Estate. After that, I was invited to attend Miss Madahavan's birthday party at the school, and a cinema show afterwards. So after rambling all day with David on the Takvar Tea Estate, getting covered with leeches and trying to peel them off in his bedroom, stripped down to our underpants, I went up to the school and celebrated Miss M's birthday party, with lots of chocolate cake. Then the picture show started at about 6 p.m. I think it was "The Red Shoes" that was being screened.

After the show, I looked around for any day-scholars, and to my dismay found none. So I walked up to Mr. Stewart, who was rewinding the last film spool on the projector. He looked at me. "James. Why are you here?" he said. I explained. "We don't send the driver into town to pick up the day-scholars for the film show," he said, "as it's the driver's day off." I was embarrassed. "Anyway," he sighed, "I suppose I will have to take you back to town." However, as it was Miss Madahavan's birthday, he invited her to accompany us, together with Mr. Jones and another couple of other teachers, as they intended to go onto the Gym Club afterwards and celebrate.

The drive back was a hair-raising experience! The evening was dark and misty and Mr. Stewart drove us round the twists and turns at breakneck speed. We ran over a pariah dog in the Darjeeling Bazaar ("Stupid thing. Just dashed right in front of me," was Mr. Stewart's only comment). Anyway, he dropped me off at the motor stand, (wasn't I grateful to get out of the vehicle with all my limbs intact!) and the rest of the party went on to the club.

The following Monday when I got to school, I noticed one of the goalposts on the upper playground was broken. Then when I got into class, Miss M said "James. I'm so glad you were stranded at school and Mr. Stewart had to take you back to town. We had a lovely time at the club, so thank you very much." Then she added with a giggle, "When we got back to school, Mr. Stewart drove the Jeep around the upper playground, going through the goalposts and we all shouted 'GOAL.' But unfortunately on one attempt he missed, and hit the goalpost instead!"

Other experiences of Mr. Stewart's driving took place when our faithful old driver fell sick for about a week, and Mr. S took over this duty. What a week that was. Woe-betide you if you were a minute late, and worse if you played hookey for the day. Once, it was a simply beautiful sunny day – unusual during the Monsoon season, and Thomas suggested to Mr. Stewart that we have a "sunshine holiday." This was a big mistake! I could see the back of Mr. Stewart's neck reddening as he shouted "What! How dare you suggest such a thing! Your parents are spending good money to give you an education, not to loll about in the sun all day." He was furious, and poor Thomas looked so abashed.

So that was the life of a day-scholar back in 1954-55. Although I was happy enough being a day-boy, I felt I missed out a lot on school life. Yet, I had more freedom, and would tell the boarders about any recent film I had seen, and weren't they envious! So – "Farewell School Days. Farewell to you ….."

62 "I Love Darjeeling Because It Was My Home"

Batch of 1969 reunion in Darjeeling.

Anon

Darjeeling is a hill station in West Bengal, India, set mile-high in the foothills of the Himalayas. It was formerly part of Sikkim and its name derives from Dorje Ling, abode of the thunderbolt, a monastery built for the Chogyal of Sikkim in the mid-nineteenth century. Its diverse population of about 130,000 includes Gorkhas, Lephchas, Bhutias, Bengalis, Marwaris, Anglo-Indians, Chinese, Biharis, and Tibetans. It is justly famous for its flowery, faintly orange-scented tea, its cool climate, its ancient narrow-gauge Darjeeling Himalayan Railway that chugs up from the plains, its botanical garden, its Himalayan Mountaineering Institute (founded by Tenzing Norgay), and, when the mists clear, its stunning views of Kanchenjunga, the third-highest mountain in the world.

I love Darjeeling because it was my home for two and a half years during my teens, when my parents sent me to boarding school there, to Mount Hermon, where the snows of Kanchenjunga were the view from our dormitory window. Keeping in touch with my MH friends and classmates (Batch of '69), drinking whole-leaf Darjeeling tea, lifting my voice and my eyes to the mountains as we did every day, and recalling the awe-inspiring beauty of the Himalayan landscape, all continue to bring me joy.

Some 17 years ago the Batch of '69 celebrated its 30th anniversary in Kathmandu, hosted by Lobsang, our classmate who is settled there. Three of us, Tsognie, Marianne, and I, being based in the U.S., were unable to travel to Nepal at that time, and so we got together at the same time for a mini-reunion at my house. We made a video in which we reminisced, sang MH songs, and sent our greetings to everyone. In it, Marianne, who has the clearest, purest voice I have ever heard, sang To Sir with Love, that she had first learned as a tribute to our class teacher, Mr. Mellor. In short order, we converted the videocassette from the U.S. NTSC format into the Indian PAL, and sent it to Kathmandu by *Global Express Mail*. (This was before Skype or YouTube were founded (2003 and 2005, respectively) and email, even if some people had access to it, was slow and unreliable.)

Our video got to Kathmandu on time, but on that day it was either a long weekend or the post office was closed due to a strike. Our classmates celebrated without us while it languished in the mailroom. Months later, Mr. Mellor, who was retired back in Australia by then, visited Calcutta (just before it became Kolkata again), where we believe that members of our batch of '69 showed him the video. We hope it meant half as much to him to receive it as it meant to us to record it for him. Mr. Mellor passed away not long afterwards, and so did dear Santosh, our classmate who had brought us all together on an email list after many years.

I realize that my tone here is nostalgic; but Darjeeling is a place of such sublime natural beauty that, even half a century later, it is still able to cast its mountain mists upon my inward eye, bringing with it that emotion recollected in tranquility so treasured by the Romantic poets.

I had to leave Darjeeling a year before the rest of my class graduated. While it was a wrenching parting for me, Darjeeling itself was devastated almost immediately afterwards by the terrible landslide of 1968. It was not until twenty-five years later that I returned again, and I haven't been able to return since. How is it that a place lived in for such a short time, and that too so long ago, still means so much to me?

63 The Woods Are Lovely, Dark And Deep

Jigme N. Kazi, SC 1972

    Work load piles up at home. But MH beacons me one more time and I cannot resist the temptation of not visiting Darjeeling next week. Out ex-Principals (1964-1978), Mr. G.A. Murray, and his wife, will pay a brief visit to Darjeeling and MH (Mt. Hermon School) in the third week of this month. This could perhaps be their last visit to Darjeeling where they spend so many happy and memorable years in the '50s, '60s and '70s. The visit calls for another reunion of all Hermonites in Darjeeling. At such time the mind must take a break. Matters of the heart naturally takes precedence.
    Nostalgia and a sense of love and deep feeling and appreciation of the past 16 years in Darjeeling (1963-1979), once again, filled me even as we braved incessant rains,

landslide-scarred roads, and vehicle breakdown to attend a crucial meeting at MH last week. Eight Hermonites representing four alumni associations from Darjeeling (Anup Chachan and Pawan Saraf), Siliguri (Jagjit Singh), Delhi (Krishna Goenka), Sikkim (Tobgay Dahdul, Punam Agarwal and myself) were present during the short meeting presided over by the new Principal, Mr. P. Das. The agenda: Murray's visit. The objective: give them a warm welcome and a fond farewell.

We are anxiously looking forward to the Murrays' 4-day visit to Darjeeling next week. We had plans to invite them to Sikkim this time but due to shortage of time and uncertain road condition we felt that a combined reunion in Darjeeling would be better. Apart from meeting former and present Hermonites, Mr. and Mrs. Murray would love to spend their short time visiting old friends and places that meant so much to them during their 24-year-long stay in Darjeeling.

Mr. Murray wrote to us in June this year from New Zealand: "So far as our time in Darjeeling is concerned, we have already made some suggestions to the Principal at MHS… Our main purpose in coming to Darjeeling (possibly for the last time, although that's hard to believe!) is to see as many Hermonites as would like to catch up with us, to renew acquaintance with folk in town like Fr. Leclaire and David Howard (St. Paul's Rector – Ed) whom I mentioned last time I wrote. And we want to take some time to look around some of our old haunts in the town and around the nearby hill, as I am sure you will understand."

We now hear that Fr. Leclaire of St. Joseph's College will, unfortunately, be away in Canada and will be back only in October. However, Mr. and Mrs. Gibbs (St. Paul's Rector 1964-73) may be in Darjeeling sometime this month. It would have been wonderful if the three giants of three great educational institutions of Darjeeling come together this time. That the three of them chose to be in the hills of Darjeeling at the dawn of the 21st century means so much to those whom they taught and worked with in the past so many decades. Had the heads of these institutions maintained a close rapport with each other as witnessed during our time we could have made their visit more fruitful and meaningful.

Mr. Graeme Armstrong Murray and his wife, Mrs. Patricia Murray, first came to MH in 1955 when the school was just beginning to come up under the leadership of Rev. David G. Stewart of New Zealand, who took over MH as its Principal in 1953. Mt. Hermon almost closed down during and after World War II as most of its students, who were foreigners, left India. However, Mr. Halsey E. Dewey of the United States, managed to keep the school going until Rev. Stewart came along. With Mr. Murray as the Senior Master to assist Rev. Stewart, MH not only pulled through this critical period but the school progressed in all respect, including its enrolment. After Rev. Stewart left at the end of 1963, Mr. Murray took over and steadily build on the firm foundation laid by his predecessor.

Mr. Murray, sometimes referred by his students as *Bhuntay* (a Nepali term for a fat person with a big stomach – he was actually not fat but bulky), was not only an efficient and an able administrator but also a friendly person who got along well with almost everyone he met. Apart from being the 'big boss' at MH Bhuntay was also a familiar figure in Darjeeling. He had many friends outside the school from almost all walks of life.

After spending nearly two and half decades at MH the Murrays finally left for New Zealand at the end of 1978, which was also my second last year teaching at MH. Their four children – Adrienne (missionary) in Bangladesh, Bronwyn (musician) in Germany, Stephen (lawyer) in Singapore and Johnnie (chef) in New Zealand will not be with the Murrays next week. But they will be with us in spirit and we will remember them.

I spent 16 short years in MH (if relieved of my burden in Sikkim I'd be ready to spend more time in MH) but the last year, 1979, wasn't as good as the previous years. Perhaps this was partly because Mr. Murray was not any more at MH. I think 1978 was perhaps my best year in MH as a teacher. There were at least 13 ex-students on the staff. We had lots of fun and created a better and more friendly environment in the school. Mrs. Murray often used to tell us, "It is not Mt. Hermon School but Mt. Hermon Family." Very few schools on this planet can boast of the strong family spirit that was in MH for nearly a century. Unfortunately, things are not the same now but we are hopeful that Mr. Das will do his best to regain MH's past glory in all respect.

While Mrs. Murray buried herself in the chapel or in the music rood/cells (MH to this day has maintained strong tradition in classical and western music) preparing for class plays, Sunday services, operas etc., Mr. Murray not only ran the school with a touch of dash and enthusiasm, but also taught geography, preached on Sundays, coached as well as played both football (as a former rugby player he was a terrific goalkeeper) and cricket (he once scored 203 during the Edinburgh Shield match against St. Paul's in late sixties). I enjoyed his history lessons during my two-year teachers' training at MH's Teachers Training College and ever since history has become my passion.

As one who was actively involved with development of sports and games in Darjeeling district, Mr. Murray was one of the main persons chiefly responsible for starting the annual Gold Cup Football Tournament in Darjeeling. To this day, this Tournament remain perhaps the most popular and prestigious tournament in the hills of Darjeeling and Sikkim. It is, therefore, not by accident but one of his pupils, Mr. Tempo Bhutia (Managing Director of State Trading Corporation of Sikkim), who heads the Sikkim Hermonites Association (SHA) as its President, is also the President of the Sikkim Football Association (SFA – affiliated to the All India Football Federation), which organizes the annual Governor's Gold Cup Football Tournament in Sikkim.

According to Mr. Namgyal Wangdi, ex-Hermonite and Vice-President of Sikkim Cricket Association (affiliated to Board of Cricket Control in India), the SCA has now decided to make the Murray Cup Cricket Tournament an official tourney of the SCA for the under-19 team in the State. This is indeed a great achievement for the Sikkim Hermonites who initiated the tourney in 1986 and thus contributed a great deal in promoting cricket in Sikkim.

The MH Centenary (1895-1995) bash in Darjeeling three years back in 1995 not only witnessed the presence of many ex-teachers from abroad, including almost all the ex-Principals from Mr. Stewart to Mr. Jeff Gardner, but many ex-students in the region also participated in the historic reunion. The Sikkim Hermonites Association, which played a major role in making the centenary celebrations more meaningful, memorable and a grand success, invited all ex-staff members and students to Gangtok for another get-together in the State capital. They went back in high spirit and with happy memories of Sikkim and Sikkim Hermonites. Some of them had spent more than a decade in Darjeeling but had not visited Sikkim at all.

The Sikkim Government responded positively to the Association's request for help during the centenary celebrations. While the Sikkim and West Bengal Governor, Mr. K.V. Ragunatha Reddy, inaugurated the function in November 16, 1995 the Sikkim Education Minister, Mr. Kedar Nar Rai, was the Chief Guest in one of the major functions in MH. Another contribution from Sikkim was the unique cultural show at the playground which was performed by artistes of the Culture Department. "This is perhaps the best cultural show that I've seen in years," Mr. Murray is believed to have said during the celebration. Hermonites all over the world, particularly the Sikkim Hermonites, are deeply grateful to the Chief Minister, Mr. Pawan Chamling, for all his help and cooperation during the centenary celebrations.

As we look back we find that ex-Hermonites have made tremendous contributions to Sikkim in many fields. While two Hermonites, Mr. Athup Lepcha (SC '69) and Mr. O.T. Bhutia (SC '72) were former Ministers, Mr. N. K. Pradhan (SC '67) is presently the elected member (MLA) of the Sikkim Legislative Assembly from the prestigious Gangtok constituency. Had he not dithered, Mr. Lepcha could have been the Sikkim Chief Minister in 1984 instead of Mr. Bhim Bahadur Gurung. Mr. Murray often used to say, "He who hesitates is lost." Athup cannot forgive himself for not paying heed to this advice.

Tempo seems to be doing well at the STCS. While most government departments are either showing losses his unit, last year, made a profit of Rs. 0.52 crore for the State. This is a notable achievement. As Secretary, Tourism Department, Mr. Tashi Densapa (SC '63) heads perhaps one of the most important departments. If Mr. Tashi Namgyal (IPS (Rtd)), had not resigned as Inspector General of Police (IGP) a few years back he would definitely have become the DGP (Director General of Police), the highest post in the State Police Department.

Mr. J.K. Thapa, perhaps one of the oldest Hermonites who passed away recently, was Secretary to the State Government for many years. Another old-timer, Mr. Madan Mohan Rasaily, who retired as Secretary, is now in active politics. Had he stuck to the ruling Sikkim Democratic Front he would definitely have played a vital role in the State as Cabinet Minister. However, Mr. Rasaily has chosen to float his own political outfit and today he is the President of Sikkim National Front. So much for Hermonites in the field of politics and administration.

In the judiciary, we have Mr. Udai P. Sharma (SC '72), who is a senior advocate and the State Government Public Prosecutor. There are many other Hermonites all over Sikkim government service, private institutions and doing their own business. For instance, Mr. Thentok Lachungpa (SC '71) is the Branch Manager of the State Bank of India in Chungthang, a remote town in the tribal-dominated region of north Sikkim. And the list could go on and on…not forgetting myself in the Fourth Estate whose role in the State has visibly increased in the last one and half decade that I have been in the profession.

Sikkim badly needs a fiercely free and independent Press and if it hadn't been for this I would have spent a year or two at MH. Both my wife, Tsering Tso, who is currently teaching at Tashi Namgyal Academy (TNA), and I are trained teachers with some teaching experience and a year's break in MH would do a lot of good to us all. However, I've said my last goodbye to the school in December 1979 with these words and there's now no possibility of turning back in the near future:

> *"The woods are lovely, dark and deep,*
> *But I have promises to keep,*
> *And miles to go before I sleep,*
> *And miles to go before I sleep."*

But MH beacons me, and every time I climb up the steep slopes of Peshok from Teesta to Darjeeling and go down to MH I feel fresh, alive, relaxed and at home. Words from the Old Testament of the Bible fills my heart even as I deeply cherish and long for things of the past. I quote from this passage (Psalms 121) from my small black leather-bound Bible given to me by my class teacher, Miss P. Russell, in 1971:

> *"I lift up my eyes to the hills.*
> *From whence does my help come?*
> *My help comes from the Lord,*
> *Who made heaven and earth."*

Perhaps it's the centenary hangover, perhaps its just plain nostalgia – funny thing is that it has lasted for nearly two decades now! – or perhaps its just a deep longing for the days gone by. Whatever it may be, all Hermonites, all across the globe, share similar feeling. And this is the main reason why all of us to this day bind ourselves together as 'Hermonites.'

And together, irrespective of whether all Hermonites are present in Darjeeling next week or not, let us say a big 'Thank You' and 'Godspeed' to the two persons who have meant so much to each one of us in the words of William Shakespeare from Julius Caesar:

> *"For ever, and for ever, farewell, Brutus.*
> *If we do meet again, we'll smile indeed;*
> *If not, 'its true this parting was well made."*

But Mr. Murray is an incorrigible optimist. During the centenary session he hinted that he would come back for the 125th anniversary which falls in 2020! By then he would be well over 95 I guess. But along the way something of *Bhuntay* has been rubbed into each one of us. If *Bhuntay* is there for the 125th we'll certainly not miss the 150th in the year 2045!! Till we meet again. Au Revoir.

(*Sikkim Observer*, August 29-Sept 4, 1998.)

64 Memories Of Another Time

Prava Rai, SC 1970

Prava Rai is seated at the centre.

It was sometime in mid-March 1960 two of us from Sikkim arrived in Mt. Hermon School. We were the first girls to be admitted into the school under the Colombo Plan programme. On our arrival we were introduced to Miss Watson, a delightful lady from New Zealand who worked in the office and also doubled up as our matron. She took us firmly by our hands and marched us to the dormitory – a beautiful large room lined with pine panels and lit by numerous skylights. After ascending the cold wide steps through equally daunting corridors it was a relief to arrive at the cosy room with rows of neatly made beds and filled with many girls who looked so different and interesting – girls so different from the ones in my village. There were girls from all over India, Bhutan and also some from England, Australia and New Zealand.

The first few weeks were both exciting and difficult. I knew very few English words, so communication was restricted to "yes" and "no". Every time I got a chance to enter into the chowkidar hut, I would go in and gaze through the little window at the hills of Sikkim. I was particularly pained when I saw the river flowing way down in the valley and imagined retracing my steps across that river to Sikkim and my village beyond the hills. I would fight back tears. But as weeks slipped by and my vocabulary grew and made friends life became easier and, even enjoyable.

The writer at work: 1970 batch Hermonite Prava Rai at her home in Namchi, South Sikkim.

Memories of another time come to me in flashes of joy, pain, friendship and the excitement of discoveries. Among all my teachers two stand out to this day and in my mind I bow to them in gratefulness and wonder.

In 1963 our class teacher was Mrs. Patricia Murray. She was a beautiful young woman, sometime a little unpredictable when dusters flew out of the window when she became angry with the unruly 36 brats. But that year is indelibly etched in my memory as the year so filled with wonder and discovery.

For the first time the English language came alive for me when she read out a poem, it was about snow-flakes falling (I don't remember the name of the poem) she gestured with her hand and made the snow fall ever so gently. The connection between words and gesture came to me in a rush of epiphany. Language from then on acquired in my child's mind a resonance so rich that it has continued to add magic to my life even today. Mrs. Murray introduced us to the 15th and 16th European explorers and suddenly horizons opened up: endless miles of oceans and wide open skies. She told us about Magellan, Christopher Columbus and so many others. She pushed the boundaries of our imaginations and the sense of the world. She narrated stories from Greek mythology, Jason and the Golden Fleece, about Medusa and the travels of Odysseus, about the Roman and Greek gods and goddesses. It was a heady year.

Equally important for us was the music lessons she gave us. We sang; she taught us how to read music, introduced us to different musical instruments through the delightful "Peter and the Wolf" record. Every instrument was a character having a very specific voice.

We were encouraged to compose musical phrases which she would play back to us adding the base. We were wonderstruck at the possibilities that this opened up for us.

Then she taught us to listen to music, our eyes closed and follow the stories through different movements of melodies and harmonies. "William Tell" I still recall how I imagined the action in the story, the heroes and the villains.

Mrs. Murray gave us so much in that one year and though I never had the opportunity to acknowledge her contribution to my growth before, whatever she taught me has remained with me all these years. Thank you Miss.

The second teacher who helped me navigate through a difficult academic decision was Mrs. Valerie Johnston. In my last six months into my final exams I realised with horror that I had made a terrible mistake by opting for Science stream. I was unable to cope with Physics and had to change course. It was then Mrs. Johnston, who was also my class teacher, assured me that she would help me. And, she did. In six months, we covered two years course material and I managed to secure a good grade too! That spurred me to study English Literature in college.

Other teachers, friends crowd in as I relive those days in memory. I grieve still for my friend Indira who passed away shortly after we finished school. Recently, I heard about Sushil Sarogi's passing away. I miss another friend Padma Vangala, I am unable to trace her and often wonder where she is.

I will always remember Michael Johnston's blue eyes, the impact they made on me when I saw them the first time. They were so beautiful and I remember asking myself, "Can he see with those eyes?" I remember Mrs. Rongong, Mr. Murray, Mr. Lewis, Miss Pradhan, Miss Vaz, Miss Raju, Miss David and of course many of my friends. We have reached that time in our lives (in spite of WHO's recent declaration that the 60s are not old age!) when remembering becomes so important.

65   Down Memory Lane

Pratap Rai

It is not often that I get the itch bug to sit by my desk and peck at the key board even after so much repeated bugging by Jigs. However, with no offences to Jigs (Jigme N. Kazi), circumstances are such that there is nothing else better to do. We are stuck with a strike for over a month for Gorkhaland with everything shut down and leaving me very little options but to remember Jigs and peck away. Sometimes I feel that many governments missed a trick when they locked their political adversaries and I can well imagine their predicament being cooped in for months and years on end – not to say that I belong to that elite group.

I really don't know where to start even after rambling around so much so I come to the conclusion that the best place to start is at the starting, pretty wise "ain't" I?

This leads me to Mrs. Williams, may her soul rest in peace. Such a darling mother to me, so firm and yet so tender. It was in UKG and it was a serious matter of a Spelling Test and I forgot how many times a U had to go up to become a U and I ended up by writing "IP" instead of "UP". The way she got me to overcome this hurdle I have not forgotten till date.

But seriously, it would not be possible for me to write the whole history (and geography) of me and MH so let's just jump around. For this I would like to take a story of Prabir, or was it Johar, any way they were all my seniors while they were at Fern Hill and Mr. Darr was their warden. It was the late 50s and Tiger Hill sunrise was a real proposition. No regular pitched road which was anyway only up to the nonfunctioning golf link. So adventurous Mr. Darr and a few handpicked lads were to walk up late in the night to greet the sun the next morning.

So off they marched loaded with food, maps and compass to boot. Come next dawn neither were they there to greet the sun nor was the sun to be seen anywhere; they were caught in the thick foliage where glimpses of the sky could be discerned with great difficulty. Undeterred Mr. Darr says, "Don't worry boys all we need to do is get to a vantage point." Sure enough after much hard plodding they do make it to a vantage point and Mr. Darr takes out his compass and map and after much accurate identifications he proclaims, "According to the map we are on that hill, so buck up boys." The veracity of the journey may be authenticated by the seniors.

Next, may be the enthusiasm of THE BOSS, Mr. Stewart, should be recalled. It was the year of the new swimming pool. All was readied and everybody was itching to take a dip except that the Darjeeling Municipality could just not get the water even after many requests and promises. The monsoons had set in and water was everywhere except in the pool. It was then – may be even in the global context – for the first-time water harvesting was resorted to by MH. The carpenters were busy and soon all the water from the main field found its way into the pool and no sooner said than done the pool was full, full of murky water. The filter house worked endlessly 24 x 7 for "ages" and THE BOSS' patience wore thin as it was for the boys at Fern Hill and Minton. So, one fine day the gates are thrown open and without a second invitation the pool is finally alive with humanity. Alas the episode reached Dr. Master's (RIP) ears and it is believed that our Boss got such a rocket that it rocked the very roots of MH.

Next comes a very revealing facet of Mr. Murray's unquestionable ability at handling students. It all started with a Helen of Troy background. Of course, who the Helen was is still a mystery and some even claim her to be a him or as better referred sh(e)+(h)im= "shim". As the whispers spread tempers flared and soon we had two big groups on full blooded war paths. One group was an amalgamation of foreign boys from overseas and the other was also the newly domiciled foreigners from north of the mighty Himalayan range and their allies.

We the other local Indian boys were far in the minority and were just mere spectators with may be a few commentators. Whatever, I think it was the break just after we had finished lunch or may be just after tea that the whole area in front of the school was filled with pugilists and grapples. (I do remember it was after a meal because the jostling started as we were leaving the dining hall). Mr. Murray also must have been having his lunch or tea and it took him quite some time before he could make his appearance. To make himself seen (and heard) he stood up on one of the cement flower pots and hollered, "Are you really men?

I think you have fighting for ten-fifteen minutes and I don't see even one flattened on the floor," and that's it, not a word more not a word less but the message was loud and clear. I don't know if he met any of the warriors afterwards but Helen of MH never appeared again.

I have already given a glimpse of what a fantastically endowed student I was (cf. Spelling Test) and the pattern endured throughout my school days. I was in absolute no hurry to get over my golden days and they actually extend from 1953 to 1967. At MH it started from 1954 till 1960 and resumed from 1964 till 1967 and still I did not "pass out". I actually completed Class 10 in 1969 privately. For courtesy's sake no teachers' names will be mentioned but I do remember being able to turn some teachers from blue to red to livid white with my academic skills especially pertaining to spellings and hand writing. It was only in 1984 while doing my TTC these hurdles were overcome, if at that. For this I am eternally indebted to Mrs. Johnston and her very dexterous handling. I still fondly remember her gentle words of praise and encouragement as I finished my final (black) board work.

This walk would be incomplete without at least a mention of my (last) batch mates and me. I still could possibly still run through the list of +26 with something or the other to say but that would turn this into a thesis rather than a loaf around. Apologies to those that do not find their space in the following lines.

My musical endowment was and is also limited to the love of music, full stop. I distinctly recall turning Mr. Wilde really wild when I had the audacity to enter the audition for the Senior Choir. To come back to the point, I enjoyed listening to the Green Grapes consisting of Raja Sen (RIP), lead guitarist and vocalist, Sonam at the rhythm guitar and Binod Yonzone at the bongo. Beatles was the then the in thing but they strummed many others and also composed a few of their own. The only one I can recall is the "Night Creatures".

Then there was Lundhup the physical and health personality. Sleeping in the bed just next to his was quite an experience and hazard. When in the mood we would be whispering away into the wee hours of the morning. Lord knows what we gaffed about and till date I still cannot remember even a word we exchanged the night long.

There was a taciturn Tapas but a phlegmatic Athup takes the cake. His stoic stance had crossed all limits and enough was enough we had get some emotional response out of him. Some, (names withheld) decided on a perfect ploy and after night study rushed up to the dorm. A whole pitcher of water was spilled in between the bed sheets and the wait began. In strolled Athup, changed into his night suit, went and relieved himself and finally got into bed as though to sleep in a fully soaked bed was the most natural thing to do.

The toppers of our group were usually Rajendra, Kavita and Preet (RIP) to name a few but there are always a few at the opposite end like me. I had a special contender (name withheld) and in one MoV period had amongst others him and me reading at the same time. With great difficulty I managed to stumble over my lines but he got stuck at his. Ms. Hawke had reached her tolerance level with me and now let fly volumes at him. Suddenly, with a stroke of genius he managed blurt to out his line and was pleased as punch.

Ms. Hawke on the other hand almost had a stroke and gave him another salvo much to the bewilderment of my friend (and me) who had just proudly read out, "Now come to the full stop."

Then there was another Sonam (RIP), a footballer. Besides being able to kick a football from one post to the other he had a special natural knack with ALL the girls. It was in one of the House matches, he being in Fisher and me being in Stahl I got a ball kicked full bloodiedly on my face and almost did a complete back flip.

I would also like not to miss out on Sunil as it is a great reflection of life in MH. It started at the basketball court in the gym. He was almost a head taller than me and as I jumped to reach the ball the best I managed was to slap his face. Nothing much could be done in public and so a challenge was set up at the dorm. As soon as the match was over, I dashed up to the dorm and awaited his arrival. Others walked in and Sunil strolled in almost the last. As soon as he entered, I jumped on the bed closest to the door and took my stance. There was pin drop silence for a moment and then a burst of laughter from almost everyone present. I must have looked ridiculously comic like David facing Goliath without the sling. After a while he smiled and I could not help but smile back and hug him and he carried and shook me like a rag doll. Here I recall another senior Anup (RIP) who broke his arm in one of these altercations and (I might be wrong) Biswanath (RIP) or Bao (RIP) the antagonist took him to the infirmary saying that he had slipped in the bathroom. (Note the plural noun)

Our batch may also make claim that we were the first class to bring in Nepali as a fully scheduled subject at MH. Senior to us there was just Munna who was taking the subject but more on the private lines. I feel it is Sonam of the Green Grapes that first floated the idea and soon we had Binod, Lundhup, Athup, Yankey and Sonam and yours truly in front of Mr. Murray's (BHUNTAY) office. There could have two or three more but I cannot recollect fully. To cut a long story short he finally relented on the condition that we find our own teacher and study after school hours. Courtesy my late father, then posted at NCC House, Ashley Dale, Mr. Gabriel Rana (RIP), a regular language teacher at St. Robert's School, became the first Nepali Language teacher at MH. (Now that's what I call history for MH and the Gorkhaland agitators folks.)

Now, coming near to the end let's talk some about the girl friends and if that does not sound right you may read as, "girls who were friends". There were some whom you wished had given a little more of their time to you and then again there are others whom you wished you had given a little more time to them. Two have been mentioned above for their academic excellence but Mohini was not too far behind. Then there is the already mentioned Yankey whose sir name was Donka but we boys, much to her displeasure, would call her something else that rhymed with her first name. There was also a Kiran and how so faithful friends were we. During the course of the years so many friends had deserted us but we were still together. Would also like to include Kusum but go on to Topu. Topu and me were never that close at school but that distance has never stretched and now after 50 years we are still as close if not closer.

Hang on a minute. This would be most incomplete without the mention of my last mentor – the one and only Ms. C. Hawke. I know many of my seniors and may be an equal number of juniors would have coinciding opinions or otherwise and I would like request you all not to begrudge me as I lay open mine.

Her fiery nature which amplifies her zeal in her mission has already been dealt with but that is just an infinitesimal molecule of her totality. One MoV period while explaining one of the Casket Scenes dealing with appreciation she slipped into a small episode of a few days before while she was supervising the junior boys swimming. The Fern Hill boys were moving up to school and a junior boy saw his House Captain in one of the groups. The small boy excitedly shouted out, "Hey, I have just completed my first lap of the pool!" The Captain barely managed an, "Oh yah," which left the unappreciated child almost in tears. Being a teacher she was, she quickly intervened showering the child praises. She could not enjoy her winter holidays without making sure we were burdened with writing to her at least three letters to her in the three months.

Many plays were performed under her direction but the two that stands foremost are The Trial Scene of MoV and The Prodigal Son in full Sunday suit. I think it was for this we had also perfected the hymn "Jesus Walked This Lonesome Valley" which I still catch myself humming. But what stands out most in memory's lane of Ms. Hawke may be slightly incongruous with what others have to say. It is her tenderness shown in her "Remarks" in my Terminal and Final results. I quite understand her inability to find any lofty words regarding my academics but there was always lots of encouragement, praise and appreciation reflecting other abilities she saw in me thus showing her love, concern and may be faith in me – "Miss, I hope I have not belied your trust"

(Sorry Tilak, Mani, Achint, Ashok, Bijay, Bhusan:- just saying you are still with me. And thanks Jigs for the opportunity of this walk which I am sure many have not completed with me but I don't grudge you. And for those that have "Thank you")

Now that I am down and dusted let's share a secret and the last of my mates. Like Topu we too were never that close during our school days but this is the only mate who takes time to meet me when in and around Darjeeling and thus compels me to do the same while I am at Kolkata. If distance has made the heart grow fonder it is true for Mono and me. Introduction over let's get to the secret. He has a whole lot of episodes, anecdotes, and howlers than I would ever imagine and he has a knack of telling them. Am sure his writing would be very red-able!

The entrance: If only we had a moat and a small wooded draw bridge at the entrance, MH would have surely looked as an enchanting-magical place. The arch of the gate propped on about two feet by two feet and may be five feet high brick work, a simple arch, with the words MOUNT HERMON SCHOOL, glimmer in golden (brass) capital letters. Simplicity at its best!

Drive in: No guard. While the left side of the drive way was marked by dancing ferns reaching out to touch every visitor, and to the left was a steep khud side, which terraced down to the neat, and well maintained tennis court; where I learnt the lexicon, deuce and volley. And also found out the true weight of a tennis racket!

Come March, the terrace was crowded with small white and pink flowers playing with the mild sunshine and rolling their heads with mirth and joy in the gentle breeze. Even these wild blooms knew March 11th was not too far!

The Quadrangle: 1960s; I was both enchanted and awed by the huge chiselled stone structure of grey sand stones - the Quadrangle side of the Main Building. And large arch ways reminding of entrance to many magical paths and riddles yet to unfold (in the next 10 years)! In fact, the quadrangle, and especially the verandas on the ground floor and the top two floors looked like the battlements of some medieval English castle. And the small snug circular balcony - tucked on one side - seemed like a place reserved for an expected royal entrance. And soon the knight may come riding in to show the skills with a lance and sword!

Parapets and Portcullis at the main entrance - Principals office - would have given it the truly magical look of any Castle from the Harry Potters books. The three-sided arch way was an almost a sacred place with silence both weird and sacred! No work here - no place to loiter here; written on the invisible silent atmosphere. Hush was the language - in the foyer - and only via raised eye brows could you question the meek standing student; if the trip was for pleasure or punishment?

The Keep/donjon: The main kitchen was located at the present dinning hall. Mr. Wainwright, a master baker, always coming up with new and tasty pastries and cakes.

Who can forget the short-bread of that crafts man? The whiff of fresh bread always travelled up to the study hall above, and the dinner menu was known much before it was served!

Another flight of steps; close to the kitchen passage led to a magnificent high – sound proof chapel cum entertainment hall. Here, all Hermonites (especially of the 1960/1970 batch); had had the good fortune to watch the dainty small fingers (Mrs. Murray) create astonishing music on the grand piano. And who can forget the small Bible skits of the Saturday morning; also the anticipation of a classical picture in the evening. Here, the characters from Shakespeare's, Othello, Shylock, mingled with the nymphs and goblins created by the junior section. And, hello! How come I forgot to mention the magic of going home day's school…..friendly walls?

The front of the Main Building faced the grand Kanchanjunga, almost challenging each other to the grandeur of the other. Many an evenings I noted the mighty Kanchanjunga blushing when looking into many of the Main building's window glasses.

A miniature garden kissed the feet of the Main building. A small moss covered log gate - covered with passion flowers - led to many well tended rows of flowers. Here pansy-violet with streak of yellow-knocked their head against the dainty poppy; while many hues of yellow marigold danced at a slightly higher level. Small fresh green shrubs marked the boundary of the miniature garden; and in between the dry brown legs of wild shrubs white and pink flowers glowed with joy. And almost centrally located stood the blue oval shaped pound; where gold fish swam in out of moss filled rock. Sometimes we took a stole – though out of bounds - by being pal with Mrs. Davidson or Mrs. Mukand.

A few feet further down, a red corrugated roof marked the basketball, court. In those days it was covered only on the wider side. While one side was flanked by green grass, the other marked by the long rough plank facing the main field. Turn inwards, and you were watching basketball, let by Mr. Mathai; twist around, and cricket match under the wily wicket keeper Mr. Murray.

There was also a Kiran and how so faithful friends were we. During the course of the years so many friends had deserted us but we were still together. Then there was the one and only Thai representative, Sajee, so silent and unobtrusive that she almost blended into the furniture. She was great on the piano but it worried me ever so much that her slim delicate fingers would snap as they pressed on the keys.

I did not know that my dear Jigs as such a severe task master. In fact, he reminds me in a way of our one and only Ms. Hawke. After wracking my numb brains to its limits, the "Down Memory's Lane" was laboriously done, dusted and submitted and what does Jigs say? "It is incomplete!" He knowing my history and geography further presses, "What about your school and some report of the Hermonite movement in Darjeeling?"

Well, I am no scribe like Jigs and his troop who can scribble off a thousand words per hour and continue doing so for hours on end. For me my fingers fly over the keyboard at about fifteen to twenty words per minute and that too is too fast for my composing skill and I have to take a break after every sentence or two. Whatever it be there are no excuses Jigs will take so let me see what hodge-podge can be delivered this time round. It is doubtful if too many will be interested in my personal affairs and the school so maybe it is more advisable to rack my brains, or whatever is left of it, and get along with the Hermonites of Darjeeling.

Having left school in 1967 but however living on just the adjacent spur of Lebong MH was never too far away and visits there were frequent. However, it was only after 18 years that the need of an association was felt. In 1984 an honest search for easily accessible Hermonites was made and Mani Kumar Lama, being the eldest, was installed as the President. The Treasurer was a junior boy with a whole sale sweets store just across Pawan's hardware store. Yours truly was coerced to float the Secretaryship. Honestly, not that I did not enjoy it.

We dubbed ourselves as the Hermonites Association Darjeeling (HAD). We had a couple of non-starters but managed to keep together until the MH Centenary came round the bend. 1993 saw a flurry of activities. Even two of the very elderly Hermonites lent support to our enthusiasm. Mrs. Thendupla (Rose to her contemporizes) of the Windermere Hotel was there with ideas while Mr. Charles Dunne (Charlie to almost everybody in Darjeeling) was there physically, attending meetings and running around bureaucratic circles meeting the District DM, the SP, Col. Commanding 107 TA Batt., and even liaisoning with friends and dignitaries of the North East.

He was thinking on the lines having the Police and Army Bands playing at least three of four times at MH during the year. He was thinking of having artistes local and from the North East (mainly of Assam and Nagaland) performing cultural shows staggered throughout the year. Unfortunately, nothing in these lines could be done, period. There was a wild rumour that the Thai Hermonites were planning of bringing a Centenary Birthday Cake all the way from Bangkok in a chartered helicopter.

Though it was unofficial, we, the HAD members, remained alert and contacted Air Vice Marshal Pratap Rao who was the second highest placed Indian Air Force man of India – besides being a Hermonite. He promised all help and guidance should the occasion arise. This plan too did not see the light of day. We are not aware of the Siamese letdown nor plan but it may be more advisable not to delve on the local debacle.

Next was the Hermonites' Directory failure. Though I had sent personal apologies to those who had shown faith in me and sent in their bio-data along with their fees may be this a good time to re-tender my apology and reason. At a MH 99th Birthday Celebration on stage the total file with 281 names, addresses etc., along with the fees which amounted to a little more than Rs. 3,500/- was handed over to MH on assurance that they were the better and better placed body to bring out the Directory in the Centenary year. Needless to say that was the last of it.

Next was the Ailina Project fiasco. For those not familiar with it – it was a project to rebuild the Ailina cottage and use it as a Guest House. Much effort was put into it and the Project submitted to MH. However, a small landslip just below Ailina made us shift the project to Bright Side which is opposite the Ailina and had burnt down. More time and effort was invested into it and it seemed the Project was finally going to see the light of day and all Hermonites, national and international, were informed that should the green light be given then there would be a call for donations and subscriptions.

Unfortunately or may be fortunately, the light never blipped. The 80s and 90s being days before the internet era it was rather difficult to stay in the picture of Hermonites of India forget around the world. Thus HAD worked on its Newsletters. It started off with just 85 copies for Darjeeling circulation and finished off with over 200 copies for Darjeeling, Siliguri and Sikkim, about 80 for the rest of India and 60 for USA, GB, Australia and New Zealand. It was a happy note when MHUSA also sent a few of their Newsletters to us.

With the advent of the electronic media the NLs died a natural death. All these papers, files, addresses were handed over to the junior Hermonites when I stepped down from my post as Secretary. Trust they still have it. Along the way there were many get-togethers, in fact too many to count and a few farewells. Most of them went off well but some left sour tastes. Mr. Johnston's farewell is one that can now face the light of day. Presents of carpets and rugs were bought from the Hayden Hall were given to him.

About three months later when I had to go there for personal reasons I was reminded that the payments were still due!!!!! Then there was a get-together at the Planters Club. Then Kamal (daju) was the President of both HAD and the Club. After much foot slogging thirty members had confirmed. Unfortunately, come the time and only Kamal Daju and Bhauju and yours truly and wife, were present. As a last ditch effort, I walked around town and could rope in only Amar, my brother, and Mukesh. Needless to say that was the last of Kamal's presidentship and it was left to me to make good the rest of the 24 dinners.

One more unfortunate incidence was at a reunion at Kolkata. I quite forget the occasion but I remember it was at Calcutta Rowing Club. Being an early bird, I was just loitering around when Prabir met me and said he had something personal to tell me. We walked out of the club and he told me very candidly, "I don't believe what I have heard but maybe you should clear your name during the party." What he had heard was that I had collected tons of money and ---!

I am still ever so grateful to Prabir. Be what may, we also had wonderful times at Gangtok, Siliguri, Kathmandu and Delhi, especially in the mid-90s when we were warming up for the Centenary. The best I feel was at Delhi at the Sunflower something or the other. The youngest present was Samden who had just passed his ICSE and joined Class 11 in Delhi while the second eldest was our Air Vice Chief Pratap Rao. The eldest was his sister Mrs. Pereira the wife of the just retired Naval Chief of Staff. After the formalities of dais seat warming, introductions and blah blahs when it was announced that the partying begin she walked right across the floor and started talking with Samden – the floor was not broken, it was shattered.

So, whatever it be it was great to don the garb of secretary ship of such a wonderful association under late Kamal Pradhan, late Mani K. Lama, late Jagdish Singh and not so late Anup Chachan. Coming to the last part, namely my school, Bhadra Sheela Memorial Institutions, School Wing, I feel most awkward. The subject being so subjective however I will try to keep it as objective as possible.

To help me I will touch on points only where it pertains to Hermonites and such affiliated topics. We started BSMI in 1981 with 22 students and then keeping the style of MH alive they were divided into two Houses, Red and Green, the School Colours. Then in 1984 when the school crossed the 150 students mark, they were re-divided into the four Houses that we have till date. Needless to say where the inspiration for the names of the first three Houses came from, namely Stewart House, Murray House and Johnston House.

The fourth House was dedicated to late Mr. Clifford Hicks, Principal of Calcutta Boys' School in the 60s. Till 1988 we used to make our students run only short distance cross-country races not more than 5 kms but in 1989 when the school was bordering the 400 mark it was decided that we start running the marathon, the full marathon ever odd year and the half marathon every even year. Around that time June Dewsberry, Secretary Mount Hermon Students, USA, walked in and helped us in it as her brother was also a marathon runner.

Every year she sent us 100/- and tons of trophies her son had won in bowling! They all served the purpose well enough. The 91 and 93 (full) marathons were also dedicated to her as the "J. Dewsberry Marathon". Unfortunately, after 1999 we have restricted to the half marathon. Next comes Archery and it pertains to Mr. Stewart and his help. During one of his visits to school he very kindly offered us Rs. 5,000/- to be used in the way I thought it was best.

For me, what was a better way to use it than to commemorate his name in some way. Thus the "Joy Rongong Inter-House Archery Shield" was made. Unfortunately, names of Houses or Individual Winners have yet to be inscribed onto it because Winner House has to have a minimum of 60% points while Individual Winners must have 80% points for such an honour. Unfortunately, Boss did not seem too pleased when he told me that the amount should have been used for the School.

In his last visit to MH, though he did not visit BSMI, he once more referred to the shield when he said, "May be some people back in Australia would be happy to know about the shield." Next I would like to thank and appreciate Rosemary. She had sponsored children of our school for quite some time till 2010. Unfortunately, that year I had to undergo a cancer operation that kept me out of the school office for quite some time.

When I returned to office by then the students had left school and that made me forget Rosemary's help towards our school. Andrea is another name that must be included as she too came forth to help us in what was termed as the Students' Fund. Due to difficulties in foreign money transfers it has not materialized but we are still very grateful for the thoughts. Finally, with the help and guidance of some Hermonites we have two more projects in the pipe line. The first is a Yoga Centre and the other is an Old Age Home. I will blab no more and just let the future unfold itself.

66   *Bhuntay* Will Be Missed

"There was nothing left behind except a pile of memories"
Vedprakash Agarwal, SC 1971

    There have been two sad moments in my life. Convulsions might be the right word. The first was within a day or two of Senior Cambridge week. The second only a few weeks ago.
    I was sitting in the dormitory writing little farewell notes to kind friends, when the packers came. Books, clippings, magazines were put in boxes. The hangings and the pictures came down from the walls. The linen and the bedsheets were packed. The mattresses were carted away, the beds placed one upon the other and piled in the corner of the by-now-desolate dormitory. I watched all my effects being taken out and an overwhelming sadness threatened to engulf me. I stood motionless before one of the large windows, staring beyond the tree tops of MH Estate, to savour a moment of lost years.

Bhuntay Will Be Missed

Birds came homing to their nests and there was a twitter in the solemn air. Lights began to come out in the servant quarters below, a reminder of the MH staff coming home after supper. My mind was in a swirl. Then my loneliness hit me until tears, long withheld, came to my eyes. I do not remember how long I stood there in the empty darkness of my depleted dormitory. I turned away from the window, watched mutely with a heap of towels and *dhobi* bags, and made for the door. There was nothing left behind except a pile of memories. I closed the door softly behind me, not daring to look in again, and walked out into the cold air seeking a friend and a warm dinner…that was the first sad moment of my life.

Today, eight years later (1978), I have again returned to my Alma Mater. It is like coming home. They tell me that this is Mr. Murray's last year in school…and that brings me to the second sad moment of my young life.

I try and recollect. I can picture him standing behind the cricket stumps, rocking back in his boots, laughing at the success of a strategy that has made a fool of the batsman just dismissed. He laces his fingers over his bellow without taking his hands out of his wicket-keeping gloves. Yet I know how big and beat-up his hands are. His voice loud and full of life. Blonde hair and a tangle of locks coming out from under his cap, been needing a cut for a long time. He's broad and tall – broad across the shoulders and jaw and chest – with a broad devilish grin. He's hard in a different kind of way, like the cricket ball he's handling is hard under the scuffed leather. He laughs till I have walked up to my bowling mark, then squats behind the wickets…even when he is not laughing, the laughing sound hovers around him, the way the sound hovers around a bell just stopped ringing. It's in his eyes, in the way he smiles, swaggers and in the way he talks.

I did not know that this would be his last year, but somehow I was not surprised. I respected him as most children respected their teachers, and I suppose I was a bit infatuated with him. As a man I liked him and I hope I look at him honestly, good points, warts and all. I have never known him anything but honest, abrasive certainly, aggressive and blunt always, be it on the cricket field, in the classroom, or in the chapel where he is expounding a theory on the current trends of discipline among students.

Mr. Murray is one of those most casual and immediately likable persons I have ever met. He knows character instinctively and is always in a hurry to impose the force of his own which is considerable. Perhaps the secret of his rugged good nature is that he is an incurable individualist, certain of himself that he can afford to be sure of others. This trait has always invited comments and he has been described by an NP (St. Joseph's School) teacher as petulant, rude and stubborn. However, there is one yardstick about people I know. The ones who don't change are the genuine ones. *Bhuntay* (a Nepali term for a fat person) has not bothered to change. He is always going to be his own man and do his own thing. He is loved by his students and although he endangers more arguments, more fury, more passing than others, he definitely is the most intriguing man I have ever met.

Mr. Murray was at his best on the cricket field. Perhaps the best captain on the Darjeeling cricketing scene. I always like playing under him. He was firm but kindly, knew what he wanted and was intent on being obeyed. His brilliant wicket keeping so camouflaged our fielding that he made a second-rate team seem outstanding. He got the best out of us with a poor combination. Every change in the bowling or in the field placing was made with the express purpose of squeezing the batsman. It was impossible to fault his schemes. Whilst batting he was the complete player, steady, determined, faultless. Spotlessly turned out, he was attractive in his batting that even his struggles had elegance. Moreover, he had the undefinable quality of personality. Somehow he caught the eye, even if he was not playing well.

One of the most sweet sounds I have heard is *Bhuntay*'s reassuring voice hollering from the pavilion, shouting advice to us playing in the middle. His voice was loud and free and it came out of his mouth in rings bigger and bigger till it lapped against the fences all over the ground...with his departure the voice will be heard no more. It will be like watching a film on television, with the sound turned off.

Of all the incidents that I can recall, the one that sticks out most in my mind is when he put a harmless grass snake in my bed, knowing the human aversion for the loathsome reptile. Luckily, the timely intrusion of a friend, who was more worried about the snake's welfare than mine, prevented the calamitous union with such an unwelcome bed-mate. I duly returned the petrified snake to him with a note which said, "A snakes makes a lovely bed companion...if you don't know its there."

On another occasion he reprimanded an erring friend: "At some time perhaps, in your childhood, you may have been allowed to get away with flouting the rules of society. When you broke a rule you knew it. You wanted to be dealt with, you needed it, but the punishment did not come. That foolish leniency on the part of your parents may have been the germ that grew into your present shortcomings. I tell you this hoping that you will understand, that it is entirely for your own good that we enforce discipline and order. One more mistake, and I am afraid I will have to give you your marching orders." The erring friend now is a very successful and honest businessman. It has been seven years since Mr. Murray told him that. He hasn't forgotten...yet, nor do I think he will...ever.

Mr. Murray has been here for twenty-four years now. Thousands studied at his feet, united in reverence and love for him. I don't know what he taught us and I don't really care. He taught us to think and that was enough. That was the heart of it all, *Bhuntay* made us think. He was his own man. *Non Scholae Sed Vitae Discimus* (Not for school but for life we learn). That was his legacy to us – he made each of us want to be his own man.

(Hermonite 1978, annual school magazine.)

67 Hail Mount Hermon!

Hail Mount Hermon! A Tribute

Jigme N. Kazi, SC 1972

"He seems to me to be one of the few Christians who walked in the fear of the Lord, and, therefore, feared no man."

- Mahatma Gandhi on Bishop Frederick Bohn Fisher

"I will study and get ready, and perhaps my chance will come."

- Abraham Lincoln

"Each one of us, who has had a part in Mount Hermon, has a responsibility placed upon us to continue to promote not only education but peace and goodwill everywhere."

- Halsey E. Dewey

I had just entered the huge school building when someone who greeted me at the main entrance gate welcomed me and asked me, "Do you like this school?" Though I did not know much English, I understood what he was saying and promptly replied, "Yes, Sir". The gentleman who so warmly welcomed me to Mt. Hermon School thirty years back in 1963 must have been either our Principal, Rev. David G. Stewart, or the Senior Master, Graeme A. Murray.

My association with Mount Hermon School (MHS – most of us refer to our school as simply 'MH') in Darjeeling started in early 1963 and ended seventeen years later in 1979. I not only like the school but fell in love with it, and the love affair lasted for sixteen short years. I think I established some sort of a record by graduating from the school, going through the two-year teacher's training college of the school, and finally becoming a teacher in the same school. Finally in 1979, I said my last goodbye to the school which had been my home for nearly two decades.

I was almost eight when I joined MH in class 2 in 1963. Before this, I was in Tashi Namgyal Academy (TNA) in Gangtok for a year. I must have been four or five when I first went to my village school in Lachen in north Sikkim. Due to several deaths in our family, I had to move down to south Sikkim in Yangang in 1959-60, where my father's family members resided, and I spent a year there. I have many happy and vivid memories of my school days in both Lachen and Yangang.

My admission into MH was sheer luck. It was a fine Sunday in Gangtok in early 1963 when I made up my mind to quit TNA and go for studies in Darjeeling. Sunday was a shopping day, and I accompanied my uncle, Legpal Lachenpa, to the *bazaar* that day. Normally, my elder brother, Tenzing Danen, accompanied him for shopping on Sundays, but somehow it was different that day, and instead of my brother, I went along with my uncle and my brother stayed back. We were day-scholars staying at my uncle's place beside the India Press building near Balwakhani in Gangtok.

While we were at the Lal Bazaar, we met the Lachen *Pipon* (village headman of Lachen), Cho Ngopon, an elderly gentleman, who was related to me. He told my uncle that the Sikkim Government was providing scholarships for two students from Lachen and Lachung for studies in an "English school" in Darjeeling. He wanted to know whether I would be willing to go as a candidate from Lachen.

"The government is providing a scholarship for a student from Lachen to study in Darjeeling. Would you like to go?" my uncle asked me after talking to the *Pipon*. "It is up to you to decide and you have to give the decision right now," he added. My parents were in Lachen at that time and it was impossible to contact them for advice and consultation. For us in those days, Darjeeling seemed a far off place and going there for studies was like going to the end of the world. But something in me gave me the courage to make a bold decision and I accepted the offer on the spot. "Yes, I want to go," I told him. And then the ball got rolling and I was all set to leave TNA for Darjeeling.

Apart from my brother, Tenzing Danen, I was the only Lachenpa studying in Gangtok and I guess it was proper for the *Pipon* to give the first preference. Being quite studious and more competent in studies, I was given preference over my brother. Though he had joined TNA much earlier than me, by 1963 I caught up with him and we were in the same class (class III). *Azo* Ngopon, the Lachen *Pipon*, could have easily given the seat to another candidate and ignored me. I was later told that someone from Mangan in north Sikkim was trying for the Lachen seat. However, I was the lucky one. My grandfather has now been dead for many years but I shall never forget the fact that he opted for me. The only real way of repaying my debt to him and to my people in Lachen, has been for me to make the best use of the education that I received from MH. My uncle, too, had put considerable pressure for my selection for which I'm truly grateful.

There were more than a dozen students from Sikkim who were admitted into MH in 1963 on government scholarship. One of them was my friend from Lachung, Thentok Lachungpa, who is now working in the SBI (State Bank of India). He, the candidate from Lachung, was previously a Deputy Superintendent of Police (DSP) in Sikkim, but later resigned from government service. Apart from Thentok, my other TNA friends, who joined MH along with me, included Udai P. Sharma and Bhupendra Thapa. While Udai, till recently a practising lawyer in Gangtok, is now the State Government's Public Prosecutor, Bhupendra, a Superintendent of Police (SP), was till very recently in-charge of the Special Branch, the intelligence win of the State Government, in Gangtok. On my first day in MH, I was pleasantly surprised to find out that Krishna Kumar Chettri, my friend from Yangang school, who is now working in the State Forest Department as a Block Officer (BO), was also in MH. He had joined the school one year before me in 1962.

Throughout our schooling, the Sikkimese students played an important role in the life of the school. Whether in the classroom, on the stage, or in the playing field, the Sikkimese students made outstanding and valuable contributions to the school which have been greatly appreciated. Most of my Sikkimese friends, including myself, held responsible positions in the running of the school. As school monitors, prefects, House captains etc., Sikkimese students were outstandingly prominent and excelled in most activities they chose to undertake.

In 1971, our school XI football team, which reached the finals of the prestigious Herlihy Cup Football Tournament in Darjeeling for the first time, had at least seven Sikkimese students, and I was proud to represent the team as its captain. A Calcutta daily labelled us as the "Giant Killers" when we knocked down the 2nd Gorkha Rifles team (previously representing the Kumar Sporting Club of Gangtok) – perhaps the best team in the region during that period – in the quarter finals of one of the football tournaments in Darjeeling.

The majority of Sikkimese students who were in my class completed their SC (Senior Cambridge – class 11) or ISC (Indian School Certificate), in 1972 and by the end of 1973 almost all Sikkimese students of my batch had left the school. Only my friend and classmate, Dhruba Rai, and I returned to MH in 1974 to undergo two years teacher's training at the Mount Hermon Undergraduate Training College for our Teacher's Training Certificate (TTC).

After successfully completing the two-year course in 1975, Dhruba and I taught in MH until he left at the end of 1978 while I stayed back for another year. Dhruba, originally from Chakung in west Sikkim, married Sandra Riley, a New Zealander of Indian origin, and left us to settle in New Zealand. Both of them have now become full-fledged teachers in Auckland. I went to Bombay to study law in 1980 and returned to Sikkim three years later in 1982.

Thirteen may be considered an unlucky number but Mt. Hermon first started with only thirteen students! The school, then known as Arcadia Girls' School, was founded on March 11, 1895 by Miss Emma L. Knowles (1840-1921), and was located below Chowrasta on the other side of the town facing Lebong in Darjeeling. Miss Knowles, an education missionary under the Woman's Foreign Missionary Society of the Methodist Episcopal Church of America, had already spent many years in India in establishing the Wellesley Girls' High School in Nainital and the Calcutta Girls' High School before coming to Darjeeling.

Deeply religious and a committed Christian, Miss Knowles was convinced that it was God's will to establish a school for girls in Darjeeling. Within three years of the founding of the school a terrible landslide in 1899 completely damaged one of the cottages of the school where some of the students lived. Ten students died in the tragic disaster.

Undaunted by the terrible disaster, Miss Knowles reopened the school in a new location just above the railway station on the Hill Cart Road on March 1, 1990 and continued with her mission in two rented houses named Queen's Hill and The Repose. By 1902, the school had four dwelling houses, including a three-storeyed building. The enrolment of the school rose to fifty and the school was renamed Queen's Hill School for Girls (QHS).

In 1978, while I was working on the special historical edition of the annual school magazine – *Hermonite* – my friend, Ved Prakash Agarwal (SC 1971), who was then living in Darjeeling, and I took several shots of the old school buildings, which lay just above the cart road. These photographs are now recorded in the 1978 *Hermonite* magazine, which has now become a valuable historical document of the school. One of the ex-students OHS whom we were able to contact during the course of our research for the magazine, was the wife of Thondupla, owner of the posh Windemere Hotel in Darjeeling. She apparently knew

Miss Stahl, who succeeded Miss Knowles as Principal of QHS, quite well. Unfortunately, we could not locate the original site of the school located below Chowrasta. A second effort to spot the site must be made before the school celebrates its birth centenary in 1995.

Recalling the character and service of Miss Knowles, her assistant and the next to step into her shoes, Miss Carolyn J. Stahl, also from America and a member of the Society, said: "In her contact with young people, Miss Knowles was markedly a character builder. She had the ability in an unusual degree of bringing out and developing the best in a young girl's nature. Her pupils realised this and responded with lasting love and veneration. Scattered over many parts of India and Great Britain, are those who have received from Miss Knowles not only good education through the schools but a lasting appreciation of the highest ideals of life and service."

From the beginning of the 20th century till 1929, it was Miss Stahl (Principal, 1918-1929), who really served the school, first as an assistant to Miss Knowles, and then as Principal from 1918 to 1929. In 1914, the school was almost closed down due to shortage of funds but because of the concern and dedication of both Miss Knowles and Miss Stahl, the school survived. Miss Stahl believed that "any great task can be accomplished by the exercise of boundless faith, much intercessory prayer and ceaseless work". By 1918, the total enrolment reached 163 and the school authorities felt the need to find a suitable site for expansion of the school. And for the third time, the school was ready to shift to somewhere else. It was a clear indication that the school was forging ahead.

The present location of Mt. Hermon was purchased in 1920 during the time when Frederick Bohn Fisher (1882-1939) was elected to the Episcopacy and became the Bishop of Calcutta. Bishop Fisher – born 1882 in Pennsylvania in the USA – was a man of intense energy and conviction and came to India as a missionary and served in the Thoburn Methodist Church in Calcutta.

The present Mount Hermon Estate, which is about four kilometres away from the town, was bought from the Lebong Tea Company in 1920 for Rs. 50,000 and the Fernhill Estate (now occupied by the boys' hostels and the swimming pool), which is also part of the larger Estate, was acquired separately in the same period from the proprietor of the Grand Hotel in Calcutta and Mount Everest Hotel in Darjeeling for Rs. 35,000. Bishop Fisher himself came to Darjeeling to negotiate the purchase of the Estate.

The inauguration of the new school building, which has been described as "one of the finest buildings in the Orient", was performed by Lord Lytton, then the Governor-General of Bengal, on May 26, 1926. Initially, there were two institutions in the present campus – Queen's Hill School for Girls and Bishop Fisher School for Boys. Rev. E.S. Johnson of the Thoburn Methodist Church of Calcutta became Principal of the two institutions in 1929. In 1930, the school was renamed Mount Hermon School and became a co-educational institution. Today, Bishop Fisher is considered as one of the Founders of the school and a House (Fisher House – yellow) has been named after him in his honour.

Bishop Fisher's wife, Dr. Mrs. Welthy Honsinger Fisher, a noted educationist in her own right, visited MH in November 1967 when I was in class 7. We had the privilege of hearing her speak on the annual Speech Day as the Chief Guest. During the prize distribution on the Speech Day, I, as, Junior School Captain of Dewey House, received the Dr. Master's trophy for the best House in the junior school on behalf of Dewey House from Dr. Fisher. It was indeed an exciting moment in my life which I shall ever cherish. In 1972, Sherab Namgyal, my friend and classmate from Sikkim, and I shared the Bishop Fisher Cup, a prestigious annual award of the school for the best boy student of the school. The award is given in recognition of the student's character, leadership and sportsmanship.

Commenting on her husband, Dr. Fisher (now no more) wrote: "Fourteen years with Fred convinced me that living was an adventure. He was interested in the smallest creature and the most insignificant happening in our day, and wove them into the rich tapestry of his enjoyment. He taught me nothing is unbearable – unless we ourselves permit it to be. When we were riding on the hot dusty trains of India, the screeching of the flat wheels dinned into our ears all day long. But Fred would say, "Now, Welthy, just get into the rhythm of hot squeak!"

She described herself as "just a member of the human race" and felt that "racial discrimination is obnoxious". She wrote: "Better to light a candle than curse the darkness". Bishop Fisher knew Mahatma Gandhi and Rabindranath Tagore on intimate terms. "He seemed to me to be one of the few Christians who walked in the fear of the Lord, and, therefore, feared no man," was Gandhi's comment on Fisher, who died of a heart attack in 1939.

MH endured another major crisis in the early 1940s. The effect of the Second World War hit the school badly and it was nearly closed down in 1943. Not only were the funds low, the students' roll also dropped to only 120. The uncertainty of the future of the mission in India also had an adverse effect on the school. But it was Rev. Hasley E. Dewey, who became Principal in 1938, who was chiefly responsible for keeping the school going during one of its darkest periods. Rev. Dewey, who is the last of our Founders, visited MH sometime in early 1970s. He was then fairly old and grey. It was a great experience for to have such a renowned historical figure of our school in our midst.

Recalling what the school had to go through in the early 1950s, Rev. W.W. Jones, then one of the senior members of the staff, and later the Vice-Principal (1973-1977) of the school, wrote:

"While I was training in Hartford, Connecticut in the summer of 1951, I got further news from Mr. Mathews that I wouldn't be going to Woodstock School, because there was an urgent need for help at Mount Hermon School in Darjeeling. Mr. Dewey was the Principal, and he was barely able to keep the school open. Staff were hard to get, the student enrolment was low (less than 150 in the whole school) and Mr. Dewey had heavy responsibilities for mission work in Bengal as well as in the school.

During the winter of 1951, Mr. Dewey had seriously wondered if the School could be reopened for the 1952 session. He decided we could reopen if 100 paying borders could be enrolled. We did open in 1952 with about 110. I still can't imagine how we did the things we did, with such a small student body. He fielded teams in Senior, Junior divisions against St. Joseph's and St. Paul's, in cricket, football and hockey. (Actually, we were more afraid of St. Joseph's competition for the attention of our senior girls than we were afraid of them on the sports field) We fielded a girl's hockey team against the Convent (Loreto Convent) and defeated them once when Julie Dunne was captain (having transferred from Dow Hill to M.H.S.) I had to learn hockey, so I could coach the junior boys, who lost only to St. Joseph's in 1954, as I recall.

The senior teams did well too, with chaps like Brang Seng, Mawu Naga, and Ram Bahadur making M.H.S. a real football power. We came to the finals one year, and I made problems for the District Sports Association by preparing the whole school for American-style cheering, complete with drums, horns, tin cans and lids to be beaten, and organised cheers completely distracting the opponents. Unfortunately, this *hulla* also distracted the officials, who had to stop play until I would agree to stop the din."

When I was editing the annual school magazine in 1978, the Hermonite Editorial Committee wrote to Dewey, who then lived in the USA. He wrote back to us and said: "As the school reaches out as it does through it students and a faculty to many places around the world, we can rejoice in new opportunities, and perhaps new responsibilities, resting on our shoulders. Each one of us, who has had a part in Mount Hermon, has a responsibility placed upon us to continue to promote not only education but peace and goodwill everywhere."

But perhaps, Mt. Hermon really grew up in the best sense of the word when Rev. David G. Stewart of the New Zealand Chinese Inland Mission (now renamed Overseas Missionary Fellowship) took over the school as its Principal in 1954. From only about a hundred students in the early 1950s, the school grew to well over three hundred students by the time Stewart left at the end of 1963. The school grew not only in strength, but in standards and character. Students of the Stewart-era, it has widely been observed, had their own distinctive mould and character which appealed to many of us.

It was in 1960 that the school was divided into four Houses and named after its Founders and Heads – Knowles (green), Stahl (red), Fisher (yellow), and Dewey (blue). In the Principal's report during the annual Speech Day on November 15, 1960, Rev. Stewart said: "May the Four Houses each seek to bring honour to the name of the founders after whom they have been called...In our school where we are builders together with God, we are building not a building of wood and stone or bricks or mortar, but of flesh and blood, of mind and spirit."

In a wider sense, the value of schools such as MH lies not in what we learn from the classrooms, however important they may be, but from the high ideals and standards set by those who lived and served in the school.

Rev. Stewart left MH after my first year in school in 1963, and in the following year, Murray, then Acting Principal, took over the school as its next Principal. They say "first impressions are always the last impressions", and I'm glad that I have many fond memories of my first year in MH. One of the most pleasant memories of 1963 were the times when Rev. Stewart used to casually walk into our dining room on Saturday mornings, while we were having our breakfast, and announce the name of the movie we were to see in the school hall in the evening. When he announced in his deep and husky voice, "Tonight's movie is… and it is a technicolour" (the emphasis is on the word technicolour, as most of the movies in those days shown on our 16 mm projector were black and white), we used to go wild with excitement and gave him a big hand.

Rev. Stewart's next major visit to MH was fifteen years later, towards the end of 1978. His visit also coincided with Murray's final departure from MH, where he and his wife, Patricia Murray, had spent 24 years of service. 1978 was really my last in MH; 1979 was spent looking ahead and packing up! It was also my best year after coming back to the school as a teacher in 1976. We had at least 10 ex-students on the staff in 1978 and all of us actively participated in the life of the school and had a lot of fun, too. Incidentally, in 1925, 8 of about 25 members of the staff were ex-students of QHS. 1978 was also Murray's last year in MH, and it was a great treat for us to see the Big Two (Stewart and Murray) together at the end of the year. Rev. Stewart was slightly thinner having lost some weight, but nevertheless, he was the same man we had seen one and half decades back.

What touched me most during Rev. Stewart's visit was the talk he gave to a small gathering in the school chapel on the need to have men and women of "integrity" in the world today: "Several ex-students have told me that what they gained from MH most of all was to recognize the need for integrity. To be true to themselves and their inner convictions, to be honest in business, loyal in friendship, trustworthy in word and deed, to be real people and not phonies."

Perhaps his message to the school as the Chief Guest on Speech Day in November 1978 reflects the real character and essence of school such as MH: "It's always a scary thing to come back. Especially to come back to a place that has bound close ties around your heart. After fifteen years there won't be, of course, be any students who know you. The customs will have changed. Even the buildings will be different…I don't know whether the students thought strange or not, but I felt at home. A school is not, of course, buildings and playing fields and wooded hillsides, memorable as they all may be. A school is people, and a school is a shared spirit and philosophy…And how can one described the spirit and philosophy which lies at the core of Mount Hermon School? I think it may perhaps be summed up in three words: initiative, wholeness and integrity. And central to all is the spiritual dimension of life, a right recognition of God, and a striving for the highest ideals, as taught by a Christian school such as Mount Hermon."

And as I look back to my 16 years' association with the school, I can rightly endorse Rev. Stewart's views of what MH really is and should be. For without integrity, all our education and spiritual upbringing has no real value to the world outside, which has an abundance of experts in almost all fields, but which is lacking in people who are dedicated and committed to reach out beyond themselves.

Murray was a different sort of person altogether – more open, direct, robust, tough but friendly. What impressed me most about him was his realistic down-to-earth attitude to life. There was no beating round the bush with him, and if he wanted tell you something, he'd give it to you straight between the eyes, whether you liked it or not. Of course, it hurt the person on the receiving end, but it made you tough in the process and prepared you for life ahead, which is often hard and cruel. Beneath his tough exterior, Murray, however, had a gentle, loving and a caring heart. He was full of energy, enthusiasm and had natural zest for life. He often counselled us on the need to become 'responsible' persons and to take up responsible roles in society. And as I look back, I'm convinced that Murray had the greatest influence on me and prepared me most for the tough years that I have had to go through in this past one decade.

Murray's character and personality were more discernible on the playing field of which I have rich and happy memories. He was a born fighter and made us go all out till the very last minute of the game. He, of course, wanted us to win, but one of his chief concerns was not whether we won or lost, but how well we fought. He was pleased with the team even if we lost the game, provided we put up a good show. Scoring a boundary with a bad stroke in a cricket match was sheer "Junk!" for him. He preferred that we made the correct strokes even if no scoring was done.

In his last few years in Darjeeling, Murray devoted much of his time to the development of sports and games for the public. He was the Chairman of the Darjeeling District Sports Association and successfully ran the Gurkha Brigade Gold Cup Football Tournament for four years before he finally left Darjeeling at the end of 1978. As a player, (he was a terrific goal-keeper in his early days in Darjeeling and was superb in cricket – both as a batsman and a wicket-keeper), coach and organiser of many sporting events in Darjeeling, Murray left his unforgettable mark on the field.

Rev. Johnston, who first arrived in Darjeeling in 1959 and who was well-acquainted with Murray, had this to say about his friend and colleague: "Graeme Murray is one of those people who cannot easily be fitted into any neat category. Some say, 'he is mad on sport' – which no doubt would be true, but hardly adequate as a description of someone who is also mad on History and a walking encyclopaedia on the causes and pattern of current affairs. He is always busy in the wider community – Chairman & the guiding spirit of such diverse activities as the Gold Cup and the Darjeeling and Dooars Medical Association. But he is also the man willing to lay aside his business to give individual attention and loving counsel to someone in need."

Recalls Charles Dunne, one of the most popular and colourful ex-students of MH, who till very recently was still very active in many a social circle in Darjeeling: "I know Mr. Murray best on the sports-field. We all know how he personally participated by playing cricket and football for Mt. Hermon. Although he was one of the best New Zealand rugby players, he had to take up football as there were no turf grounds in Darjeeling. In cricket, he led the Darjeeling team against the Visitors' Team for many years, and he was always a terror when playing for the school in the Edinburgh (cricket) tournament. I would always dread being an umpire when Mr. Murray played wicket-keeper, particularly when he would knock the bails off and appeal to me with a loud 'How's that!'

Charlie Dunne, whom many of us referred to him as just 'uncle', passed away quietly in Darjeeling on June 8 this year (1992), the day Rev. Stewart arrived there for his visit.

His death was a great shock for those of us who knew and loved him dearly. He will, of course, be dearly missed by us all and will remain rich in our memories, not only as a true friend and a great companion, but as a landmark of Darjeeling itself.

One of the most remarkable and unforgettable personalities of the school during my time was Mrs. Joy Rongong. Miss Joyce Stewart, sister of Rev. Stewart and mother of Roslyn Namgyal (wife of Sherab Namgyal – ex-student-SC 1972), who was teaching in TNA (Gangtok's Tashi Namgyal Academy) till June this year, came to India in 1944 and married D.G.K. Rongong, a senior teacher of the blind school in Kalimpong in north Bengal, in 1954. Having taught in Dr. Graham's Homes school in Kalimpong for some time, she later joined her brother in Mt. Hermon as the Junior School Supervisor in 1960.

Mrs. Rongong was the Jn. School Supervisor when I was admitted to MH in 1963. She was also the main lecturer when I joined TTC eleven years later in 1974. Later, when I joined the junior school teaching staff in MH in 1976, she was again my boss as the Junior School Supervisor. Mrs. Rongong lived a full and active life right till the very end. She died in Darjeeling in 1987, still at the helm of her latest project – looking after 80 orphans in Kalimpong. Heather, her younger daughter, is married to Michael Prickett and is now living in Australia.

Perhaps it was in TTC that I got to know Mrs. Rongong most intimately. She was a superb lecturer, and with all the experience and training that she had in the teaching line, she was the ideal person to train the young would-be-teachers, most of whom were Anglo-Indians from Calcutta. In TTC, there was also quite a sizeable section of students from our hill community, including Tibetans and Bhutanese. The TTC commenced in Darjeeling in 1972, when the Under-Graduate Men's Training College at the St. Thomas's School in Kidderpore, Calcutta, was transferred to the management of the Mount Hermon College of Education Society. The transfer of the college from Calcutta to Darjeeling was initiated with a view to training local teachers in the hills for English medium schools in the region.

Mrs. Rongong really made us slog and squeezed out every ounce of energy that we had. I realised, under her, that unless you exerted yourself to the maximum in any work, you would not be able to realise your own potentials and limitations. She herself was a perfectionist and somewhat of a workaholic.

If in school I was able to receive an education which catered to the all-round development of my personality, it was in TTC that I grew up mentally. Although I still kept myself busy on the playground, I gradually became more interested in reading and writing and spent much of my leisure time indoor. History and Psychology became my favourite subjects. Ever since, I have continued to enrich my knowledge in these two subjects which then was fairly new to me.

If during my school days Mrs. Rongong was regarded as a strict disciplinarian, as a colleague, I found her to be very helpful, concerned and caring sort of person. She gave me complete freedom in teaching and never kept a tag on me as it is usually the case with other heads. I remember the times when she used to come to my classroom and fire somebody for something; and when she had finished and before closing the door to go out, she would give me a gentle smile as if to say that she wasn't firing me indirectly! She had perfect control over her emotions and her stern action against students was not an outburst of her uncontrolled emotions. It was part of her disciplinary action.

In 1981, after she left MH and was managing the Albella Boys' Home, a hostel for orphans in Kalimpong, she, in an article in the *Light of Life*, a Christian growth magazine, wrote: "March 1963. Sikkim, the little kingdom surrounded by West Bengal, Nepal, Bhutan and Tibet was aglow with color. The richness of satin, silk and brocade in magnificent shades of purple, blue, gold and green was breath-taking. Excitement filled the air as the crown prince of the kingdom was united in marriage with the American heiress, Hope Cooke. In the midst of all this splendour, I found myself a guest. My purpose in visiting Sikkim was not to attend the royal wedding, but to test children who were seeking admission to Mount Hermon School, Darjeeling.

As I faced the 300 young hopefuls with my simple intelligence and aptitude tests, I asked my Lord to lead and direct so that I might select the twenty-four of His choice. I asked that He, who knows the end from the beginning, would guide me to select children who would respond, not only to the good English education we would give them, but to the call of the Lord Jesus Christ of whom they would learn at Mount Hermon School. There were 300 little village children and double that number of adults.

I set to work with my apparatus and with faith that He would lead. So, early in 1963, twenty-four little fellows from Buddhist and Hindu homes were enrolled in Mount Hermon. The years passed rapidly and happily. There were two or three disappointments, but with what joy we watched the seed of God's Word taking root in individual hearts from time to time. Of course, there were some who needed to be spurred on to harder work at times, but never did we have any difficulty in getting them in front of a wicket or behind a football!"

Although very few of those who became Christians in the school are still clinging to their faith, many, I'm sure, are nevertheless, consciously or unconsciously influenced by the great teachings of the Bible and the high ideal and values that were taught MH. There is definitely a marked distinction between the outlook and attitude of those who receive their education in Christian missionary schools such as MH, St. Joseph's, Goethal's etc. and the products of other private and government schools. This distinction, which is lacking in today's society, is worth preserving.

For a while, MH faced a leadership crisis after Rev. John Johnston left in 1989-90. Rev. Johnston, who took over the school after Murray left in 1978, was an old-timer in MH and his association with the school went as far back as 1959. I was lucky to renew my contact with the Johnstons in 1979, when Rev. Johnston became Principal after Murray left. They had left MH in 1970 and were returning to the school after a long gap. One of their daughters, Carol, was my classmate. She has now become the wife of another ex-student, Benu Chatterjee, and they are now settled in Australia after being on MH staff for several years.

Most students of my days would remember Rev. Johnston (nicknamed Johnny) as a quiet, soft-spoken gentleman, who taught Bible and Biology, and also preached in the school chapel on Sundays. "Coming home" to MH "was the most exciting day," recalled Mrs. Val Johnston when the Johnstons returned to Darjeeling in 1978. They're now back in Australia where Rev. Johnston heads the Flinders Christian Community College, a small Christian school south of Melbourne.

Jeff Gardner, an ex-teacher of MH and the Rector of St. Paul's School, Darjeeling, took over the school in 1992 as its new Principal. The school's uncertain future after Johnston's departure in 1990 cause some worry to many of us, but Gardner's takeover was good news to all Hermonites. I personally felt the school was in safe hands. Gardner, originally from Sherwood College, Nainital in Uttar Pradesh, came to Darjeeling in 1970 when I was in class nine. Being well-acquainted with all the recent heads and teachers of MH, and having lived in Darjeeling for the past two decades, Gardner is perhaps the ideal person to look after the school at this critical juncture.

To me and to most people, who have spent some time of their life inside the old and friendly walls, MH was more than just a school. It was one big, happy family where we lived through many of our ups and downs in preparation for the life ahead. It will take a few volumes to recall in detail my days in MH, and perhaps there will be a time for me to do just that. But in this book, which is basically about myself, I want to recall and record a few instances of my school days, where I saw my attitude and character taking a distinctive shape which influenced my latter years.

Speaking up for others and getting into trouble is nothing new to me. I remember three specific instances in school when I got into trouble for conveying to the authorities what the students and the staff felt on certain things.

For instance, during one of our football practices, most of the boys were against a certain method adopted by our new football coach, Bill Moore, a footballer-turned-preacher from Northern Ireland. Being a football enthusiast and a keen footballer, and having witnessed football matches and training sessions in Ireland and England, where the standard of the game is very high, Moore perhaps wanted us to adopt the same methods during our training. Instead of having the traditional practice matches which lasted about an hour or so, Moore wanted us to have short practice matches with about 6-7 players on each side.

I actually wasn't disagreeable with the new training session, but there were some who were against it and were quietly grumbling and muttering something on the sidelines. This went on for quite sometime and when Moore found out that some of us were uncooperative, he asked for an explanation. When nobody spoke up, I told him, "Sir, we don't like this type of training. Why can't we have the usual practice matches?" There was no way Moore would listen to us and he had his way.

The matter was reported to the Principal immediately and I was called to Murray's office in the evening at around 5.30 p.m. Murray was disappointed at my behaviour with Moore and lectured me for about ten minutes. I interrupted, "Sir, I just told Mr. Moore what the boys felt. It was up to him to decide how we should be trained. Our only complaint was that he did not pay any heed to how we felt."

"Why should he listen to you people?" Murray retorted.

"If our teachers don't pay any heed to what we feel, then how can we learn? They may not agree with us, but they should at least pay some attention to what we say," I replied. "If MH is like that, then I don't belong to this place. I'm leaving," I told him and headed for the door.

Before I finally left his office, Murray advised, "Don't make any hasty decision. Take a walk around the school to cool yourself down and don't go back to the study hall. Let me know what you decide finally."

"Sir, my decision will be the same," I told him and left his office.

I really felt bad and was all set to quit MH if it hadn't been for some of my friends who wanted me to stay. I was then in class 10. I had nothing against Moore. In fact, we got along very well, both inside and outside the playing field. Both the staff and students dubbed us "football crazy". I was only conveying to him how some of us felt, that's all. I felt that he should have at least listened to us even if he wanted to have his way. Finally, all the angry clouds went away and I stayed on.

It was my class teacher, Miss Patricia Russell, who got me into trouble on another occasion. Our class had decided to go for a picnic all by ourselves without being accompanied by any member of the staff. Some of us were quite apprehensive that Miss Russell may barge in. If she did this, we would not be able to stop her. We had nothing against her but wanted to be on our own. While some of us were casually talking over the picnic programme in the Geography lab during the change of period, Miss Russell overheard us and wanted to know what was going on. When no one wanted to tell her what we were discussing, I spoke up, "Miss, we are planning to go for a picnic and we don't want you to come with us." She seemed a bit surprised and disappointed over what I said but didn't react straightaway or make any fuss in the classroom. But later in the day I was called to Murray's office. She had obviously reported the matter to *Bhuntay* (Murray's nickname).

"You are being rude to Miss Russell, I hear," said Murray starring at me sternly over his glasses. "Sir, that's what the boys were feeling. We didn't want her to accompany us for the picnic. I told her how we felt and if that means I'm rude then I guess I'm rude." This was followed by a ten-minute lecture from him on 'being rude'.

When I came out from Murray's office, Miss Russell was at the door. "I'm sorry. I didn't mean to get you into trouble," she told me. I was in no mood to listen to her consolation after Murray's lecture and I walked off – rude again?

Another heated exchange that I had with Murray was when I was on the staff. MH food wasn't really all that bad during our time. Surprisingly, the staff got the same food as the students and the only difference was the service! I ate a lot during those days when I was on the staff and so did my friends – Dhruba Rai and Robin Sengupta – both ex-students who were on the staff. As bachelors, and being ex-students, the day's schedule was always hectic – teaching, coaching, supervising games, looking after the children in the dormitory etc. We ate together, particularly during breakfast. Of course, we did grumble about the food at times, but most of the time we ate what we were given and enjoyed it.

But there were some lady staff members, who used to grumble most of the time, and their constant nagging at the table put us off at times. But we preferred to ignore them. This went on for days, and one fine day we decided to put an end to it by deciding to act on the matter. We made a formal complaint to Murray through a letter which was signed by everyone who regularly dined in the staff dining room. I submitted copies of the letter to the concerned authorities, including Rocky Gardner (Jeff Gardner's elder brother), who was in-charge of the kitchen department.

Murray was wild when he called me to his office to explain what was going on. He seemed to be convinced that I was the 'ring leader' who started everything. "We are a family here. You could have come and talked to me about it instead of writing such a note," he said. I never saw him become so angry with me or with anyone before.

"Sir, we felt that this was the best way to inform you of how we felt about the food." I sat there for a while then got up, and before leaving his room I told him: "Sir, if you think that I'm the only one who started all this, then you're wrong." Fortunately, the food improved, but only slightly, and I maintained my reputation for speaking my mind.

Not many Hermonites will know Dr. Charles M. Swan, who wrote many of our school Going Home Day (GHD) songs, sung mainly in November, just before the school ended. Perhaps the favourite GDH song by Dr. Swan starts with these words:

> "Old walls are friendly walls,
> Friendly walls, farewell!
> Old walls hold memories
> That breathe a kindly spell;
> Breathe then your benison
> On me as I depart
> I'll keep your memory
> Warm in my heart."

Sung at the end of the year, the song with its sad and melodious notes, truly captures the spirit and mood of those who were spending their last few days in the school which was their home for perhaps 5, 10, 15, or even 20 years.

Dr. Swan, an ex-student and also an ex-teacher of the school, visited MH in 1977. He was 69 then. Dr. Swan's over twenty years' (1914-1936: student, 1914-1921; teacher, 1930-1936) association with MH goes back to the time when Miss Knowles was still the Principal of the school. He joined the school on May 15, 1814 in KG and later taught in the school from 1929-1936. Because of his long association with both the students and staff, Dr. Swan and I, along with Dhruba Rai, share something in common, which is both rare and unique. He says, "When I was a small boy in old Queen's Hill, Miss Stahl had only just retired from the principalship. So my memory leads me to think of the original purposes of the school. It was patterned after the Public Boarding Schools of England, but the pattern was given an American flare, and some major adjustments were made to fit to the Indian scene."

According to Dr. Swan, the school was primarily started "to meet the needs of the Protestant and Evangelical families of the Anglo-Indian community, many of whom had been touched by Methodist revivals of the period. The children of missionaries were served well by the school but their needs were secondary. Instruction was based on the standards of British education. At that time, Britain was taking a leading role in the education developments needed for a new age of industry, science and world perspectives. In this role, however, British educators generally retained their concern for the traditional values of the Judeo-Christian heritage and moral experience of the Church. Mt. Hermon, even today, is deeply rooted in that original setting."

Referring to Dr. Swan, the October 1992 Newsletter of the Mount Hermon Alumnus of the USA, carried a tribute to him by an ex-student of MH, Linnea Sword Davenport: "He (Charles Swan) was my hero. I was about 7 years old when he knocked on our door at Bide-A-Wee, our cottage at Mt. Hermon. It so happened that the boys playing hockey on the top-flat had lost their ball in the ditch that ran along the path to Hafiz ("Half-fees") store. While retrieving it, they discovered a cobra lying besides the ball. The boys killed the cobra with their hockey sticks, and Charles had come to ask if I would like to see a snake. I was both frightened and excited, but Charles promised I would come to no harm. He even hoisted me on to his shoulders so I would be out of danger. Then he took me to see the snake, which was quite dead, but I was impressed – the fact that he thought of a little girl impressed me even more. No wonder he was my hero. I still have a painting Charles did of Kinchenjunga, which he gave to my parents."

I had the privilege of meeting Dr. Swan personally in 1977 in our school when I was in the second year on the staff. I still clearly remember talking to him of my interest in journalism in the staff-room. I was surprised to learn that he didn't give much importance to journalism but seemed to be more interested in me taking up serious writing. He suggested that I take up writing instead of going for journalism. "You are appointed" to write, he told me suddenly out of the blue while I was chatting with him. Unfortunately, I didn't know what he wanted me to write on, and because of the lack of time and rush of work, I didn't ask him either. Consciously, I didn't feel that I was influenced by what he told me at that time, but in retrospect, I feel that his three-word commandment – "You Are Appointed" – had a profound affect on me. It is interesting to look back now and note that my interest in writing took definite shape in 1977-78.

Apart from writing something on Sikkim's history, much of my time in 1978 was spent on preparing for the special edition of the school magazine. I bought a typewriter (Smith Corona) from an ex-student of MH, which I used for preparing materials for the annual *Hermonite* magazine. This book, too, is being typed on the same typewriter! And as I look back now, one of my lasting contributions to MH was definitely the 1978 school magazine of which I was the editor. Dedicated to Mr. and Mrs. Murray, the *Hermonite* was prepared by ex-students, who were on the staff in 1978. Neville Gardner, son of Rocky Gardner and one year my junior, who was then and still is on the staff, was the assistant editor.

Hail Mount Hermon! A Tribute

We wanted the magazine to become a historical document, which would truly reflect the richness of the spirit and tradition of this great institution.

I wrote in the editorial of the magazine: "It is indeed a great privilege for us, who have whole-heartedly cooperated into making this a special issue. It is special because of the variety of people who have taken part in it. It is special because it is our turn to pause for a while, and may be look back with a feeling of warmth and affection, as we come to the end of another chapter in the history of this great institution. It is hoped that something of that spirit which has made Mount Hermon great may be ever present with us as we face the future. May the dreams of our founders, and the lives of great men of the school, ever remind us of our gratitude to their service and our allegiance to the values that have had a far reaching effect. May we, too, hear the call from above and follow wherever He leads us."

The *Hermonite* was supposed to have come out by early 1979 but the printers took a long time and it was delayed by almost year. It finally reached MH towards the end of 1979, when I was about to leave the school for college in Bombay. Murray, who was then back in New Zealand, wrote to Neville and myself on December 22, 1979, expressing his appreciation for our effort: "This letter should have been written long ago, especially Jickmi as we had a letter from him sometime ago. However, the arrival of the 1978 HERMONITE today makes a letter really imperative. All of us do want to thank and congratulate you both, and your helpers, for all the work you have put in to make it such a worthwhile publication. I know that you have been very upset and annoyed over the long delay that has kept it from publication, and I guess people have been rather critical, but I hope that his hasn't bothered you. We have been pouring over the magazine since it arrived, and are just thrilled at all that you have been able to include, the research you have done, and the general layout. I am writing today to Mr. Johnston to make sure that copies are sent to all ex-staff I know in NZ who will surely want a copy."

As ex-students, our association with the school continued for many years after leaving the school. In 1986, the Sikkim Hermonites Association started a cricket tournament in Sikkim in Murray's honour. The Murray Cup Cricket Tournament, perhaps the most prestigious cricket tournament in Sikkim, is going on in its eighth year in 1991. Once we had our senior staff member from MH, Mathew Mathai, in Gangtok, prior to his final departure from MH, as the Chief Guest on the final day of the tournament, to present the trophy. Most of our team (Veterans) members have been Hermonites (Sherab Namgyal, Tempo Bhutia, Thentok Lachungpa, Pema Wangyal, Lhundup Topden, Karma Bhutia, Namgyal Wangyal and myself). We've also had ex-students of TNA, St. Joseph's and Goethal's playing for us.

Murray again wrote to me from Wellington in 1986, expressing his happiness over our initiative: "Thank you so very much for your letter and for the photos and certificates enclosed. I am very, very touched by your action in naming the cricket cup after me – it is an honour which I very deeply appreciate. I just hope that one day I might be in Gangtok to preside over a final and present the trophy." (Fortunately, Mr. Murray did turn up for one of our matches at the Palojor Stadium, Gangtok, during the centenary celebrations in November 1995)

Sikkim Hermonites, who number around more than 150, have been able to keep in touch with the school and other Hermonites over the years. Many of the children of ex-students are now studying in MH. Several of our old teachers have visited us in Gangtok in the past several years. These visits have been very memorable occasions for us all and we've had several 'get-together' on such occasions. Our school motto – "Non Scholae Sed Vitae Discimus" (Not for school, but for life we learn) – has become more meaningful to many of us after leaving MH, as we renew our friendship and extend our ties beyond the bounds of our school.

While Mrs. Rongong visited us in 1985 (just two years before she passed away), Mr. and Mrs. Johnston came to Gangtok in 1990 before they finally left MH. In 1991, Miss Cynthia Hawke payed us a short visit followed by Miss Russell in the beginning of 1992. Miss Russell is back now in England after having spent 24 years in MH. Interaction with other Hermonites keep on taking place from time to time.

In June this year (1992), we were much honoured and delighted to have with us Rev. Stewart, who was in Gangtok for just two days. The time was much too short for the visit, which some of us eagerly looked forward to; nevertheless, we made the best use of it. The Sikkim Hermonites Association (SHA) organised a reunion of Hermonites at Hotel Tibet in Gangtok on June 12, which was attended by Madan Mohan Rasailly, an ex-student of the Dewey-era, who left MH in the early '40s.

Three Hermonites from Darjeeling – Charles MacGilchrist, Pratap Singh Rai and Jagdish Prasad – who accompanied Rev. Stewart to Sikkim from Darjeeling, also joined us at the evening's wonderful get-together. Besides enjoying each other's company, renewing old ties, refreshing our memories of old times, as well as establishing new contacts, we took the opportunity to set up new office-bearers of the Association with a view to revitalise the organisation.

My classmate, O.T. Bhutia, who is a Minister in the Bhandari Government, was made the President, while I was chosen as the General Secretary. The re-union was also a rare occasion for us to sing our school anthem – "*Hail Mount Hermon!*". Rev. Stewart, whom his colleagues in MH referred to him as the 'Boss', had not changed much in appearance and personality. He was still very much the same man many of us worked under three decades back in 1963. He showed the same concern and enthusiasm for the school and its products – both staff and students – who are now scattered all over the world. We are now looking forward to seeing him again, hopefully with his wife, in 1995, when MH celebrates its birth centenary.

In the two years from now, MH will celebrate its 100th birth anniversary on March 11, 1995. Hermonites all over the world, particularly in India and the neighbouring areas, are making preparations to make the centenary year a grand success. This has led to the setting up of the All Indian Hermonites Association (AIHA) with its headquarters in Darjeeling. Pratap Singh Rai (MH 1964-68), who is in-charge of the Association's activities in this field, have been very active in his work. The ex-students in Siliguri have recently formed The Foothills Hermonites with Jagdish Singh (MH 1962-1971) becoming one of the most active members. The Mount Hermon Alumni Association Nepal (MHAAN) of Nepal led by Tom Creese (MH 1955-63), Sulee Hung (MH 1962-1970) and Annie (Gardner) Vaidya (MH 1968-1979) is also quite active and will definitely participate in the centenary celebrations.

The occasion will give us an opportunity to focus our attention on the school, which needs help and guidance in various fields. Its problems and prospects will have to be studies in depth and a concrete plan of action has to be initiated by all Hermonites, friends and well-wishers of the school to take our dear old MH into the 21st century and beyond. We live and die, but life must go on. The ideals and values and the high standards set by the school must continue to enrich our lives and the lives of those around us. March 11, 1995 will indeed be an occasion for us when we can, once more, join our hands and hearts together, and sing the school hymn in full-throated voice and mean it:

> *"Beloved Mount Hermon, we greet thee,*
> *Thy daughters and sons from afar*
> *As oft as we pause in our toiling*
> *To hail thee whose children we are.*
>
> *Hail, Mount Hermon! Hail, Mount Hermon!*
> *Safe for aye in memory's shrine.*
> *Hail, Mount Hermon! Dear Mount Hermon!*
> *Praise and love be ever thine."*

I loved MH and wanted to stay back, but something in me pulled forward and I had to finally move out. And as 1979 approached, I knew it would be my last year in MH. By then I had made up my mind to leave the teaching profession. MH had given me so much and the only way to show my gratitude was to give myself for the school for a few years.

My attitude to life has always been to give my best to whatever work I undertake. I certainly would not be able to do this if I did not enjoy what I was doing. I realised that I would not enjoy being in the teaching profession if I was not working in MH. It was partly because of this that I opted for another profession and decided to go for law studies.

My attitude to life is best described in these words from my little quotation book, which I have kept with me since 1967-68: "Behold, I do not give lectures or little charity; when I give, I give myself". I gave myself to MH fully and completely.

And as I look back now, I think the most valuable and the lasting thing that I have learnt from MH was not in the classroom, but on the playground; not from my textbooks, but from people and from everyday experiences. Taking part in the various school activities, leading various teams and finally the 1st XI football team and going through our many defeats and victories on the playing field, have been some of the greatest moments of my life. Giving my best shot and fighting till the very end, irrespective of consequences, is what I have learnt from MH. And as I look back over these fourteen years away from the old and familiar surroundings, I know that whatever MH taught me during my brief sojourn in Darjeeling has withstood the test of time.

In the final talk to the school on November 25, 1979, I said, "I venture into new frontiers with good intentions, high ideals and faith in God. To those who will be leaving us at the end of this year, let me urge you to give your life to a great cause. The kind of person we are in ten years time will reflect what we have learnt here in MH. I wish you all the very best."

And with tears in my eyes and a lump in my throat, I gave my last few words to the school, which had been my home for sixteen short years: "Sometimes when you reach out for a dream, you have to leave something behind. I leave behind my school, my friends, my home...my MH.

> *The woods are lovely, dark and deep,*
> *But I have promises to keep,*
> *And miles to go before I sleep,*
> *And miles to go before I sleep."*

I left MH at the end of 1979; but a part of me has always remained behind. And, I guess, a part of MH has always been with me. Hail Mount Hermon!

(*Inside Sikkim: Against the Tide*, Jigme N. Kazi, Hill Media Publications, Gangtok, 1993.)

ALUMNI – Part IX

68 It's Springtime For The Hermonites

Jigme N. Kazi, SC 1972

Hermonites reunion in Thimphu, Bhutan.

Beginning from mid-September last month (2014) in Kathmandu, the Hermonites – alumni of Darjeeling's co-ed Mt. Hermon School (founded by American missionaries in 1895) – are on the move. The three-day revival of the alumni in Nepal attracted at least 52 Hermonites. For the Mount Hermon Alumni Association Nepal (MHAAN) it was a rare event in recent years.

Former Mayor of Biratnagar Ram Bhattarai was one of the prominent oldies who was among the MHAAN meet in Kathmandu. Anil Jatia, Bachan Gyawali, Sangeeta Prasai and Ashoke Pokharel were among the main organizers of the reunion, whose main aim was to revive the alumni body.

Kathmandu's reunion was followed by a mini-reunion in Gangtok during Dusserah/Dassain. 1973 batch Hermonite Varongthip Lulitanond (Thip) has visited Sikkim at least 4-5 times in the recent past. This time he was accompanied by his batchmate Ravi Agarwal from Siliguri. The reunion get-together dinner on Oct 1 followed by a day-long trip to the Indo-Tibet border near Nathula in Tsangu and a rare treat by Sikkim Hermonite President Karma Bhutia at Mayfair resort was most relaxing and enjoyable.

Despite his busy schedule (Dassain) Thip's batchmate Uttam Pradhan, as always, was on the driver's seat during the Tsangu trip but missed the Mayfair treat! Arthur Pazo did well to arrange the permits to Tsangu, where the visitors were treated with sun, hail, rain, snow and a huge rainbow.

Hermonites reunion in Nepal.

Thip says Hermonites meet should always be held in the hills and not in the cities. "Thank you to all…I'll be back soon!" says Thip, who also joined the Hermonites at the Thimphu reunion (Oct 5-8, 2014). The Thimphu reunion was basically organized for the batch of 1978-79 but others, as is usually the case, joined in. Corinne Brokken, Mala Sujan, Dheera Sujan and Varongthip Lulitanond were among Hermonites from abroad who were present during the occasion. Former MP from Nagaland Apok Jamir, Mukesh Singh Adhupia, Yasmin Mukand Chung, Ratnakar Bhengra, Thinley Gyari, Geeta Bikst, Nima Dhondup, Binod Bhutra, Bebashis Brahma and Karan Anand were among those who enjoyed the brief autumn bonding that took place in Thimphu and Paro.

To Bhutan's Home Secretary and former Ambassador to Thailand Tsering Dorji, an active Hermonite, goes the credit of organizing the grand get-together in the Druk Kingdom. Autumn has returned to the hills but for the Hermonites its springtime!

Hermonites reunion in Bhutan.

Come November and we have the 1969 batch of Hermonites ascend to good old Darjeeling. I missed the Thimphu meet but will surely be one of the gatecrashers to this get-together in Darj. Had promised to have b'fast with James Lowangcha Wanglat at Keventer's, still a favourite haunt for Hermonites.

Prahalad Prasad, Om Prakash Kanwal, Raaj Kumar Bhangar (Lakhotia), Punam Agarwal, Marcus (Bappa) Dam are among those expected to be there for the occasion. A visit to MH has also been planned.

Hail Mount Hermon! A Tribute

The recently-revived Calcutta Hermonites, who seemed to be having bigger plans for MH, is planning a grand reunion in Darjeeling in December. Many from all over the region are expected to attend the get-together. Hashib Mondol is in-charge of the show.

Len Gangte and other Northeast Hermonites are planning to form the North East Hermonites Association (NEHA) in Imphal in January 2015. We are eager to form this club as there are many Hermonites all over the Northeast who are looking forward to formation of the association. "I'll be there!" I told Len. And I will be there!!

Our school motto is "Non-Scholae Sed Vitae Discimus" (not for school but for life we learn). Most of these reunions are taking place 30-40 years after we last left our alma mater. We are now more than convinced that our foundation for life, friendship and camaraderie are strong and deep.

Therefore, the Hermonites' motto "Closeness For Life!" and after life!! Hail Mt. Hermon!

(*Sikkim Observer*, **October 2014.**)

It's Springtime For The Hermonites

Hermonites International President Varongthip Lulitanond (seated on left) with Sikkim and Siliguri Hermonites in Gangtok.

Hermonites International President 'General' Thip welcomes Hermonites for the Bangkok reunion, 2016.

Hail Mount Hermon! A Tribute

Reunion in Pattaya, Thailand, 2016.

FRIENDS OF HAPPY DAYS

Senior Hermonites of early 1960s, Barid Manna (seated, Indonesia) and Tashi Namgyal (Sikkim), at a reunion in Sikkim after nearly 60 years.

Australia
69 Sherab And Roslyn Spent An Afternoon At Mount Hermon School In 2012

During their visit to MH in the winter of 2012, Sherab Namgyal and his wife Roslyn (Rongong) – 1972 and 1971 batches, who went around the school campus, give an independent account of the state of MH estate:

Sherab and I have just returned from a month in India during which we spent an afternoon at Mount Hermon School. There have been so many stories coming from the school in recent years that it was good to just go in person and have a wander around all our old haunts. Unfortunately, as it was in January, there was only one staff member (a Matron from Stewart building) we met, but we did catch up with two of the Grade 4 (servant) staff who were present at the new building site and at Fernhill.

Apart from the usual stroll down Memory Lane, we also tried to look at MH from a more dispassionate perspective and were most keen to see what damage there may have been from the earthquake of a few months ago. We also wanted to take stock of how things were looking in general. The furthest we could get to was the top of the first flight of stairs in the main building, but we walked down past Fernhill to the Sunshine Cottages, around Stewart Building and up past the new dining structure where the old Gym used to be. I hope the labels on the photos are adequate.

In short, there wasn't as much visible damage as we thought there might be, but we did not get to the upper floors (the girls' dormitories) where we were told most repair work needs to be done. However, we did notice that the desks and dining tables are still the ones from vintages long before our own!!

Fernhill, Trees Cottage and the Round Hostel looked in pretty good shape, and the damage at the corner of the main field seemed to have affected only the fence which had fallen down. We looked down at Rosebank and the other cottage (the Murrays first home in MH I think – just above Minton) and they both looked intact. Snow View looked in pretty good repair, but the other 2 remaining cottages in that line - (Mountain View and Bell View) looked shabby.

Encroachment onto the swimming pool area has been stopped by a cement wall. We also noticed there was a lot of fencing around other potential encroachment sites which seems to have halted the spread.

There was also a lot of activity on the new building site. The building has been created to mirror some of the architectural design of the main building, and there was an airiness and lightness inside the building that was very encouraging. We heard that this will temporarily be used as the Girls' Dormitory until repairs have been completed. However, in the long term, it looks like a very nice facility for a dining room and kitchen – very different from the dark dinginess of the current underground dining room/kitchen.

70 United States
Barbara's Barry In Leather Jacket

Barbara and Vinai.

They used to party with him in college. He was the guy who'd drink a few beers, maybe take a toke, stay up until 4 a.m. then excuse himself to crank out an "A" paper due that morning. Other than the toke, good training to have for someday running a country.

"He will always be Barry to us," Barbara Thummalapally says of her college friend, Barack Obama. "We can't believe that we'll be saying 'Mr. President.'"

She and her husband, Vinai, met the man who would be president at Occidental College in Los Angeles in 1979. Vinai roomed with Obama one summer and taught him how to cook Indian food.

Obama later transferred to Columbia University, but the Colorado Springs couple stayed good friends with him through the years. "We went to his wedding, and so on and so forth," Barbara says.

The Thummalapallys have been there throughout Obama's rise to fame - from his Senate swearing-in to the Springfield announcement of his bid for president. And today, the couple and their kids, Vishal and Sharanya, will be VIP guests at Obama's inauguration ceremony and ball.

Barbara opted to delay a new teaching career this year to work for Obama and open their Rockrimmon home to other campaigners. Vinai, president of a CD and DVD manufacturing company, was on the national finance committee.

The couple often get asked what Obama was like in college. Easy. He was Barry, the mellow guy in the leather jacket, dragging on a cigarette.

"The leather jacket he wore for years. The leather jacket, that's exactly him," Barbara says. "He would be sitting there smoking quite a bit in those days."

Barbara and Vinai Thummalapally with their friend and college buddy, Barack Obama.

Their close-knit circle of international students hardly rated as party animals. "There were about six of us. We'd go to Venice Beach to see all the crazy people. We'd have all these great political discussions about whatever the latest thing was."

Having a good time didn't interfere with Obama's academics. "It was so typical that he could just go and type out this amazing paper and do well after having partied all night, having drinks, beer or whatever we do at college," she says.

Obama sometimes drove her to class. "He'd sit there low in his seat, he played cool music." She has pictures of her on the beach with Obama when they met up in Hawaii on a summer break from college.

There's a photo in New York City from a reunion about 20 years ago with a few other classmates. Obama's wearing a leather jacket.

In the campaign last summer, the couple helped put on a fundraiser at The Broadmoor, enjoying some private time with Obama when they went to his room for a nightcap.

"We relaxed and chatted. He offered us some of his chocolates and cheese and the fruits he eats at night," Barbara says. "I sat on the floor and rubbed his back. I knew he was very exhausted and decompressing."

She isn't surprised he's taking the nation's top job. "He has always been such a cool character and so comfortable in his skin," she says. "He is so grounded about what is important in life and what he is made of."

Even in a tailored suit, to them he's the same Barry in the leather jacket.

(gazette.com)

(Barbara Thummalapally was previously Barbara Nichols-Roy, an alumni of Mt. Hermon School, Darjeeling. Daughter of the Late Stanley D.D. Nichols-Roy, Barbara and her two sisters, Mariane, Cynthia, brother David and mother Helen now live in the US. Her grandfather, J. Nichols-Roy, was one of the pioneers who laid the foundation of the special provisions in the Constitution of India for the tribals in the Northeast. Stanley Nichols-Roy was Tourism Minister in Meghalaya. The Nichols-Roys were one of the notable and well-respected families in Shillong. They used to live in Shillong before settling in the US. – Editor)

71 "Being The Principal's Daughter Had Its Advantages And Liabilities"

Kitty Katzell, MH – 1931-1934

Kitty Katzell (Mildred Engberg) is the daughter of Headmistress (Mt. Hermon School Principal – 1931-34), Lila Engberg. The following is an account of her growing up and schooling in India, 1930s:

How do you answer when someone who grew up in the U.S asks, "What was it like growing up in India?" How would an American answer the question, "What was it like growing up in America?"

Only now that I'm in my 90s have I figured out how to answer that question. I need to show the person the ways in which growing up in India was different from growing up in America, and the ways in which it was the same.

I had my second birthday on the Atlantic Ocean, on our way to India. My father had died when I was 15 months old. He and my mother were planning to be missionaries, he a medical missionary, she a teacher. He contracted pneumonia while he was interning, so she went forward with what had been their plans.

My mother was what was called a "contract teacher" in a Methodist boarding school in Darjeeling. She had dormitory duties, teaching duties, recreation duties, and a 2-year-old child. Needless to say, she quickly engaged an *ayah* (Indian nurse-maid) to keep an eye on me. But she also arranged for me to spend time in the school's kindergarten – at age 2. The school operated under the British educational system and its graduates were eligible to take Cambridge University entrance examinations. The kindergarten's content carried students through the American equivalent of second grade; the class levels were known as "standards", not "grades".

From the time I was two until we came back to America on furlough when I was five, I was enrolled in the kindergarten, so I learned to read and write and do arithmetic.

Back in the U.S. for most of a year, my mother set about enrolling me in a public school. To the principal of the school, six-year-olds went into first grade. My mother would not hear of that; she simply would not enroll me. The principal agreed to let me try second grade, but very soon the second-grade teacher

Mildred Engberg, aged 9.

let it be known that third grade would be more appropriate, so, at age 6, I spent several months in third grade before we returned to Darjeeling, where I entered second standard, the academic equivalent of America's fourth grade.

The climate in Darjeeling is generally cool and damp. It is reputed to get snow every ten years and, in fact, it snowed the year before we got there and the year after we left, which validated that reputation. It is also reputed to get 120" of rain a year, most of it between May and October, due to the monsoons. Because of the climate, school was open from March to November, and parents sent their children to the schools in the hills so they could escape the summer heat and humidity on the plains. When the weather was nice after months of monsoons, we sometimes were given a half-holiday, so we could play out in the sunshine.

1934

At various times in my childhood, although I lived in a boarding school, I had pets. At one time, I had a dachshund named Reggie; another time there was a cat named Saraswati, an Indian goddess's name; and later there was a pair of guinea pigs, who produced more guinea pigs. We used to take the little ones to class with us in the pockets of our pinafores. Being the principal's daughter had its advantages; it also had its liabilities, like when the teacher sent me to stand in the hall for talking out of turn and "the principal" happened to walk by.

Although we lived in Darjeeling for nine years, it was only in the last year that I lived in the dormitory with other girls my age. Before that, I roomed with my mother. During her first term, I was too young to be in the dormitory; during her second term, she was principal of the school and had a suite of rooms, so I lived with her there. During our last year in India, I lived in the dormitory with other girls in my age group. This meant getting up at 6 a.m.; washing up at a congregate wash stand; going to daily chapel services every morning; playing outdoors when it wasn't raining, and often even when it was; kneeling on the cold cement floor with all the other girls in my dorm for bedtime prayers; and so on.

Chota hazri (little meal) was tea and toast at 6:30 a.m. The tea was strong Darjeeling tea, to which plenty of sugar and milk had been added. Breakfast was at 11 a.m. It consisted of brown suji (Wheatena), white suji (Cream of Wheat), or kwakerotes (Oat Meal). The next meal was at 3 p.m. It was a light lunch called "tiffin". Supper was at 6 p.m. and often included curry, rice, and dahl, a special preparation of yellow split peas. For children who found curry to be too spicy, dahl and rice was a favorite meal. Other favorites were egg curry, chicken curry, and mulligatawny soup.

The school was situated on what was known as Mt. Hermon Estates, on a level below the main road in to Darjeeling. Part way up the hill, there was a "tuck shop" over on the right below the roadway where we could buy things like graham crackers and sweetened condensed milk – and probably lots of other things, too, but those are what I remember. Further up the hill, also on the right below the roadway was the North Point Post Office. This memory is significant because 50 years later, as my husband and I neared the school, I said to him, "Around that next curve is where the post office used to be." And sure enough, it was still there.

The old Post Office at North Point, Singmari, Darjeeling.

As principal, my mother was responsible for the school car, which was a Whippet. She drove it and maintained it. She would lie down in the driveway under the car with a flashlight and the manual and do the necessary lubricating.

She had taken a transformer with her to India, so she was able to use her American sewing machine to make our clothes, her iron to press things, and her waffle iron to make waffles when she entertained. The laundry, of course, was done by the dhobi, who picked up the things to be washed every week and delivered them the following week. Every item in our bundle was stamped with indelible ink by the dhobi using a special symbol to identify every item as ours. Our symbol was three dots in a triangle. It was years before that symbol disappeared from our lives.

So that's what it was like growing up in India. Certainly different, now that I think of it.

More about growing up in India

This article is prompted by comments of readers who read my earlier article about growing up in India. They wondered about the teachers and students at the school.

The short answer is that most of them were English, American, Anglo-Indian and some European. A better answer is to give some of their names and anecdotes associated with some of them.

The most famous person who attended the school is Tom Stoppard, but he wasn't there when I was and I never knew him.

My kindergarten teacher was Miss Balthazar. Another K.G. teacher was Louise "Louie" Cox. My third standard teacher was Louise Humphreys. My best friend, Evelyn MacTavish, and I had a serious crush on her. Evelyn's parents were Salvation Army missionaries from Scotland. Evelyn eventually married and lived in Canada, and we were in touch until quite recently.

Two Salvation Army sisters who attended the school, Betty and Anna Hannevik, were Norwegian. I later came across Anna's name in an international Salvation Army publication that was handed to me one time when I was waiting in Union Station in Chicago. From that I learned that she was an international SA figure, so I contacted Anna and, when my husband and I were on a cruise that stopped in Oslo, Anna came down to the ship to see us.

Other students whose names I remember are Reggie Stuart, Sidney Pedrick, Ardys Engel, Pali Thu, Patsy Fox, and Max Wiborg. Mention of Max reminds me of his mother, Mrs. Wiborg, who was my arithmetic teacher. She was very strict, and she drilled us thoroughly in the times tables. I can still hear her saying, "I want you to know your times tables so well that if I came to the dormitory and woke you up in the middle of the night and said 'six nines' you'd wake up and say '54'." And we did. I got all the way up to twelve, and was working my way toward sixteen, which I never quite mastered.

Another of my teachers was Annette Sookias. I think she was Anglo-Indian. She was only there for one year, as I recall. Miriam Scholberg was a teacher from America. Her parents were also missionaries.

The woman who had the title of Housekeeper was Mrs. Lottie ValDeramao. She was Scandinavian. We called her Mrs. Val. She was in charge of the kitchen. The bortchi (cook) did the cooking, but she was his boss. On one occasion, he asked for permission to plan

"Being The Principal's Daughter Had Its Advantages And Liabilities"

Kate and Tsarong with Principal Lila Enberg, 1934.

and prepare a special dessert for the teachers' dining room. The permission was given, and the dessert was served. My mother, as principal, received the first dish and tasted it, knowing it was the bortchi's special treat. It turned out to be a pudding composed of sweetened mashed potatoes. She was not favorably impressed.

The school's business manager was Mr. Sur. He was an Indian. His daughter, Annapurna, was a classmate of mine. She died of "consumption" when we were in fifth standard.

The last year we were in India, we had two Tibetan princesses at the school, Kate and Tess Tsarong. They came to the school before the other students, to give them time for some orientation. They spoke virtually no English but they learned quickly. They were members of the royal family. I am told that Kate was killed attempting to escape during the Chinese oppression. There had been other Tibetan women who had attended the school earlier, and one of them, Mary Laden-la, operated a popular hotel in Darjeeling where my husband and I stayed when we visited in 1985.

Frances Kirby, from America, was my domestic science teacher. That was the subject that is now called home science. I was not talented in that subject. I can still hear Miss Kirby saying, sadly, "Mildred, your stitches are like crocodile's teeth!" And then there was the time we were cooking pancakes over kerosene stoves with a tall flue. We were to flip the pancake so it turned over in mid-air and catch it in the pan to cook the other side. In my case, I flipped the pancake and watched it go down the flue into the flames. Well, now I can say, after all, I was only 10 years old.

We left India early in 1935, and sailed to England where we spent three months visiting my mother's sister's family. They lived at 63 Oakwood Crescent, Greenford, Middlesex. I went to school while we were there, so by the time I got to America, in the summer of 1935, I had a lovely English accent, but I soon got over that, because an American cousin told me I sounded like a duck!

North Carolina Reunion 2015
Whispering Pines And Misty Mountains

72

Nina Wason Harkness, SC 1972

 The Atlanta Party (as against the Assam party) consisting of a three vehicle caravan inches its way up the Blue Ridge Mountains of North Carolina through winding mountain roads that are oddly reminiscent of someplace else I've been. Can't quite place it. Pine trees soar heavenwards in a rich jungle of damp fronds interspersed with rhododendron. No, it still won't come to me! Would we ever arrive, I ask impatiently as the GPS' strident tones instructs us to make yet another right turn up the hillside.

 We'd assembled the evening before at Karl and Kimbi Hagen's lovely home in Atlanta, eagerly awaiting the arrival of the Senguptas from Tulsa, Oklahoma, a twelve hour drive away. I'd flown in from Naples, a short hop by comparison, and was met at the airport by Ken Hagen in his rutfut truck. Finally Robin, his wife Noella and daughter, Priya arrive and hobble stiffly out of their SUV. Sixteen-year-old Priya sees a white guy Ken, rush out to greet them, accompanied by his wife, Linda. Apparently he speaks no English, just Nepalese, a language she's never heard before. "Talae!" he insists on calling her father who has a perfectly good head of hair. Yes, this was going to be just as weird as she'd feared. How would she endure three whole days in their company? "Hey Kancha!" he addresses his brother, Karl, thumping him affectionately on the back.

Today, we turn one last corner and finally arrive at Montreat, a two storied lodging with a mossy shingle roof, nestled under the pines. Kenny Jones greets us enthusiastically and suddenly we're surrounded by warm smiling faces and offered hot cups of tea. Arun Jones appears, a shadow of his former self. He shares with us later that he'd been sent to MH because he needed to lose weight. He's accompanied by his charming wife, Yolie who he'd met in the Philippines. We're shown to our rooms, which are up a steep staircase and along narrow corridors. I sniff the aroma of pine outside my window, strangely evocative of another time and place. Can't quite put my finger on where.

Back downstairs, Marianne Nichols-Roy smothers me in a bear hug. We figure it's been 45 years since we last met and she hasn't aged a bit. I would have recognized her anywhere. She introduces me to her hubby Steven Schwartz, to Josna Rege, bubbly as ever and to Tsogie Hamilton who all represent the Class of '69. JoJo later shares that, unlike Arun, she was sent to MH because she was too thin! We are privileged to have among us Gordon Hostetler who was at MH between 1941-45 as a kid in junior school. He's accompanied by his wife, Phyllis: brave people to join our throng after a period of seventy, yes seventy years! They fit right in and bring a new perspective to the gathering. I turn around and suddenly there's Cynthia Nichols-Roy, my dorm roommate and confidante of yore! How we'd whispered confidences deep into the night, long after lights-out, about boys who'd broken our hearts and the punishments meted out by teachers who'd caught us kissing them! With her is Ed Austin, her stalwart spouse (spice) who braved the Colorado Reunion of 2004, and is therefore somewhat prepared for the onslaught of singing and reminiscing that's to be an integral part of the reunion.

Lalrinpuii Changte, marathon driver, arrives laden with old sepia photographs, song-sheets and ancient copies of the Hermonite Magazine. What joy to flip though those pages and read our earnest and comical poems and articles! David Nichols-Roy, chai-walla, brews awesome pots of tea with the milk mixed in, MH style. He and his wife Minette have flown across the country from California to be part of this. At Mount Hermon and in our homes in Shillong he'd been the Nichols-Roy's puny kid brother and therefore beneath our notice. Now towering over me, I consider it prudent not to boss him around. Besides, he resembles his father, Stanley, more and more, a person we'd all respected greatly.

"When's dinner?" someone asks. It seems no one has lost their boarding school hunger! We're told Barbara Nichols-Roy is bringing it in her car all the way from Arlington, Virginia. Without her, there'll be no dinner. All of a sudden she arrives, accompanied by her lovely mother, Helen, aged almost ninety. We swarm around them, delighted they'd arrived safely, reassured that there would now be food! Some things never change. Barbie has brought everything but the kitchen sink. Apart from coordinating the reunion, she has taken on responsibility for cooking and organizing dinner on two nights as well as accompanying the singing on piano. She brings song-sheets she's typed with the words of Going Home Day Songs and our favorite anthems. She and Kenny have put in extraordinary effort to make the reunion happen.

Hail Mount Hermon! A Tribute

Some of the US Hermonites: Kenny Jones, Mrs. Nichols-Roy, Barbara Nichols-Roy, Margaret Mapley (Jackson), Sharon Jones, Arun Jones, Ken Hagen, Sunita, Josna Rege, Mariane Nichols-Roy, Karl Hagen, Puii, Nina Wason.

(www.oldmhs.com)

Margaret Mapley who left Darjeeling back in 1972 arrives with her "air-head" husband, Nigel Jackson all the way from Canada. And in time for dinner! "I'm fascinated by anything to do with flying," he laughs, "so you can legitimately call me an air-head." He's obviously good MH spouse material. She's hungry for news about everyone and later reads an email sent to her by Lucinda Gibbs. It brings disquieting news of the current situation in Mount Hermon. We pause in our revelry and reflect on what, if anything, we can do to help.

Fui Chung Li and his wife June, who attended Goethals in Kurseong, a smoking hot couple, arrive the next day, also from Canada. They're followed by Michal and Michael Ashkenazy, also amazingly youthful, from New York. Michal was another brave soul who'd attended MH for only one year to do her HSC in 1976 but felt sufficiently inspired to attend the reunion. We discover that Michael is a Khasi and he's quickly inveigled into participating in the Talent Night scheduled for Saturday. Nalini (Nelly) Jones arrives with her five-year-old son, David. She reports that her mother, Beulah, wife of Mr. Bill Jones, is now home from hospital and doing well. Nelly's South Indian husband, Jude Joseph, roars in on his motor cycle. Nelli confesses that when her big brother Arun was sent to MH because he was fat, she was afraid to eat for fear of being sent there too! Eventually the entire Jones family moved to Ailina and Nelly was able to eat again.

Last but not least, Barbara's husband, Vinai Thummalapally, arrives from DC. He co-hosted the Colorado Reunion of 2004 and is well-honed in the art of indulging old Hermonites. The party is now complete! We do all the things we came here to do. We sing our hearts out, we catch up on each other's experiences, we trek up the mountainside, we exchange phone numbers and email addresses. It's a magical time. Despite singing about how "We said we wouldn't look back," we do little else.

The more active among us wake up before the rising bell (siren) to take a hike, Priya included and I'm impressed that she's keen to join us, leaving her parents sleeping in their beds. She's roughly the same age we were when we created many of these memories we're trying to recapture. She walks with the Hagens, ahead of the pack. Apparently, Ken does speak a little English. They're kind and funny and she feels included. Suddenly she sees how cool they are, and that maybe there's more to this reunion thing than she realized. Does she perhaps even feel a twinge of jealousy? How is it that these people still have so much in common? What type of bond could have them hurtling across countries and continents after so many years just to get together to share a few old jokes (come by running??), to look at old pictures and sing the same old songs? She wonders if she'll want to get together with her school friends half a century later in another country. Probably not. (Sorry, Priya! We identify with you more than you realize!) Tsogie forges ahead without leaving so much as a footprint, much fitter than she's any right to be, but what else can you expect from a Himalayan? The view from the top is stupendous. We are above a shroud of mist that enfolds the valleys below. I rack my brains for where I might have seen this phenomenon before.

We assemble later to formally introduce ourselves to the group and tell each other what we've been up to since we "passed out" of school. We learn new amazing things about each other. At an ecumenical gathering the next day presided by Rev. Arun Jones we pay homage to those who have recently passed away. Tragically, we've lost three school principals this past year, Rev. Davis Stewart, Rev. Bill Jones and Mr. Graeme Murray. We share in a time of reflection and sing "Lord of all hopefulness" in loving remembrance of Mr. Murray. We each believe we were at MH in its heyday. Perhaps everyone thinks the same, but we're eternally grateful for the blessings bestowed on us by our beloved school.

Saturday afternoon is set aside for momo making with Robin and Noella Sengupta in charge. We all have guilty memories of "bunking" to North Point to indulge in momos and soup…mmm delicious! We consume dozens of these culinary masterpieces and I serve fresh mangoes for dessert. But Barbie informs me we have yet to eat dinner, and the momos, apparently, were just the appetizer. Seriously? The Talent Show follows with Barbie nipping into the kitchen between performances to see to the rice. Cynthia has already cooked her famous *dahl*.

The Talent Show is living testimony to the skills fostered in Mount Hermon. It's a feast of music, comedy, literature and drama that I am privileged to compere. The Khasis, (not the Kardashians - we have slightly less money) kick off with a sad lament about a deer. Marianne's voice is clear as a bell in her rendering of "As long as he needs me" from Oliver Twist. Nina delivers a lesson in sex-ed from her novel, "A Sahib's Daughter." Robin, one of those guitar playing guys we girls swooned over (in bell-bottoms and tie-dye tees), still rocks! Marianne, JoJo and Tsogie enact the three witches from Macbeth. The long-suffering spices (spouses) valiantly enter into the spirit of things with their own performance of Red River Valley. Gordon relates hilarious tales from when he was seven. Cynthia, Barbie and Nina sing "Three Old Maids" with Helen sitting in as Sister Digby administering spoonful's of tonic. Ken Hagen impersonates Mr. Jones and JoJo reads her Blogs about life in MH. Nina reads an episode about her mother, Mrs. Wason from her book, "The Jewel Daughters" followed by a hilarious impersonation of her by David Nichols-Roy. (Did he miss his true calling?) The show winds up with everyone wearing towels on their heads (shades of Junior School Chapel Play costumes) for "The Lost Tribe of Israel" which is recited by Margaret Mapley.

And yes, we're hungry when it's time (again) for dinner! We share in our final hours together and decide not to leave it so long for our next reunion, perhaps five years? Fu Li and Vinai declare that five years is too long, we're none of us getting any younger! It's heartwarming to hear concurrence from everyone, especially the spices! We reluctantly turn in for "Light's Out."

Sadly, I ascend the stairs to my room under the eaves. I shed quiet tears as I gaze at the dark trees outside my window. And then it comes to me! The mountains, the pines, the rhododendrons and the mist! Our dear Kenny had chosen the perfect location for the reunion that brought us together to ruminate, reflect and reminisce about a place that's been instrumental in shaping our lives. We'd travelled back in time, and Montreat, for a few shining days, cocooned among the pines of the Blue Ridge Mountains became Mount Hermon!

(1972 batch Hermonite Nina (Wason) Harkness is the author of A Sahib's Daughter *and* The Jewel Daughters.*)*

73 United Kingdom
Renown British Playwright Tom Stoppard Studied In MH

Welcome to the Old Mount Hermon Students' Association (UK)! This association is made up of old students of Mount Hermon School, Darjeeling, living in the UK, Europe, America, Australia, New Zealand, India, Sikkim and Nepal. It is run by Hazel (Innes) Craig, ex-pupil of Mount Hermon and author of the well-known book about the hill schools of India, "Under the Old School Topee." A reunion lunch is organized once a year in London and attended by members living in the UK or visitors from abroad. Some of our senior members were in school as far back as 1914 as in the case of our senior-most American member, Charles Swan, (now sadly deceased) who wrote many of the beautiful school songs. We would, however, like to attract some newer members to our group. The annual subscription is £3.50, and Life Membership at £25. You can join by contacting Hazel (Innes) Craig at her address or email below.

About Mount Hermon School

Founded in 1895 in the hill station of Darjeeling India by American Missionaries, Mount Hermon School (originally Queen's Hill School) was established for the education of boys and girls in a healthy climate, away from the heat, dust and flies of the plains of India. By the mid-1950s it had a mix of children of different nationalities - American, Australian, New Zealanders, British, Europeans, Indians, Anglo-Indians, Tibetans, Nepalese, Chinese and even students from Thailand who used to fly all the way out to India for the school term. It was a friendly school, and the discipline was more relaxed than the other Darjeeling schools, and although in the 1930s and 40s school uniforms were strictly adhered to (navy-blue skirts and blouses for the girls with both boys and girls wearing blazers and badge), this was largely ignored by the 1950s and more casual dress - sometimes jeans and T-shirts - became the norm!

Tom Stoppard, the famous playwright, attended MHS during 1943-45, and wrote in the Mail on Sunday (1991) - "Mount Hermon School was founded by American Methodists and was so far from being an English public school as to include baseball among its sports." The television actress, Felicity Kendal, also had fond memories of the school which she wrote about in her book "White Cargo." The school took mostly boarders, but there were also some day-scholars from Darjeeling town.

Today, Mount Hermon is a thriving institution with an additional building, the Stewart Building, named after former headmaster David Stewart (1954-65) who now lives in Auckland, New Zealand. The boys' hostel, Fern Hill, further away from the main school building below the football field, has also been enlarged and modernized. The Mount Hermon Estate comprised several "log-cabins" built on the mountainside below the school. They were there so that missionary parents visiting Darjeeling for the summer holidays, could be near the school with their children, who attended as day-scholars for the duration.

About Darjeeling

The name "Darjeeling" comes from the Tibetan words "dorje", meaning a thunderbolt (originally the sceptre of the Hindu god Indra) and "ling," a place; hence, "the place of the thunderbolt." (Anyone living in Darjeeling during the Monsoon will tell you that this name is most appropriate!) The town, which originally consisted of a few mud huts only, was purchased by the British in 1835 from the Maharaja of Sikkim as a health resort and sanatorium for British soldiers.

The town is famous for its tea industry, started in the mid-1800s, and Darjeeling tea is famous for its delicate and orangey flavour. It is also famous for its unique mountain railway which snakes through the mountains in a series of twists, zigzags and loops. Magnificent vistas of the Kanchenjunga mountain range are visible from the town, whilst the summit of Mount Everest can be seen from Tiger Hill, on a higher elevation. A number of schools were established in the town and surrounding region: St. Helen's Convent, Dow Hill, Goethal's Memorial and Victoria Boys' School in neighbouring Kurseong, and St. Paul's, St. Joseph's, Mount Hermon and the Loreto Convent in Darjeeling itself. Darjeeling boasted of cinemas, clubs, a museum, zoo and even a racecourse, all tucked away in this remote region of the

Himalayas. It is also a place of worship, with the spires of churches, minarets of mosques, pagodas of Buddhist monasteries and sikharas of Hindu temples, all seeming to point to one universal god.

Today Darjeeling has changed from a quiet hill station to a busy market town. Yet, the snows are eternal, as are the friendly, happy hill people, who are as unchanging as the mountains themselves.

(UK alumnus)

MEMORIES OF OUR YEARS IN 'MH'

Dear Members and Visitors to our site,

This is just to let you know that I have made another update for our OMHSA website at www.oldmhs.com. I have finally completed The School of 1934 page with more photographs from the School Yearbook and Kitty Katzell's old album of school photographs of 1934 which she so kindly sent to me.

I have also included several more New Pages. Click on the Tab for "Memories of 1954-55" and that will take you to the page where you can click on further tabs to view the other new pages in this section. These are MHS Through the Years, SC 1954, School Notes 1954, School Notes 1955, Prize List 1954, Prize List 1955 and Winners of Trophies 1955. These will be of particular interest to Teachers and Students who were at school during those two happy, memorable years (for me), as several names of Teachers and Students are included in these pages.

All good wishes and happy browsing!

James (Sinclair)

74 MH Needs 'Reliable People' On The Ground

Hon. Secretary of MH's UK alumni, Lucinda (Cindy) Gibbs, who has visited Mt. Hermon several times, feels the need for "reliable people" to tackle multiple problems faced by the school. In her November 2015 Newsletter, she says:

Lucinda (Cindy) Gibbs

MH Needs 'Reliable People' On The Ground

Dear Members,

I have been asked by James Sinclair to take on the role of Hon. Secretary, which is rather daunting, as I shall have to try and follow on from Hazel Craig, which will be a hard act to follow. She is a great loss to us all.

As we have just been to Darjeeling, I thought I would write a bit about our trip, Darjeeling itself, and of course Mount Hermon.

It was my father, David Gibbs, who suddenly decided he would like to make a, possibly last, visit to India to see old boys, friends and St. Paul's (he was Rector there from 1964 -72). My mother didn't feel able to come, so remained behind (breaking her hip just before we left, but was well cared for, so we felt able to go).

We went straight to Calcutta, where several airlines and now flying direct to, bypassing Bombay and Delhi. The weather was very pleasant and we stayed in the Grand. It remains the grande dame of Calcutta hotels, and is still the haven it always was. Calcutta is no different I think, bustling, busy, but charming and full of delightful people. People complain of the traffic, which is true, but if one avoids the rush hours, it isn't so bad! We met up with a couple of Hermonites who had been at Mount Hermon in our era; Betty Bannerjee, whose father had been a doctor on the tea gardens and Miti Adhikari, who has returned to Calcutta with his wife, to promote Indian bands, after a very successful career with the BBC in London. As we had to chaperone my father it didn't leave us a great amount of time to connect with any others.

However, I had also gone to St. Paul's for a couple of years as a youngster, so did see some of my own classmates from that period too, as the Paulites put on various lunches and dinners for my father. The Clubs in Calcutta still thrive and waiting lists to join run into years! We have been lucky to visit most of the Calcutta clubs over the years, and the old rules are all still in place – dress codes, wonderful snacks – cheese chilli toasts, cheese balls, fish fingers, paneer tikka, kathi rolls and so on, along with the chota and burra pegs, pukka club food served on linen cloths in the dining rooms, old bearers who have been there for years, and so on. There is something very comforting about it all. How pleasant it is to go into a place where everyone is dressed properly for dinner.

After four days of a fairly hectic regime we had been invited to stay at the ancestral home of old Paulites, about a three and a half hour drive from Calcutta – in Maheshgunj. If you would like to see photographs of the place do look up www.balakhana.com. They have opened it as a homestay. It is a 19th century French villa. The drive was breathtaking – through the Bengal countryside – wonderful scenes of life beside the numerous ponds, paddy fields stretching as far as the eye could see, typical small villages bustling with life, villagers selling their produce on the roadside – shiny purple aubergines, short, fat cucumbers, long string beans,- bullock carts carrying heaps of jute, thatched huts, sweet shops with pyramidal piles of colourful sweetmeats, schoolgirls in crisp, starched uniforms, hair neatly plaited, carrying armfuls of books, colourful woven saris washed and blowing in the wind. It was a feast for the eyes.

Balakhana was a very special place. Set in 16 acres of gardens, fields, and fruit trees with langurs high in the trees. The Jalangi river flows close by – just a short walk through a typical Bengal village, filled with laughing children, and past people tending their crops either side of the raised path to the river. A lone boat wends its way down the lazy waters. Utterly peaceful.

We were treated to wonderful Bengali hospitality – sumptuous home cooking, and wonderful company in the most idyllic spot. Each night mosquito nets were hung over the four poster beds, as we slept with the top windows in the high-ceilinged rooms open, letting the heat out and the cool of the night in. We heard jackals howling in the near distance – and it really took me back to nights in Darjeeling.

Our next leg was back to Calcutta for the night and on to Bagdogra the next morning. Calcutta airport is no longer our DumDum but a smart and modern Netaji Subhash Chandra Bose International Airport. Bagdogra is much the same, small and informal, with its busy café with temptations such as momos, pakoras, cutlets and fish and chips!! We didn't stop but went on straight up to Kurseong, climbing rapidly out of the heat of the plains. The scenes never change; the tea gardens, lush forest vegetation, the red and white rhododendron trees, the steep climbs and hairpin bends. It was misty at Kurseong, but we stopped at the Tourist Lodge, which on a clear day has a wonderful view of the snows. It is a well-known stopping place to Darjeeling, and has a good menu, with of course plenty of Darjeeling tea! Onwards and upwards to Darjeeling.

We have been to Darjeeling regularly over the years, and were not surprised by the crush of traffic and further new buildings. My father hadn't been back for 5 years, and noticed a big difference. We were staying in the Mayfair hotel, at the far end of the Mall road, opposite Raj Bhawan. It was the old summer-house of the Maharajah of Nazargunj, and has had some tasteful additions added to ensure there is space for the restaurants etc. We have stayed here for several years, and have found the rooms extremely comfortable, with excellent bathroom facilities, good food and very pleasant staff. It has a Library, filled with photographs of Tenzing and the Everest expeditions, and a bar dedicated to the artist Goray Douglas, whose works adorn the walls. It is a nice walk up to the Chowrasta from the hotel.

The Chowrasta has also changed a little. Beneath the end of the Windamere's land they have now built a stage for performances etc. The old row of shops with the Oxford Book Store, Habeebs, Lekraj are still there – with little change. However, Lekhraj is closed, Habeebs is run by the same family, but the old man my parents bought lovely things from has died. The Oxford book store still has many wonderful publications on the hills, books by Indian authors, guide books etc., and will post on anything you buy, to save you carrying the book with you on further travels. The ponies for rides are still there, but their quarters are not in good shape. The huge expanse of the Chowrasta remains, but a Café Coffee Day (sort of Costa Coffee type place) has come up next to Jolly Arts, modern influences of course.

All the shops on Nehru Road we knew are still there – Das Studio, where Durga Das still runs the show (Mohan was visiting whilst we were there too), still has a wonderful array of photographs, postcards etc., Frank Ross the Chemist, Bata, Keventers and Glenarys, which has a wifi café and bakery downstairs, and the restaurant upstairs is as good as ever. We were in both places, and had to have our cream cones with pots of Darjeeling tea. So good. On the opposite side of the road below the D&DMA (Planters Hospital) a new construction is coming up (narrowing the road) and is housing modern fast food 'joints' – like Kentucky Fried Chicken and Pizza Hut. This, I suppose, is progress……

MH Needs 'Reliable People' On The Ground

When we were there in earlier times, there was nothing, and then a series of make shift shack type shops came up. These have now been relocated and they are erecting this new concrete building. The Planters Club still carries on and we have in the past sat out with beers on the terrace over looking the road below and life in Darjeeling. There are so many hotels now in Darjeeling that I think they struggle with bookings. However, it has its old-world charm still. There is much building in Darjeeling, and positively thousands of vehicles. Everyone it seems runs a taxi, and the streets are lined with drivers waiting for a fare. There is a one-way system round town which otherwise would become impassable. Sometimes the change is depressing, but one can still see the old Darjeeling pushing through to remind us of our happy days there.

We went down to Mount Hermon of course, leaving my father to go up to St. Paul's to see the current Rector, whom he had not met. We had spoken on the phone to Mr. Wharton to ensure he was going to be around. Sadly Aileena, the guest house just outside the gates, is now thoroughly neglected and has a fence around it. Happy times were spent there whilst I was in school, with the Mapleys. However, when we came through the gates and parked, we noticed some improvement from a year earlier. The grounds were in better shape and the malis were working away. It looked tidier and better kept. Mr. Wharton was there, and greeted us warmly and we went into his office, where we were served tea. We had met him the previous year and he had told us of how difficult things in the hills were. They now have almost an equal number of boarders to day students. It is hard with all the previous political unrest to get boarders.

Trying to get old students to send their children there it seems is difficult too. We had seen around the school last year, including the no longer used senior and junior girls' dormitories. The earthquake in 2011 caused some damage, but there was a great deal of neglect in maintenance over the years as well. All the windows in the junior girls' dormitories needed attention from good carpenters, but the rest of the dorms were more or less fine. A fresh lick of paint was needed everywhere.

I understand now the claim for the damage to the main school building is still under discussion as the insurance company are prepared to only pay around half of the claim. As we are really not privy to the detail it is hard to know where things will go. There have been discussions with various alumni groups about raising funds, but until the insurance claim is sorted out we have no idea what will remain undone. I also heard that one particular batch did do up a classroom, raising funds between them, and I think arranging the works themselves. After discussions with several people it seems that what one would really need are reliable people on the ground close by to clearly detail works required, costs, and then the safe collection of any donations, with a clear picture of how this money will be spent. Not an easy task.

As some of you will be aware a new building has come up, where the old, open gym was, above the main school field. This, I understand, had been destined to become a new dining hall, but after the earthquake the boarding girls are now in that building. The dining hall moved down to the basement of the main building some years ago, and a library is now where our old dining room was. Last year we happened to visit on the day the Junior School Musical production had its first showing – revived after 25 years I understand. It was called 'The Magic Basket' and was quite delightful. Mrs. Murray would have been proud. I think Mr. Wharton was, and rightly so. The music was very good, and the children were charming in their colourful costumes, all singing in tune. We really did enjoy it.

The outlying old Darjeeling cottages, that housed staff, are all in need of repair. They are treasures really and it is a shame they have not been able to be kept up. Some years ago, I had suggested that if places like Aileena and it's adjacent house could be restored Hermonite parents/visitors could rent the places, bringing revenue into the school, and keeping the properties in good repair. However, the logistics, money to do this etc., is always the issue. I am sure we all have ideas of where any fundraising monies could be spent, but the most difficult part is the management that end of the funds and how they are spent.

We also met Rev. Noel Prabhuraj, the Vice Chairman/Secretary, on this trip and he was the person who brought us up to speed on the situation with the insurance company. We also talked about staff, and the question of foreign staff came up. As I suppose work permits are difficult and paying a foreign staff salary would also be difficult, if people wanted to volunteer to come and teach with simply board and lodging the school would be happy to welcome the help.

Sushil, Shiv, Saroj, Cindy and Pradip at Shiv's place in Siliguri.

We took the car back up to town and met my father along with several other people in Glenary's, before driving down the hill to the Dooars, to spend a few days on a tea garden, owned by a Paulite. A wonderful, restful time, in a lovely climate, with superb garden food – taking one back to days gone past. We sat on the lawn watching beautiful birds flit through the trees, listening to the Gauhati train as it chugged through the garden, drinking excellent CTC tea, and being spoilt.

We managed to meet another Hermonite, Shiv Saria, on his garden, Soongachi, and he was most hospitable. After mouth-watering momos, we had a delicious vegetarian lunch, and then we drove around parts of the garden seeing how he had brought up inhospitable areas, learning about irrigation techniques and generally enjoying the beautiful tea garden scenery. I knew a classmate of mine, Beverley Mackie, had spent some time on Kumlai garden, which was very close by. Shiv kindly got in touch with the current Manager, and we went to visit it. The old bungalow they would have lived in was still very much in use, and I took a lot of photos to send Beverley. What I hadn't realised was they had also lived at Soongachi! After four days in the Dooars we returned to Calcutta and our seventeen-day trip with my father was at an end. He returned to Ireland, and we went on to Goa for a short break.

I hope this will have taken you back to times at school and memories of Darjeeling. Of course, much has changed, but our love of school, and the friendships we made there, will always be close to our hearts.

"The only way forward is to have a single united body of alumni"

We need people at the helm that everyone feels confident with and can trust: Cindy

In her report for the Old Mount Hermon Students Association (OMHSS) for the year 2016-17, Cindy Gibbs, Hon, Secretary of the alumni organisation, points out the only way forward for Mt. Hermon School is to seek the help and involvement of a united body of the alumni.

Dear Members,

I am quite late this year (2016-17) in getting the newsletter written. My apologies.

Once again we visited India, this year in March, travelling with a classmate of mine, Margaret Mapley Jackson and her husband, Nigel. Margaret's father, Jeffrey Mapley, had run the Maintenance Department at Mount Hermon from around 1959-71, and her mother, Rachel, ran Ailina Guest House. Margaret had not been back to India since they left in 1971 so we decided we would make this exciting trip back together. I am leaving the bulk of the Newsletter for her story of the trip.

My up-to-date information on the school is slightly sketchy but this is what I have been told, or have seen myself. When we visited this year we found that the girls who were boarding,

Cindy with Pradip and Uttam Pradhan in Gangtok.

had been moved out of the 'new' Millennium building back into the main building, and all were housed in the newly-painted, and renovated senior girls dormitories. They were looking lovely. Apparently, the Millennium building was leaking, and needed repairs. The main corridor in the Main Building downstairs had been repaired (after the cracks appeared after the earthquake), and repainted and was looking excellent. As for the renovation and contributions, Sarthak Pradhan played an important part in getting permission from the school authority allowing the renovation work to be carried out. I think they were responsible for three classrooms being repaired and the major cracks being repaired around the corridor.

We met with the current Administrator, Mr. Norton Emmanuel. As I write there still is no Principal. Mr. Emmanuel visits from time to time from his school, where he is Principal, The Methodist School, Dankuni in West Bengal. Mr. Emmanuel greeted us warmly and we discussed the situation at the school. At the time there were more boarders and day scholars than there are today. I was recently told there are only 80 boarders and 120 day students. We heard some boy students had had to be expelled for disciplinary reasons. Therefore, with so few students money continues to be a huge problem. Some classes have taken it upon themselves to renovate their own old class, and collected the money from their classmates for the renovation. This was welcomed. However, this is not really a long-term solution.

It was felt by some that a clear cut, independent, report on the school needs to be done. Mr. Emmanuel has been approached and if this is agreed things can then move forward. There are many different alumni groups, and it is all rather disjointed. Many now feel an apathy towards the school, as in the past their offers of help, or being involved have not been taken up. Possibly the only way forward is to have a single united body of alumni, but I'm not sure where this should be based. Ideally in India, I would imagine. However, what we really need is to see where all the problems lie within the school and goals set to remedy the issues and take it forward. Then people can be approached to help financially when a clear cut solution is on the table. We will then need people at the helm that everyone feels confident with and feels they can trust.

There is a huge Mount Hermon Reunion being organised by the Thai alumni in Bangkok and Pattaya, December 15-18. So far there seem to be around 277 people going - that includes Hermonites, and their families. We are hoping that the issue of Mount Hermon's plight will be raised, but we shall have to wait and see what may come of it. They have indicated there will be a slot to discuss the situation the school is in, so let's keep our fingers crossed.

As and when we do hear more news we shall try and keep everyone updated.

With warm regards to everyone.

Cindy Gibbs

75 Friends Are Forever

Ronen, James And Menno

Menno Ziessen, Ronen Ghose and James Sinclair in London, 2012.

Ronen and wife Rita in London.

"I do believe I am the founder of the Hermonites Association in the mid-sixties as I discussed such an association with Mr. Murray in Darjeeling on a visit to school and he gave me the go ahead to do so. Mr. Murray would inform me well in advance of his arrival and I would muster together whoever I could to come to the Methodist Church Hall on Lower Circular Road. I got Trincas to cater and Murray paid me to sort out. However, this was sporadic and it is good to see a proper nucleus is now in operation," says 1950s Hermonite, Ronen Ghose, originally from Calcutta, now living in London with his family, which includes his son, Ronobir, also a Hermonite.

In more than one way, Ronen is the archetype Hermonite – frank (often brash), friendly, a go-getter, spontaneous, generous and passionate. Back in the 1970s (I think), in one of the reunions, when some Hermonites from Calcutta attended the function, I heard someone say, "Money can't buy Mt. Hermon!" I think that person was Ronen, who loves to talk about his Hermonite friend, Menno Ziessen, one of the few Hermonite icons of his days.

Ronen and Nat

Ronen Ghose & Nat Indrapana going out to open the innings for Mount Hermon - May 1959 at St. Paul's, Darjeeling.

OBITUARY

IOC pays tribute to late member Nat

Long-serving International Olympic Committee member Nat Indrapana passed away yesterday after a long battle with cancer. He was 80.

Dr Nat died peacefully at Bangkok's Siriraj hospital, said Khunying Patama Leeswadtrakul, Thailand's other IOC member.

The IOC is deeply saddened by his death, its president Thomas Bach said.

In honour of Nat, who became IOC member in 1990, the Olympic flag at the organisation's headquarters in Lausanne is being flown at half-mast for three days.

"With the death of Nat Indrapana, the IOC loses a true gentleman of sports. With his outstanding gentleness he made many friends around the world, including me. Over the years of his membership, Nat contributed greatly to the Olympic Movement and the protection of its values. For this, he mobilised all his personal forces to serve the IOC even while fighting his serious disease. We will all miss him greatly," Bach said in a statement.

"The IOC expresses its deepest sympathy to his family."

With a strong academic background, Nat was a key figure in the development of sports in Thailand and Asia, holding numerous positions within sports organisations in his country and continent.

He was deputy minister of Thailand's Tourism and Sports Ministry, president of the Asian Trap and Skeet Shooting Federation, member of the Asian Games Federation and Olympic Council of Asia, vice president of the World Taekwondo Federation, and executive member of the National Olympic Committee of Thailand, among several other positions.

Patama said: "I am sure that following his long illness it is a blessing that he no longer suffered.

"Like many of you, Nat Indrapana was a man I admire dearly. Few people can be as productive as he was throughout his life."

Late IOC member Nat Indrapana.

Ronen Ghose and Sri Krishna Day – MH 1958 (photo taken in Dr. Graham's Homes, Kalimpong when the school opera, *HMS Pinafore,* was staged there.)

"In any generation and in any school you have certain individuals who stand out above the rest. Menno was one such individual," says Ronen. He then adds, "May be, I too stood out for my acting and voice as I was in the school choir and brought the house down in Darjeeling district acting as Sir Joseph Porter KCB in *HMS Pinafore, Gilbert and Sullivan*, in April-May 1959. But Menno was towering and was liked and disliked. We did just about tolerate one another in school. But in England all that changed and I feel he realised that friendship was more important than envy."

Emma Burns was Menno's partner and they lived in London in her fabulous apartment. Menno died of cancer on October 8, 2012.

Ronnen goes on to say, "He did tell me he had cancer but never told me what type. He was born in Calcutta in 1942. His father was a wealthy businessman from Holland and his mother an Anglo Indian. He was in Mount Hermon from the age of 5 till 16 and left school in 1959 under Boss and Mr. Murray's regime."

(L to R): Ronen Ghose, Emma, Cyrus Ruttonshaw, Menno Ziessen, Jim Sinclair and Freddie Ruttonshaw during a small gathering of MHS friends at the Il Portico Italian Restaurant, Kensington High Street, London on September 1, 2012.

In a message posted in UK alumni's website, James Sinclair has this to say: "It is with deep sadness that I have to announce the death from cancer of my dear classmate, Menno

Ziessen, on 8th October 2012. I had met up with Menno and some other MHS friends in London on the 1st September, and he seemed very cheery and full of life on that occasion. Sadly we did not know that time would be so short for him. Menno was at Mount Hermon from 1947 to 1959. He attended some of our Reunions in London in recent years, and was a very supportive member of OMHSA. He will be sadly missed."

Incidentally, Ronen was one of the first to open his heart and hands when we floated the idea of starting a 'Hermonite school' after we received no response from the school authorities to revive a dying institution. Ronen offered his land in Mirik, West Bengal, to help build the school. Unfortunately, due to procedural problems – as is the way in India – we could not takeover the land. Better luck next time but thanks anyway, Ronen.

Menno Ziessen's 'Journey Across India'

Extract from "The Turquoise Mountain," By Brian Blessed

For instance, a voice-over for a British Steel advertisement took me to the Saunders & Gordon recording studios in London's West End. In charge of the ad was a charming young man from British Steel named Menno Ziessen. As I looked up he softly began to sing:

Down from Old Mount Herman, on the small Toy Train,
After nine months mugging, back home again,
Teachers are so rosey, children are the same,
Everyone is happy, waiting for the train
Ghoom, Sonada, Kurseiong, are all left behind,
Though the journey's very long, I'm sure we do not mind,
When we reach Sealdah, hail it with a shout,
Pan Beeri cigarette, hop the bloomy out.

'Good God!' I exclaimed. 'That song is about the "Toy Train" that travels backwards and forwards from Siliguri to Darjeeling in India.'

'Yes. You are right,' said Menno. 'And I travelled in my childhood many times to school in Darjeeling, and that is the traditional song of the "Toy Train" that we sang on our journey.'

'But this is a million to one,' I said. 'I mean, me being here with you, who went to school on this unique little train. It's absolutely amazing! You do realize I'm going to Everest in the footsteps of the twenties expeditions, and this is exactly the train they took!'

Menno laughed loudly at this, and begged me to try and get him on the expedition. I was completely nonplussed.

Back: Benu Chatterjee, Nat Indrapana, Ronen Ghose, Noel Long, Akbar Sadique, Cyrus Ruttonsha, Aulis Aho, Kishore Gandhi, Ho Shan Ying. Middle: Somkiat Gantanant, Menno Ziessen, Gordon Whyte, Anup Banerjee, Ram Bahadur, Suraphat Krisadaphong, Lim Hong Tatt. Front: Lynda Martin, Chhanda Datta, Rev. D. Stewart, Mr. M. Mathai, Rosalind Thutyakul, Anne Hunt, Nilima Raichoudhury.

Ronen Ghose and Cyrus Ruttonshaw with Menno Ziessen (seated).

76 Canada
My Return To India

Margaret (Mapley) Jackson

In 2016, Margaret Mapley took a walk down memory lane after 45 years and recalls her fond memories of her birthplace and alma mater.

Margaret, Nigel, Pradip and Cindy in Gangtok, 2016.

My Return To India

My return to Darjeeling, my birth place, took 45 years! It was bitter sweet, an emotional rollercoaster. My memories of India were those of a 12 ½ year old, aware of what was of interest to me as I tagged along behind my parents! I have wanted to make this trip for a very long time, as I still consider Darjeeling 'home'. I wanted to create memories as an adult.

My husband Nigel and I flew into Delhi, where we met our friends Lucinda and Pradip Verma. A side trip to Agra to see the Taj Mahal was not negotiable, as was the tour to see the Qutub Minar, the Bahai Lotus Temple, the Birla Temple, and Humayun's Tomb. I really have no memories of Delhi, but the Taj lived up to what I remember it to be – magnificent. One thing that stuck out for us was the incessant horn honking! Nigel shared with our tour driver that he had whiskers like a cat – that even though traffic was crazy, he knew exactly where the surrounding vehicles were. We shared some time with another Hermonite, the 'Queen of Delhi', Anita! She cleared her schedule to spend time with us and to help us find things that were on our 'to buy' lists!

I had the best seat on the plane as we flew to Bagdogra – the Himalayan Range was on my left almost the whole flight! The drive up the hills to Darjeeling was an experience my husband has never had – windy, narrow roads, and all the switchbacks! I remember riding the train up and down from Darjeeling to the plains, maybe the only time we drove by Jeep was when we left in May 1971. It was hard to recognize for the most part, as the roadsides are now mostly built up and inhabited. When we travelled by train, there was wide open space, hills to one side and the drop to valleys below on the other.

The shell or skeleton of Darjeeling is still the same – the roads up and down from the Chowrasta to the New Dish, the Mall to the Himalayan Mountaineering Institute. Das Studio, Keventers, Glenarys. BUT, it is so built up – the hillside from the Planter's Hospital to the Chowrasta now covered with structures. It was very hazy for the time we were in Darjeeling, so a clear view of the Kanchenjunga Range was elusive – even from Tiger Hill! I remember the walk from MH to Tiger Hill when we raised funds for the floods in Bangladesh, but the look-out is nothing like it used to be – a building is half taken down and rebar sticks up in many places. I tried to walk as many places as I remember walking with my Father – the Himalayan Mountaineering Institute to see the display of Tenzing and Hillary's gear from their first climb to the top of Mt. Everest, around the Mall, to

Glenary's for tea. Nigel and I went for a 'joy ride' on the Toy Train, to Ghoom and back. It too seemed to be much smaller than my childhood memory!

Beloved Mount Hermon – what more can I say! It was great to walk once again in the halls, up the steps to the 'hospital', up the path to the top field, out the school gates and home to Ailina. I had been warned by many that it was in bad shape, and I thought I was prepared, but I don't think anyone could have said anything more to prepare me for the state it is in. It was exciting to walk through 'Wayside' where we lived, telling everyone where things were when we lived there (the bedrooms, the add-on Dad built, the bathroom, the hiding spot in the chimney enclosure).

Everyone was surprised that I could recall it all so vividly. It is sad that many structures at MH have not been regularly maintained – the staff cottages below the playing field, the hospital, the classrooms, the chapel. We were able to go up to the junior girl's dormitory (although they are not in use at this time due to lack of enrollment), and were taken round the dorms that are in use now (senior girl's dorm being one now in use again). It was amazing to see the same lockers and cupboards that were in use in the senior girl's dorm – my Dad built those! It was funny to walk beside the concrete water towers above the hospital – I am sure they were 50 feet tall when I went with Dad to check on the water levels! I was struck with how small things are in reality – when I was younger, it seemed like a long walk from school to Ailina, the yard in front of the study hall (where there used to be a BIG tree) is really not very big!

It was a fluke that we were actually in Darjeeling for Mount Hermon's 121st birthday! Pradip, Cindy, Nigel, Thangi, Sarthak and I met with Mr. Emanuel on March 10th to talk about concerns, and we were invited back for Chapel celebrations the next morning. Unfortunately, Cindy and Pradip both were ill, so Nigel, Thangi and I went back for Chapel. We were invited to speak to the students and share our thoughts as alumni. I wish I had known ahead of time that we would be called on, as my thoughts were whipped together in a matter of 5 seconds and I feel I could have been more eloquent if I had planned it out beforehand!

We stayed with Shiv Saria in Siliguri for a night before our flight to Kolkata. It was great to share a meal with some fellow Hermonites, one classmate, Narendra Saraogi! Nigel, Pradip, and I joined Shiv for his morning walk. Nigel sure got to see what happens on the streets on a normal day – a family of pigs hoofing it down the median, a Holy Cow laying in the waste from the stalls chewing its cud. Shiv's complex was like an oasis in the middle of it all!

We stayed in Kolkata for a couple of nights at the Grand before Nigel flew home to Canada. Once again, I was struck with the contrast between what lay inside the walls and what was on the outside. This is truly a beautiful colonial building that has been well maintained. I don't have many memories of places in Kolkata, but the activity on the streets was familiar. Another Hermonite friend, Betty, opened her home for visits and cleared her days to make sure I found a saree! She had connections to get my saree blouse made in 2 days! We joked about Betty being the "Queen of Kolkata."

Lucinda, Pradip and I took the train to Maheshgunj for a couple of days. We stayed at a beautiful colonial plantation home. It was on an indigo plantation many years ago. It was interesting to see another part of life in rural India.

The three of us went on to Bangkok to visit some of our Thai classmates. I stayed with Kuruvin and her husband. We were taken out for a wonderful Thai meal with the group, and shared many memories and laughs! This was the first time that I had seen my classmates in 45 years!

There is such a contrast in India - people who are employed and live well, and others who rely on the local water spigots on street corners for their morning showers. Beautiful colonial buildings, some clean and well-kept while others right beside them are in ruins. I must say that it still tugs at my heart! It was great to finally see what I left behind – what was my whole world, the only place I had ever known as home. Whenever we watch movies about India, Nigel always asked "Is that really how it is?" Now he knows – the beauty and the filth, the busy cities and the slow-paced villages, the advanced and the behind times. All of it somehow manages to work side by side and creates the country that it is – my home.

GLOBAL HERMONITES – Part X

77 'MH Revival' Campaign 2012

Hail Mount Hermon!

When many of us realised that our school was gradually going 'down the drain', due to many reasons, we decided to do something about it. The downhill slide began soon after Mr. Johnston's retirement from principalship (1979-1989). In response to our (Hermonites) concern the school's Managing Committee appointed Mr. George Fernandes, a senior member of the staff, as Principal around 1999-2000. When Fernandes's tenure was nearing its end the Hermonites, including ex-teachers and principals, made an appeal to the school authorities, including the Chairman of the Managing Committee, to appoint me (Jigme N. Kazi) as the next Principal. For more than a year in 2011-2012, Hermonites from all over the world appealed to the school authorities to appoint a capable Hermonite to lead the school during its trouble times.

The endeavours of Hermonites led by Roslyn (Rongong) Namgyal (Australia), Shiv Saria (India), and Deepak Mirchandhani and Lucinda Gibbs (UK) and other active Hermonites for the 'MH Revival' campaign in 2012 and thereafter have been documented as a record of how Hermonites from all over the world and ages expressed their concern for their alma mater. Their hopes and aspirations for their beloved school is a unique and an eloquent testimony of their love and loyalty to MH.

HAIL TO THE HERMON-KNIGHTS
"We Shall Overcome"

Dear Hermonites,

First of all on behalf of the alumni let me wish our beloved alma mater Mount Hermon School and all Hermonites everywhere a very Happy Birthday! Today it is MHS's 117th Birthday.

Ever since the first week of the New Year (2012), when the Sikkim Hermonites Association (SHA) took the initiative to involve all Hermonites to campaign for 'MH Revival', there has been an overwhelming response from the alumni of all ages and places on the school's future. The concern for our beloved alma mater – Mount Hermon School (MHS) – from Hermonites of the '30s, '40s, '50s, '60s, '70s, '80s, '90s and right down to the present generation is not only very encouraging but also very inspiring. This is great! Which school in the world can boast of the 'Hermonite spirit'? Hardly any. It is, therefore, our honourable duty to preserve this rich and unique heritage of MHS.

Barry Ison – former MH student and teacher – once explained this unique phenomenon: "It is not emotion; it is passion."

In the past so many decades since I left the old and friendly walls I never failed to think and even dream of MH! This is but natural for all Hermonites but more so for a person like me who did his schooling (1963-1972), Teachers Training College (TTC – 1974-1975), and even taught at MH for four years (1976-1979).

Ex-students of the school under Rev. Mr. D.G. Stewart, who not only revived MH when he took over in 1953 but actually placed it among one of the best boarding schools in India – MH was on top of the list in 1961-62 – are still showing great concern for the school. This is amazing and an inspiration to us all.

"We Shall Overcome"

Ever since its inception in 1895 when the school (then called Arcadia or housed in Arcadia cottage, located on the Lebong side of Chowrasta in Darjeeling) was born MH has had its ups and downs. But we pulled it through. With faith in God and missionary zeal our founders – Miss Knowles, Miss Stahl, Mr. Dewey and Bishop Fisher – made sure that failures and obstacles were stepping stones to success.

After shifting the school from near Chowrasta to above the railway station in Darjeeling and calling it Queen's Hill School the school grew in leaps and bounds leading to the acquisition of the present premises for further expansion.

Fifteen years after the school was renamed Mount Hermon School in 1929-30 MH almost closed down due to dwindling enrolment. The cause of this was the Second World War when many of its foreign students and staff members of the school left MH. It was Mr. Dewey, Bishop Fisher and finally Mr. Stewart who helped MH to pull through the crisis and regain its past glory. Mr. Graeme A. Murray, who stepped into Rev. Stewart's shoes in 1964, built on the foundation laid by his predecessors. There was no looking back for MH after Mr. Murray's takeover.

However, in the 1980s MH and many schools in the hills passed through a very difficult and trying period due to uncertain political situation in Darjeeling. But Rev. Mr. John Johnston from Australia and later Mr. Jeff Gardner (India) kept the school going. Thereafter, MH faced a crisis of another sort as those who headed the school stayed only for a brief period.

The present Principal Mr. George Fernandes, who worked under Mr. Murray, Mr. Johnston and Mr. Gardner and who is also married to an ex-Hermonite (Saroj Pradhan), was able to stabilize the situation when he took over in 2000-1. We are, therefore, grateful to Mr. Fernandes for his contributions to the school.

Hermonites all over the world have expressed their apprehension of MH's future after Mr. Fernandes retires this month. Damages caused by the recent (Sept 18, 2011) earthquake to the main school building and falling enrolment, coupled with Mr. Fernandes' departure and doubts over who is to step into his shoes, have prompted Hermonites to play a leading role in the choice of the next Principal.

Hermonites now want an able and trustworthy Hermonite to head the school during this very trying period. They have backed Mr. Jigme N. Kazi's (Sikkim) candidature for the post and want the Managing Committee to appoint him as the next Principal.

MH Revival

Several names were floated for the post of MH Principal last year. However, during Mr. and Mrs. Johnston's visit to Darjeeling and Sikkim in December – January 2012 it was revealed that though Mr. Barry Ison, Mr. John Glasby and Mr. and Mrs. Sherab (Roslyn) Namgyal – all ex-students and teachers of the school – were willing to help the school they would not be able to take the top job at the present juncture. Mr. Kazi's name was then proposed and the Sikkim Hermonites Association (SHA) passed a resolution on this and urged all Hermonites to support his candidature and other resolutions on 'MH Revival'. Sherab and Roslyn (SC 1972 & 1971), who were on a visit to Sikkim from Australia during this period, supported this move.

One of the suggestions of the Hermonites is to have at least two active and credible Hermonites in the Managing Committee, which not only frames policy matters of the school but also appoints the Principal. Two other suggestions made by the Sikkim chapter and endorsed by global Hermonites was allotment of a space for the alumni to function from the school premises and also to route all Hermonites-initiated projects and funds of the school through Hermonites International (Hi!), a global body conceived during the centenary celebrations in 1995, when many ex-principals and teachers and students were present, and formed in 2005-6.

No matter what the future holds for MH the resolution on 'MH Revival' must go on. It must not begin or end if and when Mr. Kazi gets the top job. The campaign for MH Revival is led by Roslyn & Sherab (Australia), Dipak Mirchandhani and Lucinda Gibbs (UK) and Shiv Saria (India). They are being assisted by a group of active and concerned Hermonites from all over the world.

The Methodist Bishop, who resides in Bangalore and who is temporarily the Chairman of the Managing Committee of the school, has been briefed on the prevailing situation. We are eagerly awaiting his response to our proposals. However, irrespective of what the Managing Committee decides on MH's future the campaign for MH Revival must go on. The present crisis has motivated us into action. This is a good thing and must go on.

We must say and sing the hymn "We Shall Overcome" and mean it and show the world that we can triumph over all our trials and tribulations.

They may succeed in taking a Hermonite out of Mount Hermon, but they will never succeed in taking Mount Hermon out of a Hermonite!

We must continue to believe that the Almighty is on our side and that He has a great future for MH and that while the past has been great and small the best is yet to come!

Hail Mount Hermon! And Happy Birthday to MH and All Hermonites!

(Jigme N. Kazi)
President
Hermonites International (Hi!)

Email: jigmekazi@gmail.com
+9434630097
Gangtok, Sikkim
March 11, 2012
(see my blog: jigmenkazisikkim.blogspot.com)

The Awakening: Future of Mount Hermon

December 2011

From: barry ison <barrydison@hotmail.com>
Date: 6 December 2011
Subject: RE: Johnston Visit | Reunion 05/01/2012
To: Sujit Kumar MHS <sujitskumar@gmail.com>
My Dear Friend,

I would love to be at the Johnston's dinner .... but a thought!! If as much effort went into trying to get a friendly new MH principal (I am available but I am too old) - then MH would have a secure future.

What do you think? Surely MH in Calcutta has enough clout to pressure the Board (or give them death threats if necessary) to make sure our wonderful experiences growing up and learning in MH will be sustainable?

I'm so pissed off at hearing time and again about the corrupt Board ... guys not do anything about it. I can see the next principal tearing down our beloved building and putting up a concrete brick monstrosity - and once it has been done - what then? 'Fait accompli' - a la Gillson .... we will be lower than a busti school!! ... and there will be no turning back!

I know we can't say much as our Dhaka alumni is rather non-existent - but there are 3/4 of us who would commit Banzai - to make it happen - but of course we can't because we are in the wrong country. Corruption will turn our amazing historical heritage into garbage! We really need to do something now and you guys in Cal, Siliguri and Gangtok are the ones to do it ... whatever I can do - just ask and I'll come with all my 'aggression and logic' to help make a positive change take place.

With an earthquake-wrecked building, an imminent new principal - we Hermonites are in a position where we have to do something urgently - or else all we will be able to say is "oh me oh my" like Eh Aw - I can't emphasize enough that if we do not do something urgently and really mobilize some dialogue with the Methodist Church - then all we have held dear in terms of what MH has meant (and still does) and hopefully will in the future - will simply die!! I mean really die!!!!!! I have lived in this part of the world to know when urgency becomes a necessity.

Please pass this around - because it is very very urgent.

My very best to all my MH colleagues - we are a great family!!!

Barry

From: barry ison <barrydison@hotmail.com>
To: Bijay Hermonite <bpalriwala@yahoo.com>
Sent: Friday, 9 December 2011
Subject: RE: [HERMONITES50s60s] Fwd: Johnston Visit | Reunion 05/01/2012

Hi Bijay,

I'm sending you a copy of an email I just sent to Tammy and Sujit. Let me know what you think and whether you would want to be involved and to mobilise people and other resources to make a convention/conference happen? Because that I think is the first thing we need to do to get everyone on board and working in the same direction.

Here it is:

"I agree with you Tammy - about the re-hashing. Last night I dreamt about MH and saw many faces old and current and on waking I spent a lot of time thinking about MH. There have been many alumni meetings and a lot of suggestions and a lot of words - and some plans.

I think the earthquake and the damage and the likelihood that some irresponsible person(s) may think about tearing the whole building down - has energised me to consider the whole MH set up.

Its a school and a teacher's college and has a massive estate with all kinds of potentials like a conference centre, a seminar, tourism, and guest houses for alumni and parents, botanical gardens, etc. etc. But at the moment it is simply crumbling because the main players - both the Board and the power brokers of the Methodist Church are not in Darjeeling and therefore do not see its potential and have no real feelings one way or another about the place.

We the alumni do - but we are scattered and busy with our own lives and therefore we simply continue talking.

When we consider the world-wide interest through ex-students - the numbers are significant. And I am sure the resources for doing something in terms of developing MH's full potential is also significant.

So what to do?

MH cannot be handled simply by one Principal. It needs an academic head - say a Superintendent to look after the academic side; it needs a building supervisor for repairs, renovations and new projects; it needs a chef to supervise the kitchen and not simply serve the slop that even we had to put up with; it needs an estate manager (perhaps an ex-Gurkha officer) to come to terms with its neighboring community and consolidate the estate; it needs a Counsellor to work with students and teachers in terms of personal needs and professional development; it needs a high quality medical team (like Sister Digby) .... and so on.

Now how can this happen?

Somehow the Methodist Church of India needs to become aware of the potential of MH and its estate and its program - perhaps also a representative from the Methodist Church of the US. Once they can see the potential they may buy into the development of a short term repair and renovation plan as well as a long term development plan.

I have just returned from Washington DC where I attended a Social Studies conference (it was the National annual SS conference) - and was excellent and productive and inspiring.

I would recommend that such a conference be planned and held and representatives come from all over the world - we have UK, US, Australia, NZ, Kolkata, Siliguri, Sikkim, Thailand, Bhutan, Nepal, Delhi and Darjeeling - to mention a few. It would take maybe a year to plan such an event if it was to be done properly. We would need a liaison person from each of the places mentioned - and include the Methodist Church of North India and the US - with the end product being a plan and a commitment to go ahead and make MH a great centre of learning.

I would think the Johnstons would be keen coordinators in Australia along with the Canberra contingent; Mr. Stewart and the Murray family (Adrienne etc), and John Eade for NZ. You for the US, Sujit for Kolkata - and so on.

I have a ton of ideas as to what MH could become and as I have been a student, teacher and a parent in MH (you know my ward recently passed out from year 12 as School Captain, prefect etc etc - and is now in University here in Dhaka), I'm still a teacher at the American school, I run a business including the contract for catering at the American school - and so on!! So I would be happy to help.

But first we need a gathering, a commitment and a plan. Then we mobilise the (I'm sure) many resources that our MH community could offer.

I am at the stage where I could do this part time or full time - because I really think that now (with the damage and Mr. Fernandez's imminent departure and a new Bishop in the wings - and all kinds of changes that could effect MH and its future) is the time we who have been talking and planning could do something practical and meaningful. But we need to get everyone on board.

What do you and Sujit think and what next? Do you think this idea would work or are there too many obstacles?"

Cheers Bijay

Date: Tue, 6 Dec 2011
From: bpalriwala@yahoo.com
Barry,

I think that's a great idea (finding a new Principal!) and I would be willing to do everything I can to make it happen, so I will wait for your (or anyone else's) suggestion(s) for how to go about it and what, keeping in mind that I currently live in London.

May I suggest some candidates besides yourself: Ranjit Dasgupta, Alka Ganesh (nee Sinha), Ronen Ghosh, Roger Griffiths, Cherry Hall (nee Williams), Sujit, Prabir Manna, Alan Mills, Pradip Nath, Anne-Marie Pender (nee Stevels), Andrea Porter (nee Phillips), Mahendra Prasad, Pratap Rai, Anjali Sengupta (nee Kundu), Anwar Sheikh (Mohammed), Dipkantha Sinharoy, Namlha Namgyal (nee Tsarong), Menno Ziessen, Mr. Darr, Miss Hawke. I have not sought approval/of any of the previously listed people!
Bijay

From: Sujit Kumar <sujitskumar@gmail.com>
To: HERMONITES50s60s <HERMONITES50s60s@yahoogroups.com>
Cc: Namlha <namgyaltaklha@gmail.com>; Humayun Kamal <kamalhumayun@hotmail.com>; Virginia Wenzel <virginiawenzel@wasteresources.com.au>; Shanta <shantamathai@hotmail.com>; Dipak Dutta <hi_dipak_dd@yahoo.co.in>; Iqbal <hayatexp@gmail.com>; Dibyendu Banerjee <dibyendubanerjee57@yahoo.com>
Sent: Tuesday, 6 December 2011
Subject: [HERMONITES50s60s] Fwd: Johnston Visit | Reunion 05/01/2012

Thanks Barry ... most of us are aware of what you have said; these coupled to political innuendos have added to the woes and raised the bar of difficulty.

Nevertheless, I shall bring it up in our next Alumni meeting.
wkr
Sujit.

From: Namgyal Taklha <namgyaltaklha@gmail.com>
To: bijay palriwala <bpalriwala@yahoo.com>
Cc: Sujit Kumar <sujitskumar@gmail.com>
Sent: Monday, 12 December 2011
Subject: Re: FUTURE OF MOUNT HERMON!!
Dear Bijay and Sujit,

I am really sad to read about the reality of Mt. Hermon at present. About 4 or 5 years back my sister Norzin and I visited MH with our brother, Jigme who was at North Point. We did not stay too long as the Principal was out and we did not have much time, but it looked ok.

North Point was blooming and I believe the Rector, an ex-NP from Bhutan made all the difference. As the Gurkhaland movement is still simmering, I think Roslyn having close touch with that area of the world, I think she would be very suitable. To be a principal is one thing, but to have some loyalty to the school and working amicably with the local government and the people side by side is very important.

With the right principal and a strong, transparent board who cares of the school (maybe some ex-Hermonites from W. Bengal and Sikkim can be on the Board) then I am sure getting funds would not be a problem.

Hoping a good solution of a school which has meant so much to so many of us.
Namgyal (Namlha Tsarong class 61)

From: Ron at minibus2000 <ron@minibus2000.co.uk>
Dear Menno,
   I do not know whether you are aware of the grave situation of our old school in its present physical condition. I do not know what the financial situation is. Evidently, the condition of the school building is dire and something will have to be done. Barry Ison is quite upset and rightly so. I wonder what are the views of Mr. Fernandez? Perhaps he could throw some light on the subject.
   There is vast potential with the school provided there is sound planning and the Methodist Big Bosses are taken on board. I would appreciate your constructive ideas please.
Ronen

Hi Barry,
   Thanks for the time you have taken and effort you have made with respect to trying to "revive" old MH and its (mis)fortunes.
   I am in agreement with most of (if not all) the concerns and issues you have raised and/or addressed in your email. All I will say (write) at this time is "I am ready and willing (if not completely able) to do anything and/or take responsibility for anything that is within my capability to at least get a "plan" going and/or implemented. All anyone has to do is tell/ask me!
   I am copying this to ALL HERMONITES whose email(s) I have with the hope that some will respond with ideas and/or suggestions or even just comments!
   Come on, Hermonites! Your old school needs you NOW!!
Bijay

From: bijay palriwala <bpalriwala@yahoo.com>
Date: 13 December 2011
To: Namgyal Taklha <namgyaltaklha@gmail.com>
Cc: Sujit Kumar <sujitskumar@gmail.com>
   Thanks Namla! It's great and encouraging as more and more people get involved! I'm circulating this to encourage more people to do so!

Ronen,
   Thanks for getting involved and for your input. ONLY COMBINED, SUSTAINED EFFORT CAN HOPE TO IMPROVE THE SITUATON SO I AM HOPING THAT OTHERS WILL JOIN IN THE EFFORT!
Bijay Palriwala
London

From: bijay palriwala <bpalriwala@yahoo.com>
Date: 12 December 2011
To: barry ison <barrydison@hotmail.com>
   Thank you, again, Barry and Ronen! I'm circulating this so hopefully everyone can get to realise the seriousness of the situation and get involved.
Bijay

Sent: Sunday, 11 December 2011
Subject: RE: FUTURE OF MOUNT HERMON!!

Hi Ronen,

Great to hear from you ... I have heard back from you and Bijay and Mr. Logan (I'm not sure you remember him - he is from NZ).

Otherwise I have had an email from Tammy and from Sujit but with no reference to my email.

You may not know, but I became a ward to a Bangladeshi orphan about 6 years ago and sent him to MH. He did a great job and ended up School Captain (though these days they call them Chairman of the prefects) - plus first in class and Cricket Captain etc. So I had many occasions to go to MH.

As you say, the Methodist big bosses must be involved and although the US has given everything to the Methodist Church of North India, I would think they should be involved as well. And ..... its a very comprehensive thing - all aspects need to be covered - including a wide range of management skills which one person would find hard to do. Some teachers are great, but others are appalling. The Teacher's College also needs help - I talked to Mandira and she was very keen on getting professional help.

But we do need a rather universal response from Hermonites who, up to now, have really been keen on reminiscing, digging up old photos and having re-unions. We are going to lose MH if we don't do something serious and soon.

Keep in touch - very best wishes
Barry

Jigme Kazi to Rajendra Lakhotia, Dec 15
Dear Hermonites,

Its good to exchange views and feelings on MH. Within Dec-Jan (2011-2012) we have to come up with a concrete agenda for MH. The visit of Mr. and Mrs. Johnston and Hermonites Sherab and Roslyn (MH 1963-1978 - as students and on the staff) to this area in December would act as a catalyst. We have to take advantage of the situation. I'm ready and eager to do my part.

We need to create our own blog or website on this as many of us don't know or feel lazy to go on Facebook etc. Direct and speedy interaction is needed. A get-together on the issue in Darj or Siliguri or Gangtok would be ideal.

Cheers, Merry Christmas and Hail Mt. Hermon!!
Jigs (Jigme N. Kazi)
Student (1963-1972)
TTC (Teachers Training College at MH) (1974-1975)
MH Teaching Staff (1976-1979)
Dec 2011

Hail Mount Hermon! A Tribute

Dear Mick and Kristine,

First of all, let me wish you all a Merry Christmas and Happy New Year.

I'll be at MH with Namgyal Wangdi (SC 1971) tomorrow at Christmas - we've been invited by our workers there for a Xmas function. We are taking a small contribution from Sikkim Hermonites and some booze to cheer them up.

During my brief talk with Kristine we felt the need to start a website for MH Revival. K was to talk to John on coming back to MH for a year or two to help the school. The present Princi George Fernandes will leave in March next and we desperately need a good man to take over.

Mr. and Mrs. Johnston and Sherab and Roz will be here this month-end and the main topic for discussion will be MH Revival. It would be good to know what you have decided on the matter and share with us at the earliest.

As usual I've been too busy with my newspapers and could not spend much time during your recent visits.

Take care

Jigs

'MH Revival' Campaign 2012

HAIL BIJAY PALRIWALA!

Bijay Palriwala, 1963 batch (!!), who passed away in London in November 2019, was one of the key Hermonites to inspire the Hermonite fraternity to realise the situation at Mt. Hermon and to do something about it. This is what he wrote to Ronen Ghose in the winter of 2011: "Thanks for getting involved and for your input. Only combined, sustained effort can hope to improve the situation so I am hoping that others will join in the effort!"

Bijay (seated) with Rajendra and Kavita Lakhotia and Savita behind him in London, 2019.

The efforts of people like Bijay Palriwala, Ronen Ghose, Barry Ison, Namla Tsarong, Tammy Dalal, Kamal Haque, Sujit Singh etc. - all from the Stewart era - galvanised the global Hermonites into action, leading to "MH Revival" campaign in 2012. Today, Hermonites all over the world are united as never before. Thanks to their guidance and inspiration.

Bijay Palriwala (back row left) with his 1963-64 batchmates.

We are very sorry to hear this very sad news and offer our heartfelt condolences to the bereaved family, including Kavita Lakhotia and her sisters.
Bijay's efforts and hopes will not die in vain. May he rest in peace.

January 2012

WE SHALL OVERCOME!

Inch by inch
Step by step
One day at a time
WE SHALL OVERCOME!

> And so, my fellow Hermonites
> Ask not what Mt. Hermon can do for you
> Ask what you can do for Mt. Hermon!

Jigme N. Kazi, MH (1963-1979), Chairman Emeritus, Hermonite International (Hi!).

The Initiative: Sikkim Hermonites Take The Lead

The Sikkim Hermonites Association (SHA), formed in 1983-84, took the initiative on the issue of "MH Revival" when in January, 2012 it passed a number of resolutions on the subject. SHA President, Karma Bhutia (1972 batch), appealed to all Hermonites to take a serious note of the issues raised during Sikkim Hermonites meet in Gangtok on January 3, 2012, as they have "serious implications on the future of our school."

The appeal is reproduced below:

SIKKIM HERMONITES ASSOCIATION

Jan 4, 2012

Dear Hermonites,

The Sikkim Hermonites Association (SHA) has passed several resolutions on Mt. Hermon School during its meeting held in Gangtok, Sikkim (India), on January 3, 2012. The issues (MH Revival - attached) raised during the meeting have serious implications on the future of our school.

Therefore, kindly take the issues raised and resolutions passed during the meeting seriously and take appropriate action – individually and collectively – at the earliest.

We have tried to inform as many Hermonites as possible on the subjects raised during the meeting. Your feedback on the said matter and help in its circulation is earnestly requested.

As stated in the attachment we would like to request all Hermonites (individuals and alumni bodies) to share your concern and thoughts with concerned authorities on MH's future and any other matters that concern MH.

I'm confidant that with the help of global Hermonites MH will pull through the present crisis and regain its past glory.

Hail Mt. Hermon!
Happy New Year and with all good wishes,
(Karma Bhutia)
President
Sikkim Hermonites Association
Jan 4, 2012

Sikkim Hermonites Association President Karma Bhutia (standing right) with his wife and daughter and Varongthip Lulitanond and Jigme N. Kazi (left) in Gangtok.

MH Revival January 3, 2012

EMERGENCY GENERAL BODY MEETING OF 'SIKKIM HERMONITES ASSOCIATION'

An emergency meeting of the Sikkim Hermonites Association (SHA - established in 1984) was held in Gangtok, Sikkim (India) on January 3, 2012 on the following subjects:

1. Mt. Hermon School figuring at the bottom of boarding schools in India is a cause for concern for all Hermonites. The enrolment of the school has dipped to around 300 from the previous enrolment of about 700.

2. Damages caused to school buildings, including cottages, during the September 18, 2011 earthquake and the gradual encroachment of school premises.

3. Poor maintenance of the school and alleged irregularities in administrative functioning.

4. Search for new Principal of the school as the present Principal Mr. George Fernandes retires at the end of March 2012.

5. The need to have a credible and competent Hermonite as Principal of the school and Hermonite representations in the school's Managing Committee.

6. The need for the Methodist Church of India, which owns the school, to review its policies towards Mt. Hermon School in the light of changing situations.

7. To bring Mt. Hermon School back to its past glory with help of Hermonites all over the world. Hermonites should have a base (office, cottage or a site) at the school premises to help the school in every respect.

After a thorough discussion on the above subjects the Sikkim Hermonites Association passed the following resolutions:-

1. Resolved to propose the name of Mr. Jigme N. Kazi, ex-student, ex-college student (TTC) of Mt. Hermon Undergraduate College of Education, and former teacher of the school as the next Principal of Mt. Hermon School.

2. Resolved to propose that two Hermonites be included in the school's Managing Committee with a view to ensuring that Hermonites are actively involved in the running of the school and framing its policies.

3. Resolved to establish an office for Hermonites at the school premises. It is proposed that the global Hermonites body, Hermonites International (Hi!), conceived during the school's centenary celebrations in 1995 and formed in 2005 under the Presidentship of Mr. Jigme N. Kazi, take up all project works for the school sponsored directly or indirectly by Hermonites on behalf of the Hermonites.

4. Resolved to form a high-level Hermonites panel to probe into various problems faced by the school and its prospects. The panel is to submit its findings by end of January 2012.

5. Resolved to urge all Hermonites organizations, including Hermonites International, to make a thorough study of the above subjects and make representations to the school authorities and the Managing Committee at the earliest.

Members of the Sikkim Hermonites Association raised the above issues with Mr. J. A. Johnston (former Mt. Hermon School Principal and staff) and Mrs. Val Johnston (former MH teacher and TTC lecturer), of Australia and Mr. and Mrs. Sherab Namgyal (Sherab Namgyal and Roslyn Rongong – daughter of late Mrs. Joy Rongong of MH - are former teachers of MH and ex-students of the school. They are now settled in Australia and are active Hermonites there) during their visit to Darjeeling, Kalimpong and Sikkim in December-January 2012.

Representatives of Sikkim Hermonites Association, who attended a Christmas celebration function at the school premises in Darjeeling on December 25, 2011, organized by group D employees of the school, also discussed the issues relating to MH Revival with Nepal and Darjeeling Hermonites in Darjeeling.

(Suresh Sarda)
General Secretary
SIKKIM HERMONITES ASSOCIATION

Members present and endorsing the above resolutions:-

1. NK Pradhan – Minister, Govt of Sikkim
2. OT Bhutia – Ex-Minister, Govt of Sikkim
3. Karma Bhutia – Secretary, Govt of Sikkim
4. Nim Lhamu – Secretary, Govt of Sikkim
5. Tempo Bhutia – Ex-MD, STCS and President, Sikkim Football Association
6. Udai P. Sharma – Ex-Judge, Advocate, Secretary, Rotary Club of Gangtok
7. Jigme N. Kazi – Editor, Sikkim Observer
8. Thentok Lachungpa – Sr. Manager, SBI, Gangtok
9. Uttam Pradhan, Chief Engineer, Govt of Sikkim
10. Ram Gopal Pradhan, Deputy Secy, Govt of Sikkim
11. Punam Agarwal – businessman
12. Suresh Sarda – contractor
13. Kamal Sarda – contractor
14. Namgyal Wangdi - Civil Defence Warden and social worker
15. Arthur Pazo - Photographer and designer
16. Ujjal Gurung – Joint Secretary, Govt of Sikkim
17. Pintso Chopel – businessman
18. Gyurmed Yousal – MD, SITCO
19. Shuva Pradhan – social worker
20. Tashi Densapa – Director, Namgyal Institute of Tibetology, ex-Secretary, Govt of Sikkim
21. Tenpa Lachenpa – contractor
22. Tsetop Ragasha – businessman
23. Ramesh Lakhotia – businessman
24. Karma Thinley – businessman
25. Sonam Shengdarpa – senior bank official, SBI
26. B. Thapa, Inspector General of Police (IGP)

The Sikkim Hermonites Association and Hermonites International are two alumni organisations of Mt. Hermon School, Darjeeling, which is owned by the Methodist Church.

We would like to make a representation to the Managing Committee of the school on matters regarding Mt. Hermon. We would be most grateful if you could kindly provide us with the names and addresses, including email addresses and phone nos, of the school's Managing Committee members, including the Chairman. Most of them reside in Calcutta.

Many thanks,

(Karma Bhutia)

President, Sikkim Hermonites Association

Secretary, Govt of Sikkim

Hermonites back Jigme Kazi for post of Mt. Hermon School Principal

Gangtok, Jan 7: Author and journalist Jigme N. Kazi is likely to say "yes" if he is asked to be the next Principal of his alma mater Mount Hermon School, Darjeeling.

George Fernandes, the present Principal of the school, retires in March 2012 and Hermonites all over the world want a "Hermonite" to head the school to pull through this very difficult period for the school.

The Sikkim Hermonites Association headed by Karma Bhutia, presently Secretary, Sports Department, has urged global Hermonite fraternity to support Kazi's candidature. The Association has passed a resolution urging the authorities to make Kazi the next Principal of the school and also to nominate two Hermonites in the school's Managing Committee, which not only appoints the principal but also frames all policies of the school.

While most alumni bodies in India and abroad are likely to back Kazi's candidature the decision to appoint the new principal lies with the Committee, whose members belong to the Methodist Church of India.

Kazi not only did his schooling in Mt. Hermon he also did his teachers' training at the school and also taught there for four years.

Prominent among the former principals who are likely to back Kazi are Rev. DG Stewart, Mr. GA Murray (New Zealand), Rev JA Johnston (Australia) and Mr. Jeff Gardner (India). Apart from ex-students of the school Kazi will also have the backing of influential former teachers of the school.

While Kazi edits two English weeklies owned by him, *Sikkim Observer* and *Himalayan Guardian*, his wife TT Namgyal is a senior teacher at the prestigious Tashi Namgyal Academy.

(*Sikkim Observer*, January 2012.)

Hail Mount Hermon! A Tribute

Active Sikkim Hermonites (L to R): Uttam Pradhan, Namgyal Wangdi, Punam Agarwal, Udai P. Sharma and Jigme N. Kazi with Mrs. and Mr. J.A. Johnston in Gangtok in October, 2010.

Dear Jigme (and all the others concerned).

I can only say I am delighted about all that has been suggested.

It has been on my heart very much for two years now, who should succeed George Fernandez as Principal. When Roslyn's name came into focus, I thought she would make an excellent Head, perhaps for 10 years, and her husband, Sherab an excellent side help either for Comptroller of the School (kitchen and other staff, and spending of money), or whatever the appropriate name is (I forget now), or in charge of the Estate, where his years of experience in Sikkim, and his law qualifications would help him deal with the problems that are plenty there. But I know that Roslyn (excellent choice though I think she'd be, with two strong, utterly loyal and incorruptible men in these two positions alongside her) is very uncertain about whether she should move..

Jigme, if you get appointed, I would be very, very, happy. I remember when I first met you, I warmed to you so much, and right from then wondered if you might again contribute to the School, and fit in with, and continue, a genuine Christian tone. From the sound of letters I have read, many, many, Hermonites think the same.

Now I think the Hermonites Associations should get solidly together, and put strong pressure on the Bishop, and the whole Board, to agree with the proposals. It is a disgrace, in my opinion, that the Board governing the School, I believe, has no "old Hermonite" on it at all. Yes, any Board of a School that developed Mount Hermon's reputation, in the 50s, 60s, and 70s, should have sizable old students' representation.

Let the Methodist Church continue the ownership of the land, if they so desire, and let the Bishop himself be ex-officio member (not necessarily Chairman – he wasn't Chair of our Managing Committee in the 50s and 60s), but a new Board must be formed fairly soon.. I think the suggestion of a joint letter from all the Chairmen of the various Associations should be going quick smart to the current Board, appealing for quick action. I believe that Hermonites over the world would contribute as they are able, if they knew right changes were being made, and an absolutely loyal Hermonite like you, with some strong help, was running the show. Not otherwise!

I'll attach for your personal interest a copy of my notes on my recent cruise.
Bless you, Jigme. Consider that the Lord may well have brought you "to the kingdom" for such a time as this. Read Esther 4:14
With love, Jigs, David "Boss"

To: Mr. Stewart, Jan10, 2012
Dear Sir,
   Greetings from Sikkim and Happy New Year!!
I hope this note finds you as I had send two other mails and Roz tells me that you email add has changed. James (UK) had kindly given me your new add and so I'm attaching something that concerns MH and which is dear to your heart.

Roz updated us about you and I hope things are OK. Would love to hear from you.
With warm regards and much love,
Jigme and family

Dear Jigs and Karma,
   The Sikkim Hermonites Association rocks!! I am all for Mr. Jigme Kazi to be the Principal. That would be the best news for MH for this decade.
   Karma – it was really good to see you in Delhi. Where is my daughter?
Warmest regards,
Joy (Nalinee Taveesin), Bangkok.

Joy (centre) with Karma and Jigme in Gangtok, 2014.

Joy with Chinese President Xi Jinping, 2015.

Dear Jigs,

I have just received your mail about school. This is marvellous news that there is now a great feeling of wanting to do something. It would be fantastic if you would become the Principal and I think everyone will then feel positive about helping and getting involved to get the school back on track. We need people who feel a connection with the school and who are keen to have it back up the top of the list.

This note was forwarded to me and I thought you might like to see it too. Maybe you already have. It is interesting reading. As it was on the Hermonites site I suppose he would not mind using it if you wish - you can check with him if you feel it would be useful.

We also visited school in November and were very worried and upset about everything and did take a lot of photos also. I suppose now you all will have seen the state of the school but if you wish for photos to circulate we can forward them to you.

We hope to visit the hills again in the Spring and will let you know when it is likely to be. For now you have my support and I am sure everyone else's too!!!
Lots of love
Cindy (Lucinda Gibbs), UK.

Thank you so much for this news, Jigme.

No better news than that the Hermonites of the area, and of the world, should take a very firm line with the owners/policy makers of the property, and lay down conditions, in every respect, should this excellent idea of your election to the post come to pass! All the legal side, and everything. This is my feeling - so that what you and your committee say, comes to pass too, and far-away owners in Lucknow [or wherever] should not have too much of a veto.

[They will have to keep some, of course, to protect their property, and there has to be a balance, as we know, so that even the Principal will have to take No for an answer from his committee on occasions - no human being is safe as a despot, as we also know, am I right?]

(Are we not too fallible, as human beings, to expect to always have it right, no matter what our experience, earthly wisdom, expertise, amazing personality, etc might be - what do you think? Ask Mr. Murray [as being your contemporary], Mr. Stewart, Mr. Johnston, Mr. Fernandez, or whoever??)

And that brings me to one further point, that may be difficult for a number of us to go along with, but that is, the 'great days' of MH were very much the fruit of ten years of earnest prayer on the part of Mr. and Mrs. Stewart [and maybe of many earlier Principals and their families too, only the God of Heaven knows that] - a Christian foundation, based on the name of the Lord Jesus - and please do ask all your 'believing' bible friends and supporters (plenty in Sikkim, and elsewhere, not only on the committee, but in so many other quiet spots) to be behind you every day in prayer to God to give you His wisdom (good sense, knowing what is right in His eyes, not only in the eyes of the world), to do this task as we would all love it to be done!

Some of us will start asking God right now, that if this is of Him, His idea for MH, that He will direct every step of the way!

Bless you, dear Jigme.

In prayer, with much love, from Miss Russell

Dear Jigme and former Hermonites,

First of all I congratulate you for taking this initiative to revive our old school to whom we owe much for the way our lives have panned out.

The nomination of Jigme as the next Principal of the school sounds great especially for his continued interest in the school and generally keeping in touch with the former students of the school.

The idea of creating a separate cell/department for alumni of the school is a good idea. I know of at least one school where there is a full fledged department where the Alumni Office actively solicits advice and help from former students and teachers keeping the network alive. And there is a regular meeting in the school where some of them are also on the committee.

As I see it I think we will have to approach the school management (Methodist Church in this case) to start the ball rolling. Without the support and consent of the legal management we can do little.

It seems there is a lot to be done in medical parlance the school has to be admitted in the ICU for rapid revival.

All the best and if there is anything I can do, please count me in.

Prava Rai

Hail Mount Hermon! A Tribute

Hi Everyone,

Greetings and Happy New Year!

Many of you will know that there have been concerns as to the future of Mount Hermon School, as enrolments have dropped alarmingly, and Mr. George Fernandez (who has held the fort faithfully for many years) now leaves in March of this year.

There have been many ideas and suggestions from alumni around the world as to what could or should be done, but while we were in Gangtok just last month, we did meet with Jigme Kazi, and talked over one of the most viable possibilities to date. Jigme has been the heart and energy behind both the Sikkim Hermonite Association and the International Hermonite Association. He has regularly visited the school over many years, and most recently attended a 2011 Christmas party in December organised by the Grade 4 staff at Mount Hermon. He is perhaps the best known ex-student/teacher in Mount Hermon today. Jigme has agreed to apply for the Principal-ship of Mount Hermon once Mr. George Fernandez leaves in March 2012, and in our minds, Mount Hermon School will be extremely blessed to have him in this role.

Jigme has always been the most loyal and committed Hermonite we know. He joined MH in 1963 and completed his SC in 1972. He then completed 2 years of Teachers training at Mount Hermon TTC, and taught in the Junior school for 5 years. He went on to do his Bachelor of Arts, and his LL.B. degree from Bombay University. He started his own press in Sikkim, and has been an ardent supporter of freedom of speech, accountability of leaders, and an advocate for truth and fairness for people for many years.

Jigme has always been passionate about anything he undertakes and he gives everything he has to the job at hand. His character is above reproach – many of us have experienced his loyalty, friendship, fairness and compassion. He has always been a leader, even when things have been difficult - and he leads by example.

At the heart of things:

Jigme has always loved people – his family, ex-students and myriad friends will attest to this. This love has been reciprocal and he has friends all over the world who are willing (and in some cases able) to lend a hand if needed - MH needs this right now.

Jigme will always give any task his absolute commitment and energy – his work will not be dictated by the clock, but by the job that needs to be done – MH definitely needs this right now.

Jigme will be truthful, fair and honest. He never looks down on people but will always stand up for the underdog and see that justice is done. His concern for, and rapport with the current Grade 4 staff in MH attest to this – MH certainly needs this right now.

Jigme has always been keenly interested in holistic education, and the limitless possibilities that can be unleashed for children as future citizens of India – MH will be blessed to have this right now.

Of course, the way ahead will not be easy, and a lot of assistance and support will be needed.

While we were in Gangtok we talked with Jigme's wife, Tshering, and his twin daughters who are completing their studies and are still at home. They have very generously offered Jigme the time to undertake this new role should he get it – so he has every blessing from the home front.

'MH Revival' Campaign 2012

Mr. and Mrs. Johnston with Sherab and Roslyn and Jigme, Gangtok, 2011.

One of the questions that may arise will be to do with his faith. Jigme was brought up as a Buddhist, but became a Christian while a student at Mount Hermon and was later baptised in the swimming pool. He is not a member of a church, but he knows and affirms the Christian faith and values, and certainly attests to these in his own life.

We who have been welcomed, nurtured and sent out from the wonderful heart of Mount Hermon, have known God's richest blessings during our time there. I believe that we now have the chance to re-vitalise this spirit, by offering our support to Jigme at this time.

The Managing Committee for Mount Hermon will need to be approached. However, given that enrolments for the school are at an all time low, they may be encouraged by this new possibility, and to this end we (the alumni of MH) want to send a letter to the Managing Committee endorsing Jigme as a suitable candidate. We would like to get as many signatures from Hermonites in Australia and New Zealand as possible. There are alumni chapters in Sikkim, Siliguri, Kolkata, Darjeeling, and some in the UK and USA who are doing the same thing, and while it is not a usual occurrence we would like to voice our concerns for the future of the school along with support for Jigme in this venture.

If you would like to support Jigme, please could you reply to this email. Also, please forward it on to others whose email addresses I don't have. I will then put together a single

document for our signatures and forward it to the Managing Committee and other Hermonites around the world as soon as possible.
Thank you all very much,
Kindest Regards,
Roslyn Namgyal
Canberra
14 January 2012

Dear Jigme,

I am John Lee, ex-MHS student 1941-1945. I am touched by your letter regarding the current plight of MHS, and will see what I can do to help.

Mr. Hal Dewey was the Principal when I was at MHS. I live in Hollywood, California, where until recently I was a cameraman in the studios.

Meantime, I wonder if you can solve a problem for me please? I have not been able to contact my very good friend Madan M. Rasailly, who was also a student at MHS when I was there, and whom I visited several years ago in Gangtok. Can you possibly find out what has happened to Madan and how I may reach him please? I have tried email and telephone, both to no avail. He lived at Sichi Busti (I'm not sure of the spelling!!)

Many thanks, and I wish everything good for you, especially so far as MHS is concerned. Please stay in touch!
Warmest personal regards,
John (John D Lee), US.

Dear Jigme,

Greetings from California! Thank you for sending me this information about our old beloved school.

I have some questions first.
Who holds title to the property?
Who pays the bills at this time?
Who is on the board of trustees? Is there still a board?

It seems to me that you might consider forming a board if there is none, and then identifying exactly what the various problems and needs are both for the physical plant itself and the state of the governing board.

Next would be trying to identify sponsors. Repairing an ancient set of buildings can be a costly enterprise as I am sure you know.

Also if there is a need for serious shoring up of land that has slid away, or building retaining walls, that in itself will take a lot of money to accomplish.

Simply replacing a principal and hiring teachers who are qualified would be much further down the list, I would assume, unless you have the first things taken care of already.

I was not aware that MH was in trouble and this comes as a sad shock.

I wish you the very best with this daunting task.

Sincerely,

Marianne (Nichols-Roy) Schwartz (1968 batch), US.

Marianne Nichols-Roy, Chuni Wangmoo and Jojo.

Hi Jigs,

We last met at Delhi a few years ago along with Thinley. You were staying at Sikkim House then and your son was to visit Japan probably. I was amazed to see how trim and fit you were despite being many years senior to us!

I am really glad to know that you are willing to take on the mantle of turning around the school to its past state of glory. It is a gigantic task and a long road ahead. Most importantly, apart from funding, the critical factor would be to have a dedicated core team with the passion, vision and drive to bring the institution back on the rails. Needless to mention that transparency will be crucial to have the support of Hermonites around the world. The electronic form of communication is a powerful tool.

However, nothing works better than walk the talk....one to one.... face to face across the generations that have walked through the portals of the institution. The energy is dormant, but it takes a small spark to burn the fire in all....It can be infectious if managed with a clear vision and strong networking. I believe you can do it....coz you have the grit, passion and sincerity to make things happen apart from the fact that you will be well accepted among the local community. But first, we have to take you on board and this is something which has to be worked out on priority.

If you visit Kolkata, please do not hesitate to get in touch. We can start the ball rolling here too.

We can get the support of the Bhutanese alumni too. Dowa Penjore is a big timer in Bhutan...probably First Secretary in the Government. Tsering Dorji is the Ambassador to Thailand. They can make a difference in the Bhutanese circuit.

I am at Kolkata and my cell no is 9163485587. (Left The Doon School, Dehradun last February after a stint of over 4 years).

Look forward to being in touch with you more frequently.

Regards,

Brahma (Debashis), India.

Dear Hermonite,

I have taken the liberty of accessing your email address from the Hermonites Unite Website: http://www.success.co.th/mthermon/contact.asp

Please find attached a document entitled Boarding Schools in India showing MHS at the absolute bottom of the list.

Towards the end of November, this was widely circulated among some of us who graduated in the 1970s and it is heartening to see that the Sikkim Hermonites Association has taken a proactive step in proposing the name of Jigme N. Kazi to be appointed as the next Principal of Mount Hermon School after the retirement of George Fernandes in March 2012. Please see the SHA's report below.

This move has the support of the present Principal, Mr. Fernandes. The Murrays, Johnstons and Rev. Jones endorse Jigme's candidature as well and Rev. Stewart, wholeheartedly gives his support to Jigme.

The Management Committee will need to be approached and a dialogue has to be opened in order to make this appointment happen.

To this end, Roslyn (Rongong) Namgyal has proposed a signature campaign which we can then forward to the Management Committee to seriously look into Jigme's candidature. For those who do not know Jigme personally, she has also written a few words about him (please scroll down).

We have seen how an alumnus of St. Joseph's, Fr. Thinley has revitalized his school and I am confident that, with the right support, Jigme could bring MHS back to its former glory.

Should you wish to support Jigme please reply to this email (with copies to: roz.namgyal@gmail.com and jigmekazi@gmail.com) with your full name, year that you left MHS, and your present country of residence, all in the following format:

- Jigme N. Kazi, 1972, India

A letter can then be addressed by Roslyn to the Management Committee with a list of all of you who support Jigme's candidature.

Meanwhile, other Hermonites in India are making moves to figure out how best to motivate the Management Committee to make the right choice and some of you might have heard of this from them already.
Best Regards
Dipak Mirchandani, MHS 1976
London, UK.

Dear Roz, Dipak and Jigs,
Well done Roz. A mammoth task. Maybe the idea of putting Principals first, then teachers and then students would be a good idea. Also mentioning the fact they were teachers and Principals. I did forward you everything that came in to me in support so am sure you have got them all. Do we have time to send the list to key people i.e. Varongthip, etc to see if there are more who would want to have their names down? It might though take too much time at this stage as he would have to mail anyone not on the list etc etc. Not sure what you think.
Love
Cindy (Lucinda Gobbs), UK.

Dear Jigme,
I've just got back from Tas and saw John over there. Kris had posed the question to him of returning and his reply was that we can no longer really conceive of the outsider helping in this situation.

However, is there any consideration for anyone on the current staff to be coached into the head job? What are your requirements for advertising and interviewing?

Someone like John would be more interested in a support scenario but no politics. He would hate to deal with any church or state issues. He has had to work at a high level in the NT govt and was subject to a fair amount there.

Anyway happy New Year and we'll keep up a dialogue.
Mick Glasby, Australia.

Dear Mick and Krissie,
Happy New Year. We've just posted a message on MH. Immediate and effective reaction needed.
Jigs

Whole heartedly support the choice of Jigme Kazi as the next Principal of Mount Hermon School. He would surely be a great asset to the institution and I am confident that his managerial abilities, coupled with his unquestioned loyalty and concern for the well being of MH will put MH back on the path to regaining its old glory.

Hail Mount Hermon! A Tribute

Vedprakash with his family.

I remember with pride, working with him, in trying to unearth the places where Queen's Hill stood and I still remember the determination, commitment and pride he put into his work. It would be a step in the right direction. Moreover, being such a lovable person, he would command respect from all quarters and people would love to work with and for him - I for one would gladly give my voluntary services, if he needed them.

With warm personal regards,
Vedprakash Agarwal, India.

Dear All,
I am forwarding this on as you do not appear on Jigme's list. I thought you might find this interesting and very positive. If you find there are other Hermonites not on the list you would feel would like to know about this please do pass this on to them.

Happy New Year and Hail Mount Hermon!
Cindy

Dear Roz and Jigme,

Today I received the second batch of forwarded messages with more details. I hereby endorse the proposal. My brothers and sister were at MHS in the early 40s.

I am Ira R. Dash, 1947, U.S.A.

Thank you, and GOOD LUCK!

Ira R. Dash

I support Jigme Kazi for the candidature. I knew him during my days at MH.

Hope that his successful nomination will usher in a new great chapter for MH. Roslyn "Rongong", please include my name in your letter to the MC.

Thanks.

Om Prakash Kanwal

MH 1963-1969, '69 batch.

Hello Roslyn and Sherab

I would like to lend my support 100% for Jigme Kazi. Did not know MHS was such a bad state. I have been living in Japan for more than 20 years.

Palden Sherpa

Hey Jigs!

I have just heard about you being principle of Mt. Hermon, how wonderful for Mt. Hermon and a huge congratulations to you!

I am teaching music part time and still play in a band, otherwise things the same. Anyway once again and big congrats-wow!

And good luck with sorting the place out.

Corinne Brokken (1977 batch), Perth, Australia.

Barry Hi,

I too am supportive of Jigs; but our every move needs to be thought out carefully. I do not think there is anyone (here) who does not want to see a strong and vibrant MH; its just that there are too many areas of conflict and tying one end might unravel another.

So, let me think, discuss and tell you how the Cal. Hermonite can contribute.

wkr

Sujit, Kolkata.

Good to know that there is an association of Hermonites. We must now work quickly and get everything in order. There is a vast untapped resource out there, experience, knowledge and financial potentials.

I am sure if we could work together we could pull the school through and breathe new life into it. It would be so good if we can do this. We owe much to the school.

Any help you require, count me in as I said before.
With all my best wishes.
Ani (Prava Rai – 1970 batch), Sikkim and Goa.

Dear Hermonites

You have most probably received this email either directly from Jigs or from the Sikkim Hermonites or been forwarded this mail by your Hermonite friends who have received it and forwarded it to you.

I have recently visited Mt. Hermon twice, once with Jigme and I am forwarding this to you just in case my mailing list of Hermonites happen to have someone on it that has not yet received the original email below. I hope you will do the same and spread the word.

For those of you who have already received this and might even have replied to Jigme, my apologies. It is a worthwhile cause. I hope you will respond with your own opinions regardless.

Jigs, all the best.
Navin Wongsejullarat, Bangkok.

LETTER TO BISHOP SAGAR

We got the address of Bishop Sagar through Kitty Katzwell (Mildred), an old alumnus of the school and daughter of a former Principal of MH in the thirties, Mrs. Lila Enberg. Kitty had contacted the United Methodist Information Service and United Methodist Communications in Nashville, Tennessee, USA, (Mary Lynn Holly InfoServ/United Methodist Information Service, infoserv@umcom.org mholly@umcom.org) when approached about Bishop Sagar's whereabouts.

With Mildred's help, 'MH Revival' campaign manager and 1971 batch Hermonite from Canberra, Australia, Roslyn Namgyal, sent all materials connected to the issue of MH revival to Bishop Sagar to the following address:
Methodist Church in India
South India & Madras Regional Conferences
Bishop Taranath Sagar
Bishop's House
Baldwin Methodist Educational Ctr,
13 Convent Rd,
Museum Rd,
Bangalore 560 025, India;
TEL: 080-222 49 827 - FAX: 080-224 84 776
EMAIL: Bishop_sagar@hotmail.com

LETTER TO BISHOP SAGAR FROM 'MH REVIVAL' CAMPAIGN MANAGER

Dear Bishop Sagar

My name is Roslyn Namgyal, and I am an ex-student and ex-teacher of Mount Hermon School (Darjeeling). My family has a long history with the school as my Uncle was the Principal from 1954 to 1964, and my mother (Joy Rongong – editor) was the Junior School superintendent for 19 years. My sister and I studied there from Kindergarten to HSC, and I later went back to the school and taught for 7 years. I now live and work in Australia, but I return to India every year or so.

I am taking the liberty to write to you with an unprecedented request, as I believe that the care of the school has now come to you. I was unable to locate the names and contacts of the existing Mount Hermon School Managing Committee during my brief visit to India in December/January, and as time is of the essence, I do hope you will forgive my coming directly to you.

Mount Hermon has always been much more than an educational institute - it has been a deeply loved community and home for thousands of people now scattered around the globe. The motto of the school is "Non scholae sed vitae discimus" – Not for school, but for life we learn. People in myriads of jobs around the world today give credit for the success of their lives to the love, discipline and nurture that was given to them in Mount Hermon. Teachers gave themselves whole-heartedly to the task of guiding and inspiring young children from all communities within India, as well as from other countries. Mount Hermon School has always been a place of acceptance, love and equality – wonderful foundations for peace and justice.

From the 1980s to the mid 2000s, political upheaval and unrest made the task of the principals (most recently Mr. Fernandez) difficult and challenging to say the least. Darjeeling suffered as a tourist destination, and parents started looking to safer areas for their children. Teachers too were less inclined to choose Darjeeling as a career goal. There has been a steady decline in enrolments, and this year they hover around the 400 mark (down from 700 is past years). Added to this is damage to the main building of the school after the recent earthquake (2011, editor). All this makes one wonder at the viability of the school should numbers sink much lower.

A recent survey has placed Mount Hermon School last on the table of India's 48 best Boarding Schools league for 2010 - and (while I cannot vouch for the rating scales that have been used), it is a public document that has caused much dismay and sadness to the alumni around the world. (see attachment) (http://educationworldonline.net/userfiles/file/Boarding-Top%2010.pdf)

While ex-students and teachers from Mount Hermon continue their friendships for life, the alumni of Mount Hermon exist formally in Associations and "Chapters" around India – in Sikkim, Kolkata, Siliguri and Delhi as well as in the UK, USA, Australia and New Zealand. There is also an International Hermonite Association. These groups meet for friendship and support, always with a great deal of good will towards Mount Hermon. However, these associations do not have any formal link with the School, and no known representation on the Managing Committee of the school either. It would seem that at this point in the history of the school where there are many people willing to engage and offer support to the school, it may be timely for the Managing Committee to engage with alumni groups. There is still a deep interest in the continuation and success of Mount Hermon School as a premiere institution in the development of future leaders and citizens of India and the rest of the world.

This brings me to the crux of this letter, and that is to formally request you and the Managing Committee to consider an ex-student and ex-teacher of Mount Hermon School for the position of Principal when the current Principal Mr. Fernandez leaves in March 2012. The person is Mr. Jigme Kazi from Sikkim, and he comes with the support of Mr. Fernandez himself, three ex-Principals, and many teachers and students of Mount Hermon School, whose names are listed on the attachment.

My husband and I were in Gangtok (Sikkim) just last month, where we met with Jigme Kazi. Jigme was a student at Mount Hermon from 1963 to 1972 and has always been the most loyal and committed Hermonite we know. After school he completed 2 years of teacher's training at Mount Hermon Teacher's Training College, and taught in the Junior school for 5 years. He went on to do his Bachelor of Arts, and his LLB degree from Bombay University. He started his own press in Sikkim, and has been an ardent supporter of freedom of speech, accountability of leaders, and an advocate for truth and fairness for people for many years. He is also the author of several books on the political history of Sikkim. Jigme has been the heart and energy behind both the Sikkim Hermonite Association and the International Hermonite Association. He has regularly visited the school over many years, and most recently attended a 2011 Christmas party in December organised by the Grade 4 staff at Mount Hermon.

Jigme has agreed to apply for the Principal-ship of Mount Hermon once Mr. George Fernandez leaves in March 2012, and in our minds, Mount Hermon School will be extremely blessed to have him in this role. Mount Hermon School is of course strongly Christian. Jigme became a Christian while a student at Mount Hermon, and while he is not a member of a church, he knows and affirms Christian faith and values, and certainly attests to these in his own life.

Jigme has always been passionate about anything he undertakes and he gives everything he has to the job at hand. His character is above reproach – many of us have experienced his loyalty, friendship, fairness and compassion. He has always been a leader, even when things have been difficult - and he leads by example.

At the heart of things:

1. Jigme loves people – his family, ex-students and myriad friends will attest to this. This love has been reciprocal and he has friends all over the world who are willing (and in some cases able) to lend a hand if needed – Mount Hermon needs this right now.

2. Jigme will always give any task his absolute commitment and energy – his work will not be dictated by the clock, but by the job that needs to be done – Mount Hermon definitely needs this right now.

3. Jigme will be truthful, fair and honest. He never looks down on people but will always stand up for the underdog and see that justice is done. His concern for, and rapport with the current Grade 4 staff in the school attest to this – Mount Hermon certainly needs this right now.

4. Jigme is a good teacher and has always been keenly interested in holistic education, and the limitless possibilities that can be unleashed for children as future citizens of India – Mount Hermon will be blessed to have this right now.

In summary here are some of Jigme's strengths for the role:

1. Family: Jigme has the support of his wife Tshering and children who have very generously offered Jigme the time to undertake this new role should he get it – so he has every blessing from the home front.

2. Connections with the local community: Throughout his schooling, and into his career, Jigme has forged and maintained good and fruitful relationships with people in his locality. This has extended to people in local government both in Sikkim and in Darjeeling. He is fluent in Nepali (the lingua franca of the area) and will not be seen as an outsider. Given the intricacies of the political climate in Darjeeling, this could be a real advantage.

3. Connections with Mount Hermon alumni: As stated earlier, Jigme is the best placed person I know to liaise with the many alumni associations around the world. He is a person who is already trusted, and this could be a powerful commodity if the school ever needs to seek assistance. In fact, assistance has already been offered to him both financially as well as in time and expertise from past teachers and students who may have skills that could be of service to the school.

4. Leadership: Jigme possesses strong and charismatic leadership qualities. I can speak most confidently about his school and early teaching career when we worked together. He was a natural leader – the Prefects chairman, the football and cricket captain and the leader of the Christian

Youth Group. As a teacher he has made an indelible mark on his students, and I can forward you recent emails to attest to this. Jigme has been at the heart of two of the most active alumni groups in India – the Sikkim Hermonite Association, and the International Hermonite Association. The overwhelming affirmation we have received in support of his current bid for the principal-ship is also testament to the fact that many who know him, know that he is very capable of rallying people together and getting the job done.

5. Organisational skills: For a number of years Jigme was the journalist from the North East for the Telegraph as well and the Statesman newspapers. He is still the editor and producer of a weekly newspaper in Sikkim – the Sikkim Observer. As stated earlier he has authored three books that trace aspects of Sikkim's journey from being an independent kingdom to becoming a state of India. He is well used to meeting deadlines, and will be able to take responsibility for the multiple tasks that will need to be juggled in this position.

6. Availability: As he is self-employed, he will be available at any time should he be called. Of course, the way ahead will not be easy, and a lot of assistance and support will be needed. However, if any one person can rally others around him, inspire them, lead them and forge ahead, it will be Jigme.

Please would you give this request your prayerful consideration. Many of the people listed on the attachment are ex-colleagues, teachers or students of Jigme who would be more than happy to talk with you if required. I will send their email details if you wish.

Thank you - I really appreciate you having taken the time to read this, and look forward to hearing from you.

Yours very sincerely
Roslyn Namgyal
Canberra, Australia.

Some words about Jigme Kazi: Sherab & Roslyn Namgyal

I just want to say thank you to all of you who have so kindly done us the honour of suggesting our names as possible Mount Hermon leaders. We have carefully considered the possibility, but at this stage we are not in the position to move forward in this direction.

However, while we were in Gangtok, we did meet with Jigme Kazi. Jigme has agreed to apply for the Principal-ship of Mount Hermon once Mr. George

Fernandez leaves in March 2012, and in our minds, Mount Hermon School will be extremely blessed to have him in the role.

Jigme has always been the most loyal and committed Hermonite we know. He joined MH in 1963 and completed his SC in 1972. He then completed 2 years of Teacher training at Mount Hermon TTC, and taught in the Junior school for 4 years. He went on to do his Bachelor of Arts, and his LLB degree from Bombay University. He started his own press in Sikkim, and has been an ardent supporter of freedom of speech, accountability of leaders, and an advocate for truth and fairness for people for many years.

Jigme has always been passionate about anything he undertakes and he gives everything he has to the job at hand. His character is above reproach – many of us have experienced his loyalty, friendship, fairness and compassion. He has always been a leader, even when things have been difficult - and he leads by example.

At the heart of things:

Jigme has always loved people – his family, ex-students and myriad friends will attest to this. This love has been reciprocal and he has friends all over the world who are willing (and in some cases able) to lend a hand if needed - MH needs this right now.

Jigme will always give any task his absolute commitment and energy – his work will not be dictated by the clock, but by the job that needs to be done - MH definitely needs this right now.

Jigme will be truthful, fair and honest. He never looks down on people but will always stand up for the underdog and see that justice is done – MH certainly needs this right now.

Jigme has always been keenly interested in holistic education, and the limitless possibilities that can be unleashed for children as future citizens of India – MH will be blessed to have this right now.

Of course, the way ahead will not be easy, and a lot of assistance and support will be needed.

While we were in Gangtok we talked with Jigme's wife, Tshering, and his twin daughters who are completing their studies and are still at home. They have very generously offered Jigme the time to undertake this new role should he get it – so he has every blessing from the home front.

The Managing Committee for Mount Hermon will need to be approached. However, given that enrolments for the school are at an all time low, they may be encouraged by this new possibility, and to this end we (the alumni of MH) want to send a letter to the Managing Committee endorsing Jigme as a suitable candidate. We would like to get as many signatures from Hermonites in Australia and New Zealand as possible. There are alumni chapters in Sikkim, Siliguri, Kolkata, Darjeeling, and some in the UK and USA who are doing the same thing, and while it is not a usual occurrence we would like to voice our concerns for the future of the school along with this solution.

One of the questions that may arise will be to do with his faith. Jigme was brought up as a Buddhist, but became a Christian while a student at Mount Hermon and was later baptised in the swimming pool. He is not a member of a church, but he knows and affirms the Christian faith and values, and certainly attests to these in his own life.

We who have been welcomed, nurtured and sent out from the wonderful heart of Mount Hermon, have known God's richest blessings during our time there. I believe that we now have the chance to re-vitalise this spirit, by offering our support to Jigs at this time.

Sherab and Roslyn (Rongong) Namgyal
Ex-students and teachers of Mt. Hermon School

Curriculum Vitae: Jigme Namgyal Kazi

DOB	05 August 1953
Address	Observer Building
	Nam Nang Road
	Gangtok SIKKIM – 737101
	INDIA
Marital Status	Married with 4 children
Nationality	Indian
Email	jigmekazi@gmail.com
Home	03892 - 220409
Mobile	94346 - 30097

EDUCATION

1982	L.L.B. (General), Government Law College, Mumbai
1982	Diploma in Business Management (DBM), Davar's College of Commerce, Mumbai
1980	Diploma in Journalism, Mumbai
1979	Bachelor of Arts (BA) North Bengal University
1975	TTC (Trained Teachers Certificate) Mount Hermon Undergraduate Training College, Darjeeling
1972	Indian School Certificate (ISC) Mount Hermon School, Darjeeling

SKILLS AND ABILITIES

Proven excellent leadership skills
Excellent people skills
Ability to work with people from varied backgrounds
Excellent team player
Ability to adapt to new situations
Ability to learn new tasks quickly and easily
Professional and mature
Displays sound judgment
Excellent rapport with children and young people

TEACHING EXPERIENCE

1976 – 1979   Primary school teacher in Mount Hermon School for all subjects.

Roles and responsibilities:

- Hostel Warden
- House Master
- Coach – Football and Cricket
- Played for school IX – Football and Cricket
- Edited School Magazine – "Hermonite"
- Held charge of providing spiritual guidance to students via Sunday services and Hi-Crusaders

OTHER CREDENTIALS

- Represented Darjeeling District – Football 1975
- Represented Mount Hermon School in Football, Hockey, Athletics and obtained school Colours for Football and Cricket
- Participated in Debates
- Participated in school dramas
- Camping/hiking with school students

AWARDS

1972   Bishop Fisher Cup for Best Boy Student (Mount Hermon School)
1975   Principal's Award (Mount Hermon Teachers' Training College)

POSITIONS HELD IN SCHOOL

1972   House Captain
1971 - 1972   Captain – School Football XI
1972   Prefect – Senior School
1967   Monitor – Junior School

JOURNALISM EXPERIENCE

EDITORIAL
1986 - 2012	Editor – *Sikkim Observer*, Gangtok, SIKKIM
1992 - 2012	Editor – *Himalayan Guardian*, Gangtok, SIKKIM
1995 – 1996	Editor – *Hill People* (Magazine)
1983 – 1985	Editor – *Spotlight on Sikkim*, Gangtok, SIKKIM
1983 – 1985	Sub-Editor – *Eastern Express*

CORRESPONDENT
1987 – 2000, 2001	*The Statesman*, Kolkata
1995 - 1996	*United News of India* (UNI)
1991 – 1993	The Independent, Kathmandu, Nepal
1983 – 1986	*The Telegraph*, Kolkata

ARTICLES
Sunday Magazine - Kolkata
Caravan (Magazine now known as "Alive") – New Delhi
North-East Sun Magazine
North-East Daily – Guwahati (Assam)

PRESS EXPERIENCE
1986 - 2012	Proprietor and Manager of Hill Media Publications. Experience in printing and publication work, and running an off-set printing press.

POSITIONS HELD
1989 – 1993	President – Sikkim Press Association, Sikkim
1981 – 1982	President – Sikkim Students Association, Mumbai
1990 – 2012	President – Hermonites International
1995 – 1998	General Secretary – Federation of North-East Journalists
1983 – 1985	General Secretary – Sikkim Tribal Welfare Association
1985 – 2004	General secretary – Sikkim Hermonites Association
1991 – 2004	Steering Committee Member – Sikkim Bhutia – Lepcha Apex Committee (SIBLAC)
1994 – 1999	Chairman – Organisation of Sikkimese Unity (OSU)
1994 – 2004	Convenor – Inner Circle of Sikkim (ICS)

AUTHOR
"Inside Sikkim: Against the Tide": The book was released by the External Affairs Minister K. Natwar Singh at the Press club of India (New Delhi) 1993 and subsequently launched in Gangtok, Sikkim, in 1994 by Chief Minister Dr. Pawan Chamling.

"Sikkim for Sikkimese – Distinct Identity Within The Union", published 2009.

REFERENCES
Mr. Narendra Pradhan	Minister, Government of Sikkim
Rev. Dr. David Stewart	Ex-Principal Mount Hermon School (1954 – 1964) (New Zealand)
Rev. Dr. Bill Moore	Ex-Teacher Mount Hermon school (1970 – 1973)
Email	billandlizmoore@talktalk.net
Mr. Sunirmal Chakravarthi	Principal La Martiniere School Kolkata (1954 – 1964)

Attachment: Support for Jigme Kazi from ex-students and teachers from Mount Hermon School

Profile of Hermonites International

Hermonites International (Hi!) is an old Alumni body of all Hermonites internationally which was formed in year 2005 under able leadership of Mr. Jigme N. Kazi, and had been actively in communication with various bodies of the school in the past.

A. Introduction:

It has been proposed that all Alumni, Hermonites get together to form/revive a mother body known as Hermonites International, which will represent all Alumni, Hermonites irrespective of individual countries or states having their local Alumni body. The enclosed profile will act as an initial guiding philosophy for Hermonites International and will act as handbook to represent Hermonites International in any or all platforms may it be reunions, representing and communication with School Managing Committee and others. Thereafter, once Hermonites International is in full function they will work within the principles of the constitution.

The initial Hermonites International body will consist of reputed, intellectuals, legal entities and other abled Hermonites to initially revive Hermonites International.

B. Primary Objectives:

1. To introduce Hermonites International as a primary body representing all Alumni and Hermonites.
2. To request all Alumni body to join Hermonites International as chapters from their individual constituency.

3. To form sub-committees and revive the old Executive Committee.
4. To define, prepare an agenda, make objectives to help Mount Hermon to revive its lost glory in cooperation and guidance of the Managing Committee of the Methodist Church in India.
5. To bring about unity among all Hermonites.
6. To form/draft a universal constitution for Hermonites International.

C. Proposal for Mount Hermon School Managing Committee:
1. To discuss and explore all avenues about how to revive the school.
2. To help increase enrolment/students for the school.
3. To have joint study with the school management for refurbishing, repair, prepare budget, financial implications, find solutions and prepare a master plan to repair and refurbish the school in line with other international schools in India.
4. To prepare a financial feasibility study for funds required, fund management, budgeting and transparency contingencies to be enforced for both the School Management Committee and Hermonites International.
5. To review existing faculty, appoint new Principal, additional staffs in line with knowledge of top leading schools running today in India.
6. To help prepare a positive campaign, publicity to help in getting more students to enrol in the school.
7. Study the possibility of Hermonites International members representing in the School Managing Committee.

D. Immediate Objectives of Hermonites International:
1. To draft a constitution, memorandum of articles and association, Executive Committee format.
2. To appoint, select highly able individuals to the Executive Committee under abled guidance of Mr. Jigme N. Kazi, which will act as the representing Executive Committee of Hermonites International until a constitution is drafted and put into effect.
3. To form sub-committees as below:
    a. Establish communication channel with the School Managing Committee.
    b. To communicate with all Alumni body, individuals to invite to join Hermonites International.
    c. To create an initial seed fund to bring about the existence of an active Hermonites International and create a common communications centre.
    d. To appoint key office-bearers, invite as patrons Murrays, Johnstons, Gardners etc., to give goodwill to Hermonites International.

E. What Hermonites International will bring to the table during meeting with the School Managing Committee:
1. Exchange, discuss issues what a body like Hermonites International can play an active role in reviving the school's glory and putting back Mount Hermon on the map as a leading education institution.
2. To discuss the financial and funding issues and where Hermonites International can play a role from its network of ex-students, Alumni, Hermonites and other sources.
3. To jointly discuss goals and objectives to achieve the above.
4. The importance of representation of Hermonites International in the School Managing Committee, its role and benefits.
5. To develop a communication channel between the School Managing Committee, Principal and Hermonites International.

F. Key Proposal from Hermonites International:

Appointment of new Principal: MH will highly benefit with our proposal to appoint one of most respected and loved Hermonite Mr. Jigme N. Kazi. His vast knowledge and also insight of the school and his leadership qualities will attract many Alumni and Hermonites to unite to help in process of reviving our Alma Mater to its past glory. There are many testaments by Hermonites to support this.
Sherab and Roslyn (Rongong) Namgyal
Ex-students and teachers of Mt. Hermon School

Dear Dipak, Roslyn and Jigme

Your mails below were deeply saddening and yet pointed to a silver lining. It was saddening to hear of the state of Mt. Hermon today and its perception in the eyes of others. Those of us who were privileged to be students in its heyday, can only grieve with a heavy heart to know how our wonderful alma mater has deteriorated over the years.

I have absolutely NO HESITATION in endorsing Jigme's candidature for Principalship. Not only was he my classmate for over a decade, but his humility, good nature, sporting abilities and helping hand at every turn, were examples to us all. Old friend - my complete support goes to you.

I would also be delighted to help/serve in any way to bring the standards of the school back to what they were.

One last thing, which Roslyn has mentioned in her mail, regarding Jigme's faith. I think we have all now experienced the world as a wide open space where all faiths meet and mingle and eventually become one. The only true dharma is our own actions - and there can be no one better to demonstrate what true religion is than Jigme.

Warmest regards

Chandralekha (Lahiri) Maitra (Class of 1972), Mumbai.

Hail Mount Hermon! A Tribute

Class of '72: Chandralekha Lahiri is seated front row second left.

Hi Jigme, Roslyn, Dipak,

My sister, Chandralekha, kindly forwarded me your messages. I was Class of 1970, and now live in Muscat, in the Sultanate of Oman. Needless to say, I was deeply shocked to hear of the state of our dear old School, of which, like you, I have such fond memories. I would love to do anything possible to help restore its fortunes to what they once were.

I remember Jigme well, and have absolutely no doubt at all that he would make the best possible Principal for Mount Hermon. I have no hesitation in supporting his candidature in the strongest possible terms.

By the way, who are the folk on the Management Committee these days?
Warm regards to all,
Chandrashekhar Lahiri (Class of 1970)

Hi Jigs - yes, I have already spoken to my cousin (the Bishop's daughter) to furnish the names of the chairman/committee members. Once I get it, I intend talking to the chairman to get his take on the proposal and to push this forward. Despite my best effort I have not been able to get in touch with the Justice. Will do once he surfaces.

I think time is important and this whole thing has to be done with utmost urgency but at the same time we need to tread cautiously so as to take them along and not appear as if we are, in any way, impinging on their domain. The church, as you know, is very protective about their turf and unless convinced that basic principles on which the Methodist church functions is not compromised they will not give in so easily.

That brings me to the most important question - Are you a Christian? That is - is Christianity your declared religion. Forgive me for asking this stupid question but this could be one of the mandatory eligibility criteria. Absurd but that's the way it is with all Christian institutions. About my trip to Sikkim it all depends on getting leave and that is very difficult. That's the price we pay for being senior level public servants. But do let me know if you guys are planning some reunion - will try to make it despite the odds. Take Care.

On Wed, Jan 11, 2012 at 7:01 P.M., Ashish Bhengra wrote:

Jigs - I couldn't agree with you more. I was born into a Christian family and have been baptized but true to my secular credential I have never let religion be my USP. My wife is a Hindu and my daughter has the freedom to practise any faith or none if she chooses to. While the world has changed so much the church has remained frozen in time, shackled in it's own old age dogmas which has little or no relevance today. Sadly that's the situation today. But the important thing is - you have been baptized and that should make you an eligible candidate. I am meeting the Johnstons for dinner tomorrow along with Shrobanshu Roy. I propose to discuss this with them and get some insight as to how to take this forward. Bye for now. Will be in touch.
Ashish Bhengra
Jan 12, 2012

I have looked through Jigmi's CV. I don't think we can get anyone more suitable or so highly qualified and able, to steer the school in the coming critical years. I would thoroughly endorse Jigmi's candidacy.
To all and the new Principal,
I sincerely hope and pray that the old school will return to its 'natural' status and bring back the stature it was known for. Please let me know how - can help. Abu Rauff (1946-54), US.

Dipak,
Thanks for the email.
MHS deserves a committed principal who can catalyze the changes required to bring it back to the top.
Given that he has the support of many former Principals, I would be happy to support Jigme, and his initiative to revitalize our beloved Mt. Hermon.
Arka Mukherjee, 1982, US.

"THANK YOU!"

"You can take a Hermonite out of Mount Hermon, but you cannot take Mount Hermon out of a Hermonite."

Dear Friends,

Roslyn (Rongong) Namgyal (Canberra - Australia), who is coordinating with Dipak Mirchandhani (UK), has sent a letter to Chairman of the Managing Committee of MH (Bishop Sagar of Methodist Church of Bangalore) regarding the campaign for MH Revival and my candidature for the post of Principal.

The application, which has the backing of global Hermonites, including several principals and teachers of our school, was sent yesterday (Jan 26, 2012).

Sherab and Roslyn.

While we wait for the response, I want to share with you and other Hermonites of the joy and strength we get from our efforts and enthusiasm for trying to save our beloved Alma Mater. The enthusiastic manner and the spirit in which we have shown our love and concern for MH is something the world does not know and understand but badly needs. So keep up the pressure; back it with faith and prayers.

Dipak and Rekha.

I would also like to thank you personally and the Hermonites who have supported me for the job. The support from past students and teachers of the school - from 1930s and down to the 21st century - is overwhelming.

Shiv and Saroj.   (L to R): Jigme, Saroj & Shiv, Cindy & Pradip.

This in itself is a wonderful experience. A big hug to all and a "Thank You" from the bottom of my heart.

The campaign for MH Revival must continue no matter what the Bishop and the Managing Committee decide. My class friend (SC 1972) and fellow Hermonite Sunirmal Chakravarthi (Chuck - Principal of La Martiniere Boys School, Calcutta) rightly said: "You can take a Hermonite out of Mount Hermon, but you cannot take Mount Hermon out of a Hermonite."

Thank You and Cheers! Hail Mount Hermon!

Jigs

Dear Cindy and Roslyn,

Thank you for forwarding this note on Jigme. What a splendid endorsement of Jigme's capabilities and character.

I happy to give my support for his candidature for the next Principal of MH.

With love.

Prava (Rai – 1970 batch)

Dear Jigme

Wonderful indeed to touch base after so long. I am particularly thrilled to know that you took to education and may one day, God willing, lead our alma mater. May positive energies follow you always.

Yes, I have lived in Mumbai for the past 35 years. Brij must have seen someone else who looked like me at Wankhade as I avoid the crowds at matches like the plague and prefer to watch them on TV! I have had an unusual parallel career - in Publishing and in Human Resources. I am presently Executive Director, Editorial and HR at a six-year-old publishing house based in Mumbai, called Leadstart Publishing. I look after the Non-Fiction and Children's Lists completely.

If I can contribute anything towards the efforts to lift MH back to its former glory, please do not hesitate to ask.
God be with you.
Chandralekha

Jan 16
Dear Jigme,
Sorry for the delay in response. Of course we are all happy to hear about you being the possible principal of MH. I hope you can do at MH what Kinley did at NP.

I think the reason why Nepali Hermonites are so quiet is because we really do not see much hope for MH. There have been too many false dawns. Very few Nepali Hermonites have put their kids back in MH, exceptions being Rijals and the Pokharels. We are not so far away as not to know the gory and unpleasant details nor are we inured by proximity. So perhaps that is the reason for the lack of response.

I had made a draft email in response to Ved's email but I too did not feel like sharing my thoughts of MH because they are very direct and question the very ownership and thus the management structure and philosophy. So you will excuse me for not responding to the group. However, I am copying and pasting the draft reply. (see the message in blue after this message to you) However, I will make a CC of this to Ved as he is someone I greatly admired and respected in school and later. He was very fond of me and treated me very well when I was in MH. I will also make a copy of this to Lucinda and a few others whom I trust and communicate with often.

We would be the happiest if you can take over as the principal of MH and make it the best school in India. After all Nepalis would be the biggest beneficiaries of such a development.
When you meet Sikkim Hermonites please give them my greetings, specially my old friend from Delhi University days, Shuva Pradhan.
Love
Lochan, Kathmandu.

Hi Ved,
My take on this issue is slightly different.

Surely the owners ought to take full responsibility for the shambles that MH finds itself in. This rule applies to me in my business as well as my home. I am sure it applies to everyone here. As an owner of my business units and I take full responsibility. I just cannot pass the buck. It becomes my responsibility to pump in more funds if and when necessary. Or to find new partners if I cannot do it; or take outside consultants to sort out the mess or lease it out or sell it if I cannot run it or if I am not interested to run it. As Ian Chappell famously told the visiting Indian cricket team to Australia, "If you can't stand the heat, get out of the kitchen." The same should apply to the current management/owners of MH.

Having said that we can talk as much as we like but if the owners of MH don't want change, nothing will change.

There is a dictum, "You break it, you own it". From the stories that I have heard in the past 2 decades unfortunately it seems to me that in MH's case the reverse of the dictum is true: "You own it, (so) you (can) break it". These stories and the shabby and run down condition of MH do not inspire much confidence. In such a situation I just don't see how we can help. I don't think financial and other help will be forthcoming from the alumni unless the basics are sorted out. Astronomers can spot all devouring black holes billions of miles away but I think I can see one some 500 km east from where I sit.

As it is MH probably has the worst record for keeping good relations with its alumni. It is incredible that we still have this soft spot for our beloved school despite total disregard for the alumni. In this age of instant connectivity, this neglect borders on the criminal.

I hope Jigme or whoever is ultimately chosen as the principal has incredibly thick skin and good political skills and connections to roll back the squatters and all the wrongs of the past 20-30 years. Up the road from MH, Father Kinley, an alumni of NP, was able to pull NP out of the slump. So I am sure it can be done in MH too but I think Kinley had incredibly good support from the Catholic church/Jesuit order. Will that sort of support be forthcoming from the owners of MH? Best of luck to the next principal.

Love and Regards,
Lochan

Jan 17, 2012
Hi Jigs,
Here is Tehmi's forward of Bill Jones' response. I hope this helps you open windows?
wkr
Sujit.

Sujit,
Here is Bill Jones' reply - go ahead and forward it to Jigme and others. It may still be worth visiting Donald Kessop in Calcutta.
Cheers,
Tammy

From: William Jones
Sent: Sunday, January 15
To: Tammy
Dear Tammy,
I taught and baptized Jigme Kazi, and have followed his journalistic career with pride & joy. However, I wonder if he has the qualifications and experience in educational administration that's necessary. AND: Would the Methodist bishop accept him? The even bigger question is whether the Association of Anglo Indian Schools would accept him

as a school principal. And then the Government, which oversees the Anglo Indian Schools, has to approve.

Does Jigme now have a master's degree in education? That's necessary. I can see Jigme as a manager, which the School certainly needs. The loss of Mr. Mathai was almost as drastic a blow as the failure to find good principals. Maybe Jigme could fill that managerial slot.

The American church has no influence whatever with the Methodist Church in India. The MCI and American Methodists washed their hands of each other a generation ago.

Donald, lives on Beniapukur Lane; but he is now out of circulation since his wife died and his daughter's marriage arrangements have preoccupied him. He has changed in outlook and interests since his wife's death last February.

The only way I can see to save Mt. Hermon is to get it out of the hands of the Methodist Church and other churches in India. This has been done with other failing church institutions by selling the institution and its property to another organization, usually a for-profit entity. The soybean processing industry that Methodist missionaries started in U.P. (the first soybean processor in India) was hopelessly mired in corruption and debt. It was finally sold to a Marwari firm. The first women's hospital in Asia, Clara Swain hospital in Bareilly, was a leader in the missionary era, but ran down just like Mt. Hermon has. It was finally sold to a consortium of doctors: non-Christian doctors but including a clever Christian business consultant (whose mother and father I married: the very first Methodist Christian marriage in that rural district). Some group has to make an offer for the property, an offer that the MCI authorities can't refuse. I see two possible buyers:

1. The Jesuit order of the Catholic Church. The Mt. Hermon campus could be an expansion and diversity campus for St. Joseph's and St. Michael's.
2. The State Government. The Darjeeling Nepalis very much want to expand their educational opportunities. They could run a successful school or college there, and they could get the money for it.

These ideas both depend on the extinction of Mt. Hermon as we have known it. The church authorities will give it up if that is more profitable to them than keeping it going downhill, as it is at present.

We have to realize that (1) the churches involved in Mt. Hermon never had any local base, and have no real interest in the local people there; and (2) the charm of hill stations for education has waned and practically died in India. The people who are interested in English secondary and higher education now can get it in all the major cities of India. They have no great desire to escape the heat; and they no longer fear the tropical diseases that used to threaten life on the plains.

[There is excellent medical service now available throughout most of India; the places where it is hardest to find are the hills and jungle areas.] The only people now interested in hill station education in numbers are the hill people themselves. That's why St. Joseph's and Loreto were so wise to localize their schools and preserve their high quality. It's interesting that the best person we now can find with an interest in managing the school is Jigme: a Sikkimese.

Mt. Hermon came into being as a girls' school for Europeans and Anglo-Indians. Its campus was in Darjeeling town at Queen's Hill. The campus changed; and then after Independence the mission of the School changed. In our time the School served Indians and other Asians who wanted quality English education. Now Mt. Hermon has to change drastically to have any relevance to contemporary conditions.

It is always hard to give up any person, culture or institution that Nature or History render obsolete. But it has to be done. Missionaries find persons around the world whose religion no longer serves their deepest needs, and they bring major changes into these peoples' lives, often against strong and principled opposition. Visionary businessmen find financial systems obsolete and embrace new models, sometimes through violent revolution, as in American history. The same goes for political systems. I think the Mt. Hermon alumni have to recognize that the school that so beautifully met their needs now has to change its mission in a basic way.

I wish I had an easier and brighter message.
Let me know your reaction.
Ever fondly and gratefully,
Bill (Jones), US.

Jan 14
Hi Bill,

Hope you and Beulah are both doing well. It looks like the MH body of students is on a roll and have narrowed down their search for a successor to George Fernandes. It is Jigme Kazi, an ex-student who has pretty impressive credentials.

Anyway, the latest question now is: Is the Methodist Church in India totally divorced from the American Methodist church? Or, does the US church carry any influence with the India church?

Is this address for Donald Kessop still good?
Rev. Donald Kessop
Flat # 4
172/25-A AJC Bose Road
Beniapukur Lane
CALCUTTA

Jan 16
Thanks Sujit,

Mr. Jones's views are interesting and we need to take them seriously. I had mentioned in my emails that extraordinary circumstances demand extraordinary acts. We, including the Methodist Church, cannot get stuck in the past and wake up to new situations with equal zest and vision.

I am presently in Siliguri to talk to Foothills Hermonites Association to know their views and get their support. They are positive. Also met Pratap Rai (left school in 1967), who is undergoing medical treatment. Pratap has been one of the most active Hermonites in the region and is an Invitee Member of the Managing Committee.

He has supported me and will continue to do so. Will go and meet Mr. Fernandes, MH Principal, when he comes back from Bangalore at the end of the month and then come down to Cal. By then we should have names and addresses of some of the Committee Members of Cal.
Jigs

Hi Jigs,
This was my response to the email from Bill Jones. I think he is a little out of touch with what is happening in Darjeeling and I still think MH could be revived into an elite school, though maybe a little smaller.

Keep being positive and keep pushing ahead with your plans. I am available if you need any assistance.
Cheers
Barry

Jan 16
Hi Sujit and Tammy and my other Hermonite friends,
Thanks for sending this on to me Sujit. I fully agree that times change and that what MH was for us years ago can maybe not be repeated. However, I do not agree that the only interest in 'hill schools' is local. MH has until recently had a reasonable contingent of Thai students as well as Kolkata, Nepal, Bhutan and Bangladeshis. This will continue as Darjeeling, despite its complex political situations, has still attracted large crowds during the tourist season - from all over the world. It is still Queen of the Hills and hundreds of new schools have sprung up.

The system of accepting Jigmi as a principal and having to go through the various Boards and associations could be tricky - but at the end of the day, if the Methodist Church of India accepted him, if only on an interim basis because of his interest in the school, his capacity to lead and the support of the alumni, which could raise funds etc., that would be a start.

So my response is that the momentum that so many people have started should be followed through as far as possible - hopefully until we hit a brick wall - and then we try and find a solution to get through or over that brick wall.

MH will become something different, but lets still proceed with the idea of restoration and revival into whatever the education market shapes it into becoming.
Cheers to all
Barry

Hi All, this is the best thing that can happen to MHS. I am fully in support of Jigme.
I knew him personally and vouch for his capability and his integrity. But we must support him any way possible and required. Hope he accepts the responsibility.

Regarding the committee, if possible guys who stay nearby can meet them personally or if their mobile nos can be obtained we can call them. This is over and above the proposed letter signed by all.

Regards
Suresh Chatlani
ISC 1971, Lagos, Nigeria, Africa.

I fully support Jigme's nomination. His heart has always been with MHS. He has been a leader during and since his scholarship at MHS. He commands respect from all who know him and from the wider community too.

Save for the return of a Mr. Murray or Mr. Johnston, I can't think of a more suitable or worthy captain.
Ian Hastings (1973 batch), UK.

Jigme to Mr. Ison
Dear Sir,
Fully agree with your reactions on Mr. Jones. Am as positive as ever and will stay the same till the goal is achieved. Did you get Sherab and Roz's note? It has been circulated to get Oz and NZ Hermonites support. Am here in Siliguri for Udai's daughter's marriage and am meeting Shiv Saria, Jagdish Saria, Lamba etc. They will pass a resolution on the issue. Also met Pratap Rai here, he is undergoing stomach cancer treatment. He is an active Hermonite and is presently 'invitee member' of the Managing Committee. Pratap is fully behind us and have already supported me and will urge the Committee and Fernandes to pay heed to the Hermonites and support me.

Namgyal Wangdi and I will be going to Darj at the end of this month to get briefed by Fernandes who is presently in Bangalore. We hope to come down to Cal in Feb first week to meet committee members. However, we still have no idea who the members are. It would be good if you come down when we are there. I don't think I should be with the guys when they meet them. What do you think about it? Fernandes has extended his support to me and said he would advise the committee members to listen to us.
Jigs

Hi Jigs,
Coming to Cal in the first week will be a little tough for me mainly because I won't be able to get a visa by then, but also its school time. I could take a personal day off and combine it with a weekend (Friday and Saturday - 3rd and 4th), but I still think it will take longer to get a visa. The new system on line takes forever as there are so many Bangladeshis trying to get into India and the computer system is constantly busy. In any event, once you have the dates when you will be in Cal let me know. Yes I did get Ros's email and have replied.
Cheers – Barry

'MH Revival' Campaign 2012

Dear Ros,

This is good. I have made a couple of repairs and have added something at the bottom which you should check to see if that is what you want to say. If we could only see him and talk to him and show him that we are people of reason and cooperation. I might even be able to get away if it fits into my holidays. For example, I am free April 6th, 7th and 8th or 12th, 13th and 14th.

One thing - Bishops are called something like "Your Excellency" or "Your Worship" .... there is an appropriate term. Can you find that out from your Pastor and use it down the bottom. It would sound like we are making an effort to get alongside.

Keep it going. But we need to emphasize that we only want to work with the Church not against them, not in competition. So the dialogue that is going around needs to be tempered and not aggressive. Also, I don't think it a bad idea if we put out a call to prayer, to whomever we pray to. Because we as Hermonites should know that all things are possible with Divine intervention.

Love you guys.
Barry

Nina Wason (third from right) is with her mother Mrs. B. Wason (ex-MH teacher) and Siliguri Hermonites: Ravi, Charlotte, Shiv and wife Saroj and Sushil.

Roz,

I wholly support your efforts to have Jigme appointed as Principal of Mount Hermon. Given his personal achievements at school in addition to his own experience of Mount Hermon in its' heyday, I am sure he will do an excellent job in restoring the school to its former glory.
Good luck, Jigme!!
Nina (Wason) M. Harkness, Naples, Florida.

Dear Roslyn,

I would be personally very pleased if Jigmi Kazi is elected as next Headmaster of Mount Hermon School when Mr. George Fernandez retires.
Sincerely,
James Sinclair (of OMHSA), UK.

I certainly support candidate Jigmi Kazi as he considers becoming principal at Mt. Hermon.
G. Richard Kern, '49, Findlay, Ohio, USA.

Hi,

This is Andre Strong, Jigmi Kazi's classmate, you might remember me, I was good friends with Robin Sengupta and Mike Gomes. I currently live in the good ole USA, and have been looking into the Hermonite website, hence the Hermonite address. Well how are you doing, I know you married Sherab Buthia.

My daughter lives in Melbourne and has just finished her MBA and works at the Crown Casino. Anyway I definitely will support him. And I'm glad to know that an old student will be taken the reigns and hopefully change things around. What Mount Hermonite taught us remained with me thru out my life and those found memories we always cherish, so do keep in touch, will tell Robin you emailed, we talk often, in fact we spoke overt Christmas, so take care,
Andy Strong

Andre Strong, Darjeeling, 1971. (Pic: Hemant Lama)

I fully support your campaign to propose Jigmi Kazi as the new headmaster of Mount Hermon. I was a pupil there from 1936 -1938 and 1941 - 1944. The years missing I was back in the UK.
Best wishes
Doris White (nee Hunt), UK.

Dear Mrs. Namgyal,

I just came back from India and was very sad to hear the current state of affairs at MHS. Every Hemonite I meet attribute their school days at MH as the foundation for success in life. All of us remember our school days very fondly. I am so glad to hear that Mr. Kazi is willing to undertake the rebuilding of MH and I am sure that he will take it to its glory days.

Thank you also for initiating this email to gather support for Mr. Kazi. I will be forwarding this to all the Hermonites I know and I know your inbox is gonna be full soon.
Tien Hsi Chiang

Dear Roslyn and Lucinda,

We support Jigme's candidature all the way. I shall get at least 7 - 8 names for this campaign.
Hail Mt. Hermon!
Best wishes,
Amode Yonzone – 1973 batch, Kalimpong.

Dear Lochan,

Thank you for your support and sharing your thoughts. I fully agree with you. MH is a great institution and if it is going down the drain then accountability must be fixed. How we go about doing this is a matter of strategy. Secondly, the church needs to rethink and adapt itself to changing times without compromising on its basic values and principles.

I firmly believe that we should be given a chance to pull MH through this crisis. No one can do it. Therefore, we are the natural 'guardian deities' of our beloved alma mater. We must come to its rescue. No one, including the church, can do it.

Like you, I too, feel that the school has not taken advantage of the tremendous goodwill of its alumni. The Hermonites spirit, however, can and should overcome the apathy and attitude of vested interests connected to MH. I think we can and should share your views given to me and Ved with other Hermonites. If you okay it then I will circulate it. Rare insights into MH situation will enlighten those who do not know what is going on behind the scene.

So, thanks for the response which I had expected from the Gyawalis. How's Bachan? Your friend Shuva is still a bachelor and looks the same.
Take care and stay in touch,
Jigs

Dear Jigs,

Thank you for your mail. If you feel it is ok to share my views then please go ahead and do so. I have no problem with that.

My only fear is that failure condition already exists at MH. If without addressing this root cause should you jump into the ring then even you will fail. If you fail then we all fail because you and people like you are the last hope for MH. We all were so happy when Miss Russell was re-attached to the school some years ago. We had all expected her to do well and pull up the school out of the rut it was in. With her dedication and love for MH it would have been possible. As per the information that I have unfortunately it did not happen despite her best efforts. The underlying failure condition existed and that was never addressed.

Unfortunately, that failure condition is the church itself. Or at least the manpower looks after the affairs of the school in the church.

If the church is not up to it, then the school can become a non-religious institution. I really see no great benefit from keeping it as a school controlled by one religion if the office-bearers of that religion neglect such a fine institution. If the church is (only) more interested in saving souls for the next life and not so interested in saving fine institutions in this life then it is time for them to get out. Let them be in the business of saving souls and let others who can run schools be in the business of running schools.

I for one see absolutely no benefit of having owners who neglect such a fine 125 year old institution or owners who cannot pump in funds. After all churches are some of the richest institutions in the world and if they cannot fund the revival of one fine school then it is an unpardonable sin, to use their language.

Thank you for the news about Shuva. He was always a great looking guy. I am happy that he looks the same. It is a shame that he is a bachelor because if such a good looking and fine person has remained a bachelor then it does not reflect too well on the female population of Sikkim! Please ask him and the female population of Sikkim to rectify this situation. Please do give him my regards as and when you meet him.

Love
Lochan

Dear Jigs,

Just saw your mail, and with it, all the other attachments and I must admit I am a little shocked, and like all of you, very concerned about what is happening at MH. I had been hearing distressing reports of declining numbers but I really did not know it was this bad!

I do not have ready access to the contact details of the members of the MH Managing Committee but I could ask around and fetch them up.

Give me a day.

While I share everyone's concern and (perhaps anger) at the recent downturn, as a serving School Principal myself, I would advise great caution about some of the measures that have been suggested by friends (many of whom I remember very fondly). For instance:

1. Whereas the idea of nominating your name for Principalship is an idea I would heartily endorse because of your commitment to MH; I think it would be in the best interest of the school to go about doing it the right way, which is to go through the Management Committee. Also, do keep in mind, that the Government of

West Bengal (and the ISC Council) have certain terms and conditions for appointment of Principals.

2. Also I think there is no harm in the MC considering the inclusion of former students to the Committee; but to demand that the old boys and girls should have a say in the day to day running of the school is a very suspect idea. It does however make great sense to create a liasoning group who will interact between the School, the Alumni and the School Management Committee!

3. I don't really know how the numbers have declined so badly but all this would surely have had a terrible impact on the finances of the school. We have a situation here: Without numbers, it won't be possible to improve the finances, and without strong finances at the moment, we seem to be not able to improve infrastructure etc., which will attract students. May I suggest that you get someone who is strong on financial fundamentals to advise you in this area so that a blueprint of some kind can be worked out which would help you in your meeting with the MC.

As I scrolled down your mail page, I was struck by all the names there. I haven't met so many of them since leaving school in 1972. Though I must say I was over the moon when I bumped into Sherab and Roslyn in Darjeeling early this month. It would be great to catch up with you all soon.

Take care and here's wishing you the very best in the effort to resuscitate MH. I promise to get back to you on the details of the School MC within a day.

Cheers!
Chuck
Mr. S. Chakravarthi
Principal
La Martiniere for Boys,
11 Loudon Street,
Kolkata

Dear Chuck,

Thanks for the support and your suggestions. We are in Siliguri to attend Udai Sharma's daughter's marriage and will have some Hermonites from our class and 73 batch during the wedding. Firstly, hope you are ok there, we've heard and read so much. Anytime you need our support we are there now that we have resumed our contact. So proud that you are the chief there!!

Now please send us the names and email add of the members of the Managing Committee members straightaway even if you have to stretch a bit. I'm told that the Principal of Cal Boys and Girls school are members, so you can send theirs first.

Also with whom do we need to contact in the government on the issue, guide us with specifics.

Thanks for your help and we count on you,
Jigs

Hail Mount Hermon! A Tribute

(L to R) Former Cal Lamart Principal and 1972 batch Hermonite Sunirmal Chakrabarti (Chuck), Gorkha Territorial Administration Principal Secretary Hermonite Choten Dhendup Lama and Senior Master Partho Dey at MH, 2018.

"RESOLUTION PASSED BY THE DELHI HERMONITES"

To,
The Chairman,
Managing Committee,
Mount Hermon School,
Darjeeling-734 101.
(W.B).   Dated:- 17.01.2012

Sub: Delhi Chapter of the Hermonites, supports the candidature of Mr. Jigme Kazi, for the Principal-ship of Mount Harmon School Darjeeling.

Dear Sir,

This is to invite your kind attention to the good news which is in circulation amongst the Hermonites and the well wisher of the school that Mr. Jigme Kazi has been recommended by the Sikkim Hermonites Association for the Principal-ship of Mount Hermon School Darjeeling. Thus, in support of the Resolution passed by the Sikkim Hermonites Association, we the Hermonites settled and living in Delhi do hereby fully endorse and give our full support to the candidature of Mr. Jigme Kazi as the next Principal of Mount Hermon School, Darjeeling.

The Delhi Chapter of the Hermonites Association, who met at Delhi on 17.01.2012, passed a resolution in support of Mr. Jigme Kazi as the next Principal of Mount Hermon School, which is quoted below:-

Quote:

"The Hermonites Association of Delhi do hereby resolve that we fully support and ratify the Resolution passed by the Sikkim Hermonites Association in favour of the Candidature of Mr. Jigme Kazi as the next Principal of Mount Hermon School, Darjeeling and we are sure that he will prove to be an asset to Mount Hermon School and will fulfill all it's needs, because a Hermonite can only understand and appreciate what Mount Hermon needs at present".
Unquote.

Conti..."2"

The above Quoted resolution was passed in the presence of the following Hermonites at Delhi on 17th day of January, of the year 2012:-

"RESOLUTION PASSED BY THE DELHI HERMONITES"

To,
The Principal,
Mount Hermon School,
Darjeeling-734 101.
(W.B). Dated:- 17.01.2012

Sub: Delhi Chapter of the Hermonites, supports the candidature of Mr. Jigme Kazi, for the Principal-ship of Mount Hermon School Darjeeling.
Dear Sir,

Kindly find enclosed herewith, the copy of the Resolution passed in the meeting of the Delhi Hermonites, living in Delhi.

> Please do the needful by forwarding the same to the Managing Committee of Mount Hermon School, Darjeeling, inviting their kind attention to the Resolutions passed by the Delhi Hermonites.
>
> The Delhi Chapter of the Hermonites, who met at Delhi on 17.01.2012, passed the following Resolution in support of Mr. Jigme Kazi as the next Principal of Mount Hermon School, Darjeeling.
>
> Quote:
>
> *"The Hermonites Association of Delhi do hereby resolve that we fully support and ratify the Resolution passed by the Sikkim Hermonites Association, in favour of the Candidature of Mr. Jigme Kazi as the next Principal of MOUNT HERMON School, Darjeeling and we are sure that he will prove to be an asset to Mount Hermon School and will fulfill all it's needs, because a Hermonite can only understand and appreciate what Mount Hermon needs at present".*
>
> Unquote.
>
> With Regards, for and on behalf of Delhi Hermonites.
>
> Mahesh Singh and Others
> J-3/36, First Floor,
> Rajouri Garden,
> New Delhi-110027.

Hi Jigs!

My whole hearted support to you. I wish you all the best in whatever initiatives you take to revive the Glory of MHS!

Best of Luck!

Mahesh Singh, 1973 batch, Delhi.

Dear OMHSA Members,

I'm forwarding these messages on to you concerning Jigmi Kazi's candidature for Headmaster of MHS once George Fernandez retires in March this year. I believe the school is in a bad way at the moment and it is hoped Jigmi can restore it to it's former glory. If you would like to support him, please respond to Roslyn's email.

Sincerely,

James Sinclair, UK.

Dear Roz,

My mother was Lila Engberg, principal of Mt. Hermon School from 1931 to 1935. The school has a scholarship in her name. I know she would want me to support your efforts to preserve and protect the school she dearly loved, and I certainly share that sentiment. What you have written about Jigme makes him sound eminently qualified and suitable for the position being vacated when Mr. Fernandez leaves in March.

Supreme Court lawyer and 1973 batch Hermonite Mahesh Singh with Jigme N. Kazi, New Dehi.

    I hope those who must make the decisions about the future of the school will give serious and favorable consideration to his application. After such a long and presitigious history, it would be a tragedy for Mt. Hermon School to disappear as an educational institution. It must be preserved. Let me know if I can help.
Mildred Engberg "Kitty" Katzell, US.

Hi again Jigs!!

I don't know if things have changed since when I was Vice Principal of St. Paul's Mission School in Calcutta - but at that time there was a requirement for Principals and Vice Principals to have Masters' Degrees.

Do you have a Master's degree? If you do - it will make it easier for the Board to consider your application.

If you do NOT - that doesn't necessarily mean that they will not consider you - but if they are against giving it to you - that would be something they can use as a valid reason for not considering you.

Either way, I wish you well and I wish MH well. When I was a Vice Principal in Cal - I often thought that I would like to be back in MH in an administrative position.

With the situation in the school now, however, with people squatting on school property and I don't know what other local tensions relating to Gorkhaland etc [I am out of touch with Darj politics], I think someone FROM Darj/Sikkim might be in a much better position to deal with local, administrative and estate issues.

You would be at an advantage there. However - there is also the internal aspect - dealing with teachers, managing academics, sports programs, dealing with other staff. These are the heart of the school and need as much, if not more, of a Principal's attention.

Pulling the school out of its current slump will not be a cakewalk - as you probably know. In short - this is not just about being Principal of MH.

It is a political, legal, cultural, administrative, educational, emotional - and above all - Spiritual - endeavour. Consider carefully and prayerfully whether it is God's will for you to embark on this path. If He is behind this, He will guide you to success.

I got to know you quite well while I was up in MH as a teacher - and I want you to know that you have my vote of confidence.

But I also want to caution you [as someone who has been in school administration from 1987-1993 in Cal] pursue this only if God is leading you in this direction.

I consider you a friend and a brother in Christ - or I would not feel the freedom to speak so freely to you of this.

You know that you have the support of all the Hermonites from our days and that is because of the great respect you earned from all of us who knew you.

Still - very few of our Hermonite brothers and sisters have any knowledge of the workings of school administration - or of the MH Board of Governors - or, sadly, of the perfect will of God.

Make your choice not on what you hear man saying - but what you hear God saying. I hope you are already doing this and it would not surprise me in the least if you have been seeking God's will in this matter already.

Either way - you will always be a precious friend to me and have my support if this is where God is calling you to set your hand to the plough.

Let me know if I can help in any way. This situation will be in my prayers.

With Love and blessings in the name of Jesus!

Robin Sengupta, US.

Dear Roslyn,
Happy New Year!

You most probably wouldn't remember me. Was too junior but I was in the first batch of students that Mr. Rai (class 5R) had as he started his teaching carrier with Mr. Kazi in MH.

Have met Mr. Kazi when he visited Bhutan a few years back, it was memorable and a pleasure to be sitting with your teacher as a friend and family with all due respects.

MH has been going through rough times and Bhutanese Hermonites have been trying our best by having our own children and encouraging other Bhutanese to join MH by even recruiting a Bhutanese language teacher to be as part of the teaching staff there with all due support from Mr. Fernandes as the Principal. (I am not sure if the language teacher is still there though).

With all due respect to Mr. and Mrs. Fernandes and what they have been doing for MH all these years, which definitely wasn't easy, I guess things have to and should move on and maybe for the better too. They hung on through all the rough days!

To know that Mr. Kazi and his family that supports him, is now the new candidate to take over from Mr. Fernandes, sounds absolutely perfect! Being born a Buddhist and baptized as a Christian should be the least of importance is what I personally feel. What is most important is getting a capable, initiative human being with a good soul and positive thoughts.

I am sure the other Bhutanese Hermonites will be as happy as I was to get the great news. What do you think of this? @ Father Taki

Best Rgds
Thinley Dem,
Thimphu, Bhutan

We support your candidature, Jigme!
Deborshi Hazra, 1996, India
Rajarshi Hajra, 1996, India
Arindam Roy, 1997, India
Goutam Roy, 1996, India
Hail Mount Hermon!

Dear Sir,

I full support and endorse the candidature of Mr. Jigmi N. Kazi for the post of Principal of Mount Hermon School.

I have forwarded this email to many other Hermonites who are there in my mailing list. I hope to get many more Hermonites to respond this matter and pray that Mount Hermon reaches back to its past glory.

If there is anything more that I can do in this regard please let me know.

Thanks.
Prakash Mundra

Hail Mount Hermon! A Tribute

Bhutanese Hermonite Thinley Delma, Barry Ison and Jigme N. Kazi in Paro, Bhutan.

Hello Bijay,
 Would you kindly send me Roslyn's e-mail address so that I can add my endorsement. (Hope I haven't been negligent in seeing it on the message!)
 Thanks and while I am about it, "Thanks" for the many messages you take the time to send, which I enjoy.
Keep well.
Cherry

Dear Roslyn,
 Please add my name to the list of those endorsing Jigme Kazi for Principal of Mount Hermon.
 You have given him an excellent recommendation and MH would be fortunate to have a leader like him. Give him my best wishes.
 Hope you and your family are well. All the best to you all and a Happy New Year.
 Cherry Hall (Williams)

Dear Cindy and Roslyn,
 Thank you for forwarding this note on Jigme.
 What a splendid endorsement of Jigme's capabilities and character. I happy to give my support for his candidature for the next Principal of MH.
With love.
Prava Rai, Sikkim.

 I absolutely support Jigme as Principal of Mount Hermon School. Please let me know what else I can do. I fully support the idea and I hope that we can do something about it.
Vinij Khureya (Hermonite-1976), Bangkok.

 I think its an excellent idea and I fully support it.
Aamir Tarique
1979-1987

Hello Rosylyn
Thanks for the update. I support Jigme Kazi for principalship for MH.
Regards
Fui Chung Li, ISC 1975, Canada.

 Hello fellow Hermonites. Received this email regarding support for Mr. Jigme Kazi for principalship for MH. Wonderful news indeed. Just when we all are in despair for the current state of MH, we know Mr. Kazi as principal for MH will take it to its glory days. Please reply to Mrs. Namgyal personally...see email for her add.

Happy new year to all and hope the year of the Dragon bring love and peace to all.
Tien Hsi.

Dear Hermonites,

Thank you for your effort to SAVE MHS.

I on behalf of the Class of 1988 do support Mr. Jigme's candidature for the next Principal of MH.

We the batch of 1988 have had the privilege of being under both the present Principal Mr. Fernandez who taught us passionately in our Senior School and my memories date back to 1979-80 when I joined MH and Mr. Jigme was a person who helped me in my early days in School.

We give our full support to Mr. Jigme and request all concerned to do the same.
Pramod K Sirohiya, 1988, Nepal/India.

Hi Roslyn

On receipt of your forwarded message, thought I would reply and let you know that both my sister Sandra and I are delighted that something is being undertaken to revitalize the spirit of MH and get the school up and running to it's former glory. We both have very fond memories of our time at MH (1959 - 1961) and were horrified at it's decline over the years.

We would be happy to add our names with all the other signatures on your document to the Management Committee, in support of endorsing Jigme Kazi as a suitable candidate.

Thank you for your very informative message regarding this situation and hope that all our 'small voices' together will create a 'big noise' to be heard by the Mount Hermon Management Committee, and hopefully acted upon!
Kindest regards
Andrea Porter
(was Andrea Phillippe)
also Sandra Robinson (was Sandra Phillippe), UK.

Dear Roslyn and all other Hermonites,

First of all Happy New Year.

Thank you very much Roslyn for the very informative and encouraging message about the future of Mount Hermon. I fully agree with all the qualities of our very good friend Jigme, you have my support all the way and please advise any assistance required.
Take care and rgds,
Thip (Varongthip, 1973 batch), Bangkok.

Dear Jigme,

Thanks for your prompt reply. As I read some of the mail sent to you more recently I was really encouraged to read Roslyn's recommendation of your case. I can only hope that the MC of the School can see not only the groundswell of support for you but also discern that it makes best sense to hand over MH to a Hermonite!

Before I go any further let me thank you for expressing your support for me. Much of all that has happened is the result of La Martiniere being a high profile school. The nuisance persists and I keep visiting the court from time to time; and I have learnt to take all this in my stride. But let's get back to MH.

Sunirmal (Chuck, centre) with Mahesh (left) and Jagdish (right) in Darjeeling.

I was able to speak to Mr. Raja McGee, Principal of Calcutta Boys School. This is what he told me:

After the last Methodist Bishop of Lucknow passed away, the responsibility of looking after this area and MH was given to the Methodist Bishop of Bangalore. He, in turn, set up a committee to oversee matters concerning the School. But I got the distinct impression that this committee has not really met in a long, long time. Yes, Mr. McGee is on the Committee and is worried to death about MH.

My suggestion is that you should talk to him as soon as you can. I have told him about your sincerity, commitment and resolve and also requested him to take your call. He has agreed to take your call. I will sms his mobile number as soon as I finish writing this mail.

The reason, if you don't mind, for not sharing the number over the mail is that given his busy schedule as Principal I don't want too many people calling him up (in spite of their sincerity). It might just annoy him and we surely do not want that.

Regarding the qualifications bit let me share this with you: The MC will definitely want the candidate to be a Christian. I should think they will prefer a Methodist but I am not too sure about that. The WB Government and the ISC Council expect that the minimum qualification to become a Principal is for a candidate to possess a Post Graduate Degree (MA/M.Sc) with a professional qualification (i.e. B.Ed).

Now, if you don't have this, one can still work around it with the School MC asking you to complete the necessary qualifications within a specified time limit (say the next four years). I know for certain that the current Rector in St. Paul's Darjeeling has also been appointed under these same conditions. So one can work around this.

I have read some of the more recent mail attached to your letter and found some really hard hitting truth in there - none so more than Lochan's opinion of the current MC!! He has hit the nail on the head; yet, one has to work within the system and I hope that if the MC has its heart in the right place, they can throw you the challenge and MH begin to walk the path of recovery.

Let me know if there is anything else I could do. Do keep me posted of developments.
Hail Mount Hermon!
Cheers,
Chuck

Dear Jigs,

They have a saying here in La Martiniere which I would like to paraphrase and pinch and share with you: "You can take a Hermonite out of Mount Hermon, but you cannot take Mount Hermon out of a Hermonite." True, I am very loyal to my current School, La Martiniere, but I cannot forget that I am here today because there was Mount Hermon yesterday. I owe it all to my alma mater.

Thanks for calling, it was great to talk to you. Let's all resolve to fight the good fight.
Cheers,
Chuck

Absolutely support Mr. Jigme Kazi to be the next principal. Who better than a qualified Hermonite to be at the helm. Go Mr. Kazi!
Sebanti Chatterjee Chadha, 1982 Canada
Sebanti Chadha

Dear Fellow Hermonite,

It would be an excellent idea to have Mr. Kazi as the next principal of Mount Hermon. Much can be expected from him. The alumni need to perhaps write direct emails to the Methodist Bishop of North India. If anyone has the address please post it. Also, mails to the individual managing committee members may be helpful.

On another note, I would ask you not to take the Boarding Schools of India report too seriously....it has no sound scientific methodology in the way the schools are graded. The "marks" appeared to be based on hearsay and reputation. I was tickled to read the column on "alumni participation"...we were at the bottom of the heap and perhaps rightly so.

Except for the 'Old MHS' website, all other websites/social networks have a preponderance of negative comments by the alumni. Let the alumni start thinking positive. Maybe start by trying to raise funds to fix the leaky chapel roof?

Finally, 35+ Hermonites had expressed their willingness to attend the reunion in Las Vegas for the 27th to the 28th of Jan. That number has dwindled down to 10. I will collect their signatures and forwad them to Mrs. Namgyal (who was my class teacher in 1982, class 6R).

Kanchan Koirala, 1989, USA.

I support
Vinay Kedia,1998, Dubai U.A.E
Regards
Vinay Kedia
Simpsons batch

Dear Dipak,

Many thanks for your didactic e-mail to me. I fully support the candidature of Jigme and sincerely hope the managing committee see the light of day and not appoint a failure. It is imperative that Mount Hermon has the proper calibre of person to head and drive the school forward. I believe that Mr. Stewart and Mr. Johnston are the heavy weights that count and am sure they will do everything possible in the matter.

It really saddens me to see how my beloved Mount Hermon has gone down the pan and I blame the present management. I am honestly hoping that good sense will prevail in the selection of the next head. Do keep in touch with me as I live in Milton Keynes, Buckinghamshire.
Best wishes,
Ronen Ghose, UK.

Dear Deepak Mirchandani,
Name: Ritwik Baidya
Years at Mount Hermon School: 1974 - 1982
Residence: Saba, Dutch Caribbeans, Kingdom of the Netherlands

I fully support Jigme N. Kazi's candidature for the post of Principal at Mount Hermon School. I believe with his background and sincerity he is best person for this post and will do a marvellous job.

My sisters (Ruma and Soma Baidya) and I know Jigme very well from our MHS days and so did our parents. My father (Late Dr. Rabindranath Baidya), who was a member of the school Managing Committee, was a great fan of him. He would be always there either at the MHS or NP grounds to watch him play football. In fact, he provided medical assistance on the field when he broke his forearm in one of those matches at the NP field. (I am not sure if Jigme will remember that).

Ronen (left) with Kishore Gandhi (centre) at Mount Hermon, 1958.

I do not remember him teaching me in any class, but he was my warden in one of the dorms, he coached me at football and cricket, he was my house master for Dewey and he was very active in scripture union and High C.

I wish him the very best and do hope he is appointed.
Best wishes to you Deepak and your family.

PS:
Best wishes to Roslyn - you were my class teacher in grade 7 or 8. Say Hi to Sherap from me. Best wishes to Jigme and his family.
Ritwik Baidya
Saba University School of Medicine
Dutch Caribbeans

Yes from my side (for Jigme Kazi to take charge as Principal of Mount Hermon School, Darjeeling) - Arnob K. Mondal, MHS 1976, India.

Hello Dipak,
Please accept my support to your campaign towards taking the first, but a firm step, in getting our school to the top of the table/survey. We are truly disheartened to be at the bottom.
Please let me know in case you require any other support from me. Even if I require to come up to the school, I am ready for the same.
Thanks,
Rajesh Nath Mehta

Hi,
PFB my details. Hope this is the start to a brighter future for our beloved Mount Hermon.
Aditya Keshav, 2002, India
Thanks and Regards,
Aditya Keshav
MHS 2002
Mysore, India.

I left MHS in 1980 after completing 6th grade. Mr. Kazi was my teacher in 5th grade, and a big influence on who I am today. I fully endorse Mr. Kazi and wish him all success in his endeavors.
Omar Choudhary

I completely agree with you, that MH now requires someone with true passion & vision for the school to turn things around. I visited MH in Oct '11, and was saddened to see the dwindling number of students, the bad shape of the overall infrastructure (further devastated by the earthquake), and the numerous encroachments that have claimed the Top Flat and other school boundaries.
Yes sir, Mr. Kazi should be appointed the new Principal, and just as Fr. Kinley has turned things around for his alma-mater, we pray and hope the same for ours.
Shalini Sinha, 1995, India.

Dear Mr. Kazi,

I was at the Kolkata reunion this Jan 2012. Met with the Johnstons and fellow Hermonites. I was very sad to hear the current state of MH. MH holds a dear place in all our hearts and I personally attribute all the success in my life to MH and the all round upbringing we had there. I try to bring up my 3 kids with the same all rounded outlook on life.

David (right) at a Hermonites reunion in Gangtok, 2018.

After the reunion, I was genuinely sad at the prospect of MH disappearing into the history books. Being here in Canada makes it also impossible to garner any revival movement for MH. Then, I get this email from Mrs. Namgyal and Dipak....I am smiling. You, Sir are the perfect choice to get our dear MH to back to its glory days.

I know you will revive MH. I am going to send this email to all the Hermonites I know and I am sure they will share the same sentiments. Thank you for personally undertaking this huge responsibility and once you take principalship of MH we should discuss how the alumni can help too.

Sincerely,
David Tien Hsi Chiang (Class of 1988), Canada.

I support Jigme Kazi
Prithviraj Dasgupta 1994 India

Hi Jigs!
Good to hear from you.
    May God be with you in your desire to restore MH to its former health and success. I have been a computer programmer [mainly Database programming] since 1997.
    I tried teaching here but soon decided that it wasn't what I wanted to do. My main problem was that discipline is very different here from what it was in India - and you have to almost 'negotiate' with students to even do simple things like 'take out books', 'be silent in class' . . .
    I have been in charge of the music we do in church [it is not hymns like we did in Chapel at MH - but very contemporary music].
    I have written several songs that we have done in church. My son Ryan plays bass in the church band. He also swam in his school swimming team and when he was in 9th grade, he broke all my MH swimming records. Can you imagine??
    Of course - he had a Swimming Coach who was a full-time employee of the school and did nothing BUT Swimming.
    And . . . they practised 5 days a week for about 2 hours a day - all year - 12 months a year. Have you had any contact with the MH Board?
    Please let us all know how things progress and if there is anything we can do to help MH. Here's a Christmas 2011 photo of my family at a friend's house.
Robin Sengupta, US.

Dear All,
    Greetings & Love for 2012
    It is truly a matter of concern and pain to read the contents in the forwarded mail.
Anything for Beloved Mount Hermon.
Mary Ann (1969 batch)
Sultanate of Oman

Dear Rozlyn and Jigme,
    I do hope we can help bring the ranking of Mt. Hermon back up. I support whoever is chosen to do so.
    I am a past MHS student. I was there from 1948 through 1954. My brother, Subhash Khare graduated from MHS in 1954. I was a year behind but left that year.
    I live in the US. What is it that we can do to help there? I support Jigme in his efforts. I wish you all the best of luck.
Sincerely,
Mina Gupta nee Khare, US.

Dear Jigs
I fully support your post of Principal of Mount Hermon School.
Santosh Rijal, Nepal.

Hermonites International President Varongthip (Thip, right), Santosh Rijal (centre) and Jigme N. Kazi in Bangkok, January 2020.

Dear Jigs and all Hermonites,

We are enthused with the response of all the Hermonites. We, at Siliguri, are certainly happy with the overwhelming support that Jigme Kazi has got from Hermonites all over the world. I know Jigme very well, an UPRIGHT and HONEST person, a sportsman, a friend par excellence and a choice for the job beyond compare. He will succeed in bringing glory to this cherished institution. I am a product of MHS and I am proud to be a Hermonite.

I beg the Managing Committee to take a sincere and honest decision so that the school returns to its former glory days. I am sure MHS students from all over the world will pledge funds and time to revive this edifice of excellence if Jigs is given this responsibility. He is the person capable of fulfilling this responsibility.

I am willing to travel to Lucknow to talk to the powers-that-be so that this happens.
Thanks and regards,
Shiv (1972 batch), Siliguri

Dear Sir,

I endorse my full support to my Class 5K teacher (1979), Mr. Jigme N. Kazi. And I do feel a Hermonite can only bring my school's past glory back.
Yours,
Prashanta Pradhan, MHS 1984
Darjeeling.

Dear friends,

Thanks for the email and it is quite shocking to see where MHS has been rated presently. I very much agree with the suggestion of Mr. Jigme Kazi's name being proposed for the post of principal of MH. I support his candidature and wish him all the best.

I am Dr. Rajat Kumar Agarwal - a general Surgeon in the department of surgery, as an additional professor of surgery, at B.P. Koirala Institute of Health Sciences. Dharan Nepal. - A medical university.

I was in MH from 1978 - 1990. ICSE - 1988, ISC - 1990.

Presently I am in Dharan A city in Nepal about 160 Km west of Siliguri.
Thanks and regards,
Dr. Rajat Kumar Agarwal, Nepal.

Dear Mr. Dipak,

Thank you for your mail. It really is sad and disturbing to hear about the status of MH on the boarding scale of schools in India. However, I am extremely glad that initiatives are being taken by genuinely concerned Hermonites to try and address this sad situation, the most important being the proposal to appoint Mr. Jigme Kazi as the next Principal of MHS.

'MH Revival' Campaign 2012

I have known Mr. Kazi personally during my happy years at MHS from 1976-1981 and without any reservation, I can vouch that there will be no better candidate to be the next Principal of MHS than Mr. Kazi to bring MH back to its former glory.

My best wishes to Mr. Kazi and my hope and prayers for the success of him becoming the next Principal of MH.
Thuji Tshering
Thimphu, Bhutan.

Dear Mr. Kazi,
This in in continuation of Deepak Mirchandani's mail.

I would like to support your candidature for the position of the Principal, Mount Hermon School, Darjeeling. I am an ex-Hermonite; Dr. Narottam Pradhan, ISC 1989, Mount Hermon.

I am presently: Immunization Officer, UNOPS, Delhi
With warm regards, best wishes and sincere prayers,
Narottam

I strongly feel Jigme is the right choice, as he has been associated with Mount Hermon School since childhood, as a student & member of the faculty and his concern and feelings for Mount Hermon is immense. I am very confident in his ability to turn things for the better for MH.
Rajibendra Narayan Choudhury, 79, India.

GO FOR IT!!! Really sad to know about the situation....
Abhirup Dhar, 2003, India.

Also: Teacher at MH: 1978 & 1985.
All the best with your efforts towards helping MH. Let us all know if there is anything else we can do.
Roz - please say Hi to Sherab for me.
Robin Sengupta, US.

Dear All,
It would be brilliant to have Jigme Kazi at the helm of things in MH. If these is anything to be done to mobilize the Nepal Hermonites, do let me know.

Perhaps this can also be moved to Facebook, where there are thousands of Hermonites?
Ashok Pokharel, Nepal.

My support for MHS new principal:
Jigme N. Kazi, 1972, India
From: Kitiphorn Krisanalome, 1974, Bangkok.

Robin Sengupta

Dear Jigmela,
    We will be most happy if you become the PRINCIPAL of Mt. Hermon school. You are most eligible and it will be a big change for Mt. Hermon and if there is anything we can do please let us know.
Best wishes,
Thinley Gyari, New Delhi.

Hi Jigme
    Congrats...and u know that I am always in support of u and will stand in support of u..
God Bless u.
Yasmine Naomi Mukand Chung, Kolkatta.

Mr. Kazi,

All the best in your new possibility of being Principal of Mount Hermon School.

I have many memories of Mount Hermon School from 1970 to 1979.

Gil Engen, Canada.

Dear Jigme,

Mr. Rockwell Gardner and I pledge our support to you for the post of Principal. MH badly needs help and you are the right person with your enthusiasm to do a great job. Best of luck!

Regards,

Charlotte Gardner, Siliguri.

Dear Mr. Kazi,

Great to hear that you are going to be in Kathmandu at the end of the month. I have talked to Pramod Shrestha (Goofy), our young and dynamic leader of Nepali Hermonites, copied here, who was a few year behind me in school and he suggests we get the Nepali Hermonites together to meet you and talk with you on in the evening of Monday the 31st of January. Venue to be decided.

Ashok with his family.

Please let me know when and how you are arriving and if there is anything that Goofy, I or any of the other Hermonites can do to make your stay in our city more comfortable.

By the way, both Goofy and I have kids in MH currently and we would be happy to share ideas about what is right and what is currently wrong with MH and help in any other way we can. I agree with you that revival of MH does not end with you in the chair, but must contain a clear map of continuity. This is something I pressed Mr. Fernandez about starting some years ago without much success. Anyway, I look forward to seeing you soon. My cell number is +977 9851021563 and Goofy's is +977 9841251636.

Once again, please let us have your arrival details, etc.

Ashok Pokharel, Nepal.

Hi there,

We have been following all the emails regarding this and wholeheartedly throw our support behind Jigme Kazi's candidature as next Principal of Mount Hermon School.

I give below my name, and also my sister's name (when at MHS) in the format requested, for Roslyn to add to her letter:-

- Andrea M Phillippe, 1961, England, UK
- Sandra D Phillippe, 1961, England, UK

If you need our present names on the list and not our maiden names, then that would be Andrea Porter and Sandra Robinson.

Hope the above helps for the campaign in bringing back our beloved Mount Hermon School to its former glory. All the very best in this most worthwhile endeavor.

Kindest regards
Andrea Porter
Maidstone, Kent, UK
and also Sandra Robinson
Nr Bideford, North Devon, UK.

Dear Dipak

I not only endorse the candidature of Mr. Kazi but also appreciate the effort all of you are taking to revive the school. I am also marking a copy of this letter to all the Hermonites whose mail id is with me so that they can react too.

I wish the best for all your success in this aspect.

Regards
Achyut Chandra, ICSE 1981, Kolkata.

Dear Dipak,

Thank you for taking the initiative to get the Hermonites involved in the process of lifting up MH.

I would like to support Jigme's candidature for Principalship.

Lanusungkum Aier, 1986, India.

Hi Dipak,

I have had the pleasure of being a student of both Mr. and Mrs. Kazi and I fully endorse Mr. Kazi as the next principal of Mt. Hermon School.

Thanks

Suvabroto Roy, ICSE '81

Hi Jigme,

I was present along with Binod Bhutra (79 batch) when Hermonites International was formed in Siliguri.

I have full faith and confidence in your ability to take on the responsibility and the herculean task of MH revival. I know its not easy but your willingness to shoulder the responsibility is in the right direction.

If there anything I can do from here in Malda, then please do let me know.

Regards,

Raj Choudhury, India.

All the best, Jigs!!
You, and MH - will be in my prayers!
Let us know how things progress!
Robin Sengupta, US.

Dear Jigme,

Thanks for the prompt reply. You are right about Mr. Stewart. He did make a difference. I am in touch with him and Mr. Jones. Tammy Dalal has put me in touch with a lot of MHS past students. Tammy went there after I left. Her mom was friends with my mom.

Anyway I do hope you are successful in making Mount Hermon come back up in the rankings.

I was in touch with the Ex-Hermonites in the US but dropped out as I got busy with a lot of things. I am in touch with Tammy who keeps me in the loop.

I wish you all the best.

Regards,

Mina (Gupta), US.

Greetings, all.

I remember Jigme Kazi when he was my teacher back in like, what, World War Two? I remember him as a good man, and I'm sure he'll be a good principal for MH.

If I may just add my two cents' worth - does he know what he's getting into? The problem with our beloved alma mater is not just about management and money. The school started going downhill when the Gorkhaland agitation started in the '80s and we had hoodlums running loose on the premises, shutting down classes and setting the stage for rampant encroachment on campus land with *khukri*-brandishing intimidation. I was there, sliding downhill with the school.

Yonden is Chief News Editor at the *South China Morning Post*.

The protected and pristine set-up we had going there is history. The last time I paid a visit, there was a thriving slum around the swimming pool with local residents' clothes drying on the net fencing. You can never drive them out. They're there to stay. Compare that to St. Joseph's School which has now been turned into a Fort-Knox-style...well, fortress. What's worse, my understanding is that the leaders of the new Gorkhaland movement were running admissions at MH before they even came into power. Now they ARE in power. If that's not clear enough for you, they were taking money and dictating who would get admission. In OUR school. I wouldn't be surprised if they still are. It's a lucrative business. How do you tackle something like that in Darjeeling's basket-case political atmosphere where everything runs on corruption, intimidation and violence. Does Jigme Kazi know how to use a bazooka? He might need it.

Sorry to rain on your parade. The truth is harsh. Having said that, you have my vote for Mr. Kazi. I'm not on Facebook or Twitter or whatever, but there are quite a few Hermonites here in Hong Kong and some of them are social networking sluts, so I'll pass on the message to gather more signatures.

Yonden Lhatoo, Hong Kong.

Dear Roslyn,

Thank you for sharing this news with the alumni of MH. Very sorry to hear about this situation of Mount Hermon School. I would surely like to support the candidacy of Mr. Jigme Kazi for the position of principal of Mount Hermon School.

Kind regards,
Shoma Baidya
Brisbane, Australia

Hi Dipak,

Nice to hear from you. While in India I visited MHS several times and felt that everything did not seem well as before.

Therefore, I heartily support Jigme for whom I have the utmost faith and confidence that he will do a fantastic job as the head of the school. I am not just endorsing him, I knew him very well and personally throughout the many years I spent as a student at our beloved MHs. He is a good leader, a good family man, religiously faithful, kind hearted, honest, a gentle man but firm and committed and a man who will not fail in his task or job.

I also did my college in Bangalore with Fr. Kinley and I was very glad to hear he is doing a good job at north point.

I am sure Jigme will do just as well or even better.

Sincerely,
Jigme Taythi (Jimmy) MHS 1973, US.

Hail Mount Hermon! A Tribute

Jigme Taythi (formerly Jimmy Tsewang, left back standing) at a batch of 1973 Hermonites reunion in Siliguri, 2019.

Dear Dipak and Roslyn,

Yes it is indeed sad that MH is currently at the bottom of the league table for boarding schools.

However, I am optimistic that this could be reversed by dedication and hard work of the next Principal, students, teachers and well wishers like ex-Hermonites.

I totally support Jigme Kazi for the nomination of the next Principal of Mount Hermon and wish him the very best to take our dear school forward.
Kind regards and Happy New Year
Smita Prasai- Upadhyay, ISC year 1981
Currently residing in Hull, United Kingdom.

Thank you for all your efforts.

I visited MHS with my family in June, 2011, and I was very concerned with the situation. In fact, I was so discouraged that I affirmed I would not return. But now I see a light, a light that I pray will get brighter and brighter.....

I support Mr. Kazi - you were my teacher once upon a time.
God Bless Mount Hermon!
Kimi Hmar Zook, 1986, USA.

Dear Dipak,

Here is my support for Jigme to run for MH principal's post this coming year and as long as it is necessary. Also would like to request Roslyn and Sherab to join MH in the management capacity to help Jigme and to oversee the true spending of school yearly budget.

My name is Mr. Varongthip Lulitanond – from Bangkok Thailand, (SC 73).
With kind regards,
Varongthip, Bangkok.

I was a student in Mount Hermon School when our beloved Mr. Murray was the School Principal.

Mr. Jigme Kazi was a Senior, Prefect and Dewey House Captain to which I belonged. Jigme Kazi was someone we loved and respected and looked up to even then, a man of character a natural born leader, a very friendly person with a positive and sunny disposition.

I want to endorse his candidature to become the Principal of my beloved Alma Mater. I can think of no one better and whom I would like to see, and in whom I can be fully confident has the capability to unite Hermonites to revive Mount Hermon School so that once again it can be one of the best schools in India and in the world.

Thank you to all the Alumni who have poured their passion and are working so hard to help revive Mount Hermon School

> "Beloved Mount Hermon we greet thee
> Thy daughters and sons from afar
> As oft as we pause in our toiling
> To hail thee whose children we are
> Hail Mount Hermon, Hail Mount Hermon
> Safe for aye in memory's shrine
> Hail Mount Hermon Dear Mount Hermon
> Praise and Love be every thine"

David R. Chhangte
MHS 1981, United States of America.

Dear Mr. Kazi,
It is indeed a privilege for me to be able to be in touch with you. I am sure you will be able to take MH to its former glory. If I am be of any support do will be happy to do so. May be my boys now 7 and 13 can go to Mount Hermon too!
Warm regards
Sincerely,
Aparna Basu Mallik (Chaturvedi)

Hi Dipak,
Thanks your email. I am writing in support for Mr. Jigme Kazi for Principal of MHS.
Dekyi Zingkha, 1987, USA.

Jigs

Thanks for sharing. You have got endorsements from all corners of the globe!! Many Catholic schools especially the Christian Brother Schools have now made it a practice to appoint lay people preferably ex-students and old staff to head their institutions and they are doing pretty well. It is time the Methodists took similar steps.

MH would be truly lucky and blessed if you were to take up the post. The job would be extremely demanding and challenging, given the present state of the school and the political upheaval in the Hills but if anyone could take up the challenge AND WIN that man is YOU!!
Cheers
Lenny (Northpointer), Darjeeling.

It is good that Yonden has spoken up and explained the situation because many of us do not know the inside story. Nevertheless as an ex-Hermonite I would definitely want something good to happen there, if it is possible so Mr. Kazi definitely has my vote as the next Principal. He knows the school and also the local language and culture so I guess he is the best for the job at this moment.
Kausik Bose, India.

Thanks Jigme. I know you must be extremely busy working for the cause which has my full support, but if you can make it, nothing like it! Wishing you all the best and looking forward to visiting MH when you are the Principal soon.
Fond regards, Tarun (Sarkar), India.

Dear Jigme

Nice to hear from you. Just to clarify that I am Smita, Sangeeta Prasai's sister. Sangeeta is at present in Kathmandu, Nepal

We remember you very well and you certainly deserve to be the Principal of Mount Hermon School.

I hope to join the UK Hemonites group sometime and have been out of touch with such events for a long time.
Kind regards and best wishes always.
Smita. UK.

I do support Jigme Kazi for this candidature, whom I know personally since my days at MH. Hope that his successful nomination will usher in a new great chapter for MH. Roslyn "Rongong", please include my name in your letter to the MC. Please do not reply to this mail. Thanks!
Laifungbam Debabrata Roy (Bobby), 1970 Batch, Manipur, India.

Mr. Jigmi Kazi, Sir....I have seen you way back in the 70s, in my childhood days. A fine sportsman and a charismatic person you were, though age physically changes the qualities of a person, I can still bet that you are still the same. My sincere vote for you for the post of a highly dignified post of the "principal" of the school which I still love so much.

"If your actions inspire others to dream more, learn more, do more and become more, you are a leader" John Quincy Adams quotes
My sincere regards & best of luck,
RAJENDRA KUMAR SINGH, BHADRAPUR (JHAPA) NEPAL
1980 ICSE batch

I endorse and support Jigme's candidature as Principal.
Savita Maynard (nee Palriwala)
Left MH 1969
Currently reside in London, UK.
Kind regards
Savita Maynard, UK.

Dear Dipak,
I fully endorse the views of the Sikkim Hermonites Association and am in favour of their proposal to have Jigme Kazi appointed as the Principal of Mount Hermon School, Darjeeling. I was in the batch of 1979 ISCE. Presently based in Kolkata India.

Incidentally, I also happen to have worked at The Doon School, Dehradun as the Head of Human Resources (rated as the no. one School in India). If any advice/suggestion is solicited, I would gladly support the move to steer my Alma Mater from troubled waters.
Regards,
Debashis Brahma, Kolkata.

Thanks Sondhya for your prompt action and thanks Vikas for your "getting along with it" so fast.

The only thing I would like to add on is to make explicit that which is already there. Jigmi spent not only his school life at MH but went straight on with 2 more years at the MHTTC. He then continued without break into the MH staff, albeit in the Juniors, for another 5 or 6 years.

Even after spending about 20 years of his prime life at MH he was not satisfied and remained in touch with MH and when it was time for the Sikkim Hermonites to form he was one of the founder-members and continues to be an active members. He has been many times to MH on purely Hermonite affairs like meeting the different Chairpersons and Managing Committee members.

Pratap

It seems that he has just not had enough of MH as yet which is more than I can say for myself! So why begrudge him?
Pratap Singh Rai (54-67) (though I never did actually pass out of MH), Darjeeling.

Hail Mount Hermon! A Tribute

Hi Friends,

I was at MH for the last couple of years and I can't really place Jigme Kazi but I do trust Vikas's judgement in the matter and wholeheartedly support his mandate.
Regards
Sondhy Dutta
ISC 1981

Dear Sir

Thank you for contacting me. The decision is a wise one. My family has been in MH for 30+ years starting with Hena (1976?) my cousin to Sarfraaz my nephew (2009?).

I fully support Jigme as the new principal. May I suggest involvement of politically oriented Hermonites or those in WB government (eg. Choten Lama DM) to especially be roped in.
Dr. Syed Tanveer-ur Rahman 1979-88, Jhansi, India.

Dear Jigmela,

It's wonderful to hear this news. I feel there is hope now for Mt. Hermon to rejuvenate and regain it's long lost glory! I remember all the great times I spent there during my teachers training program. I highly recommend you for the prestigious post of principal. With your experience and qualification and most of all your love and dedication towards the school, I have no doubt that there will be a great future for the school and all the students! Hail Mt. Hermon!!

With warmest regards,
Chime Lhatso (TTC 1974), India.

I truly support Mr. Jigme N Kazi's candidature to bring back MHS to its former glory. Will spread the word...
Hail Mount Hermon!!!
Barbara Lama, 2000, India.

Dear Roslyn,

I appreciate your efforts on behalf of Jigme. I think that someone needs to contact Mr. Jones in the States as he has contacts with Methodists both in India and the States and make an appeal to him. I don't know if you have already done this but if not, then you need to do that and forward him your letter of support plus the letter from the Sikkim Hermonites and ask for his help.

I don't have his email address but here is Kenneth's email. I hope this is still correct: kensunitajones@frontier.com. Unfortunately, I don't have his phone number. It was on the phone that I lost last year but I can see if Puii has their number as she has visited them in North Carolina a few years back.

Wishing you all the best for 2012 and praying that your efforts to get Jigs as the next MH Principal succeeds.
Cheers,
Rothang (Rema), US.

Dear Mr. Kazi,

Like all Hermonites, I am also quite worried about the future of our MHS. I fully agree with the vast majority that you should take control & save MHS from gradual oblivion.

Although I did not have the pleasure of meeting you (joined in 1954 & graduated/left in 1961) I know how much you love MHS. I still retain an article you wrote (now yellow with age) which was published in "The Sunday Statesman" on November, 12, 1995, captioned "Hermon on the Mount", on the occasion of the year-long centenary celebrations of MHS. At the conclusion of the above article, you said how you have been "emotionally attached to the school". You concluded by declaring & I quote "....And as I look back over these 14 years away from the old and familiar surroundings, I know that whatever MH taught me during my brief sojourn in Darjeeling has withstood the test of time. I left MH at the end of 1979-- but a part of me has always remained behind. And I guess, a part of MH has always been with me. Hail Mount Hermon." Unquote

You have the qualification & experience. But much more than that, you love MHS & this is what is needed to save our dear MHS.

Good luck. You have our blessings.

With warm regards,

Humayun A. Kamal ("Kamal Haque", India).

Hey Jigs,

Keep on trying and tell us if you need us to bombard the Bishop (and Management Committee) with emails. Mr. Fernandez will have all the Management Committee names and emails - and we can start a campaign on polite but persistent emails to them all.

I am with you - as are many Hermonites. Once you get in - re-building is the first agenda - i.e.: re-building (repair) both the buildings and the credibility of MH. You'd be amazed at how many Hermonites are talking to each other about the future of Mount Hermon. It will, of course, never be what it was - but what it can be .... a quality institution that teaches both academics and life values and skills .... is what we want it to continue to be.

All the best

Barry Ison, Dhaka, Bangladesh.

Dear Hermonites,

Greetings from Sikkim and Happy New Year!!

Its been a week since the Sikkim Hermonites Association emailed you on "MH Revival" and the response from Hermonites all over the world on issues raised has been very positive and encouraging.

I am forwarding the reactions for your information and response. I want to thank all those who have supported our proposals and reposed so much faith and trust in me.

However, the fact is that I'm not the boss as yet! We are yet to approach the Managing Committee and as of now we have not been able to contact them. It is the Managing Committee that appoints the Principal and takes important decisions regarding MH.

However, since the Committee members will surely give top priority to problems and prospects of the school they will, I am sure, take the right decision at the right time and allow the school to be run by the Hermonites for a while until things are stable.

MH is likely to close down if things do not improve. We need to chip in and do our part to revive the school and restore it to its former glory.

Looking forward to hearing from you.

Hail Mt. Hermon!

Jigs (Jigme N. Kazi)

Gangtok, Sikkim.

Dear Jigme

Thanks so much for writing. Yes, losing anyone is very difficult, let alone our mothers. It was really good to have Rajendra and Kavita visiting; at the time they planned the trip they had hoped to meet my mother too. And their visit was followed by Naren's.

Thanks again for your mail.

God bless.

Love

Shanta (Mathai)

PS. I see they have nominated you to the MH Principal post???

Dear Sir,

Received this wonderful offer finally from a Hermonite and sending it immediately to you (along with copies of some of the PERSONALLY KNOWN active Hermonites round the world). Unfortunately Ms. Jane Dewsberry of MHUSA address has got deleted but I am sure it should be in some others computers, so please forward it to her.

Please Sir, do make this known to the Managing Committee members so that the needful can be done.

As is Karma, President, SHA, confidant of total support, I too am equally sure his faith will not be belied.

Pratap Rai, Darjeeling.

Jigs,

I've been a bit busy over the Christmas and New Year period and these emails have brought me up to speed. So disappointing to hear of the decline in enrolments and I think it entirely appropriate that something be done as a matter of urgency. Having someone like yourself, an ex-Hermonite and a local resident to take up the challenge is a very good step. Your strength of purpose, strong moral character and dedication will stand you in good stead mate .... and Dallas and I wish you all the best in your endeavours. If we can help, please let us know.

Kind regards

John (Glasby), Australia.

'MH Revival' Campaign 2012

Dallas and John Glasby.

Dear Jigmi,

Thank you for your New Year greetings and I heartily reciprocate the same. I am so pleased that you have been offered the post of Headmaster of Mount Hermon School when Mr. Fernandez retires this year, and I look forward to hearing the good news that you will be taking up the position.

I am forwarding a copy of this to "Boss" (Mr. Stewart) as his email address has changed and is now davidgs@xtra.co.nz I am sure he will be very pleased as under his stewardship he too made many improvements during his term as headmaster, as the school was in a rundown condition when he took over.

With my kindest regards and congratulations,
James (OMHSA), UK.

Dear Jigs,

So much for all our comments and good wishes and the desire to see you as the next Princi. It seems that things are still not quite clear as to how one should go about approaching the Managing Committee. One way could be a joint mail from the MH Alumni through an association like the Sikkimese one, which currently seems to be the most active, and certainly "up there". Additionally, one could write and seek help from the UK Association OMHASA. James Sinclair, the secretary, is very active, and I am sure would be horrified to know the state of affairs of the school presently being in. Their mail to the Managing Committee could be a good follow up to the initial one from the Sikkimese one and perhaps if both these mails are acknowledged by the Committee, then it would certainly be appropriate to forward your CV and set up an eventual interview.

I am not sure how your relation with Mr. Fernandez is, but since he is going to retire and not seeking an extension, you might seek his assistance to open up a door for an interview with the Committee. His word could matter in a case like this, and above all he knows the committee members from his dealings over the years. You do know that education these days is fraught with politics at every level. I did hear from a pretty reliable source that for the earthquake North Point was given 50 lakhs from the Govt as assistance, whereas MH got nothing. Our Calcutta friends can play a significant part in all of this, and currently the timing is just about right. The school is closed for the winter vacation, and by the time it opens Mr. Fernandez will be on the verge of retirement and therefore, it needs a new Princi to begin providing a new lease of life.

I know some of us have expressed a thought about seeking repairs and funds to be raised for it, as a priority over and above the establishment of a new Principal, however all that will amount to naught if there is nobody at the helm of affairs to oversee such repairs/construction and find funds to carry out these tasks. I am sure we all know that it is easier to raise money, but seeing that it is spent correctly and for the rightful purpose is harder. You as a known quantity, will immediately enlist the kind of trust that people will seek (including the managing committee).

You have sought a mandate not so recently in the political scene and therefore realise that dealing with the people who have the final word requires more than a sense of diplomacy, and it would be good if you found an excuse to meet with the Committee in Calcutta, along with a small delegation from Sikkim, and let them know that they do not have to look beyond the Hills for the right candidate. Anybody who does not belong to the Darjeeling Hills will find it very hard to deal with the local influential political group that has become so integral to the proper functioning of a school in Darjeeling. People like Karma, Ogni, Udai, who are all in reasonably influential position in the Govt of Sikkim, might just provide the right impetus to the delegation.

I do sincerely hope that time will see you sitting across the table and completing that interview that will allow our favourite school to have a Principal that it deserves.
Pradip (Verma), UK.

Jigs,
I have attached a contact list for Hermonites in Calcutta (unfortunately, the list is perennially work-in-progress).

The reason I am passing this on, is two ex-Hermonites, Sunirmal Chakravarty (wife is a Nepali - owner of Orient Restaurant, Darjeeling) and Sonia Pradhan (Saroj Pradhan's sister) are Principals of La Martinere and Pratt Memorial School respectively.

Sadly, our Alumnus has not been able to get either to attend the get-together(s). Anyway, these two are likely to be in touch with the Bishop. May I suggest you come down to Cal. We do have a few persons who could be of some assistance to your quest, and I can put you on to them.

Meanwhile, do feel free to call me on +91-99038-50331
wkr
Sujit, Kolkata.

Okay, this is how it is ...
I spoke to Tehmi in the US this morning, and asked her to talk to Bill Jones (formerly MH). Bill Jones is married to Beulah Kessop and Rev. Donald Kessop's sister. Donald Kessop, would know the composition of the Managing Committee.

I am not very sure if the American Methodists did a complete retreat and left total control with their Indian counterparts? We need to find an answer to that first. Bill Jones, maybe one of the few who can tell us the whys and wherefores from the admin point-of-view. There are a few bumps. Bill Jones is old and not very comfortable communicating by e-mail. So, I have got Tehmi (MH-1956-64) to interact on our behalf, seek advice and if possible put us on to Donald Kessop.

I have opened a second track here in Calcutta. Anjali (MH-1957-64) who is organist and Choir Director in St. Paul's Cathedral, Calcutta (her father, Rev. L. Kundu, after retirement, was attached to St. Paul's Cathedral, Calcutta) will ask to her friend, Beulah Raju (formerly, Principal, Calcutta Girls School) for friendly opinion. At the end of the day, we need to meet Donald Kessop, and thro' him, the Methodist Bishop.

I suggest Jigs open a third track, one to Bimal Gurung, thro' an ex-Hermonite … maybe? Now, lets just make a start and see how far we go … good luck all.
wkr
Sujit, Kolkata.

Hi Jigs - I am extremely happy to know that the Sikkim Hermonites Association has taken the initiative to revive the school and that you are the fore runner for the top job. I am fully confident that with you at the helm the school will get the transformation it so badly requires. Hope the management see merit in the proposition and complete the required formalities before the next academic year.

I propose to talk to Justice Indrajit Mohanty who was a member of the governing body not many years ago and should have a good idea about the nuances in selecting a suitable principal. Unfortunately my uncle, the erstwhile Bishop of Darjeeling is no more but his daughter should be able to help. Hope to revert once I get more information.
Ashish Bhengra. Tamil Nadu, India.

Ashish Bhengra in Gangtok, 2019. (L to R) Tsetop, Ashish, Uttam, Anup, Lamba and Jigme.

Dear Jigme,

I was happy to hear from a Hermonite but was rather distressed to learn of the present state of MH. Many years back I was in contact with Kishan Goenka, Apok Jamir and others in Delhi and was under the impression that things were going well with our school.

We do have a number of Hermonites in Bhutan who have all received so much from this great institution and would be happy to help in any small way to revive the old MH.

I hope you will take up the post to head the school. We have all seen how Father Kinley has transformed North Point School which shows how individuals can make the difference.

I am sure all the Hermonites in Bhutan will be fully behind you if our support is required to be conveyed to the management board. Please count on us.

Last month Pradip Nazari was here in Bhutan, we met after almost 37 years!
With warm regards,
Daw Penjo, Class of 75, Bhutan.

Dear Jigme,

You have just received an email which you had sent. I hit "reply" instead of "forward". I was forwarding it to Rosemary Mitchell (now Rosemary Lowe) who wanted to be brought up to date with MH news and get a few addresses.

The reason I was phoning her is that her 33 year old son has died and I was offering condolence. I will not give you her address as I think it might be better to hear from her first, but if you haven't had anything from her shortly then let me know.

Sorry to be the bearer of sad tidings but she spoke so warmly of you I just felt I should.
Blessings
Bill Moore, Ireland.

Dear Jigme,

This may sound very superior but think about it please. Since you knew me I have done some more study and am now Dr. Bill Moore. I know it should not make any difference but it DOES. So if it would help for the Methodist Mission to receive a letter of commendation from Rev. Dr. William D. Moore, M.A. (TCD), B.D. (Edin), D. Min. Theol. (Sheffield), then all you need do is send me their address and even write the letter if you wish!! We both know these things are unimportant but people can be impressed and, let's face it, sometimes it means the person is not stupid... Ha, ha.

There it is. Don't worry! I'm still the football daft ordinary guy you knew so well.
Blessings
Bill, Ireland.
P.S. you can leave out the Sir next time. Robin Sen Gupta managed after a day or two when he visited!

'MH Revival' Campaign 2012

Mr. W.D Moore with HSC students, 1973.

Dear Jigs

I am late into the fray, but here's sending you all the warmth and encouragement of someone who lived and breathed Mt. Hermon as home for so many years. Thank you for the courage and willingness to put your hand up - we are all delighted in Canberra! The world is round Jigs - who would have thought so many hearts and minds would meet all these years later! Can't wait to see Ros and Sherab again to hear all about it.

I know MH has gone through tumultuous times. No doubt there will be a myriad things to do and fix in ever changing lists of priority, but I will be thinking of you and your lovely wife as you start out on this journey together and praying for the wisdom and strength you will need each day. I guess you first have to locate the Board!! It is heartening to see so many old friends (old!!!) gathering in support - use their skills and good will wherever you need - I offer mine too...
Much love,
Heather (Rongong) Prickett, Canberra, Australia.

Dear Roslyn,

I was so wonderful to get your mail from Kristine, and also appreciate your promptness in taken up this vital issue in the interest of the School to have Jigme be appointed as the Principal of our beloved School.

I re-confirm the discussions we had on the subject during meeting you & Sherab just before you left India. I along with many many other fellow Hermonites would like to have Jigme head the school.

We need to convince the Managing Committee to accept and appreciate our concern for the school and students.

With warm regards,
Ravi Agarwal, Siliguri, India.

Dear Jigmee,

Thank you for your letter explaining things. Saroj and I will always support you. Am enclosing a print out of best schools in India. Kindly share it with everybody. Am so happy that there is so much love and support for the school. Hail MH. I would like to laud the Hermonites whose children are with us, Mr. Ashok Pokharel and Mr. Rajesh Chettri, Mr. Santosh Rijal, Mr. Pranab Kalita, Mr. Rajesh Singh and a host of other Hermonites who are happy with the School.

The buildings have suffered extensive damage in the earthquake on 18th Sept (2011). But this has happened before. In 1943 the whole School was destroyed but was rebuilt. So with God's grace MH shall be built again and will shine once more...it will take a little time and a lot of effort.

Leaving for Bangalore in the morning. Will give you all support and information when I get back.

Regards
George (Fernandes)
Principal, Mt. Hermon School.

Dear Jigs,

The support you have and are getting is encouraging.

About "American Methodists" - there is no harm in finding out if they are in the picture (at all); might make it a bit easier for you. Please do remember it is the Methodist Bishop (in Calcutta) who is relevant to our interest; he is not the same Bishop Sunirmal is answerable to!

I am not aware who the Johnstons met. They are in Chennai just now and guests of my classmate, Subhrangshu (Roy) if you remember him? They will return to Tasmania (via, Adelaide and Melbourne) on Sun 15/01.

wkr
Sujit, Kolkata.

I am sure everyone will want a change, and wrest control from the managing committee in Calcutta, and to have more active participation from the school alumni in the matters of the school. I know someone has to begin the level of dialogue with the committee, to show serious intent, and then in due course let the placement sub-committee, if there is one in place, be forwarded your CV through the association. I am sure all this will definitely have an impact and will open up doors for you to be interviewed for the position. I really do look forward to that day.

Think about all this, I am sure a door can be made to open.
Robin Sengupta, US.

Hi Jigs and Sujit,
You've made a great start Sujit .... somewhere we'll erect a statue to you one day - maybe near Black Rock!!

Seriously - its a good strategic start.

I have understood that Ghising is back in control in Darjeeling and while Gurung is still important because he lives near Patlibas (below Fernhill), I think Ghising can make more things happen as his kids went to MH (I seem to recall).

Part of negotiating with the Bishop and Board (Management Committee) should be Alumni representation on the Board as well as Jigs as Principal.

Whenever I start something new Jigs, I put pressure on myself to be accountable - so you may want to put an initial time limit on your Headship - say two years to get things in order and if the Board (by which time there will be alumni on it) is happy you continue as Principal long-term.

You could also offer a Consultancy Committee (or group) whereby people like myself, Ros, Sherab, Sujit and one or two more with appropriate experience will support and advise you and provide the Board with regular progress reports. I can do a flying 2/3 days visit at a moment's notice from here - via bus and the Changrabandha border.

Remember Jigs - you were also a Bishop Fisher Cup holder and that Cup has not been given to anyone for the past 14 years (Fernandez tells me).

All the best guys and just call if you need help. Maybe a weekly or bi-weekly news update to all those who have expressed interest would be good and once the ball starts rolling we can start talking about raising resources to re-build and revive.
Cheers.
Barry Ison, Dhaka, Bangladesh.

No thank you Barry. There is one thing I dream of though -- a 'garden of silence' dedicated to all Hermonites (students and teachers) who have passed on.

I spoke to Tehmi (in Florida) this morning and expect her to get back in a week?
wkr
Sujit, Kolkata.

Thank you, Sir (Mr. Ison),
Will just do what you have proposed when I'm there. I have lots of plans and we all have great dreams...beside the Bishop Fisher Cup I also got the Principal's Award in TTC.

Apart from sports and leadership role in other areas I came second in the final exams in TTC, where I got to realize my academic potentials which was untapped in school due to so many extra-curricular activities.

Stay posted,

Jigs

Dear Jigme,

    I sincerely pray that the email I received regarding appointing/nominating you as Princi of MHS comes true as only a GOOD ex-student can understand the problems & work about a solution so that the Glory we shared in the past is brought back to the Present & carried forward to the future.

    I pray & wish you get the post.

Best wishes always.

Abbas Ahmed, 1979 ISC, India.

Dear Jigs

    Great news from your end - especially about George's support!

    We arrived yesterday and as yet have not had time to sit down and write. Lost luggage on the way and had a few minor hassles, but are safely back now. It was wonderful to see you and Tshering and the lovely girls - even though so briefly. Anyway here's where we are up to.

1. Will be sending out a detailed letter to all Australian and NZ contacts possibly by tomorrow. I'll give some details on yourself in case there are any who do not know you. I will send you the copy before I send it out so you are happy with my wording.

2. Will also include photos of the damage we saw (in the places we could access), the new building, and the fencing that now seems to have put an end to further encroachment.

3. Met 2 Grade 4 staff who have grave concerns for the future of MH, and I will also mention that.

4. Have not had any word from the Johnstons either, but will include them in on my email.

5. Mr. Stewart is currently on a cruise with his best friend and will not be back in Auckland until Jan 18 - however, I will also send him a separate email requesting that he write something in support of you.

6. Had a very good meeting with Saroj and Suren who think that you coming would be the best thing that could happen. Saroj also mentioned her Uncle (Mr. Dewan) and his interest in MH (from many years ago). They will be very useful contacts with regard to local support.

'MH Revival' Campaign 2012

All in all, Jigs, Sherab and I feel very positive along with you!! Will send you my letter that is going to the Australia NZ folks shortly. I will be asking them to send their support via email, and will keep an updated list of their contacts. Once this has happened, we could forward it to all the old MH contacts on the Yahoo website too.

Will be in touch shortly.

Much love and best wishes,

Roz and Sherab, Canberra, Australia.

Dear Joy,

I've tried unsuccessfully to get onto the Hermonite website today.

The site has a goldmine of a database of email addresses that I would like to use to send out Roslyn's message to support the candidature of Jigs as the new Principal of MH. This would ensure that we have access to a wider range of Hermonites than just our bunch from the early to mid-70s.

If you can ask your guys to send me all the email addresses of Hermonites who have submitted their names and details to the site, I could engage with them to follow through on Roslyn's signature campaign to ensure that Jigs does indeed fill the position that becomes available in March.

Considering that the Management Committee has allowed the school to become what it is now, we will have to ramp up the campaign and put enormous pressure on them.

Take care and enjoy your trip to Delhi.

Love

Dips

Hi Jigs, Dipak and Cindy,

I think sending your resume with copies of the emails we've already sent to the bishop and the full spreadsheet with all the support will be a good package to send given that we have not had a single word of communication - what are your thoughts?

I think it would be good if we could all help out with the CV - what do you think? At least to give it a critical check before it goes off.

I guess we still need to mindful of what your contact has said, Jigs, about not antagonising the committee etc., too much, but as you say - time is also of the essence…

Anyway I'm working on the list tonight - and maybe you'll hear something more concrete from Ashish before too long.

Thanks everyone!

Roz

SILIGURI HERMONITES' ENDORSEMENT

MH REVIVAL

GENERAL BODY MEETING OF FOOTHILLS HERMONITES ASSOCIATION, SILIGURI

A telephonic discussion of the Foothills Hermonites Association was held in Siliguri on Janary'22, 2012 on the following subjects:-

1. Mt.Hermon School figuring at the bottom of boarding schools in India is a cause for concern for all Hermonites. The enrolment of the school has dipped to around 300 from the previous enrolment of about 700.
2. Damages caused to school buildings, including cottages, during the September 18,2011 earthquake and the gradual encroachment of school premises.
3. Poor maintenance of the school and alleged irregularities in administrative functioning.
4. Search for new Principal of the school as the present Principal Mr.George Fernandes retires at the end of March'2012.
5. The need to have a credible and competent Hermonite as Principal of the school and Hermonite representations in the school's Managing Committee.
6. The need for the Methodist Church of India, which owns the school, to review its policies towards Mt. Hermon School in the light of changing situations.
7. To bring Mt. Hermon School back to its past glory with help of Hermonites all over the world Hermonites should have a base (office, cottage or a site) at the school premises to help the school in every respect.

After a thorough discussion on the above subjects the Siliguri Hermonites Association passed the following resolutions (by circulations):-

1. Resolved to propose the name of Mr.Jigme N.Kazi, Ex-student,Ex-College student (TTC) of Mt.Hermon Undergraduate College of Education and former teacher of the school as the next Principal of Mt. Hermon School.
2. Resolved to propose that two Hermonites be included in the school's Managing Committee with a view to ensuring that Hermonites are actively involved in the running of the school and framing its policies.
3. Resolved to establish an office for Hermonites at the school premises. It is proposed that the global Hermonites body, Hermonites International (HiI) conceived during the school's centenary celebrations in 1995 and informed in 2005 under the Presidentship of Mr.Jigme N.Kazi, take up all project works for the school sponsored directly or indirectly by Hermonites on behalf of the Hermonities.

Contd....2

Page No.2

4. Resolved to form a high-level Hermonities panel to probe into various problems faced by the school and its prospects. The panel is to submit its findings by end of January'2012.
5. Resolved to urge all Hermonites organizations, including Hermonites International, to make a thorough study of the above subjects and make representations to the school authorities and the Managing Committee at the earliest.

Members endorsing the above resolutions:-

Sl.No.	Name	Years	Signature
1	Hrishikesh Saria	1985-1989	
2	JAGDISH P. SARIA	1965-1972	J.P.Saria
3	SHIV K. SARIA	1961-1972	
4	BIJAY KUMAR SARDA	1960-1970	
5	SUSHIL SARAOGI	1960-1970	
6	SUSHIL MITTAL	1963-1972	
7	ANIL KR BHARTIA	1967-76	
8	Er. R.P.S. Chowdhry	1970	
9	KAILASH SANEWALA	1966-76	
10	Arun Sadaswala	1966-72	
11	Binod Chawdhry	1960-1970	
12	RAVI AGARWAL	1962-1973	
13			
14			
15			
16			

Contd.... 3

Hi Jigs Roz n Cindy,

Yes we should all help to edit Jigs' resume. Jigs please send us a first draft. Roz, you're right, we should send a full package to the Bishop through Ashish's contact. Please send me the list of whatever names you can put on Excel before you call it a night and I'll try and complete it during the rest of the day (just woken up:).

Time IS of the essence so we do need to move things along. Maybe the same package can be sent to Chuck to have an informal word with Raja McGhee and ask him if he could consent to meet with a delegation of Hermonites.

Take care
Dips

Hi everyone,

It seems things are really moving along now. You all seem to have great contacts and hopefully it will all now come together. If there is anything I can do please ask, but I don't have any contacts I'm afraid that could help in any way. Please let me know if there is anything else I can do though.

Take care
Cindy (Lucinda Gibbs), UK.
Ps. I wrote to James Sinclair and he wishes to communicate directly with his OMHSA members directly rather than have them be included in the larger mailing that eventually we will put out. He feels as they are older he will screen and send what he feels appropriate. I said we would of course be happy to go along with that wish.

Dear Sir (Mr. Stewart),

Greetings from Sikkim and Happy New Year!!

I hope this note finds you as I had send two other mails and Roz tells me that you email add has changed. James (UK) had kindly given me your new add and so I'm attaching something that concerns MH and which is dear to your heart.

Roz updated us about you and I hope things are OK. Would love to hear from you.

With warm regards and much love,
Jigme and family

Dear Jigs and Roz,

I have over 1000 email addresses sent over by Joy's office and am looking to send the following email to all of them tomorrow.

Please feel free to comment/or edit below before I send it out.

Regards
Dipak Mirchandhani, UK.

MEETING WITH MH PRINCIPAL GEORGE FERNANDES ON FEB 11, 2012

Principal George Fernandes's U-turn surprised and alarmed us

Dear friends and fellow Hermonites,

After we informed you of the 5-Point Resolution on MH Revival adopted by the Sikkim Hermonites Association on Jan 3, 2012 we contacted MH Principal Mr. George Fernandes and sought an appointment to seek his views, advice, suggestions and information on the subject. He said he would not be able to give any information on MH, including the Managing Committee, then as he was going down to Bangalore and would be back on at the end of Jan. He promised to meet us after his return and do the needful.

George Fernandes with his wife Saroj Pradhan.

A meeting was fixed with Mr. Fernandes on Feb 11 (Saturday). Present at the meeting were Mr. Fernandes, Namgyal Wangdi (SC 1971 - Sikkim), Anup Chachan (ICSE 1977 and former member of Managing Committee - Darjeeling), and Jigme N. Kazi (SC 1972 – Sikkim and global Hermonites). Although we wanted to talk to Mr. Fernandes only Mr. Simon (Senior Master) and Mukund Goyal (ex-Hermonite and a local contractor who is constructing the kitchen-cum-dining room building at school) were also present during the hour-long meeting. The gist of the meeting is as follows:

1. As soon as we three entered his office Mr. Fernandes started complaining to us on the subject on "alleged irregularities in administrative functioning" discussed during the Sikkim Hermonites Association meeting on Jan 3, 2012. He was visibly agitated and upset on the issue and said he was deeply hurt on passing such a "resolution." When we told him that we had merely "discussed" on the subject of "alleged irregularities" and had not passed a "resolution" on it he would not see the point and refused to listen to the voice of reason. He said his image and reputation were harmed because of our reference to the issue. He asked us to delete the reference on "alleged irregularities".

2. He said the Hermonites, excluding Pratap Rai and Anup Chachan (both from Darjeeling), had done nothing for the school and even doubted and almost ridiculed our love and concern for MH.

3. When told that we had come to him to seek his advice, views on MH's future and information on the identity of the Managing Committee members and their addresses, phone nos and email addresses Mr. Fernandes said we had no right to seek information about them which is a "secret". He refused to give the information. Hermonites want to make representations to the Methodist Bishop, who is the

Chairman of the Managing Committee, which runs the school, and also inform other members of the Committee on MH's future.

4. When told that we may be forced to file an RTI to seek information concerning Managing Committee members' whereabouts Mr. Fernandes said we are free to go to the court but he will not reveal their names and contact numbers as it was "secret."

5. When told that we would inform all Hermonites that he refused to give us the list of Committee members and their particulars Mr. Fernandes said he had no objection to this.

6. As soon as we were seated in his office Mr. Fernandes "fired" us like a bunch of junior school kids who had bunked classes for about 15 minutes. We maintained our composure and took things at our stride. When we asked for a cup of tea Mr. Fernandes said there was one in school to do the job. However, after sometime Mr. Simon called someone who got us tea and biscuits. The meeting was official and on an important subject. It was not a gatecrash but an appointment was sought in advance.

7. Namgyal Wangdi said he was sorry to hear from Mr. Fernandes that Sikkim Hermonites had done nothing for MH even though they had done a lot for the school in the past so many years. "From now on I will not help MH," Namgyal said.

8. Anup, Mr. Simon and Goyal said Mr. Fernandes should not be agitated by reference to "alleged irregularities" as the Sikkim Hermonites had not passed a resolution alleging that there was administrative irregularities but merely discussed on the subject. But Mr. Fernandes kept on rattling on the same issue again and again and refused to hold the meeting in a calm and cordial atmosphere.

9. At one point Jigme pointed out that he was tolerating Mr. Fernandes' unjustified abuses and allegations against the Hermonites and his "immaturity" in holding a meaningful meeting on such important issues that concern the school in a proper manner simply because he was a Hermonite who had come to the school in the best interest of the school and that MH was a family and that discussions should be held in true Hermonite spirit.

10. Jigme said he had come for the meeting on behalf of Hermonite International, a global Hermonites body of which he is the Founder-President.

11. Mr. Simon said he would not accept anyone if the Managing Committee fails to appoint a Principal as per the school's constitution and government guidelines. He threatened to approach the court if the appointment was illegal and unconstitutional.

12. Mr. Fernandes said MH was guided by its constitution and governed by the Church and no one had the right to question how the school was run. Jigme reminded him that India was a democratic country and its constitution guaranteed fundamental rights and no one was above the law. Jigme said there should be openness and transparency in the administration.

13. Both Mr. Fernandes and Mr. Simon appealed to Hermonites to give funds to the school for various projects. Mr. Fernandes said he was the Committee's Secretary and any application to the Committee should be routed through him.
14. Mr. Simon and Mr. Fernandes had a dig at Hermonites' aspiration to restore MH's "past glory". "When you say "past glory", which period were you referring to?" they asked.

Our observations after the meeting:

1. Mr. Fernandes and Mr. Simon's views may or may not be the views of the Managing Committee. If it is their views only then the Managing Committee ought to let the Hermonites know what their views are. As such meeting Committee members in Calcutta next week would be pointless. Accordingly, our trip to see Committee members in Calcutta next week has been cancelled. Hermonites are urged to think seriously on filing RTI (Right To Information) in the court to obtain relevant informations on MH.
2. A tough posture needs to be adopted with the administration as it has taken serious matters of MH lightly.
3. Inform everyone, including the Managing Committee, of what transpired during the meeting.
4. Since Jigme is the candidate for the principalship he cannot be expected to lead the campaign at home front although Roslyn (Rongong) Namgyal (Australia) and Dipak Mirchandhani (UK) are presently incharge of the job. Someone in Darjeeling or nearby needs to head the campaign committee.
5. School begins on Feb 23 and Mr. Fernandes' term ends in March-end. The process of appointing the next Principal is most urgent.
6. Mr. Fernandes has completely or deliberately misunderstood the minutes of the meeting of the Sikkim Hermonites Association held on Jan 3, 2012. Views expressed during the meeting were not against Mr. Fernandes or MH. However, Mr. Fernandes said the Sikkim Hermonites had completely destroyed his image and contribution made to MH in the past 35 years that he served the school on the staff. The Sikkim Hermonites regret Mr. Fernandes holding such views despite the fact that they had done nothing against him during the meeting. The content of the meeting has been emailed to all Hermonites to see for themselves. The Sikkim Hermonites also noted that the Sikkim chapter had rendered great contributions during the centenary celebrations of the school in 1995 and thereafter. The Sikkim chapter was at the forefront in making Mr. Fernandes MH Principal.
7. Jigme, a senior journalist presently edits two English weekly newspapers from Gangtok, Sikkim. As there was no one among the Hermonites to shoulder the responsibilities in MH after Mr. Fernandes retires he agreed to become the candidate for the post of Principal as requested by Sikkim Hermonites and whose decision was unanimously endorsed by global Hermonites.

8. The Bangalore Bishop, who is said to be incharge of the Managing Committee, has been apprised of the situation by Roslyn (Rongong) Namgyal on Jan 26, 2012. We have reports that a meeting of the Committee was called in Calcutta on Feb 2 but the meeting did not take place.

9. The Hermonites are hopeful that the Methodist Church and the Managing Committee will take the final decision on the issues raised by the Hermonites after careful thought and deliberation in the best interest of Mt. Hermon School, the Church and in memory and honour of our founders and all those who studied and worked in MH in the past 117 years.

Greetings from Sikkim!!

Dear Jigme,

To say the least, I was distressed by the account you gave of the meeting with George Fernandes, the retiring Principal. I agree totally with what Sherab has written. It is vital always in our discussion of controversial issues, and especially at this present time, to make sure that all we say must be truthful, honest, and gracious. While I agreed totally with the points listed by the Sikkim Committee, I would have preferred wording which would not seem to George totally critical of his Principalship. But having said that, I was very disappointed in the totally negative reaction shown by Mr. Fernandes. A bigger man would have more humbly admitted that at the moment things are not going well, and that the appointment of a suitable new Principal is a vital and urgent question. And in my mind, Jigs, you are a very acceptable choice.

Some of the things George said are, in fact, incredible to me. I think the names of a Board, or Managing Committee, should always be public property, and Hermonites should have a right to throw into the ring the name of a nominee for this most important post, at least for the Managing Committee to consider it.

What a tragedy if the graduates of the School have no contact with the governing body. I would hope this might be recognised without having to appeal to law. Does India have an Ombudsman system like we have in NZ? Alternative approaches should be (very gently!) to the Bishop who is Chairman, and to the Inspector of Anglo-Indian Schools, West Bengal. Not criticising the present Principal, but indicating how many Hermonites have signed their desire to present your name as a candidate for the urgently needed Principal. Should Hermonites not have a right to present their feelings to the School's Governing Body?

Jigs, speaking personally to you, I can only imagine how this meeting must have distressed you personally. Jigs, don't give way to grief, and DON'T withdraw your candidature.

I also hope that Namgyal Wangdi will withdraw his threat. Mr. Fernandes made his comment on the Sikkim Hermonites in anger. Don't reply in anger. I think God will yet over-rule the situation.

With fatherly love,
David (Stewart), Australia.

Thanks for circulating, Jigme,

A very frustrating situation, obviously but as a Hermonite for 10 years, all I can say is "Lage Raho! (Keep at it!)"

Circulating to all my Hermonite contacts (worldwide) for their knowledge, information and any action anyone deems fit.
Tehmi

It was saddening and maddening to read Jigme's report on the meeting. The short-sighted arrogance that the Principal Mr. Fernandes displayed epitomized everything that is wrong with Mount Hermon today. His comments are silly and ridiculous and it is very depressing and hurting that the management preferred to forego and forget even the basic courtesy of offering its guests a cup of tea.

I am sure my old friend Namgyal must have restrained himself greatly and vented his frustration by merely saying that he won't do anything for MH henceforth. A stronger reaction would have been justifiable and perhaps more desirable we can see why the school, counted

amongst the best not too long has slipped down the ranks so quickly. The poise and dignity with which the team maintained its composure deserves to be applauded there is no reason why Mr. Fernandes should feel slighted or hurt? His unpardonable and unacceptable behaviour shows that there is more than meets the eye and if time has given him wisdom to mull over his deplorable behaviour, he should apologize to Jigme and his team for his insensitive remarks.
Ved Prakash, India.

Dear Jigs and Hermonites Worldwide,
   Sorry to hear of the posture adopted by Mr. Fernandes. We need to rally around Jigs and see that the school is properly revived.
   Can the Church be requested to break their silence and let everybody know what is in their mind and how they propose to look after MHS without milking it to death?
   Thanks and regards
Shiv Kumar Saria (1961-72), Siliguri.
PS: I commit to make a donation of Rs 1,00,000 per year for the next 5 years if Jigs is installed as Principal.

Hi Shiv & Ved,
   Very heartening to know of your support for Jigs. Shiv you have started the ball rolling with your generous financial offer of support. I am sure Hermonites of all generations will be prepared to put their hands in their pockets for MH.
   To all of us (including myself) – let us all remember in all our communication with each other that our words should be truthful, honest & gracious. I don't believe that careless use of words & hurtful comments will ever promote the Hermonite spirit. Our motto is "Not for school but for Life we Learn". In this forum of public engagement let us speak words that build up others in spirit & body, not destroy and damage.
   Siliguri and Sikkim Hermonites – you are the people physically on the spot. Give your continued support to Jigs on the ground. We will continue to do whatever we can from our end.
   Hail Mount Hermon!
Sherab Namgyal (Bhutia), Canberra, Australia.

Hi Jigs
   So sorry that the meeting with George went so badly, however, we would really re-iterate what Barry has said and encourage you to keep going forward. Certainly cancelling the Cal trip is a good move - Sherab and I think the following:
   *I am going to get all the emails onto a single document for when it is needed.

Hi jigs
Sorry the last email went off before I had finished it! Anyway, I think we should do the following:
   * I'll send a follow up letter to the Bishop just to confirm where things are up to with him.

* I'll consolidate all the emails from around the world onto a single document for when it is needed.
* We think it would be really helpful for you to meet some of the people with political influence and introduce yourself to them - hopefully Rudra etc., will come to the party.
* We think that Barry is right - and the Bishop is the key - so we need to try to organise for you to meet with him accompanied by a support group - I wonder if Barry could be part of that group?? To that end it probably would be good to source some Hermonite support in the Bangalore region....any ideas? - What about Mon Mathai?
* Finally, I think that some of the points Barry made about approaching the Bishop with a plan are excellent. I'll start drafting some words, and will get them to you to have a look at as soon as I can.

Jigs - we always knew it would be a fight. We are praying - as are many others - and if it is to be - then it will be.

We tried to ring you, but the line wasn't very good.
Take heart, Jigs - we are with you.
Roz (Roslyn Namgyal), Canberra, Australia.

Dear Jigs,

Thank you for such a detailed account of what has happened in the past few days. Don't be discouraged Jigs. Fernandez is on his way out and so he is going through lots of strange emotions. His early days were questionable in that he was probably still learning and a little self-serving. Now he is seeing an ex-student as a potential successor and feels threatened. Anyone coming in (if they are not his *chora*) will discover many irregularities and he is worried. So he is going to try and make sure a 'friendly' takes over - never mind whether they are efficient or committed.

He will never understand the commitment of MH students (he was never one and anyone who has not experienced being a student there can never understand our passion) and should not denigrate what Hermonites have done for him and the school. I spent a lot of time trying to support him and give him credibility over the past 5 years.

Anyway, now it is time to start playing the game (and I say that from a positive standpoint). I think we should start mobilizing the influence of Hermonites especially in India (particularly Bangalore and Kolkata). We need to have the Bishop in Bangalore in agreement as well as the Committee. For a start, the Committee should understand that Hermonites do not want to appear as a threat. They can continue as a Committee (for now - but we don't tell hem that) ... and still get their free trips to Darjeeling every year. All we want is their approval of you and their agreement to let a couple of Hermonites sit on the Committee.

Then there is the Bishop. We need some influence to get him on side. He also needs to understand that appointing you as principal will ensure the safety and security of MH as a Methodist institution. You will consolidate the boundaries and re-build the school. That is a huge plus. Who else could do it? Certainly not a South Indian!!

Can you call on your political influence such as Sonia Gandhi? Do we have any Hermonites in Delhi, Mumbai or even Bangalore that can bear influence? Once you get the influence started especially with the Bishop - then I would think you plan a trip to go and see him - in a specially selected (and appropriate) group. I do think the Bishop is the key. I would suggest you put together a proposal (written in detail with facts and figures and perhaps a number of letters expressing support from influential persons - some of whom you have mentioned - including Gurung). This proposal will outline your plan for reviving MH - rebuilding and recruiting and how it can be sustainable.

Lastly, maybe a call to all Hermonites for prayer - to recruit God's wisdom and support for our wanting to revive the institution which gave us so much and which we hope will give many more students from all over the world - just as much. For those skeptics who say, let MH go the way many redundant institutions go - we should be saying "we want others to share in the wonderful experiences and life determining preparations that we received and have enjoyed".

Keep on believing my friend and keep in touch.
Barry Ison (Dhaka)

Mr. Barry Ison (left) with Ken, Karma, Nina and Jigme during the Centenary Celebrations in Darjeeling, November 1995.

Feb 16, 2012
Hi,
   Further to my extended conversations with Cindy and then Jigs yesterday, following the abortive meeting with Mr. Fernandes last week.

The strategy that we might want to take is:

- That Jigs should not be seen as leading the initiative, nor be the front man at meetings. We now have confirmation that OT Bhutia has consented to front the team in India.
- Arrange an immediate meeting in Calcutta where Chuck, OT and a select few Calcutta (e.g. Debasish Brahma) and Siliguri Hermonites can meet with Raja McGhee. I suggest that Jigs not attend the first meeting.
- It seems that Raja McGhee is not too happy with the Committee and is concerned about MH. We need to turn that concern into action by strategizing with him about what would be the best way forward rather than saying outright that we want Jigs to be Princi.
- Our concerns should be voiced to him and then let us hear him out and ask him to spell out his concerns, options, possible solutions and hurdles so that we can co-opt him into working with us. It is at this stage that the candidature of Jigs should be brought up with him and see if he would be willing to divulge the contact details of other committee members or contact them on our behalf. The team members can then ask Jigs to join in the meetings if deemed fit and correct by all parties involved.
- A second team could try and do something similar by making an appointment to meet with Bishop Sagar in Bangalore. Ashish Bhengra is in Chennai and George Mathai is in Bangalore and I can write to them do try and initiate this.
- Concurrently we should try and get past principals and faculty to write to committee members (Raja McGhee and Bishop Sagar are the only ones we know of at the moment) voicing their concern and supporting Jigs' candidature. Roz, could you speak/write to them and see if they would be willing to do so.
- Write to each other regularly with updates on any initiatives or developments plus new strategies and actions that we might undertake.

Roz, do you think that we should share the contents of the letter you wrote to the Bishop with the 100 odd Hermonites who wrote back in support. It's been almost 3 weeks since their emails of support started pouring in and we ought to give them some feedback. If so, please send me a copy.

I'm not too sure if we should write to them about the meeting with Fernandes but if you guys think it's Ok, then I can circulate that to them as well.

Cindy, as discussed, please gather our emails into one mailing list so that we can hit "reply to all" and be sure that all who wish to be on this active list are in the loop. We should also give people the option to opt in or out from this active list.

Best,
Dipak Mirchandhani, UK.

Feb 2, 2012
Dear All,

I, Abinoam Panu Rong, former student of Mount Hermon School, Darjeeling for 13 years (1992 to 2005, i.e. from Class KG to 12) do hereby propose the name of Mr. Jigme N. Kazi for the position of Principal of Mount Hermon School, Darjeeling subsequent to Mr. George Fernandez's retirement from the said position.

At present, Mount Hermon School, Darjeeling desperately requires a dynamic, outgoing and dedicated Principal who possess excellent managerial and leadership qualities along with excellent communication skills in order to regain its past glory. I feel only a Hermonite can revive Mount Hermon School out of its present pitiful state.

Therefore, once again, I propose Mr. Jigme N. Kazi's name for the position of Principal of Mount Hermon School, Darjeeling.

My best wishes and prayers to Mr. Jigme N. Kazi along with all the Hermonites in and around the globe and my dear Mount Hermon.

Warm regards,
Abinoam Panu Rong, India.

If it comes to it Jigme you might not know but John Johnston didn't have a masters when he became principal!! He however got it done somehow as soon as he could.

As you know the biggest issue is that the board won't get kickbacks from you and they would expect that from anyone else that they post. I don't know how u get around that!

Unless you have support from other Hermonites and basically have a personal support group who can work out how you manage the corruption that normally goes with that position in other principal jobs and what the board has got used to in the last while.
Regards
Mick Glasby, Australia.

Dear Jigs

Mick has just let me know he discussed with you some aspect of my Dad's qualifications for the Principalship in terms of doing his MA. Is there a requirement for Principals to have their "MA" anyway?
Regards
Kris Glasby, Australia.

Hi all,

I sure would be delighted to have Mr. Kazi as the next principal of our school. Let me know what I can do, here in California, to get this done.

As you know, we will do anything for our beloved MHS.

Rahen (Msskey), US.

'MH Revival' Campaign 2012

Dear Hermonite well wishers,

Yes I do support Jigme's candidature for the position of Principal. I am positive he shall do justice to his position & restore our glory.

Warm wishes to all,

Hail Mount Hermon,

Abbas Ahmed, India.

Thanks for your note Jigme...I am quite in support of the proposal being made that you be approached to take on MH....am waiting to see what kind of reaction there is from the Bishop, and I must say I am not very hopeful of a sensible response if my own experience is anything to go on. I fear the "powers that be" with whom I have zero influence, will have their own agenda. We'll keep hoping.

Glad you enjoyed K/M Ashok was one of my prefects; gained the Fisher cup in 1986...... Mona a great senior girl////her kids were recently at MH and she should have been able to give a fair picture of how things were with George F. I feel he is not being given a fair go in general comments......whoever takes on a school in Darj is going to have problems with the politics. Sinnee Hung would also be worth talking to as she has had nearly 20 years on the staff, and "is loving it". Keep us informed about how things go. Yours JJ (John Johnston), Australia.

Mr. and Mrs. Johnston with Jigme N. Kazi in Gangtok, 2010.

Hi,

I think your ideas are great Dipak. How do you feel about it all Roz, Sherab and Jigme?

When do you want these conversations to go 'live' to the smaller number of people that has been suggested? Can we agree on the final list of names for the smaller group (which in itself is now growing) - the following have been suggested:

The Bishop, Jigme, OT Bhutia, Ros, Sherab, Dipak, James Sinclair, Varongthip, Navin, Joy, Prava Rai, Shiv Saria, Ved Prakash, Sujit Singh, Pratap Rai, Barry Ison, Cindy.

I suppose these people initially could be asked if they are happy to be on the small contact list. We do need an email id for OT please Jigs unless you will pass all on to him.

I did try to add more names to the original main Hermonite list that Jigme wrote to and my computer would not let me send the message. I guess there are just too many names. Maybe we will have to have another couple of lists for the large MH group of students. You have all the names Dipak of those who wrote in support, then there is the original list of 105 Hermonites from Jigs, and there is the OMHSA list from James Sinclair and a few stragglers not included, and I think Varongthip has a separate list for the Thai Hermonites too.

I guess when an informative mail is sent out we could simply ensure it is sent to these groups individually. If you have a better idea and are more techy let me know what I could do!!
Love
Cindy, UK.

Dear Jigme,

Thank you for writing. I have already been thoroughly aware of the truth as you write it. And, like you, I have been sure of George's personal honesty, and I believe he tried his honest best, but things were perhaps beyond him.

But in what he said to you, I think he was unwise. He should encourage everyone who is seeking MH's good, and any school board should be public, and available. Probably in his personal distress he made angry and wrong judgments.

I am praying for you, and for the whole school, that at this critical time, what is God's will may be done.

DEO SOLI GLORIA! ("To God alone be glory" – if your Latin is not that good!) David (Stewart), Australia.

Dear Jigs,

Your suggestion to me personally is most attractive, but I must say No. You see, I'm at the stage where I need to have medical help available on the spot, and I can't really manage stairs and slopes any more. But I was deeply moved by your loving suggestion.

Do you remember long ago, when the Central Govt of India offered 10 full scholarships for 10 years from young people in Sikkim? I think back to when my sister Joy, and Mrs. Williams were going to Gangtok, to give tests and make the choice out of 400 applicants (the Sikkim Govt had reduced this to forty).

Joy was especially concerned, and asked some of us to pray very earnestly that they would make the right choices. She felt that the two of them were so inadequate to decide rightly, when they had to judge independently of English language skills. Boy! The answers to some prayers stick out like sore thumbs. Did God guide? I think especially of Sherab. And Dubs, and you. And you will know what has happened to others.

Sometimes there are key points in our lives, and we only long after realise how wonderful they were. Yes, I'm glad Esther spoke to you. And there will be many who are praying hard for you, now and when you hold the reins of Principalship. Of course, Mount Hermon is a Christian School. This does not mean that it is not tolerant and open to those of all faiths, or none. Far from it. But it will be a school marked by unity, uprightness, and love. The School that I believe I saw God developing wonderfully in "my era", and years beyond.

Well, Jigs, be at peace in your own spirit. I pray that God will heal George's spirit beautifully. I am praying for this, as well as everything else, Managing Committee, and all. Love, David (Stewart), Australia.

'MH Revival' Campaign 2012

My wife Tsering and myself with Mr. and Mrs. Stewart and Mr. and Mrs. Murray at the Centenary Celebrations at MH, November 1995.

Dear Jigme,

Thank you for your greetings at Christmas. I am sorry I have not contacted you long before this but my hand still has a long way to recovery and it hurts to type on the computer - hence my silence for so long.

How sad to read of all that is happening in MHS or about MHS.

The main thing we can do in all this is pray and you can be sure I am praying for you, for you all and for the future of MHS.

That trip with you and Namgyal was so special, as was our time with you all. Please give my love to everyone and urge Namgyal not to give up on MHS.

Blessings be upon you, upon you all

Love from Miss Hawke, Australia.

Thanks for sharing this, Sujit.

And wishing you luck and complete success with all your endeavours for and on behalf of Mount Hermon and all Hermonites, Jigme.

Will be waiting with abated breath to read more developments, hopefully all positive!

Circulating this to ALL my Hermonite contacts for their knowledge and information.

Bijay Palriwala
(MHS 1954-64)

Dear Jigs and Dipak

Thanks for the updates - it is very encouraging news, and we will be thinking of you Jigs as you and others meet with George today.

I think that our thoughts at this stage are that it would be prudent to proceed gently. As you say, if the Bishop has received our letter and has called a meeting he must consider that it is worth looking into in more depth. Jigs - you present as a really viable and strong contender at this stage, and the fact that you have such tremendous support behind you will speak for itself. I don't think anyone else will come so highly recommended by such an array and diversity of people. That speaks for itself - and one thing that I think we could do, Dipak, would be to collate the testimonials of all the Hermonites who have written in - maybe on a single document rather than a myriad of emails.

It is good and appropriate to meet George at this stage, but I think that if he becomes alienated that could cause problems. Even if he voices concerns and maybe even objections, I think that a courteous and gracious meeting will actually be best. We don't know the kinds of pressures that he might have been, or continue to be placed under, but the reality is that he is leaving, and this presents an opportunity for a new chapter to begin.

Our best bet is the Bishop, and whatever remains of the Committee.

One thing - do you think I should write again to the Bishop as a follow up to my original email.

Jigs, I am really sorry we are physically so far away at this time - but please do know that you and Tshering are always in our thoughts and prayers.

Dipak - thanks for your generous and practical support!
Love and best wishes
Roz (Roslyn Namgyal), Canberra, Australia.

Dear Jigs and people concerned,

Yes I could not agree more to what have been commented on the meeting with Mr. Fernandez. However I am not surprised at his reaction to the meeting, this comment comes from my own experience with the other Thai Hermonites on our visit to MH, we were not treated well and Mr. Fernandez did not show interest in our visit. I am not surprised at the present state of MH with such principal and management committee.

We will continue to support Jigme all the way and please let us know what is required from our side in Thailand.
Kind regards,
Varongthip (SC73), Bangkok.

Bijay,

I am very happy to learn that something constructive is happening to revive MHS. Jigme seems very enthusiastic and I wish him and others all the success in making our old school even better!!
Namgyal (Namlha), India.

Jigmi: go for it!

Although I must admit I didn't like the way you were first introduced, I do like your energy and fervour, and you seem to hold out some hope that things might begin to change for the better.

With the very best wishes.
Pradip Nath (Graduating class of 1963)

Dear Jigs,

I am just opening this email and by now you are probably in Cal. I'm with you my friend - all the way. Let me know if I can help in any way - such as sending a letter to the Bishop, or to Committee members etc.

I'm afraid I cannot come to Cal at this time as school is full on. But I am free for about 6 weeks from the middle of June. I will be going to Australia on the 26th/27th June and then back about mid-July. so could come across then if necessary.

I was wondering about the politics of Darjeeling. I heard that Ghising is back in power and that Gurung is on the out. What is the situation? I'm sure you can work around it. Both of these guys will probably be crucial in the future of MH as Gurung is a neighbour and Ghising had his kids go to MH.

Keep me in the loop and every blessing on your very adventurous but hopefully fruitful path. You have a lot of support.
Best wishes
Barry Ison, Dhaka.

Wishing you all the best in your efforts to make Mount Hermon the best that it can be. I was at MHS last week with a group of people I had brought from the UK. Such happy memories, such a secure and loving childhood despite being separated from our parents for a long time, from a young age (6). I would wish it on more people. Mrs. Norbu, at the Dekeling Hotel, also said without prompting that MHS has always produced happy cheerful children, as well as high achieving ones.
Yours Karen Hastings, UK.

Dear Sir,

I had replied in the positive to your email and have asked many more Hermonite friends to follow suit. By now there must have been thousands like us who expressed similarly but now the question is what the managing committee is thinking.

Please let us know the exact status of our suggestion/demand and the views of the Managing Committee as people including me want to know. We want the revival of MH and a U turn in its conditions.
Prakash Mundra, Sikkim.

Dear Jigs,

I had also forwarded all the info to Dipak in London and his classmate, Ashish Bhengra, knows Mahanty and I think is going to contact him as Mahanty was on the Board of MH till 99 (as you will see from stuff I sent). Maybe this way we can find out who is on the rest of the Board currently. If we can do that maybe we can glean some information. Maybe it would have been worthwhile seeing McGee as he may have been on our side it seems. Was he not keen to divulge the other Board members details?

Who can lead the assault from the Darjeeling/Cal side? Is there anyone you can suggest to do the job? What about Udai as he is also a lawyer or Namgyal who was with you in Darj or Anup who has been so involved with the school for so long and is in Darj? How do any of them feel about taking charge of this?

I am copying this to Dipak too so he is up to date. I suppose Ros and Sherab are aware of where we are to date with this? Do they have any views?

Not sure what else I can do right now, but we are right behind you. Keep me posted.
Cindy (Lucinda Gibbs), UK.

Jigs

I'm sure everyone will contribute if you take over - that is for sure. I'm sure it is unlikely any of our batches will be happy to pass cash over to anyone that is not known to us. As far as the Main Building is concerned a thorough, unbiased report from a professional needs to be put forward before anyone would want to cough up to build a new building. I think the last quake and poor maintenance has put the building under strain, but I could not see (when we visited) the need for it to be pulled down.......but I am not a professional.

My only other suggestion then as far as someone to head this assault, but pass this by the others you are communicating with, is what about writing to the whole group of Hermonites and ask for someone to come forward to lead this from the Cal/Delhi/Darj/India end. If someone does come forward then this can be again passed to the list and see if everyone is happy for that individual to go ahead. I can't think of any other way forward. Is there no one in Cal interested???? What about Sinnee Hung - she is on MH staff?

I will keep an eye on what is happening but am away a couple of days, but will take the lap top anyway.
Take care
Cindy (Lucinda Gibbs), UK.

Dear OMHSA Members,

I'm forwarding this to you regarding the outcome of the meeting with Principal George Fernandez which took place on February 11th 2012 which may be of interest. I sincerely hope that something will be sorted out to appoint a new Head for Mount Hermon (hopefully Jigmi Kazi) so that the future of the school is assured.
James Sinclair, UK.

'MH Revival' Campaign 2012

Dear OMHSA Members:

Can't we do something? Does the United Methodist Church still have ultimate responsibility? And if so, what group within the church? Is it a committee, or an individual? Is there anyone there we can address? There must be enough of us that we could have some influence. Do let's stay in touch and keep one another informed.

Mildred Engberg "Kitty" Katzell, US

Thanks for your work and time and effort Jigs, and to others on the front line.

Am I wrong in thinking that Mr. F is certainly about to leave? That he will cease to be committee's secretary? That he has no say in a successor? What is it to him? A golden handshake at stake?

Isn't the managing board the people 'we' have to approach? Isn't there a constitution, or public records that identifies this board - or at least the chair of the board? What is their agenda for the appointment of a new head?

Am I to presume that M. F wouldn't be willing to forward a letter from Hermonites to the board or better each board member, to arrange a meeting?

I don't think we are being confrontational - we are a concerned body of people, many who have children at the school I understand, and many more would go if we felt the school was achieving satisfactorily.

We personally have nothing to gain. We are voicing our dismay that our children - more likely grandchildren for some of us now - won't be able to enjoy the level of education and camaraderie we enjoyed. There are other schools of course, but who in society forsakes their own family in distress in order to look for a better family instead?

Please keep us updated.

Yours,

Ian Hastings, SC73 batch, UK.

Dear Jigme:

Thank you for supplying all that historic information. I had not been in touch with the school since my husband and I visited there in 1985, 50 years after I had left. I got to make a speech in the Assembly Hall and I was quite feted during my visit.

However, I am not the grand-daughter; I'm the daughter of Lila Engberg who was principal from 1931 to 1935. I attended what was Queen's Hill School from the time I was 2 years old (in 1926), through its renaming in 1934 as Mt. Hermon School and we left India during the winter of 1934-35.

With the information you have supplied, I'll see if I can contact anyone in the World Council of Churches and/or the United Methodist Church of USA. I'm now 88 years old, and don't know how much influence I might have, but we shall see. I'll keep you informed.

Peace and God's blessings to you.

Kitty (Mildred Engberg Katzell), US.

To: United Methodist Church, USA
I'm trying to reach someone with whom I can discuss a situation involving UMC in India.

At one time, my mother (Lila Kehm Engberg) was a Methodist missionary teaching and later principal at Mt. Hermon School in Darjeeling, India between 1926 and 1935.

As I understand it, the school is currently overseen by a board of managers under the Methodist Bishop in Bangalore. There seem to be some problems, and I would like to find out whom I could contact here or there to see if American alumni of the school can be of assistance. There are international organizations of alumni all over the world who have concerns in this matter. Can you give me that sort of contact information?
Mildred Engberg Katzell
56 Medford Leas
Medford, NJ 08055-2221

Jigme:
Below is the response I got from them. Are you familiar with Bishop Taranath Sagar? Should I or you or someone else contact him, or their organization?

You'll note at the end there was an invitation to respond to their evaluation survey, which I did.

They were very prompt, but of course I don't have any way of knowing if the Madras Regional Conference has anything to do with Darjeeling.
Cheers! Peace! and God bless!
~Kitty (Mildred Engberg Katzell), US.

Greetings from InfoServ, the United Methodist information service!
Your message reached our offices at United Methodist Communications in Nashville, Tennessee, USA.
Hello Mildred,
Thank you for writing. We suggest that you contact the:
Methodist Church in India
South India & Madras Regional Conferences
Bishop Taranath Sagar
Bishop's House
Baldwin Methodist Educational Ctr,
13 Convent Rd,
Museum Rd,
Bangalore 560 025, India;
TEL: 080-222 49 827 - FAX: 080-224 84 776
EMAIL: Bishop_sagar@hotmail.com
https://www.surveymonkey.com/s/VPDQV3V

InfoServ welcomes each and every opportunity to assist those seeking information about The United Methodist Church.
Mary Lynn Holly
InfoServ/Find-A-Church
United Methodist Information Service
infoserv@umcom.org
mholly@umcom.org

Jigs he gave you verbal support in Sikkim according to him and Roz. Muscling in with a letter to committee members he does not know may not be appropriate. Apparently the person he did look up in Calcutta is no longer on the committee. You personally had his support. He had stressful complications through the 1980s that none of us understand with all that political stuff going on.

His dealings with the committee may have been fraught, I don't know. Also their dealing with the outgoing Principal may not be able to be affirmed.... I don't know, but I would not want him to be dragged into a bun fight. Roz is the person to talk this over with as she understood his perspective I'm sure.

He may not have your previous correspondence if you are still using his wrong email address as it was wrong in your fwd list.

I'll forward this to Roz who has been talking with him
Regards
Kris Glasby, Australia.

I will prepare a SWOT analysis of MH as best as I can and also a few other points that we can present to the committee. However, most of it will be based on whatever reports I have. An onsite visit would have been great. But you can fill in the blanks.

I will send it to you by this weekend - I have a scrutiny report to present at the Regional office of AICTE in Bhopal on the 17th and that is taking all my time at the moment. I will send the SWOT report by this weekend. Finances will come and we will also think of other means of raising revenue - we will cross the bridges when we come to them. For this moment our priority is to somehow be put in charge of MH and initiate the resurrection process.
Ved Prakash Agarwal, India.

Don't give up. Keep at it. I smell trouble ahead.
Ronen Ghose, UK.

It's very disturbing that Mr. Fernandes presented with such a defensive stance. Is he not ready to retire? Does he have a preferred successor for the principalship? This situation brings up too many questions.
Bijay Palriwala, UK.

Hail Mount Hermon! A Tribute

Feb 22, 2012
Dear Bishop Sagar

I was wondering if you have received my earlier email to you dated 26 January 2012. Since then there has been a lot of email activity around the world from alumni and ex-teachers of Mount Hermon School. Last week there was also a meeting between Jigme Kazi and George Fernandez (current Principal of Mount Hermon) that did not go well. Since then there has been even greater uncertainty because it has not been possible for anyone to meet with, or talk to anyone on the Managing Committee.

One of our alumni, who later taught in the school and who had a ward studying back in Mount Hermon School until last year has said the following, and with his permission I quote from his letter to Hermonites around the world. These words encapsulate our thoughts:

"....I'm sure you will join with me in expressing to the Administrators of the school and the Leaders of the Methodist Church that it is not a case of 'Us' and 'Them'. For example, the only way sustainability can be maintained is to ensure that the ownership of the school stays with the Methodist church. We are only saying that we want to be part of the process though which our school can be revived and regenerated.

Because I have had a ward studying in Mount Hermon over the past 5 years, I am reasonably familiar with what has been happening there, including knowing about some of the teaching and administrative staff. While many of the teachers in Mount Hermon today work hard and contribute positively to the student's studies and well-being, there is no one there who could take over the Principal's position.

After witnessing 'outsiders' trying to lead and manage Mount Hermon over the years, I am convinced that for now, the ideal person for this position would be someone from the region – being Darjeeling, Siliguri, Sikkim, Bhutan or Nepal. Currently we have someone who grew up in Mount Hermon, having significant achievements during his school years including the Bishop Fisher Cup (which is quite rare these days); has attended the Teacher's College; has taught at Mount Hermon; is a writer and communicator; and over the past decades has earned a name for himself in the political and social scene in Sikkim and the Himalayan region, who is willing to take on the task of rejuvenating Mount Hermon and mobilizing the significant support that the alumni represent. I also suspect that he could possibly mobilize Central Government support as well. He is, of course Mr. Jigme Kazi and to those of us who know him and respect him, he is someone whom we are confident in and know (with the support of so many of us) will do an excellent job.

I trust that we will all throw our support behind Jigme and continue to promote him and his vision for a new and invigorated Mount Hermon which will be a source of pride to all those; Committee members, Administrators, Students and Alumni, who have a vested interest in its future." – Mr. Barry Ison 1951 to 1961 (student) at Mount Hermon, 1971 to 1972 (teacher).

There are representatives of the school throughout India, and if it were possible, Jigme Kazi, and other alumni would really appreciate the possibility of coming to Bangalore and meeting with you.

I realise that this may be a real imposition to you, given that the custodianship of Mount Hermon School seems to be something that you have just recently inherited, and it is a long way away from where you live. However, given that there is no way of identifying or getting in touch with the present Managing Committee of the school, I do hope you will give us some response, or at least guide us in the right direction so that we can have some communication and dialogue with the people who hold the future of this precious institution in their hands.

Thank you very much,

Yours sincerely,

Roslyn Namgyal, Canberra, Australia.

Dear Kitty

Thank you very much for following up on the information about Bishop Sagar from Bangalore. It confirms that the email address I sent the original email too is correct. Last night I sent a follow up email to him asking him to acknowledge my email and requesting him to consider meeting with Jigme. We believe that he has only recently inherited the responsibility of Mount Hermon as the previous Bishop of Lucknow had passed away - however, with the deafening silence from all quarters, even this is hear-say.

We do now have phone numbers thanks to you - so if we don't hear back in the next day or so we will try that method of contact.

It is so heartening and encouraging to have your wonderful support, Kitty - As one ex-student put it – "You can take a Hermonite out of Mount Hermon, but you can't take Mount Hermon out of a Hermonite!"

Hope to get back to you with good news soon.

Warmest Regards,

Roslyn Namgyal, Canberra, Australia..

Thank you, Roslyn. I was thinking earlier today that I should write to that bishop whose address I received, but I've decided to wait till I hear more from you. Let me know what you think I can do to be of assistance at any time. I have plenty of time to write emails. I don't really want to be phoning them, because I don't feel well enough informed, but if a phone call will help, let me know and we'll see what we can do. ~Kitty

Dear Jigs,

I am only addressing this mail to you and you alone, with a copy to Thip because you asked us not to be negative or use unkind language when commenting on your report re your latest visit to MH and your encounter with Fernandes. Thip and Ian are both right. So is Shiv and everyone else who have written and whose e-mail I was privileged to read.

I support you 100%. I agree with Thip. You let us know how, when and what kind of support you want at any given time and we will be there. I agree with Ian. MH is family.

I don't want to go looking for any other family. I may not have kids but many people I know do, both kids and grandkids. And I have given my fair share of advice regarding schools.

Since my first visit back to MH, which both you and Namgyal so kindly came all the way from Sikkim to play gracious hosts, I saw what has become of our beloved MH and how both Fernandes treated us. Subba and Sinnee were the only 2 who gave us any kind of welcome from our old school. Never thought I'd ever return after that but I did, because of my wife Eiam who went with me on the second trip and wanted to see my "roots". Again, the Fernandes couldn't care less.

When you wrote about how he treated you, his friend and collegemate, and all because of some alleged irregularities comment in the Sikkim Hermonites minutes I found it most intriguing. In my experience, the GUILTY make a big thing out of nothing. Sorry but that is my experience dealing with shoplifters, pickpockets and petty criminals when I worked at the Mall Shopping Complex. I was not there with you to witness first-hand his actions (reactions) but your description fits the bill. If he was not guilty and wanted to clear the air, he would have asked you what made the Sikkim Hermonites write such a thing and if they had any proof so he himself could initiate an investigation but he believe all his staff to be innocent. Something like that. (please pass this on to Namgyal as well)

Not bad. I have not used any swear words once and I was mostly polite in my language. I was presumptuous and accusatory but I explained my reasons for being so. However, I did not have any positive comment to add so I think it best if this e-mail is between just the 4 of us.

Thanks and keep fighting
Navin (Khuria) Wangsejullarat, Bangkok.

Dear Jigs, Cindy and Dipak,
Sorry for the delayed response from our end. Things have been very busy, and I've only managed to get back to my emails this evening.

We agree that there should now be smaller groups able to meet and take decisions on the spot - we also feel that they should be based on the ground there in India - so we definitely support that move.

I have not heard anything back from the Bishop, but someone we know in Bangalore rang his phone number tonight and found out that he is out of station until Monday.

Dipak and Jigs, I think that it may be wiser at this stage not to flood the bishop's email box with messages from all of us. Barry Ison also thinks it would be wise to proceed more cautiously on that front until we have had some sort of response to know where he might be coming from. I think that if nothing has come by Monday - I'll give a phone call from here and try to talk to him.

On a different front - what do you think about us approaching Raja MacGee - (we understand he is on the Managing Committee) - do we have any email contact for him?

The deafening silence from anyone involved in the management and running of the school is a very big concern.

Please let us know what you think.

All the best

Roz (Roslyn Namgyal), Canberra, Australia.

Dear all,

Contacted Ashish Bhengra, who is trying to garner support for our case with the Bishop. He has a guy who is in touch with top Church leaders in Bangalore and will meet the Bangalore Archbishop. He wants my resume. What is to be done?

Jigs

Dear Dipak Mirchandani:

Thank for the notice about the critical condition of Mount Hermon High School. I was saddened and shocked to receive the news.

As you suggested, I sent an E-mail to Ms. Rosyln Namgyal as shown below. I hope Jigme Kazi is appointed principal. His credentials are outstanding. My preferred E-mail address is: ThomasRobertson@verizon.net

I hope to visit Darjeeling in the not too distant future.

Kind regards,

Thomas Robertson, US.

Dear Roslyn Namgyal:

I am Thomas Lee Robertson, M.D., former Head Boy and a graduate of Mount Hermon School (MHS) in 1950.

I was alarmed and saddened to learn that MHS has fallen on bad times. I have fond memories of my years at MHS. I agree that Jigme Kazi has the credentials, experience, and commitment to lead MHS back to the former glory that it had. The education I received at MHS was outstanding and thereafter I easily achieved top placement in college, Medical School (University of Virginia in Charlottesville), and specialty training (internal medicine and cardiovascular disease).

Please add my name to those who highly recommend Jigme Kazi.

Sincerely yours,

Thomas Lee Robertson, M.D.

10625 Rock Run Drive, Potomac, Maryland 20854-1701, USA.

Dear Uncle David and Dear Friends,

Thank you for your email, Uncle John, and apologies for my delayed response. There have been hundreds of emails flying around the world, either from individuals who have then made their own lists, or from the Yahoo 50s and 60s group. Sherab and I don't write on the Yahoo web-site, but Bijay Palriwala forwards things to us and we have kept up with some comments from that source. Therefore, our communication has all been via emails to and from individuals. We have your correct email address, but will keep an eye out for correspondence that has incorrect addresses for both you and Uncle David.

It might be best to go through this sequentially:

1. How Jigme Kazi became a name to put forward to the Managing Committee:

    For a number of years, various alumni groups have expressed concern with the way in which Mt. Hermon has gradually been degenerating under successive principals, although most were relieved that George had managed to hold things together in recent years. Some of these people however, have sent their children to school and some we know have later withdrawn them for various reasons. Others have visited, only to feel they were cold shouldered etc.

    When it became known that George Fernandez was retiring, there was an understandable interest (and anxiety) in knowing who would be taking over from him as Principal. This was coupled with local views in Darjeeling that things were at an all-time low and that the school was in danger of collapsing altogether (it is also the expressed opinion of some of the school's longest serving Grade 4 Staff (servants) who stand to lose complete livelihoods should this happen). There was also a much publicised report placing Mount Hermon at the bottom of a list of 40 Boarding Schools in India.

    As you know, Uncle David first suggested that I apply to the Board to see if Sherab and I might join the school again, even that I might apply for the Principalship. It became clear to us that this was definitely not an option as you know but it is the point at which Jigme Kazi's name was raised as being someone who might be a suitable candidate.

    Jigme's willingness to consider this was not a direct threat to anyone in the school to 'take over'. It should have been a simple matter to have approached the school board and to have been able to submit an application. However, it has been impossible to even find out who is on that Managing Committee, let alone approach them.

2. How the Managing Committee have (not) responded:

    We did hear from "a reliable source" that the Bishop of Bangalore recently "inherited" Mount Hermon, so on January 26th I sent an email to Bishop Sagar of Bangalore, asking if he was the person we should be addressing and acknowledging that, if he was, we were making an unprecedented request for him to consider Jigme as a potential candidate.

    Because the Bishop was so new to the position, I tried to explain something of the history of the school, the passionate interest of alumni all over the world, and the dismay with which many had seen MH ranked lowest in a recent publication listing the top 40 boarding schools in India. I also gave a personal reference for Jigme's character and explained that he would come with the support of many people who wanted to help the school in any way they could.

There was no response from Bishop Sagar, although it would have been perfectly acceptable to have received a polite 'no thanks, we have already made our choice!' I have since tried again (about 10 days ago) but until now have heard nothing back. We have had confirmation that the email address is correct – so all I can assume is that he either doesn't read his emails, or he doesn't want to engage with anyone on the subject.

3. How everyone else got involved:

As part of understanding whether Jigme would have broad support for such a move, I also sent an email to my Australian and New Zealand contacts. They must have forwarded this email on because things spread like wildfire and people started responding from everywhere. Within the day I was getting responses from places as remote as Oman and Africa!!

Early on in the conversations, it became apparent that some people were using emails as a place to vent past angers and frustrations which was helping no one and doing an alarming amount of damage on the way – hence Sherab's email. Thank you for your comments once again, Uncle John.

Certainly since then, the tone of emails has become much more measured and helpful. Because it became impossible to marshal what has been flying around, a group of us - Dipak Mirchandani, Lucinda Gibbs, Jigme and I, started to collate all the email responses into a single spreadsheet. We have not written any response to these Hermonites apart from letting them know that we are waiting on some response from the Managing Committee.

4. How Jigme approached George Fernandez:

Jigme talked to George some weeks ago and was of the understanding that George thought it was a good idea for him to put his name forward. So in late January/early February Jigme, and two other Hermonites asked to meet with George to discuss the matter further. No one was expecting the reception they got - the meeting turned out to be acrimonious and humiliating and left everyone feeling stunned.

George was furious that the Sikkim Hermonites had met and discussed supposed "irregularities" in the school and it was obvious that he and Mr. Simon were far from supportive. They also clamped down and said that the Managing Committee members' names were secret and that everything to do with the future of MH was already decided. For want of a better description, Jigme reported that they felt like 'a bunch of kids who had been caught bunking!!' Jigme sent a report to all his contacts regarding this meeting. So things are a mess at present, and until we hear something from this elusive and secretive Managing Committee/Bishop, things are at a standstill.

5. Questions:
   a. If nothing else, one serious concern for everyone is the fact that the Managing Committee is so hidden and secretive. Where does their accountability lie?

I have looked at St. Joseph's College and St. Paul's websites, and they clearly specify their Board or Managing Committee members - and in one case, even have their pictures on-line! In this day and age this lack of transparency only raises further suspicions for everyone.

b. Why would Bishop Sagar be refusing to answer an email? He could so easily have thanked Jigme for his interest, but declined the offer politely saying they had already appointed someone else. Incidentally, George could also have said this too – more politely than he did. Instead, George retires in March and nobody seems to know who is taking over (several of the alumni still have children in the school). This lack of coherency and transparency has meant local gossip is rife - not at all helpful to anyone.

c. The people most able to ask for information (ex-Principals, teachers etc) are all retired, living overseas or out of contact. Those (who) left in India have tried their best to offer help to a place that has meant hearth and home to them for many years. There was no crime in this, although the passion has been difficult to contain!

Anyway, I thought I'd write to all of you to let you know where things are up to from our perspective.

I'll keep you in the loop as anything develops, but would really like to ask if you might pray for Jigme and Tshering, and for all those at Mount Hermon - staff, students and servants, and for all the alumni around the world who still hail Mount Hermon as home.

We think of you all often and hold you in our hearts.
Love
Roz and Sherab, Canberra, Australia.

Dear Jigs

Did this reply to you from Dad not reach you? I have your note to me dated 14/2/12 so not sure if you had already seen his reply or not as you state you had not heard from him... In it he does reiterate his support of yourself and various other comments. I got him to forward it to me so am re-sending. I'm sure a separate letter of his support would be fine if that is what you want.... let him know. He is back home now and sounding much better healthwise.

I do hope it works out in your favor and it sounds like "they" are a difficult committee to deal with, and its hard to see why GF was so defensive??? Maybe he recognises the furor that the rating of MH at the bottom of the heap has caused and it reflects on him???

But he has done the hard yards in terms of the 35yrs I guess.
Sincerely all the best
Kris (Glasby), Australia.

'MH Revival' Campaign 2012

Dear Jigs

Kris is concerned that I should see the notes that are going round MH....unfortunately, my ID is wrong in the emails circulating! (it should be bigpond, not bigpong.)

In any case you can use this note from me, to say I feel the committee would be well-advised to approach you to consider taking on the difficult task of stearing MH out of its present problems. A person with some political connection with the area, personal integrity, and experience in dealing with difficult business problems, would be more valuable than one with direct experience in running a school.

Unfortunately, I do not have personal contact with any on the Committee.....in fact they completely left me out of any information loop as soon as I left at the end 1989..... even Jeff Gardner did not keep in touch when he had that year or so in the 90s. Did you see Bill Jones' comment? It seems to me he makes good sense.

I shall want to have all the information available as time goes by. What did Ashok and Mona have to say about their experience with their own kids?? And what does Sinnee have to say about her own experience in the past years?

Yours sincerely

(Rev) J Johnston, Principal 1978 to 1989, Australia.

Dear Sir (Mr. Johnston),

I read your account of your visit to India and was surprised to note that you had a hectic time. If I can do that at that age then it would be fantastic.

Sir, I and other Hermonites feel that I need just 2-3 years to pull the school through and do all that we can to do all repair works, including the cottages and main building, get rid of old furniture eg. beds and desks and make new ones. And also lay the foundation of future construction works as the old building cannot last long. The other thing is to ensure that Hermonites play an active role in helping the school and the Managing Committee.

Extra money can come only when a Hermonite takes charge at the moment. Already Shiv Saria has pledged to give Rs. 1 lac annually for five years if I become the Princi. Dipak Mirchandhani (76 batch), who is leading the UK MH Revival campaign, said he would give US$ 5000 (Rs. 2.5 lacs) if I head MH. The Nepal guys said they were willing to dish out Rs. 1-2000 initially to help with repair works if I take charge. There are around 600 Hermonites in Nepal alone and this means around Rs 7 plus lacs.

The Managing Committee and the Church need to know that Hermonites really care for the school. For instance, Kitty (88) from US who is the daughter of Mrs. Enberg, one of our Princis from the 1930s, is actively involved in the revival campaign. I have around 200 pages of email messages of support from Hermonites all over the world. This is unprecedented.

Ashok, one of my students, and Mona are very eager to help the school. They have their kids there and are very disappointed with George. "School starts in two week and we don't know how much we have to pay," said Ashok during our reunion in Kathmandu on Feb 1. Mona said she did not take out the deposit and gave it to the school. "But at least they should let me know how the money was used," she complained.

One of my classmates in Cal said, "Simon is a crook and he is very cunning." When I told Sinnee how George treated us she said, "I'm surprised." Pratap Rai, who has just finished his 4th chemo treatment for his stomach cancer, said George should be more cooperative. Incidentally, Pratap is one of the Committee members but he does not have any details of the members.

Politics: We have 3 MLAs from the hills from Bimal Gurung's party and they are all educationists and able administrators. I have put Rudramani Gurung and two of my Gurung friends to deal with Bimal, who will meet me at an opportune time. In Kalimpong, Amod and Binod Yonzone and some other locals will tackle the Kalimpong MLA, who is a lecturer. I will be seeing him in a week's time to brief him.

Besides MH I have this vision thing on all schools in Darj like ours eg. Homes, SAS, Goethals, etc. Before I finish with MH, I hope to have helped these schools in a similar manner. In Darj the MLA is Saroj Rongong's uncle, who seems keen on helping MH. Saroj is on the job since Sept 2011. And the Minister of WB for the hills who lives in Siliguri is another friend who can and will be approached. Karma Bhutia through Bhaichung Bhutia (Indian foota capt from Sikkim) will tackle with WB govt's Home Minister and in Delhi I have a few big shots, including Sonia Gandhi. I was in Congress for 4 years and they know how much I did for the party and who I am.

Roz and Dipak and Lucinda Gibbs are incharge of the campaign. Presently, we have formed teams for Cal and Bangalore to tackle with the Bishop and Committee members. I'm amazed to see how keen and cooperative the Hermonites are. As you know the stumbling block is the Church. In St. Joseph's Father Kinley from Bhutan has been able to do a lot for the school mainly because the Jesuits are solidly behind him. If the Protestant Methodist-Baptists does the same thing for us at MH then we can not only save this great institution but also place it on a higher ground. We are blessed and I'm sure God will understand our aspirations and do His part. If God is with us, who can be against us?

Losar begins on Feb 22. Happy Losar.

Jigs

A school which can't even provide a decent meal to it's student which greatly hampers the future health of that individual, doesn't require politics at this stage.

Let there be a Principal who is honest and has character, who will work for the best interest of the students.

Your's sincerely
Sudhir Rajbhandari
Final Year MBBS
Kathmandu Medical College, Nepal.

'MH Revival' Campaign 2012

HERMONITES International (Hi!)

Newsletter Vol 1 No 2 March 11, 2012

CAMPAIGN FOR MH Revival

"You can take a Hermonite out of Mount Hermon, but you cannot take Mount Hermon out of a Hermonite."
- Hermonite Sunirmal Chakravarthi
Principal
La Martiniere for Boys, Calcutta

HAIL TO THE HERMON KNIGHTS

"We Shall Overcome"

In response to Sikkim Hermonites Association's appeal on the issue of "MH Revival", Jigme N. Kazi, President of Hermonites International (Hi!), initially conceived soon after the school's centenary celebrations in 1995 but formally launched in 2005, made another appeal on MH in March 2012: "...irrespective of what the Managing Committee decides on MH's future the campaign for MH Revival must go on. The present crisis has motivated us into action. This is a good thing and must go on. We must say and sing the hymn "We Shall Overcome" and mean it and show the world that we can triumph over all our trials and tribulations."

Dear Hermonites,

First of all on behalf of the alumni let me wish our beloved alma mater Mount Hermon School and all Hermonites everywhere a very Happy Birthday! Today it is MHS's 117th Birthday.

Ever since the first week of the New Year (2012), when the Sikkim Hermonites Association (SHA) took the initiative to involve all Hermonites to campaign for 'MH Revival', there has been an overwhelming response from the alumni of all ages and places on the school's future. The concern for our beloved alma mater – Mount Hermon School (MHS) – from Hermonites of the '30s, '40s, '50s, '60s, '70s, '80s, '90s and right down to the present generation is not only very encouraging but also very inspiring. This is great! Which school in the world can boast of the 'Hermonite spirit'? Hardly any. It is, therefore, our honourable duty to preserve this rich and unique heritage of MHS.

Barry Ison – former MH student and teacher – once explained this unique phenomenon: "It is not emotion; it is passion."

In the past so many decades since I left the old and friendly walls I never failed to think and even dream of MH! This is but natural for all Hermonites but more so for a person like me who did his schooling (1963-1972), Teachers Training College (TTC – 1974-1975), and even taught at MH for four years (1976-1979).

Ex-students of the school under Rev. Mr. DG Stewart, who not only revived MH when he took over in 1953 but actually placed it among one of the best boarding schools in India – MH was on top of the list in 1961-62 – are still showing great concern for the school. This is amazing and an inspiration to us all.

"We Shall Overcome"

Ever since its inception in 1895 when the school (then called Arcadia or housed in Arcadia cottage, located on the Lebong side of Chowrasta in Darjeeling) was born MH has had its ups and downs. But we pulled it through. With faith in God and missionary zeal our founders – Miss Knowles, Miss Stahl, Mr. Dewey and Bishop Fisher – made sure that failures and obstacles were stepping stones to success.

After shifting the school from near Chowrasta to above the railway station in Darjeeling and calling it Queen's Hill School the school grew in leaps and bounds leading to the acquisition of the present premises for further expansion.

Fifteen years after the school was renamed Mount Hermon School in 1929-30 MH almost closed down due to dwindling enrolment. The cause of this was the Second World War when many of its foreign students and staff members of the school left MH. It was Mr. Dewey, Bishop Fisher and finally Mr. Stewart who helped MH to pull through the crisis and regain its past glory. Mr. Graeme A. Murray, who stepped into Rev. Stewart's shoes in 1964, built on the foundation laid by his predecessors. There was no looking back for MH after Mr. Murray's takeover.

However, in the 1980s MH and many schools in the hills passed through a very difficult and trying period due to uncertain political situation in Darjeeling. But Rev. Mr. John Johnston from Australia and later Mr. Jeff Gardner (India) kept the school going. Thereafter, MH faced a crisis of another sort as those who headed the school stayed only for a brief period.

The present Principal Mr. George Fernandes, who worked under Mr. Murray, Mr. Johnston and Mr. Gardner and who is also married to an ex-Hermonite (Saroj Pradhan), was able to stabilize the situation when he took over in 2000-1. We are, therefore, grateful to Mr. Fernandes for his contributions to the school.

Hermonites all over the world have expressed their apprehension of MH's future after Mr. Fernandes retires this month. Damages caused by the recent (Sept 18, 2011) earthquake to the main school building and falling enrolment, coupled with Mr. Fernandes's departure and doubts over who is to step into his shoes, have prompted Hermonites to play a leading role in the choice of the next Principal.

Hermonites now want an able and trustworthy Hermonite to head the school during this very trying period. They have backed Mr. Jigme N. Kazi's (Sikkim) candidature for the post and want the Managing Committee to appoint him as the next Principal.

MH Revival

Several names were floated for the post of MH Principal last year. However, during Mr. and Mrs. Johnston's visit to Darjeeling and Sikkim in December – January 2012 it was revealed that though Mr. Barry Ison, Mr. John Glasby and Mr. and Mrs. Sherab (Roslyn) Namgyal – all ex-students and teachers of the school – were willing to help the school they would not be able to take the top job at the present juncture. Mr. Kazi's name was then proposed and the Sikkim Hermonites Association (SHA) passed a resolution on this and urged all Hermonites to support his candidature and other resolutions on 'MH Revival'. Sherab and Roslyn (SC 1972 & 1971), who were on a visit to Sikkim from Australia during this period, supported this move.

One of the suggestions of the Hermonites is to have at least two active and credible Hermonites in the Managing Committee, which not only frames policy matters of the school but also appoints the Principal. Two other suggestions made by the Sikkim chapter and endorsed by global Hermonites was allotment of a space for the alumni to function from the school premises and also to route all Hermonites-initiated projects and funds of the school through Hermonites International (Hi!), a global body conceived during the centenary celebrations in 1995, when many ex-principals and teachers and students were present, and formed in 2005-6.

No matter what the future holds for MH the resolution on 'MH Revival' must go on. It must not begin or end if and when Mr. Kazi gets the top job. The campaign for MH Revival is led by Roslyn & Sherab (Australia), Dipak Mirchandhani (UK) and Lucinda Gibbs (India). They are being assisted by a group of active and concerned Hermonites from all over the world.

The Methodist Bishop, who resides in Bangalore and who is temporarily the Chairman of the Managing Committee of the school, has been briefed on the prevailing situation. We are eagerly awaiting his response to our proposals. However, irrespective of what the Managing Committee decides on MH's future the campaign for MH Revival must go on. The present crisis has motivated us into action. This is a good thing and must go on. We must say and sing the hymn "We Shall Overcome" and mean it and show the world that we can triumph over all our trials and tribulations.

They may succeed in taking a Hermonite out of Mount Hermon, but they will never succeed in taking Mount Hermon out of a Hermonite!

We must continue to believe that the Almighty is on our side and that He has a great future for MH and that while the past has been great and small the best is yet to come!

Hail Mount Hermon! And Happy Birthday to MH and All Hermonites!

(Jigme N Kazi)
President
Hermonites International (Hi!)
Email: jigmekazi@gmail.com
+9434630097
Gangtok, Sikkim
March 12, 2012

Dear Jigmi, It was a pleasure going through your letter and I agree that something should be done for the school and it is grt that you are working towards that goal. All the Best and yes I am with all your suggestions. Lots of Love and God's Blessings in your endeavour.
Ronita Edwards, India.

Hail Mount Hermon! A Tribute

Dear Jim,

Thanks for the wonderful report from Hermonites International. The review of the history was certainly impressive. You may recall that my mother, Mrs. Lila Engberg, was principal from 1931 to 1935, after having taken her predecessor, Miss Adele Stahl, home to America when she retired.

It always distresses me when my mother is omitted from the history of the school. She was principal when the school was destroyed in a major earthquake on January 15, 1934 while the school was on holiday. She was in Calcutta when she received a telegram, which I will never forget (I was 10 years old). It said "School extensively damaged. Come immediately." And she went.

School had been scheduled to open the first week in March. The two wings of the school had been virtually destroyed, and all of the interior partitions were down. The managing committee said they could not afford to rebuild it; they were already in debt. She said the school had to be rebuilt and they would get the money somewhere.

School opened two months to the day after the earthquake, and only ten days later than scheduled. All the partitions were in, and work continued on the outside until August. Mrs. Engberg used her connections with Indian government officials to get a substantial amount of Indian Relief money to help rebuild the school.

Classes began immediately and were held wherever there was space:– in the library, an unoccupied office, the sewing room, the art room, anywhere. Two dormitories had been destroyed so beds were crowded into the usable dorms. The Assembly Hall had been destroyed, so students were crowded like sardines into the teachers' parlor where benches had been placed. And so things went on. There's much more to the story, but this will suffice to justify her inclusion in the history.

This may also be the time and place to comment on the name of the school. When it opened in 1926, it had the name of its predecessor, Queen's Hill School. The new school was built on land that had been known as the Mount Hermon Estate. As the number of male students increased, many of them expressed their disapproval of what to them was a "sissy" name. Gradually, the name Mount Hermon School crept into usage. So when the school was rebuilt after the earthquake, its name was officially changed, and the new name was emblazoned on the rebuilt wing.

I hope the foregoing historical information can be added to the record. The 1934 Blue and Gold, Mt. Hermon's yearbook, carries a report of the earthquake and its impact on that year's activities. In 2006, my mother's biography was published: "Lila", by Kitty Katzell. One chapter is devoted to the 1934 earthquake.

Thank you for reading this.
Mildred Engberg "Kitty" Katzell
56 Medford Leas, Medford, NJ 08055, USA.

Dear Kitty,

Thank you for the historical update. I will make sure that it goes down in history. Besides being a Hermonite I am also a professional journalist and have also authored two books: *Inside Sikkim: Against the Tide* (1993) and *Sikkim for Sikkimese* (2009). While in school in class 10 I was in the Hermonite magazine committee and in 1978, when Mr. and Mrs. Murray and most of our foreign teachers left MH, I edited the Hermonite magazine which had a lot of history.

After the 1995 centenary celebs I wanted to bring out a Souvenir on MH with lots of pictures and historical updates. This project is still on and I was glad to here something more about your late mother. In fact, I wanted you to write something about her and also yourself so that the records can be preserved. Please send me all materials and photos of your and your mom's stay in MH. Also how do I get her book? Longing to read it.

Please send me your telephone/mobile nos so that I can talk to you.
With much love and affection,
Jigme

Jigme,
Hello! Thank you for the email. I am Gil Kern and attended Mt. Hermon for a year, in 1949. After my Senior Cambridge I moved up to St. Joseph's to begin my college career. Through the hard work of James Sinclair in England I have been kept informed with respect to the problems facing Mt. Hermon.

I would like to help, of course. When it comes to funds needed is it possible to send American dollars to help out? I realize that there are several issues here, but I note that St. Joseph's alumni have been able to financially support their school by sending funds to a Jesuit province here in America. Fr. Van at St. Joseph's is an excellent source of information about such things.

Thank you for your efforts.
Gil (Richard) Kern, '49
docdick17@aol.com, US.

Dear Richard,
Thank you for your very positive response. Besides MH I would also like to help in reviving other schools in Darjeeling, Kurseong and Kalimpong which were once started by missionaries and which are facing multiple problems. I will seek St. Joseph's Fr. Kinley's help on this matter since North Point has become some sort of a model where the alumni can pitch in to save the school.

As far as funds from foreign countries are concerned I will get back to you after contacting the concerned persons in the Hermonite International (Hi!) which deals with finances. Your and Hermonites' help in mobilizing funds is the need of the hour as we need to do a lot for our 80 acre odd land.

Once again, thank you and stay in touch.
Jigme N. Kazi

Jigme,

I thought that was an excellent letter on the School Birthday. You will have received a copy of Roslyn's letter, and I think I will make a copy of my letter to her in reply, hoping something urgent can be done. You, as a candidate, may need to have others with you in any approach to the Bishop, and the Inspectorate. Keep calm, brother Jigme. David (Stewart), Australia.

CONFIDENTIAL

When 1973 batch Hermonite from Bangkok, Navin (Khuria) Wongsejullarat, sent this note through email it was marked "CONFIDENTIAL". Now that nearly 8 years have passed it is safe, I think, to place the letter in the public domain.

March 27, 2012

Hi Jigs, Roz,

How are you? I haven't heard much since you e-mailed us about the 2012 returning boarders and your attempts to contact the Bishop and the Board. I was most delighted to read the outpouring of good intentions and support for your efforts, even Shiv's financial commitment.

Which started me thinking - daydreaming more likely - I am, after all, an Aquarian. Many Hermonites we know own schools, some much larger than MH. Ronita Edwards (Patricia Ismail) to name one right off the bat, but there are many more. Some own more than one.

Again, just my thinking out loud (just for your two pairs of ears) IF the Bishop is disinclined to listen to you and you are unable to persuade a reluctant or even a stubborn Board to hear your ideas for WHATEVER reason.

1. Can we purchase the school outright?
2. If yes, what would be the price (a reasonable price business-wise, considering assets, potential earnings, etc. against liabilities). And the current political climate in Darjeeling.

I might be crazy but to my thinking, we Hermonites love our school and among us have enough funds to buy the property AND through our own network of children and relatives supply sufficient students AND quality teachers to profitably operate the school for the foreseeable future AND we have sufficient integrity to rebuild our school in our image as the best school we can.

Ranking be damn but a school, our school, we can be proud of again and feel confident to send our own children to as well as to recommend to anyone. Then the ranking will take care of itself. I don't care much about ranking. I care very much about what I now see in my two visits and what was when I attended MH. Ours is a worldwide network. It is in our power to do what we believe best for our school.

Of course, your course is the LOGICAL course of action. It should be pursued to the max. Mine is only a pipe dream - a possibility IF so many things can come together. Meanwhile MH is going through another downfall but, like the proverbial Phoenix, will rise again as it has done in the past. Even if it has to start again from scratch. Quality education is not something to be discarded lightly.

Again, may I ask you to keep my e-mail only among us. However, the idea can and should be explored as you see fit. The idea is passed on to you who are at the forefront and can act should you feel all other avenues have been exhausted. If it comes to that, we have so many lawyers and businessmen who are Hermonites and who can give us the best possible counsel.

I salute you both for changing intention into action. I support and will continue to do so always.
Navin Wangsejullarat, Bangkok.

Dear Navin,
Thank you for sharing your thoughts on MH. Many Hermonites are seriously thinking of purchasing the school to save it and give it the necessary boost and right direction if the Methodist Church is not interested in running the school as it should be run. When the time comes we will certainly raise and take up the issue.

Roz had sent the third reminder to the Bishop in Bangalore on MH Principal. This time she sent it through registered post and we think he got it as he had called a meeting of the Managing Committee on March 24. MH Principal Fernandes attended the meeting. We are yet to hear the verdict. Fernandes's term ends this March and no one knows for sure who will step into his shoes. We are told that he is trying for an extension. We also hear that Senior Master is trying for the post. I've also learnt that several applications for the post have been rejected. Surprisingly, our application, which has the stamp of approval of Hermonites (students, teachers and principals) dating back to 1930s and 1940s has neither been rejected nor accepted.

Will keep you posted on this. Meanwhile, you all stay in touch and take care of each other. Hi and love to Eiam.
Jigs

My full support to Mr. Jigme Kazi to bring MH back to its glory!
Name: Vivek Karmaa Subba
1981-1987 Left MH during the agitation times at Darj.
Present location: Gangtok, Sikkim, India.

Roz, you're right about a delegation, since the Bishop does not deign to respond to written communications.

Jigs, I understand from your email that your source in Cal says to stay put and things will work out but we do need to put a Plan B in motion as well, or at least lay the groundwork for one, so that it can be put into action immediately if the need arises.

So it might be a good idea that you start making plans for an Alumni Delegation to meet with the Bishop face to face and put forward our concerns by:

- Coming up with a list of people who might be suitable and who might volunteer (Cindy+Pradeep and Ashish and George Mathai come to mind – do we know of any others in South India).
- If Prava Rai would not be in the right state of mind, then finding another representative to seek an appointment with the Bishop.

Take care
Dipak (Mirchandhani), UK.

Jigs,
    Here is something you can look forward to doing to report that you have 342 boarders.
    In 1971 there were 360 boarders - total enrollment 460
    In 1964 there were 290 boarders - total enrollment 350
    Best wishes to my fellow editor of the 1971 year book!
Puii, US.

Hi Puii,
    Thanks for the record. Its amazing! that you have these. While we wait for the Managing Committee's verdict we need to make our global alumni body - Hermonites International (Hi!) - formed in 2005 but conceived during the 1995 centenary celebs and approved by some of our ex-teachers, princis and students, strong and powerful so that it not only endures the test of time but also initiates and inspires future generations of Hermonites yet to come.
    I hope you and some like you in the US can make your own body strong. The 1940-50s in the US batch have already an alumni body which is quite strong. You people can get in touch with each other and make it strong. We will do the same with other alumni body throughout the world.
    Did I tell you that Pema Wangyal died a few years back? I miss him still.
    Take care and stay in touch.
Jigs
March 3, 2012

    You should try and get a copy of the 1971 Hermonite as you were on the Editorial Committee!
    I also have the 1975 yearbook and this has a "history of MHS". The school celebrated it's 80 the Birthday. Back in the 60s the school was under new management when Mr. Stewart was the principal he brought up the enrolment from 200. Mr. Murray told me when I met him during his last visit to the states that Mr. Stewart saved the school. The Methodists (Americans) were ready to close the school due to

declining enrollment. We have Mr. Stewart to thank as there would not have been a school for us to attend.

There is just a handful of us here from the 70s and we are not close to each other. Some are on the east coast, west coast, the south etc. The last time we had a "reunion" was in 2003 in Colorado but none of us are in regular contact.

I think the 40s-50s group no longer meets as they are all elderly and some may be in nursing/retirement homes.

Best wishes to you and the alumni who are working to hard for the school.
Puii, US.

Dear All,
Something to cheer us at this moment of time!

Ex-students of St. Paul's in Sikkim are thrilled to know that Hermonites are backing me and trying to revive MH. I spoke to Ravi Pradhan (Cindy knows him well) the other day and he said he was wanting to meet me to say that the Paulites will back us to rebuild MH. He will get in touch with their alumni in Cal and get back to me and will officially support our MH Revival campaign.

What is their motive? Having seen NP revived under an ex-student (Fr Kinley) they want a Hermonite to do the same in MH and hopefully the same thing should happen to SPS. That's a fair deal and I have always been trying to rejuvenate all such schools in Darj.
Jigs

Dear Jigme,
Am certain that the board of Mt. Hermon will definitely agree to you becoming the Principal of your old ALMA MATER. This will definitely become another feather in the cap of your illustrious career. Am getting a regular supply of your publications. All the best and hopefully I will see you in Darjeeling next.
Yours most sincerely
Yambem Laba (North Pointer), Manipur, India.
March 8, 2012

Dear Jigmi Kazi La,
What a shame on me, I only noticed your mail just now. I was away in India for about two weeks and then on a lecture tour. This morning I came to mu university office, anyway these are only excuses, I must apologise. What is the result? How can I express my support? Please advise me, as there are a few more Hermonites here in Japan if it is not too late, I can inform them.
With best wishes.
Pema Gyalpo, Japan.

Pema Gyalpo (MH 1963-1966) with Jigme N. Kazi, Gangtok, 2014.

Hello Hermonites,

Sorry to read this from Puii but let us pray that things change for the better. Surely, this is the worst phase that we are seeing and the situation can only improve from here, God willing.

In the meantime, I would like to put my thoughts for the consideration of all Hermonites:

1. Some of our Hermonite friends, from Sikkim and other North Bengal areas have been running around for quite some time and meeting the management of MHS towards revival of MHS. At times this may involve them expending a considerable amount of money.
2. I have received some requests from some Hermonites, especially from abroad, to open a bank account where donations can be parked and used for the benefit of MHS so that some of the people doing most of the running around don't end up spending all the money as well.

My thoughts on the above are as follows:

1. A bank account, authorised by the Hermonites International be opened in Siliguri, or Darjeeling, or Gangtok and this account be used for collection of donations and transfer of funds by bank draft or RTGS "AUTHORISED SUMS OF MONEY" towards expenditure incurred for the revival of MHS.
2. The bank account must only be operated JOINTLY by at least 2 (if not 3) authorised signatories.
3. No cash money will be drawn from the account.
4. The expenditure incurred by any individual or Hermonite association must be vetted by the core committee. Upon authorisation by them the funds can then be transferred to the association or individual who has incurred the amount.
5. Individuals/groups/associations willing to contribute/donate money can then begin depositing money into the account.

This is an initial suggestion/draft. Hermonites can suggest amendments and improvements which can then be incorporated by the core committee into the final draft before the resolutions are passed and implemented.

Thanks and regards,
Shiv (Saria), Siliguri.

Thanks Jigs. Will keep you posted. I won't begin my new job until July as I have commitments at my current job that I need to take care of first before I can leave.

You should contact Thangi and ask her if she can get in touch with some of the Methodist church leaders regarding MH. As she's there in India it'll be easier for her to do it.

I talked to her this morning and told her that with the help of my Dad she can set up a meeting with the Bishops and some MH alumni who are involved in Christian ministry (like Pradeep Pradhan who is working with the Boro Baptist Convention and heads their medical work as a doctor) so that they can see some strong Christian leaders and maybe get a few others as well like Ashish Bhengra and others who are in secular work. My Dad just had eye surgery and he also has back problems and is in constant pain so he's not able to do things like he used to but he could help chair such a meeting if Thangi can call around folks and help set it up.

Do you have her cell phone number? It's 943-611-9350 I believe. Her email is lthangi@yahoo.com. Still praying that things will work out. Maybe one needs to shut the school down and revamp everything and re-open it again. Other schools have done that. I think St. Joseph did that many years back and now its thriving.

Good luck and don't lose hope. Just got to trust God!
Rothang (Rema), US.

Dear Friends

Thank you, Shiv and Cindy, for your emails and the wonderful practical step of encouraging us to take leap of faith at this point in time, and put our hands in our pockets. We will be using Western Union initially as it is a great way to get money to India quickly. Thank you for spelling out the details of how the account will operate - it sounds very good. I think that even the smallest amounts will be of great value - and for those of us who live overseas and want to be able to show our support and assistance, it is a very important step.

It appears that the time has come for Jigme and other local supporters to visit Kolkata and maybe Bangalore to seek a face to face meeting with members of the Managing Committee - and most especially with the Bishop. (On that front, last week we printed all the paper work of the email correspondence to date and registered it to the Bishop's Bangalore address so that there can be no claim that it was never received.)

The deafening silence is unnerving. We have had confirmation that the email address is correct, and can now only surmise that the powers that be in Mount Hermon do not want to engage with us. At the very least we would have expected an acknowledgement of our interest and ideas - even if it was a "No thank you".

However we are not going to give up. Let us continue to pray for the school and move ahead with any opportunities that come up.

We will keep you informed of things as they eventuate.
With warmest regards,
Roz and Sherab, Canberra, Australia.

Hi Jigs,

Below is something I just wrote to Ros - so I will share it with you. It is in response to the email she sent me - below!

The deafening silence is rather scary (i.e.: from the non-response of the Bishop). I believe there are only one hundred students in MH right now - so it is going broke. Does that mean the Methodists may want to sell? That would be an interesting option and I am sure we could muster the funds with the thousands of Hermonites around the world.

I wonder how much they would want? Lets say we could identify 5000 alumni and see if we could get an average of $1000 each (some will give less and some will give more). That would give us $5 million. I am sure many would give anywhere up to $5000. Maybe I am over-optimistic - but I am sure the idea of MH being owned by the alumni would be an attractive proposition and we could have the opportunity of turning it into the top school in India - what a project!! I'd almost want to give up my job here to be part of that - part - not head!!! I'd love to be an Education Consultant to help academically in the school and teacher's college.

Menno and Ronen seemed pretty aggressive - which they can be from a distance - and were proposing a legal approach. If it got bad - we could threaten legal and let them realise they would end up with nothing - then negotiate!!

Anyway - we do have options!

Love
Barry, Dhaka.

Dear Jigme:

I sent most MH materials to Jim Sinclair a year or so ago. I'm 88 years old and feared everything would be destroyed or discarded when my time comes, so I was trying to find homes for things that might be of use. You can check with Jim. He was going to do something with the pictures, too.

I'll send you a copy of "Lila". I have a few left that I got when it was published. So you must send me your snail mail address for the book. My snail mail address is 56 Medford Leas, Medford, New Jersey 08055-2221 USA. My phone is 609-654-3056. I do have a cell phone, but never turn it on except when I'm traveling, which I don't do any more because of my relative frailty. So I won't give you that number. I live in a retirement community, so I'm here most of the time.

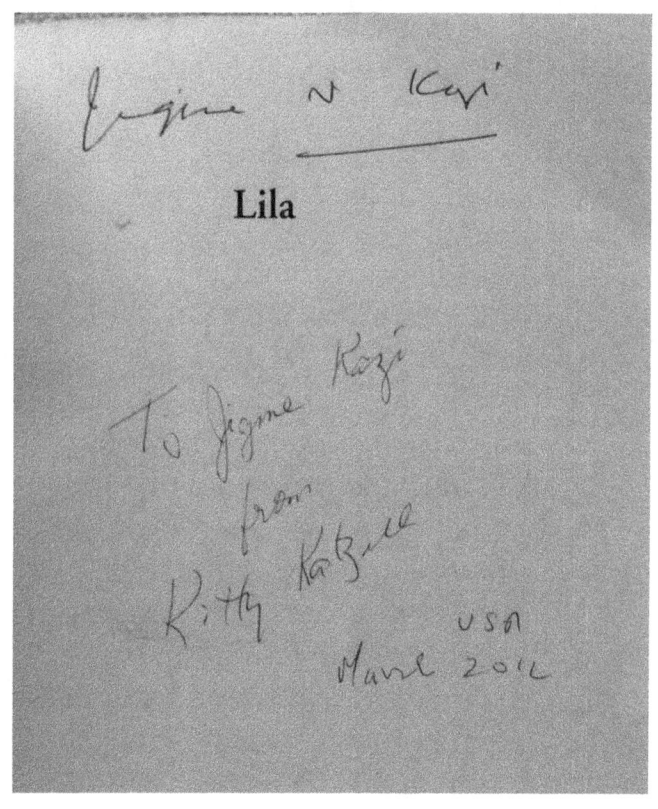

I've added Mt. Hermon to an international prayer list and trust things work out for the best, though of course what I think is best is not always what God thinks is best.

Thank you so much for writing. I look forward to hearing from you further. I go to email several times a day, so you can always expect a prompt response.

~Kitty, US.

Kitty Katzell passed away in September 2014

"She will be missed"

Kitty Katzell (Mildred Engberg)

"It is with great sadness that I have to announce the death of Kitty Katzell (Mildred Engberg) on 6th September 2014. I was concerned about her as I had not received any emails from her since earlier in the year, as she was such a regular correspondent, reports James Sinclair, UK chapter Secretary.

"Gordon Hostetler very kindly searched and found her Obituary published in the *South Jersey Local News*. She was very much involved with Mount Hermon School, where her mother, Lila Engberg, was Headmistress in the 1930s, and Mildred recalled many happy memories of her school days, which is published under the tab "Growing up in India" on our Home Page. She sent me School Yearbooks of the 1930s which has enabled me to publish many of the photographs they contained. She also set up a Scholarship Fund for MH students, and sent in a large donation for this some years ago. She will be sadly missed," adds James.

Obituary – Mildred Kitty Katzell

MILDRED "KITTY" KATZELL Mildred Engberg "Kitty" Katzell, of Medford Leas, Medford, NJ died Saturday, September 6, 2014 after living a full and blessed life. Kitty was born in Chicago. Her childhood was spent in India and she went to high school in Iowa. She attended Carleton College in Northfield, MN, and earned BA and MA degrees at Syracuse University, and a Ph.D. in Psychological Measurement at Columbia University.

During her career, she worked for several prominent testing companies engaged in testing for allied health professions. She was president of the New York Lung Association and was active in psychological and counseling professional associations, having served on the Board of Directors of the American Psychological Association. At Medford Leas, Mrs. Katzell was elected president of the residents association three times, and was editor of Medford Leas Life for nine years.

Her husband, Raymond A. Katzell who pre-deceased her, taught industrial psychology at New York University. Before moving to Medford Leas in 1989, they lived in Manhattan and Glen Cove, NY, where they were active in the antique car hobby. Mrs. Katzell is survived by many cousins and friends.

(*South Jersey Local News*, Sept. 24, 2014)

Hi Everyone,

We are in full agreement too. It is our understanding that Shiv is willing to help out and has followed this up with his email regarding the funds. We did talk with him when we were there, and he is certainly the right person to co-ordinate any funds at this stage.

Cindy - your help with secretarial work has already been so valuable - I really appreciated your getting the email list co-ordinated. I was thinking along the same lines, but hadn't got around to it. In fact, I think if you could include all the email addresses we have of anyone who has sent in an email, it would certainly help keep everyone in the loop at the same time.

Let's hope we hear something this week.

Jigs - have you heard who is in charge at MH at this time? Has George left or is he still there?

Take heart, everyone.

Love

Roz and Sherab, Canberra, Australia.

Hi again,

I'm sure Dipak will agree too as it is the most practical thing to do. Could you, Jigs, maybe speak to Shiv and I will take a quiet back seat and continue trying to get all the MH email list together. I need to go through all emails that have been sent as there are many different address books to co-ordinate together. I have asked you Jigs for names against emails that are not obvious – e.g. sikkim@gmail.com, which will help identify people. I think Dipak, you too have a list of all those who responded after your initial email, and Roz I shall incorporate your spreadsheet emails as well. Is that OK with everyone?

Once it is compiled I will send it to you all, including Shiv and then hopefully we will have everyone under the same umbrella. I know James Sinclair of OMHSA wants to handle his group himself, so as long as he is on the main list he will send appropriate mails to his ex-Hermonites. Once it is fixed that Shiv will do the job an email could be sent to all once again indicating this, so people are aware it is someone on the ground locally that is handling India. I think people will feel comfortable with this idea.

I had a feeling Mr. Fernandez was leaving around March 23? Maybe Anup can check from Darjeeling?

We must just keep going and moving forward. I know Binod Bhutra mentioned having a Reunion in Darj in mid-Nov but unless people are replying directly to him no one seems to have responded. If you, Jigme, are in charge it would I think certainly motivate people to make the trip up to Darj and would be a great opportunity for people to see what is going on and what needs to be done etc etc. It's something to be thought about once we have crossed the first bridge!!! What about Tom Stoppard as chief guest???? Prava Rai had launched this idea about contacting him - I wonder if he would be interested?????

Love

Cindy (Lucinda Gibbs), UK.

Hi Jigs,

I will keep your news confidential. There is so much potential for us Hermonites if we can establish some control over the school. Its encouraging to hear that Bimal Gurung is supportive. In a way, it is to his advantage as the school provides employment for many in the local community. It would also suggest that an agreement on school boundaries could be finalised in the future.

Do we have any good lawyers in our alumni? What about the other sources of influence - political etc. Perhaps getting your strategy and support lined up now would be good. I am sure you have thought about this. You said earlier that Sonia Gandhi knows you and is supportive.

If you can manage to get control of the school - as Principal or as a school run by the alumni - I am with you in any capacity you would need.

Very best wishes
Barry Ison, Dhaka.

Dear Jigme,

I too join in wishing the school a Happy Birthday. The present state of the school is sad and I do hope something can be done before it's too late. I fully support you as the next principal. Good luck!
Prem (Rai), Nepal.

Dear All,

Of course I am happy being at hand for anything I can do. I had read the passage from Kitty which is very interesting. Her book is also available on Amazon.

It would be nice if Tom Stoppard would take an interest. I feel sure he would at least be interested in what is going on?? Are you happy trying to locate him Dipak?

I shall get in touch with Jim Sinclair about the photos and documents. It would be nice if we could make them available for viewing by ex-Hermonites. Let's see how we could progress with that.

Let's see what happens in the next couple of weeks with Mr. F.

Love to all
Cindy (Lucinda Gibbs), UK.

Hi Jigs,

Thanks for such a detailed account of your support base. I am impressed and so should be the Bishop - if you ever get a chance to talk to him. Rudra was one of my favourite students and so hopefully your MH days with him will stand you in good stead with Bimal Gurung.

I will be having Summer holidays from June 8th and during that time will be around here and able to meet you in Kolkata or Darjeeling. I will be visiting Australia and on a couple of other trips, but maybe we can get together for some time during June and July.

Very best
Barry, Dhaka.

Topic: Very few students returned back in 2012
By: ex-Hermonite (ww@mhs.com)
At: 27/2/2012

Description: The school reopened a few days back.

Very sad to hear that only a little over 100 Boarder students have returned back after their winter vacation for the new session for the year 2012.

I am afraid whether the school will close down by the end of this year with this less students on the roll.

MHS will not be able to pay all its creditors if this is the condition and the authorities do not look into the matter urgently and this can be possible only by mass advertisement of the school through website and help of all the Hermonites around the globe.

There is no quick fix solution to a sliding lack of confidence, which is exactly what students & parents must have felt, for them not to return and look elsewhere.

It speaks volumes about the condition of the school; the lack of management, the lack of good teachers, possibly bad food and the overall poor ambiance around the school.

The rebuilding must start immediately. Starting with making excess teachers and workers redundant based on the number of students enrolled at school, finding a capable Principal, giving a new look to the managing committee with those who are capable of taking hard decisions, committed to the school and are honorable.

Unless real, rather than superficial, changes are put in place and results begin to show, there will be no confidence from students, parents and the alumni. The last group remains a potent source of endowment funds which is untapped because of lack of trust.

As an alumnus, I would rather that the school closed than see it running in a shabby, mismanaged and dishonorable way.
Tashi Bhutia

Jigs,

Eiam sends her love. She's off to Japan for a week and will be back for a day before jetting off to Europe. Ah, working in the travel and tourism industry has its perks.

I am glad to hear that like minds think alike and that I am not the first or the only one who has that thought of owning our school. Personally, I have had much reflection beyond just ICSE - vocational training and undergraduate programs that can benefit Darjeeling, Bhutan, Sikkim, Siliguri and anywhere else wherever students may come from. That's the great thing about daydreaming.

Getting back to reality and doing the things you do, now that is hard. And you know that you can always count on, not just me, but all the Hermonites in Thailand. The buzz is growing. Every time we meet the subject always comes up for a healthy discussion of ways and means to support you and your efforts - not just money but just about everything you can think of under the sun.
All the best
Navin (Khuria) Wongsejullarat, Bangkok.

Dear All,

Has anyone heard anything about what happened at the meeting on the 24th? Everything is very quiet.

Love

Cindy (Lucinda Gibbs), UK.

Dear Friends,

I'm not able to find out really transpired during the Managing Committee's meeting on March 24. However, the meeting did take place and MH Principal George Fernandes attended it.

I'm now told that another meeting of the Committee will take place in MH in mid-April. I'm not sure what is the agenda for this meet. Hopefully, our case will be taken up this time. So we need to be prepared. A group should meet the Bishop and present our case.

I suggest the following Hermonites representing Hermonite International meet the Bishop:

O.T. Bhutia, Uttam Pradhan, Udai Sharma, Namgyal Wangdi (Sikkim), Anup Chachan, Pratap Rai, Mukesh Adhupia (Darj), Shiv Saria, Sushil Mittal, Ravi Agarwal, G.T. Bhutia (Siliguri), Amode Yonzone and Binod Yonzone (Kalimpong), Santosh Rijal and Ashok Pokharel (Nepal), and Binod Bhutra, Sujit Kumar (Cal).

Santosh kindly inform Ashok Pokharel as his email add is not working. Opening of an account with a nationalised bank for Hermonite International is being arranged to collect funds for travel expenses from Hermonites.

Please be free to add more names and ideas. We'll keep on hoping.

Cheers,

Jigs

Dear Jigs,

Is the intention for this group to meet the Bishop in Darjeeling when he comes for the committee meeting in about two weeks time or to go to Bangalore prior to that?

If the team is travelling to Bangalore you might want to ask George Mathai who lives there to join in as well. His credentials are as the son of a long serving Senior Master. His email address is: george.mathai@hdfcbank.com.

Take care.

Dipak Mirchandani, UK.

April-November, 2012

Jigs,

I don't know if Rothang has contacted Mr. Jones. He does not have e-mail so you will have to contact either Arun or Ken. He lives in the same city as Kenny so it may be more convenient to ask Ken if he would be able to deliver the message to his Dad. I do know that Mrs. Jones brother was on the Managing Committee and he was in charge of the school estate. I don't know if he is still on the school's Committee. My Dad is no longer involved with the Committee and I don't think that a letter from him would mean anything.

It is very strange that the Bishop and the Committee have not acknowledged Roslyn's letter/e-mail. Wonder what Mr. F is saying to them.

I hope that they will contact Roslyn after they meet in April.
Regards,
Puii, US

Thanks for getting in touch Jigs. What's the game plan for now .... what do you plan to do next? You know we are behind you - you have been through a difficult period with a death in your family and the strain must be there. However, we must keep the momentum going. What can we do to help you and those of us who are seriously motivated will back you and support you in whatever way you need.

Has Shiv set up the account? Has there been a meeting of the Sikkim Hermonites to allow Shiv to set up an account?

Fernandez, apparently is keeping the MH fires burning (probably burning on the incriminating evidence!!) but is purportedly wanting to finish quickly. That's fine - but we need to convince the Bishop (whoever he is) to consider our plan.

Is anyone working on a business plan? Ros said that John Glasby might be willing to help put a plan together. Without a feasible and sustainable plan - we should not be talking to any Bishop.

So where are we now ... and is the Hermonite interest dissipating? It must be hard on you and for that I am sorry - but you may become the 5th House in MH in the future ... 'Kazi' House - lets say purple in color for royalty!

Let us know how we can help and what you need to do next?
Very best wishes
Barry, Dhaka.

Dear Jigme Sir,
No Sir, I was a new student in 1979 just coming to school, you were our Art & Craft incharge. I look forward to visiting MH under your guidance. Do confirm once you take over. It has been 25 years since I left MH and sure would like to come back.
Pramod

Jigs,
Good to hear from you. Please keep me up to date as things develop. But, again, I stress that you should develop a strategy SOON that will challenge the Methodist church and get them prepared to come to the negotiation table.

I was sharing with Ros and Sherab that you need a written game plan. Its all very well to have ideas and talk about what needs to be done and what you and other Hermonites can do - but it really needs to be written down as a comprehensive plan. Ros said she would talk to John Glasby and see if he would be willing to put a plan like this on paper - at least the outline of a plan. Once you have a document that outlines your plan - your road map as to how you will put MH back on track - then the Church has something concrete. I know Mr. Fernandez is already planning his road map and putting his case to the Bishop. I suspect that Mr. Fernandez also sees an opportunity to make money in case the school gets any assistance from the Central Government for earthquake repair - that is probably why some people are saying there is a lot of damage.

Your 'road map' - or proposal should look like this:

1. Introduction:
   What this document is about and why it is being written.
2. Background:
   Past History: MH and what it stands for - what it was.
   Recent History: The earthquake, political turmoil and enrollment numbers down and the school's reputation being low.
3. SWOT Analysis of MH:
   Strengths:
   Weaknesses:
   Opportunities:
   Threats:
4. Needs analysis:
   What MH needs to bring it back to being a quality institution.
5. Proposal:
   What you are proposing in terms of:
   Management
   Infrastructure
   Staffing
   Curriculum
   Estate:
   Other (?):
6. Budget:
7. Conclusion:

Summary statement of what this proposal will achieve. Hope this helps
Very best wishes
Barry, Dhaka.

Yes Sir,
   Fully agree with your strategy. Will form a team from our end - most probably it will include O.T. Bhutia, Uttam Pradhan and Udai Sharma (Sikkim), Amode Yonzone

(Kalimpong), Pratap Rai and Anup Chachan (Darj), Ravi Agarwal and Shiv Saria (Siliguri), Ashok Pokharel and Santosh Rijal (Nepal).

Will talk to these and others and go ahead with the plan.

Jigs

Dear Jigs,

I am now back in Dhaka so I thought I should send you a summary of what I mentioned to you the other evening from Canberra.

We had a small and brief meeting consisting of Ros, Sherab and myself from MH and Debbie (my wife) as observer. We thoroughly endorsed you and your efforts to revive and revitalise MH. We also thought that you need a lot of physical and financial support and so we came up with the following suggestions:

1. You need to develop a small, committed and active group around you as a source of support and advice. Perhaps one from Gangtok, one from Darjeeling, one from Siliguri and one from Kalimpong or Kurseong.

2. You could also have a larger support group who are signed up and committed to working with you and with whom you can bounce off ideas and seek other types of support such as financial. This group could include Ros and Sherab, myself, Lucinda in Goa and others in the region who are very keen and have something to contribute.

3. You need a fund and that is what Shiv is arranging for you. I trust that it is near completion so then we can appeal to Hermonites to contribute to a 'development fund' which Shiv can manage and you can access.

4. You need to identify your strategic allies whom you can depend on when the 'crunch' comes and you are challenged to 'put up' or 'shut up'. By this I mean - if you throw the Methodist church, or Fernandez a challenge and they call you out to see if you mean it - then who can you count on for strategic support? Remember that Fernandez is now under threat. I am sure he is worried that once you get into the books (and maybe the church is worried too) you will find all kinds of irregularities. He wants another year in the seat to make sure that if a 'non-friendly' gets in to be the Principal the books will look ok. He has been depending on another crony of the church getting in who would not ask questions.

5. You need a strategy now that is probably more aggressive than before. I think the Bishop needs to be challenged with a 'show cause' legal letter. Maybe the same for Fernandez. If they can be frightened into coming to the negotiation table - then that is the purpose for an aggressive strategy. I don't think you have a lot of time to do this. While it must be carefully thought out and every angle anticipated (so it does not backfire), time is limited because while we are sitting back waiting for the Bishop to reply to Ros' letter - he is having meetings and getting his 'ducks' lined up - which could be legal and fiscal and political. I am sure the church would be able to buy strategic people off in Darjeeling - and Fernandez would know whom to buy.

That's as far as we got. Hope this helps and let us know how else we can help and be involved.

As I said over the phone, I can go up to Siliguri on a Thursday evening - arriving on Friday morning and then return Saturday night. I can most likely do the same thing for Kolkata - fly across Thursday evening and return Saturday. But there should be some concrete reason for me to do that.

All the best Jigs - we're with you
Barry, Dhaka.

Dear All,

It is now quite confirmed that Fernandes has got an extension. I've heard this from various sources. I've also been told that a new Bishop has been appointed for MH and there will be a meeting of the Managing Committee in MH on May 2-3. Kindly contact your sources and get it confirmed. I was told earlier that there was to be a meeting of the Committee in mid-April but nothing has been confirmed.

Mr. Ison and our Oz chapter want us to be more aggressive now that we have exhausted our soft approach and there has been no response. I tend to agree with this. I think we need to prepare a fresh application - a short one - for the new Bishop if there is a meeting of the Committee early next month. What about the long-term strategy for MH revival? Can we prepare this now even if its a short one and then give the details later for the Bishop and Committee members to think it over? We have just over a week to do this if the meeting is on.

My uncle - Thondup Tashi (53) - also a Hermonite of mid-sixties died on April 3 and since then for three weeks we have been engaged in death rituals.
Cheers
Jigs

You are right. Mr. Fernandez has been asked to stay on a year. He told me this when I met him over the Easter break. I have no idea about the new Bishop but, I did hear that a Bishop based somewhere down south has been tasked with the old Bishop's job. This could cause more problems and delays. I will however, call my friends in Darjeeling and find out. At my brief meeting Mr. Fernandez told me that he had told the committee that he wants out as early as possible and to find his replacement. He was looking at beginning handing over beginning August or September 2012.

The short term strategy has to be to get someone appointed at MH who can share the vision of the Hermonite community-at-large and one who understands the spirit of what Mt. Hermon should be (am I making sense?). The long term vision must be one where continuity and succession at the top level must be enshrined. So MH in effect needs a new Principal and new Vice Principal.

Sorry to hear of your uncle's passing.
Regards
Ashok (Pokharel), Nepal.

Hi Jigme

Thank you so much for making the time to come and spend the evening with us in Gangtok. It was very special meeting up with you again after all these years.

Thank you also for sending us a copy of *Against the Tide*, which I read with great interest. It gave me a huge insight into the troubled history of the state and into the personal cost that you and your wife and family have had to wear for speaking out.

Since getting home I have also read with great interest Sunanda Datta-Ray's book on the annexation of Sikkim and Sinha and Subba's volume of essays, The Nepalis in Northeast India: a Community in Search of Indian Identity.

Our short visit to Kolkata, Sikkim and Darjeeling was a wonderful experience, exceeding even the high hopes I had dared to harbour for this first return in 35 years. Kishan and Jailata were very thoughtful hosts, and through them we got to meet many interesting and kind people—including some of whom we had known in the past, and quite a few other Hermonites. I took a lot of photos and have had these cycling through on the screen of our computer, so we have been reliving our experiences every day!

Is there any news about the principal role at MH, or any other MH news? For example, have you heard what the verdict is on the earthquake damaged main building?

I have just discovered from an internet item that your brother died in September last year. Please accept our belated condolences.
With our love and best wishes
Ian and Joy Reid, New Zealand.
May 15, 2012

Jigme, Can you tell me anything about the present situation? I seem bereft of information. I heard an indirect report that the school had started again this year, but with only 100 boarders, and that it was deeply in debt. Who is acting as Principal? Any further knowledge of Chairman and members of the Board? I know they keep all under a veil of secrecy, but you, not being far away, may know something. Meanwhile, what is your own position? Are you meanwhile continuing with your Press work? Greetings to your lovely family. David "Boss", Australia.

Dear Sir,

Thank you for your note. Both the school and the Managing Committee have not responded to us. Meanwhile, the Bangalore Bishop, who was the Managing Committee's chairman and to whom Roz had sent three letters, is out and is replaced by a new one. We still don't know who he is. But we feel the change is good for MH as the earlier Chairman was not responsive to our campaign on 'MH Revival'.

George Fernandes, who has been Principal for just over a decade, has got a year's extension. Sadly, the number of boarders has gone down to just over 200. This means about 110 girls and the same among of the boys who will be scattered in the main building, Stewart Building, Round Hostel in Fern Hill and the old Fern Hill hostel. If there is no change in the leadership the enrolment is likely to dip further threatening a closure of the school next year. I don't know how long I can wait as I'm nearly 60.

My son Tashi has finished his 4-year college in Tokyo and eldest daughter Yangchen is into her 3rd year in Tokyo. The two have been in Japan for over 6 years now. My twin daughters - Kunga and Sonam - have just successfully completed their class 12 and will be doing a 3-year hotel management course in Sikkim. So we are now entering another phase in our family life and look forward to some relaxing time.

We do have you in our thoughts and prayers and hope you are keeping fine.
With all good wishes as always,
    Jigme, Tsering and family

Dear Jigme,
    Thanks so much. I thought George must have been given a further extension, and at least 200 boarders is better than 100! But I am still mystified at the Chairman and Board members remaining incognito. I'm sure this must be against the law, and I fondly thought that a simple approach to the Anglo-Indian Inspector of West Bengal would divulge the name of the Bishop (new Chairman presumably) and Board members. Sparring in the dark with unknown "opponents" seems silly to me. Would a request to the President of the Methodist Church of Southern Asia reveal who these people are?

Good to have news of the family. My, both Tashi and Yangchen so well on in their University work in Tokyo, what degrees will they come out with? And the twin girls' plans.

Don't despair about MHS, it is a call to prayer for God to intervene, I believe.
    Love,
    David (Stewart), Australia.

Dear Jigme,
    Seeing this in my Inbox from long ago [Jan '12], I just wondered if anything ever came of all the good hopes, and right thoughts, and actions too? Should love to know any outcomes?
With best wishes
Miss Russell, UK.

Dear Miss Russell,
    Thank you for the short note. Despite our best efforts and despite about 200 pages of email letters to me and the MH Revival campaign, MH and its Managing Committee have not moved an inch. The old chairman of the Managing Committee, who has refused to respond to us, has been replaced a new one and there was a meeting of the Committee in MH just last month and the agenda, according to sources, was choosing the next princi.

So far we have not been formally or informally approached. How are you and how's your health? I'm busy with my two weekly newspapers.

Bishop Phillip Silus Masih, Chairman, Managing Committee.

Two of my kids (Tashi and Yangchen) are still in Japan. Tashi has just finished his college and Yangchen is into her third year. My two daughters - Sonam and Kunga - have passed class 12 and have just started their three-year hotel management course in Rumtek, about 30 mins drive from Gangtok.

Do keep in touch from time to time and stay well.

Jigs

Aug 7, 2012

Great to hear from you, Jigs. Thanks every time for telling me about yr family: those are the sort of things I really like to hear!

I have read all that you have to say in your letter with great interest. I think that that lot [the committee, etc] will never move an inch, unless a miracle moves them.

They will just go ahead and choose another one like Mr. Samuel, in 1995-6 [I tried to work under Mr. Sm for the year 1996, on Mr. Stewart's recommendation to Mr. Sm that I could be of help to him].

They will only select one of their 'own' that will do what they tell him [or her], and who will send the money from the school to the bosses in Lucknow.

The only way to get a miracle is to ask God, and if you would think about it, and consider that, then certain actions would need to follow.

The first action would be that one needs to request the strong believers in Skm to ask God what His plans for the school are - I'm meaning for you to ask Ram Gopal, and/or Mrs. Kalyani, and others, several of them, as many as possible, whoever has the same heart for the school as you and I and we all do, to take time to hear from God, the question being whether it is right to hope for the school to rise again, or whether the world has gone too far along for it ever to be possible again?

When some weeks, or however long they feel it'd take them, have passed, then they will let us know, and we can go from there: either stop altogether, or else start to pray in earnest.

[If in earnest, then we are looking at further weeks, or even more time, as the wrong at present in the school will not go out with one little prayer - it will take lots, and a dedicated group who can personally meet together, more than once, for real strength and unity, probably centring on ppl like the above, in Skm, also perhaps Darjeeling, or wherever else, any who are willing to give themselves to the task.

As we could all be in email-touch, I could talk to them on this (or by post, if any don't have email - Mrs. Kalyani??) and we could agree together.]

What do you think?

My feeling is there is no other way out, but we need to hear from those ppl about what God is saying, first, before anything else.

If it'd never work, if it seems the answer is No, then we just sadly have to give up and admit it. It's no good trying anything if it is not God's will.

MHS was founded on the Bible and prayer, and maintained in prayer, as you recall I said to you before, and I can't go any further than that!

Lots of love, I still value all my students the same as ever, from Miss Russell (UK)

Hail Mount Hermon! A Tribute

Miss Russell at MH, 2012.

Dear Jigs,
   Thanks so much for yr reply, and I do see what you mean - it is not very encouraging! I agree with you that there is nothing we [in ourselves] can do. Sad, but it appears to be the way it is.
   If after a little while, you might like to try my suggestion, after all, and approach some of the ppl mentioned, I really do think that is the only hope - at least to ask them about it?
   But if you find that too much, OK, I won't ever say it again, don't worry! Love you all very much, as always, from Miss (Russell).
PS - Thanks too for the news about Nyantara. She was such a sweet little girl: was it just one year she was in MH, in class 5 or 6, I forget: I wonder if she'd Email me, as I'd love to hear from her - I will ask Udai...
(From Miss Russell)

FINAL LETTER TO ALL HERMONITES

From: Roslyn Namgyal
Sent: Wednesday, 21 November 2012
Subject: Re: Final letter to Hermonites for 2012
(Unofficial)
Dear Cindy, Dipak and Shiv
   I hope each one of you and your families are well. It's been now 10 months since we first started the journey of looking at ways to support Jigs as a potential principal for MH.

Given the twists and turns of the year and the resounding silence of the school authorities and the Board, I think it's time we contacted our wonderful Hermonites around the world who offered their support - to let them know where things are up to. I think it is most important that we all acknowledge Jigs' and Tshering's generosity in offering Jigs' service to MHS this past year, and let the alumni know how things have panned out.

Please have a read of my attachment, and if you are happy with it, I will send it out to all our contacts later today.

With Love and Best Wishes
Roz (Roslyn Namgyal), Canberra, Australia.
Nov 21, 2012

Dear Sherab and Roz,
Its a wonderful letter - fully embodying the spirit in which we - and others before us - have worked and hoped for MH.

We should release it straightaway. The timing would be perfect for reactions as we are on our way to Darj for the Speech Day.
With warm regards,
Jigs

Dear Roz,
You have written a wonderful letter. It has been such a difficult time for Jigs, wondering and waiting, and getting nothing at all back from any quarter. It is so sad that this has how it has ended. It will be very interesting to see how things are at the Speech Day. Sadly Pradip and I are unable to leave Goa at this juncture, but do hope to get to Darjeeling and possibly Gangtok too in January, all going well, and can then catch up with our friends in that part of the world. It will be good to see you again Jigs. Maybe we shall have more news by then of what will finally happen at MH.

Love from us both to you all and special wishes for a Happy Christmas and a peaceful 2013.
Cindy and Pradip, UK.

Dear Roz,
This letter is wonderfully written and so very thoughtful.

Thanks for taking this initiative - we did get all these Hermonites excited about it and it is only fitting that we let them know that our collective effort has now come to an end and that the present Administration and Board does not really care about its alumni.

With this paternalistic attitude, it is no wonder that our beloved Mount Hermon is failing as an institution.

However, the ties that bind us are stronger than the physical structures standing on that bluff in Darjeeling and we should rather focus on building a stronger Hermonite Association and make an effort to plan a big reunion.

Jigs – Thanks for your generosity and time and I applaud the maturity that you have shown in attending Speech Day and in continuing with your commitment to Hermonites.

Winter is now setting in on these Isles and the nights are getting longer but there is the hope of Christmas in the air and we're looking forward to Varish and Deeya coming home just before Christmas. We're staying put all winter and are praying that we don't have a horrible one. Cindy, hope to see you in Feb.

Rekha joins me in sending our Love to all you wonderful folks.

Take care of yourselves.

Dipak (Mirchandhani), UK.

Greetings Everyone,

At the start of the year we wrote to you with a proposal that Jigme Kazi's name be put forward as a possible candidate for Mount Hermon School's next Principal as George Fernandez was retiring. From many of you we received messages of wonderful affirmation and support, and even now as we write these words, the warmth and sincerity of your responses resonate in our hearts. Mount Hermon has always been so much more than an educational institute. We have "talked" with each other from literally the ends of the earth, and been united in understanding, purpose and love as we have considered the future of this magnificent institution. We all continue to be part of a very blessed community – Hail Mount Hermon!

However, things have not progressed at all in this bid. It is now nearly 10 months since we first sent our letter to Bishop Sagar – followed a month later by the registered mail version of the same. We have never received anything back from him even though the correspondence would have been received by his office. If the information ever filtered through to the Mount Hermon Board, we have never been informed of it. Information from Mount Hermon School itself is sparse, and generally received through hearsay from past students visiting the school. The official web-site (http://mounthermon.co.in/) has no information on staff or Board members and there is no mechanism set up for the school to communicate with alumni.

Recent information via the grapevine is that the Board is considering 12 candidates as potential principals, however Jigme is not among them. Had the Board even acknowledged that we wanted to be part of the discussion, Jigme would have been happy to consider any sort of involvement with the school. However now that the school authorities have indicated that they have other ideas for the school, Jigme will not be pursuing any formal role in Mount Hermon School in the future.

He does, however, continue to support the alumni groups and his commitment to Mount Hermon remains as steadfast as ever. In November he will attend the Speech Day celebrations along with other ex-students. He continues to meet with the Grade Four staff (cooks, bearers and cleaners) and hopefully through his contact we will be kept informed of the situation in the school.

We are sure you will want to join us in thanking Jigme and his wife for the generous offer of his time and potential service to Mount Hermon School. Your overwhelming responses of affirmation and love are indicative of your support, and we thank each one of you for your interest, your encouragement and your warmth of expression to Jigme and Mount Hermon School. The fact that we have all rallied together and have picked up the threads of communication from all corners of the world has been a truly wonderful and blessed thing.

As we enter into the Christmas Season, may peace, love and joy be in all your hearts, and in the lives of those you love.

Dipak, Lucinda
Shiv, Roslyn

Hi All

It is demoralising to read the email below.

I would like to use this platform to appeal to Jigme not to step aside or stand back. And to continue to pursue a formal role in MHS.

Some reasons come to my mind. I request all to add their own reasons to mine and request Jigme to make himself available. Roslyn please help to forward this email to Jigme as I don't see his name on the receipents list.

- Jigme you are not doing this for your personal accomplishment - you are doing this for the love of your school, no our school
- You are the best thing that can happen to this school
- You are best suited, experienced and involved from the heart for this job
- Our hopes lie with you.

Having said that maybe some of us could take a more constructive role in persuading the board. For this we need names and addresses or email id's of board members.

Second we should add names of other Hermonites to this mail and ask them to assist by writing to the board or helping in any way possible.

If you all remember my classmate and good friend Tashi Dorjee - he visited MHS very recently. He said the school was in a sorry and shabby state. That the girls (boarding) were staying in the Gymn till their dormitories were repaired. This statement says enough about the state of the school.

Finally I request all to pitch in again as we all owe it to our school. Today we are what this school made us.

Warm regards
Suresh (Chatlani), ISC 1971, Lagos, Nigeria, Africa.
Nov 22, 2012

Suresh Chatlani (centre) with Roslyn (Rongong) Namgyal and Jagdish Saria.

Hello friends of the old grey wall,

I have been very much in touch with Hermonites around India and other parts of the world and I must agree that one thing MH has given us is we are united and dedicated for the cause of MH. People may not be vociferous but the commitment is there.

I also have a few things to put forward in this regard:

1. If given a chance the present Managing Committee and the school administration, they will ruin the school. The ground work for that has already started and MH is considered an outcast in Darjeeling where people put their children after trying for SP, NP and Loreto.

2. The school administration can plead that the agitation has had an adverse impact on the well-being of the school but how come SP, NP and Loreto are flourishing?

3. What personal benefit will a Hermonite have if Mr. Jigme Kazi is made the Principal of the school....nothing. It is just because of the love for the school for which Hermonites all over the world want him to be the Principal of the school. We can all vouch that the school has seen a steady downfall after the era of the Johnstons. I have nothing personal against any Principal. If the school would have done well under a particular Principal fingers would not have been pointed. The Managing Committee members should realize.

4. It comes to my mind at times that why is the Managing Committee not coming to the forefront, declaring their names, contact details and answering concerned voices of Hermonites. Are they trying to hide something or shield some here? Is there anything fishy?

5. If all was going on fine in the school, who has the time and energy to go around poking nose, we just want the school to flourish and do well, and this is because we love MH from the core of our heart.
6. If due to some legal/technical reason Mr. Jigme Kazi could not become the Principal of the school, I am sure rules can be amended as per the need of the hour. If the Constitution can be amended, why can't the rules of the school be amended if it is for the betterment of the school?
7. Ok if he still can't become the Principal, maybe the school could have made a post for him like Bursar or some other Honorary post which he might have accepted as long as he was associated with the school and nurtured it full time. Outrightly his application was turned down by not replying to him, at least an audience should have been granted to the Hermonites. I am not sure if anything of this sort happened but I am picking up the que from the trailing email.
8. If this opportunity is lost MH will be ruined and take my word for it. The Managing Committee is least bothered.

In the end I earnestly request all Hermonites who will be attending the reunion tomorrow and day after tomorrow in Darjeeling to have a good time, don't dig up old skeletons but at the same time ponder about what can be done for the betterment of the school and to put in a word or two here and there.

Prakash Mundra, Sikkim.
Nov 23, 2012

Dear All,

I agree with Dipak that since many Hermonites will be at the reunion, we should use this moment to lobby for Jigme (provided he's still interested). It will not be easy to get a large group gathering again in the near future, so grasp the moment. Start the campaign to pressure the Committee (whoever they are) to have Jigme Kazi involved in the running of our school. Could we sign petitions by emails? As I see it, most ex-Hermonites from Thailand support Jigme. He was a champion in his days, and 40 years later... still is. Old Champions never die.

Hail Mount Hermon

Jutatip Boon-Long (SC '76), Bangkok.

The School Song

Beloved Mount Hermon, we greet thee
Thy daughters and sons from afar,
As oft as we pause in our toiling
To hail thee, whose children we are.

Hail Mount Hermon! A Tribute

Chorus
Hail, Mount Hermon! Hail, Mount Hermon!
Safe for aye in memory's shrine.
Hail, Mount Hermon! Dear Mount Hermon!
Praise and love be ever thine.

With strong steady hand dost thou lead us,
Thy powerful arm is our stay,
Thy light is our beacon in darkness
Which ever will lend us its ray.

Chorus

O may thy fair name live forever,
Be deeply impressed on each heart,
That we, in our trials and triumphs,
May ne'er from thy guidance depart.

Chorus

78 MH Says 'No' To Global Hermonites After Assurance

Dear Rev. K. Sardar,

Good morning Sir and my respectful regards from all of us Hermonites International body. Kindly find attached Hermonites International letter of intention, which is self-explanatory and we look forward to your kind close cooperation in the future.

On behalf of Hermonites international and Hermonites all over India, I would like to sincerely congratulate your good self and Mr. Partha Dey for the tremendous effort in keeping Mount Hermon School running in good shape against all the local political turmoil. With kindest and respectful regards,

Mr. Varongthip Lulitanond (SC 73)
President of Hermonites International

To,
Rev. K. Sardar
Administrator
Mount Hermon School
Darjeeling (WB)
May 31, 2018

Subject: Mount Hermon School and Hermonites
Respected Sir,

First of all, on behalf of all Hermonites I wish to convey to the staff, students and the school authorities our greetings and good wishes.

Sir, in the past several months some concerned Hermonites who visited our beloved alma mater have expressed their appreciation of how the school has been run and maintained despite trying situations. Informal talks held with some staff members of the school have given us a ray of hope for the school's future.

Mount Hermon is now nearly 125 years old and a casual glance over our school's history proves that though we have gone through trying times we were able to overcome the hurdles with faith in God and in ourselves.

On behalf of all Hermonites I would like to say that we are deeply concerned about the present situation that the school is facing and would like to seek your advice as to how we could pitch in and help the school in whatever way possible. Hermonites from all over the world are keen on opening a dialogue with the school and its authorities to enable us to offer our assistance.

We are hopeful of a positive response to our concern and suggestion and are waiting in eager anticipation to work together for our beloved school.

With warm regards. Hail Mount Hermon!

Yours truly,
(Varongthip Lulitanond)
President
Hermonites International
Copy to: Mr. Partha Dey, Senior Master, Mount Hermon School

To
Mr. Varongthip Lulitanond
President
Hermonites International

Dear Mr. Lulitanond,

Greetings to you and to all Hermonites from the Mount Hermon School!

This is in regard to your mail dated 31st May 2018 regarding the Mount Hermon School. I highly appreciate of your concern for the school.

Let me, in brief, inform you that I have assumed charge as the Administrator of the Mount Hermon School with effect from 1st June 2017. The situation of the school, at that time, was really very challenging due to various problems including the political instability in Darjeeling. The school was suffering from acute financial anemia. A large amount was showing in our financial report as liabilities, salary of the staff along with other related payments were due for more than 3 months. On top of that the '104 days strike' in Darjeeling made the situation worse.

Due to our location Mount Hermon School campus became the real 'battle ground'. We did our best during the 'strike' to take care of our students by providing hostel facilities to our boarder students in our other schools situated in Calcutta (in Calcutta Girls' High School – for Girls and in Methodist School, Dankuni – for boys) and by introducing 'portable school' to our local day scholar students. But in spite of our best efforts many parents decided to withdraw their children, which needless to mention was a big financial blow to the school. It happened with not only Mount Hermon but also in other schools.

As a result of that a kind of 'Vulture Culture' developed in Darjeeling. Every school was (and is) trying to steal/snatch students from other schools by using unfair means. A false rumour, with an ulterior motive, was spread in the town and everywhere in our country and even abroad that management has decided to close down Mount Hermon School and has already closed down the 'Mount Hermon Under Graduate Teachers' Training College. Which is not true – neither we have closed the school and the college nor we have any intention of doing that. I am sorry to tell you that unfortunately even few of the Hermonites (former students of MHS), may be due to their ignorance about the ground reality, played a vital role and contributed greatly in spreading that rumour.

However, during the past few months, in spite of all these problems and adversities the school had to go through, we did our best to improve the physical and environmental condition of the school by revamping School Website, repairing the school buildings, improving the food quality in our school canteen, installing 40 KV green generator was installed, by renovating hostels etc. You will be happy to learn that after many years we have restarted the MOUNT HERMON Bakery. In this year, after a gap of few years we have produced our 'Major Production' on 1st June 2018 which was highly appreciated by all. The Students, Staff, Parents, Hermonites and people in the locality again started speaking good about the school and seems has gained their confidence in the school.

We are also working on having a 'Dairy Farming' and 'Organing Farming' projects in our school. There are many other things/projects that we need to do take up to maintain the legacy of Mount Hermon.

I once again thank you so much for your letter which has encouraged and motivated us a lot and made us feel that we are not alone in this struggle but the entire 'Mount Hermon Family' is standing behind us to support this noble cause. I am keenly interested and look forward for the opportunity to have a meeting with you to apprise you about the status of the school. Please feel free to write to me for any further information and/or clarification in regard to your alma mater. Before closing let me assure you that we will not spare any effort to justify your confidence in us. May God bless you all and may He bless Mount Hermon abundantly.

With thanks and regards,
Sincerely yours,
Rev. K. Sardar
Administrator & Secretary
Mount Hermon School

Dear Jigme,

Thank you for reminding me of the proposed letter that Thip could write on behalf of the Hermonites International as his role of the President.

Subsequent to my conversation with you I managed to speak with Mr. Partha Dey again after he returned from Calcutta following the sad death of his Father-in-law. He is willing to continue acting as a liaison via the administrator Rev. Sardar with the Governing body. My thoughts, and I dare say some may agree on the same line, are as follows

1. The school desperately needs a full time Principal who not only acts as the head of the Institution but is the face of the school for all prospective parents and any administrative body that the school would require that a head represent, but also someone who can function and extend discipline amongst students and teachers. Partha Dey has been the senior school master for many years and is fully aware of all the goings on at the school. In his new authoritative position, he might be able to exert some pressure on erring teachers too, as the school seems to have them. The notion of a teacher's Union body should not be encouraged.

   We were told that the school's financial condition does not allow the board to employ a full time Principal. Therefore, Partha Dey can be elevated to the post of Interim Principal till such time the school can find someone suitable. Partha Dey after so many years at MH can almost be considered a local who is reasonably aware of the various situations that exist. Therefore proposal no.

1. Partha Dey be elevated to the position of an Interim Principal till a solution is found or if he is able to do the job he be made permanent. The financial burden of new employment can be done away with (from the board's point of view) and the school immediately gets an Institutional Head.

2. If the political situation continues to be volatile then there is every reason to be concerned about boarders. Therefore, the proposal of making MH a completely day school for the moment should be taken up by the board. I guess we all should get over the nostalgic times of a boarding school and embrace the fact that if MH has to survive and continue as an educational institution, then let it become a day school. These are changing times and we have to flow with the tide.

    Let MH become a day school like St. Joseph's and Loreto. The increase in numbers (though with a lower fee structure of a day scholar) should elevate the financial crunch that the school faces today. The idea of a boarding school should not be given up completely as there is the infrastructure in place. Should the situation improve anytime soon then boarders can be made welcome.

Both North Point and Loreto alumni are keen to see that MH continues to survive and are willing to help by providing students who are unable to seek admissions at their respective schools. This does not mean that the quality of the potential student is poor. At the end of the day it is what the teachers make out of a student. The alumni's of both North Point and Loreto have tried liaising with the school but were unable to make headway. Suggest that the local committee of MH alumni's liaise with these people and take it forward with the school. Tenzin who happens to be a Hermonite of '91 batch is married to a North Pointer had come forward during our visit to Darjeeling with the suggestion that we work together with these two alumni's. She lives in Canada but frequently visits Darj where her husband is setting up a resort and is actively involved in the "Save Mount Hermon" project of the NP alumni.

3. The school needs a periodic audit of its finances and its activities. I am sure the alumni can produce a finance auditor who can advise the school of its financial progress, rather than depend on periodic injections of funds from outside when there is insufficient funds. The report generated can be reviewed by the board and any action that may be required to be taken can be done in accordance with the advice provided by the auditor. The money within the school coffers must be utilized wisely and carefully and expenditure should be prioritized with the school/principal having the authority to signs expenditure cheque on projects cleared by the school board working with the alumni committee.

That the alumni have a working committee whose role would be to monitor both financial and administrative situation together with the principal and the board and keep abreast of the situation/s on a regular basis. The alumni committee should be made up of people who are committed and are willing to spare some dedicated time to serve its function. Every Hermonite is busy, but committee members chosen amongst us and particularly local and on the ground, must be prepared to take this job on seriously.

4. The school has enough infrastructure in place to encourage outside organizations to hold their seminars or workshops during the holiday periods when the school is closed. This will bring in extra cash that the school needs. There are many such organizations that are looking for large places made available for a moderate fee. Darjeeling is now an all year round destination and a 2-3 day conference can quite easily be arranged. The New building overlooking the playing field can be such a venue. The recent Church conference held in the beginning of May, which I believe, paid MH for the use of the facilities, is just such an example of use of the existing infrastructure with some monetary returns.

Proposal: The school periodically advertises about the availability of space for seminars workshops etc. A fee structure can be devised by the alumni working committee and the school authorities with inclusions and exclusions. A lot of people amongst us who are in know of such organizations/companies, can step forward and help.

The above are some of my thoughts and others are free to have their inputs. I have a distinct feeling that the board are more than anything else looking for financial commitments from the alumni. We as alumni are acutely aware of this and therefore should be discreet in how this matter can be put forth to the board. It is a tricky question that does not have an easy answer. (i.e. who controls the money and how that money is to be spent) We would have to rely on a general consensus as to collections amongst us and TRUST the judgement of the committee to execute the expending of such funds. If we are to go down the route of raising funds then the amount of contribution should be left to the contributor (as some can afford more and others little or not at all). The contributions should always be an ongoing process and not just confined to just one time donations. It's like going to church/temple that you put in a bit of money each time you visit.

Jigme you may have contrary views to the above and please feel free to scrap any or all of these ideas and add and subtract at will. But put forth this to others whom you know and are keen to bring other ideas to the table. I spoke to Shiv while he was at school today and he felt a sense of positiveness with what was happening in school. Do liaise with him too on these ideas and maybe something can happen pretty soon.

By the way Partha Dey's email is parthadeymhs@gmail.com and his mobile number is 9547078819. In case there is a mistake in the email address, as it was dictated over a very unstable telephone line, please try parthadeymhsdarj1895@gmail.com.

I hope the above makes sense to you all and there can be merit in some ideas going forward. It should not be delayed too long as the momentum can be lost and the slight window that seems to have opened may shut with a bang!!

Hail Mount Hermon!!

Warm regards to you and all other Hermonites.

Pradip

May 29, 2018

Dear Pradip and friends,

Thank you Pradip for your long note. Please note these points:

1. A few of us visited MH recently and felt good about the school putting up a brave front with less than 140 students. We felt sad, sorry and happy.
2. Unlike before we at least were able to talk to some staff and workers. Uttam and I had a chat with P. Dey and told him we have no intention of taking over MH but just want to help the school to get on its feet.
3. Some of you know the situation I'm facing at the home front. I don't even have a decent place to call my home. My papers have closed down and no politics for me.

Therefore, I cannot make any commitment to MH unlike before as I am now committed to my family. But my 0.1 per cent is equal to ordinary Hermonite's 50%!

4. 80 per cent of MH's success even as a day school depends on Darj people and their politics. Only 20 percent is in the hands of school authorities of which our stake is about 2%. Such is the situation. It is the reality no matter how much some of us yearn for MH's revival.

5. Thip as Prez will sent a letter to the school Adm and hopefully he will place the matter before the Managing Committee and get the desired response.

6. If the response is good we will then form a committee to discuss on all things. If there is no response then formal association with the school is a closed chapter but we can still do our bit in our own ways to help MH.

7. Partha has been there for almost 25 years and 2020 is MH's 125th anniversary. He should be the next Principal. While we may help in these two things we should not be used to do their job and allow them to leave us high and dray post-March 2020. Church politics is just politics as usual.

8. Though we have Hermonite pages in FB and WA I propose to start a closed group for the very active Hermonites so that meaningful discourse takes place with our goal in mind.

Cheers to all!
Jigs

A NEW BEGINNING AT 'MH'

A new beginning has been made by concerned Hermonites to enable the Hermonites (alumni of Mt. Hermon School, Darjeeling.) to do whatever possible to help and support their alma mater.

Rev. K. Sardar, the school's Administrator and Secretary, has welcomed the initiative taken by Hermonites International (Hi!), a global body of the Hermonites, to work together in unison for the welfare of the school.

In response to a letter from Hermonites International President, Varongthip Lulitanond, Rev. Sardar, who also represents the Managing Committee of the school, while stating that the Hermonites' concern for the school "has encouraged and motivated us a lot and made us feel that we are not alone in this struggle but the entire 'Mount Hermon Family' is standing behind us to support this noble cause", has also stated, "I am keenly interested and look forward for the opportunity to have a meeting with you to apprise you about the status of the school."

On June 14, three Hermonites of the '70 era – Namgyal Wangdhi, Anup Chachan and Jigme N. Kazi – representing the global body, met the school's Senior Master, Mr. Partho Dey, at Mt. Hermon to lay the groundwork for further talks regarding the

(L to R) Jigme N. Kazi, Partha Dey, Anup Chachan and Namgyal Wangdi at Mt. Hermon, 2018.

school's welfare. Mr. Dey's response was also very positive and encouraging and the talk was very friendly and fruitful.

A team of concerned Hermonites in the region, representing the HI, are expected to have a formal meeting with Rev. Sardar shortly on the said matter. If the Methodist Church of India (MCI), which owns the school and governs it through its Managing Committee, formally gives the green signal for the alumni to pitch in then a way will be cleared for global Hermonites to participate in the school's welfare in a more organised and systematic way on a long-term basis.

Finally, after a long and arduous struggle the way is being cleared for the alumni's association with their alma mater in a deep and meaningful way. In his year-long stay at MH, Rev. Sardar and Mr. Dey, who has been on MH staff for the past 25 years, have done a wonderful job in running and maintaining the school despite trying circumstances. Hermonites who visited the school recently are all impressed by their work.

At this stage, when we see a ray of hope for the school's future success, we urge all Hermonites and well-wishers of the school to be very, very positive in their outlook and ensure a bright future for MH. Hail Mount Hermon!

Good Jigs that you finally feel that there is hope to take MH forward. Meeting Rev. Sardar will be the next more serious step.

If you recall I did mention very clearly that Rev. Sardar is not only a member of the committee but is their representative with delegated authority from the committee to work in the interest of the school.

He is very keen to right the wrong of the past for the school and move forward. He should be the major point of contact for all assistance. Be aware he speaks to all alumni on behalf of the school and more importantly the MC. He will be the main person to take into confidence if you and the alumni wish to take this any further forward. Rev. Sardar is open and sufficiently liberal minded and wants things done. Continuing to insist that you want the MC's approval for going forward will be an affront to Rev. Sardar and you can be assured that the alumni will go nowhere. The very fact that he has written an open letter to the alumni is sufficient assurance that he is speaking on behalf of the MC. So whatever you all propose please do take ALL CONCERNED Hermonites thoughts and ideas into consideration as that will be essential in the going forward mode. You and the rest on the ground can see best the reality.
Pradip Verma

When we meet Sardar this time we are going as Reps of HI and will be in response to his letter to Thip. There is no need to take a big team to meet him. As of now Anup, Namgyal, Chuck and myself should do. Pratap and Sarthak may join us. No, we may not insist that we get a formal green signal from MC if he says he represents the MC. Speaking to individuals personally on the issue is one thing and speaking to reps of an organisation in a formal meeting is another matter.

We have been very patient with MH for a long time. Let us not rush. Let us build a strong and secure foundation for MH-alumni-MC relationship that will last when we are no more. Most of us who are active and are in touch with the ground reality share these views. Hope you see the light.

Dey was very happy and pleased with our talk in his chamber which took more than an hour. He has been a long friend of Namgyal since the days when he was a warden. We indirectly hinted that we would support him as the next Princi. He said we should meet Sardar who be back next Tuesday. We want to come back next week to meet Sardar. Dey emphasised the important of meeting Sardar, who is member Secy of the Managing Committee. Dey said he would apprise Sardar of what took place during our talk and said since he was not part of the committee he cannot do much. He also agreed with us that the final go-ahead for our involvement must come from the committee but was hopeful of a positive response from the church. We also met his wife, a teacher, matron and Raj Kumar Subba. We met Chuck who was very happy with the outcome of the talks and wants to join us for talks with Sardar. Chuck said Sardar is a very influential member of the committee. We had two cups of tea, school made biscuits and cakes. We took for Dey and Sadar Sikkim's Temi Tea, Shiv's Gopaldhara tea, my book and khada. Our good feelings for MH is taking us forward. Please do not share this with others. Only for u two and Shiv.

Cindy, I wanted to get in touch with Sarthak this time but decided not to as this informal meeting was basically between Dey and Namgyal. Namgyal believes that the main reason for rejecting me was coz the school and church felt very strongly that we were going to 'takeover' MH. This misconception is now cleared for us to go ahead. Secondly, at this stage we don't want to involve other Hermonites before getting a concrete 'yes' from the church. This is our third try and we must succeed in urging the church to talk to us. Cannot at this stage give false hopes to Hermonites. I met Sarthak last year and he has impressed me and we are in touch. OK?

Cindy and Pradip, despite what you two say about going ahead straightaway in helping MH after the good response from Sardar most of us, including Thip, Chuck, Anup, Namgyal, Shiv, Dey and myself, still feel that the final green signal must come from the MC. As the Adm. Sardar is open about meeting us and Dey is arranging this meeting. Hopefully, it will be next week. In this meeting there is only one agenda: the church's response to our involvement in a collective way for MH. At the moment Thip as Prez of HI is formally in touch with the school authorities openly.

Discussions with MH on various issues can only take place if they want us to get involved in a more organised and systematic way. And these discussions must be with reps of global Hermonites and not just a few of us. I hope the silver lining will open the door soon. If not then the door is open for individual Hermonites in their individual capacity to help MH. When the church has blocked our entry for nearly 7 years those of us who still feel for MH cannot pitch in without a concrete and formal decision by the MC on the issue. Sorry Pradip and Cindy, positive chats and a letter from Sardar as Adm is not enough. I hope you now understand us fully.

Jigs

To Pradip, June 16

When we meet Sardar this time we are going as Reps of HI and will be in response to his letter to Thip. There is no need to take a big team to meet him. As of now Anup, Namgyal, Chuck and myself should do. Pratap and Sarthak may join us. No, we may not insist that we get a formal green signal from MC if he says he represents the MC. Speaking to individuals personally on the issue is one thing and speaking to reps of an organisation in a formal meeting is another matter.

We have been very patient with MH for a long time. Let us not rush. Let us build a strong and secure foundation for MH-alumni-MC relationship that will last when we are no more. Most of us who are active and are in touch with the ground reality share these views. Hope you see the light.

If you guys think that I have decided on this alone ignoring the wider Hermonite community then you got it all wrong. Those who visited MH recently are Cindy and Pradip, Shiv, Anup, Namgyal, myself and a few others. We all felt good about the school and felt that if they needed our help we could pitch in. There are many others who were informed about our feelings and they gave the go-ahead and Thip made a formal submission.

Though Sardar is part of the Managing Committee and though he has asked HI to come for talks we feel we needed to be very clear on formally obtaining the Church's green signal. This has now been agreed. If the MC says yes then the ball is in the Hermonites' court and then and then only the committee should be formed. We have also made it clear that when the talk is fixed with Sardar next week all are welcomed to join. Those who have confirmed are Anup, Chuck, Namgyal as myself. Unconfirmed participants are Shiv, Sushil, Sarthak, Pratap. If others like Thip, Cindy, Pradip, Margaret, Rekha, Len, Barry, Jagdish, Jagjit, Goenka, Annie, Mahesh, Goofy, Santish, Thinley (both), Tshering etc etc are warmly welcomed.

It would be time-consuming and unwise to call for a meeting of all these guys and others before we are formally asked to pitch in. There are many others who will be reluctant to participate on MH if the Methodist Church does not favour global Hermonites to get involved in a big way. I have already resigned as HI Prez during the Thai reunion in Dec 2016. I have already stated before in 2015 that I am not in the race for MH Princi. I only don't want MH to die when I'm alive. And if despite our sacrifice and sincerity there are those who have vested interest on MH and want it to be no more WE SHALL FIGHT and we will do it openly come what may. Got it?

Jigs

Jigs

As far as it's understood the requirements to become Principal are they require a Christian, (which has been in their bylaws for at least 20 years) a BA Ed, with min 5 years teaching experience. It seems no one was aware of this at the time. The business about the Sikkimese wanting to take over probably came about via the Hermonite alumni rumour mongering. I fail to see how, after asking the representative of the church, and MC, Rev. Sardar, for confirmation in writing that they are happy to interact with the alumni, and getting that positive response you still feel you have not got a concrete 'yes'. I think Rev. Sardar will find it very insulting if you indicate you feel he has no authority after all and you expect the Bishop to confirm. I think you are treading on very thin ice.

We met Sarthak in March 2016 and he told us all he had achieved, with the blessing obviously of the school and church. There should be no reason to fail, as we know the school and Administrator are keen on our help. This however must be seeing what they require, giving practical suggestions and ideas to help with getting more students, which in turn will increase revenue and assist in more money being available for staff, improvements in the facilities, grounds, etc. I'm sure many will come up if they feel there is a good, open minded, trustworthy committee taking this forward. We need to move forward and get a good committee together who can bring positivity to this and who represent a broad alumni base. Obviously you will meet Rev. Sardar next week and will post up the outcome.

Pradip

Just got back home after a very enjoyable and successful trip to MH and Darj. The meeting with Dey went off very well and he will now brief Sardar, who was in Cal and will be back on Tuesday. Dey said we should meet Sardar after he gets back. We told him we need concrete and formal go-ahead from the Managing Committee for us to come to MH's aid. This he agreed and admitted that he very much wants our help he does not represent the MC. But he will brief Sardar who is the Member Secretary of the MC, according to Sunirmal Chakravarty (Chuck), my batchmate and former Senior Master of St. Paul's and Princi of Cal's Lamart School, Sardar is quite powerful in the MC. Chuck is willing to go with us to meet Sardar. The meeting with Dey was arranged before you wrote to Dey. Namgyal knows Dey very well and one of the main reasons why they were reluctant engage the alumni in a big way is because they fear that we will 'takeover' MH and leave the Church high and dry. We told that this was not the case and was just a propaganda and he believed us. So all misconceptions of us taking over MH has been cleared and a way has been created for us to help MH in a big way for a long time. But much now depends on the MC response and we hope Sardar will do the needful. We took tea, khada and my books for Dey and Sardar. So far, so good. This briefing is for your eyes only. We can go open when we get the green signal from the church but not before that.

Jigs
May 30, 2018

June 14

Thinking of you Jigs, Namgyal and Co. I am praying for wisdom for all concerned that the future success of MH is everyone's priority. Just remember that the combined assets and contributory power of MH alumni probably is greater than the Methodist Church of India - just in case they would like to tap into this resource.

Barry (!!)

Just to share further on MH. I got a call from Rev. Sardar today here in Ireland, as I had been in touch with him too, confirming that he had responded to Thip's via email. Thip is now in possession of the mail (at least I hope so). I believe the tone of the letter is very positive and gives hope for all of us working together.

During my conversation with him I mentioned the possibility of Jigme, Namgyal and possibly Anup and Shiv going to school and having an informal talk with Mr. Partha Dey. Rev. Sardar may not be there as he goes to Calcutta for a meeting with the MC and as he called it's begging 'bowl' to collect funds for the school. Incase his trip is postponed he will be available at MH and it would be worth the effort of Jigs and co to induct him during the discussions. He also confirmed that he spends about 20-25 days of the month in school, so he may be the face of the head of the institution that the school is lacking. He is an easy going person and very unlike Noel Prabhuraj and keen to meet any old students and talk about the well being of the school.

Maybe all of this might allow us to open a new page in the ongoing book of MH.

All the best guys.

At the end of the day does it make a difference what the total amount is? Rev. Sardar is not looking at the alumni to cover the deficit.

One should progress from there. Do you feel and some of the other alumni feel that is what Rev. Sardar and the school is looking at? If that is the case then we should rethink on what the alumni want.

Even if it is quoted everywhere under the circumstances how relevant is it via visit the alumni and it's approach to the school. At the end of the day the amount is huge and there is no denying and Rev. Sardar is not denying either.

If people wish to gossip they can and nothing good can come out of it. Just hope that better sense will prevail on people who wish to gossip and have nothing to contribute.

Dear All, I was contacted once again by Rev. Sardar today and the outcome of the conversation is as follows:

1. He will be delighted to welcome any Hermonite to the school and see first hand what the school is doing.
2. He was very categorically clear that he nor the school is looking for money from the alumni for the functioning of the school.
3. Since the times of Mr. Fernandez he has read the audit report and mentioned the school was bamboozled into expenses of over 6cr and in that amount people benefited who shouldn't have.
4. He has pain stakeingly worked in bringing back some semblance of normalcy and all this is showing.
5. The decision making process is simple. He takes all the decisions for the school and informs the Managing Committee of his decisions, and has their full support.
6. He said that he was willing to listen to Hermonites as long as they were interested in talking about the development of the school and he was not going to be interested in being told what the school should do and not do.
7. He felt that a lot of bad publicity was also propagated by some Hermonites who had vested interests and he would not entertain such people for any discussion.

Like we hear various rumours about the viability of MH, he too hears the same and has also reasonable ideas that a lot of such bad publicity is a result of Hermonites with vested interests.

He felt that a good and constructive dialogue is essential for anything to progress further between the alumni and the school.

He has no intention of relegating the Hermonites to the background and wants them involved much like a family, after all as he says All Hermonites are extended family members how can we ignore them.

So guys we now have a semblance of his attitude and approach, we should be guided by it.

By the way in case any Hermonite wishes to stay in school he would arrange appropriate accommodation on the premises. The condition that he has sufficient information in advance.

At the end of the day does it make a difference what the total amount is? Rev. Sardar is not looking at the alumni to cover the deficit.

One should progress from there. Do you feel and some of the other alumni feel that is what Rev. Sardar and the school is looking at? If that is the case then we should rethink on what the alumni want.

If people wish to gossip they can and nothing good can come out of it. Just hope that better sense will prevail on people who wish to gossip and have nothing to contribute.
Pradip

June 17
Note to Krishna Goenka

Indirectly, you have sent a message to me? Well, this is my answer. In autumn, some of us visited MH and felt good about it. We shared our feelings. This led to asking the church to address our concern. Those involved in this effort are Thip, Cindy, Pradip, Chuck, Sushil, Namgyal, Dey, Margaret, Thinley, Anup, Shiv, Ison etc. There is no point asking for ideas and help from all Hermonites if the church, once again, shuts the door. We don't own MH, the church does. We can only sympathise and give help on ad-hoc basis if we are not allowed to intervene in a more organised and systematic way. In any case most those in the above list, including myself, have earlier decide not to become active once the church's door is open. Those who have the time, energy and resources should take charge. We have done enough. Good day.
Jigs

June 17
I think we have a lot to be grateful to Jigme for. He's been on this bandwagon for a long time, giving a 100% and investing a lot of time and energy - in fact his whole life at one point. A lot of this would have been impossible without him riding at the helm. He has been burnt numerous times and I am amazed that he is still willing to take up the challenge. He has every reason to proceed with caution - and this caution does not mean that he is not open to all the good suggestions that people are giving. I'm all with you Jigs.
Walsa (Mathai)

Note to Walsa Mathai, June 17, 2018.
Thank u Wally for your kind note and support. It was needed. A way has been made this time and although some of us have worked hard on this to happen we, including myself, have already expressed our inability to be in any team or committee to help MH if the church gives the green signal. Ever since our sincere efforts to help MH since 2012 the church has kept mum and this time it was essential to get its 'yes' formally. Only when this is given can we find a solution for MH. Otherwise it is simply a waste of time. Contrary to allegations hurled against me that I'm dictatorial, the decision to approach the Managing Committee was a collective decision of these people: Pradip, Cindy, Namgyal, Anup, Chuck, Mr. Ison, Thip, Pratap, Shiv, Sushil etc. Hope the Australian and NZ chapters continue to guide us in future also. Please remind Shanta for her article of the Mathais for my MH book. Good day and once again thank you for the support.
Jigs

Jigs - you have given a lot of time and effort in (linking) so many Hermonites towards helping MH regain its profile as one of the prominent educational institutions in India. Now you have the opportunity in taking us to the next step of acceptance by the Management Committee in mobilizing alumni involvement in reviving MH. Please, my friend, be wise in your dealings with Rev. Sardar. If he says the Committee is interested (start by saying) that we can be trusted. Let's start carrying out some simple tasks - prove ourselves - and then let's sit down and talk about serious long-term planning. I'm with you Jigs. If required, I'll come across and help you. Blessings my friend.
Barry

Hi! Barry. When this whole episode of re reviving MH came up in discussion at Shiv's house with Jigs who had graciously come down from Gangtok to meet us nothing more was mentioned except that the reality of the political situation did not help in getting boarders. The way forward was converting MH into a day school as NP and Loreto had done. On our going up to school and subsequent meeting with Mr. Dey we came away with the impression that the school authorities were interested in a dialogue with the alumni. The school looked in much better shape and the few children we met looked happy.

We thought it only proper that we share our views with all Hermonites that we could be in touch with. Shiv's visit to school was a photo essay on the improvements he noticed and realised that there was progress but sadly lacked students.

Discussions became animated. I had several subsequent telephone conversations with Mr. Dey and indeed with Rev. Sardar who is as a person very keen to listen to the alumni. Formal letters were exchanged between him and the President of HI in an effort to assure the authorities that the alumni wish to support the school's efforts in improving the facilities.

The stage is now set to try and take it forward.

Jigs and co who have volunteered to take it further must have a plan in place that is plausible and effective with a definite step forward to regaining the trust of the Church and its delegated authorities.

From Rekha's notes and conversation with the Bishop it is very evident that he is aware of what is happening amongst us alumni and continues to be sceptical and I dare say rightly so. We have never bothered to present ourselves as a cohesive whole. We have possibly approached the authorities with little or no thought process in place.

Jigs who has been at the forefront of all of this from the beginning has been left to work on his own thoughts of what the alumni should be doing, simply because nothing was out in an open forum for others interested to comment and contribute so possibly that line of action was flawed. Further some alumni in Calcutta presented another face to the church and proclaimed that they were the only authorised group who could speak to the authorities, thereby negating efforts of those people who were quietly serious about reviving the school.

The stage is now set for another meeting with Jigs and co but none of us know anything beyond the line that the church must formally acknowledge the alumni's desire to help MH.

So as you put it…what will be our response if Rev. Sardar asks the people attending the meeting to present a plan. Currently none of us have been told if there is a plan at all. So as Jigs so often says…wait and watch so we are all waiting with bated breath.
Pradip Verma

June 18, 2018

Hi Ros and Sherab, it now seems a concrete thing is taking place for MH. Please see updates in Whatsapp and Facebook for details. I was quite hurt when Pradeep and Co made wild allegations that I was doing things by myself with a handful of Hermonites. You know the facts. Those going for the meeting would be: Namgyal, Shiv, Sushil, Jagdish, Anup, Pratap, Sarthak, Dipang and a few others. Please note that TTC is on drips, in semi-coma. I would like to see that it is also resurrected. What say you? Good day.
Jigs

Got it, Sir (Ison). We are so near now in clinching the deal and it would be unwise to back away when saving MH is within reach. Cindy and Pradeep and Namgyal have done a great job in bridging the communication gap but wild allegations by Pradeep and Co that it's only me and a handful of Hermonites are involved is far from the truth. You know how the global Hermonites backed us in 2012. I have all the details and in my book it will be fully recorded for posterity to note of our endeavours for MH.

When I told Pradeep that he should back his allegations with facts he says sorry, I didn't know. His allegations that it was me, me only is supported by the juniors who are in touch him. Please advise him. Finally, those who will be at the meeting are: Shiv, Pratap, Anup, Namgyal, Sarthak, Depang, Jagdish, Sushil, Thangi and perhaps a few others. You and Co could also suggest more names. We need to focus on the fact that Thip and HI are the main players so that there is no controversy on who and which group represents the Hermonites. Meanwhile, you could jot down ideas for helping MH in consultation with Thip and others. The names of proposed committee have to be thought out. This committee must function under HI as if the MC gives the green signal HI is responsible. For your information when Thip took over me as HI Prez at the Thai reunion in 2016, I was made life-time Chairman of HI, whatever that means but at least when the talks are on I will be have a formal position of the HI.
Jigs

Jigs - you have to be confident that we are with you and cheering you on. You've done so much to date - and now the fruit is going to be there for the picking. Talk over a game plan with…anyone else who attends the meeting with you so you have a simple strategy and can be seen as having one voice. Why not start by committing to some simple projects to show we can be trusted. In the meantime HI can liaise with various alumni to talk about a small and active committee within the Darjeeling area which can be the operational committee of MHI and through discussions around the globe a longer term strategy can be developed. MH admin does not need to know of MHI operational details. We are all cheering for you.
Barry

June 18 Meet

Hi guys! Hope this week is a lucky week for us. There could be a mini-reunion in Darj: breakfast at Kevs, lunch in school, tea at Glens and dinner!!! Also start nominating names for the proposed committee to swing into action. I propose - subject to MC's go-ahead - that these Hermonites: Barry Ison, Miss Russell, Moores, Dubs and Sandy, Sherab and Roz, Glasbys and Johnstons, Margaret and Hubby, Cindy and Pradip, my TTC friends etc. should come back to MH for a while to set things in order. Got it?

Folks, just got the good news from Namgyal Wangdi, who is in touch with Sn Master Mr. Partho Dey. The good news is the meeting has been fixed for June 20 at 11 a.m. at MH. I have asked them to serve lunch for us. List of those attending the meeting are: Chuck (Sunirmal Chakrabarti), Pratap Rai, Sarthak Pradhan, Anup Chachan, Dipang, Shiv Saria, Jagdish Saria, Sushil Mittal, Jagjit Singh, Namgyal Wangdi, Thangi Chhangte Rema. The group represents Darj, Siliguri, Sikkim and Northeast. Those interested also welcome to join. Get cracking, guys. The finals are on at MH and we will let the MC win! Got it?
Jigs

Jigs - thanks for this message to us…it has been 6 years since we tried Jigs, and we do hope that you feel good about whatever happens now this time around. You always have such a good heart. You have been the archetype Hermonite right from the start through TTC then to teaching. No one has more voice in this arena than you. Take care Jigs
Roz

**MINUTES OF THE MEETING BETWEEN REV. K. SARDAR, ADMINISTRATOR, MOUNT HERMON SCHOOL, & SECRETARY TO THE MANAGING COMMITTEE
AND
HERMONITES REPRESENTING 'HERMONITES INTERNATIONAL'
HELD AT MOUNT HERMON SCHOOL ON JUNE 20, 2018**

The meeting was called to order with Rev. K. Sardar, Administrator and Secretary, Mount Hermon School, in the Chair.

The following people attended the meeting:

1. Rev. K. Sardar, Administrator, Mount Hermon School, & Secretary to the Management Committee
2. Mr. Partha Dey, Senior Master, Mount Hermon School
3. Mr. Pratap Singh Rai (1954-1967), Darjeeling
4. Mr. Sunirmal Chakravarthi (1968-1972), Darjeeling
5. Mr. Mukesh Singh Adhupia (1978-1979), Darjeeling
6. Mr. Vikramjit Dhir (1980-1993), Darjeeling

7. Mr. Sarthak Pradhan (1982-1991), Darjeeling
8. Mr. Sachep Pradhan (1982-1994), Darjeeling
9. Mr. Gyanendra Thapa (1984-1995), Darjeeling
10. Mr. Shiv Saria (1961-1972), Siliguri
11. Mr. Sushil Mittal (1963-1972), Siliguri
12. Mr. Jagdish Saria (1965-1972), Siliguri
13. Ms. Thangi Rema Changte (1970-1974), Shillong
14. Mr. Namgyal Wangdi (1962-1971), Gangtok
15. Mr. Jigme N. Kazi (1963-1972), Gangtok

1. Rev. K. Sardar began the meeting with a brief introduction on himself and stressed that his mission at Mount Hermon was to ensure that the School regained its lost glory with the active involvement of all stakeholders - the MC, the staff and students and the alumni.
2. Mr. Partha Dey, Senior Master, then welcomed the alumni.
3. Mr. Jigme Kazi thanked the School authorities for inviting the Hermonites to the meeting and conveyed to them greetings and good wishes on behalf of the President, Hermonites International, and the vast body of alumni across the world.

    Khadas (ceremonial silk scarves) and packets of tea were presented to Rev. Sardar and Mr. Dey on behalf of all the Hermonites.
4. Mr. Sunirmal Chakravarthi (1968-1972), former Principal of La Martiniere School, Calcutta and former Senior Master, St. Paul's School, Darjeeling, thanked the School authorities for taking the initiative to convene a meeting with the Alumni and commended the present School authorities on the positive transformation that had been palpable to all visitors to the School. While congratulating Rev. Sardar and Mr. Dey for the hard work they had put in over the recent past, he also noted that while, "Much has been done, more remains to be done." Mr. Chakravarthi stressed two basic issues:

A) The need to establish a system whereby the Alumni body is 'recognised and accepted' by the School, and associated with it, so that a 'working relationship' is created. He suggested that the School authorities should look into how the Alumni bodies such as the OPA in St. Paul's School and ALMA in La Martiniere are formally associated with their respective Schools. He offered to help in this matter.

B) The need to create an atmosphere of trust between the School and the Alumni body. Towards this end, he clarified that it was for the School and the Managing Committee to tell the Alumni body how they want the Hermonites to help. He emphasised the need for a deep bonding between the School and the alumni. He made it abundantly clear that the Alumni had no intention of either interfering in the day to day affairs of the School nor did they want to "take over" the School. He assured the School and the Managing Committee that all that the Alumni wanted was to help the School "move forward" after the recent troubled times.

5. Mr. Shiv Saria (1961-1972), while expressing his appreciation for the manner in which the Church has "kept the School going" in spite of all the recent "calamities and difficulties", expressed his complete confidence in the Church being 'capable' of running the School successfully. He repeatedly stressed that everything be done to create a positive outlook about the School and urged everyone not to be misled by rumours. He opined that the first and foremost task before the Alumni and the School was to increase the enrolment of students and restore the 'prestige of the school.' Mr. Saria urged Rev. Sardar to 'facilitate' the formation of an Alumni-School association so that the alumni could contribute in a meaningful way. He further emphasised on the need to strengthen the School's Accounts Office and make it transparent and accountable in order to improve the School's revenue.

6. Mr. Sarthak Pradhan (1982-1991) raised the issue of improving and School-Parent/Guardian interface so as to help build confidence among the various stakeholders. He also urged the Administration to look into other immediate needs of the school, including the need to recruit good teachers, and begin a 'cosmetic facelift' of the School buildings. He underscored the need to work on an urgent basis on the School's collapsing drainage system and the leaking roof of the Main Building.

7. Mr. Sachep Pradhan (1982-1994) focussed on improving the School's decaying infrastructure and working on student discipline.

8. Ms. Thangi Rema (1970-74) spoke of her family's close and abiding relationship with the School and suggested that the School should explore ways and means of increasing the number of students from the North East since parents of the area would be very keen on sending their children to good Christian Schools closer to the North East. Mr. Chakravarthi suggested that the School should look into the idea of doing road shows and conducting Admission Camps in the North Eastern States, Bihar, Nepal and Thailand just as some other reputed Schools in the neighbourhood have done. The Alumni in these areas would be glad to help.

9. Mr. Namgyal Wangdi (1962-1971) urged upon the Managing Committee and the School Authorities to trust the Alumni and give them the 'green signal' so that the Alumni could help the School on a long-term basis.
10. Mukesh Singh Adhupia (1978-1979) opined that a working relationship between the Alumni and the School would be mutually beneficial.
11. Jagdish Saria (1965-1972) said his only dream was to ensure that the School regained its past glory.
12. Sushil Mittal (1963-1972) stressed on the need for mutual understanding. He added that everyone should go about helping the School in a "Christian-like" manner.
13. Pratap Singh Rai (1954-1967) thanked Rev. Sardar and Mr. Dey for "bolstering" the "enthusiasm and courage" of the Hermonites in working for their alma mater. He remarked that he had heard encouraging reports of how the School was improving and he hoped that a partnership between the School and the Hermonites would see this reach greater heights.
14. Mr. Jigme N. Kazi (1963-1972) traced the background of how this meeting came about. He reported how a request from the President of Hermonites International, (HI) Mr. Varongthip Lulitanond (1973 - Bangkok) to Rev. K. Sardar culminated in this meeting on 20th June 2018.

A meeting with the School authorities had been sought to express the deep concern of Hermonites all over the world for the School's survival and future success and also to look into the possibility of the Alumni having a meaningful and enduring working relationship with the School authorities and the Management Committee in order to help the School regain its past glory and fulfill the aims and objectives for which Mount Hermon had been set up almost 125 years ago.

Mr. Kazi said the main purpose of the meeting was to seek the formal approval of the Managing Committee for the Alumni body to associate itself with the School in a deep and meaningful manner with the long-term view in mind. He stressed that if this was done, then and then only can the Alumni engage itself in an organised and systematic way; otherwise any help given by the Alumni would be on an ad-hoc basis.

Mr. Kazi briefly traced the formation of a global body which was initially conceived during the School's Centenary celebrations in 1995. The idea had had the approval of Mr. G.A. Murray, former Principal, and before long several alumni chapters were begun in various places. Hermonites International now had chapters all around the globe with a large membership. Mr. Kazi presented Rev. Sardar with a copy of the draft Constitution of Hermonites International for his perusal and comments.

He expressed the hope that the Managing Committee, the School and the Alumni would be able to work in unison in the interest of the School and concluded by saying that this would be a fitting tribute to the great Founders, Principals, teachers and students who had dedicated themselves to working for the greater glory of God and the School.

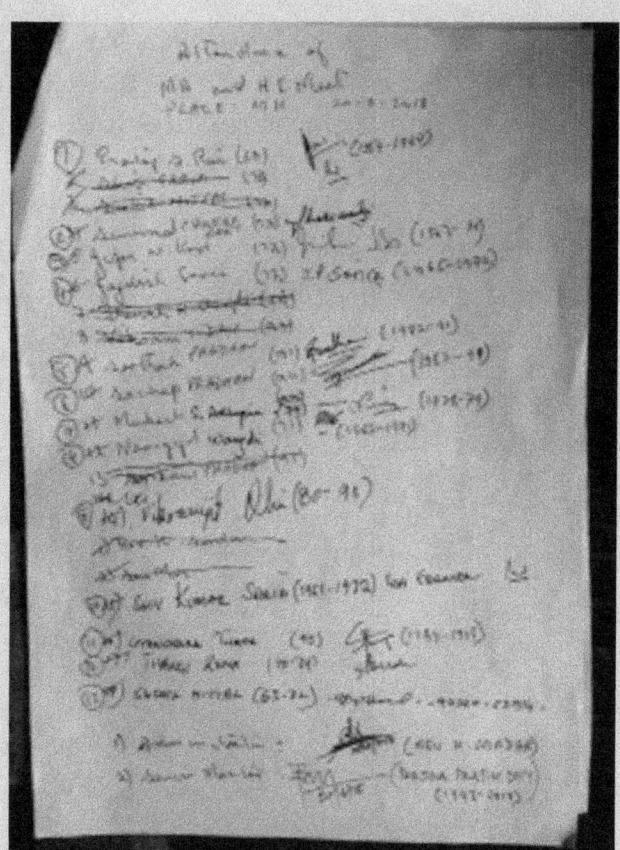

15. Rev. K. Sardar in his concluding remarks made the following observations:

   a) That his main goal is to work for the betterment of the School and also to build a healthy relationship with the Alumni.
   b) That his association with the School went back to almost ten years even though he had taken up his responsibility as Administrator only on June 2017.
   c) That though the School was undergoing great financial stress, he did not seek any financial help from the Alumni. He further clarified that the School's financial difficulties had started more than 15 years ago and he was looking at various ways and means by which this could be remedied over the next few years. Towards this end he remarked that he had re-started the School's bakery and hoped to begin dairy and organic farming in order to raise resources for the School.
   d) That apart from the recent political instability, "negative publicity" of the School had also been responsible for the School's current poor image and declining student enrolment.
   e) That he was confident that he would be able to put Mount Hermon on an even keel within the next two years.

Rev. Sardar assured the gathering that there should be no doubt about Bishop Philip S. Masih's desire and dream for Mount Hermon. He said that Bishop Masih, who is the Chairman of the Managing Committee, is deeply concerned about the School and is determined to put the School back on its feet as a leading School of this region. Bishop Masih had instructed him to clear all misunderstandings with the Alumni and Rev. Sardar was pleased to inform all concerned that he would have the pleasure of reporting a positive and fruitful meeting with the Alumni.

Mr. S. Chakravarthi, on behalf of all the Alumni, thanked Rev. Sardar for the courtesy extended in meeting former students and for sharing his time and concern with them. He also expressed the hope that this would be the beginning of a long and fruitful relationship between the Alumni and the School and wished the School Managing Committee and the Administration every success in the task they have undertaken to restore the School's old glory and pride.

The meeting was then adjourned for fellowship and lunch in the School Staff Dining Hall.

NOTE:

The meeting was held in a very free, frank and cordial atmosphere. Those present at the meeting unanimously resolved to lay a firm and strong foundation for a healthy and lasting relationship between the Alumni and their Alma Mater with the blessing of both the Managing Committee and the Methodist Church in India.

Jun 24, 2018
   Hi all, sharing the minutes of the meeting. Please pass it around.
Jigs

   Dear all, We Hermonites had a wonderful meeting with the school and church authorities at MH on June 20, 2018, on school-church-alumni matters. We think the groundwork of a new chapter on MH-Hermonites relationship has now been laid. Your feedback is vital for MH. Kindly circulate.
   Jigs (Jigme N. Kazi - MH: 1963-1972 (student), 1974-1975 (TTC college) and 1976-1979 (staff)

   Wonderful discussion friends. It seems to me that the work of Jigs and Thip, supported by many, has progressed to the point where a very positive invitation has developed by Rev. Sardar. There appears to be an expectation that the Management Committee (MC) must recognize MH alumni (whoever or whatever that may mean). What in fact is expected from the MC? A letter - a contract - a message from Rev. Sardar as it's representative? What must the MC do or say to mobilize the MH alumni? Given the history of dealings with various Bishops and the MC - at the same time we should accept that they have had (it seems) a negative perspective of MH alumni. That perspective needs to be changed into one of trust.

How can that be accomplished? If Rev. Sardar asks what is the alumni offering - what would be the response? Could it be that we Hermonites who would love to see MH the way we experienced those wonderful "Old Walls" (and more) - firstly want to prove to the MC that we can be trusted. Then in a practical way - to prove it - embark on a few small projects like Annie and Margaret have suggested. Having proved that we can be trusted - then the appropriate group or committee or whatever sits down with reps of the MC and makes some long term, strategic plans where many skills such as legal, marketing, recruitment, negotiating with local politicians re encroachment, and funds etc., can be mobilized. I'll be praying for your meeting Jigs. Let's not forget the power of prayer. Blessings to you all.
Barry

June 22
To Ison
   Namgyal and I were wondering why you were so quiet after the terrific meeting. Anyway. Just for you only: I have typed the minutes of the meeting and sent it to Chuck for his corrections. After this I will send it to Sardar and Dey to have a look before it is sent to the Bishop and before it is formally placed on record. I requested Chuck to go through our HI Constitution and SP and Lamart's alumni body and formulate a platform for MH-Alumni body to implement anything for MH.
   We will be doing this together and in consultation with a few Hermonites and the school. When this is done it has to be approved formally and then we may begin our work in a big way. Meanwhile, we need to form a team in consultation with Thip and others. The team should include all regions and age group. In the meanwhile, this team could gather ideas and suggestions for MH revival. Please, please kindly note our fear and apprehension of a possible mold within the Hermonites who may vested interest. Be alert on those who while supporting us raise contentious issues to create confusion and misunderstanding with a view to sabotage our mission for MH if we do no submit to them.
Jigs

June 29, 2018
Dear Jigme,
   Thanks so much for sharing the minutes of the meeting with me. Most interesting development and good to know that there is some dialog that is continuing with the board etc....
   I understand from Arun Jones (we were together for our mini-Hermonite reunion in North Carolina) that a key person is the bishop who has all the power and has used MH as his cash cow or something...? corruption etc., at the top levels of that church apparently. So very sad and disappointing to hear but glad you all are forging ahead and maybe something can come of it in the future. Well done on your continued perseverance and I look forward to future updates etc.
Warmest wishes,
Barbara Thummalapally

Hi Babara,

Yes, its something like that. This is the world and we need to see the ground reality and do our best to move forward to save MH with a positive outlook. There is no other way. Take care, stay in touch and hi to your hubby.
Jigs

28 June

Thank you so much Mr. Jigme N. Kazi for considering my request favourably. I just wanted to be a part of this Hermonite Family and also wanted to keep myself informed about what the Hermonites think and feel about their Alma Mater. Please feel free to ask anything you would like to know about the present status and future plans of Mount Hermon. May our fellowship and interactions with each other be a source of God's blessings to Mount Hermon. Hail Mount Hermon!
Rev. Kamalaksha Sardar

YOU ARE WELCOME, SIR

With pride and great humility I humbly accept the Facebook friend request from Rev. K. Sardar, my beloved alma mater Mt. Hermon School's Administrator and Secretary and Vice-Chairman of our school's Managing Committee, appointed by the Methodist Church in India, which owns Mt. Hermon.

Sir, you have rightly said in our June 20 meeting in MH that you have a 'dream' for MH to help the school regain its past glory. We, too, have a dream for MH, Sir.

Due to so many reasons I was not able to educate my four children in MH, but I want my grandkids to study where I studied. This is my dream and I want to seek all help to fulfill that dream. Why should our kids go down to the plains of north Bengal or travel to the deserts of north India to study when we have world-renown heritage schools in our region blessed by natural air condition? We need to give the right touches here and there to our missionary schools in the hills to get the recognition they so rightly need and deserve.

Sir, the message of yesterday's Sikkim Hermonites meeting in Gangtok is this: if you have the inclination, we have the passion!
Jigme N. Kazi

Hermonites,

Namgyal, Thip and our football cheer leaders know what it takes to win in a foota match/tourney. Physical fitness, skills, fighting spirit and team work. For the 50 and 60 plus Hermonites MH revival is a huge challenge. We must win the finals. It is not a 100-metre dash, it is a marathon. Darj, Gangtok and now Siliguri get-togethers are warming-up sessions. We must get well-acquainted with key players to build a firm foundation that will lead MH well into the 22nd century. Hermonites of these three chapters played a great role in the celebrations of MH's 100th anniversary in 1995. We will repeat the performance in 2020 under General Thip, who is paying a visit to Sikkim in October this year. Cheers and final a Goodnight to all.
Jigs

Very nice to read all exchange of views. Thank you Pradeep for the reminder, we all have agreed to wait for the school MC to give us Hermonites permission to work and propose ways and means to assist the school in the future.

My personal idea is once the MC gives us the green light we should set up One single Hermonites Alumni body. Then select the committee which will then gather ideas and filter them into a selected realistic ways and means of helping MH in the future.

One immediate action, if I may propose is to increase revenue and efficient cost control.

Good night to all. The Thai Hermonites will only meet when School MC give us the green light.

Thip

To Miss Russell

Hope all's fine with you, Miss. The outcome of the meeting should lead MH forward.

Jigs

Well done Jigs and all of you. Great to see the positive movement. Could you please send me Thangi's email? I'd like to be in touch with her again

So good to see all those familiar names!

As you perhaps know, I met Mr. Partha Dey on my visit in March, and his wife, as well as several other concerned staff members, and was much impressed with all of them.

We'll pray God's will in the matter.

Best regards and love from Miss (Russell)

June 30

Hello Jigme,

Thank you for your email.

You may know that our connection with MH was severed at the end of 1990. From this distance I have never been in a position to make any suggestions, especially considering the changing conditions in India.

Carol and I visited Darjeeling a couple of years ago and we were very saddened at the state of the school.

We are aware that you and others nearby have had some firsthand input with the Administration of the school, and seriously hope you will have success in restoring MH as a quality educational Institution.

It is quite possible of course that it may morph into a very different place from the one which you and we experienced.

All the very best with your endeavors.

Regards,

Benu (Chatterjee)

July 10
Dear Jigme,

I cannot describe the joy on receiving your positive mail regarding our beloved MHS. I convey my sincere congratulations from the bottom of my heart. You have done all Hermonites proud.

I am confident that you and your dedicated team will achieve what we have desired for so long.

I am keeping you & team in my prayers,

Hail Mount Hermon, Former secretary & ambassador of Bangladesh (Dhaka) Humayun A. Kamal, Class of 1961

Dear Sir Humayan, Its always a great pleasure to hear from the Hermonites. Thank you very much for your thoughts and kinds words. Finally, there's a small opening - a ray of hope - in MH. We will - together - embrace this opportunity and ensure that this great institution gets back on its feet. Stay in touch. Hail Mt. Hermon!
Jigs (1963-1979)

My (Jigme N. Kazi) message in Facebook on November 23, 2018

HOPE ON THE HORIZON

After months of waiting in anticipation there's a ray of hope for revival of our beloved alma mater, Mt. Hermon School. Today, we have been informed that the school authorities are likely to resume the dialogue, which formally began in MH on June 20, 2018, between the school and the Hermonites.

Inch by Inch
Step by Step
One Day at a Time
WE SHALL OVERCOME!

From: "Rev. K. Sardar"
Date: 7 December, 2018
To: "varongthip@gmail.com"
Subject: Mount Hermon School
To
Mr. Varongthip Lutinond
President
Hermonites International

Dear Mr. Varongthip,

I would like to take this opportunity to express my appreciation for all those Hermonites who feel strongly for their alma mater and are keen in lending their support. In the meantime I would also like to take this opportunity to mention a few facts that are important and relevant for an ongoing dialogue.

Many of you have visited us over recent times and are aware of our continuing efforts to revive Mount Hermon to its former glory. We are also aware of ongoing negative rumours being spread such as the school being sold, a hotel being made out of the school, the school/Managing Committee and Church are not interested in help from the alumni etc. I am writing to dispel these rumours and to inform you that none of these rumours are true. We, that is myself, the staff, the Managing Committee and the Church body itself, are working hard to get Mount Hermon back on track and do require help and support from the alumni to achieve our goals. However, we are rather mystified about the number of different alumni groups. We recognize each and everyone of you as an Hermonite, and are not overly concerned to which alumni group any of you belong to. The school looks for support from all Hermonites who can or are willing to extend a helping hand. You will be pleased to know that from the commencement of the next session we are looking to a new Principal joining us. We hope this will encourage parents and alumni alike to directly liaise with for all their needs. We hope that with the Principal in place, Mount Hermon will begin to be a place where parents and students alike, can feel comfortable.

As you well know Mount Hermon has been a boarding school and we wish to continue giving emphasis to this aspect, and to give impetus we are currently planning roadshows in Thailand, Nepal, Bangladesh and Assam in the month of January and February 2019. Again, we hope this venture will attract more students and bring in much needed revenue. I shall be in touch with various people in these places and be most grateful for any assistance you may be able to provide.

We are working on revamping our website that will allow regular updates to keep everyone informed of what is happening at Mount Hermon. We have been thwarted with difficulties over a landline/availability of broadband, however we hope this will soon be rectified.

Despite having made a certain amount of improvements, as some of you will have seen when you visited, we do have some projects at the school which require urgent attention. These are the following.

1. Roof repairs of the Main Building, including the roof of the Chapel/Auditorium Hall.
2. Repairs of the girls toilets in the Main Building.
3. Construction of a Gymnasium. Either a new construction or converting the basket ball/volley ball court by the swimming pool.
4. Repairs to the road beginning from the main gate, around the school and down to the main field.

The ideas we currently have for the Millennium building are renting it out to other schools/organisations for seminars, workshops etc., which, we hope, will bring in further revenue.

It had been mooted many times about the restoration of the cottages on Mount Hermon's land. This is another project we are looking at with the idea the renovated cottages, that are not used as staff quarters, could be rented to Hermonites and their families visiting Darjeeling. Once these are available we are considering having a small shop on site with goods from the school bakery, and basic provisions. We also hope to have some cows for our own milk, and to start our own vegetable garden to grow vegetables for school consumption.

I am hoping that the above mentioned projects and our continued efforts to rejuvenate the school will be of great interest to the Hermonite fraternity, and there will be no hesitation from your end to step up to the plate and support our efforts in reviving Mount Hermon to what each one of expect it to be. I am open to suggestions from each one of you, and, you have my assured cooperation in any endeavor that you seek to venture into at the school.

I look forward to your positive response and hope that this will bring the entire fraternity of Hermonites together to work towards a good cause.

Yours sincerely
Rev. K. Sardar
Administrator & Secretary
Mount Hermon School

Jigme N Kazi
Admin • 8 December

BREAKING NEWS! GOOD NEWS FROM MH

Dear Hermonites brothers and sisters,

It is with great pleasure to announce that I have received an official email from Rev. Sardar regarding our willingness to assist MH in any way possible.

It is a very positive email which will be circulated in the near future by HI chairman Mr. Jigme Kazi.

Kindly circulate this good news to all concerned and start all your brains working as to the manner in which we can assist our beloved Mount Hermon.

We have a lot of work ahead of us.

Kind regards to all and look forward to close cooperation in the near future.

Varongthip

From: varongthip lulitanond
Date: 9 December
To: "Rev. K. Sardar"
Subject: Re: Mount Hermon School
Dear Rev. Sardar,

First of all my apologies for late reply to your email due I was out of town.

I must sincerely thank you for your kind response and all the detailed future plans for Mount Hermon school.

I will immediately get in touch with all the Hermonites chapters on behalf of Hermonites International to take this important issue forward. We will come back to you with proper organization representing all Hermonites so that there is only one channel of communication and representation. I do understand your concern about various Hermonites bodies in existence at the moment.

We are definitely working towards the same goal for the benefit of Mount Hermon School. Please allow us sometime to reorganize ourselves and come up with a workable relationship and assistance to the school.

My respectful regards and thank you to you and to the school managing committee for giving Hermonites an opportunity to assist the school.
Sincerely yours,
Varongthip Lulitanond
President of Hermonites International

This message from me, Jigme N Kazi, was sent on Facebook on December 14, 2018

MH REVIVAL

Now that the school has responded to our call most Hermonites must be wondering what to do next. Winter holidays have begun in Darj and almost all staff members would be away for at least two months.

Firstly, we need to be aware of the fact that while many may get excited and throw up all sorts of ideas, only few would be in a position to carry things through. So, while FB and our WA groups may become hyper active we need to get connected to active and sincere Hermonites who have proved their worth down the decades/years to have a platform for active interaction on a regular basis. People will be willing to help if we have a credible group. We can start by choosing such people and start jotting down names and pass it on. Now there will be some distractors - some intentional, others innocent. Whatever the distraction we have to move ahead with a clear vision for MH. Guidelines would be unity, harmony, responsibility, transparency and accountability.

Hermonites International President Varongthip Lulitanond has made an open appeal to all Hermonites to respond positively. These are my views.

Dec 17
Dear All,

We have all been waiting for some momentum to take things forward. Jigme has been forthcoming with the exchange of correspondence with Varongthip Lulitanond, and Rev. K. Sardar, the Administrator of Mount Hermon School. We are now aware from Rev. Sardar's letter the areas where he feels the alumni can be of assistance. Some of you may be aware of Lucinda's and my recent trip to India with her parents aged 92 and 90. It was deliberately kept a low key affair, as it was all about Mr. and Mrs. Gibbs's (Lucinda's parents) and their, possibly, last visit to India. However, during our very brief stay in Darjeeling we did visit school and met Rev. Sardar and another Managing Committee member who had come from Calcutta with the Reverend, specially to meet us.

We were accompanied by Thangi who made a special effort to come from Shillong for the meeting. We felt the only way forward, at this juncture, as we perceived things had come to a standstill, was to actually meet Rev. Sardar, despite having had several phone conversations over the months post our previous visit in April. As this was our first meeting

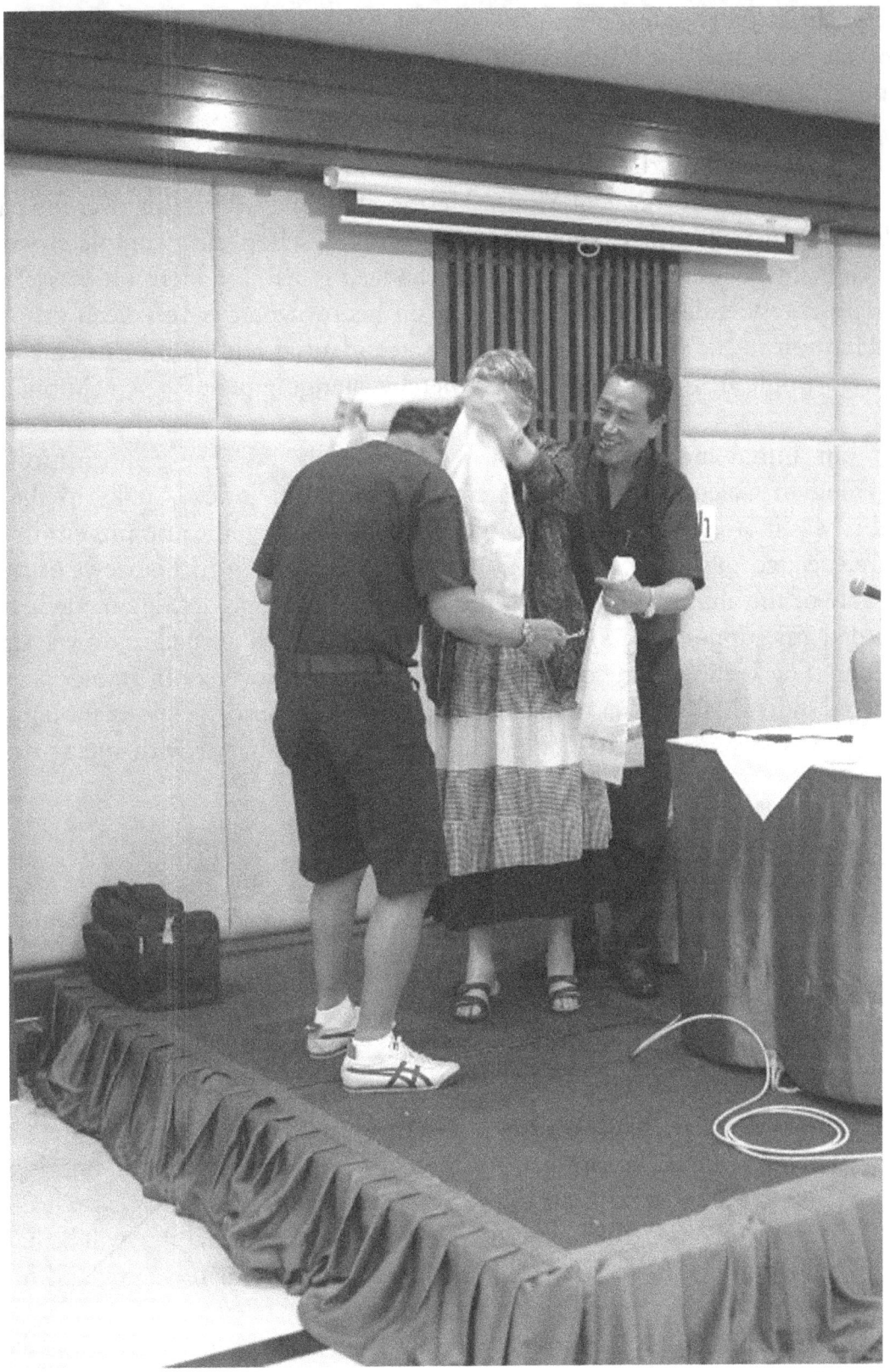

Miss Russell congratulates Thai Hermonite Varongthip Lulitanond (Thip) for being elected Hermonites International President during the Hermonites Reunion in Pattaya, Thailand, 2016.

with Rev. Sardar (not so for Thangi as she was present during the June meeting) a lot of issues were discussed including affairs of the school and, more pertinently, what role the alumni could play in helping to revive the school. We discussed and agreed upon the need to conduct roadshows in a few cities that could provide a platform and a gateway to encourage parents to send their children to Mount Hermon.

We all agreed that the image of Mount Hermon had taken a beating over the past many years. The school was neither being projected as a day school or a completely residential school. That image and perception needed change, as Mount Hermon was always and is essentially a residential school. Rev. Sardar on his own part is very keen on projecting Mount Hermon to the public and parents as a residential school. To this end we all felt the first step would be to hold roadshows, thereby changing people's perception about the school.

After our initial meeting at school I subsequently had the opportunity to meet the Reverend in Calcutta on two separate occasions and indeed spoke to the Bishop, Mr. Philip Masih on one of those occasions. Bishop Masih, while also present in Calcutta on Church related business could not join us but shared with us his views of the school and the role of the alumni and stressed the need to work together. He made it clear that if we needed any support or cooperation from the school, all we had to do was liaise with Rev. Sardar. The Bishop, and so did the Reverend, felt more comfortable in talking to a nominated individual/s rather than a huge delegation. After discussions a rough calendar of events was drawn up, and this is what the Reverend shared with me at the second meeting.

1. Roadshows

    The first one will be held in Calcutta between 5-10 Jan.

    The second and the third one will be held in Gangtok and Kathmandu between 15-23 Jan

    The fourth one will be in the North East, possibly Mizoram between 27-31 Jan

    The fifth and final one (for the moment) will be in Thailand in the first week of Feb.

For the roadshows the school needs active support in areas that they are lacking in. Publicity material - attractive posters, a decent brochure, (the current one is not only unattractive but says almost nothing about the school's heritage and its existence for more than a 100 years), and other forms of written and/or visual material that will be handy. The choice of venues would also be crucial. The number of days of the show and how far in advance should the publicity campaign start would be very relevant.

The school website needs a complete revamp. I believe somebody mentioned (Prakash Mundra possibly) that the URL is so unimaginative that the link to an educational institution like Mount Hermon is far from clear. There are many amongst us Hermonites who can easily relook at creating an attractive, user friendly (for parents and public alike to navigate), and easily manageable website. They could step forward and let that be their contribution and support for the school. Young Hermonites who have the energy and ideas can help plan and execute. They must be engaged in the whole exercise of revival. After all it is as much their school as is ours.

The first show in Calcutta, will be handled by the Reverend and his team which includes members of the Managing Committee. Any Hermonite in Calcutta who feels he or she could step up to the plate in assisting the Reverend, should liaise with him.

In Kathmandu he has been advised to liaise with Annie Gardener-Vaidya, and he will be writing to her shortly. I have taken the liberty to speak to Annie about this and she has agreed and would be willing to provide full support in terms of logistics etc., to make the show a success.

In Gangtok - anyone who feels they have workable ideas as to how they can help, I suggest could liaise with Jigme Kazi and set things up accordingly. Whatever the outcome please do let the Reverend know of your plans.

For Mizoram - Thangi is already aware and will be in touch with the Reverend directly. The Reverend on his end has spoken in Calcutta, to the Bishop of the Presbyterian Church and sought his assistance in Mizoram.

For Thailand - Varongthip has already been approached via an email, for help and guidance in conducting the roadshow, but the Reverend has not received a reply from him as yet. Maybe Varongthip can respond as soon as he can so that the Reverend is not left out in the cold and can rely on support in Thailand.

What is important to note at this juncture is. The school has no funds to conduct such roadshows as the books have been in red for many years. However, the Reverend is assured that funds from other Church related activities will be made available to him. It is therefore imperative that each region come up with an expense sheet that is just and reasonable. If Hermonites in that region are willing to pool in financial resources to ease the burden of such an activity then they should keep the Reverend informed as it would ease the pressure he will be under to keep things going according to plan. The team will consist between 5-6 people.

2. Infrastructure repairs

From the Reverend's letter it is very obvious that he is looking for support in some major repairs, like the roof. Some estimates were initially drawn up by Sarthak Pradhan and his support team. If all that is still viable then people who wish to support this endeavour can liaise with Sarthak and form a roadmap of activity. Sarthak in the past has been exemplary in his efforts of doing his bit for the school, and he gets on well with the school administration who have given their approval to him for continuing with his efforts.

People who feel strongly about doing something in the near future in terms of repairs and wish to contribute, do probably know that sending money to one person could become a problem for that person receiving the funds. I suppose the easy way out of this situation, in the interim, is to make bank drafts/bankers cheques directly in the name of the chosen contractor who will be engaged to carry out the task. These cheques/drafts which form the contributions could be sent to Sarthak directly for later disbursement to the contractor.

Sarthak hands over these cheques/or part thereof as work in progress. In the meanwhile, he can be asked to send photographs of the work in progress to all such benefactors. This way everyone concerned is taken care of without putting pressure on Sarthak. If any of you at this moment have any other way Sarthak could manage the money at this stage please do let him know.

The rejuvenation of Ailina and Wayside are to be pilot projects for the school in the first instance and cleaning up the property as a start is also going to happen in the coming month.

The roadshow dates mentioned above are all based on what the Reverend told me. They may change based on how well prepared the team is, but the coordinator/s can be in touch with the Reverend directly for confirmation and clarity. I am sure everyone knows his email id, which I shall repeat for convenience:- revk_sardar@yahoo.com.

I felt, given where we now are, it was important to share the above information with all of you. The last meeting I had was on 14th Dec, the day I left India to return home. Some of you may feel that you are not in agreement with the above roadmap as it has been laid out by Rev. Sardar, and you would be happy to help, only if it worked according to your thoughts and ideas, then please feel free to liaise with the Reverend and voice your concerns and objections. Nothing is set in stone and the Reverend is willing to be flexible to a certain extent. As time is short, from the school's perspective, the help and support provided will send appropriate positive signals to the school authorities that the alumni have their best interests at heart.

Yours truly,
Pradip Verma (1971 batch)

Pradeep,
   Despite our suggestion that we go about in a planned manner and the school deal with the global body for the long term interest of the school if the authorities do not feel the same and want to interact with each individual and chapters separately and chalk out the plans I have nothing to say. Please count me out of this kind of arrangement.
Jigme N. Kazi

Dear Jigs,
   Thank you so much for your email and your views expressed therein. I am presuming that your reluctance to be a part of the proposals put forward by the school authorities, is in an individual capacity and not as the Chairman of Hermonites International. If it is the latter than in such a case the President should write an open letter to the Rev. mentioning that the Chairman does not want to be a part of the ongoing efforts as appealed for by the school authorities. They should know as should the alumni.

   If it the former then some people will be disappointed with your decision. Anyway here's wishing you and your family a very Merry Christmas and a Happy New Year.
Pradip

Hermonites assistance to Mount Hermon school
Jan 19, 2019
Dear Rev. K. Sardar,

Here's wishing you a happy and prosperous new year.

The efforts of the Hermonites in cajoling the school into revival mode is now bearing fruits and it is now time to summarize the situation that we are in present.

The unrelenting efforts of Jigme, Namgyal and Cindy resulted in a group of seniors meeting the school Administrator, Rev Sardar, and the Senior Master, P. Dey in June 2018 to discuss how the Hermonites could help in rebuilding the school. The salient features of the meet were 3-fold:

1. Funds were not required by the school and that the school would be turned around within 2 years.
2. The Hermonites wanted HI to be accepted as the nodal agency with whom the school would liaise.
3. The Hermonites assured the authorities that they would cooperate with the authorities to revive the school if their proposal for a long-term vision, transparency and accountability was accepted.

Rev. Sardar assured the student body to take up the matter with Managing Committee Chairman, Rev. Philip Masih and back.

Since the above meet with the school authorities, President HI has received a mail soliciting financial help for repairing and rebuilding school infrastructure.

Also Pradeep, Cindy and Thangi recently met Rev. Sardar and discussed MH affairs with them.

Subsequently, Pradeep has addressed a mail to a number of us detailing the steps that the school proposes to take.

In the light of these recent happenings, the possibility of a nodal group handling the efforts of Hermonites towards the school improvement seems a remote possibility. It is a fact that the school needs help. Those willing to assist the school individually or in groups should do so on the basis of programs that they are able to formulate/execute at their individual/group level.

HI welcomes and encourages such efforts.
Yours Sincerely,
Varongthip Lulitanond

I am very saddened to see in print your dismissal of the support and work towards improvements at the school, done by whole group or small groups. I am offended that I was not approached for my input with regards to moving forward as a unified group. Some of you have acted as individuals in making the decision you put in black and white in the letter and then you have the nerve to speak on everyone else's behalf. If you (whoever was consulted to write the letter) were really committed to moving forward as a unified group you (the collective you) should have been vocal and visible in gathering everyone's

ideas, posting ideas for both the short term and long term. My interest is in the school and not my ego. I will be moving ahead with donations towards the needs identified by Rev. Sardar in his Dec letter.
Margaret (Mapley)

Dear Thip,

I was just forwarded a letter that you, as President, have written to Rev. Sardar on behalf of Hermonites International specifying that Hermonites International was not in a position to help the school. Though a copy of this correspondence was marked to me you had my email address wrong so I did not receive it. Anyway the letter is now at hand. From what I have been able to glean from the contents because a few Hermonites met up with the Reverend subsequent to the "only meeting" that took place in June 2018, these meetings and its outcome did not represent the view of Hermonites International. I do not understand why that should have been a problem.

Hermonites International did not have nor does it currently have a nominated committee who can represent the views of Hermonites to the school, so any Hermonite who goes to school and has a discussion with school authorities about school affairs is doing so as a Hermonite and not some individual. The school treats every such person as a Hermonite, since they are not aware of a formal notified representative committee. Expressing their views to such individuals/groups is as much in keeping with the prevalent norms. That alone should not have been the reason from the decision of withdrawing help. From what I understand Hermonites International is made up of a fair number of Hermonites (more than 200 or so ??), therefore your decision to not go forward, is it a collective decision of these 200 or more Hermonites? What should have been done is an open letter written by you or Jigme Kazi as the Chairman to all those Hermonites who you thought made up Hermonites International, your thoughts of withdrawal and asked them whether they agreed to this line of action, and thereafter acted accordingly.

However, now that you have chosen to withdraw from a combined concerted effort, you have effectively negated the work put in by some to have an open dialogue in the first place. What was forgotten... opening up of dialogue allowed the delegation to meet up with the Reverend and have a discussion. Nothing happened for the next 8 months, there was no follow up from you as the President and Jigme as the Chairman as to what was the school doing. There should have been follow up emails/telephone calls to the Reverend ensuring that there would be continuation of dialogue whilst a decision was being taken by them. I do not believe there was any meaningful conversation at all. It was only after our brief visit (Cindy, Thangi and myself) in late November that the Reverend wrote to you with his plans and what he thought about the various Hermonite groups that functioned separately.

You in turn wrote back to him saying that you were trying to get all the Hermonite groups under one platform and for this you needed time. We have seen no progress in this direction at all and now suddenly your letter saying that you were preparing to back out of your offer to help and left it to individuals/other groups to do what they wished, is not an excuse such a let down to all the hype that was created over the last 8 months. Hermonites International, through your letter, has proved that they are no different from any other

Hermonite group with whom the Church has struggled to liaise in the past. I am sure it has left a bad taste in everyone's mouth.

I am sure other Hermonites who feel they can support the school through these difficult times will continue without the blessings of Hermonites International. Their efforts will not only bring them satisfaction of having done something constructive but also let the school feel that they have not been let down by ALL Hermonites, and that there were some who still cared for the school. I am sincerely hoping that you will reconsider your decision and find time to write back to the Reverend accordingly.

Best wishes,
Pradip Verma

Dear Mr. Dey,

After our June 2018 meeting there has been no communication from the school authorities to our proposals. Our proposals are very clear and have been recorded in the minutes of the said meeting. I myself sought (through emails) Rev. Sardar's response to our June meeting. Namgyal Wangdi, who is in touch with you on the issue, has failed to get any response.

During the Johnstons' visit to MH in September 2018, Rev. Sardar said we would hear from him soon. We had planned for a meeting of the school authorities with Hermonites International President, Varongthip Lulitanond, in October 2018 for discussions but Rev. Sardar was not available. Thereafter, some of us had asked for a meeting with the school authorities just before the winter vacation. This too was turned down.

After six months since the June 2018, Rev, Sardar, in December first week, wrote to HI President seeking help from the alumni. This response came a bit too late to rejuvenate the school for 2019 academic session but it was good news. However, even as we were planning to respond to Rev. Sardar, Pradip Verma from Ireland starts telling us what is to be done, when and how. He said he met Rev. Sardar and had a talk with the Bishop.

It was after these developments the HI Prez, in Jan first week, wrote to Rev. Sardar informing of our decision to urge all Hermonites/chapters to help MH individually. Since the school rejected HI to be the nodal body to deal with MH-Hermonites relations we were left with no option but to urge individual Hermonites and chapters to respond to Rev. Sardar's call. You know very well that since 2012 concerned Hermonites have been urging the school to involve Hermonites in aiding the school in a big way with a long-term vision, keeping in mind the need to maintain transparency and accountability in all its dealings, particularly in matters relating to finance and construction work. Our views were highlighted in the June 2018 meeting.

But despite our submissions the school authorities have gone ahead rejecting our views and decided to deal with individual Hermonites. We have regretfully accepted this decision and have urged all Hermonites to come to the school's aid in their own way as desired by the school.

If there be any misunderstanding let us sit down face to face and clear it. We hope to continue our dialogue with the school in future in the interest of MH.

With warm regards
Jigme N. Kazi

Roof top repair scheme turned down

In response to Rev. Sardar's appeal to the Hermonites in December 2018 to assist the school on roof repair works of the girls hostel and chapel in the main school building a section of Hermonites initiated a scheme to mobilize funds for purchase of tin sheets for repair works.

The roof repair scheme initiative by 1972 batch Hermonite, Shiv Saria of Siliguri, got the support of more than 200 Hermonites from global Hermonites. Instead of collecting funds from the Hermonites the scheme envisaged that each Hermonite contribute Rs. 1,300 towards purchase of one tin sheet and labour charges for fixing the roof. Shiv Saria took this initiative with prior consent of Rev. Sardar and in consultation with a few Hermonites.

However, when the school authorities were contacted for delivery of the tin sheets there was no response from the school. When Rev. Sardar was informed of the matter he said he would meet Saria, which he never did.

However, despite these setbacks one last effort is being made to urge the school authorities to give a formal green signal to pursue our roof repair project during the 125th anniversary celebrations – March 2020 to March 2021.

As in the previous encounters (in 2012, 2015 and 2018) with the school authorities much excitement was generated among Hermonites which ultimately led to nowhere.

It may be mentioned that in the spring of 2015 there was another move to involve Hermonites to revive MH and regain its past glory. The initiative to appoint a Hermonite as MH Principal in March-April 2015 came from the Methodist Church functionaries and some Kolkata Hermonites. Despite the 2012 let-down, the Hermonites gave a positive response. However, nothing much came out of this endeavour.

Efforts to involve the school in the celebrations of the school's 125th birth anniversary has been met with lukewarm response from the school authorities, leaving the Hermonites to devise their own means to celebrate the occasion.

Epilogue

125th Anniversary And Beyond

"It is better to light a candle than to curse the darkness."

A group of Sikkim Hermonites got together over dinner in Gangtok on Christmas eve, 2019 at their favourite haunt – Hotel Tashi Delek. The main menu was, of course, MH! My batchmate O.T. Bhutia reiterated that he would host the Thai party for dinner or lunch on March 7 or 8. Tsegyal Tashi, who was in MH for several years in the '60s, has also invited the Thai party for lunch or dinner on the same dates.

In December 2019 and January-February 2020, I met a number of Hermonites and the subject of our discussion was the same – MH, more particularly the celebration of the school's 125th anniversary. In Bangkok, 1973 batch Hermonite and Hermonites International President and my dear friend Thip (Varongthip Lulitanond) confirmed that he and some Thai Hermonites would come to Sikkim, Darjeeling and Siliguri to celebrate the occasion. Navin (Khuria) Wangsejullarat, also 1973 batch and a very active Hermonite, will not be able to travel due to health reasons. We wish him good health and speedy recovery. Aphichoti (Oak) Chavengsaksongkram, younger brother of late Krisada C., will be able to come to Kolkata only to join the others for celebrations in March. This is also due to health reasons. We are getting old!! Oak has decided to write an article for this book. This is wonderful as he is a good writer. Incidentally, Oak's mother is related to Sasithorn Boonlong, the pioneer of Thai students' 'influx' into MH. In fact, Sasithorn, batch of 1963-64 (!!) came all the way from Bangkok to Darjeeling for Oak's admission in mid-1960s.

 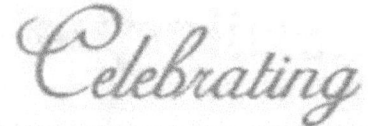 

125 GLORIOUS YEARS
MOUNT HERMON SCHOOL
(1895-2020)

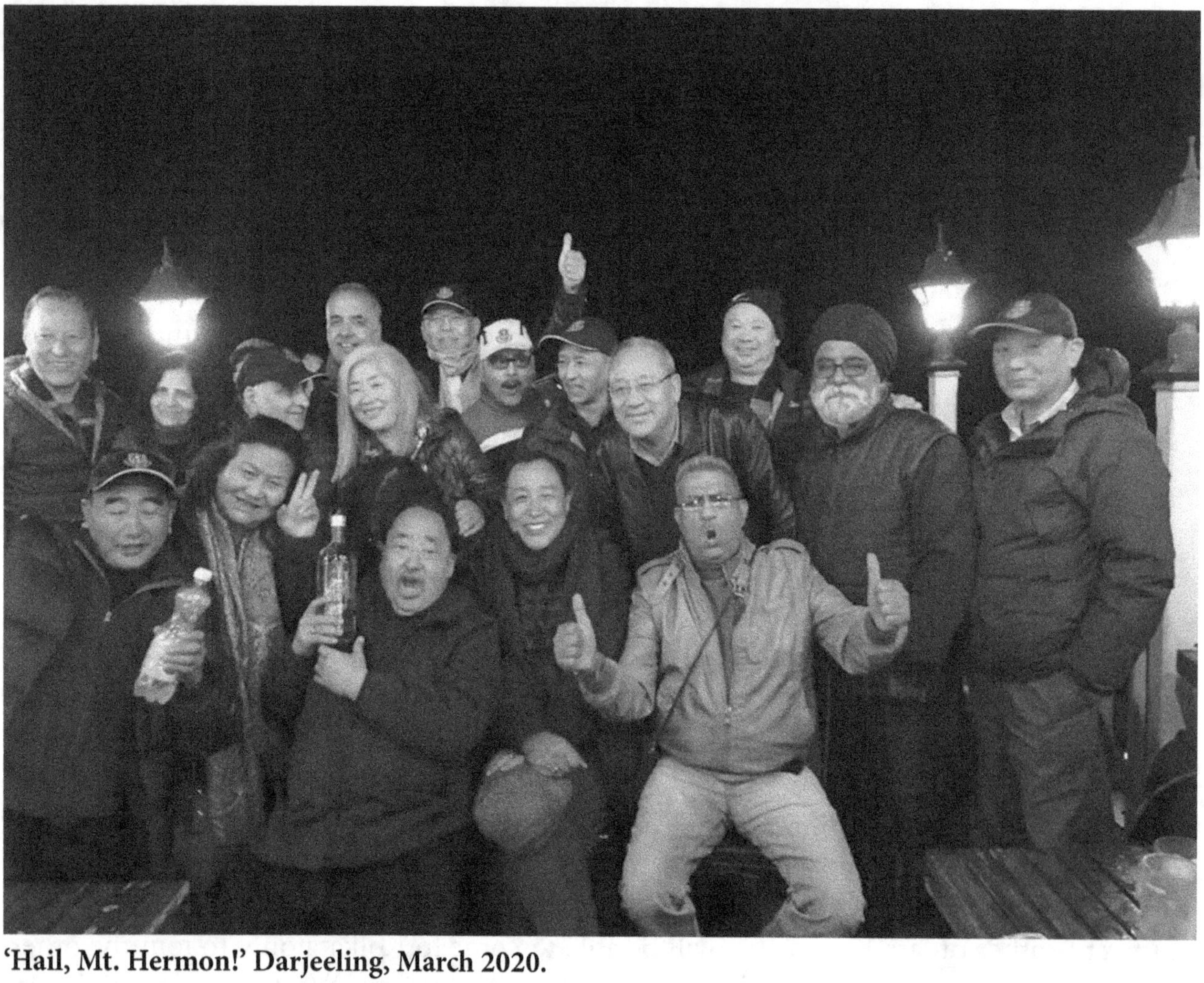

'Hail, Mt. Hermon!' Darjeeling, March 2020.

Epilogue

In Calcutta (Kolkata), the Hermonites, under Charan and Shakti, are doing a wonderful job in reviving the Hermonite spirit there. I had earlier requested Charan Chabria to 'make peace and move ahead'. They seem to be doing more than that! Keep going. When Sikkim Hermonites' President Uttam Pradhan and I met Helen Sanson and her husband over dinner in Gangtok last year she promised that during their short stay in New Zealand this year (the two work in Kolkata) they would meet up with other Hermonites in New Zealand and celebrate our school's 125th birth anniversary.

I'm sure Hermonites from all over the world and from all groups and ages are geared up to celebrate the occasion in their own way. The spirit and the manner in which some Hermonites, including some from abroad, joined the school to celebrate MH's 125th birth anniversary on March 11, 2020, is proof enough of our strong bonding and camaraderie. The spirit of MH is alive and refuses to die.

Calcutta

Hail Mount Hermon! A Tribute

Siliguri

Siliguri

Epilogue

Gangtok

Kalimpong

833

Hail Mount Hermon! A Tribute

Darjeeling

Jalpaiguri (Soongachi)

Epilogue

Kohima

Canberra

However, we are well aware that Hermonites all over the world are conscious of what's happening to their beloved MH. Some have given up on the school, others are holding on. Hopes are high but apprehensions are genuine. What can I say at such moment!? Keep going. Aim. Shoot to score!

During the celebration of the Methodist Church's 150 years of ministry in the sub-continent many years ago in Lucknow, one of the speakers reminded the delegates of what Mahatma Gandhi said about the Church in India. Bishop Robert Solomon of Singapore in his keynote address recalled an incident between Stanley Jones, an American Methodist Christian missionary, and Mahatma Gandhi. When Jones asked Gandhi, "You are an ardent practitioner of Jesus' Sermon on the Mount; why don't you join the church?" Gandhi replied, "I have no problem with Christ; my problem is with church."

When I see what has been going in our beloved Mount Hermon, the temple of learning, in the past several years I'm reminded of how Jesus Christ reacted when he saw what was happening in the Church of God in the city of Jerusalem:

"Then Jesus went into the temple of God and drove out all those who bought and sold in the temple, and overturned the tables of the money changers and the seats of those who sold doves. And He said to them, "It is written, 'My house shall be called a house of prayer,' but you have made it a 'den of thieves.'" (Mathew 21)

In 1967 when Dr. Welthy Fisher spoke at our Speech Day she reminded us how we should go about our job, particularly when things don't go our way. She, while quoting an old Chinese proverb, said: "It is better to light a candle than to curse the darkness."

Those who are concerned about MH and have displayed their love, affection and loyalty to the school need not despair "for whatsoever a man soweth, that shall he also reap". It is the law of karma. "For he that soweth to his flesh shall of the flesh reap corruption; but he that soweth to the Spirit shall of the Spirit reap life everlasting. And let us not be weary in well doing: for in due season we shall reap, if we faint not. As we have therefore opportunity, let us do good unto all men, especially unto them who are of the household of faith." (Galatians 6:8-10)

When the Chapel portion of our school's main building was restored and rededicated on August 15, seven months after the disastrous earthquake of January 15, 1934, our Principal Miss Lila Enberg in her dedicatory speech said, "We need not mourn for the greater glory of the former building that was shattered by the earthquake. Instead we all rejoice that the latter glory is greater than the former. The Assembly Hall is now more firmly constructed, more strongly bound together than before. We would now, therefore, render hearts full of thanksgiving to your Gracious God who, of His infinite mercy and goodness, has made all this possible. It was He who gave the faith and courage that enabled us to say: 'It shall be rebuilt!'"

In this hour of another crisis at MH may we, too, have the faith and courage to say: "It Shall Be Rebuilt!" and mean it.

Inch by inch
Step by step
One day at a time
WE SHALL OVERCOME!

Cheers to all! Happy 125th Anniversary to MH and all Hermonites! Hail, Mt. Hermon!

The School Song

Hail, Mount Hermon!

Beloved Mount Hermon, we greet thee
Thy daughters and sons from afar,
As oft as we pause in our toiling
To hail thee, whose children we are.

Chorus:
Hail, Mount Hermon! Hail, Mount Hermon!
Safe for aye in memory's shrine.
Hail, Mount Hermon! Dear Mount Hermon!
Praise and love be ever thine.

With strong steady hand dost thou lead us,
Thy powerful arm is our stay,
Thy light is our beacon in darkness
Which ever will lend us its ray.
Chorus

O may thy fair name live forever,
Be deeply impressed on each heart,
That we, in our trials and triumphs,
May ne'er from thy guidance depart.
Chorus

www.ingramcontent.com/pod-product-compliance
Lightning Source LLC
Chambersburg PA
CBHW081426070526
44586CB00020B/2499